SUFISM, MYSTICS, AND SAINTS IN MODERN EGYPT

STUDIES IN
COMPARATIVE RELIGION

Frederick M. Denny, General Editor

SUFISM, MYSTICS, AND SAINTS IN MODERN EGYPT

Valerie J. Hoffman

THE UNIVERSITY OF SOUTH CAROLINA PRESS

Cloth edition published by the University of South Carolina Press, 1995
Paperback edition published in Columbia, South Carolina,
by the University of South Carolina Press, 2009

www.sc.edu/uscpress

Manufactured in the United States of America

18 17 16 15 14 13 12 11 10 09 10 9 8 7 6 5 4 3 2 1

The Library of Congress has cataloged the cloth edition as follows:
Hoffman, Valerie J. (Valerie Jon), 1954–
Sufism, mystics, and saints in modern Egypt / by Valerie J. Hoffman.
p. cm. — (Studies in comparative religion)
Includes bibliographical reference and index.
ISBN 1-57003-055-3
1. Sufism—Egypt. I. Title II. Series: Studies in comparative religion (Columbia, S.C.)
BP188.8.E3H64 1995
297'.4'0962—dc20 95-4373

ISBN: 978-1-57003-849-5 (pbk)

CONTENTS

Illustrations vii
General Editor's Preface ix
Preface xi
Acknowledgments xv
Note on Transliteration xix

Chapter 1. Sufism in an Age of Change 1
Chapter 2. Among the Sufis: Experiences, Methods, and Approach 25
Chapter 3. The Prophet Muhammad and His Family in Egyptian Sufism 50
Chapter 4. The Saints: Bearers of the Prophetic Light 89
Chapter 5. The Sufi Orders 123
Chapter 6. Foundations of the Sufi Path 156
Chapter 7. Mystical Concepts and Practices in Egyptian Sufism 196
Chapter 8. Women and Sexuality in Sufi Life and Thought 226
Chapter 9. Models of Sainthood 255
Chapter 10. The Life and Influence of Shaykh Muḥammad ʿUthmān al-Burhānī 300
Chapter 11. Coptic Christianity and Popular Islam in Egypt: Elements of a Common Spirituality 328
Chapter 12. Conclusion: Sufism in Modern Egypt 357

Notes 379

Glossary	419
Biographical Dictionary	427
Select Bibliography	433
Index	440

ILLUSTRATIONS

Figure 1. Author observing dhikr at moulid of Shaykh Aḥmad 26
Figure 2. Shaykh Ṣāwī by the tomb of Shaykh Muḥammad ʿAbāṭa 31
Figure 3. Maḥfūẓ, keeper of the shrine of Shaykh ʿAbāṭa 102
Figure 4. Author with disciples of Ḥāgga Zakiyya at her tomb 106
Figure 5. Shaykh ʿIzz al-ʿArab al-Hawārī, Shaykh Saʿīd al-Daḥḥ of the Aḥmadiyya Idrīsiyya Shādhiliyya, the author, and the author's daughter 108
Figure 6. Aḥmad al-Tūnī 172
Figure 7. Rows of men doing dhikr 177
Figure 8. Men in dhikr 186
Figure 9. Woman doing dhikr 246
Figure 10. Shaykh Aḥmad Raḍwān 258
Figure 11. Shaykh Aḥmad Abū ʾl-Ḥasan leading his followers in dhikr 270
Figure 12. Shaykh Abū ʾl-Wafā al-Sharqāwī 276
Figure 13. Author with Shaykh Aḥmad al-Sharqāwī 280
Figure 14. Ḥāgga Zakiyya 292
Figure 15. Ḥāgga Zakiyya with Ḥāgg ʿAbd al-Hādī Mūsā ʿAbd al-Hādī and his family 298
Figure 16. Shaykh Muḥammad ʿUthmān ʿAbduh al-Burhāni 303
Figure 17. Muqaddasa Elīṣābāt Ibrāhīm 338

General Editor's Preface

It is common to encounter people in the West who have little interest in or love of Islam but who have a positive, accepting frame of mind concerning Sufism. And it is possible to find individuals who are engaged in supposed Sufi disiplines but who do not observe Islam's five "pillars" of witnessing to the unity of God and the apostlehood of Muhammad, daily prayers, fasting, almsgiving, and pilgrimage to Mecca. Distinctions between Islam and Sufism are not new. For many Muslims, Sufism is a dangerous innovation that was responsible for the degeneration and weakness of Muslim peoples during the modern colonialist period in Asia and the Middle East. For others Sufism is the essence of Islam, its very heartbeat.

A notable exponent of Sufism, the Persian al-Hujwiri (d. 1077), once observed that in his day Sufism was a mere name without a reality, whereas in pristine Islamic times it had been a reality without a name. It is true that Sufi spirituality has from its inception emphasized interior states and individual-personal dimensions of belief and action. The outer, practical side of Islam deals with law and behavior, whereas Sufism does not necessarily conform to the mass consciousness of official Islam. On the other hand, authentic Sufism has always based itself squarely on the fundamental doctrines and practices of Islam, as revealed in the Qur'an an elaborated in the teachings and example—known as the Sunnah—of the Prophet Muḥammad. Thus claiming to be a Sufi while failing to observe the pillars is nonsense, an avoidance of the deep accountability structures of Islamic religion that keep Muslims honest and focused.

Dr. Valerie J. Hoffman's important and arresting book on Sufis, mystics, and saints in modern Egypt looks at Sufi spirituality from a rigorous historical perspective, showing how classic texts and procedures continue to inform and inspire in contemporary contexts. In recent decades it has been widely supposed that Sufi organizations and activities have atrophied in Egypt under the pressures of modernity, nationalism, Islamic fundamentalism, and other things. Hoffman shows, on the contrary, that Sufism is alive and well in today's Egypt, providing men and women with meaning, strength, and hope in a most difficult era.

What is especially appealing and authoritative about this book is its immediacy, which has been fueled by the author's extensive experience sharing in the Sufi life under a respected spiritual guide. The human sources for Hoffman's story are as valuable as they are rare in general treatments of Sufism, which tend to be bookish and removed from actual participation in Sufi activities. Furthermore, this book provides a most valuable and unusual discussion of women and sexuality in Sufi life.

The author has modestly suggested that her book might be used as a beginning textbook on Sufism. That is surely a realistic expectation. But *Sufism, Mystics, and Saints in Modern Egypt* is much more than that. It is an original, authoritative exploration into that special and abiding dimension of Islam that both appeals to the outsider by revealing the religion's inner beauty and integrity and sustains multitudes of Muslims by keeping open the path of intimacy between God and his faithful servants. Sufism, for its exponents, is not in its essence an ism at all, but the core process in a divine-human friendship that is beyond naming.

Frederick Mathewson Denny

PREFACE

Despite the inherent limitations in any one person's perspective and information, this book aims to be a fairly comprehensive description of Sufism in Egypt today and its relationship to its own classical heritage as well as to other spiritual currents in modern Egyptian society, including Islamic fundamentalism, modernism, and Coptic Christianity. The core of this book is based on data I collected from fieldwork in Egypt from 1 October 1987 through 30 April 1989. Previous fieldwork in Egypt on a different but not unrelated subject, from September 1980 through October 1981, also provided important insights and stimulus for my later fieldwork. My undergraduate training was in anthropology at the University of Pennsylvania, but my graduate training was in Arabic and Islamic texts at the University of Chicago, and my research goals and methods combine both anthropological fieldwork and textual analysis.

I describe my fieldwork methods and experiences in chapter 2 and need not duplicate that here. Suffice it to say that my original research goals were far more modest and limited, but the extraordinary opportunities presented by my unexpected acceptance into the Sufi community led me to data and perspectives on Sufism in contemporary Egypt that are either lacking or misrepresented in our scholarly literature. The mandate simply to describe arises from that fact. Some aspects of contemporary Sufi mystical experience–the centrality of devotion to the Prophet and his family, the essentially communal nature of much of contemporary Egyptian mystical experience, and the contemporary meaning of the key classical Sufi concept of *fanāʾ* (annihilation of the ego), just to name a few–are entirely absent from previous scholarly discussions. These aspects raise the question of how Sufism has changed–not "deviated" from some ideal norm but evolved out of its classical heritage. The classical Sufi heritage of the eighth to thirteenth centuries is never far removed from contemporary Sufi experience. The texts of classical Sufism live on in the oral and written culture of contemporary Sufism, even if their meaning has undergone some transformation. The linkage of the past, examined through texts, to the present, examined through both texts and fieldwork, is a concern throughout this book. I chose not just to write an ethnographic study but to compare the contemporary situation with the past and to demonstrate the relevance of the past for the present. In most cases the texts I employ in this book are texts that are used and quoted from in Egypt today. The move between medieval texts and contemporary fieldwork is meant not to confuse but to clarify the extent of continuity as well as change in Sufism. I hope that the book will interest historians of religion, and especially of Islam.

Because Egyptian Sufism is introduced here as a total system, this book could serve as a general introduction to Sufism as a whole. For all the uniqueness of Egypt's pre-Islamic cultural heritage, Egypt is by no means isolated from developments in other countries. The Sufi Orders that developed in the twelfth through fourteenth centuries, and still form the core of Sufi life in Egypt, were usually imported from other countries, such as Morocco and Iraq. Much of what is said about Sufism here would no doubt apply to many other countries. Not having conducted fieldwork in other countries, I dare not generalize to the Muslim world outside of Egypt, but the reader should be aware that Egyptian Sufism is neither idiosyncratic nor unusual, except in the degree of government sponsorship, encouragement, and control of Sufism, a topic that will be addressed in chapter 1. What strikes an Islamic scholar in Egypt is the extraordinary richness and variety that exists in Islamic life in Egypt. The freedom of Sufism to flourish openly is part of what makes Egyptian religious life so vibrant.

In order to enhance the usability of this book as an introduction to Sufism for the nonspecialist, I have kept Arabic words and specialized terminology to a minimum, although I have provided Arabic equivalents in many cases in parentheses for the sake of the specialist in Islam. In quotations brackets will be used. I have also provided a glossary and biographical dictionary at the end of the book, although I hope that the text will read clearly enough without frequent recourse to such aids.

My fieldwork provided what many other accounts of Sufism have not: vivid first-person anecdotes by Sufis themselves that give testimony to the reality of the supernatural in their everyday lives and that flesh out what are often largely theoretical perspectives on aspects of Sufi life and experience.

Situating Sufism in Egyptian religious life means, among other things, exploring its relationship with Coptic Christianity, which is followed by as much as 10 percent of the population. Coptic spirituality is, like that of the Sufis, based on mysticism, miracles, and the veneration of saints, and an examination of Coptic Christianity allows us to examine the meaning of mysticism, sainthood, and initiatory paradigms in Egypt as a whole. The commonalities of Sufis and Copts are not always recognized among themselves because larger overriding categories such as Muslim and Christian are often given more significance. But there are exceptions, and I was fortunate to discover one particularly exceptional case of a Coptic holy woman that allows for striking comparisons with Sufism. And like the Sufis, the Copts often find themselves beleaguered in contemporary Egypt.

This study takes place in modern Egypt, in a society that has led the Arab world in embracing modernity, with all its presuppositions of bureaucratization, rationalization, and technological development. It has also led the Arab world in articulating new interpretations of Islam to make it more compatible with modern life, which in turn has stimulated the growth of fundamentalist movements that react to this modernism by calling for a reinvigorated fidelity to traditional Islamic legal texts as the foundation for social and political life. Sufism is neither modernist nor fundamentalist, and I will make some attempt to situate it in relation to these other currents that struggle over not only the hearts and minds of Egyptians but also over the right to determine Egyptian politics and law. Although Sufism is by no means a static tradition, it nonetheless presupposes continuity with the past and eternal validity for its basic precepts. This book could serve, therefore, as a case study for the dialectical relations between a tradition that presupposes continuity and a society undergoing rapid social change. It explores not only the ideas and practices of Egyptian Sufis but the relevance of their mysticism for modern society.

ACKNOWLEDGMENTS

This book could not have been written without the assistance of many people. The initial fieldwork was conducted from October 1987 through June 1988 under the auspices of a Fulbright fellowship in the Islamic Civilization Program. My husband and I decided to remain in Egypt an extra year in order to take advantage of the extraordinary research opportunities that had opened up before me. It was too late to apply for another grant, and we relied on our own funds and the loans and generosity of family and friends. To all who made it possible for us to remain in Egypt, I am deeply grateful. In 1991–92 I received a grant from the National Endowment for the Humanities to enable me to take a leave of absence from my teaching responsibilities in order to write this book. I would like to thank the University of Illinois and especially the director of the Program for the Study of Religion, Professor Gary Porton, for their flexibility in allowing me to take so much time to make this book a reality. The University of Illinois Research Board also funded a research assistant in the 1990–91 academic year, Khalil Iskarous, who assisted me in translating some of the taped and written materials I brought back from Egypt.

Those who helped me in Egypt are too numerous to mention, but I would like nonetheless to express my gratitude to those whose help was particularly critical. My largest debt goes to Shaykh ʿIzz al-ʿArab al-Hawārī, without whom this book could never have been written. He was the key to much of my knowledge and to many of my contacts. These included Shaykh Muḥammad Aḥmad Raḍwān, Shaykh Aḥmad al-Sharqāwī, Shaykh Aḥmad Abū 'l-Ḥasan, Shaykh Muḥammad al-Ṭayyib and his family, Shaykh Wāfī Muḥammad Wāfī, Shaykh Gābir al-Jāzūlī, the Sufi singers Aḥmad al-Tūnī and Yāsīn al-Tuhāmī, and Ḥāgga Nafīsa, daughter of Ḥāgga Zakiyya ʿAbd al-Muṭṭalib Badawī. To all of them I owe a debt of gratitude for their warm welcome and hospitality. I would also like to thank Alfred Hüber and Shaykh Gamāl al-Sanhūrī, to whom I owe almost all my knowledge about the Burhāniyya. For the warm welcome I received at the home of Shaykh Gamāl and his wife, Ḥāgga Mima, I am very grateful. I would also like to thank Kari Kloth for sending me a copy of her allegorical tale about her experiences with Shaykh Muḥammad ʿUthmān al-Burhānī. Laylā Shams al-Dīn Aḥmad and her husband, Mamdūḥ Abū 'l-ʿAzm, were extremely gracious and hospitable to me and my family, and Laylā patiently told me everything she could about Shaykh Maḥmūd Abū 'l-ʿAzm. I am grateful to ʿAmm Amīn for introducing me to so many Sufi friends, and escorting me to their homes. The members of Bayt ʿAbāṭa of the Rifāʿiyya Order welcomed me into their hearts and homes, and gave me my first glimpse of a moulid from the inside. The chapter on Coptic spirituality could not have been written without the assistance of Yūsuf Sulaymān Girgis, who took me to Coptic moulids, introduced me to Elisābāt Ibrāhīm, and selflessly transcribed the tapes I made at Mīt Damsīs. I am grateful to him and his wife Fifi for their hospitality. To Elisābāt and her household I also express my thanks for their openness and hospitality. My friend and fellow researcher Nelly van Doorn was also of invaluable assistance to me with her extensive knowledge of and experience with the Coptic Church. To all the friends who gave me their assistance and hospitality in Egypt, I owe a debt I doubt I can ever repay. With many of them I formed genuine friendships, and I think of them with great warmth. I never saw them solely as informants or research assistants but as people of enormous warmth and generous hearts. They trusted me to present their faith as they lived it. I only hope they will find that trust to have been well placed.

My husband, Steven Ladd, astonished the Egyptians by his willingness to leave his business in the States and accompany me to Egypt, and by his willingness to care for our baby in Cairo while I went out at night to moulids or other Sufi events and made sometimes extended trips outside Cairo. They saw him as an extraordinary man and helped me to appreciate him more. I thought it demanding enough to take him with me to Egypt for nine months and was astonished when he suggested that we remain another year. His resourcefulness in making that time productive for him is commendable, and his faith in the worthwhileness of my project was often critical.

Our three beautiful children have all been part of the making of this book. Rachel, who was less than nine months old when we went to Egypt in 1987 and more than two years old when we returned to the United States, became part of the story itself. Her sociability and fluency in Arabic were irresistible to the Egyptians as she accompanied me on many of my outings. I was called Umm Rāḥīl, "mother of Rachel." Rachel also suffered without understanding when I was frequently absent. I wish to acknowledge the price that she paid, and that I paid as well, by my absence from her and hope that ultimately she will be blessed by the baraka of her contact with so many saints. My pregnancy with Michael also became part of the story of our time there, and he returned with me to Egypt when he was a baby, where Shaykh ʿIzz, Shaykh Gamāl al-Sanhūrī, and Eliṣābāt Ibrāhīm all held him. While I worked on this book Deborah was also born, and I completed one chapter with her as a newborn on my lap. All three of them have sacrificed much time with their mother in order for me to finish this book. I wish to recognize that sacrifice and express my appreciation for their extraordinary flexibility. I hope that someday they might see it as worthwhile, and I look forward to spending more time with them in the days to come.

NOTE ON TRANSLITERATION

For rendering Arabic words into English letters, I have employed the transliteration used by the second edition of the *Encyclopaedia of Islam*, with the following exceptions: *j* for the letter ج, and *q* for the letter ق. In most cases I have retained standard rather than colloquial transliteration—for example, *dhikr* instead of *zikr*. Only when the colloquial version of a word differed considerably from the classical, e.g., *gallābiyya, sīdī,* and *moulid,* have I followed the colloquial pronunciation in transliteration. Personal names and place names have usually been transliterated according to the system here explained, the exceptions being names and places of international fame, such as Gamal Abdul Nasser, Cairo, and Khartoum, in which cases I used the more familiar variants. Arabic words have been italicized unless they appear in the English dictionary or have become so well incorporated into the text that they no longer seem foreign. I have tried to keep untranslated foreign words to a minimum in order to make the reading easier for those who do not know Arabic.

SUFISM, MYSTICS, AND SAINTS IN MODERN EGYPT

CHAPTER 1

Sufism in an Age of Change

If a servant of God dies to his passions and the desires of his soul, and his desires follow the teachings of the Prophet, he is continually elevated in this world and in *barzakh* [where the spirits of the dead await the resurrection of the body] and in the next world. Acts of worship and good deeds become a pleasure and an honor for him, not an onerous duty. This is the true Sufi. . . . To the one whose journey to God is sound, God will reveal every abstruse secret in the two worlds. He will see the perfection and beauty of omnipotence in every manifest thing. He travels until he attains to witness, and at this point he will have no need of created things, [for he will be] in the Creator. But this does not mean that a servant reaches his Lord by himself, but God frees him from his self and consumes him in His essence, so that he sees nothing but his Lord. And so the words of God according to the Prophet are fulfilled: "For him whose bloodwit I am, there is no distinction between Me and him." And in a similar saying: "I become his hearing by which he hears, his sight by which he sees, his hand with which he strikes, and his leg with which he walks." In this way the unity of God is realized. Then God returns the servant to the world, by Him, for Him, in Him. He is no longer by his former self or for it or in it, for this self has perished by being taken by God.[1]

This definition of Sufism, or Islamic mysticism, spoken in a teaching by Shaykh Aḥmad Raḍwān of Luxor (d. 1967), might appear to belong to some golden age of sincerity and devotion in Sufism, not to the contemporary setting, where the stage seems to be set for a bitter struggle between rigid Islamic legalism and secular materialism. In fact, the very title of this book might bring a cynical smile to the lips of many who believe true Sufism, mysticism, and sainthood to be a thing of the past, not of modern Egypt. Although much Western scholarship has been devoted to Sufism, it has been almost entirely devoted to the great literary works that appeared before the sixteenth century. Many scholars have been quick to declare true Sufism dead in the contemporary world, having long ago succumbed to the degradation entailed by its popularization in the twelfth and thirteenth centuries, particularly through the cult of saints. Perhaps the noted scholar on Sufism A. J. Arberry put it best when he wrote,

It was inevitable, as soon as legends of miracles became attached to the names of the great mystics, that the credulous masses should applaud imposture more than true devotion; the cult of saints, against which orthodox Islam ineffectually protested, promoted ignorance and superstition, and confounded charlatanry with lofty speculation. To live scandalously, to act impudently, to speak unintelligibly—this was the easy highroad to fame, wealth and power. . . . Though the Sufi Orders continued—and in many countries continue—to hold the interest and allegiance of the ignorant masses, no man of education would care to speak in their favour.[2]

Arberry found it remarkable that "even in its death-throes," Sufism could produce a man of the caliber of ʿAbd al-Wahhāb al-Shaʿrānī (1493–1565).[3]

Another Englishman, L. P. Elwell-Sutton, wrote, "It could . . . be argued that Sufism no longer has a role to play. In both East and West it has travelled far from the spiritual sources out of which it grew, and has for the most part degenerated into a narrow, desiccated formalism."[4]

Western scholars have merely echoed the opinion of many Muslims, including some who were involved in the Sufi Orders. Even those who have defended Sufism from its critics, arguing that those who attacked Sufism were looking at the peelings and not the kernel, nonetheless felt that Sufism had degenerated from the pure discipline of its early years to a focus on its more popular outer trappings: moulids, miracles, legends, fables, and amulets.[5] A recent Egyptian scholar on Sufism in Egypt during the Ottoman period pinpointed the end of the period of Baḥrī Mamlūk rule (1403/4) as the time when Sufi centers, formerly the center of Islamic learning and piety, deteriorated into a movement of the masses, including many charlatans and illiterates, who were more interested in worldly gain than asceticism.[6]

Dr. Abū 'l-Wafā al-Ghunaymī al-Taftāzānī, head of the Sufi Orders today, commented in an interview, "I'm afraid to say there is a gap between the old Sufi tradition and the contemporary one. Most members of the Sufi Orders are not educated. They don't even know about Islam."[7]

Among the ordinary, even illiterate or semiliterate Sufis, there is sometimes also a sense of loss. A middle-aged housewife I visited rattled off the names of Sufi shaykhs she had known or heard of in earlier years who were, in her estimation, real shaykhs. "Real Sufi shaykhs don't exist anymore," she said. "What you see today are only the peelings." An old man gently corrected her: "There are real shaykhs today as well. But they are few."

However, it must be noted that the sense that Sufism has declined, that the age of true Sufism is a thing of the past, may be observed in the writings of earlier Sufis as well. The eleventh-century Sufi writer al-Hujwiri quotes an authority as saying, "Today Sufism is a name without a reality, but formerly it was a reality without a name." Hujwiri explains that in the Prophet's generation people in fact practiced Sufism, though the name did not exist, whereas "nowadays the pretence is known and the practice unknown."[8]

Another famous Sufi writer, whose treatise is perhaps the mostly widely used of all in Egypt, Abū 'l-Qāsim al-Qushayrī, writing in 1045/6, complained, "In our time only a trace of this group [i.e., the Sufis] remains."[9]

French scholar Michel Chodkiewicz comments, "Such complaints, which continue today, seem by their very existence to contradict themselves, although it is true that Sufism reached its peak at about the time of the martyrdom of Hallaj, who made the famous declaration 'I am the Truth' in 922 (A.H. 309)."[10]

It should be noted that Sunni Islam as a whole is marked by a nostalgia for the past and a perception that the generation of the Prophet Muhammad and his Companions represented the pinnacle of pure spirituality and morality for all humanity, and that each succeeding generation has marked a new step toward inevitable degradation, alleviated only by the coming of a "renewer" at the beginning of each century. This perception has bolstered more rigorous demands for a segregation of the sexes and for the veiling of women than what obtained during the life of the Prophet, on the logic that such precautions were unnecessary in that time, when hearts were pure, but have become a social necessity in later times of moral decline.[11]

The idea that true Sufism no longer exists has been vigorously disputed by Martin Lings, who wrote, "It has to be admitted that the semi-official verdict of Orientalism on latter century Sufism is mainly based on inadequate information. Sufism is by its nature secret, and it may take time for its depths to become manifest, whereas the scum rises at once to the surface." He notes that Arberry himself retreated from his earlier position (which from Lings's point of view marred an otherwise admirable work) when his attention was drawn to Shaykh Aḥmad al-ʿAlawī of Algeria, who died in 1934.[12]

But if genuine spiritual depth is occasionally ascribed to individual Sufi shaykhs, the general verdict on Sufism in modern Egypt, among both Western scholars and many Egyptians, is that its spirituality is decadent and its popularity on the decline. There can be no doubt that organized Sufism, represented in what are usually called the Sufi Orders (in Arabic, *al-ṭuruq al-ṣūfiyya*), has suffered a considerable decline in its political power and social role in the modern period. Sufism was perhaps the most important aspect of Muslim spirituality throughout the medieval period. Through the Sufi Orders, beginning in the twelfth century, Sufism became a mass movement, with its distinctive rituals and devotion to spiritual masters (shaykhs) and deceased saints. The Sufi Orders came to dominate popular religious life. In the cities, each trade guild had its patron saint and sponsoring Sufi Order. Sufi shaykhs were the most effective religious teachers of the masses and also functioned as healers, counselors, and writers of amulets for protection against evil spirits. In rural areas, entire villages and tribes became associated with particular saints and Orders. Many important Muslim politico-religious movements had their roots in Sufi Orders.[13] Sufism undergirded Muslim literature, ethics, popular religion, and intellectual life.

Combining intense personal relationships with ecstatic ritual, the Sufi Orders allowed ordinary, even illiterate Muslims access to a spiritual power and communal experience that granted new meaning to everyday Islamic ritual acts, and embraced participants in a circle of holy love and loyal obedience to a Sufi shaykh. The shaykh counseled his followers on matters both spiritual and mundane and was a carrier of baraka, a spiritual power that he derived from his spiritual teacher, and that teacher from another, and so on in an unbroken chain that went back to the Prophet Muhammad himself.

Because one of its main strengths is accommodating itself to local traditions and belief systems, Sufism has been instrumental in spreading Islam beyond the boundaries of conquest. Under the umbrella of Sufism, indigenous beliefs and practices have been incorporated into Islam. The saint cult is the most obvious point of accommodation, as many ancient local holy sites and visitation customs have been transformed into Islamic shrines and rituals.[14] Visiting tombs to appeal to the dead for intervention in worldly matters is an ancient Egyptian custom that has persisted among both Christians and Muslims in Egypt. On the other hand, this custom is widespread throughout Islamdom and cannot be seen as uniquely Egyptian. In Egypt, the saints' shrines are often maintained by the various Sufi Orders, who also handle the money that is collected in the offering boxes where visitors make contributions, perhaps in fulfillment of a vow for an answered prayer.

Criticism of popular Sufism precedes the modern period and is best represented in the writings of Ibn Taymiyya (d. 1328) and his student Ibn al-Qayyim al-Jawziyya (d. 1350). Despite their polemics against popular Sufi practices such as saint veneration and worship at tombs, they did not object to Sufism as a whole. Some aspects of popular Sufism were criticized even by learned Sufis in the medieval period: dabbling in the occult sciences, the use of music in religious ceremonies, and aspects of the *mawlid* (*moulid* in Egyptian pronunciation), or saint's day celebrations. The moulids, which were regarded as heretical innovations by some, were especially denounced for the mixing of men and women at these public festivals. The Malāmatiyya, a Sufi movement based on the premise that the highest virtue is to avoid seeking the praise of people by publicly performing reprehensible acts and avoiding religious ostentation, naturally invited public censure. Yet Sufism as a whole did not come under attack for such excesses.

The criticisms of medieval Muslims had no appreciable impact on the status of the Sufi Orders, but in the modern period the Sufi Orders suffered setbacks on many fronts. Some of these are related to changes in the social and economic structure—for example, the introduction of a new elite educated in a system based on Western secular models and of an urban economy based on modern industrial techniques and a pervasive government bureaucracy rather than the traditional trade guilds. These changes eroded the intellectual status of Sufism as well as the economic base of the Orders. A new military and intellectual elite was educated in schools introduced in the nineteenth century that emphasized mathematics and the sciences and taught in European languages. The newly emerging social and political elite derived its moral and spiritual values from Islam, but their intellectual outlook was largely secular and embraced the values of modernism derived from the European Enlightenment.

Bruce Lawrence defined modernism as "the search for individual autonomy driven by a set of socially encoded values emphasizing change over continuity; quantity over quality; efficient production, power and profit over sympathy for traditional values or vocations."[15] The modernist intellectual, epitomized by the modern university professor, should be "above creedal claims," aiming for "affective neutrality or dispassionate unconcern with the consequences of the truth."[16]

Such an intellectual stance undermines not only Sufism but Islam itself. For Muslims who wanted to rescue the place of Islam at the center of Egyptian social and political life, the responses to Western modernism have generally been either Islamic modernist or Islamic fundamentalist. Islamic modernism, epitomized in Egypt by the scholar Muḥammad ʿAbduh (d. 1905), aimed at the reform of the Islamic educational system headed by the University of al-Azhar in order to bridge the dangerous gap between Western-oriented intellectualism and Islamic tradition. If Islam did not provide the spiritual foundation of change, ʿAbduh argued, it would lack moral orientation, and the largely pious but ignorant masses of Muslims would be led by a secular intellectual elite driven merely by aspirations for scientific discovery, technological improvement, and the power and prestige that they bring. What was needed, he felt, was for Muslim religious scholars to reexamine the Qurʾan for its general moral principles and spirit and to reinterpret Islamic law in light of the moral thrust of the Qurʾan and the needs of modern society. Although ʿAbduh's efforts to reform al-Azhar did not succeed, he acquired enormous prestige among Egyptian intellectuals, and his impact on Muslim intellectuals in Egypt and other countries has been substantial, if often unacknowledged. It became accepted among many Muslim intellectuals that Islam was originally a dynamic, progressive religion that, if properly understood, would lead to social reform and progress rather than stagnation.[17]

The fundamentalist response to Western modernism was led in Egypt by the Muslim Brotherhood, founded by a lay schoolteacher, Ḥasan al-Bannā, in 1928. By 1948 it achieved a membership in Egypt of one million, with another half-million in other Arab countries. Other fundamentalist groups emerged in its wake, especially after the early 1970s, and by the 1990s fundamentalists (or "Islamists," as they like to be called) succeeded in shaping much of Egyptian public opinion. Fundamentalists of all religions endorse and use modern technology and are, Lawrence argues, a product of the modern age, but they nonetheless staunchly oppose the ideology of modernism. In opposition to an ideology of individual autonomy, cultural relativism and progressive change, Islamic fundamentalism insists on rigid conformity and adherence to the literal meaning of Islamic legal texts. If Islamic law were faithfully applied in Egyptian social and political life, they argue, the moral problems that lie behind Egypt's vast economic, political, and social woes would be solved, and Islam would regain its position of world ascendancy. British interference in Egyptian politics before Nasser's 1952 "revolution" led many Egyptians to become suspicious of liberal parliamentary governments, and in the wake of the defeat of the hero of "Arab socialism" in the June 1967 war, an ideology based on Islam appeared to be the best option to many young people.

Sufism did not engineer a concerted response to the challenges of social change and Western modernist intellectualism. The reasons for this failure, says Gilsenan, lie partly in the structure of the Sufi Orders. With a leadership based on charisma that was difficult to institutionalize and with a tendency toward fission, the Sufi Orders lacked a common base on which to organize a response.[18] Islamic modernists and fundamentalists blamed the Sufi Orders for a lethargy born of excessive introspection and lack of concern with vital social issues. Furthermore, they blamed Sufism for much of the spiritual degradation and intellectual backwardness that were, in their opinion, at the root of Egypt's domination by the West.

At best, Sufism is deemed by most Muslim religious reformers and secularists as irrelevant to the processes of social change. At worst, it is considered a cause of the backwardness of modern Muslim society. At times Sufism is attacked as un-Qurʾanic and elitist, promoting passivity instead of social activism and denigrating the intellect.[19] Although many of the religious leaders of modern Egypt, including Muḥammad ʿAbduh, his disciple Rashīd Riḍā (d. 1935), and Ḥasan al-Bannā, received much of their early religious formation from Sufism, they criticized popular Sufism for practices they regarded as deviant. Maḥmūd Muḥammad Khiṭāb al-Subkī, after graduating from the Islamic University of al-Azhar in 1895, led one of the first campaigns to reform the Sufi Orders. He targeted practices like the solicitation of contributions from gullible adherents and the demonstration of baraka by eating fire, snakes, or glass. He called the Sufi Orders "a black spot spoiling the beauty of the Islamic religion, causing foreigners to have contempt for it."[20] This particular criticism reflects the concern many Muslims had in the late nineteenth and early twentieth centuries with Islam's image in the West.

It is perhaps this concern more than any other that has led to criticism directed against the Sufi ceremony of *dhikr*. Dhikr means "remembrance" or "recollection," and the Qurʾan urges Muslims to "remember God often," especially by means of His Most Beautiful Names. Sufi adepts make dhikr the focus of their spiritual life, both privately and communally. The communal dhikr usually includes music played on the lute, tambourine, flute, drum, and violin and is often accompanied by praises sung by a *munshid*. The participants in the dhikr chant or breathe one of the names of God and move to a common rhythm. As the participants are swept up in the movement of dhikr, the utterance of the names may be reduced to a grunt, and some participants may lose all consciousness of their surroundings and appear half-crazed. This performance of the dhikr has been intensely ridiculed by many Muslim reformers as epitomizing the ignorance, deviation, and introspection of Sufis at a time when Muslims needed to be on guard against the advance of secular ideologies. Rashīd Riḍā wrote that nothing remained of true Sufism but "noises and movements which they call dhikr, which every [genuine] Sufi keeps himself from" and criticized Sufis for the "religious glorification of the tombs of the shaykhs with the belief that they possess hidden power."[21]

Ḥasan al-Bannā's attitude toward Sufism was nuanced, distinguishing between contemporary Sufism and the "pure" Sufism of the time of the Prophet and his immediate successors. This Sufism, which consisted of the recollection of God (dhikr), asceticism, worship, and the intuitive and mystical perception and knowledge of God, was of "the core and essence of Islam." But the Sufi heritage was contaminated and corrupted by the philosophy of the ancient nations, and the Sufis divided the Muslims into "factions" by their various Orders.[22] Ultimately, Bannā emphasized a more activist approach to Islam, exemplified by a focus on jihad, whereas Sufism's more inward focus rendered it irrelevant in a changing society. Bannā's followers did not imitate his appreciation of the finer aspects of Sufism but felt that the very origin and teachings of Sufism were un-Islamic.

Some groups, such as Jamāʿat Anṣār al-Sunna 'l-Muḥammadiyya, have made Sufi ideas and practices a particular target of their religious reform. A contemporary preacher, Dr. Muḥammad Gamīl Ghāzī, formerly of that group and later head of Jamāʿat al-Tawhīd in the Cairo suburb of Zaytūn, denounced Sufism as a whole as un-Islamic and labeled Sufis as "*qubūrīs*"—worshippers of tombs—which, he said, is pure *kufr* (unbelief).[23] There is no shortage of books that attack Sufism, especially as embodied in the ideas of the famous mystic, Ibn ʿArabī (d. 1240), whose works are occasionally banned in Egypt.[24]

In the first half of this century, the Egyptian government, influenced by the reformist movement headed by Muḥammad ʿAbduh and Rashīd Riḍā, tried to curb popular practices associated with the moulids. J. W. McPherson's book on the moulids, published in 1941, not only documents much information on many Egyptian moulids but also constitutes a plea against the puritanical legalism that would destroy what he regarded as popular joyous celebrations that in no way infringed on morals or religion.[25] Nasser's regime, however, evidently decided there were advantages to be gained by allowing such harmless expressions of piety. The number of moulids for which permits were granted substantially increased under his regime, and Gilsenan's description of the moulid of Sayyid Aḥmad al-Badawī (d. 1276) in Ṭanṭā in 1964 gives humorous evidence of the prominence of the Arab Socialist Union and Nasserist propaganda.[26] At the same time that Nasser's regime appeared to encourage a revival of Sufism, it sought to subordinate and control it, as it did all aspects of public religious life, by appointing a head over all the Orders sympathetic with its purposes, using the Orders for distributing propaganda, requiring a local Arab Socialist Union committee member to approve appointees to Sufi offices, and requiring permission from the Ministry of Religious Endowments for the staging of Sufi ceremonies in mosques.[27]

The government first established a Sufi Council (now the Supreme Council of Sufi Orders) in 1903, and the first official regulation regarding the Sufi Orders was approved in 1905. The second such draft document, made in 1976, reflects the concerns of the government and the educated elite to reform Sufism by suppressing all practices deemed deviant under Islamic law as they understood it. The goal was to promote a more intellectually enlightened and ethically oriented religion among the masses affiliated with the Sufi Orders, and to present Sufism to both Egyptians and Westerners in a manner that would in no way damage the reputation of Islam or allow deviation from its standards of reverence and solemnity. Law No. 118, issued on 9 September 1976, defines the goal of the Sufi Orders as "religious and spiritual education in accordance with the laws of the Islamic Sharīʿa, and to promote such by preaching, guidance, and organizing Sufi dhikr. . . . No members of the Sufi Orders may profess beliefs or perform deeds or hold a moulid or celebration of dhikr contrary to the rules of the Sharīʿa."

The responsibilities of the Supreme Council of Sufi Orders, as outlined in Law No. 118 and Executive Decree No. 54, issued on 30 January 1978, include supervising Sufi activities; recognizing new Orders; issuing resolutions warning against activities by any group or persons claiming to be part of the Sufi Orders but not officially registered; recognizing the appointment, punishment, or removal of shaykhs and their deputies; granting permits for moulids and Sufi processions; representing the Sufi Orders at international conferences; and setting up offices for the memorization of the Qur'an in Sufi centers and shrines. Besides the "shaykh of shaykhs" *(shaykh al-mashāyikh)*, who is president of the council, the council consists of ten elected members who are shaykhs of the Orders and sit for three-year terms; a representative of the Islamic University of al-Azhar chosen by the Rector of al-Azhar; a representative of the Ministry of Religious Endowments, chosen by the minister; a representative of the Ministry of the Interior, chosen by the minister; a representative of the Ministry of Culture, chosen by the minister; and a representative of the public security of the local government and the people's organizations, chosen by the minister. The "shaykh of shaykhs" is appointed by the President of the Republic from among those shaykhs elected to the council.

Among the qualifications stipulated for the shaykhs of the Orders is that they have excellent reading and writing abilities and that they know the basics of Islamic Law. They must be of good character and reputation, pious, and educated. Preference is given in the selection of a new shaykh to the eldest son of the deceased shaykh or some other close relative.

Everything pertaining to Sufi processions and celebrations must be done with sobriety, dignity, and reverence.[28] Law No.118 and Executive Decree No. 54 aim to present a blameless Sufism to a critical, educated Muslim public and demonstrates the degree of control the government has placed over the activities of the Sufi Orders.

Majallat al-taṣawwuf al-islāmī, the monthly magazine of the Supreme Council of Sufi Orders, published since 1979, is marked by a particular consciousness of the criticisms of Sufism and emphasizes its compliance with the Shari'a and the heritage Sufism shares with other aspects of Sunni Islam. It scrupulously avoids controversy, publishes information on general Islamic activities, interviews scholars from al-Azhar who also issue legal opinions in the magazine, and reproduces portions of the legal opinions of the popular Qur'an interpreter and television personality, Shaykh Muhammad Mutawalli al-Sha'rawi. At times the journal is constrained to defend Sufism against public accusations of being un-Islamic, but even then it does so with typical restraint. Dr. Abū 'l-Wafā al-Ghunaymī al-Taftāzānī, vice president and professor of philosophy at Cairo University and shaykh of the Ghunaymiyya Khalwatiyya Order, was a favored spokesman for official Sufism even before he assumed the position of "shaykh of shaykhs" in 1982. He emphasizes that the Qur'an and Sunna (the deeds and sayings of the Prophet) are the arbiter of all truth, and he quotes Abū 'l-Ḥasan al-Shādhilī (d. 1258), founder of an Order popular in Egypt, as saying that any personal illumination that contradicts these authoritative sources is to be rejected. Dr. Taftāzānī defines true Sufism as "the science of stations and states" in character and conduct and the purification of the soul in order to attain moral perfection.[29] Although this is certainly an essential aspect of Sufi tradition and a legitimate Sufi concern, he gives no hint that this purification of the soul is a preparation for a higher goal or a deeper experience, whereas traditionally it was just that: the purification of the soul was necessary to enable it to receive progressive and direct illumination from God, by which the Sufi would experience the annihilation of the separate ego and a new existence "in God." But public expression of these teachings exposes Sufism to criticism that it acknowledges a source of revelation other than the Qurʾan and that the Sufi has failed to distinguish between the Creator and His creation. Sufism as publicly expressed today reflects contemporary preoccupations with the Sharīʿa, ethics, and fidelity to the literal meaning of sacred texts. The Qurʾanic exegesis printed in *Majallat al-taṣawwuf al-islāmī* has nothing to distinguish it from any other Qurʾanic exegesis. Dr. Taftāzānī justifies this emphasis by the fact that the majority of the members of the Orders lack a basic knowledge of Islam itself, which must take priority. To go directly to mystical illumination without grounding first in the Shariʿa is acknowledged by most Sufis as dangerous, promoting contempt for religious obligations in the name of knowledge of a higher truth. Significantly, an Institute of Sufi Studies founded in 1981 by the Supreme Council of Sufi Orders to enhance the academic knowledge of Sufi shaykhs emphasizes Islamic law, standard Qurʾan interpretation, and Islamic history as much as specifically Sufi areas of study. The goal is to train a group of shaykhs to propagate Sufism in a sound manner within their Orders. The two-month course attracts about twenty to twenty-five shaykhs at a time.[30]

But it is precisely the appearance of being the same as all other aspects of Islam that may be a problem for Sufism. For if Sufism has nothing different to offer, why join a movement associated in the minds of so many with medievalism, ignorance, and backwardness? Michael Gilsenan analyzed the position and ideology of the Sufi Orders in modern Egypt in his 1967 article, "Some Factors in the Decline of the Sufi Orders in Modern Egypt," and made the startling comment that there is nothing that distinguishes Sufism in Egypt today from any other aspect of Islam. In his study of the Ḥāmidiyya Shādhiliyya Order, which he wrongly labels "the only Order in modern Egypt which has succeeded, in however limited a way, in expanding its membership and activities,"[31] he chronicles the steady decline of Sufism in modern Egypt. Although he credits the founding shaykh of the Ḥāmidiyya Shādhiliyya with unusual foresight in establishing a solid organization, he ultimately faults him for choosing to organize a religious movement along such traditional lines that were bound to decline in significance and that appealed only to the traditional classes. He contrasts the moderate success of this order with that of the most famous religious movement of modern Egypt, the Muslim Brotherhood, which at its heyday in 1948 claimed one million adherents in Egypt.[32]

When I went to Egypt in 1980–81 to study the religious life of Muslim women in Egypt, at first I found much to confirm Gilsenan's perspective. I attended weekly women's meetings held by a popular voluntary association, al-ʿAshira 'l-Muḥammadiyya, founded in 1930 by Muḥammad Zakī Ibrāhīm, a well-known Sufi shaykh who has close contacts with the Azhar establishment and insists on close adherence to the Shariʿa. The only real evidence of the group's link with Sufi tradition was the shaykh's outspoken defense of the visitation of saints' tombs. There was nothing in the group's teachings that could really be called mystical, and the group's attractiveness to the educated and well-to-do and its friendly relations with non-Sufi Islamic organizations appeared to reflect its loose ties with Sufi tradition. This was evidenced by the shaykh's denunciation of the use of music in dhikr and his insistence that there is no distinction between the Shari'a, God's will as revealed in the Qur'an and embodied in law, and the *ḥaqīqa,* which in traditional Sufi understanding is the Truth that is the essence of the Sufi's experience, transcending the letter of revelation and constituting its true meaning. This has been a major point of controversy among Sufi shaykhs and the ulama: although many eminent ulama have also been Sufi shaykhs, their different spheres of authority represent the conflict between glorification of the revealed text and mystical experience, which allows the Sufi to "taste" what is beyond the letter of revealed scripture. Shaykh Muḥammad Zakī strove to convince the critics of Sufism that the distinction between these sources of authority did not entail real conflict; the mystically revealed, transcendent Truth of the Sufis was none other than the truth of revelation. He denied that Sufism was somehow removed from the concerns of daily life—and thereby irrelevant to the problems of society—and said that Sufism grapples with society's most crucial issues. The Order's celebration of the Prophet's birthday featured a speech by Dr. Taftāzānī, whose efforts to purify Sufism received high praise from the shaykh. This did not, however, prevent Shaykh Muḥammad Zakī from instructing some of his young men to raise responsive chants of "May God bless him [the Prophet] and grant him peace" and "there is no god but Allah" during Dr. Taftāzānī's speech at the Order's celebration of the birthday of the Prophet, in order to force him to keep it short!

However, further contacts with Sufis, first in 1981 and much more extensively from 1987 to 1989, led me to conclude that observations on the decline of Sufism and the absence of true mysticism in modern Egypt, while based on some genuine facts, also suffer from misunderstandings and at best only a superficial knowledge of Sufism in Egypt today. From October 1987 through April 1989, I spent a great deal of time among Sufis of a number of different Orders and spiritual teachers. Many of them were ordinary men and women who held regular jobs, and whom I visited in their homes to talk about Sufism and their personal experiences. Others were entirely devoted to the Sufi way, and their lives revolved around dhikr, worship, and the circuit of moulids. I attended Sufi meetings and interviewed a number of shaykhs, but my single most significant contact was with a Shādhilī shaykh who took me on as a quasi disciple and spent countless hours teaching me, allowing me to accompany him and his disciples on their travels, introducing me to other shaykhs and Sufis all over Egypt, and allowing me to have an unusual glimpse into the inner life of contemporary Egyptian Sufism. In this very different context, I met a disciple of Muḥammad Zakī Ibrāhīm and was shown a booklet entitled "Keys to Nearness [to God]," containing a summary of the shaykh's life that emphasized his possession of esoteric knowledge *(ʿilm al-bāṭin)*. That this aspect of his spirituality should be emphasized only within his inner circle is entirely compatible with Sufi tradition, which endorses a gradation of instruction ranging from the strictly Sharīʿa-based teachings for newcomers and outsiders to the secrets of gnosis for a close circle of disciples. My experiences with Egyptian Sufis led me to conclude that there is far more depth and vitality to Sufism in Egypt than Western scholarship suggests.

MEMBERSHIP OF THE SUFI ORDERS

Gilsenan notes in his book, *Saint and Sufi in Modern Egypt*, published in 1973 and based on research conducted in 1965–66, that although there were still some sixty Sufi Orders in existence, the actual number of adherents in any real sense is only a very small percentage of the population.[33] He contrasts this with the unsubstantiated statement of J. Heyworth-Dunne that in the eighteenth century virtually every Muslim man in Egypt belonged to at least one Sufi Order.[34] Although no reliable statistics are available on membership in the Sufi Orders, a few observations concerning estimations of the vitality of Sufism in contemporary society may be made.

First, the number of Orders has continued to increase since the time of Gilsenan's writing, as it has continuously since the beginning of this century. Seventy-three Orders were registered with the Supreme Council of Sufi Orders in 1989. However, the number of Orders is not in itself an indication of the number of adherents because the Orders vary greatly in the number of their members and because new Orders may arise as easily through the fission of old Orders as through the appearance of a new charismatic leader.

Second, the Sufi Council's estimate of the membership in the registered Orders, three to five million, is in itself a significant percentage of the population, even in Egypt, which in 1989 had an estimated population of fifty-six million. Furthermore, Dr. Taftāzānī and other shaykhs assured me that in the present atmosphere of religious awakening and social upheaval, many well-educated people have turned to the relatively safe alternative of Sufism rather than the more politically charged Islamic associations. Not only are the numbers in Sufi Orders growing in the city, said Dr. Taftāzānī, there is not a single Egyptian village that lacks a large number of men in the Sufi Orders.[35]

But the figure of three to five million, already extremely speculative, is no indication at all of the number of adherents to Sufism in Egypt, for it includes only men—women are denied official membership in the Orders, although they do take oaths from shaykhs and participate in many Sufi activities—and also excludes the vast number of Sufis who are not official members of a registered Order. The assumption that Sufism in Egypt is limited to the officially registered Orders is a gross error. The bifurcation of recognized and unrecognized Orders, according to Fred de Jong, dates from the early nineteenth century.[36] The most outstanding recent example of an unregistered Order is the Burhāniyya, which in 1976 conducted a census of its own membership in Egypt and arrived at a figure of three million, three times as many as the Muslim Brotherhood claimed in their heyday. Even if we allow for the possibility of exaggeration, the fact that this Order, which suffered a government campaign against it and was denied official recognition, attracted such a large membership outside the rubric of official Sufism should give us pause before we draw conclusions regarding the vitality of Sufism in modern Egyptian society. Beyond the existence of the Orders, registered or unregistered, some of the most important, well-known, and influential shaykhs of modern Egypt never founded a named Order, yet they drew disciples from all over Egypt and outside Egypt, and their teachings are perpetuated by disciples who have now become shaykhs in their own right. The personalities featured in chapter 9 of this book are all of this type, although I did not specifically look for saints who were outside the registered Orders.

In fact, many Sufis I met openly derided the Supreme Council of Sufi Orders, particularly those members who claimed expertise in Sufism but who lacked, in their opinion, true spiritual experience. Many expressed the opinion that true Sufism was really to be found outside the registered Orders. Some shaykhs felt that registration brought nothing but a morass of bureaucratic procedures and limitations on shaykhs, who have no need of any link with the government whatsoever. While no one can deny that the Sufi Orders have suffered a considerable decline in their political influence and social prominence in the new social and economic order, such comments call into question the idea that political prominence is an advantage for the Sufi Orders or that the lack of overt participation in the political process signifies a decline in Sufism itself. In its origins, Sufism was at least partially a withdrawal from the political and materialistic concerns of the Islamic Empire under the Umayyads. One might argue that the political prominence of the Sufi Orders under the Ottoman Empire represents a perversion of Sufism. If Sufism's popularization in the thirteenth century is commonly associated with its degradation, corruption, and lack of purity, can the retreat of Sufism from politics and visibility actually point to its revitalization as a true spiritual movement? Sufism has always emphasized the reform and spiritual elevation of the individual, and its influence on society has been through charismatic and reformed individuals rather than through the exercise of political power. It is interesting to note that it is precisely Shaykh Aḥmad Raḍwān's links with Gamal Abdul Nasser that have led some Sufis to criticize him (see chapter 9).

Finally, the issue of multiple membership in the Orders must be addressed. If this is the extremely widespread phenomenon claimed by Gilsenan,[37] then the estimates of membership in Sufi Orders are made yet less reliable because what is counted as two men may in fact be one man who has joined two Orders. However, it is questionable whether multiple membership is as common as presumed.

Although association with more than one shaykh is extremely common, actual membership, as represented by the giving of an oath to a shaykh, should only be to a single Order. When I asked Sufis about multiple membership, I was told repeatedly that it is extremely rare (some even said nonexistent) and basically wrong. No shaykh should administer an oath to anyone who has given an oath to another shaykh, unless that person renounce the former oath. The *awrād*, or daily prayers of the Sufi, are recited only by permission of the shaykh, and, in theory, it is not permissible to recite the awrad of more than one shaykh at a time.

It is interesting, in this regard, to note that Ibn ʿArabī, the thirteenth-century mystic, wrote, "A disciple cannot have more than one shaykh who guides him *(shaykh tarbiyya)*, any more than one can be burdened with the laws of two prophets or a wife can have two husbands, though he may keep the company of as many shaykhs as he likes. This is called 'the companionship of blessing' *(ṣuḥbat al-baraka)*, which is insufficient to produce a man in the way of God. The sanctity [of the shaykh-disciple relationship] is the foundation of [spiritual] prosperity."[38]

Although it is extremely common for spiritual seekers to take whatever benefit they can by attending the teaching sessions of numerous shaykhs—and indeed Sufis often speak of having a "spiritual mother" or "spiritual father" besides the shaykh to whom they gave their oath—there should be only one guiding shaykh to whom each disciple gives an oath. Many Sufis maintain some contact with a shaykh to receive baraka, but this too is quite different from a true shaykh-disciple relationship, which will be described in chapter 10.

THE PLACE OF SUFIS IN EGYPTIAN SOCIETY

Although there is no doubt that Sufism is marginal to the modernization process and has little impact on the political and intellectual life of the nation, this does not mean that Sufis themselves exist on the margins of society. Although they share a worldview that is distinct from modernism, a worldview that enables them to form a subculture within Egyptian society, they are nonetheless neither separated nor alienated from that society. Their differences with the ideology of modernism are not expressed as open or defiant opposition, like that of Muslim fundamentalists. They share in the life of modern Egypt and generally approve of government policies. They generally enter the educational system in a manner similar to others of their social class, whichever social class that may be, and pursue the same careers as other Egyptians. It is true that wholehearted devotion to the Sufi way of life may interfere with such activities, but most manage to live the Sufi way while very much participating in the life of the nation.

The stereotypical Sufi is poor, and the Sufi way of life undoubtedly finds its largest number of adherents not among the new educated elite but among the more traditional classes, in rural areas, in provincial towns, and among the urban poor. Such people may be marginalized from the centers of power and prestige, but they are not marginal to Egyptian society itself; they form its very core. It is for this reason that Sufism should not be dismissed merely because its presence is undetectable on the political scene. Neither should the fact that the majority of Sufis belong to fairly traditional sectors of society (as do the majority of Egyptians) lead one to assume that Sufism is unattractive to the wealthy, well-educated, and powerful. I encountered many Sufis who were not only wealthy and well-educated but politically well-placed as well.

Can the Sufi Orders attract new adherents from the new middle class of modern-educated Egyptians, or are such educated Sufis merely holding on to a family tradition that will ultimately die out? When I asked a representative of the Burhāniyya whether, during their phenomenal expansion in the 1970s, they drew their members from those with or without a background in Sufism, he insisted that they had nothing to do with those who had previous contact with Sufism, certainly not people who had given their oaths to a shaykh. The goal of the Order was to reach those who had "apostated from Islam"—that is, the Westernized segments of the population—and had no understanding of Sufism whatsoever. The Burhāniyya's ability to attract socially ascendant and prominent individuals was one of the hallmarks of its success.

Some of Sufism's new success in attracting such people may be credited to the Sufi Orders' self-reform: providing instruction in the Sharīʿa as well as in Sufism, and emphasizing orderliness, sobriety, and propriety. Many Sufis distinguish true Sufism, which they claim to propagate, from *darwasha,* dervishism, which calls to mind images of dirty, half-crazed, ignorant beggars indulging in frenzied dances under the guise of dhikr and improper behavior of all kinds. The Muḥammadiyya Shādhiliyya Order, which prohibits musical instruments in its dhikr and performs its dhikr in a highly coordinated, well-ordered fashion, defines itself explicitly as intended for the elite of society, not the masses.[39] The Ḥāmidiyya Shādhiliyya has a written charter that prohibits emotional displays, musical instruments, unintelligible sounds, or the presence of women or babies during group dhikr.[40] Both Orders explicitly prohibit beliefs or sayings that would cast doubt on the orthodoxy of their members. Members of the Jāzūliyya Ḥusayniyya Shādhiliyya Order take pride that their tent at the moulids is cleaner and more organized than others, that their dhikrs are orderly and reverent, and that the majority of those who come are well-educated and upper middle-class, though not necessarily very wealthy. Yet in many ways this Order, like the Burhāniyya, is extremely traditional, both in doctrine and in practices. The phenomenal success of the Burhāniyya will be examined in chapter 10, but it alone calls into question the notion that an Order must be "reformed" and antitraditional in order to attract the educated elements of society.

In short, despite the fact that there are Egyptians who have never heard of the Sufi Orders and have never been to moulids, assumptions of the marginality of the Orders and their activities in contemporary Egypt should be reexamined. I am inclined to agree with Nicolaas Biegman, who, in his recent book on moulids, saints, and Sufis in Egypt, first describes this as "a world apart, which can easily be missed by those who find themselves in the top levels of society, and by foreigners who do not know the language," but then corrects himself by saying, "perhaps it is the upper-crust and the foreigners who are the world apart, for what is described here is nothing short of a mass phenomenon."[41] The moulids are popular festivals attracting up to a million pilgrims apiece, and Sufi shaykhs are often highly respected members of society, functioning as counselors, healers, and mediators in disputes. Some hold respectable upper- and middle-class credentials—Sayyid ʿUways, writing in 1980, mentioned two major generals, three holders of doctorates, a former ambassador, and a public administrator among the shaykhs of the Orders[42]—but regardless of such factors, their social influence is undeniable though impossible to calculate. In a private conversation, one shaykh estimated that about 50 percent of Egyptian society had some connection with the Sufi Orders. Although such a statement is impossible to verify, it is certainly safe to conclude that Sufism's social impact goes well beyond the three to five million members of the registered Orders.

This said, it is nonetheless true that Sufism exists at a number of levels of commitment, and the core of shaykhs and their committed disciples do feel that they are a society apart from Egyptian society, at the same time as they participate in it. They form a subculture with their own distinctive norms, values, language, and behaviors.

WHAT SUFISM MEANS TODAY

Not all members of the Orders have equal awareness of their distinctiveness from the surrounding society, and even the term *Sufism* (in Arabic, *taṣawwuf*) is not intelligible to everyone. One illiterate young man denied that he was a "Sufi," although he showed me his card identifying him as a member of "the Rifāʿī Islamic charitable association." He had never heard of the term *taṣawwuf* and did not know what I meant by the Sufi Orders, although he clearly belonged to the Rifāʿiyya, one of the largest Orders in Egypt, particularly popular with the lower classes. One complicating factor is the popular definition of *taṣawwuf* as "extremism." Although this is certainly owing to a misunderstanding of the term, it should be noted that among the lower classes, both Sunnis and Shiʿa—terms that normally refer to the two major divisions of Muslims worldwide—are denounced as militant Islamic extremists, although Egypt's Muslims are all Sunnis. Because "Shiʿa" popularly connotes the Iranian revolution, widely condemned by Egyptians for its violence, and "Sunnis" connotes members of the "Islamic associations" responsible for the politicization of Islam, its propagation as rigid legalism among young people, and such infamous deeds as the assassination of Sadat, both terms connote fanaticism and extremism to the humbler classes of society. *Taṣawwuf* is sometimes interpreted as "being religious," which in the contemporary setting often has political overtones, although Sufism is mostly apolitical. So it was that an illiterate young woman, who was very deeply involved in Sufism, nonetheless mistakenly defined her "Islamist" brother as "*mutaṣawwif*," which properly is a term applied to someone aspiring to be a Sufi.

But if such misunderstandings persist among some, but not all, illiterate members of society, there were still plenty of Sufis who provided me with an answer to my constant query, "What is Sufism?" In light of the efforts of reformers to redefine Sufism simply as ethics, and therefore to dilute its illuminationist aspects, I wondered how ordinary Sufis today would respond to this question.[43]

The most frequent emphasis in the answers I received was indeed on ethics and the purification of the soul. Some respondents were clearly conscious of attacks on Sufism as un-Islamic and emphasized its orthodoxy. One shaykh said, "Sufism is based on the same source as the Sharīʿa;[44] it comes from the heart of Islam itself." A woman who headed a women's Sufi group replied, "Sufism is obedience to God and the Messenger and those in authority," echoing the famous Qurʾanic verse, "Obey God and obey the Messenger and those in authority among you" (4:59). She interpreted "those in authority" as the guiding shaykh.

On the walls of the Jāzūliyya Ḥusayniyya Shādhiliyya's regular meeting tent in a Cairo cemetery hang many sayings designed to instruct those who might entertain false ideas about Sufism: "Sufism is religion without heretical innovation *(bidʿa),* work without laziness, a soul without lust and a heart without anxiety." "Our Way is not by (intellectual) proofs, but it is patience in work and certainty *(yaqīn)* in love." "The servant cannot come to his Lord with any lust or selfish thought." "Sufism is the education of the soul and its training according to the sound ethics brought by the Sharīʿa." "Don't consider love easy; it requires renunciation." Various disciples of the Order gave speeches during a meeting that praised the way Sufism was taught by the Order: it includes work in the world and is not escapism, as so many claim; it encourages the use of the mind rather than neglecting it.

But many who emphasize Sufism's esoteric aspects also hold that the essence of Sufism is morals, self-denial, and the attainment of purity. Shaykh Muḥammad Raḍwān, son of Shaykh Aḥmad Raḍwān (d. 1967), told me that the term *Sufism* comes from an Arabic root meaning "purity"[45] and involves sincere devotion to God, doing everything for the sake of God, desiring his face. The ulama fall short of the Sufis, he said, for they act out of desire for paradise, but the Sufis act purely for the sake of God. This purification of the soul is the key to the real distinctiveness of Sufi teaching, because when Sufis purify themselves, they receive inspiration and revelation of the secrets of God.

In response to my question about the essence of Sufism, a Shādhilī shaykh in Cairo said, "When a person surrenders *(yuslim)* himself to God, he chooses by his will, with all his strength, to be in harmony with the universe." This response links the act of self-surrender, which is the very meaning of the word *Islam,* with a mystical regard for harmony with the universe, which might seem at first blush to be almost Hindu. However, it is also quite Qurʿanic, for according to the Qurʿan, all of the universe is naturally "muslim," that is, in submission to God, with the exception of humans and jinn. The linking of the will of the individual to submission to God is unique to them; the message of the prophets is therefore directed only to them. The one who is Muslim is indeed in harmony with all of nature, which is muslim.

Regarding the essence of Sufism, a Shādhilī shaykh from the province of Asyūṭ said, "The ulama have collected more than two thousand definitions of Sufism, but they all come down to one thing: the servant's purification of his heart with his Lord. He purifies his outer and inner aspects. Purification of the heart from defects. . . . The Sufi empties his heart and remains for his Lord. It begins with repentance. Any Order, whether Rifāʿī, Shādhilī, or Mīrghanī. Just as the different schools of Islamic law rely on the same principle, so do the different Orders rely on the same foundation. And the end is gnosis."

Some respondents, though seldom those in the rank of shaykh, gave me answers that defined Sufism as sincere worship of God. Conscious, perhaps, of the increasing tendency to wear one's religiosity as a badge, a middle-aged housewife said, "Sufism is worshipping God in secret, not for show. It is sincere worship." One young woman doctor, in a departure from the typical answers that defined Sufism as a lifestyle, reflected the usually transitory nature of genuine human sincerity and spiritual awareness when she said, "Sufism is a phase in the devotional life, a moment when the world ceases to have any meaning, and there is nothing but God."

Another broad category of response emphasized that Sufism is love. Sometimes the focus of love was God, but, as one man explained to a potential Sufi initiate, right behavior and love for the brethren are also a type of worship. Often the songs sung by Sufi singers *(munshidīn)* during dhikr reflect the pain and longing of love, and the object of love is left unspecified.[46] Other times the songs are clearly expressions of love for the Prophet and his family, and the centrality of love for the Prophet and his family in Sufi devotion was expressed by a number of respondents. One representative of a Rifāʿī *bayt* clearly defined Sufism as love for the family of the Prophet and said this is the love that purifies the soul. I elaborate on this point in chapter 3. This lifestyle of devotion to the family of the Prophet *(ahl al-bayt)* is expressed by attendance at the moulids of the members of his family who are buried in Cairo. The moulids of the *ahl al-bayt* and of other holy personages who are recognized as saints not only express Sufi devotion to the person for whom the moulid is celebrated, as well as for the Prophet, whom that person represents, but they also form a central aspect of Sufi sociability, which in itself is regarded as an expression of Sufi love.

CONTEMPORARY SUFISM AND CLASSICAL TEXTS

The link of contemporary Sufism with the past is maintained not only by passing on disciplines of recollection and meditation but also through the recitation of sayings and incidents from the lives of earlier Sufis. When Sufis gather, formally or informally, anecdotes, poetic lines, and pithy sayings form a large part of their teachings and conversations. Favorite anecdotes are often about local or personally known recently deceased or living saints, but sometimes the tales are about Sufis of earlier generations. Significantly, the most widely read Sufi books in Egypt today are books that are largely collections of brief biographies of Sufi saints. *Al-Ṭabaqāt al-kubrā* by the sixteenth-century Egyptian ʿAbd al-Wahhāb al-Shaʿrānī, *Ṭabaqāt al-ṣūfiyya* by Muḥammad ibn al-Ḥusayn al-Sulamī (d. 1021) of Nishapur, and *Al-Risāla 'l-Qushayriyya fī ʿilm al-taṣawwuf,* the first half of which is biographical, by his disciple Abū 'l-Qāsim ʿAbd al-Karīm al-Qushayrī (d. 1072), form the main core of Sufi literature that my respondents said they had read. A few had also read some of the biographical works written by the late Shaykh ʿAbd al-Ḥalīm Maḥmūd (d. 1978), former Rector of al-Azhar University, as well as his book on the Shādhilī Order and its founder.[47] The biographical genre continues to produce new works on the lives of the *ahl al-bayt* and the saints, and many recent saints are also included in books like Farīd Māhir's *Karāmāt al-awliyāʾ* (Miracles of the Saints) and Shaykh Fāris' *Min faḍāḥ'il wa khaṣāʾis āl al-bayt* (Some of the Virtues and Special Characteristics of the Family of the Prophet). This natural interest in the lives of holy personages is also promoted by the Supreme Council of Sufi Orders as part of its effort to transform the celebration of moulids from superstitious attachment to tomb visitation to reflection on the pious example of the person being celebrated.

Other Sufi works that were cited by respondents as influential in their lives included *Al-Ḥikam,* a book of Sufi aphorisms written by the Egyptian Shādhilī Ibn ʿAṭāʾ Allāh al-Sakandarī (d. 1309); *Iḥyāʾ ʿulūm al-dīn* by Abū Ḥāmid al-Ghazālī (d. 1111), a massive work typically absorbed selectively in pamphlet form; *Al-Ibrīz,* a collection of the teachings of the Moroccan saint, ʿAbd al-ʿAzīz al-Dabbāgh (d.

1717), by his disciple Aḥmad ibn al-Mubārak al-Sijilmāsī; *Al-Nafaḥāt al-ʿaliyya* by Abū 'l-Ḥasan al-Shādhilī (d. 1258); *Ādāb al-Darāwīsh* by Abū Najīb al-Suhrawardī (d. 1168); and *Qūt al-Qulūb* by Abū Ṭālib al-Makkī (d. 909), which Annemarie Schimmel calls "the first comprehensive manual of Sufism . . . a systematic treatise on the degrees of love, intimacy, and proximity."[48] More often than any of these famous classics, Sufis tend to rely on more narrowly distributed literature composed or distributed by their own shaykhs.

Sufis also share an interest in the broader Islamic literature. Many read the Qur'an daily and consider it and Ḥadīth, the narratives of the Prophet's sayings and deeds, the only books they need. Others share the general public enthusiasm for the Qur'anic interpretations of the former Minister of Religious Endowments turned television star, Shaykh Muḥammad Mutawallī al-Shaʿrāwī. Yet although the reformists have imposed a certain amount of textualism on the Sufis, most particularly noted in the public teachings of the Burhāniyya, in which sources, right down to the page numbers, are carefully noted,[49] it must be admitted that most Sufi teaching is orally transmitted, and the role of reading in the spiritual formation of the majority of members of the Sufi Orders is minimal.

This is well illustrated in an anecdote from the life of Shaykh ʿIzz al-Hawārī, the shaykh with whom I was most closely associated. He said, "For fifteen years I have not opened a book or read, because the words mix together and move, except one book: the glorious Qur'an. The one who caused this was Sīdī Abū 'l-Ḥasan al-Shādhilī. I was holding a book, and something happened, and I daydreamed. I saw Sīdī Abū 'l-Ḥasan standing before me with a stick of the Prophet and wearing a cloak and a red turban. And he tapped me with a stick and said, 'Don't be Sufi in speech, but be yourself a Sufi word.' "[50]

I do not know whether Shaykh ʿIzz was aware of a very similar tale that is told of his spiritual mentor: Abū 'l-Ḥasan al-Shādhilī asked his teacher about the greatest name of God, a traditional Sufi secret that is thought to be the key to all knowledge. His little son retorted: "You wanted to ask the shaykh about the greatest name of God. It is not important that you ask about the greatest name of God. What is important is that you yourself be the greatest name of God," that is, that the secret of God be deposited in his heart.[51]

The great Sufi saints all claimed to receive their knowledge not from books but directly from God. Such knowledge encompasses and goes well beyond what is written in books. In earlier years, Shaykh ʿIzz gave inspired teachings to his disciples, in which he was able to recite, word for word, from books he had never read. In this respect, the illiterate shaykh, although perhaps representing a diminution in the literary dominance of Sufism, follows the prototype of the illiterate Prophet, whose revealed scripture was considered miraculous at least partly because its human author was unlettered. The illiterate shaykh may, therefore, be superior in some respects to the well-read shaykh. Both the illiterate and the intellectual shaykhs command great respect among Sufis today, and each represents an acceptable model among the models of sainthood discussed in chapter 9 of this book.

The fact that Sufi teaching is transmitted in a mainly oral fashion should not make us lose sight of its connection with the literary tradition. I have frequently heard illiterate Sufis quote extensively from literary sources. Muslim society is still a society in which sacred texts are memorized from a young age. Virtually all praying Muslims have memorized at least some portion of the Qurʾan for use in their prayers, whether or not they can read. Many Muslims have memorized the entire Qurʾan as well as a large number of ḥadīths. Sufis are especially fond of biographical anecdotes, aphorisms, and poetry and are capable of reproducing these with often extraordinary precision. William A. Graham has argued that the oral life of texts plays an important role in the life of most religious communities and observes that even as the dissemination of printed Bibles has made the written text more available to people everywhere, its centrality in the daily lives of Christian communities enjoying such dissemination has diminished. Memorization and recitation of texts more effectively internalize their contents than printed dissemination.[52] The frequency with which texts are recited in private conversations and public teachings among the Sufis indicates the degree of internalization these texts have acquired among them.

CHAPTER 2

Among the Sufis

Experiences, Methods, and Approach

When I arrived in Egypt in September 1980 to research the religious lives of Muslim women in contemporary Egypt, on a grant from the American Research Center in Egypt,[1] I was not a stranger to that country. I had participated in an intensive advanced Arabic language program at the American University in Cairo for twelve months in 1975–76. I had sufficient language skills to move immediately into my research. For that project, I aimed at the broadest possible spectrum of Islamic religious activities for women. I spent a good deal of time with young, educated women who were part of the Islamist movement that was steadily gaining in momentum. I visited a number of Islamic voluntary associations either founded by women or providing services to women. I visited saints' shrines and observed activities there. And, of course, I was interested in whatever role women played in the Sufi Orders. But when I visited the headquarters of the Supreme Council of Sufi Orders opposite the Ḥusayn mosque, the assembled shaykhs gravely informed me, as they sipped their coffee and offered me tea (coffee, I learned, is considered too stimulating for a proper young woman to imbibe), that there were no women in the Sufi Orders. The prohibition against female membership was designed to preserve propriety and morality, they said, for the mixing of men and women is prohibited in Islam. Ironically, even as the various Islamist associations were maintaining sexual segregation among themselves by providing separate meetings and services for women, the Sufi Orders, traditionally more open to female participation than mosque-centered Islam, felt that the only way to maintain propriety and morality was to exclude women altogether. Dr. Taftāzānī at that time professed ignorance of the existence of any activities for women in the Orders.

Yet if women were not officially allowed into the Orders, they were nonetheless very much in evidence at the weekly dhikrs held at various saints' shrines around Cairo, especially at the dhikrs at the Fāṭima al-Nabawiyya shrine on Monday afternoons and the ʿAlī

Figure 1. Author observing dhikr at moulid of Shaykh Aḥmad al-Ṭayyib (d. 1956) on 9 November 1988. This dhikr was performed entirely by men in orderly rows, with responsive chanting and no instruments.

Zayn al-ʿĀbidīn shrine on Saturday afternoons. Later I discovered that an entire world of informal female participation and leadership exists in the Sufi Orders.

My research method, both in 1980–81 and again in 1987–89, depended mainly on personal observation and, to whatever extent was possible without either compromising my research or constituting a type of deception, personal participation. Although formal interviews had their place in my research, particularly when dealing with people in responsible positions, the variety of situations and people with which I dealt required considerable flexibility and adaptability on my part. Some questions that are readily comprehended and concisely answered by an educated respondent simply do not make sense to an illiterate respondent. A too-structured, pre-prepared set of questions risks imposing the interviewer's own priorities and perspective on the interviewee, whereas I aimed first of all to understand the worldview and perspective of my subjects. My questions invariably led to other discussions that had not been on my agenda but that reflected the concerns of my subjects far more than my own questions did. During my research in 1980–81, I felt annoyed at first by the frequent digressions on the disintegration of morals in Egypt or how difficult life was in Egypt these days, until finally it dawned on me how significant it was that these topics came up unsolicited in conversations again and again and were themselves an indication of something that perhaps lay at the root of the rise in interest in religion during the 1970s and 1980s.

On the other hand, the inadequacy of interviewing lies in the fact that interviewees express their ideal, or what they would like the interviewer to believe. Particularly on religious matters, educated Egyptians are extremely conscious of the need to make a moral, theological, or political point, to convince the foreigner of the superiority of the Islamic system or to claim that what they hold as a norm actually exists. The truthfulness of such statements can only be tested by direct observation. For example, during an informal interview in her home, one woman went on at length about how Islam promotes loving relationships, mutual kindness, and courtesy between a husband and wife and how this characterized her relationship with her husband, which she described as very peaceful. When her husband came home, however, it was not long before a dispute arose over finances, until finally the husband yelled, "Do we have to have a fight over this every night?" At that point, the wife looked at me self-consciously and composed a serene face. It is only by long-term acquaintance that these barriers of self-consciousness and deliberate presentation are partially overcome, until finally the researcher's presence is hardly noticed.

Participant observation goes a step beyond mere observation. It presumes that insofar as is possible, the observer will become a part of the society being observed. It means getting alongside a person, living in that person's environment, rather than just placing the person under a microscope, so to speak. In order to enter as unobtrusively as possible into the environment I wished to study, I adopted Islamic dress, covering my hair entirely with a scarf, wearing long sleeves, a high neckline, and long skirts. This facilitated my entry into mosques and shrines, often unnoticed. It also communicated a good deal of cultural understanding and acceptance to Egyptian Muslims. It is difficult for a Westerner to understand the extent to which morality, particularly a woman's morality, is judged by the way she dresses. My dress communicated to Muslims that I accepted their moral standards and was myself a moral woman. Since Egyptian impressions of Western morality are almost entirely negative, based on American television shows such as *Dallas, Knots Landing, Falcon Crest,* as well as a genre of Islamist literature designed to depict Western society in the most unflattering light in order to promote an Islamic social order, I had to be extremely conservative in my dress and behavior in order to counter the weight of assumptions about my morality.[2] In Cairo, where a sizable foreign community holds jobs in the academic and business community, my dress was outstanding enough; in the Luxor area, where millions of scantily clad tourists descend constantly to get a glimpse of the wonders of ancient Egypt, my dress stood in such sharp contrast to the other foreigners that the local people wondered how I had learned to be so moral. In either case, Muslims were greatly assured by my manner of dress and more readily accepted me as one of them.

Personal relations with Egyptians can be a surprisingly warm and intimate experience for a foreigner, for Egyptians are generally extremely hospitable and open to foreigners, regarding them as guests to be welcomed and honored. On the other hand, Egyptian hospitality can be an overwhelming experience. Egyptians freely advise each other, and their foreign guests, on what to do. Although they mean well, I found myself worrying whether I looked comfortable enough, knowing that if I did not, I would get scolded and told to rest. While traveling with a middle-aged Egyptian woman friend to her hometown of Ṭanṭā for the moulid of Sayyid Aḥmad al-Badawī, I stood up slightly before the train pulled into the station. It seemed as if the entire carload of people yelled at me at once to sit down and relax! When my friend's brother, an important official in the province, escorted us to the moulid, he was excessively worried about my comfort. I wanted to be out seeing Sufi activities, but instead we spent a long time sitting in a large tent the governorate had set up for the comfort and rest of the people. In Egypt, as in most Arab countries, offers of food must be either accepted or refused with much more vigor than seems gracious by Western standards. In their desire to be hospitable, Egyptians were constantly giving food to my baby daughter that I did not want her to eat, either because her diet would consist entirely of chocolate or because the food was likely to choke her or make her sick. The need to be ever-vigilant against such overtures (because the Egyptians seldom asked my permission to give her the food) added greatly to my stress level, which was also often exacerbated by unsolicited tidbits of advice and criticism on how I was raising my daughter.

Personal relationships in Egypt carry with them expectations that appear excessive to an American. Once welcomed into the bosom of a family, guests are expected to prove the reality of their friendship by returning again and again, bringing occasional gifts and not hastening to leave too soon. Especially during my research in 1980–81, when I was still single, families that had accepted me into their midst expected me to visit at least twice a week. They also tended to try to possess me somewhat, to claim me for themselves. Although I constantly disappointed them, because of time constraints and the difficulty and fatigue involved in traveling around Cairo, I nonetheless did make some attempt to maintain regular relationships with a few families that I decided really did have a claim on me or that made me feel particularly welcome. It was only after eight months of visits with one such family—rural immigrants who had settled in one of the newer slums that now concentrate large populations of poor immigrants from both the Delta and Upper Egypt on land that twenty-five years ago was still agricultural—that I discovered their connections with Sufism. ʿAmm Amīn, a very old and rather strange man who was a daily visitor at that apartment, became my first contact with the world of Sufism that exists just out of sight from most observers.

What a strange sight we were: a young American woman with this ancient man, almost blind with age, his right wing bone protruding, as he walked along carefully, but not unenergetically, with the aid of a walking stick. (Even very young men often use walking sticks in rural villages at night, in order to ward off the dogs.) ʿAmm Amīn was taking me to the home of Umm Fatḥī, his "spiritual mother." He explained that much of his time was spent visiting various Sufi friends. He hailed originally from the Upper Egyptian town of Jirjā. "The home of our lord Jesus," he said.[3]

"Is it?" I asked. "Was he there?" Many sites in Egypt claim to have been visited by the Holy Family during its flight to Egypt, and I thought that perhaps this was what he meant.

But he utterly confused me by replying, "He is still there."

"What do you mean?" I asked.

"Aren't you from your brother, and your parents from you? Where does *kashf* [mystical illumination] come from?"

"From God," I replied, still not comprehending.

But he went on about the oneness of spirits that transcends the boundaries of our individuality. Since there were those who personally knew Jesus in Jirjā, Jesus might still be said to be there, for his spirit was present. "This is something those whose vision is veiled *(al-ahl al-maḥjūb)* do not understand," he said.

I let the matter drop, because I was no doubt among those whose vision was veiled. Only years later, after much time spent with the Sufis, did I understand something of the communal nature of mystical experience in contemporary Egyptian Sufism, so that the focus—indeed, the very essence of mystical illumination—often lies in transcending the boundaries of individuality.[4]

That day spent with Umm Fatḥī and her spiritual sons was a genuine eye-opener. Simply by talking with them and listening to them, I discovered a type of mystical Sufism that cannot be discovered in the pages of *Majallat al-taṣawwuf al-islāmī.* Here were people who ranged from illiteracy to only modest education but who nonetheless were aware of the great early Sufi saints and quoted Sufi poetry allegedly composed by them. They openly defended such controversial Sufis as al-Ḥallāj (d. 922) and Ibn ʿArabi (d. 1240) and embraced a lifestyle that mocked the materialistic concerns and obsession with social status that characterized so many of their countrymen. Although they lauded the spread of education, they emphasized that no amount of book learning could substitute for divine illumination.

Tantalized by this brief glimpse of unofficial Sufism, I turned once again to ʿAmm Amīn when I returned to Egypt on a Fulbright grant in 1987, specifically to study the role of women in the Sufi Orders and the function of moulids in Sufi life. I came this time with husband and baby in tow, intending to stay only nine months, which was sufficient, I thought, for the rather limited project I had in mind and was about all I expected my husband to be willing to endure of residence in Egypt. ʿAmm Amīn was delighted by my new focus on Sufism and eagerly introduced me to various Sufis he knew, all very humble, even poverty-stricken, individuals, often ordinary housewives who nonetheless sometimes had extraordinary spiritual experiences. ʿAmm Amīn tended to exaggerate the spiritual insight and powers of his friends, but the experience was fascinating, for it revealed to me the world of miracles, visions, and mystical devotion hidden beneath the surface of ordinary lower-class life.

At the same time, I ventured out on my own to the various saints' shrines on their visiting days, hoping to talk to people there and make some valuable contacts. Some people, almost always extremely poor, regularly make the rounds of shrine visitation to the major shrines of the *ahl al-bayt* on their visiting days: Ḥusayn and Sayyida Zaynab, the grandson and granddaughter of the Prophet, on Fridays; ʿAlī Zayn al-ʿĀbidīn, Ḥusayn's son, on Saturdays; Sayyida Nafīsa, a great-great-granddaughter of the Prophet's other grandson, Ḥasan, on Sundays; and Fāṭima al-Nabawiyya, a daughter of Ḥusayn, on Mondays. At each shrine, there is a public *ḥaḍra*, or Sufi assembly of prayers and dhikr, usually after the *ʿaṣr* prayer in the midafternoon and often again in the evening. There were two dhikrs that took place concurrently in the square behind the Ḥusayn mosque and another within the mosque, each performed by different Sufi Orders, whereas the *ḥaḍra* at the Sayyida Zaynab shrine is a rather ad hoc affair performed without musical instruments by visitors on a crowded street adjacent to the mosque.[5] The *ḥaḍras* at the Zayn al-ʿĀbidīn, Sayyida Nafīsa, and Fāṭima al-Nabawiyya shrines, however, are all officiated by the same musical troupe, which accompanies the dhikr with music and praise singing. These are the main shrines of the *ahl al-bayt* in Cairo, and their shrines are regularly visited by crowds of the faithful.

Figure 2. Shaykh Ṣāwī, trustee of Bayt ʿAbāṭa, standing by the tomb of Shaykh Muḥammad ʿAbāṭa in 1989, in front of a drawing of Shaykh ʿAbāṭa (right, d. 1941) wearing braids during his period of *gazb*, and a photograph of his son, Shaykh Hāshim ʿAbāṭa (d. 1985).

The other days of the week belong to saints of varying degrees of eminence, none of whom draws the crowds of the *ahl al-bayt*. Tuesday is the visiting day of Abū 'l-Suʿūd, who particularly caters to women's fertility needs. Near his shrine, public *zār* (spirit possession) ceremonies take place, but no *ḥaḍra* takes place at this shrine.[6] Wednesday belongs to Shaykh Muḥammad Ḥasan ʿAbāṭa (d. 1941), patron saint of a branch of the Rifāʿiyya, and Thursday is the visiting day for Muhammad Demirdash, the sixteenth-century founder of the Demirdāshiyya Khalwatiyya Order.

In a 1976 article on Cairene shrine visitation, Fred de Jong recorded that ever increasing numbers of visitors and merchants went to the Shaykh ʿAbāta shrine on his visiting day.[7] I decided to visit the shrine, which did not appear to be particularly well known among visitors to other shrines. The shrine turned out to be a rather humble affair in the cemetery across a busy intersection from the mosque of Sayyida ʿĀʾisha, set off from the surrounding crumbling structures only by a tattered, threadbare black flag, the standard of the Rifāʿiyya. The interior of this small shrine was painted with crude Islamic designs and the names of Allah on all walls. There were three tombs inside: Shaykh ʿAbāṭa, his wife Zaynab, and his teacher, Shaykh Rīḥānī. Each of the sarcophagi was surrounded by a little green picket fence and draped with green silk, with old Qurʾans on top, and over each of the corners was a white silk handkerchief. Green is the color of the Prophet's family, and on the wall was an attestation from the Ministry of Religious Endowments that Shaykh ʿAbāṭa was a descendant of the Prophet. The name "ʿAbāṭa," which means "stupidity," was a nickname attached to him because of his foolishness during his years of *gazb* (a mental derangement induced by mystical revelation) at the end of his life.[8] The letter of attestation was addressed to Shaykh ʿAbāṭa's son, Shaykh Hāshim, in his capacity as head of the Qushayriyya Hāshimiyya Order. Shaykh Hāshim founded an independent Order after a disagreement with the Rifāʿiyya but later became reconciled, allowing his Order to be reincorporated into the Rifāʿiyya as a semi-autonomous branch, or *bayt*. The rosary of Shaykh ʿAbāṭa hung on the side of the tomb, and nearby were a drawing of the elder shaykh, wearing braids like a woman (during his periods of *gazb* he sometimes wore women's clothing), and a photograph of his son, Shaykh Hāshim, as a young man. Hāshim is buried nearby but not in the shrine itself.

Much to my surprise, only a handful of people were in attendance. No anonymity here: I was greeted with curiosity and enthusiasm by the small circle of devotees who belonged to Bayt ʿAbāṭa, and they quickly came to consider me one of their group. My attendance was expected every week, and as my presence was also observed at other shrines on their visiting days, it came to be expected that I was a regular shrine visitor and lover of the *ahl al-bayt,* as they were. Although I explained my project to them, they persisted in understanding me in these terms, seeing it as a miracle of the saint that I had been drawn to him all the way from America. They all belonged to the lower classes, and some of them were desperately poor. They knew each other very well, often pooled their meagre resources for various projects, shared meals, and visited each other. Many of them were illiterate, and only a few had much awareness of Sufi tradition. As an entrance into the world of Sufi mysticism they had little to offer, and they had few significant contacts beyond their small circle, but they did allow me to experience the world of moulids and shrine visitation from their point of view. During the moulid of Fāṭima al-Nabawiyya in November 1987, I spent many evenings viewing the moulid from where the women sat in their *khidma,* or hospitality tent, from which they dispensed meals to any and all visitors.

I learned that Shaykh Hāshim had died two years before and that the fortunes of Bayt ʿAbāṭa had since declined. Although the position of shaykh passed to Hashim ʿAbāṭa's son, Sayyid, he was only twenty-three years old at the time and clearly had little enthusiasm for the position. He went abroad to work as a confectioner, first in Jordan, then in Iraq, not because of any great economic opportunity there but simply to avoid having to spend most of his time taking the responsibilities of a shaykh. Bayt ʿAbāṭa shared many of the social characteristics of the very poor of Cairo: men and women were extremely informal with each other, even playfully hitting each other or slapping each other on the bottom, and loud arguments frequently erupted among members. Such arguing is commonly regarded as antithetical to Sufism, and some members told me that when Shaykh Hāshim was still alive, there were no fights. He had great charisma, they told me, and encouraged the women to join in the dhikr. "Since his death," said one woman, "I never join the dhikr anymore." The decline, both in numbers and morale, of Bayt ʿAbāṭa since the death of Shaykh Hāshim, is extremely common in Orders where adequate succession to a charismatic leader cannot be found.

Often, in my conversations with Sufis who did have personal spiritual experience and sufficient awareness to be able to articulate what Sufism meant to them, they were reluctant to speak. The question "What is Sufism?" was confusing to some, because the meaning of Sufism was too vast to answer in a succinct fashion. When I changed the question to "What is the essence of Sufism?" I sometimes heard the answer, "That is a secret," or "You would never be able to understand." Many Sufis feel keenly their separateness from the broader society, and the deep spiritual truths they believe they have experienced are secrets, not meant to be revealed to society at large, both because of the fear of persecution (one shaykh said, "If you say the truth openly, they will accuse you of unbelief") and because it is assumed that the truth must be experienced before it can be understood. The secretiveness of the Sufis obtains vis-à-vis fellow Egyptian Muslims; how much more with regard to a foreigner and non-Muslim!

It was ʿAmm Amīn who unexpectedly brought about the major breakthrough in my research. As we were on our way to visit a Sufi housewife, we passed by a new mosque, the interior of which was still incomplete. ʿAmm Amīn suggested, "Let's see if Shaykh ʿIzz is here." At that very moment Shaykh ʿIzz appeared at the door, a slim man in his midforties, wearing a turban on his head and a plain grey *gallābiyya* (robe). He immediately welcomed us in. Later I learned that ʿIzz regarded it as a sign of divine guidance and spiritual connection between us that he appeared at the door just as we were about to pass his mosque, that God Himself had sent him in order to meet me. Through all the vicissitudes in our relationship, he never failed to believe that God had ordained and planned it.

We were escorted through the mosque to a room off an area open to the sky. This area behind the mosque, I later learned, was called the *sāḥa,* was intended as a place of dhikr and hospitality, and was serviced by a kitchen. The small room in which we sat, Shaykh ʿIzz explained as we drank tea, would be set up as a bedroom and would serve as a place of Sufi retreat for fasting and meditation for those who wanted to see Khiḍr. Khiḍr, the prototype of the mystical teacher, is believed to have drunk from the fountain of eternal life. He is identified as the servant of God who, according to the Qurʾan, received special knowledge from God, and baffled Moses with his seemingly irrational and immoral acts that were performed at the command of God, by virtue of his higher wisdom (18:65–82). Throughout the history of Sufism, many mystics have claimed to have seen Khiḍr and to have been instructed by him. Shaykh ʿIzz claimed that Khiḍr had pointed out to him the place where he was to build his mosque, although the location had been a garbage dump. The mosque and *sāḥa* were intended as a place for people to come to pray and meditate or just to spend the night, if they needed a place to stay. "A service for the sake of God," he said. The construction was undertaken through his own funds and through private donations.

Shaykh ʿIzz is an extremely intelligent and articulate man. A former preacher in the army, he had been given early retirement when he began to be subject to divine inspiration that might lead him to say things inappropriate to say from a pulpit. Even in his own mosque he did not preach but hired a preacher appointed by the Ministry of Religious Endowments. After two months of trying to interview Sufis on their own experiences and the meaning of Sufism, I found ʿIzz extremely refreshing: direct, clear, sharp, and open.

Astonishingly so, in fact. I asked if he had read books in order to learn Sufism, and he told me the story of how Abū 'l-Ḥasan al-Shādhilī had commanded him not to say Sufi words but to be himself a Sufi word. Important knowledge, said ʿIzz, comes not with words but is without voice, letter, or speech. The eye sees, but there is another eye in the heart that has true vision *(baṣīra)*, whose knowledge comes from a manifestation in illumination *(ishrāq tajallī)* from God, just as rays from the sun make manifest the things that are visible to sight *(baṣar)*. The human mind is limited, he said. There are things it cannot know or embrace, but the human heart can know directly from God. The essence of Sufism, he said in answer to my question, is morals and self-denial. Morals concern only external behavior, but self-denial is the realization that the essence of man is spirit and that one should not be concerned with earthly things.

On ʿIzz spoke, erasing any doubt that I might yet have entertained that true Sufism still existed in Egypt. As if sensing my surprise at his openness, he explained that he usually did not talk about such deep things with people who visited him for the first time; usually he just talked about the rules for worship and other basics of Islam, but he sensed that I understood much and was ready to know these things. Months later he went much further, telling me that at that first encounter he had seen the lights of God descending upon me, and his spirit responded to this, so that he spoke to me openly and under inspiration *(ilhām)*.

I liked Shaykh ʿIzz personally. He impressed me as a very warm, unassuming person whose depths of spiritual understanding were communicated in very clear language. After talking for some time in the room at the *sāḥa*, he said, "Now that we have talked about spiritual things, let's go to the material ones." The three of us went and had dinner at his home nearby, where I met his wife, mother, sons, daughters, and sister. The atmosphere was warm and relaxed, and in the months to come I was to become a frequent visitor and friend to all of them.

In America we might say that Shaykh ʿIzz and I "hit it off" and think of it as no more than a stroke of luck for my research. From a Sufi perspective, however, it meant much more. Sufis believe that God gathered our spirits together on the day of the Primordial Covenant, when, according to the Qurʾan, He "drew forth from the children of Adam, from their loins, their descendants, and made them testify against themselves: 'Am I not your Lord?' they said, 'Yes, we testify.' Lest you say on the Day of Resurrection, 'We were heedless of this' " (7:171). The spirits were able to meet each other on that day, and a preformed affinity between two people is interpreted by the Sufis as a sign that their spirits had indeed met and liked each other on that day.

A shaykh and his disciple should always have such a preformed affinity; a natural mutual attraction is considered a prerequisite for a proper shaykh-disciple relationship. In this sense, ʿIzz and I conformed to the pattern that was expected of a shaykh and his disciple. Although I never became a true disciple of his—indeed, that was impossible without my conversion to Islam—ʿIzz came to hope and even expect that ultimately we would experience the spiritual connection that typifies a good shaykh-disciple relationship. Although ʿIzz believed that Muhammad was the only gateway to God, in contemporary Egyptian Sufism it is "annihilation" in the shaykh, effected through intense love and identification with the shaykh, that brings a person into the Prophet's presence. ʿIzz hoped this would occur with me, even without my conversion to Islam, because he believed that the realm of the spirit goes beyond the forms of official religion, and he believed my spirit was open to the spiritual realm.

Being a practical man, however, ʿIzz also checked with friends who worked in state security to see what information they had on me, to make sure his spiritual discernment was not incorrect. He told me about this only much later, when a friend in state security also let him listen to tapes they had made of one of our conversations. Although some of my questions had initially alarmed them, ʿIzz said, eventually they had decided I was harmless. In any case, he added, they were not really interested in me but in him.

ʿIzz also performed the prayer of *istikhāra,* seeking God's guidance and confirmation concerning me. After performing the ritual prayer and the formula of seeking guidance, he slept and had a "vision"—a dream—concerning me that to his mind confirmed that God had ordained our relationship.

The moulid of Abū 'l-ʿAlā' (Abul Ela) was coming up that week, and Shaykh ʿIzz offered to escort me. Moulids are extremely crowded all-night festivals that last anywhere from a few nights to two weeks. They require a good deal of physical endurance to push through the crushing crowds, particularly in the immediate vicinity of the shrines, and despite their religious significance they offer enough secular attractions to draw huge, unruly crowds. Most pertinent to me as a woman researcher, they draw entire caravans of young men out looking for a good time, and an unescorted woman is subjected to a frightening amount of sexual harassment. Few women attend the moulids unescorted, and many avoid them altogether, especially on the culminating, and most crowded, "great night" *(al-layla 'l-kabīra).* Until I met ʿIzz, I had been forced to attend moulids only in the daytime, although the activities take place chiefly at night, or else to confine myself to sitting in the *khidma* of Bayt ʿAbāṭa, where my perspective on the activities and people at the moulid was necessarily very restricted. Shaykh ʿIzz offered me the opportunity to wander freely over the entire grounds of the moulids with him and his disciples, visiting numerous hospitality tents (*khidamāt,* the plural of *khidma*) and meeting Sufis of many different Orders from all over Egypt. He told me, "People will respect you to the extent that they respect the man who is with you." Much as I might regret this state of affairs, I nonetheless gratefully accepted the opportunities ʿIzz's presence offered me. By virtue of my relationship with ʿIzz, I made many very valuable contacts. Because ʿIzz's funds were concentrated on building his mosque and *sāḥa,* he did not host a *khidma* himself at the moulids but wandered from *khidma* to *khidma,* greeting old acquaintances and making new ones. He was still a relatively young man, considered very young for a shaykh, and was still free to visit other shaykhs in their *khidamāt.* The older, more established shaykhs tended to stay in one place and receive visitors. In the moulid environment, ʿIzz often shone. It was not unusual for him to take over a *khidma* he was visiting, transforming it into an arena for teaching, holding his audience spellbound by an undeniable charisma. On one memorable occasion, he taught for five hours to a group that wandered in to listen. By the end of that time, some of the young men were rubbing his legs, which had fallen asleep from sitting on the ground all that time, and others hastened to bring him water or to escort us through the moulid crowds, beating a path before us.

ʿIzz told me that he knew most of the shaykhs in Egypt and would be able to help me a great deal in my book on Sufism. Although he no doubt exaggerated somewhat the extent of his contacts, he nonetheless did prove an invaluable resource, so invaluable, in fact, that my husband and I decided to remain in Egypt an extra year on our own resources, so I could broaden the scope of my research to a comprehensive study of contemporary Egyptian Sufism. After the first few months of knowing ʿIzz, I began to travel with him outside Cairo into the provinces, most often to Upper Egypt, where he had grown up in the province of Qinā. There I had the opportunity to meet a number of spectacular personalities, either famous shaykhs in their own right or sons of famous shaykhs. Whereas some shaykhs might try to monopolize a researcher, claiming that it was unnecessary to talk to other shaykhs because the totality of necessary knowledge rested in them, ʿIzz shrewdly understood what I was about. He introduced me to shaykhs whose feet he would gladly have kissed and to shaykhs he thought were nothing but "empty kiosks" so I could get a sense of the entire spectrum of Sufism in Egypt, its luminaries and its fakes.

ʿIzz also spent a good deal of time with me, especially early in our acquaintance, teaching me and answering my questions. Because he was preoccupied with the building of his mosque and *sāḥa,* he had suspended his weekly sessions for his followers, and whatever teaching he did at that time was on a purely ad hoc basis. Our sessions were frequently interrupted by people asking for money, or advice, or a healing amulet, and I also accompanied him on errands to help various people, so I was able to witness a good deal of the daily routines of a neighborhood shaykh. People came to see me as his disciple and usually no longer found my presence strange. On the other hand, I spent a frustrating amount of time during my research simply waiting for ʿIzz to finish errands. It was not at all uncommon for me to wait in his house for two or three hours for him to show up for an appointment.

Oddly enough, one of ʿIzz's closest followers, with whom I became fairly friendly, in a polite way, worked in the Arabic department of the American University in Cairo, fetching tea and coffee and running other errands. He had worked there when I was a student there in 1975–76, and I recognized his rather unique face immediately. At that time, my position as a foreign student at the American University virtually sealed me off from any meaningful contact with this man, whose acquaintance I would have regarded in any case as inconsequential. In this entirely different context, he became a frequent and trusted companion in group expeditions to visit various saints, both living and dead. The irony of the change in my own situation frequently struck me. Sufis are fully integrated into society, yet the high degree of class consciousness in Egypt, as well as the esoteric nature of Sufism, help maintain an often impassable social distance.

Yet not all of ʿIzz's followers accepted my presence gladly. It was only a year after my initial meeting with ʿIzz that I became aware that some of his followers hated me intensely because I was a Christian and felt that I did not deserve a minute of ʿIzz's time. They blamed me for the fact that ʿIzz was often too busy to see them, although in fact I seldom saw ʿIzz more than two or three times a week and I was experiencing the same frustration as they. I was frequently pressed to reveal my own beliefs, and if I gave in to their pressure I was usually complimented on my honesty, in contrast to the Egyptian habit of flattery and dissimulation. The Egyptians were usually less than honest with me themselves, appearing friendly but inwardly seething, and sometimes they would privately vent their anger at Shaykh ʿIzz, because he was sponsoring me. A few of his disciples simply deserted him during my stay in Egypt, although they returned to him after I left.

My most disturbing experience of anti-Christian sentiment came when I visited a women's group without escort. I had been invited by one of the women over the phone, but my presence provoked a protest from other women who felt that Christians were no better than polytheists, and the fact that I had not performed the Muslim ritual of ablutions meant that I was not in a state of ritual purity and should not be allowed in the precincts of the mosque. The selective and varied application of norms of sanctity concerning mosques and shrines can be very confusing to the outsider. While tourists are paraded through the courts of al-Azhar mosque, the sanctuary of Ḥusayn is closed to them. My own presence in Islamic dress rarely provoked protest, but sometimes, unexpectedly, in very ordinary and humble mosques, it did.

Most encounters with people eager to question me about my beliefs and convert me to Islam, as exhausting as they were, were rarely actually hostile. Although I was frequently questioned about my beliefs and occasionally subjected to long harangues on the superiority of Islam over Christianity, typically the desire to be hospitable outweighed the zeal to convert me. This was especially true of the Sufis in contrast to the Islamists, who are much more anti-Western in their ideology and sense their mission in the broader society much more keenly than the Sufis. Attitudes among the Sufis toward non-Muslims vary widely, but rarely did I encounter animosity because I was American.

Most of the Sufis I met seemed willing to believe that I had a spirit that was open to God, even if I had not embraced Islam. ʿIzz, in fact, encouraged people to see me in this light. For a while it seemed he genuinely believed I was secretly Muslim but was afraid to convert for fear of losing my husband and child because marriage between a Muslim woman and a non-Muslim man is prohibited and the children of such a union are regarded as illegitimate. I often allowed people to come to such conclusions because it was difficult for Egyptians to understand how a person could remain a Christian and yet gain a genuine understanding and appreciation of Muslim spirituality.

Yet gain one I did. Whereas the Islamists during my 1980–81 research insisted on maintaining my identity as an outsider, even as an enemy, the Sufis, by virtue of my relationship with Shaykh ʿIzz, often accepted me as one of them. Gradually I came to share some of their delight and sensations in spiritual sessions and to see the beauty in the Islamic prayer ritual. ʿIzz tested me constantly, on my memory of what he had taught me before, on my powers of observation and understanding of Arabic and of people, but also on my spiritual discernment and intuition. After meeting a shaykh and talking with him, ʿIzz would ask my opinion of him. Although I tried not to be dominated by my personal feelings toward people, ʿIzz explored my insights and encouraged me to express them. I came to realize that whereas I had been trained to approach things in an intellectual manner, often suppressing my first impressions and emotional reactions to people, ʿIzz believed that spiritual discernment arose from cultivating and eventually learning to trust those feelings. He asked me, for example, which shaykh I thought had a higher standing, or which Sufi singer was more inspired and sang "in the spirit." To my surprise, after forcing me to give an answer, he almost always validated my response as correct.

One night he and I were the guests of a man in a town in the province of Asyūṭ, and in the morning I was summoned to hear an account of a dream the man's wife had had of me that night. Dreams are often regarded as a type of vision because during sleep the spirit leaves the body and communes with the spirits of the dead. The woman told me she had seen me lying on a bed surrounded by a decorated curtain, with lights and flowers descending on me, as if I were a bride. I asked whose bride I was, and ʿIzz replied, "God's." He added, with a laugh, "You will become a shaykha [the feminine version of 'shaykh']." Later I asked him if he thought the vision was true, and he said, "Yes, absolutely. I wouldn't have let her tell it to you if it weren't true. You are indeed a bride." ʿIzz also surprised me by telling those present that I had a spirit that could see beyond what was apparent *(rūḥ shaffāfa)*. Later I asked him why he flattered me in this way, when it was not true. He replied, "But it is true. You can tell a good person from a bad one right away." I felt there was nothing unusual about this, it was simply a matter of character discernment. But ʿIzz replied, "It is not ordinary. And that is how *shafāfiyya* (clairvoyance) begins. You still haven't achieved all you will. And you entered with doubts, but you did enter in! You are greater than you think."

This was not the only affirming vision a Sufi had concerning me during my research. Often people claimed to be able to see evidence of God's light on me. After one conversation with an extremely aged shaykh at the moulid of Sultan Farghal in Abū Tīj, as I was leaving with ʿIzz and a group of his followers, two of our company excitedly told me that this particular shaykh hardly ever spoke at all. They were astonished that he had sat and spoken at length with me and took this as a sign of God's hand on me. Another shaykh, whom perhaps I respected more than any other I met during my stay in Egypt for his gentle honesty and his humble, reserved demeanor, complimented me during our last session in March 1989, saying I had a mature and enlightened mind and a spirit filled with the light of God. Since one man of our group had just spent several hours berating me for my narrow-mindedness for failing to convert to Islam, I felt somewhat vindicated. On another occasion a man excitedly told ʿIzz that in the spirit he had known me for some time, and I was his "sister." ʿIzz told him not to speak of this, for such things are secret.

To a certain extent perhaps ʿIzz and I did obtain some spiritual connection. I enjoyed sitting next to him during dhikr because I could sense the movement of his spirit, and my own perceptions of what was happening seemed to be heightened. On one occasion, ʿIzz was deeply moved during dhikr and occasionally uttered an inarticulate cry in an almost involuntary manner. I found myself able to feel when that cry was about to burst forth. ʿIzz later told me he was aware of this and took it as a sign of our "becoming one."

But on other occasions ʿIzz found reason to rebuke and upbraid me for my lack of faith in him and for letting my intellect get in the way of fully entering into the things of the spirit. He explained that the first stage in the spiritual journey was the lifting of internal obstacles, opening the self to spiritual things. The second stage was that of tuning the spirit in to the spiritual realm, so one can sense things that are happening beyond ordinary perception. I had begun to enter this stage, he said, but then I kept raising intellectual objections and doubts and kept returning to stage one. Of course, the very nature of my identity as a researcher precluded the possibility of simply giving in to a purely spiritual or emotional experience, and I maintained a certain amount of critical distance. But this very fact caused ʿIzz a good deal of frustration. From my point of view, he seemed to vacillate between understanding and accepting the nature of my research and wishing I could become a true disciple.

My relationship with ʿIzz caused problems with other relationships, specifically with ʿAmm Amīn and some of his friends. ʿAmm Amīn became very jealous of the time I spent with ʿIzz and began to tell me that ʿIzz was a bad man who lied, cheated, and stole for his own personal use money that was donated for the mosque. He also spread rumors concerning ʿIzz to his friends and complained to them that I was neglecting my relationship with him and his friends because of my relationship with ʿIzz. Whereas he had formerly praised my character, he began to denigrate me in front of his friends, although he reserved his real venom for ʿIzz. This development was extremely distressing to me. A researcher attempts not to influence her environment but merely to observe it, but the very nature of fieldwork, with its network of personal relationships, does have an impact.

This impact was not always negative. On one occasion, I was the link by which ʿIzz came to meet an entire group of Sufis who lacked a leader. ʿIzz quickly became a natural teacher among them. Although they did not adopt him as their shaykh, again I was struck by my own inadvertent impact on the people I was studying. I was also called upon on occasion to mediate between ʿIzz and the women of his family, particularly when ʿIzz's sister was being forced to marry against her will. It was also assumed that ʿIzz's niece would marry ʿIzz's older son, despite the girl's expressed aversion to the plan. The older son also appeared to be quite incompatible with the girl, whereas the younger son shared his cousin's intelligence, spirituality, and ambitions. When I articulated these observations to ʿIzz, I found to my surprise that the family began to consider marrying her to the second son rather than the first.

During the second year of my research, ʿIzz and I both became more openly critical of each other. I began to see him as somewhat vain and personally ambitious, qualities I felt were incompatible with real Sufism, although they are not particularly uncommon. He began to see me not only as shackled by my intellect but also as rather weak, having an excessive need for regular food and sleep, and unduly attached to my baby daughter, whom I often insisted on taking with me on our lengthier trips outside Cairo. These shortcomings did not really impede our friendship but marked a new phase beyond the first one of mutual admiration. Our relationship had progressed to the point of familiarity, allowing us to criticize each other. My criticisms were usually kept to private conversations, except for a few humorous barbs in the presence of his family or closest friends. To a certain extent, he enjoyed my boldness with him because his position as patriarch and shaykh prevented most people, certainly most women, from such forthrightness. He once told me, "I like hearing you say what nobody else would dare to say to me." His criticisms of me, however, were sometimes deliberately made in front of other people. During one phase, he studiously ignored me and belittled me openly. Later he explained that God had ordered him to test me, and this was a way that a shaykh tests his disciples, subjecting them to humiliation and apparent rejection in order to see how they react and thereby reveal their hidden defects. Apparently, I did pass that test to his satisfaction. However, his frustrations with my lack of spiritual progress mounted as my time with him went on. Toward the end of my research period, ʿIzz departed from his earlier defense of me and openly argued with me about the superiority of Islam in front of some of his followers. When one of those present gently advised him to let me alone, for "You have your religion, I have mine" (Qurʾan 109:6), ʿIzz heatedly replied that I had a high spirit, and if only I accepted Muhammad I would go directly through the seven heavens into the presence of God, but without Muhammad I would get nowhere. He added, to me, "If you want to get into my spirit, you must [symbolically] enter the Kaʿba."

Often the circumstances of my research were extremely frustrating and uncomfortable. I had to put up with lack of sleep, intense heat, bug bites, caring for my little daughter under very difficult conditions, and worst of all, feeling totally at the mercy of other people. During our trips into Upper Egypt, where I had no resources of my own to go anywhere by myself, I was occasionally simply left behind in a room while Shaykh ʿIzz went out with his disciples, because of the extremely rigid segregation of the sexes that obtains in the smaller towns and villages of Upper Egypt. I am not a particularly patient person and found it difficult enough to wait for hours at ʿIzz's home for him to show up for an appointment. But there, at least, I always had the option of leaving and returning to my own home. My worst experience was in ʿIzz's hometown in the province of Qinā, where he left me at his uncle's house while he went to the mosque to pray, which should not have taken more than a half hour. He told me to be ready to go out and visit some shaykhs after his return. He did not return for five hours. By then I was nearly beside myself with anger (did I travel twelve hours stuffed into the back of a hot station wagon, just to be shut into a house when I arrived?) and frustration, greatly compounded by anxiety, acute exhaustion, flea and mosquito bites, and the fact that my little daughter found all too many dangerous things to try to do, for there was no safe place I could let her roam or play. As usual, ʿIzz had a good excuse: he had come across two funerals of people he knew, and of course he had to sit through the entire Qurʾan reading for each one. To his mind, no amount of fatigue, discomfort, or frustration would ruffle the spiritual person, and my reactions to this and other situations were all indication to him of my low spiritual stature. "You are not a Sufi," he would say, as if this were an accusation, although I had never claimed to be a Sufi or even an aspiring Sufi.

ʿIzz mixed his criticisms of me with acts that, in the context of his culture, can only be described as extremely gracious. During our first trip, circumstances deprived us of sleep for two nights in a row, and I became desperate and increasingly impatient with my daughter, who had had no trouble sleeping whenever she wanted and had no intention of sleeping when I was finally given a time and place where I could. ʿIzz had warned me that he would never be seen holding or taking care of Rachel in Upper Egypt because this was against the dignity of a man in that culture, let alone a man of his noble family and status as shaykh. Yet although he mocked me for wanting to sleep, saying that if sleep were a good thing there would be sleep in Paradise, he gave in to my need, ignoring his own, and offered to take care of Rachel so I could sleep. All night long he walked about with a very alert baby girl, finally returning at dawn in a state of complete exhaustion. He also expected me to carry the luggage, food, or anything else we had, for such is the role of women in Upper Egypt, but when I complained about this, particularly when I became pregnant with my second child, he again condescended to a weakness he could not fully understand and carried the bags.

When, in the second year of my research, ʿIzz hosted a great celebration of the Prophet's birthday at his mosque, to which hundreds were invited to a meal and dhikr, I found that I personally knew many of the invited guests, including the singers and others who had traveled great distances in order to attend. Although ʿIzz's wife and some other women had been working hard in the kitchen for hours preparing the meal, and my own husband and daughter were in attendance, I felt somewhat like a hostess of the event, as I rose repeatedly to welcome guests who had just arrived.

My position as woman was rarely a real obstacle in Cairo or the Delta, where women work outside the home and where the strength of character of Egyptian women is almost legendary. But my entire relationship with ʿIzz was colored by the fact that he hailed originally from Upper Egypt, as did most of his followers and the people in his immediate neighborhood. Despite the enormous progress in the social role of women in Cairo, the position of women in Upper Egypt is frankly subordinate. Women are expected to serve men, keep out of sight, and maintain silence in their presence. In Upper Egyptian villages and small towns, many of which I visited during the course of my research, women are kept secluded in the home, tending to the animals in interior rooms and courtyards but not working in the fields, in contrast to the Delta.[9] Even veiled or with an escort, they rarely venture outside. Men who spend half the year in their home village for the harvest and half the year in Cairo manning small shops allow their wives to go out freely in Cairo but keep them strictly secluded in the village. Such women understandably have a harder time enduring such strictures than women who spent their entire lives in the village.

In this context, my position as a woman researcher, traveling in the company of men, attending moulids and dhikrs, and visiting shaykhs, was a great anomaly and occasionally aroused the jealousy of village women but more often aroused their curiosity. In deference to my intellect, discipline, and spiritual potential, ʿIzz jokingly referred to me as his "brother," since such characteristics were regarded as rare, though not entirely absent, in women. Most shaykhs did not find my identity as a woman to be a personal problem or source of discomfort. In fact, Shaykh Muḥammad Raḍwān, son of

Aḥmad Raḍwān, invited me to sit among the men rather than outside with the women and children during a dhikr in a village and arranged for me, ʿIzz, and Rachel to travel with the followers of Aḥmad Raḍwan on a great pilgrimage to the Sīdī Shādhilī shrine. He even ordered that Shaykh ʿIzz and I be placed in a single room, both at his *sāḥa* outside Luxor, and again at the *sāḥa* at the Sīdī Shādhilī shrine. ʿIzz later explained that since there were no other women present, he was in a position of protector for me, and Muḥammad Raḍwān trusted him implicitly. But although the spiritual man might not yield to or even feel sexual temptation, ʿIzz declined to sleep in our common room, preferring the floor of the mosque, "in deference to the intellects that are present," that is, out of respect for the spiritual limitations of those who would naturally assume impropriety.

Ordinary men did not share the shaykhs' unconcern for the presence of a female. As one of ʿIzz's followers said to me, "You consider yourself a man, but we see you as a woman." It was only by virtue of ʿIzz's insistence on including me in many activities that I did not spend much of my time in Upper Egypt shut away in a room with women and children. Indeed, I became so irate with ʿIzz if I were left alone that a good deal of his insistence derived from his fear of my anger! On one occasion the arrival of the famous shaykh we had come to see averted a rising crisis of confrontation between ʿIzz and the shaykh's followers. Later the men told me they were indeed glad of my presence because it was my interview with the shaykh that allowed them to derive some spiritual benefit from the occasion. "Otherwise, we would have spent the whole time in compliments and formalities," one man said.

But even ʿIzz's influence was insufficient to avoid my isolation from activities on certain occasions. This was extremely frustrating for me, especially since I had traveled so far to conduct observations and interviews. I tried to take advantage of the presence of any women that were there, but most of the time I found that the strict segregation of the sexes did indeed result in frank deprivation of the women's spiritual lives. Their time was usually spent talking about children or food, or in raucous jokes. In Upper Egypt in particular, they were often extremely shy with me. When Rachel became too noisy and active to accompany me on my journeys anymore, I often agonized over leaving her behind, missing her all the more intensely when I was forced to stay with other women and their children.

My journeys into Upper Egypt with Shaykh ʿIzz allowed me to gain a glimpse of that stern society, in all its complexity, richness, and cruelty. In Upper Egypt, far more than in Cairo or the Delta, traditional norms pertain. There, hospitality and etiquette reach a pinnacle of elaboration and formality, and nowhere more than among the Sufis. To sit in the company of such a society is in itself a liminal experience. Whereas middle-class Cairenes tend to divide Egyptian society simplistically into those who wear Western dress and carry a pen in their pocket, on the one hand, and those who wear traditional robes—the "peasants"—on the other, Upper Egyptian society is far too complex to allow for such simple distinctions. A genuine hierarchy of tribes obtains, in which the most recent nomadic arrivals lord it over the others. The word *peasant (fallāḥ)* is rarely used by Upper Egyptians to describe themselves; that word is reserved for the inhabitants of the Delta. All classes of people prefer to wear traditional robes and only wear Western-style clothing if they are in a government position that requires it, and then only during work hours.

Traditional vendettas continue to exist, in varying degrees, in many of the Upper Egyptian provinces. During a stay in a village in Asyūṭ province, I was startled to hear the men commenting with satisfaction that there were no battles today! When I questioned them about this, they said real armed conflict was frequent, but they complimented themselves that they contented themselves with killing only one person to avenge the death of one of their own, whereas in the province of Qinā revenge is indiscriminate and bloody, with perhaps eighty being killed to avenge the death of a single person.

On one trip to visit a shaykh in a village by night in Qinā, I observed that the men in the car had become extremely and very visibly nervous and the driver began to speed even beyond the normal recklessness of the Upper Egyptian driver, who apparently sees the speed at which he drives as a test of his masculinity. I asked Shaykh ʿIzz what was happening, and he explained that two villages in the area were engaged in a raging battle. Any cars passing after sunset were assumed to be carrying weapons and were shot at. Only the night before a car traveling along this road had exploded when it was shot at, killing all those aboard. Among those in our car, only Shaykh ʿIzz was unconcerned, assuring the others that his baraka would prevent anything from happening to us. He had seen the Preserved Tablet on which the fates of humans are written, and it was not yet time for us to die. Rachel, then sixteen months old, was with us, but by then there was nothing I could do to protect her. At one point two men tried to stop our car, but the driver planted his foot on the accelerator and forced his way through. When we arrived at the house where the shaykh was staying, it was surrounded by guards armed with automatic weapons, who were clearly nervous about the arrival of such late guests. They searched my tape recorder to make sure it did not contain explosives. The shaykh, whose normal residence was in Asyūṭ, was staying in the area specifically to try to defuse the conflict and function as mediator.

Middle-class Cairenes are largely ignorant of Upper Egyptian society. Although they have heard of Upper Egyptian vendettas, they assume such to be small-scale, private affairs, not the major battles they really are. They openly questioned my veracity when I told them about my experiences in Upper Egypt and assumed that if I was right about the existence of women who were secluded in their homes from the age of eleven, this must be an isolated case, for such things do not happen in Egypt anymore. One Christmas, when ʿIzz expressed an interest in accepting an invitation to a Christian celebration, I arranged for him to attend a potluck dinner with our family at an American friend's apartment, at which many other Egyptians, both Copts and Muslims, were in attendance. ʿIzz rarely gets lost in a crowd, and soon he was holding court, answering the other guests' questions on spiritual matters. Yet despite the fact that he and his wife clearly speak Arabic with an Egyptian accent, the guests later asked, after ʿIzz had departed, whether he was Saudi. They were puzzled by the presence of such an intelligent and articulate man wearing a traditional white robe, which among Egyptians they presumed was reserved for the lower classes! ʿIzz's dress, however, is entirely typical not only for the men of Upper Egypt but for the entire community of millions of Upper Egyptians resident in Cairo. The isolation of the Western-oriented Cairene middle class from the communities of rural migrants was striking.

When I expanded my research somewhat into the Coptic community for the sake of comparison with Sufi spirituality, things were not necessarily any easier for me than they were with the Muslims. My modest dress, which had helped me so much among the Muslims, often provoked negative reactions among the Copts. Although traditional women of both faiths dress very similarly, middle-class Coptic women do not cover their hair except to attend church, and even then do not cover it completely, as do the Muslims. While many Muslims were suspicious of my intentions as a non-Muslim studying Islam, the Copts were equally suspicious, accusing me quite openly of having committed cultural treason by abandoning my faith. It was difficult for me personally to identify with the very saint-based form of Christianity that obtains among the Copts, or to appreciate the spirit of exclusivity and hostility toward the Muslims actuated by their minority status and fears of persecution. They berated me for spending so much time listening to Muslims and for demonstrating so much respect for their spirituality. Indeed, by then my association with the Sufis had become so close that I was almost considered one of them, although I still occasionally encountered hostility and resistance from the more legalistic Muslims among them. At one point I complained bitterly to Shaykh ʿIzz, "The Muslims hate me because I am a Christian, and the Christians hate me—" "—because you are a Muslim," he finished with a smile.

I originally intended to keep ʿIzz anonymous in this book, by altering his name and perhaps some of the details about him, but it was his specific request that I report his name and life accurately. Well aware of the effect he had on people when under inspiration, he felt that it was inevitable that someday he would become a famous shaykh. He hoped, he said, that my book would simply hasten the coming of that day. At first I told him I would not do this, because a researcher must try not to influence the field she describes. He brought up the issue repeatedly, and I decided to consult other scholars. They sympathized with my dilemma but ultimately felt that if ʿIzz wanted to be exposed, I should not try to protect his identity. As one told me, "To change his name under the pretext of protecting him against his wishes is patronizing." I came to agree with this point of view.

By the time I left Egypt with my family, I felt that I had probably derived as much benefit from my relationship with ʿIzz as I could. Financial difficulties, problems with our landlady, my husband's frustrations dealing with Egyptian workers and bureaucracy, and my own advanced pregnancy all converged to create a sense of urgency about returning to the States. My husband had worked as a consultant for an Egyptian contractor, and by the end of our time there the relationship had become somewhat strained, as his pay, which would enable us to leave Egypt, became tied up in a seemingly endless tangle of red tape. When at last we left on the last day of April 1989, it felt like a great escape. Yet it was with nostalgia and some sadness that I reflected on the unique and intimate experience I had among the Sufis. Their friendship and spirituality had affected me far more profoundly than I could have anticipated.

CHAPTER 3

The Prophet Muhammad and His Family in Egyptian Sufism

Egyptian Sufism is not an abstract mysticism. It is, typically, a deeply personal relationship of love and veneration, and the most frequent immediate object of this love and veneration is the Prophet Muhammad. This strongly Muhammadan orientation is no less central among those Sufis who, like Shaykh ʿIzz, believe that spiritual experience goes beyond the forms of religion. Although some early Sufis, like Rābiʿa al-ʿAdawiyya of Basra (d. 801) and Kharrāz of Baghdad (d. 899), believed that their love for God left no room for focusing on the Prophet,[1] for the Sufis of modern Egypt, Muhammad is the way to God. Love for God is expressed as love for the Prophet, God's Beloved, whose presence is sought and desired, whose virtues are sung and on whom blessings are prayed with great frequency.

Love for the Prophet and the prayer of blessings on the Prophet's name are, of course, not uniquely Sufi features. Muslims everywhere embrace the Qur'anic description of Muhammad as "a mercy to all creatures" (21:107), and believe fervently in his intercession for them on the Day of Judgment. All over the Muslim world, any reference to Muhammad, whether or not his name is actually spoken, is followed by the formula, "May God bless him and grant him peace" *(Ṣallā Allāhu ʿalayhi wa sallam).* The Qur'an itself says, "God and His angels bless the Prophet *(yuṣallūna ʿalā 'l-nabī).* You who believe, bless him and give him the greeting of peace" (33:56).

Among the Sufis, however, prayers of blessings on the Prophet have reached a height not attained outside their community. The daily prayers of every Sufi Order contain a significant segment of prayers of blessings on the Prophet, and such prayers are widely believed to be extremely beneficial to the person who prays, returning blessings to the believer. Sufi shaykhs, writes one modern Egyptian Sufi, require their followers to pray such blessings at least three hundred times each day.[2] As the contemporary Egyptian Sufi singer al-ʿArabī al-Farḥān al-Balbīsī sings, "Whoever blesses the beloved Prophet, what joy and felicity will be his! . . . Every time you bless the beloved, the Prophet, it will accrue as capital in the spirit . . . Praying blessings on the Prophet gives a person rest."[3] The very lengthy prayers of blessing on the Prophet that follow the call to prayer in Upper Egypt may be seen as a sign of Sufism's penetration into the popular piety of that region.

The love and veneration of the Prophet and preoccupation with praying blessings on him are not uniquely Egyptian features and have perhaps nowhere been elevated to such heights as in Morocco, where devotional booklets of praises and blessings on the Prophet are numerous. The most popular of these, *Dalāʾil al-khayrāt*, has been described by Martin Lings as "perhaps, after the Qurʾan itself, the most widely distributed book in Islam."[4] This booklet is widely used in Egypt. The religious significance of prayer for the Prophet is evident in the following selection from that book: "Make my prayer for him a light, a bright [light], perfect and perfecting, pure and purifying, dispelling all obscurities and darkness, all doubt and association *(shirk)*, all unbelief, falsehood and sin. Make it a cause for the forgiveness [of sins], and a ladder whereby I may attain the highest position of election and special regard."[5] The specific blessings pronounced in the *Dalāʾil*, as in the regular daily prayers of the Sufis, enumerate Muhammad's virtues. In one brief passage from the *Dalāʾil*, Muhammad is extolled as the Prophet of mercy, intercessor for the people, solver of difficult problems, and light in darkness.[6]

Although the Prophet is the object of love and veneration, he is not worshipped. Prayers are not made to the Prophet but to God for blessings on the Prophet. Blessings on the Prophet, according to Shaykh ʿIzz, are of three types: through prayers, through love, and in the spirit. Prayers of blessings on the Prophet, he assured a group of devotees assembled at the shrine of Abū 'l-Ḥasan al-Shādhilī near the Red Sea, are heard by the Prophet himself from his burial place in his mosque in Medina, a place which is always referred to in Islamic discourse as "the noble garden" *(al-rawḍa 'l-sharīfa)*, because the Prophet allegedly said, "The area between my tomb and my pulpit is one of the gardens of Paradise." The blessing of love, he said, is by way of the worshipper's heart, and is higher than the prayer of the tongue. The blessing of the spirit, however, is to have true spiritual connection with the Prophet, to be in his presence at all times.

The Qurʾan describes the Prophet as a "beautiful example for all who desire God and the Last Day and remember God often" (33:21).

It commends him with the words, "You have a great character" (68:4). The Prophet is seen by all Muslims as a perfect model of morality. As he said in a ḥadīth, "I was only sent to perfect the noblest morality." The imitation of the Prophet is a concern for all Muslims and is the rationale behind the fundamental Islamic legal concept of Sunna, which may be defined as the exemplary behavior of the Prophet. It is second only to the Qur'an in authority on matters of belief and behavior, and because of the obscurity and insufficiency of the Qur'an as a sourcebook for law, the Sunna of the Prophet has been made the interpreter of the Holy Book. The Prophet's sayings and behavior, recorded in Ḥadīth, grant us the surest guide to the interpretation of the revelation that was given to him. Given present scholarship on the dubious authenticity of many ḥadīths, it may seem dangerous to give such weight to this literature.[7] However, the authority vested in Ḥadīth is merely an extension of the authority granted to the Prophet himself. "Obey God and His Messenger," says the Qur'an (3:32), and "whoever obeys the Messenger obeys God" (4:80).

Ḥadīth literature was built upon Muslims' interest in Muhammad's daily habits, as well as his interpretations of scripture. It is considered virtuous, though not mandatory, to imitate the Prophet in all his habits. The fast of Ramaḍān is broken every sunset by a sweet drink with dates, in imitation of the Prophet. Those who ardently love the Prophet refrain from drinking milk on Wednesdays, because the Prophet did so. Shaykh ʿIzz believed it was significant that his preferred sleeping position was identical to that of the Prophet. Interest in minute details of Muhammad's appearance, manner, and habits is reflected in the questions posed by the author of *Al-Ibrīz* to his shaykh, the seventeenth-century Moroccan, ʿAbd al-ʿAzīz al-Dabbāgh.[8] According to one Sufi writer, spiritual connection to the Prophet grows according to the seriousness with which the Sufi adept imitates him.[9] According to a ḥadīth, the Prophet said, "None of you believes until his desires follow what I have brought." Building on that idea, Shaykh Aḥmad Raḍwān (d. 1967) said that through devoted imitation of the Prophet's example, the very nature of the individual worshipper becomes transformed into his likeness.[10]

Despite all this, the Prophet is, according to Sufi belief, in many ways inimitable, for, in his own words, "I am not like any of you." Not only is he believed to be sinless but some Sufis also believe that his physical attributes are beyond the realm of ordinary human life. According to Shaykh ʿIzz, when Muhammad's disciples wished to follow his example in constant fasting, he responded, "You are not like me. I spend the night with my Lord, who feeds me and gives me drink." The meaning of this, according to ʿIzz, was that the Prophet's body was luminous like the bodies of the people in Paradise, and so he ate and drank the nourishment of the people of Paradise.[11] Even his urine, ʿIzz said, was pure enough for his wife, Umm Salama, to use to perform her ablutions.[12]

Although the Qurʾan depicts the prophets as righteous and courageous men, they are nonetheless subject to entirely human doubts and errors. Abraham originally mistook the heavenly bodies for God (6:76–79); Moses could not keep patient at the apparently senseless deeds of God's servant (18:65–82); and Moses' murder of the Egyptian who was fighting with the Hebrew is interpreted by the Qurʾan as a sin that needed God's forgiveness (28:15–16). David was also forgiven for an unnamed sin (38:24–25). The Muslim exegetes were aware of the biblical story of David and Bathsheba, a story that is nonetheless rejected by many Muslims as not befitting a prophet. Regarding Muhammad himself, the Qurʾan rebukes him for turning away from a blind man while conversing with a prominent Meccan (80:1–11), Muhammad is told to ask God's forgiveness for his sin (40:55), and God assures him that all his past and future sins are forgiven (48:2). Islamic theology, however, embraced the doctrine of prophetic infallibility *(ʿiṣma),* which is usually interpreted to mean that the prophets are immune from any error. Many Muslims are willing to allow that the former prophets made some minor lapses but do not include Muhammad. Sufi shaykhs in Egypt explain that he was commanded to ask forgiveness for his sins simply as an example to the believers.

The Qurʾan does not depict Muhammad as in any way superior to the previous prophets. It describes Muhammad as the "seal of the prophets," which may well have originally meant that he confirms the messages of the previous prophets, a teaching perfectly consistent with the Qurʾanic text as a whole. Muslims, however, believe that "seal of the prophets" means "last of the prophets."

Popular belief regarding Muhammad is that he is superior to all his predecessors. Muhammad is the Beloved of God. In Sufi songs and prayers he is called "the best of God's creation." In a public teaching at the moulid of Ḥusayn in December 1988, Shaykh Aḥmad Abū 'l-Ḥasan said, "If all of humanity were placed on one side of a balance and the Prophet on the other, the Prophet would outweigh them in virtue." His uniqueness is emphasized by the story of his ascension through the heavens to the Throne of God: no other creature, not even Gabriel, could approach God's throne, but for Muhammad the veils of light surrounding God were raised. According to the popular poem, the *Burda,* or "Mantle Ode," by al-Buṣīrī (1211–94), possibly the most frequently chanted poem of praise to the Prophet, he surpasses all the prophets in both physical aspects and moral excellence; they do not approach his knowledge or generosity. He is the one "whose form and essence are complete," and "he is beyond having partners in his good qualities *(munazzah ʿan al-sharīk fī maḥāsinihi).*"[13] This description verges on blasphemy: in Islam, it is God who is beyond comparison; He is the one to whom no partner should be ascribed; He is the one who, according to the Qurʾan, is unlike any other thing. Indeed, the very essence of the Islamic declaration of God's unity *(tawḥīd)* is *tanzīh,* "exalting Him above all others," the verbal noun that corresponds to the passive participle, *munazzah.* This glorification of Muhammad in such divine terms is paralleled by Sufi songs of the attributes of the Prophet, corresponding to the chanting and singing of the attributes of God.[14]

Sufi belief in Muhammad's superiority to the other prophets is intimately linked to the doctrine of the Muhammadan light. The Qurʾan says, "A light and a clear Book have come to you from God" (5:17). Even in the exegetical work of al-Ṭabarī (d. 923), one of the most authoritative and complete commentaries on the Qurʾan for Sunni Muslims, the "light" that came from God is interpreted as Muhammad.[15] Sufis believe that Muhammad is the light that clarifies the truths for all creatures. Commentators on the famous "Light passage" of the Qurʾan (24:35), which begins, "God is the Light of the heavens and the earth," have often identified the light of God with Muhammad, as early as Muqātil (d. 767), a Zaydī Shiʿi.[16] The early biographer of Muhammad, Ibn Isḥāq, wrote of a literal "light of prophethood" that appeared as a shining white spot between the eyes of Muhammad's father, ʿAbd Allāh, which disappeared from his forehead when the Prophet was conceived.[17]

The doctrines of the Muhammadan light were developed fairly early among the Shiʿa, who, in the Twelver and Ismāʿīlī branches, taught that this light was transmitted to each of their Imams, as a spiritual core granting mystical insight and knowledge. Among the Sunnis, the doctrine of the Muhammadan light was first expounded by the Sufi ascetic Sahl al-Tustarī (d. 896), to whom a number of works are attributed, though they were probably actually penned by his disciple, Ibn Sālim.[18] Some sources say that it was Khiḍr, the immortal mystical teacher, who taught Tustarī that Muhammad was created from the light of God and was formed by His hands. This light remained in the presence of God 100,000 years, in pure praise of God, and every day God gave it some of His light, increasing its honor. From this light all other things were created. Tustarī taught that the light of the Prophet is comprehensive, and all the lights of the prophets are derived from it, as are the lights of the angelic realm in this world and the next. Of all God's creatures, only Muhammad was created for the pleasure of God Himself. Recalling the divine saying *(ḥadīth qudsī),* "If humanity is preoccupied with what I created for them, I will veil them from what I have created for Myself," Tustarī interpreted what was created for God as the Reality of Muhammad, an eternal spiritual essence that later became incarnated in the man born in Mecca in 570. It is this Reality that is the beginning and end (or seal, *khātam*) of creation. The Reality of the Prophet is the *alif* and *yā'* (the first and last letters of the Arabic alphabet) of creation and existence—a teaching that exactly parallels the biblical description of the Christ as the Alpha and the Omega (Revelation 21:6). According to Tustarī, the name of Muhammad is written on every leaf in Paradise, where no tree is planted except in his name and in his honor.[19]

Whether or not all of these ideas are original with Tustarī, or even fully formed by him, it is clear that he lived at a time when the doctrine of the Muhammadan light was being formulated in both Sufi and Shiʿi circles.[20] Tustarī exercised a great deal of influence on the famous Sufi al-Ḥallāj, who was executed in 922, and was also frequently quoted by the influential Ibn ʿArabī (d. 1240). The doctrine of the Muhammadan light became enshrined in several ḥadīths that, though of dubious authenticity, are popular among the Sufis and grant them textual authority for their distinctive doctrine. In one of them, Jābir, a Companion of the Prophet, asks him what was the first thing created. Muhammad replies, "The light of your Prophet, Jābir."[21] In some versions, Muhammad asks Gabriel how old he is. Gabriel replies that he does not know, "but in the fourth veil there is a star that would appear once every seventy thousand years, and I saw it seventy thousand times." This star was Muhammad.

These centuries-old texts form the scriptural basis for the contemporary Sufi doctrine of the Muhammadan light. From this primordial Muhammadan light, said Shaykh Aḥmad Raḍwān, all other things were created: the Pen that wrote the fates of all creatures, the Throne of God, the Chair, or footstool, that stands before the Throne, the heavens, the earth, and all that is on the earth—all are an extension of that light. He concludes, "God has ennobled the whole world with this light," which is of divine origin. The fullest manifestation of the divine light is Muhammad, but ultimately it pervades and ennobles all of creation.[22] Aḥmad Raḍwān admits that some authorities, such as Ibn Taymiyya (d. 1328) and his disciple Ibn al-Qayyim al-Jawziyya (d. 1350), categorized the ḥadīth of Jābir as "weak," that is, lacking the authority that is granted to ḥadīths with sound chains of transmission.[23] Aḥmad Raḍwān even goes so far as to admit that "there is weakness in the chain of transmission," but nonetheless he holds that the text of the ḥadīth is sound, for its meaning is corroborated by another ḥadīth, in which the Prophet said, "I was a prophet while Adam was between water and clay," that is, before the creation of Adam.[24] Although doubt may be cast on the soundness of a particular ḥadīth's chain of transmission, the doctrine of the preexistence of the Muhammadan light remains sound, from his point of view.

Muḥammad ʿUthmān ʿAbduh (d. 1983), Sudanese shaykh of the Burhāniyya and center of controversy in Egypt in the mid-1970s, was criticized by Egyptian religious scholars specifically for using ḥadīths and other sources of suspect authority as the basis for his book, *Tabriʾat al-dhimma fī nuṣḥ al-umma wa tadhkirat ūlī al-albāb li 'l-sayr ilā 'l-ṣawāb.* The main focus of the book is the Sufi doctrine on the Prophet. Regarding the Jābir ḥadīth, Muḥammad ʿUthmān acknowledges that many scholars do not rely on it because it is insufficiently substantiated from more than one source (it is *āḥād*), but nonetheless he concludes that it is a "sound ḥadīth."[25] In a letter to the semiofficial daily newspaper, *Al-Ahrām,* former mufti of Egypt, Shaykh Muḥammad Ḥasanayn Makhlūf, wrote that "the strange ḥadīths in this book are not found in the books of sound Sunna."[26] The general director of the propagation of Islam in the Ministry of Religious Endowments said in an interview that "the book destroys the method of judging sound ḥadīth from what is forged. Thus they open the door to the attribution of many superstitions and fables to the Messenger."[27]

On this topic, in his taped discourses, Muḥammad ʿUthmān recalls a conversation he once had with a leading Egyptian shaykh visiting Khartoum, who told him that in his book he used ḥadīths whose chains of transmission were incomplete and therefore not judged sound. Muḥammad ʿUthmān acknowledged this but added that ḥadīths judged to be weak or with incomplete chains *(mursal)* could nonetheless be used to good effect if they do not detract from observance of religious duties and if they encourage love for the Prophet, which is the greatest act of worship.[28]

In another teaching, Muḥammad ʿUthmān told his disciples that one can rely on Sufi ḥadīths, regardless of how they are judged by scholars, because the Sufi saints correct their ḥadīths or know of their soundness by virtue of their access to the Prophet's presence.[29] Although the Burhāniyya are known for giving explicit references, even page references, to document their statements in public lectures, this does not really guarantee authenticity, as Muḥammad ʿUthmān demonstrated in a story in which a shaykh cited a ḥadīth, down to the page number of the volume from which it was derived, but a pupil consistently disputed the validity of the ḥadīth. Finally the pupil explained, "The Prophet is standing behind you, and he says that he did not say it." The shaykh turned, saw the Prophet, and fled.[30]

The great Sufi writer Ibn ʿArabī (d. 1240) likewise held that only mystical illumination *(kashf)* enabled one to verify the validity of ḥadīths.[31] Here we see that the confrontation over the validity of using these ḥadīths is really a confrontation between the methods of the ulama, based on scholarship, and those of the Sufis, based on mystical insight. However, Muḥammad ʿUthmān finds textual support for the doctrine of the prior existence of the Muhammadan Reality not only in Ḥadīth, but in the Qurʾanic verses, "I am the first of the worshippers" (43:81) and "We created man from a drop of mingled sperm, in order to try him" (76:2); this latter verse cannot refer to Adam, he says, because Adam was made from clay.[32]

The public furor over Muḥammad ʿUthmān's book indicates that this doctrine of the preexistent Muhammadan light is a watershed issue dividing popular Sufism from the official, reformed version endorsed by the government. In fact, Muḥammad ʿUthmān writes in his book that he was motivated to write it because of the alleged diminution of the Prophet's stature in modern religious circles: "Some people have diminished the stature of the Messenger of God, peace be upon him, and have claimed that he is only a man to whom God gave a revelation with a Law and ordered him to deliver it, so he did, and his importance ends after he delivers it. They have claimed that there is no benefit to be derived from him. . . . Indeed, they go further . . . by claiming that he, peace be upon him, was ignorant before Gabriel brought him the revelation."[33]

In an interview in *Al-Ahrām*, Shaykh Muḥammad al-Suṭūḥī, then head of the Supreme Council of Sufi Orders, denounced as idolatrous the doctrine that God created the world from the light of Muhammad, because it contradicts standard Islamic theology, which says that God created the world from nothing. Suṭūḥī labeled Muḥammad ʿUthmān's doctrine as emanationist, likening it to the teachings of the Ismāʿīlī Shiʿa and medieval philosophers like al-Fārābī (d. 950) and Ibn Sīnā (d. 1037), whose views, according to Suṭūḥī, were "destroyed" by the theologian and mystic Abū Ḥāmid al-Ghazālī (d. 1111) as well as the Ḥanbalī scholar, Ibn Taymiyya (d. 1328).

Al-Ghazālī is frequently held up by official Sufism in Egypt as the model of orthodox Sufism, in contrast to the doctrines of "extremist" Sufis such as Ibn ʿArabī (d. 1240). The contrast, however, may be more apparent than real. Ghazālī saw himself as a teacher of the masses and therefore was extremely circumspect in his writings that were addressed to the masses. In his later mystical works, such as *Mishkāt al-anwār,* Ghazālī espouses doctrines that appear to contradict some of his earlier positions. There he asserts that in fact the Mover of all is not God but a being described as "the obeyed one" *(al-muṭāʿ),* who is God's vicegerent, the supreme controller of the universe, and is comparable in its relationship with God to the relation of the impalpable light-essence to the sun, or of the elemental fire to a glowing coal.[34] Reynold A. Nicholson comments, "It looks to me as if Ghazali's esoteric teaching, which he keeps back from his readers because they 'cannot bear it,' was not different in substance from the Logos doctrine of the *Insānu 'l-kāmil* ['The Perfect Man,' by ʿAbd al-Karīm al-Jīlī]. His allusions to ineffable arcana, centring in the tradition that Adam was created in the image of God, are extremely significant."[35] It is unlikely Ghazālī would have objected to the writings of Ibn ʿArabī, which were directed at a Sufi audience and which were apparently greatly influenced by Ghazālī, whom he describes as one of the elect among Sufis.[36] Perhaps it is significant that while many Egyptian Sufis describe Ghazālī as a great teacher, Ibn ʿArabī's title remains "the greatest shaykh."

Ibn ʿArabī is often credited with the concept of the Perfect Man *(al-insān al-kāmil)* and the Muhammadan Reality as a Logos-type spiritual essence that is both the consciousness of God and the medium of creation. His doctrines were, however, partially anticipated by previous Sufi thinkers such as Sahl al-Tustarī, al-Ḥallāj, al-Ghazālī, and Qāḍī ʿIyāḍ. For Ibn ʿArabī, the Perfect Man, identified with the Muhammadan Reality,[37] is a manifestation of the totality of the divine names and attributes, which are also manifested in the created world, taken as a whole. The Perfect Man, then, is the microcosm, and is the mirror by which God knows Himself. For this reason, "to see God in the Muhammadan form through the Muhammadan vision is the most complete vision possible."[38] According to ʿAbd al-

Karīm al-Jīlī (d. 1408), who further elaborated on Ibn ʿArabī's ideas in his book, *Al-Insān al-kāmil,* both the Perfect Man and the Qurʾan may be characterized as manifestations of the Divine Essence.

It is but a small step from the idea of Muhammad as preexistent light from which all else is derived to the idea that his knowledge embraces the entirety of the Preserved Tablet, from which the heavenly scriptures are derived. This teaching, which was first associated with Sahl al-Tustarī's disciple Ibn Sālim (d. 909), came to be expressed in a ḥadīth in which Muhammad said, "The Qurʾan was revealed to me as one whole," rather than in piecemeal fashion, as described by Muslim biographers and historians. Another ḥadīth depicts Gabriel as receiving the revelation from the heavenly Kaʿba and bringing it to Muhammad, only to find that inside the heavenly Kaʿba was Muhammad himself, who delivered the revelation to him in the first place. When Gabriel asked Muhammad why he should tire himself out performing this mission if it all came from him and to him, Muhammad replied, "For the sake of giving the law" *(li 'l-tashrīʿ).*[39]

However much some Sufi spokesmen would like to dismiss these ideas as extremist and unrepresentative of true Sufism, belief in the preexistent Muhammadan Light and Muhammadan Reality is reflected in the prayers and songs of many of the major Sufi Orders in Egypt, which are registered with the Supreme Council of Sufi Orders. In the prayer of Aḥmad al-Rifāʿī (d. 1178), used in devotions by the Rifāʿiyya Order, probably the largest Order in Egypt today, Muhammad is described as

> the pre-existent *(asbaq)* light of God, . . . the dot of the *bāʾ* of the primordial sphere, the secret of the secrets of the pivotal *(quṭbiyya) alif,*[40] by which the turbidity of existence was clarified. . . . He is Your primordial, pervading secret, and the water of the essence of flowing essentiality *(jawhar al-jawhariyya 'l-jārī)* by which You gave life to the existents, be they mineral, animal or plant. He is the heart of hearts, and the spirit of spirits, and the knowledge of the good words, the first highest Pen, and the encompassing Throne; spirit of the body of both worlds, boundary of the two seas, the second of two, the pride of both worlds, Abū 'l-Qāsim, our lord Muhammad ibn ʿAbdallāh ibn ʿAbd al-Muṭṭalib, Your servant, Your prophet and Your apostle, the illiterate prophet.[41]

In the *ḥizb* of Aḥmad al-Badawī (d. 1276), recited by his Order, the Aḥmadiyya, which is strongly represented in the Delta of Egypt, Muhammad is described as "tree of the luminous origin, the brilliance of the handful of the Merciful, . . . mine of the divine secrets

. . . owner of the original handful," that is, the handful of divine light from which the Muhammadan light was created.[42] In the prayer of Abū 'l-Ḥasan al-Shādhilī (d. 1258), founder of the Shādhiliyya Order, which is represented by many branches and derivative Orders throughout Egypt, Muhammad is described as "most noble of beings, the secret penetrating all the Names and attributes," that is, the Names and attributes of God.[43] The prayer of his teacher, ʿAbd al-Salām ibn Mashīsh (also known as Ibn Bashīsh), which is included in the prayer books of the Shādhiliyya Orders, describes Muhammad as the one "from whom the secrets burst forth and the lights emanated . . . he is Your comprehensive secret who gives evidence of You and Your greatest veil standing between Your hands."[44]

The similarity in doctrine among the major Orders of Egypt is not surprising when one considers how intertwined they are in their origins: Ibn Mashīsh of Morocco (d. 1228), the teacher of al-Shādhilī, was a disciple of Abū Madyan al-Tilmisānī (d. 1197). Abū Madyan was also a teacher of the Iraqi, Aḥmad al-Rifāʿī, as well as great-grandfather of Aḥmad al-Badawī, and spiritual grandfather of both ʿAbd al-Rahīm al-Qināwi, the famous saint of Qinā, in Upper Egypt, and Yūsuf Abū 'l-Ḥajjāj, the equally famous saint of nearby Luxor. Ibn Mashīsh was allegedly recognized as *quṭb* (Axis) of the age by Abū 'l-Fatḥ al-Wāsiṭī, the disciple of Aḥmad al-Rifāʿī who was responsible for introducing the Rifāʿiyya from Iraq into Egypt in 1237 and who was also the maternal grandfather of Ibrāhīm al-Dasūqī, founder of the Burhāmiyya Order, popular in the Egyptian Delta. The Moroccan and Iraqi influences on Egyptian Sufism and the connectedness of the Orders in their origins argue against overemphasizing the local character of Egyptian Sufism.[45]

Although Egyptian Sufis consider the doctrine of the light of Muhammad to be esoteric, kept hidden from the minds of ordinary people who are incapable of grasping the magnitude of the Prophet's greatness, it is frequently the subject of Sufi teachings and was often articulated to me by ordinary Sufis as one of the greatest mystical truths. Sufis believe that their acknowledgment of Muhammad's true greatness is one of the things that sets them apart from other pious Muslims.

The cosmic significance of the Prophet, a doctrine that many Muslims find blasphemous, is nonetheless represented even in Orders that are known for their adherence to the Shariʿa and their appeal to intellectuals. One of the more respected such Orders today is the ʿAzmiyya, an offshoot of the Shādhiliyya. Although the main articles of their magazine, *Al-Islām waṭan*, are scrupulously orthodox and aim to appeal to reform-minded Muslim youth, in its November 1988 issue in commemoration of the Prophet's birthday, it employs the ḥadīth, "I was the first of the prophets in creation, and the last to be sent," and reproduces lines of poetry by Sayyid Muḥammad Māḍī Abū 'l-ʿAzāʾim (d. 1937), founder of the Order and former professor of Islamic law at Khartoum University, that describe Muhammad as leader of all other prophets, made from the light of providence, the secret of existence, light of God, secret of the beginning, from whom the angels, prophets, and rational beings were formed and obtained their knowledge. A sermon by Shaykh al-Sayyid ʿAbd al-Ḥamīd al-Ṣayfī reproduced in the same issue says that God created all things for Muhammad, who is the First Intellect that illuminated the worlds of luminous spirits by the light of his preexistence.[46]

According to the Neoplatonic philosophy of al-Fārābī and Ibn Sīnā, which became influential in much of Sufi and Shiʿi intellectual tradition, the first thing to emanate from the Necessary Being (God) was the First Intellect, from which emanated both the Second Intellect and the first heavenly sphere. A ḥadīth, clearly reflecting this Neoplatonic idea, states that the first thing God created was the First Intellect. In the thought of Ibn ʿArabī, the Muhammadan Reality is the rational principle of the Godhead, mediating the creative process. This identification of the Muhammadan Reality with the First Intellect reflects the merging of Sufi speculation with Neoplatonic thought. The dissemination of such doctrines by an Order known and respected for its orientation toward modern-style intellectualism and its adherence to the Shariʿa is significant.

Despite the Prophet's exalted position, he is not removed from the spiritual experiences of ordinary believers. On the contrary, his presence among them is readily available, and he continues to appear to those who love him in visions, offering guidance, correction, and reassurance. Vincent Cornell believes that the Prophet's preeminence as spiritual guide and model of esoteric spirituality dates from the twelfth century and that through the "Muhammadan Path" *(ṭarīqa muḥammadiyya)* movement of the sixteenth century, Muhammad took the place of Khiḍr, the former shaykh of shaykhs and supreme spiritual guide.[47] In fact, Khiḍr continues to play a role in spiritual guidance, but he does not elicit the love, passion, and devotion that the faithful direct to their Prophet. Love for the Prophet is a spiritual duty on all Muslims, but it is one that need not be imposed on the Sufi, for whom spontaneous outpourings of intense love for the Prophet are entirely natural. Sufis believe the Qur'an commands Muslims to love the Prophet in this way when it says, "The Messenger is more worthy of the believers than themselves" (33:6).

"Increase your love for him," Aḥmad Raḍwān (d. 1967) exhorted his followers, "and love him more than yourselves, your wealth and your children! Be greatly excessive in this *(taghālaw fī dhālika kathīran),* for it is better for you than nightly devotions. Do we have anything other than his love?!"[48] Aḥmad Raḍwān depicts the Prophet as full of concern for his people: "He is the first to open Paradise, but he doesn't enter it, because he is running here and there until he is sure of the salvation of his nation."[49]

Said Gamāl al-Sanhūrī, the former head of the Burhāniyya in Egypt who still resides in Cairo, "The one fundamental thing that is asked of all people is to love the Prophet Muhammad, for he is the Beloved, and the foundation of all Islam is love."[50]

Muhammad is the Beloved par excellence, beloved by God and beloved by the Muslims. Some Sufi sayings and ḥadīths that were formerly interpreted to apply to humanity as a whole are today sometimes interpreted to apply exclusively to Muhammad. Consider, for example, the famous *ḥadīth qudsī,* in which God says, "I was a hidden treasure, and I longed to be known, so I created the world, and by it they knew me." Some contemporary Sufis interpret the object of God's longing not, as earlier Sufis did, to be His human "lovers," those who devote themselves to His worship and become endowed with the knowledge of God, but rather to be Muhammad alone, who is the Beloved, the locus of all of God's love and acceptance. The way to God, therefore, is to be found only in Muhammad. By loving Muhammad and eventually achieving a mystical union with his spirit, the Sufi hopes to attain ultimately to the presence of God. But the immediate object of love and devotion is not God, the Beloved of early Sufism, but Muhammad, the Beloved of later Sufism. The ardent longing of the modern Sufi is somehow to attain to his presence, to enjoy sweet communion with a figure both human and touched with the divine, reflecting the pure light of God.

Likewise, the divine saying, "The heavens and the earth cannot contain me, but the heart of my believing servant contains me," a saying cherished by the Sufis, was typically interpreted to mean that the hearts of all believers may serve as God's Throne, if they are adequately purified. Not so, says Shaykh ʿIzz. The phrase "believing servant" is in the singular, and this refers to only one man—Muhammad. As he said during a Sufi *ḥaḍra:*

God said to Muhammad, "If all the peoples came to me and tried every door, they will never come to me unless they come behind you," because the heart of the Messenger of God, blessings and peace be upon him, is the locus of the manifestations *(tajalliyāt)* of the Real One *(al-Ḥaqq)*. "The heavens and the earth cannot contain me, but the heart of my believing servant contains me." One servant. Only one is meant. . . . Because God created him and poured out His manifestations upon him and placed him on the Throne of Unity and looked at him and created the creation from his light. . . . No one can have contact with God except through the heart of the Messenger of God. God the Exalted reveals Himself to the hearts it is true, but through the heart of the Beloved.

Therefore, God is loved through love for His Beloved, the Prophet. If the ultimate goal of the early Sufi path was *fanāʾ*, or annihilation of the separate ego in the Godhead, today it is annihilation in the Prophet. His is the presence that offers sweet consolation, great joy, and mystical transformation. Most Sufi songs express this ardent desire, and perhaps none better than this:

May God bless Muhammad, may God bless him and grant him peace
My longing arrives at Medina,[51] out of love for our Prophet *ṬāHā*
My entire goal is to see him, to attain the clear light
Perchance to attain to union *(waṣl)* with him, and be firmly rooted in his presence
The Beloved is the light of guidance, by him we are guided to God
He is my goal and my desire, he is the best of messengers
Oh Messenger of God, a glance, oh mercy to all creatures
Take me to you, my intercessor, and fill my heart with certitude
You are the light, you are the guide, oh beloved of the believers
The light of your face has captivated me and has captivated the lovers
The light of your knowledge, oh Muhammad, taught the people the religion
I said to my heart, "Rejoice and sing, this is the light of Trustworthy *ṬāHā*"
This is the light of Aḥmad Muḥammad, oh Lord, be my guarantor
I asked God by you, oh Prophet, to forgive the rebellious
And to release me from my troubles and worry, and to be my helper
We have none but you who is desired, oh Intercessor of sinners
You are my goal, my love, you are the light, you are the religion
Seal for us all goodness, and let not our enemies rejoice at our misfortune
God my Lord has blessed you, the Muslims bless you.[52]

Another song exults, "Love of the Beloved is my *Ḥaqiqa* and my Sharīʿa," resolving in a religion of love the old debate over the relative authority of revelation and transcendent mystical truth.[53] One poem elevates love of the Prophet beyond the performance of the ritual duty of the pilgrimage, when it says, "*Ṭāhā* is the greatest Kaʿba around which the lofty ones circumambulate."[54]

When I asked Shaykh ʿIzz why praises are so often addressed to the Prophet and the saints rather than to God, he replied, "There is no difference. Whoever honors the Prophet honors God." Indeed, during dhikr, as participants chant the Names of God, they are urged on by a singer, who typically sings praises to the Prophet and calls on the spiritual help of Muhammad, his family, and the saints of God. On another occasion, ʿIzz said that desire and longing are nothing other than a desire to return to one's origin, which is the light of Muhammad, out of which everything was created. Once the origin has been reached, there is no more desire.

The concept of *fanāʾ fī 'l-rasūl,* annihilation in the Messenger of God, is certainly not unique to Egypt and appears to be widespread in later Sufism. The Indian mystical poet Khwaja Mir Dard (d. 1785) described his father as having achieved perfect annihilation in the Messenger.[55] The Sanūsiyya Order, founded in early nineteenth-century Arabia and Libya, made concentration on the Prophet's essence the focus of their spiritual life. Constance Padwick describes the spiritual life of the founder of the Sanūsiyya as based on "absorption of the inner life" in "the spectacle of the Very Self of the Prophet." By practicing constant invocations of blessing on the Prophet, love for the Prophet dominated his heart, "so that no created being other than the Prophet had any weight with him."[56] Evidence of the concept of annihilation in the Messenger of God may be found as far back as a text by ʿAbd al-Karīm al-Jīlī (d. 1408), an important expositor of the doctrines of Ibn ʿArabī. Significantly, this is one of the texts included by Muḥammad ʿUthmān in *Tabriʾat al-dhimma.*[57]

The texts employed by Egyptian scholars on Sufism predate the development of *fanāʾ fi 'l-rasūl,* and both they and many shaykhs continue to discuss the concept of *fanāʾ* in its classical sense of annihilation in God, although in practice the means toward that goal typically is annihilation in the Prophet. Annihilation in any sense is rarely discussed openly, being reserved for the private spiritual guidance of those who have sufficient spiritual preparation. My questions on the subject met with varied responses, not necessarily in substance, but in willingness to discuss something considered too deep for a novice or outsider to contemplate. Sometimes my association with ʿIzz encouraged openness, but other times my questions met with evasion tactics. Whether or not theories and methods of outright concentration on the Prophet are taught, much of the practice remains: meditation on the Prophet's attributes and invocations of blessings on him are regular aspects of Sufi life and fill the hearts of the Sufis with longing for his presence. And indeed, his presence is available. Aḥmad Raḍwān urged his followers to seek and expect a vision of the Prophet. Failure to have such a vision indicated "spiritual sickness" and was even cause for fear at the time of death.[58] Shaykh Gābir al-Jāzūlī likewise assured his followers that Muhammad's presence remains "as long as the heaven and the earth, and fills the hearing and sight and heart."[59]

Shaykh ᶜIzz loves to tell the story of how the Prophet honored Aḥmad al-Rifāᶜī (d. 1178) when the latter visited his tomb in Medina, by extending a hand to him from the tomb that was visible to all those present. Such physical manifestations of the Prophet's presence are indeed extraordinary, but they are possible because the "subtle body," as opposed to our "body of clay," may appear in a number of places at a time. This subtle body is obtainable, says Shaykh Gābir, "by every servant who has familiar companionship with his Lord and loves His prophet and does what is right." But the pervasiveness of the Muhammadan presence is of another order: Aḥmad al-Rifāᶜī said, "God unveiled my sight and I saw the Prophet fill the heavens, the earth, the Throne, the Chair, and all regions."[60]

Spiritual connection with Muhammad is an everyday experience for some of the elect. There is a sense of intimacy in some of the anecdotes Sufis tell about their experiences with the Prophet, although it is an intimacy hedged by deep reverence. As Shaykh Gābir said, "None of the saints achieves perfection but by his [Muhammad's] permission and his purification. They meet with the chief of messengers while awake or asleep. One of the gnostics, Khalīfa ibn Mūsā, saw him often, seventeen times in one night, and the Prophet said to him, 'Do not be bored of us, for many of the saints died in grief over not seeing us.' "[61]

In some of their sayings, it seems as if faith or even life itself hinge on constant access to the presence of Muhammad. Sayyid Abū 'l-ᶜAbbās al-Mursī (d. 1287), successor in Egypt to the Order founded by Abū 'l-Ḥasan al-Shādhilī (d. 1258), allegedly declared, "If I am veiled from the vision of the Prophet for one second [literally, a blink of an eye], I do not consider myself a Muslim!"[62] Shaykh ᶜIzz quotes Aḥmad Raḍwān himself as saying, "If the Prophet were away from me for fifteen breaths, I would kill myself!" This, according to ᶜIzz, is true prayer for blessing on the Prophet, when the spirit does not separate from the Prophet but lives always in his presence. Verbal invocations of blessings on the Prophet enable humans, who are bound in matter, to overcome their material boundaries and attain spiritual connection with the Prophet.

Dreams offer a form of vision that is accessible to all believers, as well as the promise of visions to come in the waking state, for the Prophet said in a ḥadīth, "Whoever sees me in his sleep will see me while awake." Sufis acknowledge that dreams may be of Satanic inspiration or simply the thoughts of one's own soul, but they may also be true windows into the spiritual realm. Muslims are vouchsafed regarding their visions of the Prophet in dreams, for according to a ḥadīth, Muhammad said, "Satan does not imitate me." Not merely Sufis but the broader Islamic tradition has innumerable tales of visions of the Prophet to believers in their sleep, usually to offer guidance or correction. The theologian al-Ashʿarī (d. 935) allegedly attributed his conversion from Muʿtazilism to Sunni doctrine to such a vision of the Prophet. Sufis believe the Prophet continues to appear to Muslims today, especially to those whose hearts have been purified.

In view of the volume of Muslim endorsement of the idea of visions of the Prophet during both the sleeping and waking states, it is surprising that, during the controversy over Muḥammad ʿUthmān's book in 1976, Shaykh Suṭūḥī of the Supreme Council denied the possibility that the Sufi might have a vision of Muhammad while awake. The reality of such visions is affirmed even by such well-loved "orthodox" Sufi teachers as al-Ghazālī and is well attested in the teachings of the revered founders of the Orders. In fact, although many Sufis today interpret the end of the mystical path as attainment to the Prophetic presence, Ghazālī described the *first* stage of the Sufi way as the beginning of revelations and visions: "The mystics in their waking state now behold angels and the spirits of the prophets; they hear these speaking to them and are instructed by them. Later, a higher stage is reached; instead of beholding forms and figures, they come to stages in the 'way' which it is hard to describe in language."[63] Nonetheless, it appears that belief in visions in a waking state may be another issue that divides the bulk of Sufis from their official spokesmen. Perhaps these spokesmen fear that this essential aspect of Sufi experience is too extremist to win acceptance among the country's educated elite.

Regardless of official attempts to contain popular beliefs concerning the Prophet within acceptable norms, it would be difficult to overstate the centrality of Muhammad in Sufi experience in Egypt. Although Sufi beliefs fall short of deification of the Prophet, his special relationship to the divine light and essence, his exemplification of the divine attributes, and his roles as moral exemplar, intercessor, and spiritual guide all contribute to inspire enormous love and devotion. Most Sufi songs are directed at the Prophet, and speak of his greatness and the devotee's intense love, longing, and devotion. The devotee is described as "lover of the Prophet" (*muḥibb al-nabī* or, more extravagantly, *ʿāshiq al-nabī*). When the *munshid* sings, "I want to see you, Beloved" or "I long for your presence," it is easy for the uninitiated, particularly those familiar with classical Sufism, to assume the reference is to God. But when the devotees themselves are asked to whom these songs refer, they reply that it is the Prophet: he is the one beloved by God and by the believers, he is the one for whose presence they long. The Qurʾan says, "All that is on earth will perish [*fānin*—entering into *fanāʾ*/annihilation], but the face of your Lord remains" (55:26–27). These verses have inspired a great deal of mystical contemplation and are ultimately the source of the Sufi concept of *fanāʾ*. Yet when a *munshid* sang "Everything is perishing in the Beloved, the Prophet," no one found his words strange or objectionable.

Poetry and song are an important means of expression in Sufi life, so it is fitting to end this section with a few samples of Sufi songs in honor of the Prophet.[64]

The lights of Muḥammad shone and the full moons have disappeared
We have never seen anything like your beauty, oh face of joy
You are a sun, you are a moon, you are light upon light
You are an elixir and expensive, you are a lamp of happiness
Oh my love, oh Muḥammad, oh Imām of the two *qiblas*[65]
Whoever sees your face is happy in heaven and on earth
Jesus foretold your coming, Aḥmad, oh bringer of good news to the faithful
My intercessor, my bondsman with the Lord of all creatures
You have been blessed by God and all the angels
The Light is on you, oh *ṬāHā*, oh gift, oh Trustworthy One[66]
You have been blessed by God and all the angels.

My love, how beautiful you are! Glory be to Him who perfected you,
And how much He has favored you! He gave to you and did not withhold from you
My love, my love, my love, the Prophet is my love
Oh sun of the daylight, oh light of the perplexed
All goodness is in you, it follows you with every step
My love, how good you are; He adorned you with goodness
He created you from light, and made you happy with nearness[67]
My love, my love, my love, you are my love and my portion
Oh joy of joys, oh spirit of existence,

Oh best of God's creation, your light is on whoever travels (your path)
My love, how favored you are over men and jinn and angels
He sent you with love, a sun illuminating the sphere
My love, my love, my love, oh light from my Beloved
Oh light of the Throne of God, oh most noble of God's creatures,
Oh light of the niche of guidance, are you a man or an angel?[68]

The day of your birth, oh Messenger of God,
    The light shone forth in Mecca.
The joy of the hearts of all servants,
    The joy of the hearts of all mankind
The world rejoiced, oh Prophet,
    When they said, "The Light has come."
The good news descended from Heaven
    That the Prophet appeared in Mecca.
The Beloved is born, guidance is born,
    The one who was foretold is born.
Oh mercy to all creation,
    Oh best of those born of Mudar!
Oh gift from a generous Lord,
    Welcome to the lord of mankind
Oh possessor of great stature,
    Whoever takes refuge in you is victorious.

THE FAMILY OF THE PROPHET (AHL AL-BAYT)

Sufis believe that when Muhammad died, the world was not left bereft of his light. Its tangible presence was perpetuated, first by his immediate descendants, who are called the *ahl al-bayt* or *āl al-bayt* (literally, "people of the house"), and second by those who came to be known as the "friends of God" (*awliyā' Allāh*, which is most commonly translated as "saints"). As Shaykh ʿIzz said, "When God created His Beloved, Muhammad, He created him from His own essential light. Out of His love for His Beloved, He created from this light those who would love him and be dear to him, and they are the *ahl al-bayt* and the saints." Of these, the *ahl al-bayt* are those with the greatest portion of divine light and the greatest proximity to the Prophet.

The term *ahl al-bayt* is found in the Qur'an in reference to the families of both Abraham (11:73) and Muhammad (33:33). The verse referring to Muhammad's family warrants quotation here in full. At the beginning of the verse, the wives of Muhammad are being addressed, and the grammatical form of address is the feminine plural.

At a critical point, however, the pronoun shifts to the masculine plural, as indicated by "m.pl." in parentheses: "Remain (f.pl.) in your homes, and do not display yourselves in the manner of the former times of ignorance. Perform the prayer, give alms, and obey God and His Messenger. God only wishes to remove all filth from you (m.pl.), people of the house, and to purify you." In Arabic, the masculine plural may include either all males or both male and female subjects. Who, then, are the "people of the house" being addressed here?

A number of different ḥadīths seek to answer this question. In one version, Muhammad was about to engage in a test of strength with a Christian delegation from Najrān, in which each was to call down God's curse on the party that did not have the truth. He emerged from his house with his daughter Fāṭima; her husband, ʿAlī, who was also Muhammad's cousin; and their two sons, Ḥasan and Ḥusayn, and identified these as the people of his house. The Christian delegation was so struck by their countenances that they feared their entire community would be destroyed if they went on with the contest, so they withdrew.[69]

In another ḥadīth, given on the authority of Muhammad's wife Umm Salama, ʿAlī, Fāṭima, Ḥasan, and Ḥusayn are taken by Muhammad, embraced, and covered with a black shirt. Muhammad said, "My God, to You, not to hellfire, I and the people of my house." In a variant of this ḥadīth, also given on the authority of Umm Salama, the Prophet covers these same four with a cloak and says, "God, these are the people of my house and my special ones; remove filth from them and purify them," at which point the above-quoted Qurʾanic verse was revealed. Umm Salama asked whether she was not included in the people of his house, and Muhammad replied that she had an honored position as his wife, but the implication is that she is not one of the *ahl al-bayt*.

Although some Sunni authors include the Prophet's wives in the *ahl al-bayt*—and the Qurʾanic context would appear to warrant this interpretation—most agree with the Shiʿa that the designation *ahl al-bayt* is limited to ʿAli, Fāṭima, and their descendants. As Ibn Taymiyya explains, "Ḥadīth clarifies and explains the Qur'an, so although the context of the Qurʾanic text would seem to imply that the *ahl al-bayt* includes Muhammad's wives, for they are indeed of his house, the ḥadīth specifies that ʿAli, Fāṭima, Ḥasan and Ḥusayn are meant—for the bond of kinship is stronger than the bond of marriage."[70]

Both Sunni and Shiʿi Muslims interpret the Qurʾanic verse to mean that the wished-for purification of Muhammad's family did in fact occur. For Sufi authors, this purification from all filth meant that the *ahl al-bayt,* like the Prophet, are free from sin.[71]

THE ROLE OF ʿALĪ IN SUFISM

ʿAlī ibn Abī Ṭālib, the Prophet's cousin and son-in-law, is believed by the Shiʿa to be the first Imam, or legitimate spiritual and political successor to the Prophet, although he was deprived of his rightful rule by the first three Caliphs, Abū Bakr, ʿUmar, and ʿUthmān. Sunni Muslims acknowledge ʿAlī as the fourth and last of the "Rightly-Guided" Calilphs, who include his aforementioned three predecessors and view the entire period of the Rightly-Guided Caliphs (632–661) as an extension of the golden age of Muhammad's prophethood, a time when Muslims were unified and the right religion reigned supreme in the lives of both rulers and ruled, when people's hearts were pure and looked to the interests of the community first and foremost. Both Sunni and Shiʿi perspectives on ʿAlī involve a certain falsification of history. As for the Shiʿi claim that Muhammad had designated ʿAlī to succeed him, there is no historical evidence to support this contention. Sunni depictions of the period of the Rightly-Guided Caliphs as an extension of the golden age of Muslim unity and morality overlook the fact that ʿUmar, ʿUthmān, and ʿAlī were all murdered, ʿUthmān by mutinous soldiers over allegations of fiscal impropriety and nepotism, and that the entire period of ʿAlī's Caliphate was marked by civil war. ʿAlī could not even remain in Arabia, where his opposition included Muhammad's wife, ʿĀʾisha, and made his base in the Iraqi town of Kūfa, whence he faced opposition on three fronts: insurgents in Arabia; ʿUthmān's nephew and former governor in Damascus, Muʿāwiya, future founder of the Umayyad dynasty (661–750); and a zealous group of discontented defectors from his own camp, who were known as the Khawārij or Khārijīs. It was a Khārijī who finally killed ʿAlī in 661, allowing Muʿāwiya to consolidate the Islamic empire once again from its new capital in Damascus, Syria.

It is true that the civil war has troubled many Sunnis, who feel constrained to honor all the Companions of Muhammad, including ʿAlī, his highly esteemed Caliphal predecessors, and his rival, Muʿāwiya. For the Shiʿa, the episode merely confirms their perspective that the *ahl al-bayt* have always suffered abuse at the hands of their fellow Muslims, for such is the lot of the righteous minority in this world. They freely curse Abū Bakr, ʿUmar, ʿUthmān, and Muʿāwiya as villainous usurpers, conspirators, and enemies of the truth. ʿAlī became exalted among them not merely as the most worthy of Muhammad's Companions and the designated successor to the Prophet but as a recipient of the divine light and esoteric knowledge, which makes him—and his sons who became Imams after him—the necessary spiritual guide for the entire Muslim community. In a ḥadīth popular among the Shiʿa, "He who dies without knowing the Imām of his age dies the death of an unbeliever." Acknowledgment of and belief in the Imām became, for the Shiʿa, the pivot of faith.

Among Sunni Muslims—and Egypt's Muslims are entirely Sunni—ʿAlī also came, in time, to acquire a special status, and for no one is this more important than for the Sufi. ʿAlī's special relationship with Muhammad was emphasized in ḥadīths frequently quoted in contemporary Sufi literature: "ʿAlī is a part of me, as the head is part of the body. ʿAlī is part of me as Aaron was part of Moses, although there is no prophet after me."[72] ʿAlī had been, in fact, like a much younger brother to Muhammad, who, as an orphan, had been raised by ʿAlī's father. ʿAlī was one of the first to embrace Islam and had enjoyed Muhammad's confidence throughout his prophethood. Yet ʿAlī's status became more than that of a standard-bearer and confidant: ʿAlī became for the Sufis, as he had become for the Shiʿa, the recipient of the Prophet's esoteric knowledge, through the medium of special instruction from the Prophet, direct instruction by God Himself, and his inheritance of the divine light that was in Muhammad. Ḥadīths extol ʿAlī's wisdom and spiritual knowledge: "I am the city of knowledge, and ʿAlī is its gate"; "ʿAlī is the best judge among you."[73] ʿAlī himself is quoted as saying, "I learned one thousand things from the Messenger of God, and for each one of these I received knowledge of one thousand things by inspiration from God."[74]

Most Sufi spiritual lineages go back to the Prophet through ʿAlī, who represents spiritual realization and gnosis or mystical knowledge. ʿUmar, in contrast, is nicknamed "the intellect of the community" (*ʿaql al-umma),* an ambivalent compliment from a Sufi perspective. For although ʿUmar is known for his intelligence and zeal for the law, his perception was limited to external appearances, whereas ʿAlī understood hidden spiritual meanings. The following story narrated by an Egyptian shaykh illustrates both ʿAlī's wisdom and the Sufi belief that deeper spiritual truths are often the opposite of the way things appear to be:

> A man was brought to ʿUmar for saying, "I love temptation[75] and hate the true reality[76] and believe the Jews and Christians regarding what was said to them, and I believe in what I have not seen and affirm what was not created." ʿUmar summoned ʿAlī to judge the man [in deference to the Prophet's words, "ʿAlī is the best judge among you"]. ʿAlī said, "The man has told the truth. He loves temptation, for the Qur'an says, 'Your wealth and children are a temptation' (8:28). He hates the true reality, which is death. He believes the Jews and Christians [when] 'the Jews say the Christians have nothing to stand on, and the Christians say the Jews have nothing to stand on' (2:113). He believes in what he does not see, that is, God, be He praised and exalted. And he affirms what has not been created, which is the Hour (of Judgment), which has not yet come."[77]

This same author describes ʿAlī as "the sea of the knowledge of the Messenger of God, the secret of the Messenger of God, and the lamp of the Messenger of God" and quotes the ḥadīth, "People were created from several trees; ʿAlī and I were created from the same tree."[78]

Ḥadīths included in Sunni canons indicate that whoever accepts the authority of Muhammad should likewise accept that of ʿAlī, and that God is a friend to ʿAlī's friends and an enemy to his enemies.[79] Some Sufi authors interpret this as an actual designation by Muhammad of ʿAlī as his successor and accept the Shiʿi perspective that while ʿAlī was busy with the Prophet's funerary arrangements, Abū Bakr and ʿUmar defrauded him of his right to rule,[80] although they still feel constrained to give these and other opponents to ʿAlī's rule their due as righteous Companions of the Prophet.[81] This increasing Sunni acceptance of aspects of the Shiʿi version of history and of the special status attached to ʿAlī and his descendants is not unique to Egyptians and is part of what Marshall Hodgson called "the moulding of Islam as a whole in a Shiʿitic direction."[82]

In Sufi tradition, ʿAlī is the *fatā*, the courageous "young man" who, like Abraham in the Qur'an (21:58–60), destroyed the idols of his people. According to legend, ʿAlī prevented his mother during her pregnancy from bowing before idols. He spoke with the Prophet from the womb, and his mother was unable to give birth to him until she entered the Kaʿba; hence, ʿAlī was born in the spiritual center of the earth, the point directly beneath the Throne of God. He was born clean, his face full of light, smiling and looking to heaven.[83] According to a ḥadīth, on the day of Resurrection, Abū Bakr will be on Muhammad's right, ʿUmar on his left, ʿUthmān behind him, and ʿAlī in front of him, carrying the banner of praise, and all creatures will be beneath his banner. He is qualified for such an honor, says Muhammad, because "he has patience like mine, beauty like that of Joseph, and strength like Gabriel's."[84] Some later Sunni ḥadīths adopt a good deal of the Shiʿi devotion to ʿAlī:

"To look at the face of ʿAlī is worship."

"ʿAlī will shine in Paradise like the morning star for the people of this world."[85]

These ḥadīths are reproduced in works written by contemporary Egyptian Sufis, although such glorification borders on the idolatrous from a Sunni perspective.

OTHER MEMBERS OF THE AHL AL-BAYT

Although as a historical personage she remains obscure, Muhammad's daughter Fāṭima acquired special status in Shiʿism and Sufism as the wife of ʿAlī, the mother of Ḥasan and Ḥusayn, and the single link of direct descent from the Prophet. Special signs and omens surrounded her from when she was in the womb, as they did for her father and husband. Fāṭima is known in Sunni tradition as well as Shiʿi tradition for her piety, poverty, and nobility of spirit, but among the Shiʿa and Sufis, her closeness to the Prophet is emphasized: she is a part of him, what hurts her hurts him, and what makes her happy makes him happy. She was unlike other women: she was called "the virgin" *(al-batūl),* for she suffered neither menstrual nor postpartum blood, which would render her ritually impure. She gave birth to Ḥusayn and immediately rose and prayed the sunset prayer. Concerning her, Muhammad said, "My daughter Fāṭima is a *ḥūrī* in human form. She does not menstruate or become deflowered like other women."[86] Fāṭima, the youngest of Muhammad's four daughters, is said to resemble him the most. She is nicknamed *al-Zahrāʾ* ("the Radiant One"), "mother of her father," and "chief among the ladies of Paradise." She lived only six months after Muhammad's death.[87]

ʿAlī and Fāṭima's eldest son, Ḥasan, though acknowledged by the Shiʿa as their second Imām, renounced any claim to power by recognizing Muʿāwiya as Caliph. Shiʿi tradition has all the Imāms suffering martyrdom, and Sunni authors appear to accept the view that Ḥasan was poisoned by Muʿāwiya's wife.[88] But the focus of attention rapidly shifts to his brother, Ḥusayn, who acquired a pivotal role in Shiʿi piety and likewise became important in Egyptian Sufism as a spiritual guide and, after Muhammad, the best beloved.

Ḥusayn, who was invited by the people of Kūfa, in southern Iraq, to lead a revolt against the Umayyad government of Muʿāwiya's son Yazīd, was slaughtered, along with his supporters and almost all the male members of his family, on the plains of Karbalā'. The guilt-stricken Kūfans, whose fears for their own safety had prevented them from coming to his aid, vowed to die in battle to avenge his death and to redeem their guilt by devotion to the cause of Ḥusayn and his family. The Twelver Shiʿa express their devotion by elaborate commemorations of Ḥusayn's death, especially on its anniversary. They weep, with copious tears and loud wails, at the recitation of the story of his martyrdom, and young men in procession whip or cut themselves in passionate identification with his suffering and expression of their grief. Ḥusayn's martyrdom acquired, for them, a redemptive value for those who loved him and his family. Love for the family of the Prophet acquired a deeply soteriological quality.

In Egypt, Ḥusayn is also known as "prince of martyrs" *(sayyid al-shuhadā')*, and he and his brother Ḥasan are known as the "chiefs of the youth of Paradise" *(sayyidā shabāb ahl al-janna)*. Yet his importance to the Egyptians derives primarily from his closeness to the Prophet and the existence of his beautiful shrine-mosque in Cairo. As Muhammad proclaimed in a ḥadīth written on an illuminated plaque prominently displayed on the outside wall of the mosque, "Ḥusayn is from me (or, part of me), and I am from Ḥusayn." His life is seen as a continuation of that of the Prophet. He is beloved to God and His angels.[89] A visit to Ḥusayn's mosque, centrally located across a busy thoroughfare from the Al-Azhar university mosque, has the same value, in popular pious opinion, as a visit to the Prophet's mosque in Medina. Of all the moulid celebrations, Ḥusayn's is the most important, with the exception of the Prophet's, which is, however, too scattered and diffuse in its celebration to create the same impact. All of the Orders attend the Ḥusayn moulid, even the Naqshbandīs, who shun most such celebrations. As respected as ʿAlī and Fāṭima are in Egypt, they do not elicit the same passion as those members of the *ahl al-bayt* who have shrines there. In Ḥusayn's case, only his head is thought to be entombed in the holy shrine, and some scholars doubt even this, yet even that is not necessary. As Shaykh ʿIzz explained to me, there are shrines for Ḥusayn in many countries, and in all of them his light is present.

ʿIzz taught the doctrine, unique in my experience among the Sufis, that Ḥusayn did not actually die at Karbalā'. He unveiled this doctrine in a spontaneous teaching given to a group of approximately twenty men during the moulid of Ḥusayn. He asked those seated around him, "Did Ḥusayn really die at Karbalāʾ? The history books say he did, but did he?"

The men hesitated to reply. Finally one young man said, "It doesn't seem right."

ʿIzz continued: "He did not die, but it only appeared that way to them."

These words are an almost direct quotation from the Qurʾanic denial of the crucifixion of Jesus (4:157). The connection with Jesus was deliberate. Ḥusayn, said ʿIzz, like Jesus, was not flesh and blood but was pure light. How do we know? The Qurʾan says that Mary was purified beyond all other women, which in Islamic understanding of ritual purity implies that she suffered no menstrual or postpartum blood. This being so, the child that she bore could not have been flesh and blood but must have been pure light, which was why Jesus could not have been killed on the cross.[90] Likewise, of Fāṭima it is said that she gave birth to Ḥusayn and rose and prayed the sunset prayer. This implies that she had no postpartum blood. Therefore Ḥusayn had a body of pure light, like Jesus, and like him could not be killed.

On hearing this teaching, cries of glorification to God rose from the crowd of young men. One of them was so overcome with joy that he began to massage ʿIzz's legs and feet, which were numbed from his sitting on the ground for five hours.[91]

This denial of the reality of Ḥusayn's martyrdom appears to be more compatible with Sunni triumphalism, which expects victory to be granted to the righteous during their lifetimes, than with Shiʿi expectations that the righteous suffer in this world. Nonetheless, the historical reality of Ḥusayn's death is seldom denied by Sunni authors and is universally regarded as a major tragedy. The suppression of a Shiʿi revolt by the Islamic state does not justify, even in the eyes of Sunni writers, the murder of the grandson of the Prophet. As Ibn Taymiyya wrote, "Ḥusayn was killed by miserable perpetrators of abomination. His death was one of the greatest disasters Islam has faced."[92] According to ʿIzz, only the elect among the Sufis are aware of the deeper truth of Ḥusayn's alleged martyrdom. I have, however, never heard any other Sufis speak of it; on the contrary, Ḥusayn's death at Karbalāʾ is implied in his frequently used title, "prince of martyrs."

Regardless of whether or not he was a martyr, the mood surrounding stories about Ḥusayn in Egypt is not mournful, as it is among the Shiʿa. Rather, he is joyously celebrated. He is appealed to as *Bābā* ("Daddy"), at whose gates both physical and spiritual healing are expected. He is intensely loved and venerated; often, songs addressed to the Prophet are coupled with loving words and appeals to Ḥusayn.

After Ḥusayn, his sister Zaynab, known as "Sayyida Zaynab" or simply "*Al-Sayyida*" ("the Lady"), is the best-loved and most frequently called upon member of the *ahl al-bayt* in Egypt. The authenticity of her tomb is denied by the contemporary scholar Yūsuf Rāgib, who writes that the tomb of this unknown Zaynab was identified as that of Ḥusayn's sister only in the sixteenth century in the writings of Shaʿrānī and that the real Sayyida Zaynab never came to Egypt at all.[93] Such doubts never arise in Egypt, however, where the pious are certain of her physical presence among them and where her legend passes from her heroism at Karbalāʾ, where she is credited with standing up to the Umayyad commander and saving Ḥusayn's sick son, ʿAlī, from death, to her appearance before the Caliph, Yazīd, in Damascus, to her chosen exile in the land of Egypt, where she was treated with honor and consulted for her wisdom. She is nicknamed "Umm Hāshim," "mother of [the clan of] Hāshim," for her role in rescuing the progeny of the Prophet from decimation. Sayyida Zaynab's shrine in Cairo contains a lamp, the oil of which is thought to heal eye diseases,[94] and her dome is said to radiate with light when the members of the saintly "hidden court" convene at her shrine to decide the affairs of the living.[95]

ʿAlī, the son of Ḥusayn, is nicknamed Zayn al-ʿĀbidīn, "the ornament of the worshippers," and is known for his piety and the composition of devotional poetry.[96] He is venerated by the Shiʿa as their fourth Imām (after ʿAlī, Ḥasan, and Ḥusayn), and he is allegedly buried in his shrine in Cairo, near the slaughterhouses in the southern part of the city, where on Saturdays he is visited and celebrated with public dhikrs in the courtyard before a coffeehouse just outside his mosque. The area in which his shrine is situated is desperately poor. The surrounding cemetery is littered with tattered cardboard structures that are home to many destitute people, and in the immediate vicinity of the shrine, the ground is collapsing because of the rising water table beneath it. This does not diminish the popularity of his shrine, where the dhikr is said to be particularly beautiful.

Other members of the *ahl al-bayt* who have shrines in Cairo and weekly visiting days include Fāṭima al-Nabawiyya, daughter of Ḥusayn, whose shrine off an alley near the southern gate of the old city attracts a fair number on Monday afternoons for dhikr, and Sayyida Nafīsa, the great-granddaughter of Ḥasan, who is nicknamed *nafīsat al-ʿilm,* "the precious gem of knowledge," for her reputation for wisdom and religious knowledge. She was allegedly a teacher and close friend of the great legal scholar al-Shāfiʿī (d. 820), whose tomb is likewise the focus of much veneration in Cairo, and legend credits her with many miracles and acts of piety. Her mosque near the Citadel is quite beautiful, and Louis Massignon called her "the true patron saint of Cairo."[97] Again, Yūsuf Rāgib casts doubt on the authenticity of her tomb and her legend, by pointing out that the oldest mention of her comes more than 150 years after her death, and that in a Shiʿi document. The first Sunni work on her life was commissioned by the Mamluk Sultan, al-Malik al-Nāṣir Muḥammad ibn Qalāwūn, and the biographies of Shāfiʿī do not mention her at all.[98] Rāgib likewise labels the tombs of Ruqayya, daughter of ʿAlī; Sukayna, daughter of Ḥusayn ("Sitt Sakīna"); and ʿĀʾisha, daughter of Jaʿfar al-Ṣādiq, as spurious. Ruqayya was never in Egypt, he asserts, and the existence of a daughter of Jaʿfar named ʿĀʾisha is entirely unknown.[99]

Such academic doubts, however, are unknown and irrelevant to the pious in Egypt, who are certain of the presence of these holy personages in their midst. Egyptians believe their love of the *ahl al-bayt* is greater than that of other Sunni countries, without rising to the idolatrous extremism of Shiʿism. The legends of Zaynab and Nafīsa and the arrival of Ḥusayn's head in Egypt, among others, depict the Egyptians welcoming in great throngs these venerated members of the Prophet's family who had suffered persecution and expulsion in other lands. When Nafīsa decided to move back to Medina, the Egyptians successfully pleaded with her through their sultan to remain in Egypt.[100] Egypt is unusually blessed because of the presence of so many tombs of the *ahl al-bayt,* say some Egyptians. One author writes, "Egypt will remain a land of peace, security, prosperity, love and acceptance, all by the virtue and blessing of the *āl al-bayt.*"[101]

THE BLESSINGS OF LOVING THE AHL AL-BAYT

The *ahl al-bayt* are extolled in Egypt for their purity, piety, humility, knowledge, miracles, and ability to guide the wayward back to the true faith. They are, according to one author, "the tree of prophecy, the locus of God's message, a spring of mercy, a mine of knowledge, fountains of wisdom, the treasures of the Merciful. . . . By them we are guided from the shadows. They are the repository of the secret of the Chosen One [Muhammad]."[102] Another author writes that the *ahl al-bayt* are "a people by whose recollection assemblies are perfumed, by whose speech books are ornamented, by whom needs are relieved in this world and intercession is obtained in the next. By their virtue and blessings, God answers every prayer and fulfills every hope in honor of them. They are the righteous family and holy relations, in whose veins runs the blood of the Prophet, in whose deeds radiate the lights of his spirit, and in whose hearts and minds dwell his secret and his assistance."[103] The trials they suffered refined and purified them and earned them a high spiritual rank, for those whom God loves and chooses must endure suffering.[104] They illustrate Qur'anic teachings in their lives so profoundly that one author calls them "the clear exegesis and true interpretation of the Book of God in their life, their character, their morals, their asceticism and their struggle."[105]

Therefore, love for the *ahl al-bayt* is a holy obligation for all who love God and His Messenger. The Qur'an itself commands Muslims to love the Prophet's family, when it says, "I do not ask you for a reward [for delivering the revelation] except the love of those who are near of kin *(al-mawadda fī 'l-qurbā)*" (42:23). Although some interpret this to mean that the Prophet is pleading with his own relatives not to persecute him for delivering the message,[106] or that the kin referred to are not the Prophet's, for that would mean that the Prophet is in fact asking for a reward,[107] the most common interpretation is that although the Prophet asks nothing for himself, his family is to be loved by the Muslims. As is commonly stated, he who loves God must love God's Messenger, and he who loves God's Messenger must love his family; and conversely, he who hates the *ahl al-bayt* hates the Messenger of God, and he who hates the Messenger of God hates God. Indeed, whoever loves them may expect God's mercy and whoever hates them may expect God's wrath.[108]

Sufi authors cite many ḥadīths to stress, through textual authority, the orthodoxy of their devotion to the *ahl al-bayt*. One of the most frequently cited is the so-called ḥadīth of the "two weighty burdens," which is given in several variants in different sources. The following version comes from the *Musnad* of Aḥmad ibn Ḥanbal (d. 855), who is as much a symbol of Sunni "orthodoxy" as any author: "I leave among you two weighty burdens: the Book of God, a rope extended from heaven to earth, and my family, the people of my house. The Gentle One has informed me that they will never be separated until they are returned to my Pool, so be careful how you treat them after I am gone."[109]

In another version, the Qur'an and the *ahl al-bayt* are called two things "which will keep you from going astray if you cling to them."[110] In another ḥadīth, the Prophet admonishes the Muslims, "Love God because of the graces with which He has nourished you, love me because of your love for God, and love my family because of your love for me."[111] And in yet another ḥadīth, "Any prayer which does not include a blessing on me and my family will not be accepted." Faith itself is predicated on love of the Muslim for Muhammad's family: "A servant does not believe until he loves me more than himself, he loves my family more than his own, and he loves my essence more than his own."[112]

In Egyptian Sufism, as in Shiʿism, love for the family of the Prophet has a definitely soteriological quality. It is not merely optional but is the very basis by which a person attains salvation. A number of ḥadīths convey this idea, the most famous of which compares the *ahl al-bayt* to Noah's Ark: "The people of my house are among you like the Ark of Noah: whoever rides it is saved, and whoever stays behind perishes." In a less commonly quoted ḥadīth, the Prophet is laughing, his face full of light, having been told that all those who love ʿAlī and Fāṭima will be given a leaf from the tree of Ṭūbā, in Paradise, that will redeem them from hellfire. "So my brother and cousin ʿAlī and my daughter have become the redemption of the men and women of my nation from hellfire."[113] As one modern Sufi poem says:

> The Prophet Muhammad and his legatee [*waṣī*, that is, ʿAli]
> And his brother and his pure virgin daughter
> Are the people of the cloak, and I by devotion to them
> Hope for peace and salvation in the afterlife.[114]

Indeed, the family of the prophet are a security for the welfare of the people of the earth in this life as well. In another ḥadīth recorded by Aḥmad ibn Ḥanbal in his *Musnad,* "The stars are a security for the people of heaven, so that if the stars disappeared, so would the people of heaven. The people of my house are a security for the people of the earth, so that if the people of my house disappeared, so would the people of the earth."[115]

Given this background, it is less surprising than it would otherwise be to hear a shaykh say, "They are the source from which we have everything," or for a song to say, "love for them is the best worship." Love for the *ahl al-bayt* has tremendous spiritual benefits for those who would travel the Sufi path, say many Sufis, not only because of the high stature of the *ahl al-bayt* but also because of the foundational quality of love as the basis for the Sufi path. Writes one author, "Loving them is the foundation and basis of the way to God. All the spiritual states *(aḥwāl)* and stations *(maqāmāt)* are degrees of love."[116]

According to Shaykh ʿIzz, the Prophet said in a ḥadīth, "Loving my family for a single day is better than a year's worship." This is so, he said, because God has placed love in a very high spiritual station and has said that those who love each other in God are among those who will be sheltered in His shadow on a Day when there will be no shadow but His. On that Day, even the prophets and martyrs will be jealous of the high rank of those who loved each other in the spirit of God, meeting together and separating in His pleasure without any material interests to bind them. On that day, they will stand in light, and their faces will be illuminated, and they will have no fear. There is no faith, according to ḥadīth, without love. So, said ʿIzz, the foundation of all things is love. And the first ones we should love are the *ahl al-bayt*. The Prophet said that on the Day of Resurrection, a man will be with those he loves. Those who love the Prophet and the *ahl al-bayt* in this life will enjoy their high station in the next.

Many ḥadīths accepted in the Sunni canons promise great rewards to those who love the *ahl al-bayt:* whoever dies in the love of Muhammad's family dies the death of a martyr and goes immediately to Paradise; whoever dies in the love of Muhammad's family will be forgiven all his sins; whoever dies in the love of Muhammad's family will be conducted to Paradise as a bride is conducted to her groom; God will open a way to Paradise for him from his grave; God will place light in his grave and an abode for the angels of mercy.[117]

A much-loved song sometimes heard spontaneously sung by devotees at moulids celebrates the *ahl al-bayt* and conveys the sentiment of joyous devotion perhaps better than any other:

Family of *ṬāHā,* family of *YāSīn,* the Trustworthy One,
You are our support, you are the Ark
Love for them, my friend, is the best worship (2x)
They are the salvation of the people and the gate of happiness
They are the sons of the Radiant One, they are the people of mastery
And the Prophet is the guarantor for those who love them. . . .

Love them, my friend, if you wish to arrive (at the divine presence)
They are branches from the Messenger of God, who is the root
They are the sons of the Radiant One and masters of every age. . . .
Love them, my friend, if you wish to travel this path
They are the salvation of the people, from them comes every good thing
They are the sons of the Radiant One, they are the gate of worship
A trustworthy handhold to grasp[118]
Family of *Ṭāhā*, family of *Yāsīn* the Trustworthy One,
You are our support, you are the Ark
Love them, my friend, if you wish to travel this path,
Love them, my friend, if you wish to succeed (2x)
They are the salvation of the people, they are the manifestation of (God's) secret
They are the sons of the Radiant One, who light up the plains
The people of the house, their grandfather is *Ṭāhā* the Trustworthy,
You are our support, you are the Ark
Love them, for love is a paradise in the hearts (2x). . . .
People of the house of the Chosen One, oh pure ones (2x)
You are our support in matters of the world and in religion.

When I asked Shaykh ʿIzz if such lines as "love for them, my friend, is the best worship" could not lead to laxity in the performance of religious duties, he denied that this was so. The first way to show love for them, he said, is to follow their example in morality, piety, and religious observance. Nonetheless, popular devotion to the *ahl al-bayt* is controversial precisely because it appears to many as a substitute for observance of Islamic religious requirements and because this devotion is expressed in practices that are often deemed heretical: the visitation of tombs, prayer to holy personages rather than to God, and the celebration of moulids. The Sufis, however, see their love and devotion as the very essence of their spiritual life.

This point was brought home forcefully to me by the old man who functioned as *wakīl*, or trustee, of Bayt ʿAbāṭa, in the absence of its young shaykh. As we sat in their *khidma* during the moulid of Fāṭima al-Nabawiyya, I asked him my oft-repeated question, "What is Sufism?" The old man looked at me in astonishment that I could ask so naive a question, for the members of this group persisted in seeing me as a fellow devotee of the *ahl al-bayt* rather than a researcher, despite my explanations for my presence. When he responded, it was with unexpected intensity:

Sufism means love for the family of the Prophet. The Prophet is our intercessor and the one who brings us close to God, and it is through his family

> that we come close to him, just as the Prophet said, "Ḥusayn is from me and I am from Ḥusayn. Whoever loves Ḥusayn loves me." It is love for the family of the Prophet that causes us to be purified. This is why we come to the shrines of the family of the Prophet. Whoever loves the family of the Prophet is accepted by God, because the saints of God are close to God. You love the family of the Prophet, so you are accepted by God. God listens to everyone who calls on Him, and we call on Him through our Prophet and through his family. Why else would I leave my comfortable bed and come sleep on the pavement? [He was spending the entire week at the *khidma,* day and night.] I wouldn't be able to sleep on the pavement if it weren't for my love for the Prophet and his family. It is this love which purifies us and brings us close to God. That is why we do dhikr here. That is why we come here to serve people.

Scholars writing on the moulids often fail to note the centrality of devotion to the *ahl al-bayt* and the saints in contemporary Sufi life. The moulids are usually described as great public festivals, which they are, and opportunities to obtain unusual blessing, which is also true. Their social and economic aspects are emphasized, but their role in Sufi life is rarely adequately noted. It is extremely revealing that when I delivered a lecture on my research at the American Research Center in Egypt in March 1988, an Egyptian professor of history who was present denied that the moulids have any religious significance at all. He certainly did not see them as Sufi celebrations. A student audience at the American University in Cairo was likewise cynical about religious motives for participation in moulid celebrations. But although moulid celebrations, and shrine visitation in general, attract great crowds that go well beyond the ranks of the Sufis, the special role of these celebrations in Sufi spiritual life must be recognized. Many Sufis spend most of their lives attending moulid celebrations, traveling a well-known circuit. While there can certainly be nonspiritual motives for establishing a *khidma* at a moulid, including the prestige that comes from giving hospitality and attaining name recognition within the Sufi community, typically hosts and hostesses explained to me that they were offering hospitality simply as a service to the people for the sake of God and His pleasure—and often at considerable expense. The spiritual motivations are highlighted in the *wakīl*'s response to my question. Although the role of the *khidma*s as shelters for visiting pilgrims is often emphasized, why indeed should this old man leave his comfortable bed in Cairo in order to sleep on the pavement near a shrine in Cairo, if not out of devotion to the *ahl al-bayt?* What the *wakīl*'s statement underlines is that he conceives of his entire service to God in terms of his service to the family of the Prophet, through dhikr at their shrines and attendance at moulids, where he offers food to passersby and lives in the remembrance and blessings of the saint who is present among the devotees. Furthermore, this devotion to the *ahl al-bayt* is seen as a means of purification, the way to God. This statement clarifies what Sufism really is for many Sufis in Egypt today. While outsiders may criticize their devotion to the *ahl al-bayt* and find their activities heretical and irrelevant to spiritual life, they are the very essence of spiritual life for the Sufi. Although moral purification, knowledge of esoteric spiritual truths, and annihilation of the ego continue to be major concerns of contemporary Sufism, the average Sufi hopes by means of devotion to the Prophet and his family to be purified and ultimately allowed into the presence of the Prophet, the gateway to God. The practices associated with moulid celebrations might be slightly modified in order to bring about greater conformity with standard Islamic interpretation, but the abolition of shrine visitation and moulid celebrations would be a disaster for Sufi spirituality as it is understood in Egypt.

In this context, perhaps we can understand what might otherwise seem to be a terribly conceited claim by Ibrāhīm ʿAlī ("Shaykh Fāris"), author of a book entitled *The Virtues and Special Characteristics of the Family of the Prophet*. He writes, "If you read this book often and arrive at the rank of love, you will enjoy intimate companionship, and the veils will be withdrawn from you, and you will be given the eyes of inner vision *(baṣīra)* and enter the ranks of those who witness the secrets of God *(ahl al-mushāhada)*, and then your spirit will be elevated to the rank of contentment and nearness and acceptance . . . The *ahl al-bayt* are the clear proof in the Book of God and with God. They are the way that the servant reaches his Lord, well-pleased and well-pleasing, God willing."[119] The author frequently exhorts his readers to read his book often and meditate on it and promises that great spiritual benefits will accrue as a result—benefits that are specifically the goals of the Sufi path: intimate companionship with God, attainment of inner vision, witnessing the secrets of God, and ultimately reaching the divine presence. This goes well beyond the mundane ends often associated with shrine visitation and devotion to the saints. Although it is true that ordinary people visit shrines to make special pleas for intercession regarding health, disputes, examinations, or other such matters, for Sufis, devotion to the saint him- or herself is the goal. If the *ahl al-*

bayt are indeed the way to God, then it is no vain boast for Shaykh Fāris to say that meditation on his book, which enumerates the virtues of the *ahl al-bayt,* is likely to lead to increased love and devotion toward them on the part of the reader, which may yield many spiritual fruits.

The following song, sung mainly in Shādhilī circles, extols the Sufi's love and devotion to the *ahl al-bayt:*

How wonderfully beautiful is the light of God![120]
    How wonderfully beautiful is the love of God!
How wonderfully beautiful, oh Messenger of God!
    Raise the crescent, oh men of God!
The love of Ḥusayn and al-Sayyida [Zaynab],
    love for them both is all contentment.
My heart and spirit belong to Ḥusayn,
    and all my love is for al-Sayyida.
Oh Pure One [Zaynab], your light goes
    from [the shrine of] Ḥusayn to [the shrine of] al-Sayyida
Even the visitors of Zayn al-ʿĀbidīn
    are as if they were at [the shrine of] al-Sayyida
Oh family of the Prophet, by God, my spirit
    is mad with the love of the Messenger of God.
The area around your shrines—how amazing—
    light is on it from God.
Oh people of the house, your light, by God,
    is gathering the hearts of the servants of God
In love and the remembrance of God
    and "there is no god but God!"
At the gate, oh Pure One [Zaynab], we call you,
    you who are kept by God's providence.
The people of heaven look at you,
    blessing you with light around you.
They bless you with light, mother of Hāshim,
    they bless with an infatuated spirit!
They bless in the eternal sanctuary,
    And circle round about the shrine of al-Sayyida.
I came to visit you, my lords!
    They said that visiting was beyond custom.
If I am one of the people of happiness,
    let it benefit us.
At your gate I said, "Oh commanding one,
    you are the one who helped me."
I swear to you my faithful love, oh light of my eye,
    by the right of our lord Ḥusayn.

I swear to you my faithful love, oh son of Ḥusayn,
 our lord ʿAlī Zayn al-ʿĀbidīn.
Raise the crescent, oh sister of Ḥusayn,
 oh Pure One, you are our guide![121]

The centrality of devotion to the *ahl al-bayt* in Egyptian Sufism lends itself to accusations of Shiʿism, and indeed such accusations have occasionally been made.[122] Some modern Sunni Muslims say that although the descendants of the Prophet should be honored as such, they have no particular distinction beyond their piety and their noble descent. On the other hand, some Egyptian Sufis hold views regarding the *ahl al-bayt* that are remarkably similar to those of the Shiʿa. For example, Shaykh Fāris writes that most books do not give the *ahl al-bayt* their due, that the (Sunni) Muslim community engaged in continuing conspiracies against them until the advent of (Shiʿi) Fāṭimid rule, that many of the ḥadīths honoring the *ahl al-bayt* have been lost, burnt, or otherwise suppressed because of the prevalence of hatred, envy, scheming, and deceit, and that the awaited Mahdi is none other than the twelfth Imām of the Twelver Shiʿa.[123]

More often than criticisms of being Shiʿi, Sufis are accused of outright infidelity to Islam and unbelief for a veneration that, to the minds of many Sunni Muslims, is idolatrous. Many Sufi authors feel compelled to defend their devotion to the *ahl al-bayt* by quoting such textual sources as Ḥadīth and prominent Sunni authorities. Shaykh ʿAbd al-Salām al-Ḥilwānī defended his devotion with the reckless abandon of a true lover in the following poem:

Let me glorify the family of Muhammad,
 for they are my light and the source of my devotion.
They are my most exalted support, theirs is the lofty assistance
 They are the power of piety and the sun of my destination.
Leave me in the love of Ḥusayn and his grandfather,
 from their exalted station I witness all spiritual realities.
Do you reproach me for love, although love is a grace;
 if the longing heart tastes it, it will not wander.
If my love for the descendants of Aḥmad is heresy,
 then I will be led by that heresy as long as I live.
I am not removed from their love, because I know my Lord
 through them, for they are the source of my acquaintance with Him.
My moment of ecstasy was prolonged, and I delighted in passionate love;
 my heart is the heart of a lover, on fire.
The spirit of conviction has guided me, and my destination
 is the abodes of divine manifestation; you are the best guide for me.

The wedding feasts were revealed to me; they are witnesses;
the spirits drew near to me, and conducted me [as a bride to the bridegroom].[124]

Pilgrims traveling to visit the shrines of the *ahl al-bayt* may sometimes be heard singing, "We come to you, we come to you, seeking your pleasure! Were it not for God's grace on us, we would not have come to you!"

Beyond explicit Qur'anic texts and ḥadīths supporting the requirement to love the *ahl al-bayt*, Sufis believe there are implicit references to this for those who have spiritual understanding. In a teaching at the moulid of Ḥusayn, Shaykh ʿIzz said, "The Messenger of God loved *sūrat al-qāf* [chapter 50 of the Qur'an, which begins, '*Qāf* (a letter of the Arabic alphabet) and the Qur'an'] very much. He used to recite it from the pulpit on Fridays. The first letter in it is what? *Qaf*. 'And the Qur'an.' So 'the Qur'an' is added to '*qāf*.' '*Qāf* and the Qur'an.' It is a simile for what? A shaykh sitting with someone next to him. People say, 'The shaykh and so-and-so.' The one that is most important is mentioned first. The nature of logic is this. Here the *qāf* is the *qāf* of *qurbā* (kinship). Shāfiʿī realized this when he said, 'I take love for the *ahl al-bayt* as a religious duty.' " The appeal to the authority of Shāfiʿī (d. 820), founder of an Islamic legal school widely followed in Egypt, is intended to silence critics claiming to uphold Islamic law by undermining Sufi devotion to the *ahl al-bayt*. Love for the *ahl al-bayt*, according to Shaykh ʿIzz's esoteric interpretation of the Qur'anic text, in some sense has priority even over the Qur'an, although the two are always joined together, according to the ḥadīth of the "two weighty burdens." The *ahl al-bayt* are, according to ʿIzz, "the pillars of the Qur'an."

The relationship of the believer to individual members of the Prophet's family buried in Cairo may become quite intimate and bears many of the marks of an ordinary human relationship. This intimacy is evident in the frequently shouted cries of "*Bābā!*" to Ḥusayn, and "Māmā!" to Sayyida Zaynab or Sayyida Nafīsa. Some regular visitors to their shrines claim to be able to see the inhabitants of the tombs and to converse with them. Greeting the inhabitant of the tomb is, in any case, part of the etiquette of shrine visitation. One time a man who was a frequent visitor to Sayyida Zaynab greeted her, but she failed to return his greeting. He was as incensed as a spurned lover and left angrily, vowing never to return. But that night she appeared to him in a dream and told him that she had seen the Prophet standing behind him, and she dared not speak in the presence of her grandfather. And so they were reconciled. Shaykh ʿIzz claims to receive regular spiritual guidance from Ḥusayn, as well as some special graces from Sayyida Zaynab. Shaykh ʿAbd al-Salām Muḥammad of the ʿAmriyya Rifāʿiyya Order claimed to have received his guidance from Sayyida Zaynab.[125] The "guidance" received from devotion to the *ahl al-bayt* may not be restricted to the inspiration derived from the example of their lives. They may function, in effect, as Sufi shaykhs, directly training and discipling special individuals. One song in fact proclaims, "ʿAlī, father of Ḥasan, you are our shaykh!"[126] Shaykh ʿIzz said that it is in the laps of the *ahl al-bayt* that the *ghawth,* or supreme saint, is taught.

THE DESCENDANTS OF THE PROPHET

The veneration of the Prophet's family extends to honor given to his distant descendants, those who are alive today and may claim the title of *sharīf* (plural, *ashrāf*), which literally means "noble one." Shaykh Aḥmad Raḍwān (d. 1967) said that the *ashrāf* are characterized by chastity, liberality, and courage. It is evidently quite dangerous to risk incurring the anger of one of the Prophet's descendants, for they are especially loved by God by virtue of their noble ancestry. Aḥmad Raḍwan admonished his disciples not to interfere if a quarrel broke out between a *sharīf* and anyone else, "for that is lethal poison." The superiority of the *ashrāf* over other people is expressed in a saying that the Sufi can strip a saint of his sainthood if he does not give him due honor, although the Sufi may also strip the *sharīf* of his spiritual state, that is, keep him from advancing in his journey to God.[127]

Although honor is not universally given to *sharīf*s in Egyptian society, and they no longer wear distinctive dress, one sign of a gnostic is the ability to recognize the noble descent of a *sharīf* when seeing such a person for the first time.[128] Shaykh ʿIzz, who is a *sharīf,* said that the first time he approached the tent of Shaykh Abū 'l-Maʿāṭī of the Burhāmiyya Order, during a moulid in the Delta, the aged shaykh demanded that his disciples help him to rise to his feet. He explained, "I will not sit while the grandson of the Prophet is walking toward me." ʿIzz saw this as a clear sign of the old man's gift of inner vision. Belief in the physical inheritance of the prophetic light renders claims of descent from the Prophet extremely common among Sufi shaykhs. Furthermore, the current system of passing the position of shaykh from father to son within an Order is seen as perfectly natural, rather than a corruption of the practice of recognizing as shaykh the person with the greatest piety and spiritual gifting.[129] It is expected that piety and spiritual gifting will, in most cases, follow the line of physical descent.

CHAPTER 4

The Saints

Bearers of the Prophetic Light

The Muhammadan light lives on in the Muslim community, not only among Muhammad's descendants but also among the "friends" *(awliyā᾽)* of God. The word *awliyā᾽*, which is translated here as saints, is used in the Qur᾽an most often to refer to the "friends" of the unbelievers, "friends" who are demons. But the word *awliyā᾽* with the meaning of "friends of God" is also derived from a much-loved and often-quoted passage from the Qur᾽an (10:62–64): "Indeed, on the friends of God there is no fear, and neither shall they grieve. Those who have believed and are pious will have good news in this world and the next. There is no substituting the words of God. That is the mighty victory." The "good news" given to the friends of God in the next world is the reward of Paradise; in this world, according to a ḥadīth from Tirmidhī, it is a sound vision.[1]

Who is the *walī* (singular of *awliyā᾽*)? The author of a favorite manual on Sufism, al-Qushayrī (d. 1072), quotes the famous Sufi theoretician al-Junayd (d. 910) as defining the *walī* as, first, someone whose affairs are taken over by God, and, second, as someone whose worship of God is constant, without any defect of rebellion. Both qualities are necessary for someone to be a saint.[2]

A favorite divine saying *(ḥadīth qudsī)* is thought to describe the condition of the saint, after an initial stern warning, which is also frequently quoted in Egypt today:

> Whoever harms one of my saints on earth, I have proclaimed war against him. A servant draws near to Me with nothing better than the fulfillment of his religious obligations, and he continues to draw near to me by performing supererogatory deeds, until I love him. When I love him, I am his hearing with which he hears, his seeing with which he sees, his hand with which he strikes and his foot with which he walks. Were he to ask [something] of Me, I would surely give it to him, and were he to seek refuge in Me, I would certainly give it to him. I hesitate in nothing I am doing so much as I hesitate to take the spirit of my believing servant, because he hates death, and I hate to harm him, although [death] is inevitable.[3]

Although the "believing servant" could describe a vast multitude of Muslims, popular interpretation of this ḥadīth limits its application to those holy persons who are considered particularly close to God so that their prayers are answered and whose subjugation of their passions and fleshly desires has been so complete that their spirits have become in some sense united with God, as this ḥadīth indicates. They are the ones who are indicated by the Qur'anic verse in which God addresses Satan, saying, "You have no power over My servants" (15:42).

There is no Islamic body empowered to canonize or recognize persons as saints.[4] Ḥasan al-Sharqāwī, an Egyptian scholar who studied popular beliefs regarding Aḥmad al-Badawī in the Ṭanṭā area, wrote that most Sufis identified a saint as a gnostic, one who had special knowledge of God through mystical illumination, whereas ordinary people regarded a saint as any unusual person, even an insane person or a beggar, who was close to God and whose prayers are answered.[5]

Shaykh Aḥmad Raḍwān (d. 1967) described saints as resting in a state of equanimity in the presence of God, indifferent to their physical circumstances, rejoicing in nothing but God. Under divine protection, the saint is preserved *(maḥfūẓ)* from error.[6] This protection of the saints is seen as less absolute than the prophet's immunity *(ʿiṣma)* from error. Qushayrī wrote that the saint who is truly a saint must be in a state of superior spiritual awareness, whereas the person who opposes the law of God in any way is deceived. The saint's state of "preservation" does not mean that he cannot commit an error but that he will not persist in sin.[7]

Although the Sufi definition of sainthood may depend mainly on inner, and deeply personal, spiritual attributes and an attitude of separation from the world, the average person knows a saint by his or her ability to work miracles, dispense blessing, and function in an intercessory capacity for those in need. It is no doubt for this reason that Michael Gilsenan wrote that the whole notion of sainthood "is bound up, not with vague ideas of other-worldly holiness, but with the capacity for significant action in the world."[8] In a certain sense this is certainly true. Shaykh ʿIzz also described the saint as one who is not only pious but who is given by God a task in the world, responsibility to call people to God. Yet however much popular expectations of usefulness may govern recognition of a person as a saint, the Sufis insist that one important element of sainthood is its hiddenness. The greatest saints, in particular, are hidden among

God's servants and may be serving in very lowly and inconspicuous capacities in society. They may even be despised by the general population.

Some authors emphasize the hiddenness of saints more than others.[9] Aḥmad Raḍwān, quoting from Ibn al-ʿAbbād al-Rondī (d. 1390), said that God hides the saints from the masses as a mercy, because a person who knowingly opposes saints and does not obey them will come under divine wrath. For this reason, some of the gnostics are known by no one.[10] This hiddenness poses problems: can saints know they are a saint? What happens if saints divulge their sainthood? The first question was much discussed by medieval Sufi authors, who were divided on the issue. Contemporary Egyptian Sufis, however much they might agree that the saints are hidden from the recognition of ordinary people, do not countenance the idea that saints might be unaware of their own spiritual station. From Shaykh ʿIzz's perspective, it was inevitable that saints, as gnostics (ones who "know"), know they are saints, although they must regard this as a pure grace from God and continue to see themselves as nothing. Some Sufis told me that if saints reveal they are saints, they will die, although this seems to contradict the experience of many Sufis who, under the influence of ecstatic spiritual states, have revealed their sainthood. Shaykh ʿIzz said that it is proper for saints to conceal their sainthood from other people, although sometimes for the purpose of instruction or under the influence of a spiritual state, saints might reveal their status.

However, gnostics will always be recognized by other gnostics, and the saints enjoy a communication between them that requires no words or geographical proximity. The saints, in fact, function on two levels, or, one could say, they live in two parallel worlds, an exoteric world in which they dwell with their bodies and interact with other humans in ordinary ways and an inner world of visions, contemplation, revelations, and communication without words. The death of the body in no way impedes the ability of saints to communicate with the living, as is abundantly clear from tales both old and new. Ibn ʿArabī (d. 1240) wrote that it is entirely unnecessary for saints to meet in their bodies or correspond to each other and that they do so only as a matter of custom.[11] The fact that many contemporary Sufis attribute their spiritual knowledge to instruction given through visions by saints either dead or alive is adequate indication of the continued validity of this type of communication. This may take place through dreams, but it often takes place in the waking state as well.

On two occasions when Shaykh ʿIzz and I were in private session, we were interrupted by spiritual communications. On one occasion, Shaykh ʿIzz suddenly jumped to his feet and addressed, with great respect, someone I could not see. He explained to me afterward that we had been visited by Shaykh Mūsā Abū ʿAlī, who had passed away only a month before (April 1988) in Karnak, near Luxor. On another occasion, ʿIzz suddenly yelled out, "Remember God! Remember God!" He explained to me that a Sufi friend of his in Qinā was deeply grieved because his son had just been injured in an automobile accident. He assured me that his friend had heard his admonition and was comforted by it. Far from being extraordinary, this ability to communicate over geographical distances is typical for those who have attained some measure of "inner vision" *(baṣīra)* and is a common experience for Sufi disciples who have attained spiritual connection with their shaykhs. This is just one aspect of the hidden world in which Sufis live.

The hiddenness of the saints, as we have already stated, is thought to be a mercy for ordinary people, because of the danger of opposing a saint. "The saint's anger," said Aḥmad Raḍwān, "is the anger of God, and has effect in heaven and on earth." The person who opposes or hates God's saints "dies without the religion of Islam." This is because of the saint's identification with God, as indicated by the above-quoted ḥadīth in which the saint's hearing, sight, tongue, leg, and hand become tantamount to the hearing, sight, tongue, leg, and hand of God. "So whoever draws near to a saint in this state has drawn near to God, and whoever serves him has in reality served God, and whoever hates him has hated God."[12] For this reason, the baraka or spiritual power of the saint, which is often defined as "blessing," can just as easily be a curse. As von Grunebaum wrote, "The popular saint is as quick to harm as he is to help. The baraka is a force which is provoked only with some risk. . . . Thus, depending on whether travelling saints are well- or ill-received, they will cause fountains to spring or dry up, rivers to change their course, or earthquakes to occur. Saints may even openly compete to demonstrate their own superior power or engage in (often distasteful) predictions about the end and the burial place of their 'colleagues'."[13]

Shaʿrānī records one Sufi as saying, "A *faqīr* (saint) who does not kill as many oppressors as hairs on his head, is no *faqīr*."[14] There are many stories of shaykhs who angered Aḥmad al-Badawī and were stripped of their spiritual stations or otherwise punished until they repented and apologized to him.[15] Even today, people tell stories of cars breaking down when they refuse to turn in at the crossroad to Ṭanṭā to honor him with a visit. Yet on most occasions, it is thought that the saint does not intend the harm suffered by his enemies. ʿIzz was convinced that ʿAmm Amīn had suffered a serious decline in his spiritual station because of his jealousy and slander of him. When I told ʿIzz of a story I had heard about him from one of Amīn's friends, ʿIzz insisted on confronting the woman face-to-face. He assured me that this confrontation would convince me of the truth, but in fact he kept interrupting the woman and would not allow her to speak at all. When I asked him about this later, he said he feared that the woman would bring the wrath of God on herself by opposing one of His saints.

The saints are not all equal in stature but are ranked according to function and proximity to God, in a hierarchical structure. At the top of the saintly hierarchy is the *quṭb* (Pole or Axis), as he is commonly called in Sufi tradition, or, as he is more commonly called today, the *ghawth* (help). Beyond this common agreement on the existence of a *quṭb* or *ghawth*, there is much disagreement concerning the titles and numbers of the ranks beneath him. According to a saying attributed to ʿAlī ibn Abī Ṭālib, the total number of saints in the world at any one time is three hundred, of which seventy are *nujabāʾ* (sing. *najīb*), forty are *awtād* (sing. *watad*), ten are *nuqabāʾ* (sing. *naqīb*), seven are *ʿurafāʾ* (sing. *ʿārif*, the word for gnostic), three are *mukhtārūn* (sing. *mukhtār*), and one who is the *quṭb*. Yet other traditions use different terms and give different numbers. Ibn ʿArabī, the first to elaborate a detailed, systematic hierarchy of saints, said that the number of saints in the world is always at least equal to the number of prophets that have lived since the world began, which, according to traditional Islamic reports, is 124,000. This is necessary because the saints are the heirs of the prophets, and each prophet must have at least one heir among the saints who are alive in the world. If the saints number more than the number of prophets, it is because the inheritance of some prophets has been divided among several saints.[16]

Ibn ʿArabī's teachings on the saints have found their way into contemporary tradition largely because they were incorporated into the works of the popular Egyptian Sufi author, ʿAbd al-Wahhāb al-Shaʿrānī (d. 1565). Ibn ʿArabī describes the *quṭb* as follows:

> He is the mirror of the Divine Reality and the locus of the manifestation of the holy attributes, and the master of the moment (*ṣāḥib al-waqt*). He knows the secret of divine determination. He is hidden, because he is preserved in

the storehouses of jealousy, wrapped in the garments of fasting. No doubt ever occurs regarding his religion, and no thought occurs to him that contradicts his station. He engages often in sexual intercourse, desiring it, loving women, giving nature its due within the bounds of the Sharīʿa, and giving the spirit its due within the bounds set by God. . . . He is for God alone. His spiritual state is always one of worship and recognizing his need for God. He hates what is evil and approves what is good. He loves the beauty of ornamentation and of persons. The spirits come to him in the best form. He pines away in love, he is jealous for God and angry on His behalf. . . . His spirituality appears only behind the veil of the seen and unseen. He sees things only as the locus of the glance of the Divine. . . . He is persistent in prayer and intercession, unlike those who are in a spiritual state. The *quṭb* is beyond having a spiritual state [of ecstasy that would make him unmindful of things around him]. He is fixed in knowledge. . . . He does not transcend spatial limitations or walk in air or on water. . . . He rarely performs miracles.[17]

The *quṭb* (Axis) is called such because he is the center on which the world pivots. According to Ibn ʿArabī, he is both the center and circumference of the circle of the universe.[18] Ibn ʿArabī writes that there are four *awtād*, or pillars, on which the universe rests, who are the four prophets who never died: Jesus, Elijah, Idrīs, and Khiḍr. Of these one is the *quṭb,* and that is Idrīs, who, according to Islamic tradition, resides in the fourth heaven, in the middle of the seven planetary heavens. He is assisted by two Imāms, who are Jesus and Elijah. Khiḍr is the fourth *watad.* Yet these positions are also represented among living humans. Among humans, when the *quṭb* dies, he is replaced by one of the Imāms, and if one of the Imāms dies, he is replaced by the remaining *watad.*[19]

Although portions of Ibn ʿArabī's formulation are retained in contemporary Egypt, a good deal of it is unknown or misunderstood. It is generally understood in Egypt that the *awtād* are entirely distinct from the *quṭb* or *ghawth,* and the use of the term *Imam* as representing those second in the saintly hierarchy is entirely unknown. In his manual for spiritual guides and disciples, Sayyid Muḥammad Māḍī Abū 'l-ʿAzāʾīm (d. 1937), founder of the ʿAzmiyya Order, treats the "ranks of men," with the exception of the "Imām," who is described in a manner similar to the *quṭb,* simply as functions within the Order, rather than as a hidden hierarchy of saints.[20] Shaykh ʿIzz said that around the *ghawth* are twelve *aqṭāb* (plural of *quṭb*), and each of these *aqṭāb* has forty saints.[21] Yet he also spoke of the *abdāl* (sing. *badal*), a word which means "substitutes." They are called such, according to the Sufis, either because when one *badal* dies, he is replaced by another (but that would not make them distinct from any other saintly rank), or because they are able to create a likeness, a "substitute" for themselves and appear to be in more than one place at a time. This ability to appear in more than one place at a time is commonly attributed to various saints, who are witnessed preaching in two different villages at the same Friday noon prayer, or breaking the Ramaḍān fast in two different locations at the same time, or performing the pilgrimage in Mecca while never leaving their home village. Shaykh ʿIzz said that Shaykh Aḥmad Raḍwān used to say that a saint is not a saint until he can appear in forty places at a single time!

Though Sufis may agree on the existence of a *ghawth,* there is no agreement concerning his identity. It is typical for a Sufi to hold his own shaykh in such reverence that he believes him to be the *ghawth.* Aḥmad Raḍwān said the *quṭb* is one of the saints of Upper Egypt, although it is not clear whether he meant to say that the *quṭb* is always from Upper Egypt or simply that this was true at the time he was speaking.[22]

The saints are to be found all over the world, even in countries where Islam is poorly represented, and they are the source of blessing on that country. The towns of Ṭanṭā and Dasūq in the Egyptian Delta are thought to be blessed even in their economic transactions because of the presence of the tombs of Aḥmad al-Badawī (d. 1276) and Ibrāhīm al-Dasūqī (d. 1295/6), respectively, in their midst.[23] The saints have a trust to fulfill in this world. They meet in a hidden court, presided over by Sayyida Zaynab, that decides the affairs of the living. It is appropriate, therefore, to seek their intercession. Sainthood increases and decreases, as does faith. One could be a saint, or a *ghawth,* for only a few minutes or for many years. Although, theoretically, every Sufi shaykh should be a saint and gnostic, and is likely to be regarded as such by his followers, few Sufis are willing to concede that all who take up the role of Sufi shaykh are true saints. But when a shaykh is a true saint and gnostic of God, he can dispense great blessing to his followers.

A ḥadīth sometimes cited to justify popular belief in the baraka of the saints says, "By means of the righteous Muslim, God repulses affliction from one hundred neighbors."[24] The presence of the saints provides an opportunity for ordinary people to come in touch with the baraka, or spiritual power, that came into the world with Muhammad. The touch of a saint's hand, or any object associated with the saint, conveys blessing to those who love God. Loving the saints is a way of expressing love for God, and the saints provide a means of intercession before God.

After the saints die, they are considered to be alive in their tombs, hearing the greeting of their visitors, returning the greeting, and making intercession for them. The spirits of the righteous are free to roam at will and are even more powerful to act on behalf of the living after death than they were in life. The dead saints are virtually alive, not only in spirit but often in body as well. It is not uncommon at the funeral procession of a Muslim saint to see those carrying the bier running at full speed, with the entire procession of people running behind them. It is said that the dead saint is pulling the bier, and the others are hastening to keep up with it. If there are other saints buried in the vicinity, the saint on the bier may hasten to visit those saints before hastening in joy to its final resting place. A ḥadīth says, "God has forbidden the earth to consume the bodies of the prophets." In popular belief, this privilege also applies to the saints. As one Sufi author wrote, "The saint is alive in his tomb, returning the greeting of his visitors. He knows all those who visit him, and he knows their purpose." He proves his point by the fact that the Prophet's wife ʿĀʾisha visited the graves of Muhammad and her father, the first Caliph Abū Bakr, unveiled, but when the second Caliph, ʿUmar ibn al-Khaṭṭāb, was buried with them she visited them veiled, because ʿUmar was not related to her, and she understood that the righteous dead were alive.[25] The sixteenth-century Moroccan Sufi, Aḥmad Zarrūq, said that clinging to the dead indicates a lack of faith in the living, but, say the Sufis of contemporary Egypt, the *madad* (assistance) of the dead is stronger than the *madad* of the living, for the dead are in the presence of God, and clinging to them is without ulterior motive.

Egyptian Sufis say that the bodies of those who are pure do not decompose but are merely sleeping. Although Goldziher speaks of stories of saints preventing their own exhumation, saying this is regarded as a great desecration,[26] I heard a number of stories of successful exhumations of saints whose bodies were being transferred from one place to another, in which the saint was found, after hundreds of years, not to have suffered any decomposition. ʿIzz told me that the body of one of his ancestors who died two hundred years ago was moved in the 1950s from a nearby site to a new burial place in the courtyard of his ancestral home in Farshut, where a shrine was built in his honor. He said that the man's body was found to be perfectly intact, as if he were merely sleeping, and the body of an infant who had been buried with him was in the same condition.

Not only are the bodies of the saints immune from decomposition, but, according to many legends, they actually emit a pleasant fragrance, whereas people who are attached to worldly things emit an unpleasant odor even in life. Shaykh ʿIzz complained to me that foreigners often have bad body odor, although he excepted me from this general observation. He likewise bragged that even if he went without a bath for an extended period (although he was meticulous in his personal habits) he would not emit a bad odor. The blood of people who have bad morals and worldly attachments is itself foul-smelling, according to Sufi belief, whereas the blood of those who attach themselves to God is sweet-smelling. Fragrance or aroma and fragrant breezes are metaphors that are often employed in Sufi literature. The association of the tombs of the saints with pleasant aromas is reinforced by the practice of wearing perfume when visiting saints' shrines and rubbing perfume on the hands of other visitors or showering them with cologne or perfumed water. Some visitors also rub the grid that surrounds the tomb with perfume or hang blossoms around it.

Shaykh ʿIzz related the purity of the saint whose body defies decomposition to its lack of materiality. Some Sufis, when they are very old, devote themselves solely to a life of prayer and meditation and restrict their diet to the absolute minimum necessary to remain alive. This makes their excretion processes very limited and in effect reduces the material aspect of their existence. Such ascetics acquire bodies that are said to be "luminous" and, like light, incorruptible. Shaykh Muḥammad al-Ṭayyib of Qurna, on the west bank of the Nile opposite Luxor, was of this type. In the years before his death in December 1988, he limited his daily consumption to a few tablespoons of milk, and his health deteriorated to the point that he was virtually unable to move or to respond to the many visitors who came to receive his blessing. His skin was so delicate that his hand remained wrapped in cloth for all visitors who shook it as he mumbled the *Fātiḥa,* the opening chapter of the Qurʾan, on their behalf. He was regarded by many in the region as the *ghawth,* and his lifestyle was seen as appropriate to his position. Shaykh ʿIzz indicated that the *ghawth* typically lives in isolated meditation and fasting, in contrast with Ibn ʿArabī's description of the *quṭb* as never going hungry voluntarily and giving both the body and spirituality its due.

Nonetheless, saints engage in many different types of lifestyles, and the examples in chapter 9 will provide a glimpse of the variety that takes place under the title of "saint."

MIRACLES OF THE SAINTS

Sainthood in Egypt is primarily a function not of virtue but of power. The ability to work miracles is a necessary attribute for a saint. The miracles of saints are called "graces" *(karāmāt),* whereas the miracles of prophets are called "things that render impotent" *(muʿjizāt)* because they are necessarily inimitable by anyone else, and they prove the veracity of the prophet's message, rendering impotent the criticism of his enemies.[27] The distinction is largely semantic, for miracles likewise constitute the proof of sainthood.

The inventory of miracles saints perform is almost endless. Besides appearing in different places at the same time, communicating with each other and with their disciples over great geographical distances, and "reading hearts," saints can tame and talk with wild beasts, speak any language, discern whether food was ill-gotten, banish evil spirits, heal diseases, procure passports, provide transportation, and cut through bureaucratic red tape, among other things. Not all shaykhs claim to be able to perform all of these miracles, but the miracles are impressive enough to make a mockery of Paul Nwyia's statement that Ibn ʿAṭāʾ Allāh's aphorisms "are without contest the last Sufi miracle worked on the shores of the Nile."[28]

Sufi tradition records contests of miracles between alleged saints intended to determine which saint had superior status. I heard of a similar situation in the Rifāʿiyya of Upper Egypt in the middle of this century, when a dispute over succession to the office of shaykh was settled by means of a contest of miracles. Each contender for the office slept under the other's robe. It was agreed that the weight of the robe of the superior saint would render his opponent unable to rise. It was thus that Shaykh Muḥammad Wāfī assumed headship of the Rifāʿiyya in Qinā, Sūhāj, and Asyūṭ. When he died, his followers demanded that his son, Shaykh Wāfī Muḥammad Wāfī, prove his worthiness to inherit his father's office. He was taken to a place overlooking a pit in which sugar cane was boiled into molasses. A man threw a needle into the boiling brew and said, "Get it for me." Shaykh Wāfī grabbed a boy and stuck his head into the liquid and asked him whether he saw the needle. The boy replied that he did not, and emerged entirely unharmed, although by all reason he should have been dead. Shaykh Wāfī then inserted his walking stick into the boiling sugar cane and drew out the needle at its end.

The Rifāʿiyya Order is particularly well known for their ability to perform fantastic miracles. Handling poisonous snakes and scorpions is their specialty. When the headquarters of the ʿAshīra Muḥammadiyya, a voluntary association founded by Shaykh Muḥammad Zakī Ibrāhīm of the Muḥammadiyya Shādhiliyya, was found in the summer of 1981 to be infested with snakes, a Rifāʿī was summoned. According to an eyewitness, the man called and a snake appeared, which the man put into a sack. The man informed the shaykh that there were others, but for each snake there would be an additional charge. After summoning three snakes and putting them in his sack, the man informed the shaykh that there was also a scorpion, but at that point the shaykh was tiring of the expense involved and told the man to leave it alone.

The Rifāʿiyya and the Saʿdiyya sometimes ritualize the public display of miracles during their moulid celebrations. E. W. Lane reported in 1836 that shaykhs rode a horse over their disciples' backs in a ceremony called the *dosa.*[29] Nicolaas Biegman has described and photographed contemporary versions of the *dosa* at the moulid of Abū 'l-Qumṣān in Qurna, in which the disciples held knives or swords in their mouths or on their stomachs, and the shaykh walked on top of these, after a dance during which some pierced their cheeks with pins. Asked about the purpose of the *dosa,* a participant told Biegman it was to test the sincerity of the Sufi, for only the sincere Sufi could emerge from such a trial unscathed.[30]

Frederick de Jong reported in 1976 that Bayt ʿAbāṭa used the *dabbūs* during their *ḥaḍra.* "A *dabbūs* (or *sīkh*) is a metal or wooden ball of about 4 inches diametre, attached to an iron skewer resembling a knitting needle about 15 inches long. Attached to the circumference of the ball are a number of chains at the end of which are small pieces of metal resembling razorblades. When, during the *ḥaḍra* it is not put through parts of the body, it is spun around so that the chains stand out like an umbrella. I have seen shaykhs putting it through the cheeks, eyelids, throat, tongue and shoulders, of the muridun [disciples] while saying *'madad, yā ʿamm al-ʿālamin, yā Rifāʿī'*. No blood flows whatsoever and no traces are left when it is pulled out again. This is considered as being one of Aḥmad al-Rifāʿī's *karāmāt.*"[31]

I never saw the *dabbūs* during either the weekly *ḥaḍra* of Bayt ʿAbāṭa or during the moulid of their patron saint or the moulid of

Aḥmad al-Rifāʿī, and only once did I see a single individual at any moulid piercing his chest skin with a small needle.[32] When I asked about this, I was told that Shaykh Abū 'l-Wafā al-Ghunaymī al-Taftāzānī, head of the Supreme Council of Sufi Orders, had disallowed the practice, explaining that it is improper to make a public display of baraka. (Dr. Taftāzānī, however, does personally believe in the ability of the Rifāʿiyya to perform genuine miracles. When I asked him whether he thought the miracles of the Rifāʿiyya were real, he replied, "There are miracles. There are things the mind cannot understand.") The members of Bayt ʿAbāṭa seemed to have been convinced of the impropriety of such public displays, although Dr. Taftāzānī has not been able to convince them to ban musical instruments.

Concerning the practice of *dosa* at the moulid of Abū 'l-Qumṣān, Biegman says, "Dosas such as this one and the piercing of cheeks and other parts of the body *(darb silah)* are frowned upon and even forbidden in many places. At the moulid of Abul Qumsan there is no restriction since Abul Qumsan appeared in a dream to the head of the local police, saying that at his moulid everything was permitted, with the exception of dealing in drugs and shooting with rifles."[33]

Shaykh Abū 'l-Wafā al-Sharqāwī (d. 1961), on the other hand, said that miracles are the menstrual blood of saints, from which they must cleanse themselves in order to enter God's presence and that public display "breaks the back" *(al-ẓuhūr yuqsim al-ẓuhūr)*.[34] It is for this reason, says Shaykh ʿIzz, that he and his sons display no miracles at all and are relatively unknown, whereas Shaykh Wāfī enjoys considerable renown.

Shaykh Abū 'l-Wafā's son, Shaykh Aḥmad al-Sharqāwī, told me that 99 percent of the miracle stories told in books and anecdotes are false. "People expect the perfection of a shaykh to include the performance of miracles. There are people who, by God's grace, have an ability to do such things. Some can use their spirits the way someone else can use their hands. The strength of these spirits varies from one to another. My uncle was *magzūb* [one whose mind was taken up by God]. His name was Shaykh Abū Magd. They call him Sulṭān Abū Magd. He was very famous, even more famous than my father. He had this ability. He would speak of things from the world of the unseen and knew of things that were happening far away at a time when there was no radio or television or telephone or way to know such things. He would do such fantastic miracles. The stories told about him are too numerous to be counted, and they come from truthful people. My father did not have this ability. My uncle's mind was not sound, he was not responsible for what he did."[35] Shaykh Aḥmad al-Sharqāwī appears to be intimating that miracles are more likely to be performed by a *magzūb* than by an intellectually oriented gnostic. Yet other very sober shaykhs have also performed fantastic miracles, as we will see in chapter 9.

Naturally, there are skeptics among non-Sufis, particularly among those with a deep hatred for Sufism. Muḥammad Gamīl Ghāzī, head of a religious association in a Cairo suburb, frequently denounces Sufism in his Friday sermons. In an interview with an Egyptian reporter in July 1975, he scoffed at the idea that Sufis perform miracles. "What the Sufis call miracles are only imaginary devices to deceive simple minds and fill the votive offering boxes with the money of the weak-minded."[36]

But many non-Sufis believe in the miracles of the saints and have their own stories to tell. Two educated, upper-middle-class women of Cairo told me that cars regularly break down at the intersection leading into Ṭanṭā, if the passengers of the car are intending to bypass the city instead of going in to pay their respects to Sayyid Aḥmad al-Badawī. An educated man in Luxor, who disapproved of many aspects of popular religion, nonetheless told me numerous stories that proved, in his words, that there are shaykhs who have *baṣīra* and are able to perform miracles. Belief in the miracles of the saints is well-entrenched in Egyptian society, and the availability of free secular education does not seem to have seriously undermined that belief.

SAINTS' SHRINES AS SACRED SPACES

The saints, both living and dead, play an important role in the lives of the Sufis and of ordinary individuals. The tombs of dead saints are transformed into shrines, perhaps a humble white-washed domed structure but often attached to a mosque. Such mosques may be of very large proportions, like those of Ḥusayn, Sayyida Zaynab, Aḥmad al-Rifāʿī, Aḥmad al-Badawī, and Ibrāhīm al-Dasūqī, to name only a few.

In an article on women and saints' shrines in Morocco, Fatima Mernissi described saints' shrines as primarily a social space for women rather than a religious space, as a mosque is. Shrines, she said, are not usually mosques and constitute instead an informal women's association.[37] While I am not qualified to speak about Mo-

Figure 3. Maḥfūẓ, keeper of the shrine of Shaykh ʿAbāṭa, standing by the tomb in April 1989. He holds a rosary in his hand to aid in his personal dhikr.

roccan saints' shrines, her comments raise an important question about the status of saints' shrines as sacred spaces and their use as social spaces. Here I will argue that saints' shrines in Egypt are, without a doubt, sacred spaces, and will try to explicate their meaning as sacred spaces in light of their architecture and functions in Egyptian religious and social life.

To begin with, saints' shrines in Egypt share many of the trappings of sacred space in the Muslim world: shoes must be removed before entering; in theory, people in a state of impurity should not enter a shrine, just as they would not enter a mosque; and in Egypt it is considered proper etiquette to pray two *rakʿa*s on behalf of the saint within the shrine. Often shrines are attached to mosques, but an additional *miḥrāb* (niche indicating the directing prayer toward the Kaʿba) may be built into the shrine area itself. The sanctity of shrines is indicated in the very expression used for joint shrine visitation: "*Ḥaram*," says one person, inviting another to visit the saint together, to which the response is "*Jamʿan* [together]." The word *ḥaram* implies that which is sacred and inviolable.

Although prayers may be prayed in the shrine facing toward Mecca (and it is not considered proper to pray *ṣalāt* prayers facing toward the tomb itself), it is obvious to any visitor that the spiritual center of the shrine is the tomb or alleged tomb of the saint. It is true that some shrines are erected with a merely symbolic *tābūt*, or catafalque, but in point of fact such symbolic tombs do not command the same veneration as shrines that are believed to be the actual tombs of saints. As we have seen, the dead saint is not only present in spirit but is thought to be alive in the tomb, uncorrupted and incorruptible.

The architecture of the tomb reinforces the sense of being in a sacred space. The *tābūt* is located in the center, draped in thick green cloth denoting relationship to the Prophet. The cloth is decorated with the names of the first four Caliphs and Qurʾanic verses, often in glittering gold. On top of the cloth, the saint's personal copy of the Qurʾan, or another copy, is placed, as well as a turban, blossoms, handkerchiefs, and other items left by visitors. The *tābūt* is usually surrounded by a *maqṣūra*, a high gridwork made of wood or brass, which constitutes a barrier between the faithful and the tomb. The *maqṣūra* is often reinforced by glass, sometimes tinted green, and might be decorated with small colored lights and plaques bearing the name and dates of the saint, or Qurʾanic verses. Above the tomb there is a dome denoting the opening toward heaven. All of these features converge to create an atmosphere that is, to use Rudolf Otto's expression, numinous. Indeed, many shrine visitors speak of their visitations as profoundly moving and satisfying, something quite distinct from their daily lives; it is clearly a liminal experience, and the shrines are places of spiritual power and holiness.

Perhaps no scholar has contributed more to the study of universal religious concepts than Mircea Eliade. In his book, *The Sacred and the Profane*, Eliade wrote that sacred space is always marked by a center, a concentration of sanctity, a pole that links heaven and earth. True to Eliade's description of the creation of sacred space, Egyptian saints' shrines have a sacred center, a place of concentration of holiness and most direct access to heaven. In fact it is the popular belief that prayers are more efficacious at the tombs of saints, that the saints function as conduits to God, that makes the tombs of saints shrines at all. The presence of the saints themselves confers sanctity on the shrines and constitutes a nexus of the earthly and the divine.

Like that of all truly sacred spaces, the location of saints' shrines is not arbitrary, and this too marks it as different from most mosques and indicates that a saint's shrine is more of a truly sacred space than a mosque is. If the place has not been indicated during the lifetime of the saint by the building of a shrine in anticipation of the saint's body, it is indicated after death either by a vision or by the body itself pulling the pallbearers to the burial site preferred by the saint.

The sanctity of a saint's shrine is indicated by the fact that it contains its own spiritual center, its own axis that reaches toward heaven. The mosque merely directs prayers toward the spiritual center of the Kaʿba, the navel of the earth beneath the Throne of God, whereas the saint provides a center that constitutes a more direct link to heaven.[38] This direct linkage is indicated by the prevalence of visions received at shrines. One woman who slept near the Sīdī Shādhilī shrine received a vision in which a door opened before her, leading up to a mountain full of light—a clear indication that the Sīdī Shādhilī shrine opened out toward heaven itself and was a sacred domain filled with the light of God Himself, a place where prayers were most readily answered. Pilgrimage to certain shrines, such as those of Ḥusayn and Muḥammad ʿUthmān al-Burhānī, are believed by their devotees to have the same spiritual worth as the ḥajj.

It is not coincidental that the paramount saint of the age is called the *quṭb*, the Pole or Axis (although in Egyptian parlance he is more commonly called the *ghawth*, the Succour, the one whose aid is sought). Eliade says that sacred space is established around a cosmic axis. In the Sufi saint cult that axis is not a place but a person. The *qutb* or *ghawth* is the link between heaven and earth, and he is necessary for the existence of the earth. Before Muhammad the earth was never empty of a prophet to provide that link, but since the passing of the seal of the prophets this link is the ghawth, who alone enjoys the unceasing vision of God. All other saints are arranged in a hierarchy of holiness in relation to this *ghawth*. Just as every mosque is oriented toward the Kaʿba, so is every saint oriented toward the *ghawth*, who is the Axis of the Age. The essential unity of the saints is indicated by the fact that one might enter the Rifāʿī shrine and call out *"Yā Ḥusayn!"* or *"Yā rasūl Allāh!"* (Messenger of God) as readily as *"Yā Sīdī al-Rifāʿī!"* Not all saints enjoy equal proximity to the ghawth (or to God), and these different degrees of holiness result in differential degrees of sanctity attached to their shrines.

The degree of sanctity attributed to a saint's shrine depends on the holiness of the person, indicated most particularly through proximity to the Prophet, established through kinship (the *ahl al-bayt*) or spiritual rank (the great founders of the Sufi Orders). The shrines of the *ahl al-bayt* are most holy, especially that of Ḥusayn, of whom the Prophet said, "Ḥusayn is from me [or, a part of me], and I am from [a part of] Ḥusayn." Shrines might offer a sense of sanctity that touches people more directly and instinctively than mosques or the regular Islamic rituals, for it is a well-known fact that there are people who regularly visit shrines who do not pray the *ṣalāt*. Saints' shrines exude a sense of power and tranquility, marks of being in touch with the Really Real *(al-Ḥaqq)*. While Sufis may go to shrines as a regular expression of their devotion, other visitors go to shrines in order to feel peace in their turbulent lives, to seek a place of refuge from their problems, and to appeal to the intervention of the saint. Saints' shrines are perceived as places of mercy for the oppressed, as much as they are places of power.

Visitors to the shrines greet the saint upon entering, just as they would greet a person who is alive. They recite the *Fātiḥa* on behalf of the saint, both as a courtesy and in hopes of attracting blessing on themselves. Proper etiquette calls for praying two *rakʿas*, but in the crowds of the moulids this is often impossible, and in fact is rarely done. Visitors cling to the *maqṣūra*, kissing it, rubbing it and then rubbing their faces in order to transfer some of the saint's baraka to their own bodies. The holiness of the saint radiates out to the surrounding space, conferring holiness on ordinary objects, such as water, candy, or perfume, that are distributed by pious visitors at the shrine. Visitors circumambulate the tomb, absorbing the holiness, fervently muttering prayers all the while. Although Sufi leaders who defend saint shrine visitation stress that the faithful pray not to the saint but to God by virtue of the saint's baraka, the saint is nonetheless directly addressed in verbal petitions and letters, and visitors might make a vow to sacrifice an animal and distribute the meat or some other food to the shrine visitors and the poor if their prayers are answered. Such sacrifices take place outside the shrine. Dhikr may be performed both within and outside a shrine on the saint's visiting day or moulid. Visitors also sometimes sing songs of praise to the Prophet and his family. Visiting the shrine places the visitor in direct contact with the holy power inherent in the divine light passed down from the Prophet to his descendants.

Figure 4. Author with disciples of Ḥāgga Zakiyya at her tomb on 6 October 1988.

Some visitors choose to bask in this holy presence by sitting by the shrine, whether reading the Qur'an or simply sitting. Others, particularly women, sit along the outside wall of the shrine for the same reason. In deference to the saint, some visitors consider it proper to leave the shrine backwards, just as one would leave the presence of a king. Some shrines, such as that of Yūsuf Abū 'l-Ḥajjāj in Luxor, enforce humble veneration of the saint by their architecture: the shrine can only be entered in a bent position. For this reason, it is all the more important to leave the shrine backwards.

Saint shrine visitation is a popular custom that goes well beyond Sufi circles, and encompasses the majority of the population. Many people visit saints' shrines only occasionally, in search of healing, or help in examinations, or simply to find peace of mind. Different saints have different specializations, one specializing in healing barrenness, another in healing evil spirits, another in psychological illnesses, another in eye diseases, another in children's illnesses.

Visitors to the shrines expect the saints to live up to their end of whatever bargain is struck. Rarely, one might even hear a shrine visitor rebuking the saint in residence for failing to live up to expectations. On the other hand, people are also expected to be faithful in their relationships with the saints. A story was told to me concerning a Coptic woman who was barren and conceived only after visiting the shrine of Sayyida Zaynab with a Muslim neighbor. After the baby, a girl, was baptized, she became wooden and would neither eat nor drink. The Muslim neighbor rebuked the Coptic woman for failing to take the baby to Sayyida Zaynab, for "she is Sayyida Zaynab's daughter." As soon as the mother consented to the visit, movement returned to the baby, who cried for milk. Later, through a series of dream-visions, the girl converted to Islam. The baby had been conceived by the baraka of Sayyida Zaynab. The act of baptizing her was, in a sense, a breach of contract with the saint. Even without intending malice, the baraka of the saint brought affliction on those who neglected their contractual obligations.

Not all shrines have the same impact on devotees of the saints. Many shrine visitors have a favorite shrine where they have a special sense of peace. Shaykh ʿIzz said that he felt "changed" at three shrines, those of Ḥusayn, Shādhilī, and his own teacher, Shaykh Aḥmad Raḍwān. In most shrines he disdains to venerate the *maqṣūra* but stands to the side and gazes at the shrine, anticipating that the saint will rise to greet him—and he, considering himself in the ranks of saints, would naturally be able to see the dead saint, even if none of the other visitors could. If a saint does not greet him, he does not count him a true saint, for the saints know each other and greet each other. But in the shrines of Ḥusayn, Shādhilī, and Aḥmad Raḍwān, the holiness of the saint appears to have granted a sanctity to the *maqṣūra* itself. He kisses the *maqṣūra* and rubs perfume on it. His face is one of total, almost fierce absorption. Although he readily acknowledges that it is his personal relationship with Aḥmad Raḍwān that grants this shrine its special status vis-à-vis himself, he said it was inevitable that one feel a numbing in the limbs at the shrines of Sīdī Shādhilī and Aḥmad al-Badawī because of the high spiritual rank of their occupants.

Celebrating the Saints: The Moulids

Moulids were first celebrated by the Shiʿi Fāṭimid rulers of Egypt (969–1171), who celebrated the anniversaries of the Prophet, ʿAlī, Fāṭima, and the reigning Imām. However, these moulids took place only at the court in broad daylight and bore little resemblance to the modern nocturnal carnivals.[39] Of these four moulids, the only one that continues to be observed is that of the Prophet, which is, despite considerable official support, the least spectacular of the major moulids, since it is celebrated all over the country in various locations and even on different dates, rather than being concentrated

Figure 5. Shaykh ʿIzz al-ʿArab al-Hawārī, Shaykh Saʿīd al-Daḥḥ of the Aḥmadiyya Idrīsiyya Shādhiliyya, the author, and the author's daughter Rachel on 1 April 1988 in the *khidma* of Shaykh Saʿīd's Order during the moulid of the thirteenth-century saint ʿAbd al-Raḥīm al-Qināwī.

around a shrine-tomb like the other moulids. The assumed physical presence of the saint's body is vital and has contributed to the importance of the moulids of Ḥusayn, Sayyida Zaynab, ʿAlī Zayn al-ʿĀbidīn, Fāṭima al-Nabawiyya, and other members of the *ahl al-bayt* allegedly buried in Egypt and the complete absence of the celebration of moulids for ʿAlī and Fāṭima. Sunni historians and theologians trace the origin of the moulid to a Prophet's birthday celebration in Arbela, southeast of Mosul, in 1207, arranged by Muẓaffar al-Dīn Kokböri/Kokbürü, a brother-in-law of Saladin, and this celebration, influenced by Christian rites, bore many of the features of the modern-day moulid.[40] Gustave E. von Grunebaum says that with the growth of Sufism in Egypt under the Sunni Ayyūbids (1171–1250), the moulid took root there and spread from there throughout the Muslim world.[41] During this same period, in Muslim Spain and northern Morocco, the moulid was introduced as a way of countering Christian influence.[42] The Prophet's moulid, in medieval times as well as today, was sponsored by the government and attended by prominent officials. The official celebration of the

Prophet's moulid today consists of a procession by all the Sufi Orders from the Ḥusayn mosque to a sports arena in Darrāsa, where the major Orders erect large tents and are greeted by the shaykh of shaykhs and other government officials. But the large crowds attending other moulid celebrations are largely absent. Earlier in the evening, the general populace appeared to be outnumbered by the security guards, and by 8:30 the place was largely deserted.

The word *moulid,* more properly *mawlid* in classical Arabic, literally means "birthday," but it is usually celebrated on the anniversary of a saint's death.[43] I know of two saints for whom moulids were also celebrated in their lifetimes, Mūsā Abū ʿAlī (d. 1988) of Luxor and Muḥammad Abū 'l-Maʿāṭī, a shaykh of the Burhāmiyya in the Delta, who also died in the 1980s. The death of a saint is conceived as a union with God, in the type of a marriage consummation. The saint is said to have entered his *ʿurs,* or wedding consummation,[44] and the saint who is celebrated at the moulid is called *ṣāḥib al-faraḥ,* if a man, or *ṣāḥibat al-faraḥ,* if a woman, literally master or mistress of the wedding. Despite the fact that moulids are usually attended by extremely dense crowds and the grounds rapidly become quite filthy, Muslims go to these festivals dressed in their best, and some groups light candles to celebrate the saint, just as one would do for the procession of a couple on their wedding night. The dates of most moulids follow the lunar calendar and are often celebrated on a particular day of the week rather than a particular date. The specification of the date was formerly in the hands of the Ministry of the Interior, whose permission was required in order to hold any moulid, but since 1976, the Supreme Council of Sufi Orders has been granted this authority. In any case, to speak of a particular day is only to speak of the time set for the culminating "great night" *(al-layla 'l-kabīra)* of the moulid. The festivities begin as much as two weeks or as little as two nights before the great night but build until they reach a feverish pitch on that night when the densest crowds are in attendance, and activities persist until the dawn prayer. Some moulids, especially if they are associated with a single Order, such as the moulids of Aḥmad al-Rifāʿī and Sīdī al-Bayūmī, begin with a procession of the members of the Order, carrying banners and chanting praises of God and the Prophet. A few moulids, especially in Upper Egypt, end with a procession as well. The procession associated with the moulid of Abū 'l-Ḥajjāj in Luxor is the most famous, especially for its inclusion of boats, a custom that goes back to a procession from the Karnak Temple to the Luxor Temple in Pharaonic times.[45] The procession also includes a large number of vehicles containing members of the various crafts guilds, some of whom dress as women and dance, in an atmosphere of great hilarity. The procession is concluded by a series of *tābūts* carried on camels, representing the various local saints. The sight of these *tābūts*, which are wooden frameworks covered by the cloth normally found in the saint's tomb, is greeted with great shouts of joy by the crowd. Touching the cloth is thought to bring baraka.

In some moulids, especially those in Lower Egypt, secular aspects appear to predominate. At the moulid of Sayyid Aḥmad al-Badawī in Ṭanṭā, one of the largest and most famous of the Egyptian moulids, the Sufi *khidamāt* are mostly poor affairs, relegated to the back alleys, while the main streets are packed with thousands of sellers of every conceivable ware, such as toys and knickknacks for children, funny paper hats, plastic Santa Clauses, mounds of roasted chickpeas, sweets of all kinds, clothing, and spices. Eyes are drawn to television sets set up in some of the improvised shops. The eightfold image of a Western woman dancer wearing next to nothing attracts crowds of young men. The mosque and surrounding stalls are decked with colored lights. Children swing on the giant swings that seem to appear at every moulid, while men play shooting games. It is no wonder, perhaps, that the Egyptian professor at my lecture denied that the moulids were Sufi celebrations at all.

Inside the mosque of Aḥmad al-Badawī on the "great night," the culminating night of the moulid, every inch of the vast mosque floor is covered with people—men, women, and children—literally piled against one another as far as the eye could see. They all seem to be preoccupied with their own situation and pay little attention to the stranger whose head is at their knee, even if it is a person of the opposite sex—and indeed, women are about as numerous as men. Some read the Qurʾan, some pray, some do silent, private dhikr, many simply sit, and many more sleep. The dense crowds that push their way around the tomb of the saint, prodded by four guards on platforms with sticks, are, however, remarkably quiet and engrossed in their devotions. Only occasionally does someone shout at the saint. But when Shaykh ʿIzz raised his voice, chanting, "May God bless Muhammad, may God bless him and grant him peace!" *(Ṣallā Allāhu ʿalā Muḥammad, ṣallā Allāhu ʿalayhi wa sallam!)*, the entire mosque was soon stirred to join in the chant.

In Upper Egypt, the economic activities are much less conspicuous, although they still exist, while the *khidamāt* and dhikr of the Sufi Orders assume a much more prominent role. Nonetheless, the larger Upper Egyptian moulids are more likely to display spectacles such as horse racing and mock stick fighting.[46] Women are also much less in evidence, although they often prepare the food behind the scenes in the *khidamāt*, and there are usually a few who join in the dhikr, and several in the crowd looking on. At the relatively small moulid of Shaykh al-Ṭayyib in Qurna (father of the previously mentioned Muḥammad al-Ṭayyib), many of the merchants were women, although the participants in the dhikr—a sober, carefully orchestrated affair—were all men. At the moulid of Aḥmad Raḍwān outside Luxor, women were altogether forbidden, because of space restrictions and the enormous crowding that took place there. But at the more famous moulids of Yūsuf Abū 'l-Ḥajjaj in Luxor and ʿAbd al-Rahīm al-Qināwī in Qinā, women travel long distances with their menfolk to attend the moulids. At many of these Upper Egyptian moulids, photographs of recently deceased saints of the area are among the objects for sale by the merchants.

Some people's lives revolve around the celebration of moulids. There are merchants whose livelihoods depend on the moulids, although some may be regionally restricted. There are also merchants who follow the weekly shrine visitation days of the saints in Cairo and improvise coffee shops, candy stalls, and such. Some Sufis spend much of their time traveling from moulid to moulid, either setting up a *khidma* of their own or receiving hospitality at the *khidamāt* of others. Since these are all-night affairs, and the major moulids of the *ahl al-bayt* occur within the space of five months, this is an intense time of little sleep for many who pursue this lifestyle. One woman who hosted a *khidma* told me she never slept during the moulids at all and would take several weeks sleeping between moulids. Another upper-class woman quit her job as a French teacher in a secondary school when her life came to revolve so much around the moulids, and her nights became times of devotion, while her days became necessary for sleep. Those who lead the "dervish" lifestyle of traveling from moulid to moulid, content with a life of poverty for the sake of devotion to God and the saints, are clearly a subculture within Egyptian society. In utter disregard for Egyptian sexual conventions, men and women might even sleep in the same room or side by side under a single blanket.

Yet even those who participate in this lifestyle are not entirely uncritical of some of their comrades. One Sufi singer and his wife, who lived in a makeshift shack and whose lives revolved around weekly dhikrs at Ḥusayn and the moulid circuit, spoke critically of a young man who preferred to wander from moulid to moulid rather than find a job to support his wife and four children. When I asked whether they wanted their own baby daughter to grow up to become a dervish like them, they replied that they would rather she get a doctorate like me! The extent to which middle-class aspirations had penetrated even this segment of society was striking.

Moulids have a reputation for attracting large numbers of beggars and vagrants, who can expect generous hospitality at the Sufi *khidamāt* and from individuals. Among non-Sufis, it is images such as these that are most likely to come to mind when discussing moulids and saints. It is true that beggars and mentally impaired individuals are tolerated good-naturedly among Sufis, and some such individuals are perceived as saints who are *magzūb,* that is, whose minds have been taken up by God because of the severity of their initial exposure to the divine light. However, such individuals certainly do not predominate at moulids, and most Sufis do hold jobs and manage nonetheless somehow to fit weekly dhikrs and moulid celebrations into their schedules.

Dr. Taftāzānī said the purpose of moulids is to educate the people about the life of the saint, but the educational function of moulids does not predominate. People attend moulids for a variety of motives: to have fun, to obtain blessing, to be fed, to meet people, to hear dhikr, to pay respects to the saint, and to be spiritually nourished. Hospitality is constantly exchanged among those attending moulids. People distribute candies and sprinkled perfumed water on the crowds within the shrine, and people who wander into the *khidamāt* to accept hospitality might also distribute candy, breads, or cigarettes. Any gift distributed at the moulid carries the blessing of the saint and must be accepted. When occasionally I protested that I was not hungry, as food was presented before us, often the reply, given with a tone of surprise was, "It is a *nafḥa!*" *Nafḥa,* which means "gift," also may mean "fragrance," and indeed such gifts are thought to carry the aroma, a metaphor for the baraka, of the saint. They must be accepted and consumed. Candy thrown into crowds often results in a rampage among those present, especially, but not exclusively, among the children.

Moulids are an important place for Sufis to meet each other and attract new members. More than once, when I asked people how they came to become involved with Sufism, it began by attending moulids. Usually this would lead to an acquaintance with a particular group or shaykh, addresses would be exchanged, and ultimately the person would be drawn into the life of an Order. Shaykh ʿIzz, who in his earlier years attended moulids in order to rob people, said that a person may attend moulids initially for the wrong motive, but eventually they will be touched by the spirit that is there. Some shaykhs use the moulids as occasions for teaching, and a few such shaykhs draw very large crowds. But it is more typical for a shaykh simply to host a dhikr with a musical troupe, whose music is played within deafening loudness over amplification systems into the surrounding streets. The sound is inviting and the urge to move to the music is almost irresistible. For many, such dhikrs are the primary attraction that draws and holds them all night long. Some Sufi singers attract such a following that the mere rumor of their presence is sufficient to draw large crowds. A typical round of dhikr might last at least an hour before there is any break, and some participants become deeply engrossed and unconscious of their surroundings, even frothing at the mouth and appearing to be in a trancelike state. Others are obviously aware of what is happening around them and seek to move in unison within the other participants. A few simply have fun and imitate the motions of folk dancing. Such antics are met with anything from bemusement to outrage among the observers, who typically outnumber the actual participants.

Michael Gilsenan observed, in one of the more humorous passages in his book, *Saint and Sufi in Modern Egypt,* that Egyptian concepts of holiness and reverential behavior do not exactly coincide with European expectations. He wrote, "Anyone who has absorbed Victorian notions of reverent behaviour as being synonymous with whispers and quiet decorum soon has his assumptions disrespectfully shattered. As far as the Saint is concerned reverence can be demonstrated as well by shouting as by muttered prayer. Attendants roar and push the struggling mass round the shrine using bamboo canes on those who cling too long to holiness. Those who leave must do so through those clamouring to enter. Huddled in a corner, chewing on a sweetmeat dangerously thrown over ecstatic faces by a mosque servant, the anthropologist has time to reflect on the wreckage of his own fixed ideas about proper expressions of piety."[47]

Visitors shout to the saints and address them in terms denoting familiarity: *"Yā Māmā!"* (Mama), *"Yā Sitt!"* (Lady), *"Yā Shaykh al-ʿArab!"* (Shaykh of the Arabs), *"Yā Bābā!"* (Daddy), *"Yā Habībī!"* (My love). They also shout at each other and throw candies to the crowd as a form of charity that carries the saint's blessing. Some are truly overcome with emotion on touching the *maqṣūra,* clinging to it and weeping. Women might express their joy by giving forth a *zaghrūṭa,* the shrill cries they make at weddings. Others express their joy through songs, which might include a chorus joined in by the entire throng of visitors. Mothers sit nursing their babies. Tea is served sometimes in the very vicinity of the tomb. Crowds are pushed forward rudely by attendants, who yell at them to move, correct their behavior, and whip and push people who cling too long to the *maqṣūra*. Crowds leaving the shrine are nearly crushed by those surging in, frightening the children who are perched on their parents' shoulders. Visitors who petition the saints expect them to answer their requests, especially if a vow has been made, and if they are disappointed they might even argue with the saints at their shrines. Often, however, the crowds are remarkably quiet and extremely good-natured. Food or candy received at the shrine and carried home brings a portion of the saint's baraka to people at home. This is especially important during the time of the moulid. Some moulids end with a procession in which the *tābūt*s of local saints are carried around the town. Although the saints' bodies are not carried in the procession, the *tābūt*s themselves carry the blessing of the saints to the entire town.

A Radiation of Holiness

The moulid, denoting the confluence of sacred space with sacred time, is the most important time to visit the saint. Such visitations honor the saint, and indeed a saint is considered to be dishonored if the number of visitors or the number of hospitality tents around the shrine are few. The holiness of the shrine is extended, to some extent, to the surrounding area, which during the moulids is transformed into a major festival. People who live close to a shrine say they live in the neighborhood of such-and-such a saint, and the presence of the saint in their neighborhood is believed to offer the neighborhood special blessing and protection. Baraka radiates from the shrine in ever decreasing concentration, exactly like the radiation of light from the sun or from a lamp. The Qur'anic comparison of God to light (24:35) and the natural link of light to purity and immateriality has led to the association of light with the presence of the holy. In the shrines, the presence of holiness is symbolized by the decoration of tombs with colored lights and blossoms, which create an atmosphere reminiscent of paradise. Sometimes the light is of a supernatural origin, as when light shines from the dome of Sayyida Zaynab on the night of her visitation by the other major saints.

The presence of a shrine is sufficient sometimes to attract habitations around it. Even the remote shrine of Sīdī Shādhilī by the Red Sea, which until recently could not be reached without a harrowing journey through the desert, has become the focus of a remarkable building activity. There are a number of Sufi *sāḥas* in existence or under construction in the vicinity of the shrine, which is fast becoming a popular place of pilgrimage now that a road has been built to it, there are regular buses running to it, and it has electricity. (It still does not have running water, which must be brought in each day by truck.) It is said that Ḥāgga Zakiyya, a well-known woman saint who died in 1982 and who is buried near the *sāḥa* she built by Sīdī Shādhilī, during one of her many journeys to that shrine before it was accommodated with electricity, brought with her an electric lamp and a television set. When asked why she did this, she replied that a city would grow up around Sīdī Shādhilī. Her followers recall this prophecy with pride, as its fulfillment appears to be well under way, at least in the sense of a city with an ever-changing population.

Saints' Shrines as Social Spaces

Moulids turn the saints' shrines and the area around them into a massive, sacred campground. On a more modest scale, this happens on a weekly basis at many shrines, such as those of ʿAlī Zayn al-ʿĀbidīn, Abū 'l-Suʿūd, and Shaykh ʿAbāṭa. In the Shaykh ʿAbāṭa shrine, which is quite small, meals are eaten right up against the tomb itself, separated from the tomb only by the picket fence that surrounds the *tābūt* but still on the "sacred" territory where no one wears shoes. In the larger complexes of Zayn al-ʿĀbidīn and Abū 'l-Suʿūd, food is eaten in rooms adjoining the tomb area. Whether visitors eat next to the tomb itself or only outside the shrine appears to be an indicator of the degree of sanctity attached to the shrine.

For the Sufis, besides being places of devotion, the shrines are primarily meeting places. The social aspects of moulids are of major importance to the Sufis, who spend much of the time visiting each other, consuming tea or soft drinks or hot cinnamon drinks and eating foods that may range in lavishness from meat dishes to bread and cheese. Sociability often runs across the boundaries of specific Orders because respect for shaykhs is rarely confined to a specific Order. There are exceptions, and some Sufis revere their own shaykhs so much that they feel no need to visit other shaykhs. When I attended moulids with Shaykh ʿIzz and his disciples, much time was spent looking for ʿIzz's friends and visiting their *khidamāt*, but we also often made new acquaintances, some of which developed from simple conversations into deep friendships, built largely through the continuing contact at moulids, although often this would lead to visits in homes as well. This sociability is not seen as separate from the spiritual dimensions of life, but is indeed a very integral part of it, promoting love for the brethren, mutual service for the sake of God, and mutual informal exhortation and instruction in the spiritual life. Although some of the exchange of tales, morality stories, and poetry bears the marks of competitiveness, as each tries to prove to the others the extent of his knowledge, there is also a good deal of sincerity and humble receptivity. The exchange of such conversation and hospitality, in the shadow of the saint, moving to the words of the singers and the music played at the dhikr, is the very essence of spiritual nourishment for many Sufis.

The social functions of moulids and weekly shrine visitations are not secondary features but are often mentioned by the Sufis as one of their primary purposes and benefits. Contemporary Sufism does not see mysticism as something distinct from sociability but rather perceives the mystical experience itself as best achieved in the communal setting and indeed as partly communal in its goal: the goal is not oneness with God, which is unobtainable, but oneness with the host of saints and the Sufi brethren, and ultimately with the Prophet. Sufi sayings like "there is no me or you" and "you are from me and I am from you" express not mere brotherhood but a true spiritual connection that the Sufis believe they achieve with each other, a dissolving of the boundaries of individuality. Although in its truest sense this connection is achieved only with a few close individuals, and most ideally between shaykh and disciple, this also pertains, at a less intense level, between Sufis who are involved in a good dhikr together. Their spirits influence each other and pull each other up toward greater heights than they can reach on their own. The contrast between "social space" and "sacred space" is spurious in this case.

Perceptions of Sanctity and the Use of Sacred Space

Many Muslims complain of the inappropriateness of some of the activities that occur at the moulid, and clearly the space within the shrine has a sanctity that is not entirely shared by the space outside it. Within the shrine, for example, no one would smoke a cigarette, whereas in the Sufi tents outside the shrine, the sharing and smoking of cigarettes and water pipes is an essential activity. Outside the shrines, merchants sell toys, roasted chickpeas, or other standard moulid delights, and, especially at Coptic moulids but also at some Muslim moulids, religious paraphernalia. Religious items purchased at a moulid carry a sanctity they would not otherwise have. Even these overtly secular occupations bear something of the saint's aura, and merchants attribute their success to the baraka of the saint. Some moulid activities with no apparent religious connotation are shunned by the more religious pilgrims: shooting games, rides for children, puppet shows, or singers.

Some shrines, such as those of Sayyida Zaynab and Ḥusayn, are granted more sanctity than others. This is indicated by a number of factors, such as whether the entry of women is restricted at certain times, or whether foreigners are allowed to enter. Women are not allowed into the shrines of Ḥusayn and Sayyida Zaynab after sunset, and there is a widespread feeling among the people that foreigners and non-Muslims are not allowed in these shrines. The prohibition of entry by foreigners is not enforced in any strict sense, but belief in this prohibition is widespread. Attitudes toward the presence of tourists or non-Muslims vary. Although tourists are regularly paraded around the Azhar mosque and the Rifāʿī and Sulṭān Ḥasan mosques, they are not allowed in groups into the Ḥusayn mosque, though it is located right within the Khān al-Khalīlī tourist bazaar area. The one occasion when I witnessed a woman tourist in Ḥusayn, dressed in a sleeveless, scoop-necked tank shirt and miniskirt, her presence aroused the wrath of Shaykh ʿIzz, whom I was visiting the shrine. Shaykh ʿIzz usually merely laughed at the dress of foreigners in the street, and, more than most religious Muslims, understood something of the variations in cultural norms and did not regard their less modest dress as a sign of loose morals. But here in the most sacred of shrines he clearly found it offensive and demanded to know who had let her in. Set against the Muslim shrine visitors with their intense devotion, wiping the railing, kissing the posts and *maqṣūra,* praying the *Fātiḥa,* and whispering supplications, her broad smile and her focus on the art of the shrine seemed irreverent and irrelevant, and her dress was shockingly disrespectful.

In a sense, all Muslim activities become sacralized by the recitation of *bi ʾsm Allāh al-Raḥmān al-Raḥīm,* "in the name of God, the Compassionate, the Merciful." Eliade says that modern man lives in a desacralized cosmos, whereas premodern man lives in a sacralized cosmos. In Egypt, both perspectives can be found. For the Sufis, for whom almost all events are assessed in light of divine intention and saintly power, the cosmos remains sacralized. Miracles are so commonplace that it is almost a misnomer to term them *kharq al-ʿādāt,* "rending the habits" of nature. It is true that some mystics, by their very access to the divine presence, might question the heterogeneity of space and therefore question the meaning of the hajj or any other pilgrimage. For such mystics, sacred space exists within themselves. But for most Sufis, and for most pious Egyptians, saints' shrines constitute a source, a concentration of spiritual power and divine presence that radiate out to the surrounding area. Expectation of miracles does not come in a void but is linked with contact with the sacred realm of the saints. For such people, visiting saints' shrines is a deeply meaningful act that not only affirms a relationship with the saint and offers opportunities for socializing but is the main focus of the religious life. It is through such visitations that the believer is renewed, and the sacred realm can once again touch daily life. Whether or not their activities coincide with our expectations—or the expectations of the Egyptian elite—of reverential behavior, for the majority of Egyptians, there is no question that saints' shrines are indeed a sacred space.

The Controversy over Visiting Saints' Tombs

The visitation of saints' tombs is highly controversial in Egypt. The medieval scholar and polemicist, Ibn Taymiyya (d. 1328), condemned the practices of shrine visitation as a form of idolatry, on the charge that visitors pray to the saint rather than to God and that vows made to a saint are no different from vows made to idols. He quotes a ḥadīth in which the Prophet said, "By God, do not make my tomb an idol to be worshipped after I am gone." The Prophet also said, "God has cursed women who visit graves and those who build mosques and lamps over them."[48] Ibn Taymiyya's arguments are repeated by many modern reformers, who criticize the glorification of tombs, making tombs places of worship, prayers to saints, and women's visitation of tombs. Thousands of independent Islamic associations as well as government-sponsored teachers are busy propagating "the true religion," hoping to replace devotion to saints with the study of the Qurʾan. Even illiterate and semiliterate people are aware of the criticisms of prayer at saints' shrines.

Given the specific condemnation of the presence of women at the tombs, it is ironic that shrine visitation is an especially important part of the religious lives of women. Even when worship in mosques was barred to them, they could enter the shrines of saints. Edward Lane, writing in the early nineteenth century, marveled that in a country where no proper man would ever touch a woman who was not his wife, slave, or near relation, he found himself in the shrine of Ḥusayn on the feast of ʿĀshūrāʾ "so compressed in the midst of four women, that for some minutes I could not move in any direction; and pressed so hard against one young woman, face to face, that but for her veil our cheeks had been almost in contact." He added that some men say the only reason to visit the Ḥusayn mosque on that day was to enjoy being jostled by the women.[49] It is precisely such scenes that raise cries of immorality, particularly associated with moulid celebrations. In today's society, when caravans of young men attend the moulids specifically in order to have a good time, which includes touching women in the crowd, the protestations are not without foundation. Even Sufis readily admit that many evils take place during the moulids, including theft, prostitution, and amusements that pander to the baser instincts of the flesh. Sufi practices themselves are not without criticism from within their ranks. But that does negate the spiritual benefits of shrine visitation and moulids or the essential correctness of visiting tombs.

Like many other Muslim reformers, Shaykh Muḥammad Zakī Ibrāhīm denounces many of the traditional practices associated with the saint cult: deviant or irreverent methods of dhikr, the use of music, the mixing of men and women at moulids. But he vigorously defends the visitation of saints' tombs. He has devoted a short book to that subject, the purpose of which is to "protect the Muslim masses from the sedition *(fitna)* of the Wahhābīs,[50] which destroys faith, patriotism, nationalism and high human values."[51]

The Qurʾan says, "Fear God and seek a way *(wasīla)* to Him" (5:35). Shaykh Zakī interprets the way to God as the intercession of one of his saints, whether living or dead. It is by means of a godly person's eternal essence of faith, sincerity, love and purity that one seeks a way to God. He quotes ḥadīths that prove the permissibility of praying to God through Muhammad. In one ḥadīth in the collection of Tirmidhī, one of the six "canonical" collections recognized by Sunni Muslims, the Prophet instructs a blind man to pray, "God, I ask you and I turn to you by my Prophet, Muhammad, prophet of mercy; oh Muhammad, I ask your intercession *(astashfiʿu bi-ka)* with my Lord to return my sight." Since Muhammad would be absent when the man was to utter this prayer, it is clear, says the Shaykh, that it is Muhammad's eternal essence, not his temporal person, that is addressed in prayer. After Muhammad's death, the people prayed for rain both in the name of Muhammad's uncle ʿAbbās and at the tomb of the Prophet. The majority of Muslims, even the stern Aḥmad ibn Ḥanbal (d. 855), approved of seeking a way to God by the righteous dead. This is simply a way of pleading with God by what or whom He loves. Shaykh Zakī makes a distinction between *wasīla* and *wisāṭa*, the latter being mediation, which no Muslim believes is necessary. "When a person out of ignorance or error or habit or tradition says, 'Sīdī so-and-so,' they really mean, 'Lord of Sīdī so-and-so.' He errs only in his expression, not in his faith. To call this idolatry is ignorance, and means unjustly removing the majority of Muslims from the pale of Islam."[52] Seeking the intercession of a righteous person does not imply worship of the intercessor.

Shaykh Zakī goes on to say that the interaction of the spirits of the dead with the living is proven by ḥadīths concerning Muhammad's meeting with the spirits of the former prophets during his Ascension into heaven and by his addressing the dead polytheists who were killed at Badr. When asked about this, he said, "You, by God, cannot hear me any better than they."[53] The fact that the dead Muslims are also alive is indicated by the Qurʾan itself (3:170).[54] The Qurʾan also proves that the dead benefit from the deeds of the living, for it says, "Our Lord, forgive us and our brothers who preceded us in faith" (59:10).

Shaykh Zakī states that the blessedness of praying at certain places, such as mosques and shrines, is clear from Ḥadīth, which says that there are places where and times when prayer is more blessed because of their holiness and purity. The pilgrimage to Mecca and belief in the effectiveness of prayer on *laylat al-qadr*, the 27th of Ramaḍān, when the Qurʾan was first revealed to Muhammad, offer only two of the numerous possible examples to bolster this argument. Somewhat more controversial is seeking baraka from the relics of the righteous. But this too is an old, accepted practice in Islam. Once again Shaykh Zakī appeals to the example of Aḥmad ibn Ḥanbal (d. 855), founder of the legal school to which Ibn Taymiyya (d. 1328) belonged. Ibn Ḥanbal allegedly allowed people to kiss the Prophet's tomb for baraka, and he himself drank the water in which Imām al-Shāfiʿī's (d. 820) shirt was washed in order to obtain blessing. Many other examples are cited to prove this point.[55]

Shaykh Zakī also argues that although the Prophet, in order to bring an end to the idolatry that in his time consisted of worshipping stones and deifying the dead, originally prohibited visiting graves and cursed women who visited them, later, when the faith had taken firm root in the people, both prohibitions were rescinded.[56] He counters those who object to the building of domes over tombs by saying a dome is nothing but a strong roof. The Prophet and the first two caliphs were buried in the house of Muhammad's wife, ʿĀʾishah', which had a roof. Many domes have been built over the Prophet's tomb, he said, and none of the pious ancestors, whose religion Ibn Taymiyya claimed to be reviving, objected. Although tombs themselves should not be objects of worship, there is no prohibition of building mosques attached to a tomb. The Prophet himself was buried, according to his instructions, in ʿĀʾisha's house, which was next to the mosque, and the gate remained open to the inside of the mosque. No one objected. Furthermore, Ishmael and others were, according to Islamic tradition, buried beneath the walls of the Kaʿba. If burial next to a place of prayer were forbidden, then the Prophet would not have said that prayer in that place was better than any other.[57] Mosques, he concludes, have been built by graves to grant the dead the benefit of the Qurʾan recitation, prayer and dhikr taking place there, and so the virtuous dead may be a good example to the living.[58] Shaykh Zakī provides examples of famous early Muslims who made a practice of praying at saints' tombs and found such prayers efficacious.[59]

Shaykh Zakī is clearly concerned not only with the issues pertaining to the intercession of the saints but also with the danger posed to Muslim society by a growing, frequently intolerant, fundamentalist movement. He emphasizes that all who say "There is no god but Allah" are, by the consensus of Muslim scholars and the authority of Ḥadīth, to be acknowledged as Muslims.

Fundamentalists are not the only Egyptians who have difficulty accepting the validity of seeking healing and intercession at saints' tombs. To many Western-educated Egyptians, such practices fall under the category of superstition. Many of them believe that only the uneducated, illiterate, and poor go to the saints' shrines and moulids, but this impression is certainly false. Although the lower classes often do predominate in the activities at saints' shrines, there are also many middle- and upper-class devotees, and the crowds range from shabbily-dressed beggars to men in suits and ties. But although many Egyptians might visit a saint's shrine in time of need or go to a moulid just for fun or out of curiosity, for the Sufis such rituals play a central role in their spiritual life. Like the *wakīl* of Bayt ʿAbāṭa, they see their entire service to God in terms of devotion to the *ahl al-bayt* and the saints, by attending their moulids, performing dhikr near their shrines, and offering hospitality to the people. One Sufi woman of the Musallamiyya Khalwatiyya Order told me, "If I do not go to the moulids, I feel as if I am burning up inside!" This inner compulsion is a deeply spiritual drive.

CHAPTER 5

The Sufi Orders

The word that we usually translate into English as "Sufi Order" or "brotherhood" is *ṭarīqa* (plural, *ṭuruq*), which more literally means "path" or "way." In contemporary Egypt, the word *ṭarīqa* is almost always used, but in earlier sources the related word, *ṭarīq*, was often used as well. In keeping with the meaning of *ṭarīqa* as "path," the Orders see themselves not so much as institutions or organizations but as a spiritual method, a "way" or "path" to attain spiritual refinement. The differences between the Orders, both in doctrines and methods, are relatively inconsequential. The Orders are not to be regarded as sects, for their proliferation is owing to the array of teachers, not differences in doctrine. A disciple's attachment is not to an Order but to a specific spiritual master, his shaykh. Nonetheless, the term *shaykh* is also widely used in a number of ways without necessarily meaning that the individual so designated is truly shaykh of an Order. "Shaykh" can mean someone who has passed his exams at the Islamic university of Al-Azhar, or it can refer to the head of a Sufi Order, but it is also informally applied to anyone popularly believed to have spiritual knowledge, regardless of whether or not that person possesses education or official status in a religious institution.

The spiritual elevation of the Sufi is conceived as a journey from stage to stage along a path, under the guidance of a Sufi shaykh who is a "gnostic of God" (*ʿārif bi 'llāh)* or a "divine sage" *(ʿālim rabbānī)*, that is, who has personal experience with God and who has attained a spiritual rank with God that enables him to give guidance to others. Entry into the path begins with repentance from sin and leads the disciple through the stages of purification of his soul, which vary in their formulations, until he is able to attain gnosis *(maʿrifa)*. Yet few claim to have attained that station. Most contemporary Egyptians who attach themselves to a shaykh do so to derive some spiritual benefit and hope for some spiritual guidance and refinement, but true gnosis is regarded as a grace reserved for God's elect. Some, in fact, hope to do little more than shake the hand of the shaykh for blessing or attend occasional group dhikrs. Some recite the *awrād*, or daily prayers, of the Order without understanding their meanings but hope to attain some spiritual reward as a result. Others may try to understand Sufism more deeply and attend the teaching sessions of a shaykh. But true discipleship is a deeply personal attachment to a shaykh, involving training and struggle in order to attain spiritual awareness.

THE SPIRITUAL GUIDE

A shaykh or spiritual guide is deemed essential to progress in the Sufi path—indeed, some would say a shaykh is necessary for salvation itself. "He who has no shaykh, has Satan for his shaykh" goes an adage popular among the Sufis. The Qur'anic justification for the requirement to seek out a shaykh lies in 25:59: "It is He who created the heavens and earth and what is between them in six days, then rose onto the Throne—the Compassionate One. Ask someone one knows *(khabīr)* about Him." The *khabīr*, the expert or one who possesses this divine knowledge, is believed to be a gnostic, or true shaykh.

Shaykh Muḥammad Māḍī Abū 'l-ʿAzā'im (d. 1937), founder of the ʿAzmiyya Order, writes, "The first thing one must do on the path to God is to find the 'living man' who is the Imam of his age. If he finds that one of his limbs prevents him from following the man in whom God has placed light and wisdom, let him cut off the member and flee to the guide, in fear of eternal misery."[1] Abū 'l-ʿAzā'im reasons that just as one would submit oneself to a knowledgeable guide for any worldly journey, stopping and journeying at his command and obeying his every word, "believing that if he disagreed with him he would perish or lose his wealth," so should one submit oneself to a knowledgeable guide for the journey to the afterlife. He marvels at the heedlessness of most Muslims: "It does not even occur to them that they are traveling, either to heaven or to hell! . . . By neglecting to seek the companion who would guide them as a brother, they travel the crooked path of perdition, far from arriving at God."[2]

While Abū 'l-ʿAzā'im's words seem to indicate that there is only one particular man suitable to serve as spiritual guide, in fact there is a proliferation of guides. A suitable guide is a gnostic or saint, sometimes described with deceptive simplicity as "one of the righteous" *(min al-ṣāliḥīn)*. Shaykh Aḥmad Raḍwān (d. 1967) gave his followers a stern warning: "Do not do without the righteous, and thereby cause your spirits to die!"[3] He exhorts his followers to seek out a "gnostic" and learn from him all they needed to know about earthly and religious life, before death overtook them.[4]

Shaykh ʿIzz interpreted the Qur'anic verse, "You who believe, fear God and be with the truthful" (9:119), to mean that believers are obligated to seek out the company of the saints. For the Prophet said, "Your sitting with a gnostic of God the length of time it takes to milk a ewe is better than sixty years of worship," and "[Attending] an assembly of learning is better than sixty years of worship." Since the Sufi gnostics inherited a portion of the divine light that Muhammad passed on to his descendants, it is incumbent on those who hope to attain the presence of the Beloved to attach themselves to a gnostic, who alone will be able to provide them with what they need in their journey toward God.[5] Without the presence of a gnostic, said ʿIzz, even the prayers and dhikr of the believer do not reach God, although exception is made for the five obligatory daily prayers, because the spirit of a gnostic must initially carry the spirit of the uninitiated to the Throne of God. "If he is sitting with a gnostic, the spirit of the gnostic will carry him up to the Throne of God. When his praises reach the Throne of God, living creatures [angels] are created from them which will carry him up to the Throne of God afterwards." It is not just saving knowledge that is gained from a shaykh but saving association. Such is the benefit of companionship with the righteous, or merely "sitting with" a gnostic.

Shaykh Aḥmad Raḍwān said that a gnostic, who can read human hearts, knows exactly what is the spiritual state of each person and what "medicine" would heal each person's spirit. Attachment to a shaykh, ardently loving and serving him, will enable the disciple to triumph in this world and the next. Alluding to the mythical beast that carried Muhammad to the presence of God on the night of the Ascension, Raḍwān quotes a poem describing the Sufi shaykh as "the Burāq to the Highest."[6]

The necessity of learning from a gnostic is underscored, from the Sufi point of view, by the Qur'anic story of Moses and Khiḍr. Moses was a great prophet who had received revelation from God, but he nonetheless sought out the company of a gnostic, a man who, according to the Qur'an, had been taught knowledge from God (18:65–82). This gnostic is popularly identified as Khiḍr, "the Green One," who, according to tradition, had drunk from the Fountain of Immortality. He appears to Sufis throughout the ages and is the prototype of the Sufi gnostic. Aḥmad Raḍwān says, "In order to learn the divine sciences, God commanded Moses to become a disciple of Khiḍr in order that he might combine the knowledge of revelation *(waḥy)* and conversation with God *(al-mukālama 'l-ilāhiyya)* with the knowledge which is poured out on the hearts—these are the divine gifts, and whoever has not tasted them has not entered the presence of intimacy *(ḥaḍrat al-uns)*."[7] Aḥmad Raḍwān describes the prophetic revelation as externally received through the senses, in keeping with Islamic tradition concerning the externality of the agent of revelation, and opposes this to the intuitively received gnosis which is poured out on the heart. Even a prophet must learn the divine gifts from a gnostic in order to enter the familiar companionship of God.

Association with a gnostic should lead naturally to love for him and serving him. Therefore it is said that "the service of men is the cause of reaching the Lord of lords." On the other hand, "if God wants evil for His servant, He intervenes between him and the saints and does not let him love them or understand their spiritual states. He might even oppose them or hate them, and thus die without the religion of Islam."[8] Perhaps nowhere can we find a more explicit passage on the pivotal position of the gnostic in the Sufi soteriological system. Nonetheless, Aḥmad Raḍwān admonishes his disciples not to persist in sin and expect their allegiance to a shaykh to save them, contrary to the assurances that some shaykhs give their disciples. Just as Abū Bakr and ʿUmar, the righteous Companions and Successors of the Prophet, feared meeting God at their deaths despite their closeness to the Messenger of God, Sufis should always be aware of their accountability to God.[9]

One benefit of accompanying the "men of God," according to another modern Sufi author, is that it ignites zeal and desire for God in the hearts, and causes the spirits to long for the heavenly realm from which they came. Furthermore, "The Sufi masters possess spiritual secrets which illuminate the inner vision with guidance, more than light illuminates external vision."[10]

Shaykh Abū 'l-ʿAzāʾim writes that the more one follows a shaykh, the more one loves and honors him, comes to favor the next world over this, and becomes humble. Someone who finds a true shaykh should "make him your spirit by which you live and your soul by which you stand and your imam with whom you do not disagree, and believe that with him you will be with those whom God has blessed . . . and without him you will be with the common rabble."[11]

"ʿAlī," an engineer about thirty-five to forty years old, described to me how he came to follow his shaykh, Shaykh Aḥmad Abū 'l-Ḥasan of Kom Ombo, near Aswān, in far southern Egypt. ʿAlī himself came from Jirjā, also in the province of Aswān. From his youth, he said, he had loved the *ahl al-bayt*. His search for a spiritual guide began with the Qurʾanic verse commanding people to ask someone who is knowledgeable about divine things *(khabīr)*. He felt he needed an expert to ask about the way to God. He searched, he said, from Aswān to Alexandria, and in Libya and Saudi Arabia. Then, while attending the moulid of Abū 'l-Ḥasan al-Shādhilī (d. 1258), he saw Shaykh Aḥmad Abū 'l-Ḥasan addressing a large crowd. He sat among them and immediately felt as if the shaykh were speaking directly to him—although, he added, all the others would have felt that the shaykh was speaking to them, for this is the gift of a true shaykh, that his words penetrate each heart as if they were intended uniquely for that person. ʿAlī had committed a sin of which he had told no one. But the shaykh told the crowd, "The gnostics see the sins of people as if they are written on their foreheads. By repenting at their hands, the sin is washed away." ʿAlī knew the shaykh was speaking directly to him, although everyone else heard the words in a general way. From that point on, he wanted to be with the shaykh, knowing he had found the object of his search. But Shaykh Aḥmad sent him to his own shaykh in Aswān, Shaykh Muḥammad Abū 'l-Futūḥ. ʿAlī took the oath from Shaykh Abū 'l-Futūḥ and stayed with him until he died. After that time, he followed Shaykh Aḥmad wherever he went.

Shaykh Gābir al-Jāzūlī of the Jāzūliyya Ḥusayniyya Shādhiliyya Order describes the shaykh as "the guide, teacher, and spiritual father of his disciples and those who love him *(aḥbābihi)*. He is the sound model who must be followed. With him the disciples feel security, peace and familiar companionship." The shaykh should not exalt himself over his disciples but should be compassionate with them in order to help them on their spiritual journey. He should ask no reward and accept no praise for the good that he does but should be a leader, shepherd, and servant of the Order.[12]

Shaykh Abū 'l-ʿAzāʾim likewise details the characteristics of the shaykh. He should have good morals, patience, compassion, and an ability to appeal to each person at his intellectual level. He should not engage in debate and should be kind to those who harm him. He should conceal the character flaws of other people and should only mention their good points. He should avoid anything that would cause repugnance in people and should do all things for God and in God.[13]

Traditionally, one became a Sufi shaykh by receiving a certificate of permission from one's own shaykh. This system still exists, although in many cases the position of shaykh is passed on from father to son. Ḥasan al-Malaṭāwī speaks of the importance of receiving permission from his shaykh to give guidance to a group of disciples,[14] and Shaykh Abū 'l-Wafā al-Sharqāwī (d. 1961), whose father was a famous Sufi shaykh and scholar, likewise speaks of receiving his father's permission to give guidance before embarking on his own career as a shaykh.[15] Such permission to give guidance links a shaykh with the spiritual lineage *(silsila)* of his Order, and he becomes a vessel of baraka and a link in the chain of blessing that goes back to the Prophet himself.

The Supreme Council of Sufi Orders insists on such a valid *silsila* in order to obtain recognition as an Order. However, many popular shaykhs have no official position in any Order. Shaykh Aḥmad Raḍwān was such an independent shaykh, who, although he neither represented nor founded an Order, exerted tremendous influence on the thousands who visited him, and his followers may be found throughout Upper Egypt. Shaykh ʿIzz, likewise, never received official permission to give guidance, yet he began to acquire disciples of his own, at their request, while he was still attending the meetings of another shaykh. Spiritual leadership spontaneously emerges when people discern evidences of God's grace on a person, which are manifested particularly through the ability to speak through inspiration and to perform other miracles. Sufis believe that the spiritual "secrets" of a saint may be inherited by one person or distributed among several, and this inheritance may follow the line of physical or spiritual descent. Shaykh ʿIzz believes he was among a group of five followers of Shaykh Aḥmad Raḍwān who inherited a portion of his "secrets." The one who inherited the largest portion, he said, was Aḥmad Raḍwān's eldest son, Shaykh Muḥammad Aḥmad Raḍwān. One man commented when he first heard Shaykh ʿIzz teaching, "He speaks as I would expect a 'son' of Aḥmad Raḍwān to speak."

It is generally expected that the spiritual secrets of a master will be inherited by his son, unless his son exhibits attitudes and behavior that contradict the Sufi way. The inheritance by a son of the office of shaykh is therefore not seen by the Sufis as a corruption of a system that ought to be based on spiritual stature, unless it leads to wrongful veneration of an unworthy individual or the assignment of spiritual leadership to a minor. In most cases, it is seen as an entirely natural process that follows the typical flow of the grace of God and is a natural extension of the belief that the prophetic light was distributed among his physical descendants first, and then among the saints. However, it is widely acknowledged that women may also inherit these divine secrets, although women may not officially becomes shaykhs of the Orders. I came across two examples of women who are thought to have inherited the spiritual secrets of their fathers, although their brothers inherited the positions of shaykhs of the Orders. In both cases, although the brothers assumed official responsibilities, the women exercised actual spiritual leadership.

Although, strictly speaking, a person should have only one shaykh at a time, because one can only follow one method of spiritual discipline at a time, it is not at all unusual for a Sufi to have a number of spiritual guides or teachers throughout a lifetime. Perhaps only one of these will have received the oath that makes an aspiring Sufi a disciple, but the fluid system of "spiritual adoption" allows for the possibility of a multiplicity of spiritual "fathers" and "mothers." Women typically exercise their spiritual authority in this more fluid, informal system. Shaykh ʿIzz insists that aside from the formal administration of oaths, there are oaths that are given "within," through visions, or oaths that occur through unspoken understanding, "by a glance." His own list of spiritual guides is rather unconventional. His primary spiritual training came in his youth from Shaykh Aḥmad Raḍwān, who "adopted" him when he was still a young boy. He spent a good deal of time at the *sāḥa* of Aḥmād Raḍwān and says he had unrestricted access to Aḥmad Raḍwān at any time, although no one else dared to enter his room when he was in solitary worship or meditation *(khalwa).* This formative influence of Aḥmad Raḍwān is marked on ʿIzz in both the content and style of his teachings. Many years later, in Cairo, ʿIzz received a year of weekly private instruction from the celebrated Sufi author and former rector of Al-Azhar, Shaykh ʿAbd al-Ḥalim Maḥmūd (d. 1978). ʿIzz's "inner" oath, through vision, was to the thirteenth-century Sufi master, Abū 'l-Ḥasan al-Shādhilī, and much of what he knows he claims to have learned directly through this inspired source, as well as through communications with the Prophet's grandson, Ḥusayn, and the Prophet himself. His external oath was the least meaningful of all to him, for it was administered by an independent Shādhilī shaykh in a group setting in which ʿIzz felt he was coerced by the norms of etiquette. This shaykh, ʿIzz said, never taught him anything new, and ʿIzz clearly regards him as his inferior. ʿIzz also had a "spiritual mother," Ḥāgga Zakiyya (d. 1982). ʿIzz's commission to build his own mosque and *sāḥa,* thereby establishing himself as an independent Sufi teacher, came from the immortal Sufi master, Khiḍr. This unconventional spiritual formation carries no authority or validity in the eyes of the Supreme Council of Sufi Orders, for whom ʿIzz could claim the title of shaykh only because of the preaching certificates he had earned through formal study. But such niceties do not trouble the majority of Sufis, who readily acknowledge that the graces of God transcend the boundaries of human validation.

Sufi masters since the time of Junayd (d. 910) have warned of the importance of being careful in selecting a Sufi shaykh, for there are many false guides, and following them will lead to perdition. Contemporary Sufis believe that charlatans abound, although naturally they believe in the soundness of their own shaykh. Indeed, most Sufis believe their own shaykh to be the *quṭb* of the age. Some spiritual seekers spend years following a variety of shaykhs in search of guidance, before settling on a particular spiritual guide who is truly "their" shaykh. Others are led into association with a particular shaykh through family ties or other natural means of acquaintance. Yet with surprising frequency one encounters stories of guidance to a particular shaykh through visions. For example, a middle-class woman suffering from psychological problems she believed to be caused by spirit possession was led by a dream-vision to seek out Ḥāgga Zakiyya. She had never heard of Ḥāgga Zakiyya, but, she says, the dream told her precisely how to find her *sāḥa,* and the layout of the *sāḥa* turned out to be precisely as she had seen in her vision. And so she became a devoted follower of Ḥāgga Zakiyya.

Giving an oath *(ʿahd)* to a shaykh (although, in Arabic, one "takes" an oath from a shaykh) is seen as a form of oath-giving to the Prophet Muhammad. In Muhammad's own lifetime, conversion to Islam was formalized through the administration of an oath *(bayʿa),* which the Qurʾan affirms is in fact an oath to God, "the hand of God above your hands" (48:10). Oath-taking ceremonies vary from Order to Order but generally consist of a handshake between the shaykh and disciple, recitation by the disciple of some Qurʾan passages, including verses regarding oaths and covenants, and the mutual agreement by the shaykh and the disciple to enter into this relationship. The shaykh is accepted as spiritual guide, and the disciple is accepted as a son or daughter in God. Ernst Bannerth wrote that among the ʿAmriyya Rifāʿiyya, after a period of attending the shaykh's lectures, one asked to be accepted as a *murīd* (disciple). "The ceremony of initiation consists of reciting the *Fātiḥa* five times, asking forgiveness *(al-istighfār)*, and then a group of several young people sit before the shaykh, repeating the formula after the shaykh. . . . The young men take the shaykh's hand. The women do not touch the hand of the shaykh, but a long rosary held by him."[16]

The shaykh's refusal to touch the hands of women recalls the numerous accounts of the Prophet Muhammad receiving the oaths of women, which generally stress his refusal to shake their hands, although in one account ʿUmar ibn al-Khaṭṭāb does shake the hands of the women, and in another Muhammad dips his hands in water and passes the bowl to each woman to dip her hand in turn.[17] Nabia Abbott, whose foundational research on the status of women in pre-Islamic and early Islamic Arabia remains without parallel, comments, "Not even a casual reader can escape the conviction that the strained effort to credit Muhammad with the determination not to touch the hands of the women reflects the spirit not of the first but of the third century of Islam. The handshake was a customary way of concluding an agreement."[18] Many shaykhs today do shake the hands of women, and some, like Shaykh Muḥammad Zakī Ibrāhīm of the Muḥammadiyya Shādhiliyya, regularly allow their women followers to kiss their hands, although Shaykh Muḥammad Zakī makes an attempt to withdraw his hand when he realizes that someone intends to kiss it. The withdrawal of the hand follows the traditional etiquette of humility that pertains with men as well as women, and has nothing to do with the norms of sexual segregation.[19]

Concerning the oath a shaykh administers to his disciple, Farīd Māhir writes, the disciple feels that he is "born again," starting his life anew with "a clean, pure, white page," and a determination to let nothing sully this purity.[20] The phrase "born again" recalls the experience of many American fundamentalist and evangelical Christians, and it is apparent that many Sufis experience a similar conversion when entering the Sufi path.

THE AWRĀD

Once initiated into an Order, the basic discipline that each disciple practices is the daily recitation of the *wird* (pl., *awrād*), or prayers, of the Order. These consist of prayers of forgiveness, a formula of dhikr, prayers of blessing on the Prophet, and supplications *(duʿā)*. *Awrād* are recited at particular times each day, usually after the five daily prayers, or simply in the morning and at night. A *ḥizb*, on the other hand, may be recited at any time. The *ḥizb* is a prayer asking God for spiritual blessings. Most Orders have more than one *ḥizb*, of varying lengths. *Al-ḥizb al-kabīr* (the "greater *ḥizb*") of the Rifāʿi-yya, for example, begins with two pages of invoking various spiritual phenomena before making an actual request of God. It begins, "Oh God, I ask you by the eternal truths, the divine qualities, the lordly attributes, the holy words, the high oaths, the heavenly realities, the heavenly bodies, the angels of the throne . . . the spirits burned by the disclosure of the divine presence, the pure, true, holy works, the hidden, noble, great secrets, the wonders exalted above human circumstances, the names hidden in the divine treasuries." The section of requests begins: "Hasten to me the flow of your grace, so I may see your gracious grace in everything, so I may drown in the sea of your grace, rejoicing in the sweetness of that sea, a sweetness which lets the spirits of the travelers understand your secrets. And grant me one of the names of your light, that if one appealed to you by it, you respond. Protect me from the evil of what comes up out of the ground and what comes down from the sky."

Al-ḥizb al-saghīr, the "lesser *ḥizb*," consists of the opening chapter of the Qur'an (the *Fātiḥa*) and other Qur'anic verses.

The dhikr that a person recites in the daily *awrād* may vary not only from Order to Order but also from person to person within an Order. Dhikr consists of the recitation of one of the names of God, such as Allah, *al-Raḥman* (the Compassionate), *al-Ḥayy* (the Living One), or *Hūwa* (He), or it may consist of the phrase, "there is no god but Allah," which is often counted by the Sufis as one of the Ninety-Nine Names of God. Each name of God is thought to unlock a particular spiritual secret, and the shaykh should direct the disciple to the dhikr that is appropriate for the disciple at that time. A disciple may progress from one name to another in dhikr, as directed by the shaykh, who, by virtue of his God-given insight, knows what is best for each disciple. There should also be a correspondence between the numerical value attached to the sum of the letters in the name recited and the numerical value of the sum of the letters of the name of the person doing dhikr. This is because a name is more than an inconsequential label but reflects something essential about that which is named and is in fact the key to its spiritual core.[21]

One should have the permission of a shaykh before reciting the *awrād* of an Order. This permission is mandatory as a safeguard to the potential disciple, for the *awrād* are believed to be so spiritually powerful that a person could go mad from reciting them without proper spiritual protection and preparation. Even private recitation of the Qur'an without proper supervision by a shaykh is believed to be spiritually dangerous. The *awrād* are thought to be the key to all true spiritual realization. Shaykh Gamāl al-Sanhūrī told me that the Burhāniyya were spiritually stronger than other Orders because of their insistence on the primacy of *awrād*, in a time when many Orders were neglecting adequately to teach them to their members and insist on their observance. Shaykh Abū 'l-Wafā' al-Sharqāwī (d. 1961) of the Khalwatiyya likewise accused contemporary Sufis of neglecting *awrād*. He wrote, "*Awrād* are among the most important foundations of the [Sufi] Way, in order to free hearts, tongues and limbs from preoccupation with this world. No good will come to a disciple who does not embrace and persistently recite *awrād*. . . . Anyone whose soul whispers to him that it is difficult to recite *awrād* faithfully is excluded from this Path."[22] Yet he also decried those who recite *awrād* without concentrating on the meanings of the words they recite. The *awrād* must be recited correctly, for they consist of Qur'anic verses, prophetic ḥadīths and prayers containing the names of God, and mistakes in pronouncing these things are forbidden in the Sharī'a.[23]

After reciting *awrād* for some time, it is expected that the disciple will receive visions and other forms of spiritual revelation and will develop the gift of spiritual discernment that borders on clairvoyance. The personal testimony of Shaykh Muḥammad 'Uthmān of the Burhāniyya, which is described in chapter 10 of this book, is an especially clear account of spiritual realization attributed directly to the recitation of *awrād*.

Shaykhs gather their disciples together for communal *wird*, which is thought to be more powerful than solitary *wird*, just as communal *ṣalāt* (ritual prayer) is thought to be twenty-seven times more powerful than solitary prayer, for it aids in the concentration of the spirit, and the spirits of stronger Sufis lift the spirits of the weaker. Abū 'l-Wafā' al-Sharqāwī wrote that communal *wird* should be after the evening prayer, "so two pillars of the Way may be achieved at once: staying awake at night, and the recollection of God (dhikr)."[24]

Yet not all Sufis have their communal *wird* at night, as is evident from this statement by Ḥasan al-Malaṭāwī: "My shaykh used to gather a group of his disciples between the sunset and evening prayers and teach them dhikr. We used to do dhikr with much more concentration and awareness in this group than alone. The strong spirits let the weaker spirits drink from their spiritual assistance *(madad),* just as water flows from a higher ground to a lower ground and irrigates it."[25]

Styles and formats for a shaykh's meetings with his disciples vary, some concentrating on dhikr, others on teaching. For Shaykh ʿIzz, an integral part of such a gathering with his disciples was the serving of a meal. At the time I was in Egypt, Shaykh ʿIzz had suspended his regular meetings with his disciples because he was busy with building his mosque and the atmosphere, he said, was inappropriate. But as time went on he confessed that the building of the mosque complex had so drained his financial resources that he was unable to offer his disciples meat, which he felt he must offer at a formal meeting. I pointed out that many shaykhs do not offer their disciples any food during their meetings but merely serve tea. Others offer bean sandwiches (*fūl* and *ṭaʿmiyya*) or lentils. ʿIzz explained that since he came from a family of butchers, people had come to expect him to offer meat. Since he was unable to do so, he preferred not to hold a meeting at all.

THE SHAYKH-DISCIPLE RELATIONSHIP

Visions are important not only in finding a guide but in confirming the validity of the relationship that is to be established. Such relationships are not thought to be simply a matter of human choice and preference but to have been determined by God. The shaykh and disciple should feel a natural mutual compatibility, which goes beyond affection to a deep bond. The shaykh's words should penetrate the spirit of the disciple more than the words of any other person. The shaykh and disciple should have an instant understanding of each other, almost as if they had met before, which in fact they had, according to Sufi belief, in the world of the spirits, on the day of the Primordial Covenant that God made with humanity when He asked them, "Am I not your Lord?" and they answered in the affirmative (7:171). On that day, spirits who brushed right shoulders, according to a ḥadīth, will like each other in earthly life, while those who brushed left shoulders will have an aversion to each other. This natural bond between shaykh and disciple will deepen into spiritual connection as their relationship progresses, which again is validated by communication through visions.

Sufis repeatedly emphasize that a true shaykh is one who knows the hearts and unspoken needs of his disciples and is able to teach

each disciple according to his level of spiritual development and his capacity to understand. According to a ḥadīth, the Prophet said, "We have been commanded to address people according to the capacity of their minds." As one Shādhilī shaykh from Asyūṭ told me, "Teaching is according to the capacity of the receiver, not the capacity of the speaker." All shaykhs practice this to some extent, reserving certain teachings for an inner circle of disciples, while basic religious teachings are taught to the masses. More pertinently, each disciple has distinct obstacles to overcome in the spiritual journey. As the shaykh from Asyūṭ explained, "The shaykh, in training his 'sons,' is granted inspirations from God. He knows what is appropriate for each disciple. For example, the proud disciple who is of high rank is given warnings and told to examine himself, until his high rank is removed from his soul. A person who is attached to this world is commanded to do asceticism. . . . The hearts of the gnostics have eyes: an eye that looks with hope and an eye that looks in nearness and an eye that looks in God. The gnostic dies in God and lives in God. An eye that looks at what goes from you to God, and an eye that sees what goes from God to you."[26] He distinguished between two types of shaykhs, those who teach in a straightforward manner religious knowledge that can be gained from books *(shaykh li 'l-tarbiyya)* and those who teach their disciples from their own spiritual states, in an inspired fashion *(bi 'l-aḥwāl)*.

Shaykh ʿIzz explained the Sufi shaykhs' method of teaching as follows: "The shaykh's guidance of his disciples varies depending on the disciple. Sometimes he needs to be told plainly. If the disciple has awareness, he can be directed by allusions *(ishārāt)*. If the disciple is on his way toward complete identification with the shaykh, in which he sees nothing but his shaykh, at this point guidance can be internal, either by autosuggestion *(īḥāʾ)* or by vision, by calling the shaykh before him by reciting the *Fātiḥa*, and hearing him say, 'Do this or that,' or by a dream-vision, which is the lowest level. . . . The shaykh is a stellar spirit, from whose rays the disciples absorb light. The disciple comprehends the shaykh's realizations according to his capacity. The disciple cannot take in the complete rays of the shaykh."

On another occasion, ʿIzz said, "If I am speaking to a group and I want to say something to a particular person, I speak in a riddle which only he will understand." He claimed to know the unspoken questions in the hearts of his disciples and to know what was happening in the privacy of their homes, so he would know when his intervention was needed to solve a domestic dispute, for example.

A secondary school teacher described the sweetness of sitting with his shaykh, ʿAbd al-Salām al-Ḥilwānī. The shaykh was gentle and patient, he said, and spoke little. He guided his disciples with barely an awareness on their part. "They were drawn to him in spirit, taking light from his light."[27]

ʿIzz frequently said one should teach according to capacity *(istiʿdād)*, but on one occasion he elaborated that capacity is of three types: "in the spirit, and that is something special; in the heart, which is according to the level of love; and in the intellect, which is according to the level of intelligence."

ʿIzz provided two examples that he thought indicated that the Prophet Muhammad taught different things to different people, according to their capacity to understand. Two ḥadīths that appear to be contradictory, he said, are in fact addressing different situations. For example, in one ḥadīth, "a man came and asked the Prophet whether touching the penis abolishes ablutions. He was a young man of twenty-two years, so the Prophet said that it does abolish ablutions. Why? Because a youth has strong lusts to which he responds. After a year or two, an old man of seventy years asked the same question, and he said it does not abolish ablutions. Why? Because the old man's vitality is weak, and touching his penis will not affect him. There are four legal schools in Islam. One chooses one ḥadīth, one the other, and one tries to resolve the conflict by saying the touch with the palm of the hand abolishes ablutions, but the touch with the back of the hand does not. But it is more penetrating to look at the reasoning."

During a teaching at the moulid of Ḥusayn, ʿIzz gave another example of apparently contradictory remarks by the Prophet that were in fact addressed to people who were different from each other in their spiritual receptivity. "The Messenger of God was preaching from the pulpit one Friday when he saw our lord Ḥusayn at the door of the mosque, crying. He came down from the pulpit and carried him, and went to comfort him before going back to the pulpit. And he said to the people [who follow their] hearts, 'This is the way of mercy.' And he said to the people [who follow their] intellects, 'Your wealth and children are a temptation for you, so beware' [cf. Qurʾan 64:15]. Every one is given the teaching according to his temperament." The implication is that there is a higher teaching than that of the Qurʾanic verse referred to and that this higher teaching is for the people who know the way of love, that is, the Sufis.[28]

ʿIzz pointed out how I should apply this principle to my own situation. I was continuously annoyed by the questions Egyptians asked me when they found out I had done my doctoral dissertation on the religious life of Muslim women in Egypt. I was usually asked, "So what do you think of Egyptian women?" or "What do you think of Islam?"—questions I found absurd and irrelevant. I was usually at a loss for an answer, but ʿIzz said that a superficial question deserves a superficial answer, that I was far too concerned with conveying something real and precise about the way I approached my research.

Most shaykhs teach in an apparently straightforward style, usually without apparent recourse to inspiration. Shaykh Aḥmad Abū 'l-Ḥasan of Kom Ombo, however, well illustrates the introspective style suggested by an inspired state. Tall, thin, wearing an enormous turban, he carried himself with all the eccentricity and mystery that becomes a shaykh who is in a spiritual state *(fī 'l-ḥāl),* which appears to the Western observer to be simple self-absorption. An illiterate man, with no claims to education whatsoever, a dark Upper Egyptian man fully steeped in tradition, he exerted a fascinating attraction for a very large crowd of people at the moulid of Husayn in Cairo, many of whom were very well-educated and wealthy. The shaykh pivoted, closed his eyes, extended his hand dramatically, lifted his eyes to heaven. He interrupted his teaching to order people to sit, unable to abide anyone taking time to find a place to sit. He also ordered a man who distributed water not to do so, saying, "What do people need water for?" although he himself drank from a cup at intervals. He demanded that he be the sole and total center of attention. The shaykh was quite authoritarian, yet he also demonstrated respect, with the traditional signs of humility, for various members of the audience whom he singled out. He quoted from books (despite his illiteracy), but he also frequently chose to speak through poems of praise to the Prophet, most of them known to those present. He would hand the microphone to his lead singer, and while the men all rocked back and forth and sang fervently, the shaykh stood in their midst, pivoting on his staff, his eyes closed or raised to heaven, his hand stretched out. When a man near him erred in the words to a song, the shaykh threatened to hit him with his staff, but no one seemed to find the gesture funny or strange. He often illustrated his teaching with music, in a manner not at all uncommon among Sufi shaykhs. At one point he spontaneously composed a poem, prompting his singers to respond in chorus, despite their obvious uncertainty. A man rose, notebook and pen in hand, to transcribe the inspired song. One time, when his lead singer was singing, the shaykh, feeling himself at one with the words, leaned his head on the singer's head. The man was overwhelmed by the honor and shrieked, then paused a moment to regain his composure before continuing the song. When the shaykh rose to leave, the whole multitude rose as well. Lines of dhikr were formed, the shaykh in the middle organizing them, sometimes pushing people into formation with his staff, leading the beat and the movement.

The type of teaching Shaykh ʿIzz described—that of autosuggestion and of visions—indicates what Egyptian Sufis call "spiritual connection." Shaykh ʿIzz said that the spirit of the shaykh must continue to influence the disciple even when they are separated. He interpreted the meaning of the word *disciple (murīd),* which literally means "desiring," to be "loving" the shaykh. The disciples of a shaykh are those who love him, for it is love which attains to spiritual truth. He described the process of developing spiritual connection as follows: "First he sits with the shaykh. Then he starts to think about the shaykh without knowing it: the shaykh said such-and-such and did such-and-such. He starts to think about what the shaykh said. In this way the shaykh sows in this person's heart the seed of love. Then he begins to see him in a vision. . . . He is doing something in his house and the shaykh says, 'No, don't do that.' That is, they are spiritually connected. When he goes to sleep, he has a vision of the shaykh. Because if he doesn't sleep in him, he will not benefit."

Shaykh Abū 'l-Wafāʾ al-Sharqāwī explained spiritual connection: "You will find that two friends whose love is strong and who are very attached to each other have the same inclinations and natures, and their souls are similar. A person is hurt by the suffering of the one to whom he is connected, and rejoices with his joy. The human spirit has the potential to be influenced by the states of the spirit with which it is connected. . . . Therefore the people of the Way have postulated that one should adopt a shaykh as spiritual guide and be connected with his spirit, which is linked to God. Connection with such a spirit will release the disciple from bonds and draw him near to God. . . . His spirit is the rope which can free a person from preoccupations which keep him from his Lord."[29]

Ḥasan al-Malaṭāwī describes his experience of spiritual connection with his shaykh: "I used to sit with my shaykh, and his tongue would not speak to me, but his spiritual state would speak to me. Sometimes I felt what he felt." One time while sitting with his shaykh he was suddenly seized with an inexplicable and great terror. After a quarter hour of silence, his shaykh explained that he had had a vision of hellfire, with all its horrors, and was overcome with tremendous fear. The disciple had experienced the fear without understanding its cause.[30] The Qurʾan describes the Muslims as those who believe in the unseen, and Malaṭāwī says that belief in the connectedness of spirits is part of belief in the unseen.[31]

Some Sufis find their shaykhs and receive instruction from them primarily through visions. Muḥammad, a young man of Farshūṭ, a town in the province of Qinā, Upper Egypt, said that his first shaykh was Abū Khalīl of Zaqāzīq, founder of the Khalīliyya. He had met a group of this shaykh's followers and joined their Order. He used to recite their *wird* of asking forgiveness 100,000 times a day. But then he had a dream in which Sayyida Zaynab asked him, "Are you a Khalīlī?" and he replied, "I am a Khalwatī." Behind Sayyida Zaynab stood a group of shaykhs, some of whom he knew and most of whom he did not. She gestured toward them and said, "They are all one." Later he had another similar dream, but this time only Shaykh Muḥammad al-Ṭayyib of Qurna (d. 1988) was there. Shaykh al-Ṭayyib shook Muḥammad's hand with his hand covered by his sleeve, which in fact was his habit because of the fragility of his skin. What is striking about this is that Muḥammad had never met Shaykh al-Ṭayyib nor known of this habit. In this dream Shaykh al-Ṭayyib told him, "We are all one." Muḥammad took these visions to mean that he was to change shaykhs and become a Khalwatī, so he sought out Shaykh al-Ṭayyib. He found the old shaykh to be exactly as he had seen him in his dream. Furthermore, the shaykh did as he had done in the dream, covering his hand with his sleeve and saying, "We are all one." So Muḥammad took the oath from him at once, and, at the shaykh's command, discontinued his old *awrād*. His new *wird* consisted of reciting the prayer asking forgiveness three hundred times a day. The shaykh also guided him in visions as to which name of God he was to recite in dhikr. His guidance was all "within" *(bāṭinī)*, through visions, which was Shaykh al-Ṭayyib's typical method. The reality of the visions was always confirmed in person by the shaykh, who would even correct a person who wrongly related the vision he had received. This, according to Muḥammad, was proof of the shaykh's legitimacy as a gnostic.

A woman who followed Aḥmad Abū 'l-Ḥasan told me that she was directed to follow him by her deceased mother in a dream-vision. Her mother, she said, was a saint, and she told her in the vision that Shaykh Aḥmad Abū 'l-Ḥasan was spiritually the strongest man on earth in our time. Although guidance to shaykhs through visions occurs with men as well as with women, a greater proportion of women than men among those I interviewed were guided to shaykhs and by shaykhs through visions. This might be explained by the fact that women have less freedom than men to wander about searching for a spiritual teacher and less freedom to attend the sessions of a Sufi shaykh once one is found.

One of the most striking examples of this was Anṣāf, a housewife and mother of four, about forty years old, whom I met in Imbāba, one of the recently urbanized sectors of greater Cairo. She came originally from Manūfiyya, a province in the Delta. Her husband had told me that he had learned Sufism from his wife, so I asked Anṣāf how she had learned Sufism. She said that at the age of ten a shaykh began to appear to her regularly in her dreams, instructing her in the religion, and especially in Sufism. These dreams continued to the present day. She did not know the identity of the shaykh she saw in her dreams until one day her husband returned from the moulid of Sayyida Zaynab with a group of people who included the shaykh of her visions. She recognized him immediately, as he did her. He administered the oath to her at that time, but his instruction to her continued to be through the medium of dream-visions. He was a shaykh of the Qāsimiyya Shādhiliyya Order who lived in no particular place but spent all his time traveling from moulid to moulid. Such stories challenge the methods and assumptions of social scientists seeking the social linkages and networks through which Sufism is disseminated.

Teaching through visions is not confined to those who are unable to receive it in any other way. Laylā, for example, had perhaps more access to Shaykh Maḥmūd Abū 'l-ᶜAzm (d. 1983) than anyone else, for he frequently stayed at her family's home, and he became so close to her, she said, that at the time of his death they had become one spirit. Yet when she asked him questions, he seldom answered her in person, preferring instead to answer her through dream-visions.

A concept closely related to that of spiritual connection is annihilation *(fanā᾿)* in the shaykh, which in contemporary Sufism is a prerequisite to *fanā᾿* in the Prophet, which is itself a prerequisite to *fanā᾿* in God.[32] *Fanā᾿*, like spiritual connection, is a result of love—love which is so strong that it results in intense identification with the shaykh. The disciple must love his shaykh more than anything else, more than his spouse, parents, children, or his own self, and it is part of the expected spiritual gifting of a shaykh for him to be able to evoke love in his followers. A disciple who does not love his shaykh more than anything else will never progress spiritually. This is illustrated by a story in *Al-Ibrīz,* a book popular among contemporary Egyptian Sufis, in which Aḥmad ibn al-Mubārak wrote that when he first followed Shaykh ᶜAbd al-ᶜAzīz al-Dabbāgh (d. 1717), he loved his wife so much, more than his shaykh, that God caused the wife to die. The disciple's heart then attached itself to their son, and God took the son. The disciple remarried and loved his new wife as he did the old, and God took the new wife as well. It was then that the disciple attached himself wholeheartedly to his shaykh, and his next wife remained alive. The shaykh commented, "Mixing with saints is like eating poison!"[33]

Shaykh ʿIzz said, "Little by little the shaykh must get his followers to love him, so he can influence them. As love increases, so does the influence, until they reach a point where the two become one, as if the one were speaking inside the other." The disciple sees nothing but the shaykh in every place, thinks of nothing but him, and desires nothing but him. When the disciple speaks, it is as if the shaykh were speaking through him. Concentration on the image of the shaykh, eyes closed, during recitation of the *awrād* may be used as a method to aid in the imitation of the shaykh and to activate the disciple's spiritual perception. The shaykh then functions as the gateway into the presence of the Prophet. Once a disciple has regular access to the Prophet's presence and has experienced annihilation in him, he has no further need of his shaykh. Scholars on Sufism give scant attention to the concept of *fanāʾ fi 'l-shaykh* (annihilation in the shaykh), or indeed to that of *fanāʾ fi 'l-rasul* (annihilation in the Prophet), for such concepts are often regarded as mere degradations from the earlier concept of annihilation in God, just as later Sufism is rarely studied as a coherent system but rather as a degradation of classical Sufism. The perspective of those living in the system, or even of those living close to it, is necessarily different. Seeing annihilation in the shaykh as a living phenomenon, in which the disciples live in an atmosphere of veneration and love and are exceedingly devoted to their shaykhs, is very different from seeing it simply as a symptom of decline.

The shaykh represents the Prophet to his disciples, and, although it would be scandalous to say so openly, to some extent he represents God. The perfect shaykh has become annihilated in the Prophet and is united thereby with the eternal Muhammadan Reality. He is uniquely qualified to guide his disciples by divine inspiration.[34] One time, when overcome by a spiritual state, Shaykh ʿIzz declared to a group of his disciples, "You will never prosper unless I am your only lord *(rabb)!*" One of his disciples, knowing what he meant but fearing he would alienate some of his audience by such an apparently blasphemous remark, for the *rabb* is none other than God alone, politely asked him to repeat what he had said. ʿIzz, realizing what he had said, altered his words: "You will never prosper unless I am your only teacher *(murabbī).*" On other occasions, ʿIzz glibly applied Qurʾanic verses referring to the messengers of God to himself, reasoning that he was indeed a messenger of God to his followers, although the term is usually reserved for prophets bringing a book of revelation from God.

The shaykh is regarded in a very real sense as responsible for the behavior and salvation of his disciples. He is their guardian, and he can control the spiritual progress of his disciples, delaying or advancing their spiritual realizations according to his wisdom. A disciple who is unfaithful to his shaykh, or full of doubts, falls out of favor with his shaykh and is in extreme peril. To use a phrase common among the Sufis, such a person "has lost both this world and the next." Such, according to Shaykh ʿIzz, was the case of a young woman to whom he administered the oath and taught the *awrād*. He instructed her to summon him through the recitation of the *Fātiḥa* whenever she felt she needed him, for she lived in a distant city in difficult circumstances. This summoning of the shaykh through recitation of the *Fātiḥa* and recitation of the formula of blessings on the Prophet is a routine phenomenon among the Sufis. The disciple who is spiritually connected with his shaykh will then see his shaykh, and his shaykh will be able to give him guidance and assistance. The assistance a shaykh can render his disciples can sometimes be very tangible physical assistance, such as rescue in times of grave danger, for the ability of shaykhs to see and hear their disciples and work miracles is not impeded by geographical distances. ʿIzz told me that he had "visited" the young woman through visions a number of times, but only once, shortly after her oath, did she see him. As she neglected her *awrād* she lost her ability to communicate with him in visions, and she failed to develop her love for him. Ultimately, ʿIzz told me, he shut her out of his heart, and she would be miserable both in this life and the next. For an oath to a shaykh is intended to be something precious, something cultivated for life. One Sufi author quotes Abū ʾl-Ḥasan al-Shādhilī (d. 1258) as saying, "Oh disciple, you must cling to the thresholds of your shaykh, for if you knew what was in the shaykhs, you would not leave their doors, but would come running on your face!"[35]

The danger of opposing shaykhs is reiterated in Sufi tradition. In one story reproduced in the *Risāla* of al-Qushayrī, Abū Yazīd al-Bisṭāmī (d. 874) and two other shaykhs urged a young man to eat with them, although he was fasting. The young man refused, even when they said he would acquire thereby the reward of a month's fasting. When he remained adamant, they said he would acquire the reward of a year's fasting if he ate with them. Again he refused. The young man's disobedience to the command of the shaykhs bore bitter spiritual fruit. He fell out of God's favor, became a thief, and lost his hand.[36]

The most important thing a disciple owes his shaykh is obedience. The shaykh is compared to a doctor for the soul, so the disciple should hide nothing from him and should follow his every prescription. Shaykh Muḥammad Māḍī Abū 'l-ʿAzāʾim writes, "The spiritual guide might order some disciples to do something that appears to them, because of their shortsightedness, not to be in their interests: such as giving their money to the poor, or marrying their daughter to someone beneath her station, or leaving an honored position, or abandoning supererogatory duties, or ceasing to study, or becoming reconciled to enemies and pardoning them, although they had oppressed the disciple, or migrating to another country, or doing private dhikr instead of going to Friday prayer, or going into solitude instead of meeting with the brethren, or meeting with the brethren and abandoning solitude, or serving in the mosques or carrying water in mosques or markets. The disciple must hasten and strive to follow the commands of the spiritual guide."[37]

The intimate involvement of a shaykh in a disciple's life, and his role as guardian and intercessor on behalf of his disciples, is well illustrated by this story related by "ʿAlī," the previously-cited engineer, and his experience with Shaykh Aḥmad Abū 'l-Ḥasan. He asked Shaykh Aḥmad to recommend a wife for him and presented him with a number of names of women the shaykh did not know, expecting the shaykh's superior knowledge to be his guide. But the shaykh said nothing. ʿAlī feared that, given his sinful past, God would give him a sinful wife, for it is written in the Qurʾan that righteous women are to marry righteous men, and sinful women are for sinful men. Then one day the shaykh suddenly pointed out a woman whom ʿAlī had never seen before and said, "That is your wife." So ʿAlī married her. When he was going to take his oath from his shaykh, the shaykh sought God about the sins ʿAlī would commit, for the sins of a disciple destroy his oath. The shaykh saw that it was written on the Preserved Tablet that ʿAlī would commit adultery. The shaykh asked God not to change what He had predestined, but to make it a lesser sin by having it occur in a dream. And so it did. In a dream, ʿAlī tried to commit adultery with a neighbor girl, but even in his dream he ejaculated outside her.

This too lessened the severity of the sin. Then, in his dream, the shaykh of the mosque across the street appeared. ʿAlī tried to avoid him, because he was ritually polluted and wanted to wash himself, but the shaykh called him. He told him that what had happened was by the mercy and intercession of Shaykh Aḥmad. So when he awoke, ʿAlī went to his shaykh and simply said, "Thank you."

Shaykhs regularly test their disciples by ignoring them, keeping them waiting, assigning humiliating tasks to them, and treating them rudely, just as Shaykh ʿIzz tested me for a certain period. In this manner a disciple's morals, sincerity, and determination to follow the Sufi way are tested. The degree to which shaykhs practice such methods of testing varies. Gilsenan wrote that Shaykh Salāma al-Rāḍī, founder of the Ḥāmidiyya Shādhiliyya, tested potential disciples stringently in the early formative years of the Order, but later admitted anyone who wished to join.[38] Testing might occur before or after a disciple is administered the oath, but it usually occurs at the beginning of the spiritual journey, in order to break a disciple of bad intentions and purify him in preparation for the spiritual rigors that lie ahead. Shaykh ʿIzz said that when a potential disciple approached him with an interest in learning the Sufi way, "I leave him alone, and let him walk with me and ask me questions. Then I don't pay any attention to what he says, but my interest is in his behavior and his manner of speech. After a month I sit with him, as we are, and I begin to ask him what he has learned. I remember exactly what has been said, word for word, and I see what he has forgotten, and what his level is. Then I remind him of things, and we have a second meeting, and then a third. When I feel that he has learned enough, I begin to give him moral tests. What interests me in a person is his morals. If a disciple says or does anything wrong, don't think that the blame is on him—it is on me." At the time, ʿIzz would not reveal to me how he tested his disciples, because, as I was to discover, he would use those same methods on me.

In addition to obedience, the disciple owes his shaykh attentive courtesy in his presence, speaking only when appropriate, with humble demeanor. The extreme reverence accorded to shaykhs, especially one's own shaykh, is difficult to convey to a society like ours that barely practices etiquette at all anymore. Although Shaykh ʿIzz was politely affable in the company of most Sufis and at times outright autocratic with those whose position it was to serve him, he was a changed man in the presence of the sons of Shaykh Aḥmad Raḍwān and Shaykh Abū 'l-Wafāʾ al-Sharqāwī, for he had the utmost respect for these shaykhs and their elder sons, whom he deemed to have inherited the spiritual secrets of their fathers. He would not speak without humbly standing, his head bowed. He practiced these manners even in the presence of Aḥmad Raḍwān's younger sons, who were only in their twenties and thirties and whose spiritual insight he felt was more limited than that of the eldest son, or even of himself. But out of respect for their father, he treated the younger sons with the same deference he gave to Shaykh Muḥammad Raḍwān, the eldest son.

One finds in Sufi writings a consistent admonition to "think well of" one's shaykh, even if he is seen doing things that apparently contradict Islamic law. Although the shaykh serves as a model and guide to his disciples, it is readily acknowledged that the gnostics enter spiritual states that are peculiar to them. They are under God's protection, but their behavior should not be imitated by their followers. Shaykh Muḥammad Māḍī Abū 'l-ʿAzā'im gives some examples of what a shaykh, by virtue of spiritual insight, might do. He might be so preoccupied with his meditation and teaching that he neglects his other duties. He might mix socially with people in high society. He might abandon the dhikr of the tongue in favor of the dhikr of the heart. He might give away all his wealth to the poor. He might sit with women and answer their questions. He might keep silent regarding reprehensible behavior. "In all these things," says Shaykh Abū 'l-ʿAzā'im, "the disciple should not imitate the shaykh until he knows the secret of their wisdom. He should submit to the shaykh, and acknowledge that he knows little. The disciple who imitates the guide (in all things) is not a disciple, but is a monkey or an ape."[39]

ETHICS AND ETIQUETTE (ADAB) OF THE SUFI WAY

Relationships in the Sufi Orders are governed by a lofty code of ethics and a standard of etiquette that are essential to traveling the spiritual path. This code is called *adab,* which Martin Lings translates as "pious courtesy," of which he says, "in the Sufic brotherhoods . . . it takes on almost a methodic aspect as a means of purification."[40] This etiquette encompasses first of all a Sufi's relationship with God, then with his shaykh, then with his fellow-disciples, then with the whole Muslim community, and finally with all other people. The word *adab* is closely related to the verb "to discipline" *(addab),* with the implication that one learns proper manners by being trained or disciplined by one's shaykh—or, in the case of the Prophet, by God.[41]

Traditional Sufi sources emphasize the centrality of *adab* to faith and salvation. Qushayrī supplies a number of such sayings, such as "He who has no *adab* has no law, no faith, and no belief in the one God," and "We are more in need of a little etiquette than of much knowledge."[42] Ibrāhīm al-Dasūqī, the thirteenth-century founder of one of the main Sufi Orders of Egypt, said, "Just as the people of the Sharīʿa void prayer when it is done in a corrupt form, the people of the *Ḥaqīqa* [that is, the Sufis] void prayer accompanied by corrupt morals. If a person harbors hatred, envy, a bad opinion about a Muslim, or some other such defects, his prayer is void in their opinion. All of these are signs of love of this world, and whoever loves this world is veiled from the presence of God and expelled from entering it."[43] Shaykh Abū 'l-Wafāʾ al-Sharqāwī (d. 1961) comments, "One way Satan has crushed the majority of disciples and corrupted their hearts is that they think that etiquette is merely an external matter. However, this pillar is an act for God and a way to draw near to Him."[44]

One modern Sufi author finds it natural that Sufism places such a priority on proper etiquette and good morals because Sufis are those who, par excellence, seek to imitate the Prophet in every aspect of his behavior, of whom his wife said, "His morals were the Qurʾan." The Qurʾan also commends Muhammad as having an excellent character (68:4), and according to a ḥadīth, Muhammad said, "I was sent only to perfect morality."[45] Shaykh ʿAbd al-ʿAzīz al-Dabbāgh (d. 1717) of Morocco felt that humans reflect divine qualities such as mercy according to the measure that they have been recipients of this quality from God. Since no creature has received more love and mercy than the Prophet, he excelled in demonstrating these qualities to all other creatures.[46]

The etiquette to be observed with God consists primarily of according Him due reverence and respect, giving Him praise for good things and being patient in adversity, seeking His aid, trusting in His mercy, fearing His wrath, and doing good deeds for His sake only. Shaykh Aḥmad Raḍwān told his disciples to apologize to God after prayer for their heedlessness in His presence. He also told them that if God made any of them ill, they should not hasten to seek a cure, out of respect for God, but should submit the matter to Him.[47] Some Sufis felt this keeping proper etiquette with God meant that one should not do things in private that would be considered impolite in human company—such as extending one's leg, which would show the bottom of one's foot, a sign of contempt in Egyptian culture. Abū 'l-Ḥasan al-Shādhilī said that Sufis take on the morals of God, which include extreme generosity, indulgence with those who are annoying, discernment, hospitality, and love.[48]

Observing proper etiquette with one's shaykh is a sign of spiritual success. Those who oppose their shaykh openly or in secret have departed from the Sufi Way. "The disciple must serve his shaykh, and thereby attain—in their words—the status of men."[49] Aḥmad Raḍwān told his followers, "You will derive no benefit from the gnostics unless you request permission to enter their presence, not like the people of this age who attack the people of the presence of God without etiquette and enter without permission, because of their ignorance of God and of the people of His presence."[50]

Like many traditional Orders, some contemporary Egyptian Orders issue rules for the behavior of their disciples. The following rules of etiquette are issued by the Jāzuliyya Ḥusayniyya Shādhiliyya Order, founded by the still-living Shaykh Gābir al-Jāzūlī.

1. The disciple must truly repent to God.
2. He must keep away from the company of evil-doers.
3. He should not leave undone any of the obligatory duties (in the Sharīʿa) or recommended deeds done by the Prophet.
4. He should recite a *wird* from the Qurʾan every night, even if it is only ten verses.
5. He should never abandon the *wird* assigned to him by the shaykh.
6. He should eat only legally permissible food.
7. He should not vaunt himself over others or oppress anyone with his demands.
8. He should take stock of himself to see whether he does wrong or right.
9. He should respect his shaykh and follow his teachings.
10. He should regret his past shortcomings.
11. He should love his fellow-disciples, undertaking to serve them and seeing to their well-being.
12. He should think well of God and observe due reverence with Him.
13. All his moments of spiritual realization should be based on obedience and dhikr and what yields good effects.[51]

In a poem called "The Etiquette of the Disciple," this same Order provides a far more detailed account of proper behavior in the Order. The poem was written by Shaykh Gābir, and while it lacks much literary merit, it is an interesting glimpse into the way in which the rules of proper behavior are instilled into the disciples. This shaykh regularly uses poems set to music that are learned by his disciples and sung in their weekly meetings. In this poem, the soul of the disciple is likened to "a child that must be weaned in the brotherhood" of the Order. Disciples are warned against "prohibited food," the taking of interest, vanity, and the company of immoral people. Accompanying the shaykh with pure intentions is described as necessary for spiritual success. The shaykh is "your beloved and companion" but one who should be addressed sparingly, with sincerity, awareness, intelligence, and courtesy, for the shaykh has entered God's presence. Disciples should not ask the shaykh "why" but should submit matters to God and obey without question. They should avoid visiting the shaykh in the afternoon, raising their voices in his presence, associating with those he has expelled, or making him jealous in any way. They should not even request his prayers, for he is already aware of all things. The poem also warns, "Do not keep the company of other shaykhs before you attain perfection; afterwards you may accompany whomever you like." Rather than boasting of the shaykh's virtues, the poem admonishes disciples to be an advertisement for him by their own good manners. Disciples should fear abandoning their shaykh and should be joyful when they meet him. They should "think well of him and those he loves" and beware of pursuing something he does not like.[52]

The observance of proper etiquette extends beyond the disciple's interaction with his shaykh to embrace his interactions with his fellow-disciples, and finally all other people. Shaykh Muḥammad Māḍī Abū 'l-ʿAzāʾim and Shaykh Abū 'l-Wafāʾ al-Sharqāwī are particularly concerned with the way that disciples behave toward each other. Primary tasks of the disciples are to place the interests of their brethren before their own interests, to offer counsel to an erring brother in private, with gentleness and circumspection, and to avoid slander or anything that would embarrass anyone. Likewise, disciples must learn to receive counsel and believe that it is given with the best of intentions. Shaykh Abū 'l-ʿAzāʾim even instructs his disciples on how to conduct themselves in the event that somebody does correct a brother in front of others, thereby creating a potentially embarrassing and even adversarial situation. He stresses that the disciples in his Order should consider themselves all members of a single body, in which all suffer when any one of them suffers. A disciple should offer his brothers the best food, and if any of them is of high morals, he should be honored more than one's own parents, wife, or children, "because he helps you attain eternal happiness."[53] Abū 'l-Wafā' al-Sharqāwī writes, "Love for the brethren is the sum of all secrets, and is the source of graces and lights."[54]

Shaykh Aḥmad Raḍwān, like many other shaykhs, brought the lessons of etiquette into daily behavior and relationships with family members. "Do not walk gaily on the earth, and do not go into or out of any place with pride or deception or arrogance. Say 'in the name of God, the Compassionate, the Merciful,' when you go into any place or leave any place, when you sit and when you rise. Say 'peace be upon you' to your family when you come and go, for this is the Sunna of the Prophet, and God will increase His blessings to you." He admonishes his disciples to treat their wives with courtesy, not overburdening them, not treating them lustfully, but regarding them as sisters in God. He tells them that when they go on a journey they should let their wives know when they will return. (This is a courtesy that many Upper Egyptian men feel undermines their position of authority in the family.) He tells them not to walk in on them without warning, lest they embarrass their wives, and that they should wash themselves and dress nicely for their wives, just as they want their wives to do for them. "The people of God's presence are humble and speak softly," he said, "unlike the people of the world."[55]

The attention the Sufis have devoted to proper etiquette often has a profound effect on their daily interactions, especially within their own group. It is true that not all Sufi groups follow this etiquette with the same degree of success. The members of Bayt ʿAbāṭa were extremely quarrelsome, whereas most people felt that true Sufis do not get angry on their own behalf but only for the sake of God over things that anger Him. The followers of Ḥāgga Zakiyya also acknowledged that her "children" did not behave properly toward each other. But the presence of a revered shaykh often has an effect on his assembly that instills a sense of awe and love, of being raised above the petty concerns of everyday life. The holy aura around the person of the shaykh and the acknowledged rules of etiquette transports those present to a seemingly higher plane of existence.

THE STRUCTURE OF THE SUFI ORDERS

The larger Orders are characterized by a hierarchical organization, which reflects both spiritual preeminence and administrative function. The shaykh of the Order has regional representatives, each of whom functions as "shaykh" with respect to the disciples in his district. The Shādhiliyya, Khalwatiyya and Aḥmadiyya have splintered into a large number of Orders, but the Rifāʿiyya, and to some extent the Burhāmiyya, have retained their nominal unity, although they are divided into a number of "houses" (*bayt*, pl. *buyūt*), which exercise a good deal of autonomy. In practice, when one speaks of one's "shaykh" one speaks of one's immediate teacher and not always the shaykh of one's Order as a whole. The hierarchical structure and esotericism of the Orders, and the authoritarianism of their shaykhs, are features that are regarded with some suspicion by outsiders.

The number of Orders has steadily increased in this century. There were sixty Orders registered with the Sufi Council in 1958, and sixty-four in 1964. In April 1989 there were seventy-three recognized Orders. The proliferation of Orders may not mean that more people are being drawn into Sufism, but that an Order has split in two, as two rival teachers have emerged. The Sufi Orders in Egypt are thought to be derived from the four *quṭb*s, who are great Sufi saints of the twelfth and thirteenth centuries: ʿAbd al-Qādir al-Jīlānī of Iraq (d. 1166), founder of the Qādiriyya; Aḥmad al-Rifāʿī of Iraq (d. 1178), founder of the Rifāʿiyya; Aḥmad al-Badawī (d. 1276), originally from Morocco but buried in the Egyptian Delta, founder of the Aḥmadiyya; and Ibrāhīm al-Dasūqī of Egypt (d. 1297), founder of the Burhāmiyya. Of equal importance for Egyptian Sufism is Abū 'l-Ḥasan al-Shādhilī of Morocco, who died in Egypt in 1258 and is founder of the Shādhiliyya.

Government sponsorship of the Sufi Orders goes back to the time of Saladin, who founded a Sufi retreat center called *Saʿīd al-Suʿadāʾ* and gave its shaykh preeminence over other shaykhs, with the title of *shaykh al-shuyūkh*, head of all the Sufi Orders. This position passed to the Bakrī family probably in the fifteenth century, and remained in that family until 1946, when Aḥmad Murād al-Bakrī died and the position was taken over by Aḥmad al-Ṣāwī.[56] Since 1982 the head of the Sufi Orders has been Dr. Abū 'l-Wafāʾ al-Ghunaymī al-Taftāzānī, dean and professor of philosophy at Cairo University. The function of the Supreme Council of Sufi Orders is to oversee affairs of the Orders and ensure the propriety of the doctrine and practice that is disseminated by them.

RELATIONSHIPS BETWEEN THE ORDERS

Relationships between the Orders are usually amicable, marked by a great deal of mutual respect. As indicated earlier in this chapter, there is little difference between the teachings of the various Orders, and few shaykhs would deny the legitimacy or claim to sainthood of the shaykhs of other Orders. When a great shaykh like Shaykh Wāfī, head of the Rifāʿiyya in the provinces of Sūhāj, Asyūṭ, and Qinā, attended the moulid of Aḥmad al-Rifāʿi, Sufis of other Orders were among those clamoring to kiss his hand or sit at his feet to receive his blessing. When Shaykh Wāfī visited the home of a Rifāʿī shaykh in Cairo, Shaykh ʿIzz went with a group of his disciples to visit, although they are not Rifāʿīs. One man, the gardener in ʿIzz's mosque, sat at Shaykh Wāfī's feet, kissing his hand from time to time, quite beside himself with delight at the privilege of basking in such baraka so close to its source. For most in the group, the goal of the meeting did not go beyond this. Shaykh ʿIzz uttered wise sayings, which Shaykh Wāfī, despite his old age, had no trouble completing or making better. Every time he said anything, two of ʿIzz's disciples acted as if they had been given an electric shock, startling, throwing their heads back with a look of ecstasy that was almost painful, and crying out, "Allah!" One old man recited poetry, which Shaykh Wāfī also was able to complete. Shaykh ʿIzz asked Shaykh Wāfī to pray for a troubled man, who came forward to kneel at Wāfī's feet, while Wāfī placed his hand on the man's head and prayed almost inaudibly. Shaykh Wāfī was told there was a sick man in an adjoining room, and the shaykh rose with difficulty and went to pray for him, aided at every step by the crowd, who obstructed his progress as much as they helped him. ʿIzz said to me, "That is love. Everyone wants to serve."

Most shaykhs urge their followers not to be excessively or fanatically attached to their Order to the exclusion of all others, although some shaykhs isolate their disciples from other shaykhs, fearing that a stronger shaykh might attract them—something Aḥmad Raḍwān calls a "grave error."[57] Shaykh Gābir al-Jāzūlī, as we have seen in his poem, admonishes his disciples not to go to other shaykhs until their spiritual education is complete. Shaykh Abū 'l-ʿAzāʾim encouraged his followers to receive spiritual instruction wherever it may be found, although one's oath remained to a single shaykh.[58]

Nonetheless, each Order naturally assumes that its share of spiritual power and realization is greater than that of other Orders and that its shaykh has a higher standing with God than others. The ʿAzmiyya, the Order founded by Shaykh Abū 'l-ʿAzāʾim, are in fact among the most active propagandists of Sufism. At the official celebration of the Prophet's moulid in Darrāsa in 1988, their young men cornered passersby with all the zeal of evangelists and refused to consider the possibility that any of the Sufis they confronted could possess spiritual knowledge comparable to that of their own Order.

The literary scholar Ṭāhā Ḥusayn (d. 1973) recorded in his autobiography that his province was divided between two rival Sufi shaykhs, and any intrusion by one into the domain of the other occasioned fierce disputes.[59] Despite this testimony and the natural rivalry that occurs between Orders, Sufis do not hesitate to acknowledge the validity of the claims to sainthood by shaykhs of other Orders, and the flow of visits and exchange of insight occurs across the boundaries of the Orders.

THE SOCIAL FUNCTIONS OF THE ORDERS

Although most Sufi Orders contain a spectrum of Egyptian society, the Orders do not all appeal uniformly to the same segments of society. The Rifāʿiyya, Bayyūmiyya, and Aḥmadiyya have largely lower-class followings, while the Shādhiliyya, originally an aristocratic Order that encouraged its disciples to work for a living and accepted the wearing of fine clothes rather than the traditional Sufi tattered cloak, today has the reputation of being more orthodox than most other Orders. The Khalwatiyya and Naqshbandiyya, the latter Order not numerous in Egypt, are also often associated with the higher segments of society. Some groups, such as the Jāzūliyya Ḥusayniyya Shādhiliyya, the ʿAzmiyya Shādhiliyya, and the Muḥammadiyya Shādhiliyya, deliberately cultivate an image of being intended for the elite of society and boast a mainly well-educated, middle-class clientele. Orders associated with the lower classes and rural areas are more likely to tolerate practices such as piercing the cheeks without drawing blood and walking on swords in order to demonstrate their baraka. The Shādhiliyya, Naqshbandiyya, and Khalwatiyya tend to be more restrained in their religious practices.

That Sufi Orders continue to be considered an option for religious training even for those without mystical inclinations is witnessed by the following incident, in which the *wakīl* of Bayt ʿAbāṭa successfully persuaded a young man to join the Order. The young man was considered a religious fanatic by the members of Bayt ʿAbāṭa, who felt that he must be led away from the perilous road of fundamentalism toward acknowledgement of the saints. The *wakīl* described the way of the Rifāʿiyya as a way of love and brotherhood. By virtue of belonging to the Order, he said, he had spiritual brothers in cities all over Egypt, who would offer him hospitality whenever he traveled. The young man challenged the *wakīl* about the nature of Bayt ʿAbāṭa's weekly meetings, asking what good it was to come together and do dhikr, drink tea, and leave, if there was no religious instruction. Perhaps to prove his credentials as a religious teacher as well as to emphasize the uniqueness of Sufi teachings, the *wakīl* spoke at length about the life of the Prophet, the Muhammadan light, and the importance of love for the *ahl al-bayt*. After about two hours, the young man announced his intention to join the Order. An elderly woman of Bayt ʿAbāṭa immediately yelled out, "It will cost you eight pounds, and you must say the *ḥizb* and *wird* every day!"

The young man replied, "I don't care if it costs ten pounds, what's important is that I learn. I read many books at home about religion—"

"Leave those books alone!" cried the woman. "Forget those Sunni and Shiʿi books!"

"I am not a fanatic," the young man protested. "They are books about basic things, like the rules of religion and the Last Day, the testing in the grave, the two angels that each person has, things like that."

"It's all right," the *wakīl* gently admonished the woman. "Those books teach about religion in a general way. Our Order is something extra."

Such fierce reminders of one's duties—financial and spiritual—hardly seem to constitute an ideal introduction into Sufism, yet it is striking that the ferocity of the old woman did not impair the young man's zeal to learn more about religion, nor his willingness to pursue this along the (for him) untried path of Sufism, despite his initial doubts. Religious instruction is readily available these days in Egypt, as lessons on the Qur'an and Islamic law abound in the mosques and religious voluntary associations. The *wakīl* rightly emphasized what made the Sufi way distinctive: its foundation in love, the brotherhood it created among its adherents, and the centrality of devotion to the Prophet and his family.

The Sufi shaykhs played important social roles in premodern times that went beyond the confines of their Orders. To a certain extent, this continues to be the case. Sufi shaykhs in Upper Egypt continue to function as mediators in disputes. This was also the case among the Upper Egyptian immigrants in Cairo, where Shaykh ʿIzz was frequently called upon to mediate disputes. In fact, it seems that no fight could break out in the entire district in which he lived without his direct intervention. Parties came all the way from his hometown in Upper Egypt, a twelve- to seventeen-hour journey by train, to invite his mediation. Such mediation could be a very formal affair, culminating in a reconciliation banquet at his *sāḥa*. Likewise, Shaykh Wāfī visited Fāw, one of the most dangerous and volatile areas of feuding in Qinā, in order to alleviate the situation there.

The *sāḥas*, or hospitality centers, of the Sufis play an important function in Sufi life as well as for the poor of the community. Poor people regularly came to ʿIzz to ask for money, and on special occasions and every night during Ramaḍān, meals were served at the *sāḥa* for anyone who came in. The architectural features of *sāḥas* vary, but they often include very long tables with built-in benches to accommodate hundreds of guests. At the *sāḥa* of Aḥmad Raḍwān outside Luxor, besides the long tables in the eating area, long cushioned benches allow hundreds of visitors to relax and drink tea. At ʿIzz's *sāḥa* such benches are built into the wall that surrounds the garden, in the middle of which is a long table for meals. Here, not only tea but a water pipe is regularly offered to guests. The Raḍwān *sāḥa*, known for its cleanliness, does not offer cigarettes or water pipes.

One of ʿIzz's most important functions, one not shared by all shaykhs, is that of healer. ʿIzz is an expert in "prophetic medicine," which offers prescriptions based on the expulsion of evil spirits and the use of Qurʾanic verses and natural products. ʿIzz learned prophetic medicine from a Sudanese shaykh whom he served for fifteen years, precisely in order to learn. Although other potential pupils came and went, ʿIzz persevered, and finally at the end of the shaykh's life he revealed to him his secrets. ʿIzz prides himself in his ability to heal and his power over jinn, the invisible beings who are often believed to cause physical and psychological diseases. He said all saints have this power, whether or not they are aware of it, but not all of them practice this art. Although this art is widely condemned by critics as the height of charlatanism and exploitation of the ignorant, ʿIzz does not take money for his services, which he sees simply as part of his duty as a servant of God. People often come to him after medical remedies have failed, or, more often, if the problem is more psychological than physical or too personal to entrust to the impersonal Egyptian medical system. Others come simply because they have faith in him. The cures often consist of Qurʾanic verses ʿIzz writes, sometimes in separate letters rather than the customary script. The sick person might be told to soak the paper on which the verses are written in water, drink the water, and burn the paper in incense in order to fumigate the house with it. A victim of envy was given a folded piece of paper on which ʿIzz had written the Throne verse of the Qurʾan (2:255) in separate letters, and chapters 112, 113, and 114 of the Qur'an—the latter two being incantations against evildoers, chapter 113 specifically against enviers—in regular script writing. Sometimes the paper is to be burnt with a spice such as coriander or buried with a portion of an animal such as a chicken or turkey; there is a precise prescription for every situation. Matter from the stomach of a turkey might be used because its smell is considered repulsive to jinn. Coriander, if smoked, drives out demons. The feces of a dog are burned to drive away *ʿafārīt* (evil jinn) who inhabit houses. The food of a queen bee is used against impotence, and the penis of a monkey is used to give sexual vigor to an old man. Sperm drops dried and given to a girl can make her fall madly in love with the man whose sperm it is, but ʿIzz felt such magic was evil and learned about such curses only in order to break them. ʿIzz would perform the *ṣalāt* prayer in a home inhabited by jinn in order to chase them away. In more serious cases, the jinn would be commanded to leave under threat of death through Qur'an recitation. A possessed person sometimes needs to be cured by a forceful laying on of hands or rubbing. ʿIzz sees his role in the community as not only a teacher, mediator, and spiritual counselor but also as a doctor and psychologist.

Shaykh Gamāl al-Sanhūrī of the Burhāniyya said that his shaykh, Muḥammad ʿUthmān, had taught him a secret cure for cancer, which he used but did not advertise, lest people accuse him of being a quack doctor. He told me of some specific cures he had learned from his shaykh: salt in the bathtub for easing depression; burning an amulet called *khitām al-Ghazālī,* which contains the names of God written in squares, as incense, the smoke of which heals colds; and a potion made from sulfur as a cure for liver ailments. Shaykh Gamāl said that Muslims do not need all the therapists that the West has because the answer to all psychological ills exists in Sufism.[60]

A shaykh's baraka has very practical effects in this world, and does not pertain solely to preparation for the afterlife. Although the primary role of a shaykh should be that of spiritual guide, his other roles, as mediator, counselor, benefactor, and healer, may be of even more importance to the community around him. They illustrate some of the ways that Sufi shaykhs and their Orders continue to have an impact on the daily lives of their communities.

CHAPTER 6

Foundations of the Sufi Path

The Sufi way is conceived as a path through which the disciple progresses in stages *(maqāmāt).* This conception has marked Sufism since it evolved from mere asceticism into a genuine mysticism. Sufis describe their mystical experiences using a specialized vocabulary, and many of the books of classical Sufi literature are preoccupied with defining these terms and providing the sayings of various Sufi masters concerning them. Some of these sayings deconstruct the meaning of the terms as much as construct them, such as defining gnosis, mystical knowledge, as the absence of knowledge. This no doubt derives from the realization that ultimately God lies beyond the bounds of the human ability to know, whether through the intellect or through the heart, and the knowledge of one's ignorance marks a higher stage of wisdom than the articulation of what one knows. Nonetheless, such sayings mystify as often as they clarify.

Modern Sufi writings are likewise concerned with defining Sufi terminology for the sake of novices. These definitions are often kept clear and simple, with the wise sayings of the gnostics reserved for the admiring exclamations of those who are already initiated into some of the mysteries of the way. An investigation into the meaning of a select few of these terms might unlock the door into the very nature of the Sufi mystical experience.

THE *MAQĀMĀT*

A *maqām* (pl., *maqāmāt*), usually translated as "station" or "stage" on the mystical journey, means, in the definition of Shaykh Abū 'l-ʿAzāʾim, "the practices and acts of obedience the servant is engaged in," that is, the specific disciplines and attitudes a Sufi cultivates at a particular stage of his mystical journey.[1] For almost all Sufis, the first stage on the mystical journey is repentance, the earlier stages are mostly concerned with ridding the soul of unsavory characteristics through practices of self-denial, and the later stages mark a Sufi's experience of peaceful surrender and ultimately, for the blessed few, the witness of divine glory. The term *maqām* is contrasted with the term *ḥāl* (pl., *aḥwāl*), usually translated as "spiritual state." Whereas the *maqām* is a matter of conscious discipline and spiritual concentration, the *ḥāl* is a divine grace that comes over the Sufi without preparation or striving, such as rapture, grief, constriction, expansion, longing, anxiety, fear, or joy. "The *aḥwāl* are like flashes of lightning that appear and disappear," wrote Shaykh Abū 'l-ʿAzāʾim. "The *maqām* is acquired (through striving), whereas the *ḥāl* is a gift. The *aḥwāl* derive from the *maqāmāt:* grief and constriction derive from the *maqām* of fear, expansion from the *maqām* of hope, rapture from the love which arises from witnessing the (divine) beauty."[2] Although the *maqāmāt* are an expected and important part of Sufi experience, they are not to be desired for their own sake, for that would mean preoccupation with a stage of the journey rather than with God. Ibrāhīm al-Dasūqī (d. 1297), one of the four recognized *quṭb*s or founders of Sufi Orders in Egypt, is quoted as saying, "Every *maqām* in which you stop veils you from your Lord."[3]

Sufis today use the term *maqām* generously, beyond the traditional Sufi enumeration of the stages of the mystical path. For example, certain people might be described as being in a *maqām* in which they regard religious obligations as unbinding for them, although such a condition is not widely recognized as a valid stage on the mystical journey. In this usage, *maqām* simply means the manner in which those people practice their Sufism. Others might be described as being in a *maqām ʿīsawī*, a station in which they have a spiritual identification with Jesus, but this too is not a regular station on the mystical path. Some Sufis number the *maqāmāt* at seven and have the path well-defined as a predictable journey through which the devout disciple will travel, whereas others say the *maqāmāt* are innumerable, and they include among these *maqāmāt* terms more typically associated in Sufi experience with spiritual "states" *(aḥwāl)*. Farīd Māhir, a modern Sufi, writes, "The specific *maqāmāt* through which the disciple must pass are set by the teacher, who gives to each disciple what he needs. Among them are striving, seclusion, isolation, fear of God, asceticism, silence, fear, hope, grief, hunger, abandonment of passions, humility, self-abasement, opposing the (desires of one's) soul, refraining from envy, conviction, dependence (on God), thanksgiving, certainty, patience, self-examination, contentment, worship, desire, following the straight path, singlehearted devotion, truthfulness, shyness, freedom, the recollection of God, chivalry, generosity, knowledge, love, longing and many others."[4] The names and formulations of the *maqāmāt* vary, said Shaykh Maḥfūẓ of Asyūṭ, but for all the Sufi Orders they begin with repentance and end with gnosis.

Many Sufis number the *maqāmāt* at seven, a number of symbolic significance since Babylonian times. The number seven is thought to be manifested in various phenomena in the universe, in Sufi and other medieval cosmologies. The division of the world into seven climes is ancient and goes well beyond the domains of Islam. Each of these climes is associated with a particular color and a heavenly body that was believed to control the "temperament" of that region. Niẓāmī's epic poem, *Haft Paykar (The Seven Portraits)*, is written around just such a theme, and images from this traditional cosmology appear frequently in Persian poetry. The Qur'an preserved the idea that the heavens consist of seven layers (67:3, 71:15), and Muhammad's ascension *(miʿrāj)* through the heavens serves as the model for all Sufi mystical journeys. Bisṭāmī (d. 874) may have been the first to have claimed to have made such a *miʿrāj*,[5] but many others have since conceived of their journey in just such a fashion, and it is for this reason, perhaps, that the *maqāmāt* are traditionally numbered at seven. The association of spiritual stages with the heavens is not merely symbolic. When Shaykh ʿIzz rebuked me for allowing my intellect to get in the way of my spiritual progress, he said that every time I started ascending into the second heaven, I began to have doubts and fell back to the first.[6]

The sevenfold layering of the heavens is mirrored in the sevenfold layering of the earth and of the human soul. These "layers" of the soul follow Qur'anic phrases describing various human souls and serve as the basis of a distinct Sufi psychology. Māhir lists the levels of the soul as the soul that commands evil (*al-nafs al-ammāra bi 'l-sūʾ*, Qur'an 12:53), which is the soul of a person who is overwhelmed by carnal desires; the blaming soul (*al-nafs al-lawwāma*, Qur'an 75:2), which might be likened to a guilty conscience; the humble soul *(al-nafs al-mulhama)*, which sees nothing of itself and turns toward God; the tranquil soul *(al-nafs al-muṭmaʾinna)*; the contented soul *(al-nafs al-rāḍiya)*; the soul that finds acceptance with God *(al-nafs al-marḍiyya)*; and the complete soul *(al-nafs al-kāmila)*.[7] Three of these are based on a single Qur'anic verse (89:27), "Oh tranquil soul, return to your Lord contented and accepted," which does not apparently refer to three different states or types of the soul. Nonetheless, the sevenfold layering of the human soul is widely accepted among the Sufis.

Shaykh ʿIzz numbers the *maqāmāt* at fourteen, seven of which correspond to the "earthly" stages of the journey, when the aspiring Sufi must strive against the soul and subdue it, and seven to the "heavenly" stages of the journey, when the Sufi journeys on into heavenly realm, following the pattern of the Prophet, and ultimately, if that person is to become a *ghawth,* attains to the witness of the divine. At my request, he spoke with me at length on the *maqāmāt.* Although I have not heard any other shaykhs providing precisely his formulation, it is reproduced here as a window into a Sufi conception (though not the only Sufi conception) of the spiritual journey.

1. *Asking forgiveness.* The prayer of asking forgiveness begins, "I ask forgiveness from God the Great, besides Whom there is no god, the Living, the Eternal, and I turn in repentance toward Him." If a person asks forgiveness from the heart, God senses it, and by His grace and generosity He accepts that person's prayer. All the Orders that lead to God must include this prayer for forgiveness in their *awrād.* These take different forms, such as "I ask forgiveness from God," "I ask forgiveness from God the Great," "I ask forgiveness from God the Great and He is the Compassionate Forgiver," or "I ask forgiveness from God the Great, beside Whom there is no god, the Living, the Eternal, and I turn in repentance toward Him." ʿIzz said, "The shaykh chooses a form that he has "tasted" in his inner being and has realized and felt its meanings, and he teaches it to his disciples, so they may travel with it. Some make their disciples recite this prayer one hundred times in the morning and evening, some two hundred times in the morning and evening, some three hundred times in the morning and evening, according to a shaykh's taste and his feelings for what is best for his disciples."

2. *Repentance* is higher than asking forgiveness, for asking forgiveness means regret for what one has done, but repentance means regret and not returning to sin. Those who repent from their sin are like those who have no sin. After renouncing sin, they must abandon the company of evil people. If they do not do this, ʿIzz said, they will return to their sin, for "the human satan is stronger than the jinni satan, because speech affects a person." There are three types of repentance: a) the repentance of the masses *(al-ʿawāmm),* which is repentance from sins; b) the repentance of the elite *(al-khawāṣṣ),* which is repentance from heedlessness; and c) the repentance of the elite of the elite *(khawāṣṣ al-khawāṣṣ),* which is repentance from seeing the good things they do. "If one of them does something good and feels that he is the doer of that good deed, he repents

from that perception, because in reality the doer is God, and He must be praised for granting him this good thing. Therefore Khiḍr said, 'I did not do it on my own accord, but our Lord who created me is the one who did this.' Therefore the 'sultan of lovers,' ʿUmar ibn al-Fāriḍ, may God be pleased with him, said, 'I am the instrument, and the divine determination is the fingers (which play it).' "[8]

3. *Taking refuge in God (maqām al-lujūʾ).* "When a person feels that his repentance is accepted, he turns to God. In this *maqām* he has become a dervish *(darwīsh).* The meaning of a dervish is one who has turned his face *(dār wishhu)* toward God.[9] Taking refuge in God means turning to Him in all circumstances. If something happens and he doesn't know what to do, he turns to God by praying the prayer of seeking guidance *(ṣalāt al-istikhāra),* and the answer comes in his sleep, by direct inspiration or by his own thoughts."

4. *Moderation (iʿtidāl).* "Islam tells the Muslims they are the best nation (Qurʾan, 3:110), and placed upon them the obligation of moderation, which is commanding the good and forbidding the evil (3:104). 'You are a median community,' well-balanced (2:143). [They were told neither to] be like the monks (who withdraw from the world) nor lust after the things of the world. Moderation should be maintained in all things. One should not even be excessive in ablutions if one is on a boat on the river. (Muhammad said,) 'We are a people who do not eat unless we are hungry, and we eat until we are satisfied.' As long as a person is moderate in his eating, he will not get sick. Moderation in all things is best."

5. *The spiritual state (al-ḥāl).* "When a person travels in moderation, he must become grounded in a *ḥāl.* The meaning of *ḥāl* is the feelings that predominate in a person. Every Sufi has a *ḥāl.* One might say that in every *maqām* there is a *ḥāl.* Because the spiritual state is a combination of feelings. The *ḥāl* then progresses to the interior *(baṭn)* of the *ḥāl,* which is realization, then to the secret of the interior (or innermost interior) of the *ḥāl (sirr baṭn al-ḥāl),* which is the 'transparency' *(shafāfiyya)* of the heart, then to the essence of the secret of the interior of the *ḥāl (ʿayn sirr baṭn al-ḥāl),* which is the stage of direct vision of the heart."

6. *Contraction (qabḍ),* "which is fear of sin. Perhaps a slip which results in humility is better than an act of obedience which produces pride. In this station, the dominant feeling is fear of God. Fear pervades all of one's being."

7. *Fear (khawf),* "a realization in the mind, whereas contraction is in the feelings. There must be fear, in order for it to be followed by hope. The Sufi in this station has constant fear of blame, of sin,

that he won't enter Paradise, that he will not arrive at the witness of the divine. He continues in this, until finally he yields his affair entirely to God and enters the next stage."

8. *Hope (rajā')* in God. This hope is based on God's own assurances that the servant who thinks well of Him will find Him as he imagines. In a *ḥadīth qudsī* God said, "I am as My servant thinks I am. I am with me when he makes mention of Me. If he makes mention of Me to himself, I make mention of him to Myself; and if he makes mention of Me in an assembly, I make mention of him in an assembly better than it. And if he draws near to Me a hand's span, I draw near to him an arm's length; and if he draws near to Me an arm's length, I draw near to him a fathom's length. And if he comes to Me walking, I go to him at speed."[10]

9. *Obliteration (maḥw),* "a station in which a person thinks, 'I am a mere figment of the imagination, passing into annihilation. We are nothing.' If a person obliterates his self, that is, his pride, etc., his Lord will remain. This is the ultimate humility, which says, 'I am not here. I do not exist.' Mursī Abū 'l-ʿAbbās saw a dog who was lame.[11] Those who were with him mocked the dog. Abū 'l-ʿAbbās responded, 'Do you mock him? I fear that he may be better than I in God's eyes.' This is obliteration. Complete obliteration is when a person thinks of nothing but God. The creation has no existence—he sees nothing but the Creator. He has gone beyond matter entirely. He does not perceive it. No particular deeds come from obliteration, unlike intoxication *(sukr).*"

10. *Intoxication (sukr).* "In the state of intoxication one does and says strange things, and obligation is removed. Such a person could commit a crime, but it is not a crime from the perspective of Ultimate Reality *(al-ḥaqīqa),* because he acts without will or desire. In this station, the Sufi is not absent from the divine presence, but he is absent from those who are around him. Such a person prefers isolation and dislikes the company of people. He enters into long seclusion, because he is happy with his intoxication."

11. *Presence (ḥuḍūr) with God* comes only after intoxication. It can last any length of time—minutes, months. "When he is absent from created things, he is present with God and His Messenger. The presence of the Messenger of God contains that of all the prophets and the *ahl al-bayt.* The Sufi in this station may eat nothing, but he takes his nourishment from their essences and is illuminated by their lights. He speaks from these presences. If someone asks him a question about anything—even the heavenly spheres, or other things he has not seen—he answers from this presence, as Shaykh ʿAbd al-

ʿAzīz al-Dabbāgh did in *Al-Ibrīz*. He is present with God, and God is present in his heart."

12. *Expansion (basṭ).* "After being a while in the station of presence, because he has experienced spiritual states that are beyond the capacity of the intellect to understand, the Sufi becomes annoyed. Then if God wants him to call others to Him, He gives him the state of expansion, and a smile never leaves his face. He always feels like his breast is enlarged (*munsharih*, cf. Qurʾan 39:22), and his face is joyful. This is a state that comes to a saint at the end of his sainthood, not the beginning, so he will acquire even more virtue. You will always find that people of good morals have a smile on their face.[12] He is able to make others feel happy as well. Perhaps in the middle of talking to them he will tell a joke, but within the bounds of decency, a good word."

13. *Ecstasy in love (wajd).* "This is the essence of Sufism. It is possible that a person may lose the state of expansion and enter a state of giddiness and unconsciousness in laughter. God protects the saint from this with what is called *wajd*. This *wajd* is a state of constant longing (*shawq*). He longs, with all his being, for God. Longing is higher than love (*ḥubb*). Love contains the seeds of the tree of longing. Longing has another gate inside it, which is called passionate love (*ʿishq*). If the passionate lover becomes fixed, he is created in the object of his love. If he is created in the Beloved (*al-maʿshūq*), then he is born in Him. Qays saw everything as Laylā, because he was passionately in love with her, and saw nothing but her."[13] I asked, "If a person has been born in the Beloved, doesn't longing come to an end, because it has been satisfied?" ʿIzz replied, "It is like this: 'I drank all the seas, but my longing increased.' Every drink increases his longing. Longing ceases only in witness, which is the condition of the *ghawth* only. From the beginning of repentance, the wayfarer may feel a longing, but he does not know what it is for. Only when he arrives at *wajd* does he understand. It is like a little boy and girl who play bride and bridegroom without really understanding what it means. A person may thirst after something without knowing what it is."

14. *Witness (shuhūd).* "Longing reaches its peak, until the person enters witness, which is the unveiling of the inner vision (*kashf al-baṣīra*). In this station, if the heart leans toward America, it sees it. Only the *ghawth* or a future *ghawth* reaches this stage. This is absolute, continuous witness—not the intermittent inner vision that many saints enjoy. It is in this stage that Abū 'l-Ḥasan al-Shādhilī said, 'If the Messenger of God is absent from me for the blink of an

eye, I do not consider myself to be among the living.' Aḥmad Raḍwān in this station said, 'If the Messenger of God is absent from me for fifteen breaths, I will kill myself.' These people are in perpetual witness, seeing him all the time. It is a witness of the Essence—God. God cannot be seen except by way of the heart of the Messenger of God. So the best thing is to keep company with the Muhammadan presence. As long as a saint can see the Messenger and God, he can see the whole universe. The *ghawth* can see the heavens and the very center of the earth. Complete vision, without limitation. Anyone other than the *ghawth* may occasionally have his inner vision unveiled, but for a period that may range from minutes to a year. A shaykh may see what is happening in his disciple's homes, but not all of them at once, whereas the vision of the *ghawth* is like the vision of God—he can see all at once, continuously. He is one with Him *(hūwa Hūwa)*. We don't like to say this, but it is true nonetheless. He has become his Lord."[14]

Shaykh ʿIzz said that the seventeenth-century Moroccan shaykh ʿAbd al-ʿAzīz al-Dabbāgh, whose spiritual experiences are described in *Al-Ibrīz,* was in this state when he saw light like lightning flashing from east to west and above and below him while he was above the seven heavens. ʿIzz commented, "This means that he had entered into the essence *(dhāt)* of God and had become essence himself."

On another occasion, ʿIzz spoke of this station and its relationship to the Islamic obligation to pray. "Prayer is an absolute obligation in Islam, but the manner of prayer *(al-kayfiyya)* is unknown. Didn't God say in the *ḥadīth qudsī* that if a servant comes to Him He becomes his eyes by which he sees, his ears by which he hears, his tongue by which he speaks, and his hand by which he takes? If God and the servant are one, what is the meaning of prayer? Who is praying and to whom is the prayer made? Toward the end of his life Shaykh Aḥmad Raḍwān would seldom do dhikr, because at the mere recitation of *Allāhu akbar* (God is most great), he would lose consciousness.[15] His entire being was in constant communication with God. Therefore I say that although prayer is an absolute obligation, how it is accomplished is unknown."

THE RECOLLECTION OF GOD (DHIKR)

The essential tool and method for advancing on the path of God is *dhikr,* the recollection or remembrance of God. The command to remember God often is Qurʾanic (33:41). Sufis believe dhikr is the best form of worship, for the Qur'an says that it is greater even than *ṣalāt*, the ritual prayer which is an obligation for all Muslims five times a day (29:45). Frequent dhikr is among the characteristics of the men and women who are granted, according to the Qur'an, forgiveness and a great reward (33:35). In the Qur'an, God tells the believers that if they remember Him, He will remember them (2:152), and in a *ḥadīth qudsī,* "Whoever remembers Me in his soul, I remember him in My soul. Whoever mentions me before an assembly, I mention him in a better assembly."[16] Ḥadīths indicate that dhikr is the best deed to guarantee entry into heaven, better even than jihād or lavish generosity.[17] Qushayrī (d. 1072) says in his *Risāla,* still one of the most frequently studied Sufi texts in Egypt today, that dhikr is *the* pillar of the Sufi Way, "and no one comes to God without continuous recollection."[18] Dhikr is seen as the key to the purification of the heart, for concentration on God prevents the disciple from thinking of less worthy topics, and this necessarily has an imprint on the disciple's state of mind.

The Qur'an commands Muslims to call on God by means of His Most Beautiful Names (7:180), which are traditionally numbered at ninety-nine. Each of these Names (for example, the Compassionate, the Merciful, the Living, the Creator, the Eternal) describes an aspect of the Godhead, and Sufis believe that concentrated recitation of each Name opens the disciple to a particular aspect of knowledge of the divine. By means of such concentration on God through recitation of His Names, the mind is enlightened with understanding the various aspects of the Godhead contained in them.

Techniques and Benefits of Dhikr

Qushayrī distinguishes two types of dhikr, dhikr of the tongue and dhikr of the heart. Dhikr of the tongue, an audible recitation, is the gate to dhikr of the heart, which Qushayrī calls "the sword of the disciples by which they fight their enemies and repel disasters that aim for them." Contemporary Sufis often add to this list dhikr of the spirit, and some add to that dhikr of the innermost being *(sirr).* Dhikr, says Qushayrī, is not temporary. "There is no moment that the servant is not commanded to recollect God. Although prayer is the noblest act of worship, it does not exceed certain times, whereas dhikr is continuous in the heart, for God said, 'Who remember God standing and sitting and lying on their sides' (Qur'an 3:191, 4:103)."[19] It is through dhikr that God is said to dwell in the heart of His believing servant, says Qushayrī, "for God is beyond inhabiting any place."[20]

Shaykh Abū 'l-ʿAzā'im wrote, "No one comes to God without constant absorption in dhikr. Dhikr may be by the tongue or in the heart. Dhikr of the tongue leads a servant into constant dhikr of the heart, whereas one cannot rely on dhikr of the heart." Regarding the obligation of constant dhikr, he quotes Sahl al-Tustarī (d. 896), who said, "I know of no sin uglier than forgetting this Lord." This, says Shaykh Abū 'l-ʿAzā'im, refers to dhikr of the heart, not the dhikr of the tongue.[21]

Aḥmad Raḍwān said, "The cause of sin and worldly attachment and neglect of God and sickness of the heart and spirit is lack of dhikr—not bobbing the heads, but useful remembrance which preserves a man from Satan's wiles. Remember him, so your heart has room for no other."[22]

Dhikr of the tongue—the utterance of "there is no god but Allah" or one of the Names of God—must be accompanied by awareness of its meaning and concentration on it in the heart. A person may also say the divine Name "Allah" with his tongue, while reciting in his heart the other divine Names—"Creator," "Provider, "my Lord," and so forth. The Names typically used in Egyptian dhikrs are Allah, *lā ilāha illā Allāh* ("there is no god but Allah"), *Ḥayy* (Living), *Qayyūm* (Eternal), and *Hū* (He).

Dhikr of the heart is sometimes practiced by imagining the Name "Allah" drawn upon the heart. Shaykh Abū 'l-ʿAzā'im says that this method yields five subtleties *(laṭā'if)*, each of which has its special etiquettes and special image. "This is a method appropriate for the beginning of the path of the silent, to preserve the tongue."[23]

Shaykh ʿIzz describes the way in which dhikr becomes part of who the Sufi is. "When a Name is given to a person and he becomes accustomed to dhikr, and the dhikr is transferred from the tongue to the limbs, it becomes a habit for the person's faculties to recollect it. Even if the tongue is not doing dhikr, the heart is. The Name has come to be within him, and this is then translated to the outside. He finds himself unconsciously saying '*Qayyūm, Qayyūm, Qayyūm.*' When he becomes aware of what he is saying, he is surprised at himself. The effect has been transferred from inside to outside. At first the shaykh gives him dhikr to do from the outside to the inside. But with repetition and habit, when it matures inside him, the feelings, faculties, and limbs of the person are all involved in dhikr, even if he is not outwardly doing dhikr."

Some Sufis also speak of dhikr of the spirit, which is when the heart is filled with the love of God and has no regard for any reward, and then dhikr of the innermost being *(sirr)*, a dhikr so subtle that the mind is unaware of it and "it is unrecorded by angels, and Satan cannot corrupt it—that is the dhikr of those who are nearest to God, the elect who have attained the spiritual goal."[24]

Dhikr can be done individually, as part of the *wird* assigned the disciple by his shaykh, or by a group of disciples in a private or semiprivate situation, or publicly, in which case anyone may feel free to join in. The words and methods of dhikr vary from one Order to another. With regard to individual dhikr, for example, some shaykhs guide their disciples through a graduated series of meditations on certain Names of God, each Name appropriate for a certain stage in the disciple's spiritual development, while other shaykhs use a standard set of Names for all their disciples. Still others say that in order for dhikr to be truly effective in yielding the revelation of the divine aspect hidden in the Name, the Name used in dhikr should numerically match the name of the disciple—that is, the sum of the numerical values of the letters in the divine Name should match the sum of the numerical values of the letters of the name of the disciple. In this case, said Shaykh ʿIzz, "the angels come to him and give him good tidings." If the numerical values of the names do not match, "at the very least his breast will be expanded. Even if he doesn't sense the presence of the angels or if they do not come to him, the repetition of the Name will expand his breast and he will feel peace and tranquility." All of this indicates that the name of a thing contains a key to its nature or essence and that knowledge of a name provides the possibility of mastering the thing that is named. In the case of the Names of God, mastery over God is not possible, but attaining mystical understanding in connection with His Names is possible. Most Sufis believe that the saints know the Greatest Name of God (the identity of which is a matter of dispute), and use it according to the degree of their knowledge of it. Using the Greatest Name of God grants the saint spiritual power over other things, including the ability to alter the nature of substances, an ability that led to a medieval Sufi preoccupation with the "science" of alchemy.

Recitation of a particular Name might be only one hundred times in any given dhikr session, or it may be one hundred thousand times, depending on the instructions of the spiritual guide. Shaykh Abū 'l-ʿAzāʾim recommends increasing the number of recitations daily, even if by only one. Dhikr should be performed in a state of purity (although this is not a strict requirement, as it is for ritual prayer), and if it is performed alone it should be done facing the direction of the Kaʿba in Mecca, as one would face for prayer. The disciple should open and close his dhikr with a recitation of a passage from the Qurʾan. "After finishing it he should close his eyes and recall that he is given permission to do these exercises by a Guide whose spiritual lineage goes back to the Messenger of God, so that he might attain contact with the Muhammadan Togetherness and the subtleties of dhikr might come to his heart, by virtue of his understanding the meanings of the words or the secrets of the verses, or by witnessing unseen meanings, and the revelation of the secrets of songs, or tasting the spiritual stages of the Guide, or being adorned with one of his spiritual states. All that is proof of the presence of the heart (with God) and the beginning of its awakening."[25]

Some Orders also use methods of breath control and head and body movement to aid in concentration, to send the breath containing the divine Name from one part of the body to another, and, perhaps, to induce ecstasy. Shaykh ʿIzz denied the use of breath control in dhikr but said the purpose is to say the Name with every breath. The involvement of the entire body in the process of recollection is consistent with other practices in Islam, such as the movements of the body in *ṣalāt,* and is part of the general recognition of the connectedness of body, mind, and spirit in Islam. When I asked whether the movements of dhikr help a person come to God, Shaykh ʿIzz said, "They don't help him get to God, but they help him to train his limbs to do dhikr. Because there is a dhikr of the body and its parts. There is dhikr of the limbs, of the eye, of the hand. Dhikr must be perfected in the disciple. When all his faculties are doing dhikr, then he recollects nothing but God. All his bodily parts are directed toward one goal—dhikr." Shaykh Gābir al-Jāzūlī said, "Movement is essential to life; the opposite of movement is death. It is God who causes movement and stillness. Movement and stillness, this is the rhythm of life. . . . There is a link between the body and the spirit."[26]

Although the Qurʾan says Muslims should remember God "standing, sitting or lying on your sides," the preferred posture in group dhikr is usually standing, although some groups perform their dhikr seated. Group dhikr is usually part of a larger ceremony called *ḥaḍra* ("presence," that is, invoking the presence of God and His Messenger), which is opened with recitation of the Qurʾan and closed with prayers. In this case, the commencement of dhikr is often signaled when the leader of the *ḥaḍra* rises; all the others rise with him, and the dhikr begins.

In Egypt, dhikr is usually performed in rows, although some groups prefer to perform it in a circle of clasped hands. Dhikr often begins with recitation of the divine Name that is considered to be the comprehensive Name, containing within itself the meaning of all other names—Allah. The Name is pronounced slowly and emphatically, with an elongation of the second syllable, throwing the head and upper body back and then forward with each recitation. The tempo and unity of movement are maintained by the shaykh or designated leader of the gathering, who stands between the rows of participants (or in their middle, if they are forming a circle), and signals them with his own body movements, words, and clapping. Dhikr begins with a slow and solemn beat, but typically the pace is quickened, and the participants begin to move from side to side rather than bowing forward. The movements require considerable exertion, full 180-degree turns of the body and head, a steady movement that is sustained for anywhere from twenty minutes to an hour. Witnessed from above, as women often do from the balconies of neighboring buildings, the dhikr participants create a beautiful pattern as their robes swing with them around their bodies, first one direction, then the other. At this point the recitation changes to something else—perhaps "there is no god but Allah," although some groups use this testimony at the beginning of dhikr instead. If this sentence is used at this point in dhikr, some groups say that the phrase "there is no god" should be exhaled, symbolically expelling the idols (including the idol of the ego) from the participant, while "except God" is spoken in an inhaled breath, symbolizing the participant's absorption into the divine presence. This type of breathing is a difficult feat and gives dhikr a characteristically sharp breathing pattern all its own. The recitation of the Name *Hū* (He) sometimes dissolves into a mere grunt, and indeed the physical exertion involved often forces the participants to recite ever more quietly, until all the observer hears is the breathing of the participants—and the music of the *munshidīn*.

Regarding group dhikr, Shaykh Abū 'l-ʿAzāʾim likewise provides detailed instructions. The place must be pure, "far from the rabble and markets and places of amusement." Dhikr assemblies are opened with a reading from the Qurʾan, followed by group recitation of "there is no god but Allah," correctly pronounced in a moderate voice. The leader of the dhikr should be selected for his humility and spirituality. "He must be full of concentration and self-examination. If it appears that the dhikr has awakened the heart, he changes the phrase. He should be moderate and not let the dhikr go overly long, nor let it be so short that the heart is not awakened, for the goal of group dhikr is the awakening of the heart and the removal of heedlessness. He must watch that the assembly remains orderly, all saying the same thing, using the same voice and movement. If he sees one of the brethren go into ecstasy, he must alter the words or movement of dhikr. If the entire group goes into ecstasy, he must make them sit in order to preserve moderation, for God has said, 'We have made you a median community.' "[27]

Abū 'l-ʿAzāʾim further clarifies that the transition from the opening Qurʾan recitation to the dhikr of "there is no god but Allah" is by the recitation of the Qurʾanic verse, "Know that there is no god but Allah" (47:19); the transition to dhikr of the Name "Allah" is by recitation of the verse, "Say, 'Allah,' then leave them to play in their vanity" (6:91); and the transition to the recitation of the Name "He" *(Hū)* is by recitation of the verse, "Your God is one God, there is no god but He" (2:163). During the dhikr of "Allah," the other divine Names are also brought to mind, though not uttered. The goal of dhikr, from his point of view, is to awaken the heart, but ecstatic behavior must be avoided. One way to do this is to use a divine Name other than Allah, for these other Names contain only a part of the meaning of "Allah" and therefore have a less powerful impact on the unprepared mind. If the participants are overcome by ecstasy, they should be taken on to a new Name, prefacing its recitation with the Qurʾanic verse from which it is derived.[28]

Dhikr involves considerable physical exertion, and usually a good deal of perspiration. Mindful even of the physical health of disciples, Shaykh Abū 'l-ʿAzāʾim stresses that when the dhikr is over the participants should not remove their clothes, lest they catch cold, and should not drink cold water until their bodies have settled down. They should close their eyes and turn their hearts toward God, "so they may receive the gift of the angelic realm and the lights of dhikr." One person should recite something easy from the Qurʾan, preferably verses with a soothing message. The group leader or anyone else may address the group concerning an insight obtained during dhikr or with any other edifying word. The assembly is concluded with a final recitation of "there is no god but Allah" three, five, or seven times, an invocation of blessing on the Prophet and his Companions and deceased Muslims, and a prayer for forgiveness for those present and absent.[29]

The experience of group dhikr is profoundly different from individual dhikr. The spirits of the participants affect each other and are able to communicate with each other as well as with their Lord.

Biegman quotes a Rifāʿi shaykh as saying, "In the beginning, all souls were one, and they became separated from one another when they went into different bodies. During dhikr, they again become one."[30] The more advanced Sufis can help lift up the spirits of the novices so that they will be able to experience revelation of divine lights unattainable by them in isolation. Shaykh ʿIzz said that one time during dhikr with a Sufi group, the wife of the presiding shaykh took his hand because she sensed that he was more advanced than she was in dhikr. Through his spirit she was able to enter into dhikr in a manner more profound than usual. But at one point he let go of her hand, and she fell to the floor, unable to sustain such a high level. Nonetheless, even without physical contact, the spirits of the participants in dhikr affect each other. The presence of a single sinner is sufficient to prevent the revelation of divine lights to the entire group. Indeed, the very goal of Sufi mysticism in contemporary Egypt might be said to be at least partly communalistic—penetrating the spirits of the shaykh, the saints, the Prophet, and each other. Entering into *God's* essence is a privilege reserved for the advanced gnostic.

Nonetheless admiration is reserved for the individual in the group who is able to withdraw mentally from the others and be alone with God. I asked Shaykh ʿIzz why group dhikr was important when the goal of dhikr is to be alone with God. He replied that the group strengthens concentration and creates competition between the individuals. Even the Qurʾan uses the plural when referring to men and women who do dhikr often, and the *Fātiḥa* (the opening chapter of the Qurʾan) also uses the plural subject when it says, "You are the One we worship and call on for help." When two or three work together they strengthen each other, whereas the person who works alone becomes bored. For this reason each prophet had a companion. But in the presence of God the plural is canceled out, and there is spiritual clarity between the person and God in the moment of mystical ecstasy. "So you will find that the words are one and perhaps the movements as well, but each spirit has its own experience of God in dhikr. . . . The goal is for the person doing dhikr to be absent from the dhikr, or to be lost in the dhikr from awareness of the dhikr, until he comes to be in the One who is recollected in dhikr. In this there is pleasure or clarity or harmony or solitude. I may be with you, but I am not with you in spirit or heart. The true lover says, 'I permitted my body to whoever wanted to sit with me, but my Beloved inhabits my heart.' "

Music in Dhikr: Its Methods and Purpose

Although *samāʿ*, musical concerts to induce ecstasy, have a long history in Sufism, they are controversial and in some countries are distinct from dhikr.[31] In Egypt, group dhikr is often performed with the assistance of singers and musicians, who, to give a literal translation to the Arabic term, "give life to" the dhikr. While the participants in dhikr recite the Names of God, the munshidin sing the praises of the Prophet and invoke the blessings of the *ahl al-bayt* and the saints. They serve the purpose of inspiring those in dhikr by their words and their music. They also add considerably to the attraction of dhikr as a form of entertainment and are even used in lieu of belly dancers at weddings, especially in Upper Egypt. Public dhikrs typically draw large crowds of onlookers who do not directly participate in the dhikr or who at some point join in under the inspiration of the music and the atmosphere it creates. The public dhikrs performed at the major saints' shrines of Cairo between the afternoon and sunset prayers on their visiting days draw a regular crowd of faithful devotees as well as locals. When the regulars say that the dhikr at Sidi ʿAlī (Zayn al-ʿĀbidin, the son of Ḥusayn, whose shrine lies in southern Cairo near the slaughterhouse) is very good, they are referring to a number of factors, including the attractiveness of the mosque, the ambiance provided by the terrain, and the sociability provided by the cafe that borders the space where dhikr is performed, but above all they are speaking of the skill of the musicians.

The purpose of using music is to stir people to recollect God more fervently, and with greater concentration. Shaykh ʿIzz said, "The Qurʾan says there is nothing in heaven and on earth that does not praise God. So the musical instruments also praise God, and by setting a certain rhythm they encourage a particular movement. This also helps dhikr, because God likes order." I asked about the effect of the singer's words on the dhikr participants and the degree to which they can grasp their meaning, since they are absorbed in reciting different words altogether. ʿIzz replied, "It is by feelings. The singer gives water to the dhikr participants, and they take a sip, whether of pleasure or a particular taste, and so they react. They taste the word by their inner being and their feelings, but they are unable to grasp the meaning at the same time as they are doing dhikr, except for the gnostic."

Musical instruments at dhikr typically include the hand-drum (*ṭabla* or *darabukka*), tambourine (*duff*), flute (*kawla*), castanets (*ṣakkāt*

Figure 6. Aḥmad al-Tūnī (left), one of the greatest Sufi singers of Egypt, taking a break between sets with one of his musicians on 30 June 1988.

or *ṭūra*) and violin, while lead singers acquire the status of national celebrities. Tapes of their singing in dhikr can be bought at music stores and kiosks.[32]

Opinions concerning the permissibility of listening to music have varied widely in Islam, and it seems that from the beginning Sufis have felt a need to justify their use of music and to make stipulations limiting its use.[33] Qushayri said that since the Prophet had allowed the recitation of religious poetry, religious song should likewise be allowed, for the spiritual benefit remains the same. Mālik ibn Anas (d. 795) and other legal scholars of the Hijāz all permitted singing. His disciple al-Shāfiʿī (d. 820), founder of another legal school, said singing was reprehensible (permitted, but disapproved), but, Qushayrī adds, "that is not the kind of *samāʿ* we are talking about."[34]

Shaykh ʿIzz believes that the permissibility of music, like that of many other things, depends on the attitude and spiritual state of the listener. For those who are "in the spirit," listening to music will not harm but will edify. Those who are governed by their intellects will be unable to appreciate the spiritual movements aroused by listening to music, and they are right to disapprove of it, not because of anything inherently wrong with music but because of its harmfulness for them personally. He tells this story concerning the three most prominent Companions of the Prophet, who became the first, second, and fourth Caliphs of Islam after Muhammad's death. Abū Bakr (r. 632–634) represents the attribute of humility in Sufi tradition. ʿUmar ibn al-Khaṭṭāb (r. 634–44), was "the intellect of the nation," a man of legendary harshness and righteousness. ʿAlī ibn Abī Ṭālib, the Prophet's cousin and son-in-law (r. 656–61), as we have seen, represents mystical knowledge. ʿIzz first told me this story when I asked him whether it was permissible for a woman to sing praises to the Prophet in public, as I had observed at a moulid. ʿIzz replied, "She is in the house of the Prophet," and told me this story: Some singing girls were performing in the house of the Prophet. Abū Bakr entered and protested, "Are the psalms of Satan being heard in the house of the Prophet?" The Prophet told him to be quiet and sit down. He did so. ʿAlī entered and sat down without protest. ʿUmar entered, and the singing girls fled. The Messenger said, "Satan has fled from you, ʿUmar."[35]

By virtue of his spiritual understanding, ʿAlī was able to accept and immediately appreciate the spiritual import of the singing. Abū Bakr, not as spiritually adept, protested initially but accepted the Prophet's admonition and was able to learn to appreciate their singing. ʿUmar, however, was limited by his faith in his intellect and his self-righteousness from being able to appreciate it. For him, the singing girls were indeed "Satan" and were forced to flee from his presence. What is edifying to one man is satanic to another. The eleventh-century Persian Sufi al-Hujwīrī appears to affirm this idea when he writes, "Listening to sweet sounds produces an effervescence of the substance moulded in man: true if the substance be true, false if the substance be false."[36]

Qushayrī wrote that a disciple should never intentionally move while listening to a spiritual concert, although if he is overcome by ecstasy and moves involuntarily, he is excused. "If he becomes accustomed to that, he will remain behind and no heavenly realities will be revealed to him. Movement takes away from one's spiritual state."[37] Abū Ḥāmid al-Ghazālī (d. 1111), on the other hand, suggested that imitating the movements of ecstasy can induce ecstasy, which is praiseworthy.[38] In the contemporary Egyptian setting, where Sufi musical concerts are seldom held without simultaneous dhikr, which usually includes bodily movements, the issue has become moot. Yet Sufis disagree as to whether or not ecstasy is a truly desirable goal. While, on the one hand, a spiritual experience is a mark of drawing near to God and a lack of awareness of one's surroundings is a mark of sincerity, in public settings some Sufi leaders are more concerned with maintaining a sober face for onlookers, lest they be accused of being unorthodox. The ecstatic face of a person in dhikr, the loss of control sometimes accompanied by trancelike behavior and saliva shooting out of the open mouth, is an image that has brought contempt upon Sufis by other Muslims, who fear in turn the contempt that foreigners will have for Islam when they see such sights. Furthermore, a spiritually intoxicated individual might say inappropriate things and need to be restrained or "cooled" in a public dhikr. It is for this reason that Earle Waugh observed that shaykhs exercise control over their disciples in dhikr and do not allow unbridled individuality.[39]

The enjoyment of music in dhikr assemblies (and the acquisition of celebrity status by Sufi singers) is seen by some shaykhs as a dangerous development. Shaykh Abū 'l-Wafā al-Sharqāwī wrote, "Out of ignorance some have gone to dhikr assemblies to enjoy the singing and to relax—an evil goal. They think a dhikr is good if they liked the singing of the singer, and they think the dhikr is not good if they do not like his singing. In this way this pillar has been taken lightly by people who use it for weddings and ordinary things. Some singers use dhikr assemblies to obtain worldly and filthy things. Such people unwittingly stand in the ranks of those who fight against the exalted Presence."[40]

In fact, it is not rare to see a person enjoying dhikr in an entirely secular way, using the motions of secular dancing, such as belly dancing or stick dancing. The castanet player in the musical troupe at the dhikr at Sīdī ʿAlī sometimes engages in such dancing and antics. Reactions to displays of folk dancing by the other dhikr participants and the onlookers vary widely. Sometimes they rebuke the dancers sharply and expel them from the rows of dhikr, but other times people simply laugh. The distinction between spiritual and secular enjoyment of dhikr is nonetheless apparent to even the most casual onlooker. Such displays of frivolity subject the dhikr and the Sufis to strenuous criticism from outsiders.

There are a large number of well-known *munshidīn,* but the most popular and frequently compared are Aḥmad al-Tūnī and Yāsīn al-Tuhāmī. Both men hail from the small provincial town of Hawatka in Asyut province, Upper Egypt. Aḥmad al-Tūnī is the older man, a dark-skinned man with a wild shock of frizzy hair usually tamed by a turban and sharp features that nonetheless assume a wonderful attractiveness when he sings. His songs are preferred by some Sufis for the depth of their spiritual content and insight. Although both singers draw heavily from Sufi tradition and especially the poems of ʿUmar ibn al-Fāriḍ (d. 1235), the traditional lines are delivered in often idiosyncratic style, chopped up and reinterpreted and interspersed with appeals to the Prophet and the saints and lines newly composed by the singer himself, so it is possible to say that the singers need to operate under spiritual inspiration. Aḥmad al-Tūnī's style is so idiosyncratic as to be inimitable. He intersperses his words with extraordinary gestures and inarticulate utterances, utilizing his gravelly voice with astounding versatility. Sometimes he employs two young boys, one of them his son, to sing falsetto choruses of *"madad, madad"* or repeat his lines. Occasionally their voices crack from the strain of singing at such a high pitch, but Shaykh ʿIzz said it is a sound that lifts people's hearts, and it forms an interesting contrast with Tūnī's own deep voice. Between the two sets of dhikr at a private mosque, he sang a solo that displayed the full range of his ingenuity and charm. At one point he imitated before the silent throng the motions and breathing sounds of people in dhikr, as he sang of the mysteries of divine knowledge and longing to enter the presence of God. Many Sufis regard Ahmad al-Tuni as the more spiritually inspired and penetrating of the two singers, although particularly in the Delta, I am told, people have a hard time appreciating his words.

At a dhikr in the small town of Duwayra, in Asyūṭ province, Tūnī sang the following words:

The heart longs for the heavenly realm, to see the divine manifestation *(al-tajalli),*
Whether what is said about it is true
What a wonder! My heart demands that I see Him
. . . .
God is most great; no worldly pleasure will divert us from traveling in God, oh people of the Presence!

God is most great, and the verses speak, awakening us to grace pouring forth like the ocean.
Knowledge[41] has a limit; beyond it are lights
The light is unseen, and beyond the unseen are secrets,
And the secret draws me to witness his Presence[42]

. . . .

The unveiling *(kashf)* is a grace *(faḍl),*
And beyond the unveiling are the destinies *(aqdār)*
[Musical interlude] Ah-h!

. . . .

I have a favored position granted me in the station of nearness, hidden from every spirit (4x)
And beyond that is the unseen;
But the unseen is a heavy cloud, a secret beyond the comprehension of human vision.

. . . .

Intellects cannot comprehend it in its integrity,
But a chosen young man *(fatā)* in God sees it. . . .[43]
[Interlude invoking the *madad* (gracious assistance) of various saints and members of the *ahl al-bayt*]
After annihilation, no physical trace diverts me,
I am hidden from the spirit, and the perceptible is its cover
The Real is manifested in a mountain,[44] and He covers me,
And being covered in a state of proximity (to God) is manifestation *(iẓhār)*
The walls of divine manifestation crumble,
Indeed Moses lost consciousness when the secrets appeared to him,
The fire became a light for him, and they all came to be in the Real,
And the Almighty became their guardian.
Oh servant, do not turn from our gate full of regret,
Follow the conditions of authority whenever you come,
That is the life of those dear to the Prophet—whoever serves is served.

One is astonished at the density of such songs sung before a largely uneducated audience, sung indeed by a man who lacks much formal education himself. We may well be convinced of the truth that each one will understand only according to his capacity and of the utter impossibility of the average person to appreciate the full import of the words while at the same time doing dhikr. Yet even without fully comprehending the words, one can appreciate the spiritual impact of the singing, which stirred both those involved in dhikr and the large crowds of spectators. Shaykh ʿIzz cried out repeatedly with ecstasy gained from the mystical insights imparted in these words. I recorded this dhikr, and during the next several days as we traveled with a group of ʿIzz's disciples and stayed in a home in a small

Figure 7. Rows of men doing dhikr on 30 June 1988 at Shaykh ʿIzz's mosque, with Aḥmad al-Tūnī performing at the end.

village, the men listened to the tape over and over, bobbing their heads in appreciation and issuing forth delighted cries of "Allah!" The sheer density of the words almost demands the relief of musical interludes and cries for *madad,* or other ecstatic utterances.

Yāsīn al-Tuhāmī, the younger man, is, however, the more popular singer, who has undisputed star status. A light-skinned, almost blond, slightly heavy-set man, in person he is rather shy and humble, and attributes his success to the spiritual heritage he received from his father, a local shaykh who acquired the status of saint and whose annual moulid draws considerable crowds. Yāsīn's is a gentle voice, a younger voice, and his performance, although musically excellent, lacks the fire and spirit of Tūnī's. The theme of his singing is invariably love. The metaphors of love have a long tradition in Sufi poetry; the attraction of such themes for non-Sufis as well is self-evident, for love is a universal experience and can be interpreted by each listener in whatever way he pleases. Yāsīn has many imitators. But however much money he may earn from singing at private parties (called *layla*, literally "night," because, like most Sufi festivities, they take place at night) and selling his cassettes, he sings at the moulids for free, out of love for the *ahl al-bayt*.

At a *layla* in a semirural part of Imbāba, one of the newly urbanized sections of Cairo inhabited by immigrants from the countryside, several hundred gathered to hear Yāsīn in a vast open area between two buildings. Almost the entire crowd were men; only a small group of women were seated together behind the platform on which Yāsīn and the musicians performed. Fluorescent lights had been erected in designs over the heads of those in dhikr, and Yāsīn was surrounded by a large group of admirers. He has a steady group of devotees who accompany him to all his *layla*s, and during intermission he was surrounded by eager young men. As usual, Yāsīn sang of love—sadly, punctuating his lines with cries of "Ah!" that seemed to come straight from the heart. Love kills, he sang, but he who does not know love should be prayed over with the prayer for the dead, for he has not really lived. It was not clear who was the object of love—God, the Prophet, some other person—and Sufi terminology was not used. Yāsīn's is a singing style appreciable by anyone, and its potential for secular entertainment is obvious.[45]

Dhikr and *Zār*

Many people have suggested that dhikr is very similar to *zār*, or that zārs are for women what dhikrs are for men. Scholars who see the function of both as primarily social or therapeutic fail sometimes to distinguish their very different spiritual goals.[46] Zār is a spirit possession cult in which the majority of participants are women. Participants usually suffer from some physical or mental malady that they believe to be caused by spirit possession. The goal of zārs is not to expel the spirits but to placate them, by fulfilling their demands to hold an elaborate feast, wear certain clothes, perform a sacrifice, and dance to the rhythm that belongs to that particular spirit. Although the spirits of the zārs are commonly held to be demons, some women say that the spirit who "rides" them is that of a prominent saint, such as Aḥmad al-Badawī. In this way the Sufi saints have a role in zārs. One of the Cairene saints with a weekly visiting day, Abū 'l-Suʿūd, specializes in healing women's infertility. The majority of his visitors are women, and rather than having a *ḥaḍra* performed at his shrine, zārs are performed in houses near the shrine.[47] This fact strengthens the association of dhikr with men and zār with women.

The music for these public zārs often consists of praise songs to the Prophet that are very similar to the songs of the *munshidīn*, especially if the music is provided by men. Female musical troupes for zārs tend to be of Sudanese descent and play music with a distinctly Sudanese flavor. The zār itself is probably of Ethiopian origin and appears to have entered Egypt only in the late nineteenth century by the agency of Sudanese slaves who served the women of upper-class households. The movements of the women in zār are very different from the movements of dhikr. They are much less controlled and look more like a wild tossing of the body than like dance. The women often totter over and need to be constantly supported by a friend in order to sustain their dance. They sometimes dance on their elbows and knees, giving them a strange, animal-like appearance. The zār is considered by religious authorities to be entirely illegitimate and to have no basis in Islam, although its participants see it as a ceremony through which God heals, and Islamic religious elements are included.

When I asked Sufis about any similarity or connection between zār and dhikr, most of them denied that there was any at all. Some lower-class women did say that they went to zārs "to bob our heads" and enjoy the music, just as they would in dhikr, and rarely a woman said that women dance in zārs, whereas men do dhikr. But most Sufis see no relation between zār and dhikr at all. Although zārs may provide a social function in the lives of some women that is provided by dhikr in the lives of men, the spiritual goals of the two ceremonies are entirely different, and the emotional impact on the participants appeared to be different as well. Women in zār often dissolve into tears and collapse from exhaustion, whereas the dominant emotions in dhikr are serenity and ecstasy.

Descriptions of Some Public Dhikrs

A regular group of devotees attends the dhikrs at the shrines of Sayyida Nafīsa, Fāṭima al-Nabawiyya, and Sīdī ʿAlī Zayn al-ʿĀbidīn, on Sunday, Monday, and Saturday, respectively. The Prophet's grandson and granddaughter, Ḥusayn and Sayyida Zaynab, share Friday as their visiting day. Ḥusayn is honored with a number of dhikrs put on by different Orders, while the dhikr outside the mosque of Sayyida Zaynab bears all the marks of informality. When I observed it on 27 November 1987, about twenty men and ten women were congregated on a crowded sidewalk outside the mosque. The only musician was a man who played a small drum to keep the beat. Whereas other *ḥaḍra*s are held in squares by coffee shops or inside mosques, here there was only a man with a kerosene burner who did a lively trade selling tea on the sidewalk on which the *ḥaḍra* took place. People constantly stopped participating in dhikr to call down for more tea or to pass a glass of tea to somebody. Nonetheless, the participants in the dhikr were extremely enthusiastic. A long row of men, with some women at each end, took part. The praises sung by the *munshid* were usually directed at the Prophet. He sang of *ʿāshiq al-nabī,* the one who is passionately in love with the Prophet, a love by which one hoped to be granted favor with God. At the end of the dhikr the Prophet is again honored by the entire throng who recite, *"Ṣallī wa sallam wa bārik ʿalā Sayyidnā Muḥammad"*—"Honor and peace and blessings on our lord Muhammad." The dhikr was punctuated by the cries of an old woman beside me, *"Yā sitt!"* ("My lady!"), addressing Sayyida Zaynab, while a young veiled woman on my other side muttered blessings on the Prophet. The participants in the dhikr frequently cried out, *"Madad!"*—the standard plea for spiritual aid, which also formed a part of the participants' response to the prayers of the leader. A ten-year-old girl near me, apparently unaware that I was foreign, kept poking me, laughing, and pointing to one person or other who was clearly spiritually intoxicated. One man moved so violently that he repeatedly bumped into the tea seller, who shouted, "Enough!" until he realized that the man was quite beside himself. One woman was blowing her lips in a trembling fashion, producing a sound akin to blowing bubbles in water. The old woman on my left became so unruly that one of the singers turned around to rebuke her, to which she replied with shouted praises of Sayyida Zaynab and the Prophet and cries for *madad.* The little girl had to get out of the way, she was so bothered by participants jabbing her in the frenzy of dhikr, and I also feared being pushed backward into the kerosene fire, or more likely, having my voluminous skirt catch fire.

The weekly public dhikrs at the shrines draw larger crowds in summer than in winter. One Saturday afternoon in summer at the shrine of Sīdī ʿAlī Zayn al-ʿĀbidīn, a large crowd of several hundred gathered in anticipation of the *ḥaḍra* that is held after the midafternoon prayer. When the dhikr began there were about one hundred participants, fairly equally divided between men and women, while the rest remained as spectators, sitting in the cafe or standing around the square near the shrine-mosque of Sīdī ʿAlī. Some of the women covered their faces with sheer black veils; one young girl who wore only a simple scarf over her hair pulled it down over her eyes, which while failing to perform a function of modesty, no doubt granted her a sense of separation from the other people, in order to concentrate on God. The movements of most participants were synchronized, but there were a few exceptions. One old woman was very much in her own world, moving to her own rhythm, making her hands climb as if up a ladder—the slow movements of a mime dancer, sometimes similar to folk dancing, a contented smile on her face the whole time. A man with long, wild hair held a stick in his hand as he danced. One woman danced with the movements used in the zār, and as in zār she lost her balance and would have fallen had not another woman held her up. Her movements seemed terribly out of place, but nobody seemed very perturbed by her actions. The singer was an overweight middle-aged man wearing the suit of a civil servant. The piccolo player wore a tall red fez. The castanet player was a happy fellow who bowed this way and that with a broad smile on his face, a cigarette in his mouth, joking and greeting people in the crowd. In the second set of the dhikr he was replaced with a different player, but he remained on the podium, dancing by the new player. The musical group was advertised by a plaque attached to an arch of lights (there were also flashing colored lights on the mosque itself) as a "musical troupe" called The Stars of Ḥusayn, and their address and phone number were provided for those who wished to enlist their services. There were many young people in attendance. Most of them were young men who dressed in the universal robe *(gallābiyya)* of the lower class, but the dress of others made their class affiliation less obvious. Whole families came, and groups of young women as well. A large number of beggars made the rounds of the spectators. A severely handicapped man who had no limbs save one arm with a malformed hand and skin that looked like it had been burned, demanded money from everyone, and nearly everybody gave to him cheerfully. Others moved through the crowd distributing tamarind juice or water. A short man who distributed water without charge can be seen at nearly every *ḥaḍra* or moulid. In the winter he wears his hair long and a hat with the word "Allah" on it; in the summer, his hair is shorter and he looks less strange. But he always has a cheerful smile, moving to the dhikr as he makes his rounds. Another regular was a tall, odd-looking woman with a sad face, who never spoke to anyone and was always alone. I first saw her in a dhikr here in March 1981; more than seven years later, she was still going to dhikrs. The woman next to me offered me her *ḥilba* (a hot drink prepared from grains for women in childbirth), a courtesy that of course I declined. Peddlers of peanuts, *libb* (seeds that are cracked open with the teeth in order to eat the inner part), candy, and even undershirts moved among the crowd, endangering the heads of some of those engaged in dhikr. One woman in the dhikr, who had a constant smile on her covered face, angered another woman by bumping into her repeatedly, and a fight broke out. The two women were forcibly separated, and the first woman continued her dhikr unperturbed, with the same smile on her face.

The dhikr at the moulid of Aḥmad al-Ṭayyib (d. 1956) in Qurna, in Upper Egypt across the Nile from Luxor, was entirely different. Although women constituted the majority of the sellers of trinkets, candy, and roasted chickpeas, there were few women at the shrine and none in the dhikr at all. Rows of men all faced the direction of Mecca, while the singers faced them. The singer would sing a single line, and the men responded by bowing together and clearly pronouncing, with great gravity, "Allah!" The dhikr was very structured and organized, not without emotion—one man occasionally shivered—but very controlled. There were none of the bizarre characters typically seen at the dhikrs in moulids. When Shaykh ʿIzz began to clap his hands, as he often does when his spirit is aroused in dhikr, a man monitoring the dhikr at the door stopped him. The dhikr was marked by a calm, engrossed reverence unlike the ecstasies typically seen at public dhikrs.

While some Orders, such as the Naqshbandīs and Khalwatīs, are relatively restrained in their dhikr and aim to attract the cultural elite by the propriety of their activities, the dhikrs of Orders more popular with the lower classes—the Rifāʿiyya, Burhāmiyya, Aḥmadiyya, and Bayyūmiyya, for example—are often marked by what Biegman calls "violent dancing." Among the Rifāʿīs, as the intensity of dhikr reaches its climax, the participants make a "rather frightening barking," which one Rifāʿī shaykh described to him "as an unarticulated mentioning of God, coming straight from the heart." The articulation of the Name, he explained, distracts the heart from its objective, which is God Himself.[48]

The Controversy over Dhikr

Dhikr assemblies have been the target of much scorn and criticism from non-Sufis, who see the movements of the participants as meaningless and ridiculous. Failing to appreciate the spiritual reality behind the movements, they have nothing but contempt for this bowing of heads and bodies and trance-like states. They cannot understand what benefit may be derived from constant repetition of a single word or phrase, and they criticize dhikr participants for mispronouncing the divine Names, or uttering what sound like mere grunts. They see dhikr as pandering to the basest emotional instincts of the masses, epitomizing the folly of the ignorant. They decry dhikr as a waste of time spent in introspection, time that would be better spent in useful work. It is as if dhikr were responsible for the lack of economic progress and productivity of the nation as a whole. Gilsenan appears to endorse this perspective when he describes dhikr as a narcotic for the deprived, "a quasi-institutionalized channel for frenzy."[49]

Sufi shaykhs are well aware of these criticisms and are sensitive to the possibility of creating a spectacle that would bring contempt upon the Sufis. They often distinguish between "real dhikr" and the simple "bobbing of heads" *(tafqīr)*. Aḥmad Raḍwān said, "These days we see people shouting out in dhikr, and some fall to the ground as though demented. This is a deficiency. Raising the voice is not right. God is with them wherever they are, and whoever is with God should not raise his voice. Proper dhikr is done in sincere devotion to God, observing perfect etiquette with him."[50]

Shaykh Abū 'l-ʿAzāʾim says that one of the purposes of doing dhikr in public is to spread the Sufi message by presenting a good example. This is the reason for his repeated instructions regarding removing ecstatic individuals from group dhikr or altering the method of dhikr to mitigate the ecstatic effects of the recitation of a particular Name. He likewise stresses that all potentially repulsive behaviors should be avoided, such as cursing, inappropriate movements, rivalry between dhikr participants, distorting the pronunciation of the Names, or expressing veneration for the shaykh.[51]

Gilsenan comments, "The members of every Order whose hadras I have attended constantly pointed out how superior their dhikr is to that of other groups. The latter are represented as somehow degraded, or worthy but misguided, or positively unorthodox, whether in fact they are or are not."[52] Although I have heard such criticisms leveled vaguely at popular public dhikrs at saints' shrines and moulids, I have seldom heard specific groups targeted with such judgments. Although Sufi groups all tend, somewhat naturally, to regard themselves as superior to all other contenders, this seldom translates into judgment of other groups, unless I specifically asked for comments in this regard. Most Sufis dismissed the criticism of outsiders who could not possibly understand the inner states of dhikr participants. When I mentioned to Shaykh Saᶜīd al-Daḥḥ of the Idrīsiyya Aḥmadiyya that some people appear to join in the movements of the dhikr without any apparent recitation of the Names, he was shocked by the suggestion and said, "Never! They do dhikr, but in the heart. If a person merely moves and doesn't do dhikr, that isn't true dhikr. The superficial person looks at the outer person, but God looks at what is inside, at the heart. The Sufi doesn't judge by appearances, but looks at what is inside. Some people look strange while they do dhikr, but the Sufi doesn't look at such things at all."

If the Sufi can observe the inner state of a person, on the other hand, he may be in a place to judge. Shaykh ᶜIzz claimed to have this ability, and I occasionally asked him his assessment of various individuals. In most cases, his observations simply confirmed my own impressions—a sign, in his opinion, that I also possessed the potential to develop this gift. On one occasion, while Shaykh ᶜIzz and I were observing a dhikr that appeared to be more play than devotion, I asked him whether he thought any of the people were truly "in the spirit." He replied that only one woman in the entire gathering was sincerely absorbed in God—all the others, he said, were absorbed in their own selves. Later he also commented on the words of the singers—it was all *ghazal,* he said, a word for love poetry that implies a certain amount of playfulness, not the kind of love fostered by true mysticism. But while he occasionally reserved a word of admiration for the dhikr of particular groups, either for their sober observance of Islamic Law or for the veracity of their spirit, he seldom criticized entire groups for their behavior. Likewise, I asked Shaykh Gābir al-Jāzūlī whether he considered the movements of other Orders to be *bidᶜa,* literally an "innovation," with the implication that it was an improper modification of the prophetic model. I asked him this because his Order performed dhikr seated, thereby preventing some of the more extravagant as well as the more frivolous movements witnessed in other dhikrs. Since his Order catered to the upper middle class and presented itself as Shariᶜa-abiding, I assumed that he frowned on the dhikrs of other Orders. To my surprise, he replied that he simply wanted to do something different, so people would not say they were merely imitating others, and anyway, "there is no such thing as *bidʿa*."

Some groups, like the Demirdāshiyya Khalwatiyya and the Muḥammadiyya Shādhiliyya, employ dhikrs designed to appeal to the sensibilities of intellectuals and reformists. They avoid music and emotionalism and insist on uniformity and sobriety in their dhikr. The Supreme Council of Sufi Orders officially bans the use of musical instruments, except percussion, in order to avoid attracting censure, although this ban is not enforced. On the other hand, Shaykh Gābir al-Jāzūlī employs the lute *(ʿūd)* in his dhikr, an instrument that is used in Egyptian popular songs but hardly ever in dhikr.[53] The result is a dhikr with a popularizing rhythm and melodic structure different from others. The goal in performing such a distinctive dhikr is to attract the youth—for whereas Sufism's critics see dhikr as an impediment to productive activity, the Sufis see it rather an alternative for other forms of entertainment, such as sitting in a cafe smoking and playing backgammon or going to the movies or nightclubs. Whereas these latter have no spiritual benefit, and indeed might be spiritually harmful, the spiritual benefit of dhikr is undeniable.

Psychological States in Dhikr

Dhū 'l-Nūn al-Miṣrī, one of the earliest Egyptian Sufis, said dhikr is absence from oneself [by recollecting God alone].[54] Shaykh Abū 'l-ʿAzā'im wrote, "A person immersed in the remembrance of God forgets everything else. To remember something else is a form of polytheism."[55]

For some, the ideal recollection of God is one that absorbs them so much that they become unaware of their own selves or their surroundings. This absence from one's self because of one's presence with God is called "intoxication," and early Sufis discussed at length the relative merits of intoxication and sobriety. Shaykh Abū 'l-ʿAzā'im says that thinking about the essence of God's unity and His attributes of perfection, greatness, and majesty is "a shoreless sea," and the only way to avoid drowning in it is clinging to the Rope of God (the Qur'an) and exoteric knowledge. The disciple should limit his dhikr to what his shaykh has assigned him, and if he sees anything during his dhikr that contradicts the Qur'an or Sunna or what his shaykh has told him, "the disciple must set himself against what he has seen and think poorly of himself, because it might come from

Figure 8. Men in ecstasy in dhikr on 30 June 1988. Shaykh ʿIzz raises his shawl in his hands.

the ruminations of the soul or the whisperings of Satan *(al-Khannās)*, who whispers into the breasts of people."[56] Adherence to the externals of the revealed message and the Law is often cited as a necessity to avoid being deceived by the lights of one's own mystical experience. The guidance of a shaykh is also necessary, for "he who has no shaykh, has Satan as his shaykh."

Shaykh Gamāl al-Sanhūrī of the Burhāniyya stressed the importance of receiving permission to do dhikr from a shaykh who will supervise the spiritual development of the disciple and protect the disciple from receiving too overwhelming a spiritual light at first. Otherwise, he said, a person can go mad from reciting the name of Allah. The disciple must be brought gradually into dhikr by repeated recitation of the phrase, "I seek forgiveness from God the Great," in order to cleanse himself and ready himself to receive the light of dhikr. The first dhikr of the disciple should not be "Allah," which is the core of dhikr and the source of all light but should be "there is no god but Allah." In this sentence, the negation occurs before the affirmation, allowing him gradually into the light of God.[57]

Shaykh Abū 'l-ʿAzāʾim wrote that through dhikr God illumines the heart and grants it a spiritual state from His presence. The person may be so overwhelmed that he speaks of the marvels he has witnessed. Such a person should be secluded from the assembly of disciples, and if anyone repeats something said by such a person, he "has betrayed the trust of his brother."[58]

The repetition of the divine Names is natural for the person who loves God, wrote Abū Ḥāmid al-Ghazālī (d. 1111), for "when a man loves a thing, he repeatedly mentions it." Although numerous repetitions in dhikr might be difficult for the novice, the result is intimacy and love for God. This increase in love removes the burden from the repetition, which becomes so innate that "it becomes impossible to endure without invocation (dhikr)."[59] Shaykh Abū 'l-ʿAzāʾim echoes this sentiment and adds, "Dhikr requires love, which requires desire, which requires dhikr, and so on." In dhikr, divine proofs are revealed to the disciple, and "he attains joy, intimacy and peace, after the burning of desire and agitation of amorous rapture."[60]

Dhikr indeed often includes an experience of intense pleasure. One Sufi writes, "Some Sufis say nothing in the world resembles the blessings of Paradise except for the sweetness experienced in the hearts by those doing dhikr at night."[61] The Qurʾan itself says that hearts find serenity in the remembrance of God (13:28), and many say that this is the primary benefit they derive from dhikr.

Yet I have also seen people cry out in dhikr in an ecstasy that borders on pain, calling on the Prophet or one of the great saints. ʿIzz likened the pain experienced by some people in dhikr to the pain experienced when a doctor changes and cleans a wound: it is necessary in order to peel away or extract the evil that is in the soul. Some people demonstrate aggressive behavior, which is said to result from the influences of evil spirits, who manifest themselves in dhikr when the senses are stilled and the person yields to spiritual influences. Thus the Sufis distinguish between demonic and divine manifestation during dhikr. A person with a demon may cry out when confronted with the Divine Presence during dhikr, just as the demons in the New Testament cried out when confronted with Jesus or Paul. Such a person is usually quieted through immediate prayer by the person in charge. But the person under divine influences may also do strange things. Concentrated meditation can produce a heat in people so that, like the Prophet when he received revelation, they perspire, even on a cold day. Rarely, people may even remove their clothes in dhikr. People doing dhikr appear to have very taut nerves, and fairly ordinary events, like a temporary blackout, prompt loud cries from the dhikr participants. I once observed an exploding light bulb in a moulid tent cause sheer frenzy among those absorbed in dhikr. On another occasion a man fell unconscious during dhikr, but no one seemed particularly concerned. They rearranged him so he would not get in the way of the others, and he lay unconscious on the ground for at least two hours. Shaykh Abū 'l-ʿAzāʾim wrote that the person who has achieved presence with God in dhikr "sees the lights of God in everything—indeed, he perceives the spiritual realities of the Holy with all his senses, as if they were manifest to his innermost being *(sirr)*."[62]

Although the ideal may be intense concentration in a dhikr that has a logical progression from beginning to end, in fact people join in public dhikrs at any time and stop whenever they like. Interrupted *ṣalāt* (ritual prayer) is invalid, but this does not apply to dhikr; to the extent that people have remembered God, they receive a reward. People may interrupt their dhikr to greet others, and although participants in dhikr are generally left alone, it is not always considered inappropriate to interrupt them.

LOVE

The subject of love deserves separate consideration because of its importance in Sufism, yet writing a separate section on love is almost impossible, so intimately is it connected with other aspects of Sufi life. The redemptive qualities of love for the Prophet and his family, the deep love that exists in the shaykh-disciple relationship, and dhikr as a function of love for God have all already been cited. It is almost impossible to discuss any aspect of Sufi experience without reference to love. Shaykh ʿAbd al-Ḥamid al-ʿAryān, head of the Sufi Council in Abū Tīj, Asyūṭ, said, "The essence of Sufism is love."[63] Shaykh ʿIzz said, "Love is the foundation of all [spiritual] things."

The prolific Islamic writer of the 1970s ʿAbd al-Razzāq Nawfal wrote in his book on Sufism, "The goal of Sufism is the love *(maḥabba)* of God, its Way is love, and its method is love. When the traveler on the Way begins to get to know God, so that the gates of knowing Him open up to him, he finds that the love of God pours out on him. The more he travels in the Way, the greater his love increases, and it leads him to love (*ḥubb*). Love pushes him in the Way. He remains from love, in love, to love."[64]

Love for God

Love for God is a characteristic of believers, according to the Qurʾan, a response to God's own love for them (5:54). The Qurʾan demands that believers love God and His Messenger more than their families or wealth (9:24). But if ordinary Muslims love God in the sense of obedience to Him, out of obligation and fear, the Sufi is the one who desires God for His own sake. Sufi tradition credits Rābiʿa al-ʿAdawiyya (d. 801) with the idea of selfless love for God, and her poems speak of an intimate relationship with her Lord, not unlike that of other lovers: "Oh my Lord, the stars are shining and the eyes of men are closed, and kings have shut their doors, and every lover is alone with his beloved, and here am I alone with You."[65]

Whether or not Rābiʿa was the first to speak of her relationship with God in this manner, she was certainly not the last. Sufis said the saints of God were brides, veiled from ordinary people but taken into God's presence, where they enjoy the sweetness of intimate conversations, a pleasure that equals or exceeds anything the saints hope for in Paradise. The concept of God as Beloved became standard in Sufism, yet the commonality of this theme does not necessarily make it any less sincere. Junayd (d. 910), the great Sufi theoretician famous for his advocacy of "sober" Sufism, said, "When I entered the Way of love that the Folk [that is, the Sufis] travel, I tasted a spiritual state in which I could not comprehend how anyone could ever worship God out of desire for reward or fear of punishment."[66] A popular booklet about Ibrāhīm al-Dasūqī (d. 1297), spiritual preceptor of the Burhāmiyya Order, quotes some of his lines of poetry describing the secret, intimate life of the lover of God:

> I have placed you as an intimate friend in my heart,
> And have granted my body to whoever wants to sit with me.
> For my body has assemblies for the Beloved,
> And the Beloved of my heart is sitting with me in my heart.[67]

Shaykh ʿIzz quoted similar lines of poetry to indicate the untouchability of his secret life with God, which remained unaffected by the presence of people.

The Qurʾan uses the verb *aḥabba* to describe God's love for believers and their love for Him, and the most typical noun used by pious Muslims to speak of love for God is *maḥabba,* a word that conveys altruism and affection and carries no sexual connotation. The related word, *ḥubb,* is the word that is typically used in romantic contexts, although its application to the relationship of God and the believers is not terribly shocking. *ʿIshq* is a word that connotes passionate love of a usually sexual nature, and its application to God appeared scandalous when Abū 'l-Ḥusayn al-Nūrī (d. 907) first called himself *ʿāshiq Allāh,* a lover of God; Nūrī was charged with heresy. Three hundred years after Nūrī's trial the controversy was still fresh enough for the Ḥanbalī scholar Ibn al-Jawzī to write a condemnation of both his use of the word and his claim that God loved him. God would only love Nūrī if he were destined to be saved, he argued, whereas no one can know if he is saved.[68] Even some Sufis felt that the word *ʿishq* was inappropriately applied to God. Qushayrī's teacher, Abū ʿAlī al-Daqqāq, said that *ʿishq* is an extravagant love that goes beyond proper bounds, which is impossible with God, for love for Him has no proper bounds it may exceed.[69]

Today's Sufis, however, freely use the word *ʿishq* in the sense of intense love, and they consider *ʿāshiq Allāh* a sobriquet of great honor. After all, there is a *ḥadīth qudsi* in which God says, "Whoever knows Me loves Me *(aḥabbanī),* and whoever loves Me loves Me passionately *(ʿashiqanī),* and whoever loves Me passionately seeks Me." From this Aḥmad Raḍwān concludes that the first stage in the path to God is love *(ḥubb),* followed by *ʿishq,* which is strong love, and then seeking, which is the stage of striving for the rank of divine servant. "Longing *(shawq)* possesses him, and he ardently desires the manifestation of God's light."[70] Longing, he says, is the first stage of faith in God. At the end of the path, when the lover attains the realization of certitude, desire is fulfilled and there can be no more longing.[71]

A contemporary Sufi author wrote, "Love and praise are the two ladders on which the believers ascend toward the perfection of worship. Love carries him to obey and try to please his Beloved and avoid His anger, and praise reveals to him the ways in which God demonstrates His goodness, until he feels that he cannot thank him enough for them or count them." This same author writes that real love empties the heart of everything but God; preoccupation with people is especially harmful, "a sign of spiritual bankruptcy."[72] A common metaphor for the experience of divine love in Sufism is drinking wine with its resultant intoxication. Intoxication has been mentioned as a consequence of dhikr, particularly in its communal setting, but it is, in Sufi writings, the result of the experience of God's love. Although Sufis love God for His sake alone, not out of fear of hell, the fear of God remains a legitimate state, though it should be balanced by hope. Aḥmad Raḍwān said, "Fear and love almost kill the people of the presence of God when they recall His majesty." He cautions those who are too sure of their spiritual standing that "the people of God are characterized by humility and lowly behavior among the believers," and pride is a fatal flaw.[73]

Nonetheless, Shaykh ʿIzz described love as higher than humility, because love implies intimacy, whereas humility implies distance. Comparing the posture of some Egyptian Protestant Christians in prayer to the attitude of the Sufi in dhikr, Shaykh ʿIzz commented that the Protestant position (sitting bent forward, head down, hands clasped in front) represents humility, whereas the Sufi in dhikr takes on attitudes and postures that express love. A polite, deferential conversation is dry and lacks intimacy, he said, but love "removes obligation. A person may dance or sway as long as his intention is in God. Therefore some of the people say Sufism is wrong. Because of this. Because they don't understand it. They are rigid adherents of the religion, and they are excused because their intention is good. That is their (spiritual) level. But when a person delves deep into the essence of Islam, and his heart is carried to the light of God, and the spirit is preoccupied with the recollection of God, it turns eyes away from deficiencies, the ear hears nothing deficient, and the tongue says nothing wrong. In that spiritual station, all his movements are purely for God. If the spirits long to meet with God, they dance. If the sparrow who is in fetters is put into a tree, it dances in its fetters, longing to return to the tree where it was singing. So he sings, although he is in bonds. Likewise the spirits of the lovers (of God)."

ʿIzz emphasizes that any movement in the spirit is permissible, provided it is truly an unconscious movement in the spirit. When I asked about a woman who was shrieking in dhikr, ʿIzz affirmed that it was permissible if done in the spirit, despite the general objection to women raising their voices. "But if the mind is involved in what is happening among the participants in dhikr, then it is just pretense or acting." Intoxication or unconscious actions in dhikr are not seen as a result of artificial methods of inducing trance but as the result of intense love and the movement of the spirit in dhikr—a movement that may certainly be stirred by music, the song of the *munshid*, or the communal setting, or all of these in concert, but none of these alone or together is sufficient to produce a genuine movement of the spirit without love.

The relationship of love to unconventional behavior and apparently blasphemous utterances has a long history in Sufism, and this connection continues to exist, prompting authors to explain these phenomena to the uninitiated. Nawfal writes, "When the lover drinks from the cup of love, which his Beloved has been pleased to give him, he awakens to a condition that makes him live differently than before, in a reality that is different from his physical form. He lives in firm blessing and sound awareness and profundity. When the wayfarer enters the circle of God's love, he gives him moments in which his mind is caught up with God *(jadhabāt)* from the attraction of love, and moments of intoxication. He may speak words intended to express what he sees, and words come out that will make the one who hears them imagine that there is a union *(ittiḥād)* between the lover and the Beloved, or an inherence *(ḥulūl)* of the Beloved in the lover. These are called 'rovings' *(shaṭaḥāt)*."[74]

The priority of love is a favorite theme of Sufi songs and poetry. A line of one of Yāsīn al-Tuhāmī's songs says, "Jesus is your brother, Muhammad. Moses is your brother, Muhammad. . . . Love is the only religious obligation *(farḍ)*." This line has frequently been quoted to me by Sufis I interviewed as evidence that the basis of all true religion is love, and it is precisely at this point that the distinctions between the lovers of God in Islam, Christianity, and Judaism break down. They quickly add that this does not mean that Sufis do not perform the religious obligations of prayer, fasting, and the pilgrimage—indeed, they excel in supererogatory prayers as well. The mark of love for God and His Messenger is obedience. What the song is expressing is that all things must be done in love, out of love for God. The true lover of God will do more than what is required, whereas the prayer of the one who lacks love is not a true prayer at all. Likewise, the one who is happy—that is, destined for Paradise—is the one who is loved by God. Good works do not benefit a person if he is not loved by God. A contemporary author wrote that by loving God, one is in turn loved by Him, and receives divine favor and guidance. "The lover lives at peace with himself and with a clear and spiritual conscience in all circumstances." On the other hand, "The one who loses this love is miserable, removed (from God) and veiled from the truth."[75]

Love in God

The Sufi whose heart is filled with love for God is able to see God's love for all of His creation. Such a person is able to love other creatures "in God," through his love for God. Love, said Shaykh ʿIzz, is indivisible; one cannot love a person and hate what that person loves. Love for those whom God loves is a natural outgrowth of love for God. Ghazālī wrote in his *Revival of the Religious Sciences* that when love for God becomes strong, it overwhelms the heart and overflows to every existent, since every existent contains a trace of His power. Therefore, when Muhammad was brought early fruit, he rubbed his eyes with it and honored it and said, "It has recently come from its Lord" *(qarībat ʿahd bi rabbihā).*[76]

The foremost quality of love is mercy, that quality of God that, according to the Qurʾan, encompasses all things (7:156). Ḥadīths abound urging the believers to love each other and be merciful. Of the many that could be quoted, only a few will be mentioned by way of example.

"God has no mercy for those who have no mercy on people."

"The one who serves the widow and the destitute is like the one who serves in the path of God, and gets an even greater reward."

"By the One in whose hand is my soul, none of you believes until he loves his brother as he loves himself."[77]

Sufis have often felt that love for people, especially family, was a distraction from love for God. Early Sufis often shunned the company of people and preferred celibacy. Such an attitude scarcely exists in Egypt today. Sufis extol the virtues of love in all its forms and see their love for people as a function of their love for God. Yet they readily admit that for the less spiritual man attachment to wife and children is a distraction from God, and for this reason the Qurʾan says, "Your wealth and your children are a temptation for you" (64:15).

The foundation of all love, then, is love for God. After God, love belongs first of all to the Prophet, then to the *ahl al-bayt*, and then to the saints of God, particularly the spiritual guide. Such love has, as has been explained in chapters 3 and 5, a soteriological quality, for "a man is [gathered on the Day of Resurrection] with the one he has loved," according to an oft-quoted ḥadīth. This would appear to open the possibility of entering Paradise to many who would otherwise be ineligible. In one conversation, Shaykh ʿIzz hinted that eventually everyone would enter Paradise by the gate of love. Echoing the line from Yāsīn's song describing love as the only religious obligation, ʿIzz said, "In love there is no imposition *(taklifa).* Those who come to God through love know no blame, judgment or punishment."

A contemporary author writes, "Love in God is one of the highest ways of coming to Him. The one in this rank enters Paradise with the one he loves, even if he does not equal him in deeds. This is because every good deed may be seen except those of the heart. The step of the limbs is one parasang, and the step of the heart is one thousand parasangs."[78] Numerous ḥadīths indicate that love is more efficacious for salvation in the afterlife than prayer, fasting, or charity.[79] Yet, although Sufis may sing that love for the *ahl al-bayt* is the best form of worship, they deny that this implies neglect of religious duties, any more than love for God does. On the contrary, if you love someone you will strive to be like them, and the *ahl al-bayt* excelled in their performance of acts of worship.

The basis of love, like the basis of the shaykh-disciple relationship, is the meeting of the spirits on the day when God gathered them together to ask them, "Am I not your Lord?" (Qurʾan 7:172). In communal dhikr Sufis feel that they recapture some of that sense of joining their spirits in the common affirmation of God's lordship. As one modern Sufi author puts it, "Those who do much dhikr draw each other by virtue of the resemblance between them and the meeting of their spirits on the plain of His love. Each one loves for his brother what he loves for his own soul, and he hates for him what he hates for his own soul. They wish good for all believers, and do not despise any one of them for a sin or act of heedlessness."[80] He illustrates the impact of genuine love on the spiritual experience of those in dhikr by recalling the funeral of Shaykh Muḥammad Abū Khalīl in Zaqāzīq after he died on 29 June 1930. In the funerary tent his disciples performed dhikr, and the *munshid,* ʿAlī ʿAql, was inspired to sing:

> By God, by Almighty God, the third, the shaykh is here
> He hears what you hear and sees what you see.

The author writes that the disciples engaged in dhikr went into rapture and "nearly flew into the air if that were possible," because of the strength of their connection with the strong spirit of the shaykh and the depth of their divine love for him.[81]

These, then, are the foundations of the Sufi path: love for God and in God, the recollection of God, and the stages through which the mystic will pass. Closely associated with this path are many other mystical concepts and practices that will be examined in the next chapter.

CHAPTER 7

Mystical Concepts and Practices in Egyptian Sufism

ASCETICISM (ZUHD) AND THE STRUGGLE OF THE SOUL (JIHĀD)

After the initial confession of sin and repentance from all deeds that would compromise the journey to God, the Sufi's major preoccupation is with crushing his passions, fighting, as the Sufis say, against his own soul. According to ḥadīth, the Prophet said, "We have returned from the lesser jihād [warfare] to the greater jihād." This "greater jihād" is the struggle to purify the soul of all forms of evil and negligence, for, in the words of one modern Sufi, "it is the soul that veils us from the vision of the truth and incites us to acts of disobedience and attachment to lusts and material things. By such things we become heavy and cannot enter the world of the spirit to see the beauty and light of the Truth."[1] Sufis believe that the spirit's origin is divine and by its very nature yearns to return to its heavenly home; but the soul is of earthly origin and pulls the spirit back to earth.

A time-honored method of taming the soul is to resist its desires through fasting and other forms of asceticism. Sufism in the earliest phase of its historical development was *zuhd*—asceticism and withdrawal from the world. The early Sufis performed almost incredible feats of self-denial, shunning all forms of luxury, eating only what was absolutely necessary to keep alive, and spending their nights in devotion rather than sleep. (Shaykh ʿIzz expressed his admiration for this attitude with his frequent comment, "If sleep had anything to commend it, there would be sleep in Paradise.") Ḥasan al-Baṣrī (d. 728), one of the most famous of the stern early ascetics, likened the world to a snake, "smooth to the touch, but its venom is deadly."[2] Another famous representative of early Sufism, Ibrāhīm ibn Adham (d. 776 or 790), said that one must embrace hardship, self-abasement, strenuous effort, sleeplessness, and poverty, ever anticipating death and judgment, in order to attain righteousness.[3]

Early Sufis embraced poverty to such an extent that "the poor man" (*faqīr* in Arabic, *darwīsh* in Persian) became synonymous with the Sufi, and the term remains in use today. When Abū Yazīd al-Bisṭāmī (d. 874), famous for traveling the heights of mystical knowledge, was asked how he had reached such heights, he replied, "With a hungry stomach and a naked body."[4] Abū Ḥāmid al-Ghazālī (d. 1111) insisted that the way to travel on the path to God is through fasting, night vigils, sleeplessness, and renunciation of wealth.[5] The word "Sufi" is derived from the Arabic word for wool, because the mark of the early Sufis was a coarse woolen cloak, a symbol of poverty and renunciation. For centuries a Sufi shaykh invested his disciple with authority to train disciples by giving him a patched woolen frock.

Any equation of Sufism with asceticism today is likely to prompt cynical laughter from anyone acquainted with the social reality of today's Sufis. Today the majority of Sufis work, and although Sufism continues to draw primarily from the lower classes, many Sufis have prominent positions in society and are quite wealthy. The Shādhiliyya, an Order that is well represented in Egypt, was originally a middle-class Order that departed from earlier tradition by encouraging its followers to work for a living and dress well rather than (at times hypocritically) advertising their poverty. Shādhilī interpreted poverty in a spiritual sense, allowing a person to be "poor toward God," that is, recognizing his need of God, without renunciation of all material things. Many contemporary Egyptian Orders follow this same philosophy. As Nawfal wrote, "This world is an opportunity for worship. . . . The Sufi works only that he may worship in everything he does, including working for a living."[6] Another Sufi emphasizes that renunciation of the world occurs in the heart, not "with the hand" and that physical renunciation of the world is useless if love for the things of the world remains in the heart.[7]

Sufis who dress in colorful rags, shun regular employment, and live off the charity of others may still be seen at moulid celebrations, but their lifestyle is not highly regarded even in most Sufi circles. They epitomize the "dervishism" that many Sufis feel has given Sufism a bad name with today's educated middle class. Many Sufi shaykhs, however, neither live off the charity of others nor work for a living. As Aḥmad Raḍwān said, "Some people have cut off all means of subsistence, and their Lord has been their guarantor and has not left them to anyone else. I am among these."[8] His words hearken back to the spirit of early Sufism when, commenting on the

Qurʾanic injunction to "flee to God" (51:50), he told his followers, "Fleeing to God is by having nothing to do with others and avoiding attachments to anything in this world and the next, for such an attachment halts a servant in his progress toward God. If a servant detaches from all that, God enables him to control his body, his limbs and his thoughts. . . . If a servant is in the state of togetherness with God, why should he think of anything else?"[9]

Rather than embracing hunger, Sufis today make the serving of food so central to their celebrations that Shaykh ʿIzz once joked as we observed people rush for the food served at a *khidma*, "The essence of Sufism is food." Today's Sufis rarely engage in rigorous renunciation of the world. Rather than grieving over their sins and denying themselves all pleasures, Sufis today appear to delight in the assurance of their relationship with God and enjoy this relationship while functioning quite normally in the world.

Nonetheless, Sufis insist that self-denial and crushing the passions are an integral part of the Sufi path, even today. Few may engage in a lifestyle of continuous fasting, as Shaykh Muḥammad al-Ṭayyib (d. 1988) did, taking no more than a few tablespoons of milk a day to survive, but nearly all Sufis undertake fasts that go beyond those required by Islam. Few may enter into total seclusion, as Shaykh Mūsā Abū ʿAlī (d. 1988) did, but many pursue periods of seclusion *(khalwa)* in order to devote themselves to God. As Shaykh ʿAbd al-Ḥalīm Maḥmūd (d. 1978) wrote, "In order to give strength to his repentance and confirm the sincerity of his devotion to God, the disciple should be alone with his Lord for a time spent in dhikr, self-examination, repentance and asking forgiveness. The fruit of isolation is the revelation of hidden defects, the descent of God's mercy and the attainment of love, and a tongue of truthfulness."[10]

All serious Sufis continue to regard some practices of renunciation and mild asceticism as necessary tools for the refinement of the soul. Sufi writers devote extensive space to the tools for crushing the passions and struggling against the evil in the soul.[11] The tools that are emphasized today are not fasting and other austerities but submission to the spiritual guidance of a shaykh, immersing oneself in reading the Qurʾan and Ḥadīth, devotion to dhikr, and avoiding evil companions and occasions of temptation. The Ḥāmidiyya Shādhiliyya insist that seclusion should be "of the heart, not the body." Law number 249 of their charter says, "Much fasting and hunger and much sleeplessness and dhikr will lead to dullness of the brain and will create mental illness or disturbance in mind. Or he [the student] will come by chance upon a *shaitan* (demon) in his seclusion who will harm him so that he will speak that which has no meaning. Or the devil will set forth something to him and some of the people will think that he has become a Saint of God. Or light may by chance upon him, or he will see an angel or a *wali* and he will not be able to bear what he sees and he will go out of his mind."[12]

Shaykh ʿIzz corroborated this perspective: "The Shadhiliyya consider themselves in continuous seclusion." Entering into actual physical seclusion from other people is reserved, in this Order, for a shaykh. ʿIzz insisted that his heart was constantly preoccupied with God. "He whose companionship with God is in seclusion loses it when he leaves it. He whose companionship is with God all the time has no need to enter seclusion." Nonetheless, he built a room for himself to enter into seclusion. When I pressed him concerning the apparent contradiction between his words and his actions, he said he longed for seclusion "not to be alone with God, but to get away from people."

"Why?" I asked. "If you are alone with God all the time, why get away from people?"

"Because people are an obstruction," he conceded. They keep me from attaining great heights *(sumūw)* with God. It's as if a person is high in the seven heavens and someone on earth says, 'Come down from your high place to speak to me.' He has to speak to him on his level. He has to come down to talk to him on his level. I have to leave people to free myself for spiritual elevation."

Shaykh Aḥmad al-Sharqāwī of Najʿ Ḥammādī, who belongs to the Khalwatiyya, an Order with a long tradition of using seclusion as a means of spiritual training, said, "Seclusion is helpful to understand the correct meanings of the guidance of the shaykh. It is also helpful to suppress evil impulses by distancing oneself from their sources." When I asked whether the practice of seclusion held dangers for the novice, he replied, "For some people, who are insufficiently guided by their shaykh, who should know whether they have sufficient spiritual strength for seclusion. They could suffer. Likewise with *awrād*. A good shaykh who is qualified to guide disciples must know very well the spiritual strength of every disciple, and only give him the dosage he can endure." Not all disciples enter seclusion, he said, but "only those who really want to become spiritually refined. There are people who are too lazy." He added, with characteristic cynicism, "Some might enter seclusion just so people will think they are shaykhs."[13]

Though the world as a whole may not be avoided, its evils and frivolities should be. Sufi shaykhs today rarely discipline their disciples for infractions, restricting themselves to admonition. But the strictness of early Muslims is lauded. For example, Aḥmad Raḍwān encouraged his followers to take sin as seriously as the Caliph ʿUmar did when he flogged his son for drunkenness so severely that he died. ʿUmar commented, "It is better to me that he die fulfilling God's punishment than that he meet God with sin." One of the Prophet's Companions later saw ʿUmar's son tell him in a dream, "Were it not for the punishment carried out against me, I would not have attained this rank."[14]

THE ANNIHILATION OF THE EGO (FANĀʾ)

The Sufi is led on through the process of self-purification to yet deeper forms of self-denial until, to use Sufi terminology, he has killed his soul and become annihilated in God. It is at this stage that the Sufi can become flooded with light and receive revelations of the truth. Direct vision of the truth on a constant basis, the constant abiding in God, is achieved by the very few, but even the average Sufi can, to the extent that he has purified his heart, receive ever more light. All of this must be pursued for no goal other than God, the Beloved, without self-interest. The *via negativa* is the only way to the *via positiva*. Detachment from this world proceeds to the annihilation of the ego.

Shaykh Aḥmad Raḍwān was fond of reminding his followers that the Prophet told the Muslims to "die before you die." This death is the death of the soul, or more specifically its desires. The soul is distinct from the spirit; it is the lower self. The soul that must be killed is the one that the Qurʾan describes as inciting people to commit evil (12:53). Just as St. Paul urged the Christians to "crucify the desires of the flesh" (Galatians 5:24), Sufis are urged to kill their own souls or egos. This implies not only suppressing fleshly passions but eliminating all regard for one's self. Sufis recognize that any good deeds they have done are not their deeds but have been done by God in them. They have been annihilated or passed away from their own experience—they have achieved *fanāʾ*.

Fanāʾ is a concept that is much discussed in classical Sufism. Traditionally *fanāʾ* was associated with spiritual intoxication, with the spirit's absence from this world because of its presence with God. The validity of such a spiritual state is indicated in the life of Muhammad himself, who on one occasion failed to recognize his wife ʿĀʾisha or know the names of her father, Abū Bakr, or even his own identity.[15] Nonetheless, al-Junayd (d. 910), the great Sufi theoretician, emphasized that the Sufi's final goal should not be *fanā*ʾ or annihilation, but *baqā*ʾ or abiding in God, one's own attributes transformed to reflect the divine; after the intoxication of mystical union, the mature Sufi returns to the sober state, though transformed by the experience. Qushayrī (d. 1072) described both concepts in an ethical sense: *fanā*ʾ is the annihilation of blameworthy characteristics, and *baqā*ʾ is the establishment of praiseworthy characteristics. The one naturally entails the other. Those who abandon blameworthy deeds have died to their passions, and those who renounce the luxuries of this world have passed away from their desires.[16] *Fanā*ʾ as a concept is much more discussed than *baqā*ʾ, and today little attention is paid to the latter. I believe this reflects not only the priority of *fanā*ʾ but also the permutations that the concept of *fanā*ʾ has undergone in recent centuries.

Aḥmad Raḍwān said, "There is absolutely no way to enter God's presence except through *fanā*ʾ, for the servant does not arrive at his Lord as long as he has existence." This does not mean that the ideal path is that of the Sufi martyr al-Ḥallāj (d. 922), a literal annihilation of one's existence, for, as Raḍwān explains, "the meaning of existence here is the existence of pleasures and desires for other than God in the heart. For God has stipulated that He will not enter a heart that something else has entered, and He does not manifest Himself to an eye that sees anything other than Him in the mirror." In *fanā*ʾ God manifests Himself to the Sufi, who "attains the realization of His attributes and Names," which are established in the spirit. "If a servant dies in the path of God, he remains in God, and by God, and becomes an *imām* calling people to God in God."[17]

This is perfectly consistent with Sufi tradition. Ghazālī wrote, "The purity which is the first condition of the mystic way is the purification of the heart completely from what is other than God most high; the key to it, which corresponds to the opening act of adoration in prayer, is the sinking of the heart completely in the recollection of God (dhikr); and the end of it is complete absorption (*fanā*ʾ) in God."[18]

This seeing of none other than God in the mirror has been controversial in Islam, a religion that so strongly emphasizes the transcendence of God. In the experience of *fanā*ʾ mystics like Bisṭāmī uttered apparent blasphemies indicating his union with God—sayings like "Glory be to me! How great is my majesty," "I am the Throne (of God) and the Footstool," and "I saw the Kaʿba [the shrine in Mecca around which the pilgrims circumambulate] walking around me."[19] The experience of union with God is sometimes described as an identification of oneself with the divine, or even a discovery of oneself on the Throne of God. Yet, ultimately, Bisṭāmī saw it all as illusion—"a cheat," to use Schimmel's translation.[20] Ḥallāj also spoke of the "ruse" used by God to make them imagine that they could attain union with Him. Yet the absorption of his ego into God prompted him to utter his famous "I am the True Reality" ("*Anā 'l-Ḥaqq*"), an apparent claim of divinity, for which he was executed.

No modern Sufi would dare to say such things, certainly not publicly, and especially not in Egypt, where Sufism is on the defensive against charges of insufficient orthodoxy. Aḥmad Raḍwān appears to corroborate the verdict of some Sufis in the classical period, who felt that the explicit statements of Bisṭāmī and Ḥallāj were signs of having not quite arrived: the servant who has truly entered the presence of Witness is veiled from deviant, idle talk, he said, "whereas those who hover around outside the sanctuary are annihilated and drone because they have not yet entered His presence."[21] Nonetheless, Raḍwān affirms that Ḥallāj, like Bilāl, did not feel his tortures because he was annihilated in God, just as the women in the Joseph story of the Qur'an did not feel pain when they cut their hands upon seeing his beauty. "This happened because of the pleasure of seeing and loving the beauty of a creature—so how do you think it is for the one who loves his Creator?! When Ḥallāj was crucified, he did not feel his crucifixion or his mutilations. When he was asked about Sufism while on the cross, he replied, 'The least of it is what you see.' " Raḍwān appears immediately to regret this open proclamation of the realities of annihilation in God: "By God, I did not intend to say this, but God caused me to say it; because much talk is a deficiency in the path to God." Yet he insists that his speech is not like that of those who speak out of their own will or selfish motivation, for the gnostic speaks only "by Him, in Him, and for Him."[22]

The state of annihilation in God is a living reality for the saints of God who live in His presence. In annihilation, the servant of God is happy in His love and feels no pain, "for he has become totally absorbed in the love and vision of God."[23] Raḍwān enumerates eight types of annihilation in God, the final and highest one being "passing away from annihilation" *(al-fanā' 'an al-fanā')*, for "whoever remains in his *fanā'* is deficient. . . . Whoever remains in one stage of the journey is veiled from the stage that follows it."[24] Raḍwān appears to be criticizing a continual state of "absence in God," which would prevent the Sufi from continuing to strive to go rise higher in his spiritual development.

Yet annihilation in God is reserved for the elite of the elite among the saints of God. In Egypt today, while the ultimate goal is still annihilation in God, one must first be annihilated in one's shaykh, and then in the Prophet; for the shaykh is the gateway to the Prophet, and the Prophet is the gateway to God. Although it may appear that annihilation in God has become more remote by making these other forms of annihilation its prerequisites, this secondary form of annihilation may also be seen as allowing those of lesser rank to participate in an experience that would otherwise be unattainable.

This secondary form of *fanāʾ* has little to do with spiritual intoxication or being out of touch with reality. It is possible to interpret *fanāʾ* in a nonmystical sense altogether. When I asked Shaykh Aḥmad al-Sharqāwī about the meaning of becoming annihilated first in the shaykh and then in the Prophet before annihilation in God, he replied, "Annihilation means obedience. That is what the people mean when they say annihilation. Complete obedience, and seeking guidance first from the counsel of his shaykh, then the words of the Messenger, which he learns from his shaykh. The matter does not go beyond perfect obedience, even if the expressions vary. Annihilation means exerting a great effort to understand the intentions and meanings of his speech and admonitions."

Yet discussions about annihilation with other shaykhs indicated that it is an intense spiritual and emotional identification that leads to a merging of the boundaries of two personalities. The authority of a shaykh depends very much on his own charisma and his personal ability to influence his followers. Shaykh ʿIzz explained, "Little by little the shaykh must get his followers to love him, so he can influence them. As love increases, so does his influence on them, until they reach a point where the two [shaykh and disciple] become one: as if the one were speaking inside the other. This is *fanāʾ*, one in the spirit of the other. Nothing of his own ego remains."

Since this does not happen with all the followers of a shaykh, I asked with how many it would occur. He said perhaps as many as five. The concept of *fanāʾ* in this instance is virtually identical with the spiritual connection established between shaykh and disciple. *Fanāʾ* in the shaykh is the result of absolute love and devotion, to the point where all that the disciple says and does is in reality the shaykh acting through him. *Fanāʾ* begins in the shaykh because it is the shaykh who leads the disciple to the Messenger of God, and it is the Messenger who leads him to God. This type of *fanā'* in no way implies a trancelike state.

UNIFICATION (TAWḤĪD)

This perspective on *fanā'* in the shaykh as linked to love points to the essentially communal nature of many of the spiritual goals of contemporary Sufism. *Fanā'* has long been identified as the essential Sufi goal, yet here we see that the sense of oneness and absorption that many Sufis experience is not with God but with a person—the shaykh first of all, and later the Prophet. Akin to this understanding of annihilation as a function of love is the concept of unification, the ability of Sufis to become "one spirit" with each other.

All believers are said to be brothers of each other, and Sufis most of all. But Sufis in Egypt today recognize a oneness they share that goes beyond such affirmations of brotherhood, altruism, and benign magnanimity. Some Sufis say that in love they are able to transcend the boundaries of their own individuality, to touch each other's spirits in such a manner that they deny their own separate identities. This is the doctrine of *tawḥīd* (unification) in contemporary Sufism, a secret understood only by those who experience it. *Tawḥīd* is also the word used for the core belief of Islam—that there is no god but God. Sufism has sometimes been described as a personal realization of *tawḥīd* in this sense. It is ironic that such a core Islamic term should be used to describe an entirely different doctrine that is deemed a secret among the Sufis. It is possible that this double usage of the word was originally a device to confuse those not initiated into the secret. On the other hand, when a Sufi has a personal realization of *tawḥīd* in the sense of unity of God, it implies just such a merger of personalities. As Aḥmad Raḍwān explains, God "consumes him in His essence so that he sees nothing but his Lord." Drawing on the authority of the divine saying, "For the one whose indemnity I am, there is no distinction between Me and him," and other similar sayings, Radwan says the mystic becomes one with God, and "this is the way in which the *tawḥīd* (unity) of God is realized. After that God returns the servant to the world, by Him, for Him, in Him. He no longer exists by his former self, or for it or in it, for this self has passed away by God taking it."[25]

The historical roots of *tawḥīd* between believers, says Shaykh ʿIzz, lie in Muhammad's practice of assigning each of the Emigrants (those who came with him from Mecca to Medina) to one of the

Helpers (the Muslims of Medina). The Helpers would not regard their own interests above those of the Emigrants who were assigned to them but would see their interests as entirely one and the same. This buddy system formed the foundation of all Muslim brotherhood. When perfected, two people can become one in spirit.

ʿIzz illustrates the oneness experienced by the Sufis by the following story: A Sufi went to visit a Sufi friend. When he knocked on the door, his friend called out, "Who is it?" The man replied, "I." His friend called out, "Go away, 'I'!" The man went away, considered the matter, and returned to his friend's house. This time when his friend called, "Who is it?" the man replied, "You." His friend called out, "Welcome, oh I!"

The Sufi's goal is to annihilate his separate existence. The affirmation that "I" was at the door is, from a Sufi perspective, a false claim in that it gives reality to an ego that has already been killed. Yet this annihilation of the ego leads not only to a great aloneness with God, an experience common among mystics of various religious traditions but also to an appreciation of the common existence that these annihilated souls in God have with each other. The walls that lock us into separateness are breached, indeed dissolved, when the lover kills his own soul.

This experience of mutual identification can happen in a group context, especially in dhikr, particularly (though not exclusively) between the disciples of a single shaykh. Since their spirits draw their nourishment from a common "drinking place" *(mashrab)*, it is improper to draw artificial distinctions between themselves. Thus when a Sufi requested that a piece of cake handed to him by a fellow disciple be given to him instead by their common teacher, their "spiritual mother," their teacher rebuked him by saying, "The hand of your brother is the hand of your mother." Sufis commonly say to each other, "There is no I or you." When the boundaries of their individuality break down, they say, "You are a part of me and I am a part of you."[26] This is sometimes expressed in a general sense, as a courtesy, to indicate the oneness shared by all Sufis, but it can also refer to something very special and exclusive.

There are levels of *tawḥīd*. Real *tawḥīd*, like any real love relationship, can only be enjoyed with a few people at a time, and perhaps with only a single individual. It is a lofty state, a goal not attained by many, a secret understood by few. When it is attained, it goes beyond the commonality acknowledged and experienced among Sufis in general and becomes a total merging of two spirits, the true realization of that state where "there is no I or you."

SUFFERING (BALĀʾ)

Sufis believe in the mystical significance of the letters of the Arabic alphabet. Arabic, the language in which the Qurʾan was revealed, has assembled these letters together into words in a manner that is not seen as arbitrary. The Arabic word for love, *maḥabbah,*[27] according to some Egyptian Sufis, contains the meaning of love in its very letters: the letter *mīm* stands for death *(mawt), ḥāʾ* is for life *(ḥayāt), bāʾ* means trial or affliction *(balāʾ),* and *hāʾ* is for felicity *(hanāʾ).* The Sufi experience of love is one of death and life, suffering and ecstasy. Suffering is an essential aspect of the Sufi's love for God, and a sure sign of God's favor, because it is by suffering that a person is purified, forced to become detached from worldly concerns, and freed to become a vessel for God's love.

The word *balāʾ*, here translated as suffering, also means "trial." The Qurʾan uses this word when it says that God tested the Muslims "by a gracious trial" (8:17). Qushayrī wrote, "Suffering *(balāʾ)* is a test *(ikhtibār).* God tests them with good things to see whether or not they are grateful, and He tests them with afflictions to see whether they are patient and remember Him. A 'gracious trial' is one in which God enables the believer to be thankful and patient in suffering."[28]

Suffering must be borne in patience to reap spiritual rewards. One contemporary Sufi writes, "Contentment with suffering ordained by God is one of the greatest stations *(maqāmāt)* of certainty *(yaqīn).* . . . A sign of the true Sufi is that he not complain, and that he hide the effects of suffering. . . . Patience is the key to release from suffering."[29] The true lover of God embraces patient suffering as a means of drawing closer to God. Eventually the lover loses consciousness of his trials, being totally consumed in his love.

This theme has been greatly elaborated in Sufi tradition. The tenth-century Sufi author, al-Kalābādhī, wrote that suffering is a sign of God's love, for "the love of God for man is that He afflicts him, and so renders him improper for any but Him," because it is by suffering that the lover loses his attachment to things other than God.[30] Sufis felt that suffering could actually become pleasurable, as are any attentions, even negative ones, from the Beloved. It is for this reason that Job was described as "patient" *(ṣābir)* by the Qurʾan (38:44) but not "ever-patient" *(ṣabūr),* because at times he actually enjoyed his sufferings.[31] Hallaj said that suffering is God Himself and used an image subsequently popular in Sufi poetry, that of the moth who circles around the flame out of love for it and is eventually consumed. According to the legends about Ḥallāj, he saw his sufferings and death as the ultimate exemplification of love, for his love led him literally to remove his existence so that nothing but God would exist; that is the ultimate realization of *tawḥīd,* the essence of Islam. Some Sufi stories and poems give rather strange images: the Sufi imagines his head to be like a polo ball, pummeled by the mallet of God and rejoicing in its sufferings. God the Beloved appears at times to delight in the sufferings of His lovers, who are themselves content with such suffering.[32]

Lest we think of Sufism as an exercise in sadomasochism, it is necessary to bear in mind that as essential as suffering might be, it is not desired per se. Egyptian Sufis, who are not renowned for their ascetic proclivities, emphasize instead the mercy of God. They illustrate this theme by the following story, which I heard from a number of shaykhs: A man asked God to test him with suffering, sure that he would be able to bear it. God responded by granting him urinary retention. The man's discomfort increased until he repented at the hand of his shaykh, who said one must first ask for the power of God before entering into the trial of God, or one will fail. Better yet is to enter God's presence by the gate of His mercy.

Nonetheless, according to a ḥadīth, "Those who suffer most are the prophets, then the righteous, and so forth." A contemporary Sufi writer interpreted this as a kindness from God, in that He tests with affliction those who are strongest and best able to bear it.[33] Aḥmad Raḍwān said that saints must pass through trials, for sainthood is not an easy matter. He recalls that his own family and townsfolk hated him and thought he had gone mad because of his constantly fluctuating spiritual states. After forty-five years of suffering, he says, when God looked at his heart He saw nothing in it but Himself. When he could bear no more, he called on the Prophet's family, and ʿAlī told the *ghawth,* who administers both trials and gifts on God's behalf, to lighten his burden. The *ghawth* had to obey, said Raḍwān, because "our lord ʿAlī is the teacher of every *ghawth.*" Eventually Raḍwān was purified through suffering until he was crowned *ghawth* before a visionary assembly of all the saints. He comments regarding his own administration as *ghawth,* "I have not placed a burden on any saint or dervish, and I have not asked God to afflict a saint or believer, man or woman, in any way."[34]

Nonetheless, much human suffering, according to Aḥmad Raḍwān, is the result of sin, although in this case as well it is a tool for refining the soul.[35]

MADNESS, INTOXICATION, AND INSPIRATION AS MODES OF LOSS OF CONTROL

Sufi experience appears to entail a certain amount of loss of control over one's mind and behavior. This appears most dramatically in the case of *gazb* (*jadhb* in classical Arabic), which literally means "attraction" or "pulling," that is, a divine attraction that strips people of their normal mental faculties. One might say that it is losing one's mind in God. The first vision of the light of God is a shock to the mental faculties, like a light that is so strong that it temporarily blinds the eye. Although the intellect is a necessary tool in the process of purification, for it is the intellect that inhibits passions, when entering into the spiritual realities it can be an obstacle. The intellect is limited in its understanding. The Sharīʿa appeals to the intellect, but the Qur'an itself, according to Sufi interpretation, indicates that the Law may be transcended by those with access to esoteric knowledge: for Khiḍr baffled Moses by the apparent immorality of his acts, which nonetheless had a hidden purpose and were performed at the command of God (18:65–82). The disciple, therefore, must withhold judgment when he sees the gnostics doing things that go against the apparent meaning of the Law. The spirit must be unshackled if it is to appreciate the things of God, or if one is to be a true disciple of a gnostic, for, as Shaykh ʿIzz rhetorically asked me, how can someone who only knows how to walk be spiritually connected with one who flies?

People who lose partial control over their mental faculties as a result of the revelation of divine light are called *magāzīb* ("attracted," "abducted," plural of *magzūb*). The degree of this derangement varies greatly, and it might be temporary, intermittent, or permanent. Although not everyone passes through a period of gazb, Shaykh ʿIzz felt that some such shock is necessary when a person first encounters the Lord, "because the chemical composition of a person is shaken." The Prophet Muhammad, for example, did not go into *gazb*, but he perspired and trembled. The encounter with the divine is not to be taken lightly.

The state of *gazb* is characterized by socially unacceptable behavior, and indeed some persons are accused of feigning *gazb* because it excuses their eccentricities and allows them to make importunate demands on people. The *magāzīb* have no legal obligations because they are not in control of their minds and actions. Ahmad Radwan said that for this reason they have a special paradise reserved for them.[36] They are to be seen in abundance at the public celebrations of the saints' days, where they freely avail themselves of the hospitality offered by the faithful at their various tents and service stations and join in the rows of devotees engaging in dhikr to musical accompaniment. Their very visible presence at the moulids is reason enough for the reticence Egyptian officials have of foreigners witnessing moulids or photographing them. But the *magāzīb* are often regarded as bearers of baraka. On one occasion I witnessed a tall, physically and possibly mentally handicapped man with an open mouth, walking among the crowds in front of the Ḥusayn mosque during his birthday celebration. He refused to give way when a finely dressed man in a three-piece suit came walking in the opposite direction. I braced myself for angry words, but the well-dressed man touched him gently and put his hand to his own mouth and kissed it, to receive baraka from this *magzūb*.

The *magāzīb* witness the light of God, but they are not gnostics, and they are unable to benefit other people. Money means nothing to them, and they are unaware of whether they are naked or clothed. Aḥmad Raḍwān advised his followers not to ask the *magāzīb* to pray for them, "because they will pray that you have poverty and illness, for they love these qualities for all Muslims, since by these God makes the Muslims enter paradise." He also accused the *magāzīb* of using magic to bring affliction on the saints of God.[37]

Shaykh Gamāl al-Sanhūrī of the Burhāniyya, on the other hand, said that the *magāzīb* are God's policemen among the Sufis. They have territories over which they are responsible, and though they appear to engage in bizarre and meaningless behavior, they act on God's behalf in this world and report Sufis' misbehavior to the heavenly court. Shaykh ʿIzz confirmed that this was true.

An old man called Shaykh Shaʿrāwī was a *magzūb* who was devoted to Shaykh Maḥmūd Abū 'l-ʿAzm (d. 1983). When Shaykh Maḥmūd was alive, Shaykh Shaʿrāwī refused to enter the apartment where he was staying, out of respect, but would stay outside by the stairs. He had difficulty walking and wore very little clothing, and by all reason ought to have died from exposure. L., a devotee of Shaykh Maḥmūd, brought him clean clothes every week, in which she personally dressed him, and she wiped his nose as if he were a child. He continuously bit his own hand and appeared to be in a state of constant discomfort and agitation. His behavior was preposterous, but the others at the shrine treated him with a mixture of respect and amusement. L.'s husband, M., joked with him that he would divorce L. so he could marry her, but Shaykh Shaʿrāwī did not respond. The old *magzūb* sometimes demanded ten-pound notes from M., and would accept only the older large bills, not the newer small ones. All the money he took went toward building a mosque. It was he who had built the shrine to Shaykh Maḥmūd, and he had built several others as well. He was a chain smoker, but he would not so much as bring a cigarette into a shrine, and he could sit for hours without smoking in a saint's shrine, but once he left he went back to chain-smoking. One time he spent the night at L. and M.'s apartment in an upper-class section of Cairo; M. says he never slept at all but maintained his state of agitation, biting his hand, all through the night.

L., who had driven us to the shrine, discussed Shaykh Shaʿrāwī with Shaykh ʿIzz on the way home. ʿIzz said that he was not a simple man and that he understood a great deal. L. agreed. She said that in moments of lucidity he spoke with greater wisdom than any of them and that she felt a tenderness for him that she could not really explain.

A middle-aged man, nicknamed Abū 'l-Ḥadīd ("father of iron") because he had chained himself for many years to the shrine of Ḥusayn, was a *magzūb* seen at most of the main moulids. He was a comical character who liked to dominate conversations unless hushed by people with spiritual authority. He grew his hair and beard in an unkempt fashion. When one man asked why he wore a beard, and if he wasn't afraid of being mistaken for a radical fundamentalist, he said it was appropriate for him to wear it, since he worked in the Ministry of Religious Endowments. He said that the key he wore on a cord around his neck was the key to Paradise, and when asked why he had three army stars sewn onto his vest, he said that he had been promoted to colonel. His comments were very entertaining for the men, but it appeared to me that his state of *gazb* was mild, that he was well aware of everything around him and that his antics were deliberately comical. He took advantage of his reputation as a *magzūb* to demand lentils when offered beans and to complain of the lack of meat being served at the *khidamāt*. Yet often his behavior and speech were perfectly normal. Toward the end of my time in Egypt, I was surprised to see him come to a moulid accompanied by two nicely dressed, middle-class women, one in chic western clothing, with lipstick and fingernail polish. Abū 'l-Ḥadīd himself had added to his exotic appearance by putting on *koḥl* (a kind of eye liner) around his eyes. He said he was traveling the next day to Upper Egypt because he had tired of the suffocating life of Cairo and wanted to see his children. That in itself was the mark of a man who was little affected by *gazb*. It seemed to me that he had adopted a certain type of personality that is socially acceptable within the Sufi subculture and had allowed himself to be molded by it.

Aḥmad Raḍwān himself went through a period of *gazb* during which he stripped off his clothes and walked about naked, and it appears that *gazb* is not an unusual phase through which a great saint might pass. In fact, Shaykh ʿIzz told me that because of my excessive reliance on my intellect, I would have to go through a period of *gazb* in order to enter into the spiritual realities. Ideally, it should only be temporary. In and of itself, *gazb* is not a desirable state. When Shaykh ʿIzz was *magzūb*, the former Rector of al-Azhar and respected Sufi scholar, Dr. ʿAbd al-Ḥalīm Maḥmūd, advised him to go to the movies to get his feet back on the ground.

A similar loss of control is not an uncommon experience during the performance of dhikr, although in such circumstances it is not *gazb* but "intoxication" *(sukr)* or "absence" *(ghayba)* in the presence of God. After the dhikr is over, the person "awakens," so to speak, and becomes normal again. Shaykh Gamāl al-Sanhūrī, however, said that one should be gradually trained in dhikr. If the uninitiated immediately starts reciting "Allah," he will go mad. As we have seen, people may cry out in dhikr, be unaware of their speech or their movements, or demonstrate unusually aggressive behavior. And as we have seen, saints can enter strange spiritual states, in which they feel neither heat nor cold and are unable to eat or sleep.

Among the strange spiritual experiences narrated to me was that of a low-level civil servant at the American University in Cairo, who said that the first time he had a vision of the Prophet's grandson, Ḥusayn, at his shrine in Cairo, he and his shaykh rose bodily into the air and performed dhikr over the heads of the people in the shrine. He was in a state of shock and remained in a state of *gazb* for about a month. His family thought he had gone mad and was near death, but the shaykh assured them that he was fine and would return to his senses. And indeed he did.

A housewife told me that when she engaged in the long prayers and spiritual exercises of the Sufis, she lost consciousness of her surroundings and was unable to assume her normal responsibilities for her husband and children. The experience frightened her to the extent that she now performs only the obligatory five daily prayers that all Muslims perform.

Although these may seem like extreme cases of loss of control, to a certain extent loss of control over their own behavior is part of the normal experience of shaykhs and mystics who live by spiritual impulses and inspiration. Shaykh ʿIzz has built a mosque and holds a certificate as a preacher but refrains from preaching the Friday sermon because he fears that under inspiration he will say things that are contrary to Islamic law and not meant for general consumption or that he will go on speaking for two hours even though a Friday sermon should be only twenty minutes. Under such inspiration, he used to give lessons to his disciples on the inner meaning of the Qurʾan, and, if we are to believe him, he could recite word for word exegetical books he had never read. Hearing a turn of phrase that strikes some inner chord, he shrieks out loud in a moment of ecstatic insight, then returns to his normal behavior and apologizes for having no control over his behavior.

A person who is temporarily subject to moving by inspiration alone, without any recourse to the intellect, is said to be "in a spiritual state" *(fī ḥāl).* His words and his movements are entirely controlled by God, and therefore he is not responsible for what he does. He is similar to a *magzūb* in that he may violate the norms of the Sharīʿa and bear no culpability. The teaching style of Shaykh Aḥmad Abū 'l-Ḥasan, described in chapter 10, is a study in operating by divine inspiration. He appeared to be looking into himself as if assessing the direction of his own spirit. His leadership style was characterized more by introspection than deliberation. It appeared to the non-Sufi observer that the one whose ego is annihilated in God is free to indulge in yet more introspection, trusting in the veracity of his feelings, than the man whose ego remains intact.

Yet, as we shall see in chapter 9, the models of sainthood are many. Aḥmad Abū 'l-Ḥasan, ʿIzz al-Hawārī, and Aḥmad Raḍwān belong to one model, that of living by inspired impulses. This model may be contrasted with others. Their diverse experiences and personalities indicate that Sufi saints in modern Egypt run the gamut from introspective, inspired shaykhs to sober saints quietly pursuing a life of holiness, from "mad saints" who beg, to modest models of wisdom and compassion. All have, in some sense, annihilated their egos or separate wills, the essential "negative path" before the experience of being filled with God's light. Some of the resultant personalities are social anomalies, and in *gazb* the Sufis have found an explanation for the most extreme such anomaly, madness.

The Sufi attitude toward *gazb* is that it lies within the spectrum of normal mystical experience, for the intellect is limited and unable to grasp the secrets of the Divine; it is shocked and bewildered by the divine light. The intellect must be transcended in order to unshackle the spirit. Yet Sufi attitudes toward *gazb* are notably ambivalent. The mental capacity of the perfect mystic will expand to admit the new spiritual realities without pathological manifestation, to become aware of a broader spiritual horizon while remaining in touch with the human realm. The gnostic is superior to the *magzūb*. As Aḥmad Raḍwān said, "In a single moment [the truly perfect man] might ascend more than a thousand *magāzīb*."[38] Permanent *gazb* represents a stalled mystical journey, in which the *via negativa* has failed to produce its corresponding positive results. The "loss of control" of the inspired gnostic is of a different order from that of the *magzūb*. Shaykh Abū 'l-ʿAzāʾim warns against taking a *magzūb* as a spiritual guide. Their love, ecstasy, and knowledge are for themselves alone; they are "neither leaders of the pious, nor guides for the Muslims. . . . Muslims should treat them as if they were nursing infants, and have mercy and compassion on them in honor of God and His Messenger, and not imitate them, for that leads to perdition. They have angelic ecstasies and witness, and God's might and omnipotence have been unveiled to them. They have become intoxicated and 'attracted' and have passed away from all else. Whoever imitates them will perish and cause others to perish."[39]

While the *magzūb*'s pathology prevents him from performing useful social functions, the inspired gnostic is God's perfect vessel through which His power flows into the world. Not all loss of control is a good thing. The person who enters into trance in dhikr may be God-intoxicated or demon-possessed. Clearly, abandoning oneself to spiritual forces means entering uncharted territory fraught with hazards. This is another reason that many shaykhs keep a tight rein on the behavior of their disciples in group dhikr, insisting on uniformity or even sobriety. Unbridled individualism is discouraged. Such spiritual exercises as solitary contemplation are likewise fraught with danger and need discipline and oversight. Given the dangers involved in the Sufi path, one can understand why it is said that he who has no shaykh will be taken in by Satan. Without a firm anchor, one may well drown in the ocean of divine knowledge.

VISIONS

Visions play a pivotal role in the religious life of Islam in Egypt, particularly among the Sufis. Visions may take the form of dreams, appearances of light, or apparitions. By far the most common of these is the dream-vision. Dreams are not thought of as mere products of the human mind but are believed to be windows into the spiritual realm and to provide insights that would otherwise be unavailable.[40] This belief is substantiated by the Qur'anic story of Joseph, whose dreams and ability to interpret the dreams of others provided him with knowledge of the future that both reassured him and enabled him to save the people of the region from starvation. The Qur'an also provides a justification for the belief that in the sleeping state, the spirits of the living and the dead are together in the divine presence. It says, "God takes the souls of those who die and of those who do not die, in their sleep; then He keeps those ordained for death, and sends the others back" (39:42).

Although the verse says that God takes the *souls* of those who die, not their *spirits*, most Qur'an exegetes do not distinguish between the two and take the verse as an indication that the human spirits are temporarily released from the body during sleep and that if God decides, He can make this separation permanent. Sleep is therefore analogous to death, and the condition and location of the spirit in sleep and in death are the same. The spirits of the dead and the living are able to meet in the realm of *al-barzakh*, where the spirits dwell until the resurrection of the bodies on the Last Day.[41]

The realm of the spirits is by definition that of the supernatural. Therefore, in dreams one can gain a glimpse into the supernatural realm. The validity and significance of dream experiences is indicated by a ḥadīth in which the Prophet says, "A dream-vision [*ru'yā*, spelled with an *alif*, whereas a waking vision is *ru'yā*, spelled with a *tā' marbūṭa*] is half of prophecy," or, in some more modest versions, "The dream-vision of the Muslim is one-forty-sixth of prophecy."[42]

Not all dreams are of divine inspiration, this ḥadīth explains, for dream-visions are of three types: a sound vision, which is good news *(bushrā)* from God; a vision that comes from the affliction of Satan; and a vision that occurs when a man talks to himself.[43] In another, currently more popular version of this ḥadīth, "A vision *(ru'yā)* is from God and a dream *(ḥulm)* is from Satan. If one of you has a dream that he dislikes, let him spit to his left side and seek God's protection from Satan, and it will never harm him." Another ḥadīth warns only to tell a good dream-vision to someone who loves you and not to tell a bad dream to anyone.[44] The reason for this last piece of advice might be explained by another ḥadīth, which explains that a vision must be told in order to be actualized.[45]

Islamic tradition abounds with stories of guidance given through visions, particularly dreams of the Prophet.[46] There is even an approved form of seeking guidance through dreams, a prayer called *istikhāra,* "seeking guidance," concerning a particular matter. After praying this prayer, the seeker goes to sleep, expecting the answer to be provided in a dream. Shaykh ʿIzz used this method regularly to seek the truth of a matter or to ascertain God's will. It was the results of *istikhāra* that convinced him that God had called him to guide me and assist me in my research.

As we have seen in chapter 5, visions often guide Sufi disciples in their choice of a shaykh. In fact, it is striking how common visionary experiences are among the Sufis. Far from being an unusual phenomenon in their lives, many Sufis live in the expectation of guidance through visions and most particularly through dreams.

If one allows for the possibility that dreams are visions of the spiritual world and that in sleep the living and the dead may meet and converse, it is no real surprise that in a sociological survey, some 50 percent of Egyptians interviewed said that their dead relatives had visited them in their dreams, often to ask them to do something specific for them.[47] This would not be considered a religious experience. But when the person who appears is a recognized saint, or when a person is instructed in a dream to seek the guidance or healing of a saint, such dreams are religiously significant. Dreams and visions often play a major role in the spiritual formation or orientation of people. The Sufis sometimes asked me whether I had had dream-visions, in order to ascertain the degree of my openness to the spiritual realm and the extent to which Shaykh ʿIzz and I were spiritually connected. Assurances of my spiritual status also sometimes came to them through their own dream-visions concerning me. Dreams are often the first step in the ever-deepening mingling of spirits in the relationship between a Sufi shaykh and his disciple. Some shaykhs also instruct their disciples through visions. Although I have not explored this issue in sufficient depth, it is my impression that teaching through visions rather than through verbal instruction plays a particularly significant role in the religious education of women. If this is true, it may be because women are barred by social convention more often than men from keeping the company of shaykhs.

Sufi shaykhs have often been credited with knowledge of their disciples' actions and circumstances and with the ability to intervene on their behalf. The anecdotes concerning the seventeenth-century Moroccan shaykh, ʿAbd al-ʿAzīz al-Dabbāgh, contain many dramatic stories of this type, including stories of rescue and of shaykhly interference on his disciple's wedding night.[48] Shaykh ʿIzz claimed to be able to see what his disciples did at all times, so that he knew when to intervene in their domestic problems. We have seen that a disciple may summon his shaykh through recitation of the *Fātiḥa,* praying blessings on the Prophet, and calling the name of his shaykh with the command "Come!" This is possible only after the establishment of spiritual connection and the dissolution of the boundaries of the ego through the process of annihilation in the shaykh. Sufi shaykhs are often aware of their disciples' dreams and claim the ability to interpret them. And as we have seen, for many Sufis the vision of the Prophet, whether in a dream or while awake, is a fundamental, even crucial experience.

Given such strong affirmation of the possibility and importance of such visions in Sufi tradition, it is noteworthy that when Shaykh Muḥammad ʿUthmān of the Burhāniyya published *Tabriʾat al-dhimma* in 1974, a book that aroused enormous public controversy and criticism, the then head of the Supreme Council of Sufi Orders rejected, in a newspaper interview, the possibility that a Sufi might have a vision of Muhammad while awake.[49] Despite this official disapproval, waking visions of the Prophet continue to be an important part of Sufi experience.

The ability of Sufi shaykhs and saints to see things that ordinary people cannot see might be considered just a part of their ability to transcend spatial limitations. The saints can talk with each other over great geographical distances and can appear in more than one place at one time—forty places at once, if we are to believe the words of Shaykh Aḥmad Raḍwān. I personally have witnessed Shaykh ʿIzz conversing with the recently deceased Shaykh Mūsā Abū ʿAlī (although I could not see the latter) and calling out to a friend whose son had just been in an accident in Qina, some twelve to seventeen hours' travel away. On yet another occasion, when we were spending the night at the *sāḥa* of a Sufi in the Upper Egyptian town of Manfalut, ʿIzz said that a shaykh, a saint who was buried locally, had come to him during the night and they performed dhikr together, "very loudly. I'm surprised you didn't hear us." He interpreted this experience as a sign that the spiritual life and *sāḥa* of our host were blessed. All of these experiences illustrate how visions function to extend social relationships among Sufis beyond what is possible in the purely physical realm.

Some of the most important spiritual experiences of contemporary Sufi shaykhs occur in the form of visions. Shaykh Muḥammad ʿUthmān's account of his life and spiritual development contains very few facts that relate to external reality; it consists almost entirely of visions. Visions also were of paramount importance in the conversion and spiritual development of Shaykh ʿIzz. Visions may be the agent of healing, both physical and moral. It is not unusual for people to claim to be able to see their deceased patron saints when they visit their tombs, and to cultivate relationships with those saints that are very familiar. The similarity of sleep with death has already been mentioned with reference to a Qurʾanic verse, but in the case of a saint it is the obverse: death is merely sleep with regard to the body.

On 30 October 1912, following an alleged appearance of a saint risen from his tomb, a great crowd gathered to supplicate him. The next day an old man (described by George Swan as a "madman") claimed to be that saint, and crowds followed him through the street, trying to kiss his hands or touch his garments. When the old man was arrested, the crowd rioted and had to be dispersed by water hose.[50] The incident serves to underline the strength of popular belief in the presence of saints and the possibility of their physical appearance after death.

Major spiritual commissions are also given in visions. Examples of all of these types of visions are scattered throughout this book. Shaykh ʿIzz received his commission to build his mosque on its present site by the visit of a mysterious person later identified as Khiḍr. Visions of Khiḍr are so frequent in Sufi life that ʿIzz told me that one of the main reasons to take a spiritual retreat was to receive a vision of Khiḍr.

Apparitions have even played a part in the national life of Egypt. The most famous of these are the multiple appearances of the Virgin Mary at the Church in Zaytūn beginning in April 1968, which is discussed in chapter 11, and the apparitions that accompanied the October 1973 war. During the October 1973 crossing of the Suez Canal to take the Israeli line of defense by surprise (an incident that is widely interpreted as a great victory although it was followed by a vigorous Israeli rally halted only through United Nations intervention), the Egyptian forces reported witnessing angels and the Prophet himself in the sky above them. These visions strengthened their hearts and their conviction that a country that had returned to God was experiencing the victory that God promises His faithful in the Qurʾan.[51]

Visions function in Sufism to grant guidance, healing, consolation, revelation of truth, and the bonding of spiritual master to a disciple. Whether seen in a sleeping or waking state, they are invested with great authority. What is perhaps most striking about Egyptian religious life is the frequency of visionary experiences. Although they can intrude unexpectedly into the lives of secular-oriented individuals, for Sufis they are an expected, perhaps even necessary, and in some cases everyday occurrence. The usefulness of visions is directly linked to the authority with which they are regarded. For Sufis, they are indisputably true and immune from criticism, even if their interpretation is a matter of debate. Sufis expect divine intervention in their lives on a daily basis; the boundaries between the natural and supernatural world are ill-defined, and the miraculous regularly impinges on the ordinary. Divine revelations and guidance through visions cannot be subjected to the scrutiny that can be given to ordinary human claims. Visions are therefore authoritative and sometimes indispensable in Sufi life.

GNOSIS (MAʿRIFA)

"Important knowledge," said Shaykh ʿIzz, "comes not with words, but is without voice, letter, or speech. There is another eye in the heart which has true vision, whose knowledge comes from a theophanic illumination from God, as if it were from the sun. The human mind is limited. There are things it cannot know or comprehend. But the human heart can know directly from God."

The ultimate goal, the end of the path, is gnosis, mystical knowledge, the knowledge of the heart rather than the intellect. Intellectual knowledge, which is learned through teaching or sense perception, is called *ʿilm*. Mystical knowledge is derived, in Ghāzālī's words, from "a light which God most high cast into my breast."[52] This is *maʿrifa*, translated here as gnosis, to distinguish it from ordinary knowledge. The one who possesses this knowledge is a gnostic, in Arabic "a knower in God," *ʿārif bi ʾllāh*. The gnostic is distinguished from the other type of "knower" in Islam, the *ʿālim* (plural *ʿulamāʾ*, or "ulama" in Webster's dictionary), the scholars who study and preserve the great religious literary heritage of Islam, the Qurʾan and Ḥadīth, with their commentaries in the vast exegetical and jurisprudential corpus.

The necessity of gnosis is underlined by Sufi tradition. As al-Kalābādhī wrote, "They [the Sufis] are agreed that the only guide to God is God Himself, holding that the function of the intellect is the function of an intelligent person who is in need of a guide: for the intellect is a thing originated in time, and as such only serves as a guide to things like itself."[53]

Despite the distinction between the two sources of knowledge, Sufis frequently insist that *ʿilm* is a prerequisite for *maʿrifa*. It is dangerous to trust in personal mystical insight without thorough grounding first in the scriptural sources of faith. One may easily be misled by one's own fantasies and whims. As ʿAbd al-Razzāq Nawfal wrote, the more a person increases in *ʿilm*, the more the truth of which the Sufis sing and in which they live will be revealed to him. *ʿIlm* leads a person by way of his intellect to faith in God and His oneness. Such knowledge leads the believer to fear and love God, which in turn leads to gnosis.[54] Aḥmad Raḍwān said, "God reveals *(yakshifu)* very many things to the traveler on the path, matters pertaining to the creation, and secret matters, and hidden matters *(umūr ghaybiyya)*. There is much knowledge *(ʿilm)* in the Prophetic Sunna. Therefore the believer must read the Prophetic Sunna and be firmly planted in it and delve deeply into it until God opens up to him (in mystical revelation) by virtue of that."[55]

Gnosis, however, is a result not merely of knowledge but of the purification of the heart. Nawfal writes, "When the hearts are purified, and the senses awakened, a person sees and hears and understands, and arrives [at the presence of God]."[56] Or, as a Sufi woman told me, when a person purifies himself in obedience to God, God will open up his "sixth sense" to perceive things beyond ordinary perception.[57] Shaykh ʿIzz said, "The traveler on the path of God must rid himself of the filthy things of his soul, and the spiritual realities of things will radiate from it, leaving their origins and emigrating to what is beyond created things. But the understanding of this comes through spiritual perception, not words. Sufism is reality, not speech." Gnosis is an immediate experience of God, a personal realization of a truth heard and believed, but now witnessed. The soul that is purified becomes receptive to divine revelation.

Traditionally, Sufis vaunted the superiority of gnosis over the knowledge of the intellect. Ghazālī said that divine illumination is "the key to the greater part of knowledge. Whoever thinks that the understanding of things Divine rests upon strict proofs has in his thought narrowed down the wideness of God's mercy."[58] In the modern period as well, ʿAbd al-Ḥalīm Maḥmūd devotes extensive space to arguing that it is futile for the intellect to explore the supernatural; knowledge of this must come from another source. He proves the possibility of such insight into the divine realm by Ghazālī's experiences, as well as the Qurʾanic stories of Joseph, whose "inner vision" *(baṣīra)* allowed him to interpret dreams, and Khiḍr, whose knowledge taught directly from God enabled him to perform seemingly irrational acts with full understanding.[59]

The superiority of gnosis over scholarly knowledge is demonstrated by countless stories throughout Sufi tradition, right up to the modern day, of Sufi shaykhs outdistancing the ulama in wisdom. Such stories are even narrated concerning shaykhs of Orders that are especially concerned with maintaining orthodoxy and disallowing any personal mystical "unveiling" (*kashf* or *fatḥ*) that contradicts the Qur'an or Sunna.[60] I, as a representative of the new wisdom of secular education, have also sometimes been subjected to mild derision for trusting in knowledge that is less real than the knowledge experienced by the Sufi. As ʿAmm Amīn liked to say, "There is a university beyond this university!" Shaykh Gamāl al-Sanhūrī of the Burhāniyya told me that all the book learning in the world did not equal a single drop of divine knowledge. When a person has had a divine opening *(fatḥ ilāhī)*, he said, he knows everything in an instant—not just about religion but about chemistry, astronomy, and science.[61] Significantly, part of Shaykh ʿIzz's claim to gnosis was that he knew the entire contents of the traditional works of Qur'anic exegesis without having ever read them. He claims that he used to teach Qur'anic exegesis to his disciples under inspiration, and members of the ulama used to come to test him. They were all astonished at his ability to quote traditional exegetical works word for word without having studied them. In this case, gnosis comprises and comprehends *ʿilm* and goes beyond it. It is superior to it, yet it is partially validated through it.

The definitions of gnosis, and of the actual contents of the knowledge of the gnostic, are numerous in Sufi tradition. Gnosis may be interpreted as "seeing" God, for Sufis say "the heart of the Sufi has seen God," or it may be interpreted as knowing or seeing, by the light of God, other realities that are beyond the perception of the senses or the intellect. The very phrase *ʿārif bi ʾllāh,* "a knower in God," is ambiguous, for it may mean one who knows God or one who knows through or by God. Some Sufis, both medieval and modern, say that the knowledge of God is unattainable to humans, other than the knowledge of His Names and attributes. The gnostic cannot really see or know God, but only other spiritual realities by virtue of His light. Ḥallāj defined gnosis as "seeing God's gift in all circumstances, and the inability to render sufficient thanks for His bounty in all its aspects, and realizing one's impotence in everything."[62] Others emphasize that the definition of gnosis lies in the evidence of the gnostic's relationship with God, as in the definition of Aḥmad ibn Khaḍrūya (d. 854/5): "True gnosis is love for Him in the heart, recollecting Him with the tongue, and cutting off desires for anything other than Him."[63] Bisṭāmī, however, insisted that gnosis includes the knowledge of both God and other things by his light,[64] whereas other Sufis defined gnosis as the awareness of one's own ignorance and perplexity when confronted with the divine presence.[65]

The vocabulary related to the Sufis' ability to see into the unseen is considerable. *Baṣīra* is inner vision, the vision of the heart rather than of the eye. As one shaykh told me, "The hearts of the gnostics have eyes." It is said that Muhammad was asked, after his ascension through the heavens to the Throne of God, "How were you with God?" He replied, "My sight *(baṣrī)* was exchanged for inner vision *(baṣīratī),* and I became light, and I saw nothing." ʿAbd al-ʿAzīz al-Dabbāgh (d. 1717) of Morocco defined *baṣīra* as an understanding that penetrates the spirit, just as sight penetrates all the senses.[66] *Firāsa* is a traditional term for the ability to read the hearts of other people. According to a hadith, the Prophet said, "Beware of the *firāsa* of the believer, for he sees by the light of God." In contemporary Egypt, a more common, nontraditional synonym is *shafāfiyya,* a term that literally means "transparency" but carries the sense not of the transparency of the person who possesses this gift but of that person's ability to see beyond physical limits and particularly into the hearts and personalities of people.

Kashf, "unveiling," is the term for a personal revelation given to a mystic and is traditionally contrasted with *waḥy,* revelation given to a prophet. Nonetheless, Muslim mystics have sometimes described their personal revelation as *waḥy,* and the Qurʾan uses the same term to refer to the manner in which God gave instincts to bees (16:68). ʿIzz said *waḥy* is of three types—direct, which is a revelation brought by Gabriel; audial, which is like the revelation given to Moses; and communication through thoughts and dreams. This last, he says, is essentially the same thing as inspiration *(ilhām).* Shaykh Abū 'l-ʿAzāʾim defines *kashf* as "the clarification of what was hidden from the understanding. It is unveiled to the servant until it is as if he can witness it personally."[67] *Fatḥ* (plural, *futūḥāt*), "opening," is a virtual synonym for *kashf.* If what is revealed pertains to the divine presence itself, these are *tajalliyyāt,* divine manifestations or theophanies. *Yaqīn,* which literally means "certainty," is defined by Shaykh Abū 'l-ʿAzāʾim as the unveiling of "the secrets of the unseen and the signs of God and of God's power and wisdom, making the heart tranquil, untroubled by any doubts . . . for it is beautified by a bright lamp, which is the light that God the exalted places in the heart."[68]

The Sufi's experience of the divine realities is described by a number of metaphors, including "witness" *(mushāhada)*, "tasting" *(dhawq)*, and "drinking" *(sharāb)*. ʿAbd al-ʿAzīz al-Dabbāgh said that since the human spirit is created from light, it is able to "taste" lights, just as the body can taste physical things. The degree to which the spirit can "taste" varies according to the strength of the spirit. The strongest spirit is that of the Prophet Muhammad, who "tasted" the entire heavenly realm during his ascension into heaven.[69] *Ilhām* means "inspiration." To function through inspiration rather than through the intellect is a main characteristic of many Sufis. Like the English word "inspiration," *ilhām* in contemporary usage refers to a number of potential circumstances, such as the spontaneous composition of a song, or the delivery of a particularly potent sermon, or the revelation of something from the realm of the unseen.

The mystics' claim to see into the realm of the unseen is controversial for many Muslims. A Qurʾanic description of Muslims is that they believe in the unseen (*al-ghayb*, 2:3), but knowledge of the unseen realm, according to the Qurʾan, is the province of God alone (3:179, 6:59, 10:20, 19:78, 27:65, 35:38, 53:35). God does reveal news from the unseen world to his prophets, and many of the prophet stories in the Qurʾan are said to be "part of the news of the unseen" (3:44, 11:49, 12:102), but the Qurʾan instructs Muhammad himself to profess his ignorance of the unseen world (6:50, 7:188). Shaykh ʿIzz justified the mystics' claim to see the unseen realm by the verse, "He is knower of the unseen, and He does not reveal His unseen to anyone except the one He chooses" (72:26–7). This, however, is not the end of the verse. The verse says, "He does not reveal His unseen to anyone except the one He chooses as a messenger" (*rasūl*, usually a technical term for a prophet sent to a people with a scripture). When I pointed this out to ʿIzz, he interpreted "messenger" in a broader sense to mean anyone who speaks on behalf of God—and that would include the gnostic who is a spiritual guide to others. This arrogation of spiritual authority that is typically restricted to Muhammad and a handful of other prophets is a major offense in the eyes of many Muslims.

Nonetheless, Shaykh Muḥammad Mutawallī al-Shaʿrāwī, former Minister of Religious Affairs and a popular television interpreter of the Qurʾan, affirms the possibility that some of those whom God loves may catch a special glimpse into spiritual meanings that are not accessible to other people. "We are not asked to believe in it. Whoever wants may believe, and whoever wants may disbelieve. Those who see such things shouldn't talk about them unless they want earthly fame or to use them to get wealth, or some other such things, whereas those who really see such things should be above desiring the things of this world."[70] Other non-Sufi scholars also affirmed to me the reality of divine revelation and inner vision granted to great shaykhs, although they made no claim to any personal experience of such things.

Shaykh ʿIzz's claims to see into the realm of the unseen went beyond the ability to read the character of people, a trait, after all, that he was ready to concede I shared. He claimed to have read the Preserved Tablet itself on which the destinies of all things are written. He therefore predicted with some confidence that he would live to an old age, and alluded at times to events that would happen in the future. This certainty directly affected some of his decisions. When we traveled into very dangerous territory, where two towns were in open warfare with each other, Shaykh ʿIzz alone among all the people in our party remained perfectly calm. He assured us that he had read the Preserved Tablet, and our term of life was not yet over.

Sufis believe that every true worshipper of God has the potential to receive some amount of personal revelation. Aḥmad Raḍwān said, "God will unveil to whoever travels to Him in a sound manner every obscure secret in the two worlds, and in every manifest thing he will see the perfection and beauty of God's power. He travels until He arrives at (the station of) witness, at which point he has no need for created things, [since he is] in the Creator."[71]

Shaykh ʿIzz liked to quote a saying ascribed to the Prophet: "No servant was ever sincerely devoted to God for forty days without receiving revelation *(yūḥā ilayhi).*" The verb translated here as "receiving revelation" is derived from the same word as *waḥy,* the word supposedly reserved for revelation given to a prophet. The Prophet was therefore asked, "How does he receive revelation?" The answer: "The fountainheads of wisdom descend on his heart, and his tongue speaks from it. Whoever is not like that is insincere in his worship."

Despite the apparent availability of gnosis to any wayfarer on the Sufi path who is sincerely devoted, ʿIzz guessed that no more than fifty percent of Sufis had genuine experience and mystical knowledge. He attributed the failure of others to attain such an experience to their preoccupation with receiving honor from people or making a career out of Sufism instead of pursuing it for the sake of God alone. The receipt of divine revelation is also subject to the authority of the spiritual guide, who is thought in some sense to cause the spiritual experiences of his disciples. Shaykh Aḥmad Raḍwān said that a shaykh may intentionally delay his disciple's experience of divine revelation. "The gnostic knows the right time. He may delay a man for a wise reason, just as the Prophet delayed the conversion of [a man who had fought with him in battle]."[72]

ʿIzz spoke of the progressive degrees of awareness through which the disciple progresses. "He begins with his intellect. After that he begins with his feelings *(ḥiss)*. From the information you have gathered, you begin to 'feel' [intuit] things. After intuition, there is clairvoyance *(shafāfiyya)*. That is, a person who is very sensitive to the point where he sees what is behind the walls. Such a person sees more than the ordinary man. The Sufis say he is all-seeing *(baṣīr)*, which is one of the names of God. He sees by the light of God. How does he do this? God gives him a gift so that if a thief comes to him, by merely looking at him he can sense what he has done. That is *shafāfiyya*. A man came in to ʿUthmān ibn ʿAffān,[73] may God be pleased with him, and ʿUthmān looked at him and said, 'Do you come to see the Commander of the Faithful with the traces of adultery in your eyes?' The man said, 'He is telling the truth.' ʿUthmān was far from the incident, but he could sense that the man's eyes had a lustful look. The man asked, 'Is there revelation *(waḥy)* after the Messenger of God?' He said, 'No.' That is, Gabriel will not bring any revelations after the Messenger of God. This is only the believer's discernment of human nature *(firāsa)* in that he sees by the light of God. Witness *(mushāhada)* is a higher station than *shafāfiyya*. It is like the time when ʿUmar ibn al-Khattab's inner vision was unveiled and he saw the Muslim army fighting in Iraq and he called out, 'Sāriya, the mountain!' and he [Sāriya] heard the call. This is witness, the highest thing. Therefore there are saints in Aswan who speak to their brothers in Alexandria without a telephone, because they have their own telephone and television! This is witness *(shuhūd)*, the highest honor given people by God."

At the highest level of witness, says ʿIzz, the mystic sees the prophets, messengers, saints, and angels. Yet on another occasion, ʿIzz said that the vision of prophets must precede any direct vision of the Truth, thereby admitting that a higher stage of witness exists. This is consistent with the words of the eleventh-century mystic al-Ghazālī, who defined the stage of visions of saints, prophets, and angels as the *first* stage on the Sufi path. "Later, a higher state is reached; instead of beholding forms and figures, they come to stages in the 'way' which it is hard to describe in language; if a man attempts to express these, his words inevitably contain what is clearly erroneous."[74] Perhaps this is why saints at the highest stage of witness are speechless; the glory they perceive simply cannot be expressed.

CHAPTER 8

Women and Sexuality in Sufi Life and Thought

As we saw in chapter 2, the Egyptian Supreme Council of Sufi Orders officially bans female membership in the Orders, in order to prevent the mixing of men and women, which is prohibited under Islamic law and which is culturally considered morally decadent.[1] The solution to the problem of sexual tension and temptation in Islamic society has often been simply to ban women's participation in communal spiritual life, and the Supreme Council of Sufi Orders was following a time-honored principle—a principle that was not, however, followed by their Prophet. This principle was also undergoing rapid erosion in contemporary Egypt, in which mosques and voluntary associations host religious lessons for women, and the Islamist movement that began in the 1970s has attracted broad female participation. Despite the official denial of female membership in the Orders, I discovered that women are very much involved in Sufi activities. Not only do they figure prominently at saints' shrines and perform useful services in the hospitality tents set up during the moulids but they become disciples of shaykhs and even *shaykhas* (female shaykhs) in their own right, although they have no official recognition as such.

Shaykh Muḥammad Zakī Ibrāhīm of the Muḥammadiyya Shādhiliyya circumvented the prohibition of female membership in the Orders by establishing a women's section in a voluntary association, where such are allowed. The shaykh assured me in 1981 that with an overall membership of more than twenty thousand men and seven thousand women, the ʿAshīra Muḥammadiyya was both the largest voluntary association in Egypt and the voluntary association with the largest number of women. But other Orders make no such organizational adjustments, and women participate outright in all aspects of many Sufi Orders.

The women address Shaykh Muḥammad Zakī as *"Bābā"* ("Daddy"), and the women are called his "daughters." But I soon discovered that there are spiritual mothers in Sufism as well.

WOMEN AND SEXUALITY

One day when I was visiting a family during my research in 1980–81, the woman who was head of the household introduced a visitor to me as "my mother, who lives by Ḥusayn," that is, in the neighborhood of Ḥusayn's shrine. Since I knew that her mother lived in Ṭanṭā, I made further inquiry, and she explained, "This is my spiritual mother. I am her daughter in the spirit." I had already been a regular visitor at this household for eight months, and only now did I learn that they were involved in Sufism and that the woman's spiritual teacher was also a woman, Umm Fatḥī. Umm Fatḥī invited me to visit them at their *khidma* during the moulid of Ḥusayn, which was coming up. Umm Fatḥī, I discovered, was the wife of the former shaykh of the Musallamiyya Khalwatiyya Order and mother of the present shaykh. She presided over activities along with her daughter, Ḥāgga Laylā, who is the sister of the present shaykh. The shaykh himself was inconspicuous at the moulid, and the two women were clearly in charge; the others who were present referred to themselves as the sons and daughters of these women. Ḥāgga Laylā in particular seemed to take on a role that did not fit the traditional model for women: she associated with the men as one of them, embracing them, smoking cigarettes, and giving them orders. Later I learned that she was credited with insight into the spiritual world and could see and communicate with spirits. Her mother told me, "If women were allowed to be heads of the Orders, Laylā would have been it instead of her brother." As it was, her lack of official status had no bearing on her actual situation, for she was held in high regard by all.

The case of these two women is just one indication of the potential of Sufism, or indeed any form of mysticism, to offer greater opportunities for women than the mainstream, legalistic tradition. Leadership in mosque-centered Islam requires certification from the religious school system crowned by al-Azhar, and preachers and leaders of prayer are all men. Indeed, the mosque functions as something of a men's house, in which, until recently, women had little access. But the credentials of mysticism are by definition of another order, from the grace of God, and therefore the boundaries of sex and of literacy and formal education do not apply.

Sufi attitudes toward women are bound up with a perspective on the nature of spirituality and sexuality that sets them off from other Muslims. This perspective has deep roots in Sufism and must be situated in the broader context of the position of women in Islam and Sufi tradition. Such a broad topic cannot be covered exhaustively here, but I will highlight a few points pertaining to Islamic perspectives on the nature of women and sexuality.

TRADITIONAL SUFI ATTITUDES TOWARD WOMEN

At one level, Sufis share in the culture and perspective that is common to Muslims in general. There is a great deal of interest and controversy over the proper role and status of women in the Muslim world today, and this derives in large part from Western criticisms of the way Muslims and Islam have treated women. And indeed Islam does favor men over women in a number of ways. The Qurʾan itself says that men have a rank above women (2:228) and places men in charge of women because God made the one to excel over the other and because men spend their money to maintain women (4:34). Islamic law gives men more rights than women in marriage, divorce, and inheritance. The medieval commentators on the Qurʾan believed that the rank men enjoyed over women pertained to a vast array of advantages—natural, spiritual, and social.

On the other hand, the Qurʾan in no way implies that women are less than men in humanity; God created all humanity, male and female, from a single soul (4:1, 7:189). Women are promised the same spiritual rewards as men for the fulfillment of their religious duties, although the depictions of Paradise in the Qurʾan, replete with virgins for the sexual pleasure of the believers, are obviously drawn with men in mind. Although much is made in Islamic culture of the importance of modest dress for women, the Qurʾan is ambiguous in its definition of modesty norms and enjoins modesty on men as well as women. In time, however, modesty norms for women became extremely strict: the entire body of the woman is, according to Islamic law, regarded as pudendal and in need of covering. The fear of sexual temptation often dominates all other concerns pertaining to women in Islamic discourse.[2] In Arab society, honor is conceived in a corporate sense in families, and the honor of men resides in the chastity of their women. The very high cultural value given to the chastity of women encouraged Muslims to develop rigorous modesty codes for women.

Furthermore, in most Muslim societies, as we can document from both medieval literature and contemporary ethnographic studies, men regard women as more prone to immoral behavior than men, by virtue of their diminished intellectual capacity, and women are seen as a disruptive element in society. This belief is supported by a number of ḥadīths, which, though unlikely to be the actual words of the Prophet, do reveal the thinking of Muslims in the eighth century. The frequency with which these sayings are repeated by contemporary Muslims indicates that they continue to reflect much of their thinking. These sayings include "The majority of the inhabitants of hell are women," and "I leave my community no temptation more harmful to men than women," and "When a man and a woman are alone together, Satan is the third party." One ḥadīth goes so far as to say, "When you see a woman coming toward you, it is Satan approaching."

In the generation after the Prophet's death, moves were already made to remove women from the mosque. The theologian and mystic al-Ghazālī (d. 1111), while recognizing that the Prophet ordered men not to forbid women to pray at the mosques, endorsed the historical practice of excluding them from the mosques on the grounds that morals had deteriorated since the time of the Prophet, and it was no longer appropriate for any but old women to leave their homes.[3] Nonetheless, there have always been some women who have overcome the enormous barriers of their culture and distinguished themselves as religious scholars and acquired a reputation for holiness on a par with men. Such women are found especially among the Sufis.

The most famous of the female Sufis is undoubtedly the celibate mystic and lover of God, Rābiʿa al-ʿAdawiyya (d. 801).[4] The majority of early Sufi women were celibates and practiced extreme forms of asceticism. By maintaining celibate lifestyles, they rejected the guardianship of men and the requirement of obedience to men, as well as the burdens and responsibilities of being wives and mothers. Extreme abstinence from food also inhibits menstruation, which, under Islamic law, prevents women from prayer. Fasting, then, becomes a tool for ensuring their constant access to the presence of God on a par with men.[5] There were married Sufi women as well, such as the ninth-century Faṭīma of Nishapur, wife of Aḥmad ibn al-Khaḍrūya, who was consulted by such Sufi luminaries as Dhū ʾl-Nūn al-Miṣrī and Abū Yazīd al-Bisṭāmī.[6] Sufism continued to produce great women saints in later centuries, as Ibn ʿArabī's account of the miracles of various Sufi women, including one who was his teacher, illustrates.[7]

Yet the archetypal Sufi remains a man. Sufi ethics came to be known as *futuwwa,* "young manliness," based on the word *fatā,* meaning "young man," literally a code of chivalry that demanded courage, self-denial, and heroic generosity. This corresponds to the ancient Arab ethic known as *muruwwa,* "manliness," which upheld similar virtues of courage, extravagant hospitality, and indulgence toward those who are weak. It is significant that the Sufi biographer, Farīd al-Dīn ʿAṭṭār (d. 1220), listed Rābiʿa al-ʿAdawiyya among the men, rather than among the women. He explained that it is not the outward form that counts but the intention of the heart, and said, "When a woman becomes a 'man' in the path of God, she is a man and one cannot any more call her a woman."[8] ʿAṭṭār likewise said that the first "man" to enter Paradise will be Mary, mother of Jesus. He explained that "wherever these people, the Sufis, are, they have no separate existence in the Unity of God. In the Unity, what remains of the existence of 'I' or 'thou'? So how can 'man' or 'woman' continue to be?"[9] Jamal Elias reports that "biographical dictionaries often have a section entitled 'Women who achieved the status of men' and the Indian saint Farīd al-Dīn Ganj-i Shakar could refer to a pious woman as 'a man sent in the form of a woman.' "[10] Although this "compliment" paid to Rābiʿa and other Sufi women implies the degradation of the female sex as a whole and that true spirituality is normally found only among men, it also indicates that the sex of the body is not a barrier to the inspiration and grace of God. For this reason Annemarie Schimmel comments, "One should not be misled by the constant use of the word 'man' in the mystical literature of the Islamic languages: it merely points to the ideal human being who has reached proximity to God where there is no distinction of sexes; and Rābiʿa is the prime model of this proximity."[11]

SUFI ATTITUDES TOWARD MARRIAGE

Although celibacy was preferred by many early Sufis, men as well as women, some Muslims felt that this implied an endorsement of the Christian institution of monasticism, which the Qurʾan rejects as an invention of the Christians that God had never intended (57:27). Furthermore, as the concept of *Sunna*[12] in Islamic law implies, Muslims should follow the example of the Prophet, and the model set by the Prophet was a wholehearted approval of marriage. According to ḥadīth, the Prophet declared that there is no monasticism in Islam. In one anecdote, on hearing that one of his followers had taken a vow of celibacy, the Prophet rebukes him: "So you have made up your mind to be one of the brethren of Satan! If you want to be a Christian monk, join them openly. If you are one of us, you must follow our Sunna; and our Sunna is married life."[13] And in another ḥadīth: "Marriage is my Sunna, and whoever dislikes my Sunna dislikes me."[14] Marriage came to be regarded by many Muslims as a religious duty.

Medieval Sufis were not unanimous on this issue, however. Hujwīrī (d. ca. 1071) felt that women were the source of all evils and that marriage was not necessary to quell lust, and therefore best avoided.[15] Ghazālī, on the other hand—whose works continue to be authoritative and frequently read in Egypt—regarded human sexuality as an overwhelming and potentially destructive force that must be contained within marriage.[16] Such is the value given to chastity and the difficulty of maintaining it outside marriage that "he who marries preserves half his religion."[17] The Prophet is quoted as saying, "If someone comes to you with whose religion and trustworthiness you are pleased, get him married. If you do not, there will be discord and great corruption in the earth."[18] Ghazālī quotes al-Junayd (d. 910), the celebrated mystic of Baghdad, as saying, "I need sex just as I need food."[19] Muhammad's cousin, Ibn ʿAbbās, is quoted as saying, "The asceticism of the ascetic is incomplete until he marries," because only in marriage will he be able to overcome his passion and devote himself to God. Therefore it is said that a single prostration in prayer from a married man is better than seventy prostrations from a bachelor. A saying of another Companion implies that the single state is shameful: "If I had only ten more days to live I would want to marry, so as not to meet God as a bachelor."[20] The pleasure that comes from sexual intercourse is a foretaste of the pleasures of Paradise, where, according to the Qurʾan, chaste virgins will be at the service of the believers; sexual pleasure here on earth induces men to serve God more in order to obtain those pleasures.[21]

Although marriage has its pitfalls, it also has a number of benefits, according to Ghazālī. These include procreation, a legitimate release for sexual passions, the revival of the soul after engaging in the rigors of the spiritual life, having someone to manage the household, and exercising the soul by having the care of a family, fulfilling one's obligations toward one's wives, having patience with their morals, putting up with their abuse, hastening to correct them, guiding them to the way of religion, striving to earn legitimate wages on their behalf, and undertaking the education and discipline of children.[22] To endure suffering from wives and children is equal to fighting the jihād in the path of God.[23] Nonetheless, says Ghazālī, the character of most people is worsened by the challenge of living with another person, so marriage only improves the souls of those intending to benefit by such refinement.[24]

In all cases, for Ghazālī the traveler on the path of God is inevitably a man, and women constitute either a help or a hindrance to the spiritual life of men. The spiritual life of women is scarcely taken into account, although Ghazālī says it is the duty of men to instruct their wives in spiritual matters.[25] It is also their duty to fulfill their wives' sexual needs in order to ensure their chastity, for the chastity of women is the responsibility of men. Men are obliged to seek not only their own pleasure in intercourse but also that of their wives and to have intercourse with each wife at least once every four days;[26] presumably, the legal limit of four wives was interpreted as having a logic in the sexual needs of women.

WOMEN IN THE MEDIEVAL SUFI ORDERS

Although Sufi literature is directed toward a male audience in a context in which the superiority of men over women is assumed to be the natural order, some women nonetheless did participate in the Sufi Orders in medieval Islam. There were Sufi teachers in Mamlūk and Ottoman times that catered to women, and some shaykhs admitted women into their Orders, although this and the participation of women in dhikr were denounced by other Sufis.[27] According to the Egyptian mystic ʿAbd al-Wahhāb al-Shaʿrānī of the early Ottoman period, none of the women learned anything from their husbands, so the Sufi shaykhs had to give special attention to teaching them the rules of religion and their obligations in marriage and society.[28] Ahmad al-Ghazālī (d. 1123), the brother of the previously mentioned Abū Ḥāmid al-Ghazālī, deplored the loosening of morals that had occurred over time in the musical gatherings of the Sufis, as evidenced by the fact that women and adolescents were allowed to attend.[29] It appears to have been rare for a woman to become a *shaykha*, the most noteworthy exception being Zaynab Fātima bint al-ʿAbbās (d. 1394), shaykha of the women's retreat house *(ribāṭ)* in Cairo belonging to the Baghdādiyya Order.[30] The *ribāṭ* was founded in 1285 by Princess Tadhkaray for Zaynab bint Abū 'l-Barakāt "al-Baghdādiyya" "and her women."[31] Some men's Sufi retreat houses may have included women, for Maqrīzī says that one of them had a bathroom for women in addition to the bathroom for men.[32]

There were women shaykhas and scholars of the law in medieval times, most of them widows or divorcées, who lived in extreme abstinence and worship in Sufi *ribāṭs*.[33] It is significant that only women who had already completed their duty of marriage were free to devote themselves to the mystical life. *Ribāṭs* also functioned as places of refuge for divorced women who hoped to remarry and wished to keep their reputations unsullied.[34] The Maghribi writer Ibn al-Ḥājj, who opposed popular religion in general, compared the Sufi women to Christian nuns and criticized them for raising their voices during dhikr, for part of the expected modesty of women was that no one should hear their voices.[35] On the other hand, his countryman, the famous Sufi Muḥammad ibn Sulaymān al-Jazūlī (d. 1465), after his experience with a "mysterious but crucial figure of a 'hidden' woman saint," encouraged women to participate in his Order.[36]

SEXUAL SYMBOLISM AND FUNCTION IN SUFISM

But if women were intended to be neither seen nor heard, they were nonetheless at least implicitly the subject of a great deal of Sufi poetry that employed romantic love and sexual metaphor to express the ineffable mystical experience. Among the Sufis poetry is part of normal discourse, and it is impossible to read Sufi texts or sit among the Sufis even today without hearing a good deal of poetry, whether classical, colloquial, or spontaneously composed under inspiration. The use of metaphors of romantic love and sexuality in Sufi poetry was not without controversy. Many religious scholars inveighed against the use of explicit romantic descriptions that were alleged metaphors for the mystical experience and said that listening to a description of a beautiful object that is the source of evil is as forbidden as looking at it or touching it.[37]

Early Sufis were wary of excessive indulgence in sexual intercourse even within marriage, and emphasized that modesty is part of faith. Annemarie Schimmel points out that disgust with the world leads naturally to hatred for women, since through woman this world is renewed and continued.[38] The *nafs,* the lower self which must be killed and subdued in order to free the spirit to worship God, is feminine in the Arabic, as is *dunyā,* the lower world. These become personified in images of an ugly old crone or a prostitute who entices man and then leaves him in his misery.[39] Women are regarded as impure, for menstrual blood and postpartum blood prevent both prayer and sexual union, and sexual intercourse requires major ablution, an entire bath, for purification.

Sexual intercourse in most Islamic discourse is simply the satisfaction of a physical drive and a means to produce offspring. The Qurʾan tells Muslim men that women are their fields, and they may go in to their fields whenever they please (2:223). The sexual rights of husbands are emphasized in Islamic literature: if a woman refuses her husband's advances, the angels curse her until morning. She must yield to his desires, even if on the back of a camel.[40] Wives are simply functional outlets for the untamed lust of men. As one hadith says rather crudely: "If a woman approaches you, she comes in the form of Satan. If any one of you sees a woman that pleases him, let him go to his wife; with her it will be as with the other."[41]

Sexual knowledge, however, is part of the gnosis of the saint. In his book, *Recognizing Islam*, the British anthropologist Michael Gilsenan reports his conclusion, after research in a village in north Lebanon, that true shaykhs are known by their knowledge of inner secret truth, and that, in the lives of the villagers, this mystical insight is knowledge concerning sexuality, reproduction, and pollution. That is, a true shaykh is known by his ability to discern when someone is in a state of ritual pollution or whether a person has engaged in sexual intercourse, licit or illicit. Although he qualifies himself in a footnote by insisting he is not trying to suggest that sexuality, reproduction, and pollution are always the foundation of the social logic of the inner knowledge, he nonetheless found these to be the most socially significant aspects of a shaykh's legitimacy, despite, in his view, the oddness of connecting sexuality with mystical insight.[42]

Gilsenan's realization that shaykhs are credited with knowledge of the sexual acts of people is quite accurate, and consistent with traditional tales about Sufi shaykhs.[43] However, Gilsenan's analysis is too restrictive in two different ways. For one thing, the shaykh's knowledge of the unseen goes well beyond such matters and includes knowledge of who will live and who will die, the future destiny of the living and of unborn children, knowledge of spirits and the ability to see them and converse with them, knowledge of the hidden meanings of the Qurʾan, knowledge of the secrets contained in the letters of the Arabic alphabet, especially the "mysterious letters" at the beginning of chapters in the Qurʾan, and many other types of knowledge. This is true of contemporary shaykhs as well as of the shaykhs of old. On the other hand, a true shaykh's knowledge concerning sexuality goes beyond knowledge of the occurrence and manner of the sexual acts of his disciples; it includes knowledge of the true meaning of the sexual act itself. Far from being a separate dimension of life, sexuality is linked to mystical experience in a number of ways in the philosophy of Ibn ʿArabī, which has exerted considerable influence on the perspective of contemporary Egyptian Sufis. I will present Ibn ʿArabī's views at length because they represent a significant departure from previous Islamic perspectives and because Ibn ʿArabī's influence on contemporary Sufism remains profound, though usually mediated through other Sufi authors such as Shaʿrani and through an often anonymously developed oral tradition.

IBN ʿARABĪ'S VIEWS ON SEXUALITY

The great mystical philosopher Ibn ʿArabī (1165–1240) goes beyond the merely functional view of sexuality to discover mystical significance in the sexual act itself.[44] Ibn ʿArabī offers, at least in the context of Sufism, an entirely new perspective on the meaning of sexuality. In his philosophy, the Father Heaven-Mother Earth dualism, which some believe to be absent in the monotheistic religions,[45] is revived.

Ibn ʿArabī's philosophy is monistic, holding to the essential unity of all being; all existing things emerged from the "marriage" of the divine spirit, which is male, with Nature, which is female—or, in other passages, it is the combination of the divine Names with the elemental forms. Human marriage reflects this cosmic marriage, and it is by virtue of this correspondence that human sexuality derives its sacrality. In fact, says Ibn ʿArabī, Islamic law is the best law in marriage because it alone has set the number of wives a man may marry at four, which perfectly reflects the marriage of the divine Spirit with the four elements to produce its "children," all the material existents.[46] Therefore, far from being the mere satisfaction of physical appetites, for the gnostic sexual union offers the possibility of true mystical insight.

In his major work, *The Meccan Revelations,* he states, "I used to hate women and sex at the start of my entry into this path." He continued this way for eighteen years, until he came to contemplate the hadith in which Muhammad says, "Three things have been made beloved to me in this world of yours: women, perfume, and prayer." He noted that Muhammad's love for women did not spring from his own nature, but he specifies that God had made them beloved to him. Ibn ʿArabī writes, "I feared God's wrath, for I hated what God had made beloved to His Prophet." He asked God to remove this hatred from his heart, and his prayer was answered. Indeed, he says, God "made me the most compassionate of men with them, and the most earnest to maintain their rights, because I do this out of inner vision, from God making them beloved to me, not a natural love." He states, "Whoever loves women as Muhammad did, loves God."[47] In his later work, *The Bezels of Wisdom,* he contemplates a particular wisdom contained in the divine "word" expressed in each of the prophets. His chapter on the Muhammadan word is a reflection on this hadith concerning the Prophet's love for women, perfume, and prayer.[48]

In Ibn ʿArabī's philosophy, God's Names are manifested in creation, which then functions as a mirror in which God sees Himself. Whereas all of creation manifests the Names of God, the Perfect Man, identified with the eternal Muhammadan reality, a spiritual essence that is the source of all prophethood, contains the totality of these names. All other things in creation contain only certain of the divine Names, but taken together the cosmos, like the Perfect Man, reflects their totality. The Perfect Man is therefore the microcosm—or, one could say, the cosmos is a "large man." The Qurʾan states that God molded Adam out of clay and breathed His spirit into him (32:9). God's longing for man is none other than a longing for His own Self, this divine spirit that is in man, for man is created in his external aspect and divine in his internal aspect. Therefore ḥadīth says that God made man in his own image. Just as man was made in the image of God, woman was made in the image of man (for Qurʾan exegetes learned from the Jews the story of Eve's creation from Adam). Woman is from man as man is from God, and just as God longs for man because the whole is drawn toward its part, so does man long for woman, "as something yearns for itself, while she feels longing for him as one longs for that place to which one belongs."[49] Furthermore, "love arises only for that from which one has one's being," which for man is God. That is why Muhammad said that God made women beloved to him. "His love is for his Lord in Whose image he is, this being so even as regards his love for his wife, since he loves her through God's love for him, after the divine manner."[50]

When a man loves a woman, he desires sexual union with her, because there is "no greater union than that between the sexes." The goal of the Sufi is to be annihilated in God, in order to achieve union with Him. In sexual intercourse, the man is annihilated in the woman, says Ibn ʿArabī, but this is in fact a type of annihilation in God.[51] The ritual washing that is required after intercourse is a total purification of his desire, for God is jealous that man should desire any but Him. This purification by ritual ablution enables man once again to behold God in the woman.[52] Yet, he says in *The Meccan Revelations,* if a gnostic's passion is divine and not carnal—that is, if his attachment is to God and not to a temporal being—then no purification is needed.[53] It is not the act that is polluting but carnal desire, or "seeing oneself" instead of God.

Since the divine Essence is transcendent and inaccessible, humans can only see God as He is reflected in creation, and for a man there is no better way to contemplate God than in woman. This is because God contains the totality of all the meanings of the universe, and indeed is the place where opposites are conjoined. He is, therefore, both active/male and receptive/female. It is insufficient for man to contemplate himself by himself to understand God, because he will see only receptivity in himself in relation to God. But in relation to woman, man is active, because woman was created from man. Therefore the best and most perfect kind of contemplation of God is in woman. "Because of this the Prophet loved women by reason of [the possibility of] perfect contemplation of God in them."[54]

Sexual union imitates God's relationship with man. It is a sacred act because it corresponds to God's manifestation in the forms of the cosmos. As Ibn ʿArabī puts it, God's manifestation in the forms of the cosmos has its correspondence in the physical, spiritual, and logical realms. It corresponds to sexual union in the physical world, spiritual concentration in the realm of luminous spirits, and the ordering of premises toward a conclusion in the realm of logic. All this, says Ibn ʿArabī (in Austin's translation), is the sexual union or consummation of the Primordial Singularity in all its aspects.[55] This enigmatic correspondence is explained by Abū 'l-ʿAlā ʿAffīfī in this way in his Arabic commentary on *The Bezels of Wisdom:* Ibn ʿArabī sees triplicity inherent in all things in the cosmos. Sexual union is that which, by the joining of two parts, produces a third, and thereby imitates God's creative act of "breathing" into the form of man to create him in His own image. Likewise in logic the syllogism is a three-part construct whereby the major premise and the minor premise yield a conclusion.[56] This is an accurate statement, and Ibn ʿArabī does, as we have seen, discuss the "marriage" of the spirits or divine lights with the elemental forms, which combine to produce all things in the cosmos. This is compared with human marriage, which, by the combination of male and female, produces a third, the child.[57] However, Ibn ʿArabī does not speak of procreation as the goal of sexual union here. The triplicity of which he speaks is that of God, man, and woman, "the man yearning for his Lord Who is his origin, as woman yearns for man. His Lord made women dear to him, just as God loves that which is in His own image."[58]

What distinguishes the sexual act of the gnostic from that of ordinary men is that the gnostic perceives the spirit of God in woman, and by joining himself to her becomes aware of his own oneness with God and of God in his active and passive aspects. "Whoever loves women in this way loves with a divine love, while he whose love for them is limited to natural lust lacks all [true] knowledge of that desire. For such a one she is mere form, devoid of spirit, and even though that form be indeed imbued with spirit, it is absent for one who approaches his wife or some other woman solely to have his pleasure of her, without realizing Whose the pleasure [really] is. Thus he does not know himself [truly]. . . . Such a man is [really] in love with pleasure itself and, in consequence, loves its repository, which is woman, the real truth and meaning of the act being lost on him. If he knew the truth, he would know Whom he is enjoying and Who it is Who is the enjoyer; then he would be perfected."[59]

Woman does not parallel the clay of man into which God breathed his spirit; the image here is not of a receptacle for the creation of a new being but rather the emphasis is on the proper understanding of the nature of the act and the pleasure itself. Indeed, if one engages in sexual intercourse in the realization of God in woman, the act itself is a means for his own perfection. This is exactly the opposite of the intercourse of the lustful man for whom woman is merely a body without a spirit. Elsewhere Ibn ʿArabī explicitly states that the *quṭb* engages often in sexual intercourse and loves women. He does this because the divine manifestations in sexual union exceed those of acts of worship. "He desires sexual union not for the sake of procreation, but only for pleasure. The consummation of sexual intercourse is itself commended in the law . . . and the sexual act of the one in this spiritual station is like the sexual union of the people of Paradise, only for the sake of pleasure, for it is the greatest manifestation of God—a fact that has been hidden from men and jinn, except for those servants whom God has especially chosen for it. Likewise, the intercourse of animals is purely for pleasure. Many gnostics have failed to grasp this truth, for it is one of the secrets which only a few of the 'people of providence' *(ahl al-ʿināya)* understand." The nobility of sexual pleasure is indicated by the fact that it makes a person "pass away from his own strength and pretensions *(al-lidhdha 'l-mufniyya la-hu ʿan quwwatihi wa daʿōwāhu)*." Furthermore, the person who is so subjugated takes pleasure in his subjugation, contrary to other forms of subjugation. "This nobility has escaped people, who have considered it an animalistic passion *(shahwa ḥayawāniyya)* from which they refrain—

although they have called it by the most noble of names when they say it is animalistic, that is, a characteristic of animals/living beings *(al-ḥayawān),* and what is more noble than life *(ḥayāt)?* So what they have deemed ugly with regard to themselves is the very thing that is praiseworthy for the perfect gnostic."[60]

Ibn ʿArabī's reversal of the usual Muslim understanding of "animalistic" is typical of his idiosyncratic, and sometimes outrageous, insights derived from word analysis. "Animalistic" normally refers to that which is most base in humans, catering to craven desire, devoid of all spiritual values. But the word "animal" *(ḥayawān)* in Arabic literally means "a living thing," and, as Ibn ʿArabī points out, life is a noble thing. (Indeed, one of God's Names is "the Living One"—*al-Ḥayy*). The application of this insight to his revisionist thinking regarding sexuality should be taken carefully, however, for Ibn ʿArabī continues to contrast the ordinary man's lustful approach toward the pleasure of sex with that of the gnostic. The word translated here as "causing him to pass away" could also be translated "causing him to become annihilated," to attain *fanāʾ*. The overwhelming pleasure to be found in sexual intercourse in which the gnostic perceives the divine in woman is actually a type of annihilation in God, for both remove him from any awareness of his own self. This is a far cry from endorsing sexual indulgence in its usual sense. As R. W. J. Austin comments, "The very lack of any sacred and divine dimension in modern eroticism, with all its awful ephemerality and egotism, would condemn it utterly in his eyes."[61]

It is not surprising to see that another characteristic of the *quṭb,* according to Ibn ʿArabī, is love of beauty in all its forms, for they all express the absolute beauty of the divine.[62] It is this very idea that has led some Sufis to seek out the company of that which best reflects the divine beauty, a beautiful girl or a handsome youth. The gnostic's desire for women, according to Ibn ʿArabī, is the desire of the whole for its part as well as the desire and love of the older for the younger, because it has come more recently from God.[63] Furthermore, the gnostic is motivated by compassion to keep the company of women, just as the Prophet Muhammad was motivated by compassion to marry many women, since he had seen that they constitute the greater part of the inhabitants of hellfire.[64] Ibn ʿArabī does not explain how this company benefits women, but we have seen that hadith teaches that in the afterlife a person will be with the one he loves. By securing a woman's love, the Prophet or gnostic actually guarantees her salvation, for her love for him will be counted as love for God and will save her; she will be with him in

Paradise. In this way, keeping the company of women serves them as well as the man. He concludes, "Whoever knows the value and secret of women does not abstain from loving them. Rather, loving them is part of the perfection of the gnostics, and it is a prophetic inheritance and a divine love."[65]

Disciples should follow the rule of their shaykhs concerning keeping the company of women, but if they are true shaykhs, Ibn ʿArabī says, they will not be harsh with their disciples. He implies here that shaykhs should not repress their disciples, but he qualifies his statement by adding, "The spiritual states of people differ. It could be that the very thing that is good for one person corrupts another. . . . Those who do not have spiritual intuition *(kashf)* and do not receive divine discourse . . . should avoid anything that occupies his heart with something other than God—for him it is sedition. He must exert his intellect to overpower his lust."[66] He adds that one should keep company with beardless youths or women only for the sake of God, and implies that if it is done without this goal, the person suffers.[67] In fact, he says, "The disciple should not take up the company of women until he himself becomes a woman. If he becomes female and attaches to the lower world and sees how the higher world loves it, and sees himself in every spiritual condition and moment in perpetual sexual union as a female (*mankūhan dāʾiman,* ie., assuming the passive role in an unceasing act of coition) and does not see himself in his spiritual insight as male first, but purely female, and he becomes pregnant from that marriage and gives birth—then he may keep company with women and incline toward them, and love for them will not harm him. As for the gnostics' keeping company with women, [permission to do so] is absolute, because they see the absolute, holy, divine hand in their giving and taking. Everyone knows his own spiritual condition."[68]

The ideal Sufi is, according to a popular saying, like a corpse in the hands of God and of his spiritual master, the essence of passivity, a female likeness. Is that why Ibn ʿArabī says the Sufi must become female and the object of perpetual divine coition? His frequent mention of the male as active/subject and the female as passive/object lends credibility to this point of view. Ibn ʿArabī also describes the disciples as "brides of the Absolute Reality," and for their shaykh they are "like the one who combs the bride's hair and adorns her."[69] The Sufi is female in his relation to God, but he is active, like God, in his relation to woman, for man is to woman as God is to man.

It should come as no surprise that Ibn ʿArabī's ideas became the object of attack even in his own time and that analyses of his ideas have served to undermine the legitimacy of Sufism as a whole. One recent book attacks Ibn ʿArabī's doctrine regarding women and sexuality with a section entitled "Incarnation in Women," and another, "Why did Ibn ʿArabī worship women?"[70] Such titles demonstrate either ignorance or willful distortion of Ibn ʿArabī's views, but they demonstrate the tactics of many modern-day detractors of Sufism, who see Ibn ʿArabī as the epitome of the danger posed by Sufism. In 1979 such people even succeeded in having the Egyptian People's Assembly ban Ibn ʿArabī's works in the country.[71] Ibn ʿArabī's influence on popular Sufism, however, remains profound, though usually unacknowledged.

THE GNOSTIC AND THE LAW

As we have seen, the philosophy of Ibn ʿArabī allows that the very things that must be prohibited to the masses may be of the greatest benefit to the perfected gnostic. Ibn ʿArabī even states that there are some who have been annihilated from their sins and are under God's protection, even if they appear to do something that is contrary to Islamic Law. God has said to them, "Do what you please, I have forgiven you." For them, nothing is prohibited.[72]

Indeed, mystical insight sometimes constitutes a reversal of things as they apparently are. Conventional wisdom is that modesty or shame *(ḥiyāʾ)* is part of faith. But the famous Sufi poet Jalāl al-Dīn Rūmī (d. 1273) retorted, "Shame hinders you from true faith," because it inhibits people from willingly sacrificing reputation and worldly interests in the way of God.[73] The controversial Malāmatiyya movement in medieval Sufism taught that it is the highest virtue to be seen doing reprehensible things, for in this way people would be repulsed, and one's service to God would be for the sake of God alone. Many Sufi sayings are paradoxes, even on the moral plane, and in mysticism symbols turn logic inside out. Zulaykhā, the cunning woman who tried to seduce Joseph (Qurʾan 12:23–32), becomes in Sufi tradition not a symbol of wanton women but a model of extravagant love, the love of the Sufi. Likewise, in Sufi poetry wine becomes the symbol not of sinful indulgence but of the intoxicating presence of God. The Sufis are by definition those who hold to the superiority of hidden truths and hidden virtues over external meanings, status, and religious ostentation. Thus for the ordinary

Muslim, when a man and a woman are alone together, Satan is the third party, and the mixing of men and women brings corruption. For the spiritual man, the bringing together of men and women may yield spiritual fruits unobtainable even through acts of worship.

Naturally these discussions of sexuality in Sufism tend to raise the issue of the immoral behavior that is sometimes alleged to occur among the Sufis. From a Sufi point of view, if a gnostic appears to engage in behavior commonly regarded as forbidden, the outsider should withhold judgment. Many statements and deeds that on the face of things are prohibited are, once one has entered into the transcendent esoteric Truth, right and good. We have already had occasion to allude to the Qurʾanic story of the man commonly identified as Khiḍr (18:65–82), who had received mercy and knowledge from God and who outraged Moses with his apparently immoral acts. When Moses could bear it no longer, his companion instructed him in the hidden wisdom behind each of these acts and informed him that he had done these things at God's command. Khiḍr is the prototype of the mystical guide. His access to the secrets of God made his apparently wrong deeds right. Therefore, the Sufis believe, when one has entered into the Truth, nothing is prohibited; that is, certain deeds that are normally prohibited become licit in certain contexts when one has access to a higher Truth. For the Law appeals only to the intellect and is limited by the limitations of the intellect, but love knows no limits, and the Truth of God is without limits. Nonetheless, this is a secret that must not be divulged to the masses, for freedom without killing the ego leads to indulgence and debauchery.

Ibn ʿArabī also appeals to the story of Khiḍr to illustrate his belief that believers sin only out of heedlessness or false interpretation. The deeds performed by the "people of vision" are not sin in God's eyes, although those whose vision is veiled say they are. God excuses them for their accusations, for they are ignorant and their intention is right, namely, to uphold the Law of God. But the gnostic who does the deed is not a sinner.[74]

The Sufis have often been accused of immorality. While there are some examples of curious rites involving vestiges of pre-Islamic fertility cults associated with the celebrations of certain saints' days, particularly during the moulid of Sayyid Aḥmad al-Badawī in Ṭanṭā, the accusations of immorality often derive from nothing more than the admission of women into the activities of the Sufi Orders. In the early 1980s a prominent shaykh of the Muslim Brotherhood in an interview in the official magazine of the Egyptian Supreme Council of Sufi Orders denounced the mixing of men and women among many "so-called Sufis."[75] Many Sufis whose opinions would seem to be far removed from those of the Muslim Brotherhood are equally horrified by Sufis who believe their spiritual state allows them to transcend the limits imposed by the Sharīʿa. Qushayrī stated that one of the conditions of traveling the Sufi path is abandoning the company of women.[76] Aḥmad Raḍwān said that the true Sufi is one for whom worship and obedience to God become a pleasure and an honor, not an onerous duty. "The Sufi is not the one who says, 'We have attained a station in which obligation is removed.' This is the worst sort of harm to the believers from Satan. Among them are those who mingle with strange women and say, 'I am in a state with God!' "[77] The presence of women is usually seen as a sign of the loosening of morals, and in keeping with the mores of Upper Egypt, Aḥmad Raḍwān generally did not allow women into his *sāḥa.* Sufi shaykhs sometimes may be heard echoing the vague accusations of non-Sufis, that some shaykhs abuse their authority by taking advantage of their female disciples.

However, the teaching that Aḥmad Raḍwān explicitly denies here, that the Sufi may reach a spiritual station in which he may transcend ordinary limitations imposed on male-female interaction, was taught by Shaykh ʿIzz to those he deemed spiritually prepared to receive it. Shaykh ʿIzz considers Aḥmad Raḍwān his teacher. When I confronted him with the apparent contradiction between his teachings and those of his teacher, he said that permission to mingle with women is not absolute, and extreme care must be exercised regarding the dissemination of this teaching. Just as Ibn ʿArabī taught, what is permissible and spiritually valuable for the gnostic may be deadly for the novice. Most Sufi shaykhs prefer to teach strict observance of the Shariʿa and express stern disapproval of any leniency in this regard.

WOMEN IN THE SUFI ORDERS TODAY

The policies of shaykhs toward the participation of women in their Orders vary. Some shaykhs welcome women just as they do men. Women often go to shaykhs for personal problems, especially if it is believed that evil spirits or magic are involved. Some shaykhs as a general rule do not deal with women, but make exceptions. Some offer special meetings for women, and women are as interested as men in religious matters. One women's lesson offered by the Burhāniyya attracted about one hundred women. Most shaykhs allow women to observe their group dhikr, even if they are not allowed to participate in it.

Although women and children are allowed into all saints' shrines, their presence is more circumscribed in some shrines than in others. One of the reasons women are not required to attend the communal prayer in mosques is no doubt their greater susceptibility to ritual pollution, not only through menstruation and postpartum blood flow, but also by their association with young children, who might pollute them and the ground through urination or defecation. Some of these concerns apply to shrines as well. I was told not to bring my baby into shrines for fear that she might wet herself, polluting herself, me, and the shrine itself in the process. Nonetheless, many young children are brought by their mothers into shrines.

Although saints' shrines have always been available to women, in a way that mosques have not been (so they are not men's houses, as mosques are), they are certainly not specifically *women's* social places in Egypt, as Fatima Mernissi claims they are in Morocco.[78] The exceptions are saints who are thought to cater particularly to women's needs, such as Abū 'l-ʿSuʿūd. It is significant that there is no *ḥaḍra* attached to the visiting day of Abu 'l-ʿSuʿud, as there is to the other saints of Cairo who claim one of the seven days of the week as their own. Instead, women perform the Islamically illegitimate ritual of *zār* in houses near the shrine on his visiting day. Earlier I argued that *zār*s are not a *religious* parallel to dhikr, but they do function in some sense, though not perfectly, as a *social* parallel in the women's world to the dhikr in the men's world. Some women say they don't join in dhikr, only in *zār*s, and say that *zār*s are like dhikr. But many others deny any such equivalence. As we have seen, the overt spiritual goals of the two are not the same, despite a certain confluence of terminology—*ḥaḍra*—and the use of *madīḥat al-nabī* (praise of the Prophet) music in some *zār*s, which is, however, performed by men. The more exclusively female zars, which feature distinctive Sudanese-style music, do not have this dhikrlike music of praise to the Prophet and concentrate more firmly on placating the spirit.

Women are sometimes chased away from the immediate vicinity of saints' tombs, into adjoining rooms apart, and they are simply excluded from certain shrines (Ḥusayn and Sayyida Zaynab) after sunset. In many Islamic groups, the presence of women is associated with desacralization, as in the case of the self-styled "orthodox" Sufi Order, the Ḥāmidiyya Shādhiliyya, who exclude women in order "to preserve the holiness and dignity of the mulid."[79] Nonetheless, the saint functions in some sense as a defender of the weak, which perforce includes women. Women often feel free to sit by saints' shrines and even to nurse their babies there. It is not a specifically male space. The exception to this rule is the prohibition of women from entering the shrines of Ḥusayn and Sayyida Zaynab after sunset. Mosque attendants explain to indignant would-be female visitors that this is because the time of visitation is over, and it is now time for prayer, preaching, and dhikr—specifically male activities in the public domain. The women persist in sitting outside the green door to the Ḥusayn shrine, and people pass by handing out water, tea, candy, and perfume. Some of the male visitors who come with women stand with them outside rather than leaving them unattended. At the Sīdī Shādhilī shrine, where the shrine and mosque are in separate buildings, it is more obvious that men pray in the mosque, while women pray in the shrine. Since normally women pray at home while men pray in the mosque, the shrine offers a refuge for women away from home. At the shrine of ʿAbd al-Nabī during his moulid in Hawatka, women sat nursing their babies right next to the tomb, although, true to Upper Egyptian custom, they were scarcely to be seen among the men outside. Shrines often function as havens of this sort for women, as a resting place where no one can bother them and they can nurse their babies in peace.

Unlike mosques, saints' shrines in general have been marked by a lack of sexual segregation in Islam, from the greatest shrine of them all, the Kaʿba, to the saints' shrines that dot the landscape all over the Muslim world. At the very center, the focal point of sanctity, the demarcation between male and female breaks down. On the hajj, women are *forbidden* to cover their faces, and there is no segregation of the sexes. Likewise the most sacred mosques, insofar as they function as shrines, are open to women. At a time when women were forbidden to enter the mosques during prayer, they were sufficiently numerous in the shrine of Husayn on the day of ʿAshūrāʾ for them to dominate the entire space of the mosque, even sitting on the pulpit stairs, according to Edward Lane, writing in 1835–36. In the vicinity of the shrine itself the crowd was so dense that he found himself cheek-to-cheek with one woman, and it was said that no man went to the Husayn mosque on the feast of ʿAshūrāʾ except in order to be jostled by the women in the crowd.[80] This would seem to indicate that although public sacred space for prayer is a male domain (for, according to ḥadīth, the prayer of a woman is more meritorious if performed at home), at the most sacred times the most sacred centers of spiritual power do not separate or exclude women. The concentration of holiness is such that the presence of women no longer affects their sanctity; it is in the less inherently sacred spaces of mosque or dhikr that the presence of women has a desacralizing effect. Indeed, some of these very centers of spiritual power derive their sanctity from saintly women; in the aura of sanctity distinctions between male and female break down.

This pertains to visitation, not to prayer and dhikr. Women do not participate in the dhikr inside the mosque of al-Ḥusayn on Fridays, but they may well participate in dhikrs in the square behind the Ḥusayn mosque, as they do in public squares outside of some of the more remote mosques of the *ahl al-bayt,* especially those of Fāṭima al-Nabawiyya and ʿAlī Zayn al-ʿĀbidīn. At these dhikrs women sometimes participate in the midst of the men, and no one rebukes them. The presence of women at a dhikr may be a sign of a relative lack of concern for propriety. These dhikrs disintegrate at times into an irreverent, partylike atmosphere, with people, including the musicians themselves, imitating folk dancing. It should be noted that while men may be roughly corrected for such misbehavior, they do not arouse the contempt that women arouse when they

Figure 9. Woman doing dhikr on 30 June 1988 at the side of the mosque as another woman watches the men in dhikr.

engage in erotic dancing during dhikr. The more somber the atmosphere, the more charged with holiness the gathering, the more likely it is to exclude women or limit them to the role of spectators.

Women who participate in dhikr are often more restrained than men, rarely using the same full swing of the body that men do, covering their faces with a sheer black cloth, all reflections of the shyness they feel at public exposure, particularly in the unpredictable ambiance of dhikr. Many women say they do not participate in communal dhikr because it is shameful for a woman to be seen. An anthropological study of Nubian dhikr rituals observed that women were excluded because of the difficulty of assuring their ritual purity.[81] This same reasoning has not been mentioned by any one of the many people I questioned in Egypt on this subject. In the meetings of the Jāzūliyya Ḥusayniyya Shādhiliyya Order, women are seated on one side of the shaykh and men on the other. Their dhikr is performed seated, which removes much of the distinction between men and women's participation, as frequently women are too shy to stand to perform dhikr. Although the men showed emotion more readily than women, the women also became deeply engrossed and participated as equally as the men. The women also led the procession in the Jāzūliyya Order's private celebration of the moulid of the Prophet.

Cultural mores dictate much of the behavior of men and women associated with the Sufi Orders, and distinctions among them reflect distinctions in the broader society. The men and women of Bayt ʿAbāṭa are extremely casual in their interactions. Shaykh Hāshim ʿAbāṭa (d. 1985) used to encourage women to participate in the dhikr, although since his death most of the women merely watch the men in dhikr. But women march in the processions along with the men, and one woman in their group is a pretty young flirt who loves to tease the sterner older men. Her behavior would have been regarded by most Sufi groups as outrageous. This same woman's aunt may occasionally be seen slapping one of the men on the back. The behavior of the men and women in this group reflects not Sufi thought but the extreme informality of male-female relations in the *baladī* (lower-class) quarters of old Cairo.[82] In Upper Egypt, where men and women are rigorously segregated, one may go to a smaller moulid and scarcely see a woman among the tents of the Sufis; their role is generally restricted to the back sections where food and tea are being prepared. However, at the moulid of ʿAbd al-Raḥīm al-Qināwī, I saw a group of women form a parallel dhikr to the dhikr of the men in one of the Sufi tents. In the Delta and Cairo, women are very much in evidence, although they are still outnumbered by men. On the culminating night of the moulid of Sayyid Aḥmad al-Badawī in Ṭanṭā, the vast space of the mosque is covered with thousands of men, women, and children lying close together, side by side, sleeping, sitting, reading the Qur'an, praying, or just watching the other visitors. There is no regard for the segregation of the sexes whatsoever, and no one pays particular attention to the person whose head is at his or her knee. But in the dhikr itself, it is less common to see women.

When women do participate in dhikr, they may cover their faces with a light or sheer veil. It is rare for women to have a separate dhikr where they might participate without consideration of such social proprieties. Ernst Bannerth reported in an article in 1971 that a branch of the Rifaʿiyya called the ʿAmriyya had a separate section for women, which had a dhikr of their own on Sunday afternoons.[83] The mosque where he wrote that they had their headquarters has since been taken over by Jamʿiyyat Shabāb Sayyidnā Muḥammad, an offshoot of the Muslim Brotherhood, and I am unable to say whether this group still exists and still has a separate dhikr for women. I was told by a woman in the Burhāmiyya Order that the Burhāniyya Order gives women a separate room to do their dhikr in the dark, but this was denied by a male representative of that Order in an interview. I was also told that there was a woman's *ḥaḍra* held in an ancient Egyptian tomb by the Pyramids, which an American observer swore was Sufi, but her description sounded more like a *zār* than a dhikr, and public *zār*s are, like public dhikrs, called *ḥaḍra*s. That ceremony had been banned by Egyptian authorities once it was discovered.

I finally did discover a women's branch of a Sufi Order, the Muḥammadiyya Sharʿiyya, which had its own dhikr in a mosque in Heliopolis. This dhikr was led by a woman, and was performed seated, chanted in perfect unison without music, breath control techniques, or any real emotion. Their dhikr left the impression that zeal for orthodoxy had precluded any truly mystical content. The group had a female teacher, who was proud of having studied with Dr. ʿAbd al-Ḥalīm Maḥmūd and received a certificate from al-Azhar. Her teachings were remarkably lacking in specifically Sufi content. Nonetheless, the women were proud of the fact that they are unique in having a separate section and dhikr for women.

Although the musicians and singers in dhikr are usually men, there are a few women who perform these functions as well. Such women face the burden of realization that when they sing of love, the most common theme in Sufi songs, they risk becoming the object of the romantic imaginations of their mostly male audience.[84]

On the other hand, some contemporary Egyptian Sufis believe that if a person has entered into the spirit, things pertaining to the flesh have little meaning. Although women are commonly regarded as weaker than men and closer to Satan, Shaykh ʿIzz explained, they may transcend the common concerns of their sex and become great saints of God. It is not uncommon to find a woman who is "spiritual mother" to both men and women. Although it is not usual for a woman to be named actual shaykh of an Order, people may openly acknowledge that the true head of the Order is a woman. One such example is Ḥāgga Laylā of the Musallamiyya Khalwatiyya Order, whom we have already described. Another is Sāmiya Abū 'l-Maʿāṭī of one of the branches of the Burhāmiyya. Her father was a great shaykh, and when he died his son inherited his position, but his *sirr* (secrets, insight, power) are believed to have been inherited by his daughter. At the moulids she sits at the side of the tent, smoking cigarettes, moving to the music of the dhikr, occasionally appearing to shudder. She holds out her hand to the men and women who come to hold it and kiss it to receive some of her baraka.

Both Ḥāgga Laylā and Sāmiya Abū 'l-Maʿāṭī are anomalies in the world of women. One woman described Ḥāgga Laylā as "walking with the men," and another told me that no one would marry her, because she smoked cigarettes and acted just like a man. This latter opinion, offered to me in 1981, proved to be incorrect, for Ḥāgga Laylā did marry another Sufi from a different Order. When I met Ḥāgga Laylā again in 1987, she had a three-year-old daughter. Her husband was absent much of the time, traveling the moulid circuit, which suited her very well. The only reason to get married, she said, was to have children. Her daughter was enough for her, and she had no need for further conjugal relations. Her mother, who did not remarry after the death of her husband but shared her apartment with two of her "spiritual sons," shared her distaste for sexual intercourse, saying with disgust "the smell of it is in my nostrils." The strong endorsement of sexual intercourse in the writings of Ibn ʿArabī and al-Ghazālī is evidently not shared by all Sufis. It would be interesting to know whether the revulsion felt by Ḥāgga Laylā and Umm Fatḥī for sexual intercourse was idiosyncratic, specifically female, or representative of a whole other tendency in contemporary Sufism.[85] Unfortunately, I did not have the opportunity to find out.

Not all prominent Sufi women are anomalies like Ḥāgga Laylā and Sāmiya Abū 'l-Maʿāṭī. Many women saints do not depart from the norms of feminine behavior and yet are known for their piety, hospitality, miracles, and spiritual guidance to both men and women. Ḥāgga Zakiyya (d. 1982), whom I describe in the following chapter, is an outstanding example of this type of saint.

Because they have transcended the lusts of the body and have founded their relationships in the spirit, under certain circumstances Sufis may be able to disregard some of the barriers that normally pertain between men and women in Egyptian society. Umm Fatḥī readily admitted that there are people who are scandalized by the freedom Sufi men and women enjoy in their interactions, but, true to Sufi tradition, the opinions of other people were of no concern to her. Shaykh ʿIzz was, in his younger days, a spiritual son of Ḥāgga Zakiyya. He used to sleep with his head on her lap, and she called him her "daughter," not her son (a nice reversal of the "compliment" paid to Rābiʿa), to indicate that labels of the flesh had been overcome and they had returned to the innocence of children. The true Sufi man becomes perfect, able to control his passions. Shaykh ʿIzz boasted that a pretty woman meant nothing more to him than a wall or a piece of furniture as far as her body is concerned; his love for her should be purely spiritual.

Traveling Sufi men and women often mingle with one another without concern for social proprieties. One Sufi singer met his wife at the dhikrs held by the Ḥusayn mosque every Friday. For seven years before they were married they traveled the circuit of saint's day festivals together, sleeping together on the ground under one blanket. He loved her in the spirit, he says, and there was never any lust between them. They finally married to avoid scandal, although his family does not approve of his choice of a wife.

All of this is likely to send horrified shivers up the spines of most pious Muslims, especially in this period of renewed emphasis on the need to avoid temptation by separating the sexes and covering women. In the flesh and on the level of the intellect, Sufis would agree. Likewise they would agree with a ḥadīth often heard in Egypt that states that "When a man and a woman are alone together, Satan is the third party." For this reason, although women may be welcome at exclusive Sufi gatherings, for example, they may be carefully segregated at large public gatherings. Sufis are as careful as any other religious Muslims to maintain proper decorum and modest dress. Indeed, an impressive dignity, propriety, and mutual respect pervade most Sufi interactions. But having been made free from fleshly attachments, the Sufi can interact with other people without fear of temptation. For the sake of the weak man, women should not expose themselves to public view; but for the spiritual man, there is no temptation. So the Sufis may interact with a certain freedom with selected individuals among themselves that they do not exercise with those outside their group.

This distinction was reinforced to me when Shaykh ʿIzz and I stayed overnight at the home of the famous *munshid,* Aḥmad al-Tūnī. His house had been transformed into a *khidma* for the moulids of Shaykh ʿAbd al-Nabī and Shaykh al-Tuhāmī, father of the most popular *munshid* in Egypt, Tūnī's fellow townsman, Yāsīn al-Tuhāmī. The two moulids were held back to back. As honored guests, Shaykh ʿIzz and I were escorted to Aḥmad al-Tūnī's own bedroom and told to sleep there. There were two large beds and a couch. I slept in one bed, Shaykh ʿIzz on the couch, and we left the main bed for our host, leaving the door open and instructing his wife to tell him he was free to enter. However, when our host joined us for breakfast the next morning he informed us that he had not slept in his bed because he had been told that a woman was in there. But he added, "Had I known it was a dervish, I would have come in." This incident not only underscores the relaxation of rules permissible among Sufis alone, but also let me know that I had attained the status of a dervish in his eyes!

SEXUALITY AMONG THE SUFIS OF CONTEMPORARY EGYPT

Some Sufis of contemporary Egypt also embrace a doctrine acknowledging the spiritual potential inherent in sexual union that, although not identical to Ibn ʿArabī's formulation, clearly draws on his philosophy. As we have seen, the Sufis believe that although we appear to be separate individuals born in time, our spirits have a common origin in God. Those who have spiritual vision are aware of our basic unity and can overcome the boundaries of individuality through their common access to the spiritual realm. According to the Sufi doctrine of *tawḥīd,* love provides the means of transcending individuality; the love that is shared by the disciple and his shaykh enables them to enjoy this oneness of spirit. Sexual intercourse, too, if conducted in spiritual realization, can lead to a union of spirits. The Islamic system in general does not allow that in marriage the two become one; marriage is simply a contract, and sex is usually regarded in very functional terms, as we have seen. But when a Sufi man and woman enjoy sexual union without lust and with full spiritual realization, their spirits become joined; they become, in fact, one spirit. The woman becomes the mirror in which the man sees himself, just as the Perfect Man is the mirror in which God sees Himself. Sexual intercourse performed in a spiritual way can allow the partners to participate in each other's spiritual inspiration, a rarely achieved ideal, but the logical end of the realization that the union of bodies produces effects in the spirit.

In fact, according to Shaykh ʿIzz, true oneness can be achieved only through heterosexual union; the oneness achieved between two men is actually only of the rank of "nearness," not a complete union of spirits. This is the exact reverse of the logic of ordinary sexual relations in Muslim societies, which, according to Fatima Mernissi, militates against real intimacy in heterosexual relations.[86] As Combs-Schilling put it, "He must not let her into his essence, for she might undo him."[87] For the spiritual man, the female casts away the role of temptress, and in spiritual union there is no danger of the female undoing the male in the usual sense; his annihilation in her and hers in him are both an annihilation in God.

In her analysis of ritual and power in Morocco, Combs-Schilling likens sexuality to sacrifice, and the passive bride in Moroccan culture to the sheep sacrificed at the Muslims' great feast.[88] This analysis is not irrelevant to Egyptian Sufi ideas regarding the potential spiritual fruit of sexual union. Shaykh ʿIzz said that by surrendering what is most precious, her modesty and virginity, the woman "kills" her "soul" or ego. This "killing of the ego" is, as we have seen, the very goal of the Sufi's striving, and it appears that participating in an apparently carnal act can, at least for women, accomplish the sacrifice of the carnal soul. However, whereas in Combs-Schilling's study, the groom figures as the sacrificer and the bride as the ram to be sacrificed, in the Sufi analogy the bride is the sacrificer and her ego is the sacrificial victim. The woman is not a passive participant but must willingly, even joyfully, relinquish what is most precious to her in order for the spiritual dimensions of the act to be realized.

In Moroccan first marriages, it is penetration, not ejaculation, that accomplishes the goal of "sacrifice." Blood must be shed, but the sexual act need not be completed. Those Sufis who endorse this spiritualized interpretation of sexual union likewise hold that the union is that of bodies, not necessarily of waters. This also has an interesting parallel in some Tantric Buddhist practices,[89] but we are not trying to suggest that sexual intercourse is ritually used for spiritual goals in Egyptian Sufism.

All of Islamic practice, with its emphasis on physical acts and ritual purity of the body, indicates that the body is essential to spiritual life. The incorporation of sexuality into mystical experience emphasizes this. The Prophet himself said that engaging in sexual intercourse with one's wife is a type of alms,[90] and many modern Muslims speak of the conjugal act as a form of worship. Sexual intercourse has never been purely for procreation in Islam; sexual satisfaction is one of the duties owed by each spouse to the other. Early Sufis, uneasy with physical pleasure, emphasized procreation as the goal of marriage. In later Sufism, by making pure pleasure the goal of intercourse, and its fruit spiritual realization or the union of spirits, the linkage of the sacred and the flesh is heightened. But, like the early Sufis, contemporary Sufis regard the spiritual man as one who is in control of his flesh, not one who is led by fleshly desires: spirituality is indicated by both the ability to avoid sexual arousal and the ability to sustain erection in a spiritual manner, unlike the hasty lovemaking of the unspiritual man. It is through this teaching that Sufis understand the story of Muhammad's superhuman ability to have intercourse with all of his wives in a single night. According to Ibn Saʿd, the Prophet was given a heavenly morsel by the Angel Gabriel that granted him the sexual potency of forty men.[91] While contemporary Muslims are usually embarrassed by such stories, and dismiss them as foolish fabrications of a superstitious community that wrongly regarded Muhammad as "superlative in everything, including the lusts of this world,"[92] some Sufis see this story as further evidence of Muhammad's superior spiritual strength.

In fact, contemporary Sufi terminology is replete with allusions to sexual intercourse and the female anatomy. One way that Egyptian Sufis speak of progressive spiritual realization in mystical experience is as follows: the first phase is *al-ḥāl,* a spiritual state. From there the Sufi progresses to *baṭn al-ḥāl,* the "inner part," "stomach," or "womb" of the spiritual state; it is significant that the related and more typical Sufi word, *bāṭīn* (inner), is avoided in favor of a synonym with allusions to the female anatomy. The third phase is *sirr baṭn al-ḥāl,* the "secret" or "inmost part" of the "womb" of the spiritual state. Finally, the disciple comes to know *ʿayn sirr baṭn al-ḥāl: ʿayn* can mean "source," "essence," or "eye;" in this case, it refers at the same time to the vagina that leads into the secret interior of the womb of the spiritual state, or to the essence of the secret that lies within the spiritual state. Sufis are famous for speaking at more than one level by means of a single phrase; such phrases intentionally express one meaning to some and another to those who are initiated into the spiritual secret contained in sexuality.

Mystical life and interpretation, therefore, allow for unusual roles for women, new possibilities in the relationships between the sexes, and new interpretations of the very meaning of sexuality. These illustrations from Sufi tradition and contemporary Sufi life in Egypt demonstrate that too often our discussions of sexuality in Islam poorly reflect a reality that, especially in Sufism, is far more complex.

CHAPTER 9

Models of Sainthood

Living and recently deceased individuals popularly regarded (at least by their followers) as saints in Egypt number in the hundreds at least. Choosing from among these a few representatives of that tradition is at least partly a matter of personal preference. I have chosen four different personalities that represent different types or models of the exemplary Sufi saint and spiritual teacher. Shaykh Aḥmad Raḍwān (d. 1967), perhaps the best-known recent saint of Upper Egypt, is widely recognized as an undisputed gnostic and holy man, to whom countless miracles are attributed. This man, who exerted such a critical influence on Shaykh ʿIzz, was an extremely fascinating individual, possessing enormous charisma and in many ways exhibiting the qualities most typical of traditional Sufism. The second, Shaykh Abū 'l-Wafāʾ al-Sharqāwī (d. 1961), represents not Sufi tradition but modern Sufi reformism. An intellectual with deep ties to both religious scholarship and traditional Sufism, he was highly esteemed throughout Egypt and exerted an unusual influence on the Egyptian political and religious elite of this century. The third, Shaykh Maḥmūd Abū 'l-ʿAzm (d. 1983), was a much less known figure, a reclusive, somewhat secretive and self-effacing man of extraordinary spiritual power. By making the acquaintance of his core group of followers, and especially the young woman who became his closest disciple, I learned details of his life that bear a mysterious quality befitting a legendary personality. The fourth, Ḥāgga Zakiyya ʿAbd al-Muṭṭalib Badawī (d. 1982), is best known for a quality often associated with Sufi tradition: a life dedicated to charity and hospitality. Yet she was also a woman of deep spirituality, a reclusive ascetic who offered spiritual counsel to many spiritual "daughters" and "sons."

All four of them bear an aura of holiness derived from a lifetime of prayer, dhikr, reflection on the Qurʾan, and emulation of the example of the Prophet. Each of them was a paragon of selflessness, charity, and courtesy, which earned them the intense devotion of their followers. Their charisma and piety were expressed in different personal styles. Aḥmad Raḍwān was an intense, sometimes eccentric man deeply steeped in the fear of God and love for the Prophet, speaking out of his divine impulses. Abū 'l-Wafā' al-Sharqāwī was a sober, cautious intellectual who eschewed all miraculous manifestations and made no spiritual claims for himself. Maḥmūd Abū 'l-ʿAzm rarely taught openly at all, preferring to teach a small circle of followers through example, visions, and direct mind-to-mind suggestion. Ḥāgga Zakiyya, swathed in modest wraps up to her nose, devoted her life to serving the *ahl al-bayt* through offering hospitality at their shrines.

Yet they all had something in common beyond the attribute of sainthood, something that makes them perhaps untypical of Sufi teachers and might even provide a clue as to how they achieved their spiritual greatness. None of them was actually shaykh of an Order. None of them tried to attract disciples, and they all limited the administration of oaths to a small band of devotees. They were totally unconcerned with reputation, prestige, or building up a following, and they had no Order to administer, organize, or represent. Stubbornly independent, hard to pin down, they eschewed any affiliation with the Supreme Council of Sufi Orders. Despite this unconcern with the very matters that have been the traditional focus of academic studies on the Sufi Orders, they each attracted a large following. Perhaps it is their very lack of concern with attaining status and a following that allowed them to devote themselves so consistently to simply applying spiritual values and drawing close to God.

When I selected my four representatives of Sufi sainthood, I frankly paid no attention to whether they fit the more traditional model of leadership. Among the many shaykhs and saints whom I met and whose stories I heard, these stood out to me as people worthy of enormous respect, yet representing very different personal styles. Their differences grant depth and balance to our abstractions about the concept of sainthood. The fact that none of them was head of an Order reinforces the notion, which I occasionally heard from Sufis themselves, that Sufism in its truest form might best be found outside the rubric of the established Orders.

This is not in any way to denigrate Sufi shaykhs who head or establish Orders and manifest enormous skill in administering them, delegating responsibilities, and providing for spiritual succession. Indeed, it could be argued that the spiritual person who is able to transmit his spiritual knowledge to many others is far more worthy of admiration than a reclusive figure who keeps the benefits of his spirituality largely to himself. It is partly for this reason that in the following chapter we will consider Shaykh Muḥammad ʿUthmān al-Burhānī, not as a unique model of sainthood but as an enormously successful spiritual master and propagator of an Order. Rather than shunning the official Sufi establishment, he succeeded in achieving trusteeship of the Sufi Council of Sudan, his native country, while his deputy in Egypt waged an unsuccessful struggle for official recognition for his Order by the Supreme Council of Sufi Orders in Egypt. The fact that this Order was also not registered in the Supreme Council of Sufi Orders might suggest that I harbor a bias against Orders registered with this Council. This is not the case at all. I have met many admirable heads of Orders registered with the Council, and have often felt that Shaykh Muḥammad Māḍī Abū 'l-ʿAzāʾim would likely have been another fine example of an influential Sufi reformist shaykh that could have been used as a model of that tradition in place of Shaykh Abū 'l-Wafāʾ al-Sharqāwī. My choice of models of sainthood reflects the people with whom I was able to obtain close contacts and interviews as much as it reflects people genuinely worthy of description and admiration.

"PRESIDENT OF THE MAD SAINTS OF UPPER EGYPT": AḤMAD RAḌWĀN OF LUXOR (1895–1967)

Shaykh Aḥmad Raḍwān came from a "noble" tribe, that is, one descended from the Prophet, through his grandson Ḥasan. The brief biography of the shaykh written as an introduction to the collection of Aḥmad Raḍwān's teachings, *Al-Nafaḥāt al-rabbāniyya,* says that this tribe, Āl Raḍwān, was famous for its piety and asceticism and was considered a source of baraka by the people of the area.[1]

Aḥmad Raḍwān was born on 7 September 1895 in the village of al-Baghdādi near the town of Luxor in the province of Qinā in Upper Egypt, a twelve-hour ride by express train from Cairo. Luxor is the site of the famous Pharaonic temples of Karnak and Luxor, and across the river in Qurna, on the west bank, may be found the great valleys of the tombs of the kings, queens, and nobles of ancient Egypt and other ancient temples. Luxor and Qurna receive millions of foreign tourists every year, tourists who are unaccustomed to the intense heat and bright sun of the region and parade about in scant clothing, to the amusement or disgust of the local residents. Because Shaykh ʿIzz was raised in the town of Farshūṭ, near the provincial capital of Qinā, he was well acquainted with the shaykhs of the area,

Figure 10. Shaykh Aḥmad Raḍwān (d. 1967) (courtesy of Shaykh Muḥammad Raḍwān).

and it is through him that I met the sons of Abū 'l-Wafā' al-Sharqāwī, Aḥmad Raḍwān, and Muḥammad al-Ṭayyib (whom I also met in person before he died in December 1988), all of whom are considered among the greatest shaykhs of recent decades; indeed, some local Sufis believe they were each the *ghawth* of their age, one after the other. Shaykh ʿIzz said that when Abū 'l-Wafāʾ died, he stipulated that Aḥmad Raḍwān be the one to wash his body. When he did, "the *ghawthiyya* came over him." The physical proximity of this aura of intense holiness to the center of the tourist industry, which is often seen as morally corrupting, is ironic. The tourists are entirely unaware of the existence of these shaykhs, whose *sāḥa*s attract many Egyptian visitors, and the spiritually compelling atmosphere in these *sāḥa*s seems far removed from the luxury and foreign influence of tourism.

Aḥmad Raḍwān's *sāḥa,* located by his native town of al-Baghdādī, is the most impressive of them all. One section contains long tables at which hundreds may eat at a time during moulid or other celebrations, while the adjoining section contains long cushioned benches where people retire to sip tea and relax after eating. A mosque built in the *sāḥa* in 1968 was financed by Egyptian President Gamal Abdul Nasser. A small shrine bears the tomb of the saint, surrounded by a fine *maqṣūra* of wooden *mashrabiyya.*[2] Aḥmad Raḍwān's portrait was painted on the minaret of the mosque. The *sāḥa* contains perhaps twenty good-sized rooms, each with several beds, and is famous for its hospitality and cleanliness. No one smoked in this *sāḥa* in the days of Aḥmad Raḍwān, not even President Nasser, and even today no one smokes without permission. Considering the fact that most Egyptian men smoke a good deal and consider it a necessary part of social gatherings, this is worthy of note.

On the wall looking down at the tea-drinkers are large photo portraits of Aḥmad Raḍwān's four sons: the eldest, Muḥammad, who spends much of his time in Alexandria and Medina, and has assumed headship over the spiritual progeny of his father; Ṣāliḥ, who was killed in a car accident; Zayn al-ʿĀbidīn, a civil servant who lives in Cairo; and the youngest, ʿAbdallāh, who remains at the *sāḥa* and supervises the administration of hospitality and who, at the time of my research, was only in his twenties. The sons seem remarkably different from each other. Muḥammad and Ṣāliḥ physically resemble their father—small, relatively light-skinned men with similar face structures and ascetic appearances. Shaykh ʿIzz felt that they resembled their father not only physically but spiritually. Zayn al-ʿĀbidīn is, by contrast, an unusually tall man for Egypt, an unassuming man who enjoys conversation and whose fervent devotion to God and His Messenger do not prevent him from leading what in many ways is a typical lower-middle-class urban lifestyle. ʿAbdallāh is a dark-skinned, stocky man with a serious bent and a commanding demeanor, who is nonetheless a gracious and considerate host. His softer side was brought out by my daughter, Rachel, who, at the age of fifteen months, ran throughout the spacious *sāḥa* and slept overnight with me in one of its rooms. When I decided she was old enough to be left with her father in Cairo during my trips into Upper Egypt, ʿAbdallāh expressed his disappointment.

Aḥmad Raḍwān often comes across in *Al-Nafaḥāt al-rabbāniyya* as a stern ascetic, but perhaps he also possessed a quality that might be described as a major personality characteristic of his son, Muḥammad: a wry sense of humor. Although Muḥammad teaches with authority and maintains strict discipline, one-on-one he is a most unassuming character who loves to joke and had no trouble circumventing the customary practice of excluding women from spiritual sessions in order to include me, even if this meant some rather unconventional arrangements. When I expressed my frustration at being secluded in a room apart during the moulid celebration of his father, he personally escorted me, despite his frailty, into the crowd of men. He made room for me and ʿIzz on a busload of male pilgrims to the shrine of Sīdī Shādhilī, and invited me into an all-male dhikr, where he offered me an orange for Rachel. Even when he was very ill, he attempted to joke and speak with me. In sum, he possesses that characteristic so valued in the Egyptian personality, *khiffat al-damm,* "lightness of blood," that is, a sense of humor. The dominance of this characteristic in his personality has led to me speculate that the absence of this particular feature from the depiction of Aḥmad Raḍwān in *Al-Nafaḥāt al-rabbāniyya* might reflect the genre of the literature more than the personality of the man. On the other hand, Aḥmad Raḍwān's father apparently did not possess this characteristic.

Aḥmad Raḍwān frequently mentions his father, Muḥammad Aḥmad Muḥammad Raḍwān, who, according to the biography in *Al-Nafaḥāt al-rabbāniyya,* was "a scholar and a gnostic of God, ascetic with regard to this world, performing many miracles. He knew nothing but God and the Messenger of God; his waking was dhikr and his sleep was glorification of God, and his work was blessing the Prophet."[3] The spiritual impact he had on his son is evident in his teachings. The father emerges as a man of uncompromising morality in the sternest of traditional Islamic standards, unwilling to eat much of the food offered to him, suspicious that it might have been obtained illicitly, for "most food these days is doubtful."[4] Aḥmad Raḍwān's description of his father recalls the earliest phase of Sufism, that of asceticism, sternness, and avoidance of contact with political authorities. "My father would only eat a single handful every day until he died. I never saw him sleep at night, and I never saw anyone reprove anyone else in his presence. I never saw him laugh. I never saw him shake the hand of a mayor or walk on the path that leads to their house. And I only saw him smile when his spirit left him!"[5]

His father's brother, however, was a different type of Sufi, "one of the people of divine bewilderment *(min ahl al-walah),* of whose miracles and piety all who knew him testify."[6] Both types of spirituality appear in the personality of Aḥmad Raḍwān.

After memorizing the Qur'an at a young age, Aḥmad Raḍwān studied law and theology, and he began the disciplines of Sufism at the age of twelve. "He was raised in obedience to God and His Apostle, imitating the Apostle in words, deeds and spiritual state."[7] He performed the work of a peasant and was able to do this while fasting, doing dhikr, and praying blessings on Muhammad. As a young man he began to receive divine insights.

Aḥmad Raḍwān's father was a shaykh of the Sammāniyya Order, which was the initial Order Aḥmad Raḍwān followed. Later he was initiated into the Khalwatiyya Order, studying under a number of different shaykhs before becoming a close disciple of Shaykh Muḥammad al-Ramlī. Shaykh al-Ramlī was chief clerk with the railroad in Minyā, and Aḥmad Raḍwān traveled to Minyā to be with him, achieving such a close relationship with him that his fellow disciples were often jealous. It is Shaykh al-Ramlī who is said to have granted him the epithet "president of the *magāzīb* of Upper Egypt" and to have added "there is none other in our age like him."[8] This epithet would appear to indicate that Aḥmad Raḍwān was himself *magzūb,* and indeed it seems that he was for a period in his youth, before he established his *sāḥa* and began his vocation of teaching and hospitality. Shaykh Gamāl al-Sanhūrī, on the other hand, said this epithet referred not to Aḥmad Raḍwān's own *gazb* but to the fact that many of his followers were *magāzīb,* which he attributes to his failure to discipline them properly in the Sufi way by gradual initiation into the daily recitation of *awrād.*

In the early phase of his spiritual development, his spiritual intensity sometimes produced a great heat, so that he sweated even in cold weather and could not bear to wear clothes on his body, "from the heat of his longing and love *(ʿishq).* The people thought that this was an illness that had afflicted him. He also used to set intense fires around him in summer."[9] The implication is that his spiritual state produced such a heat that fires were unintentionally ignited in the hot, dry climate. Biegman, drawing on a biography written by Al-Ḥāgg Aḥmad ʿAbd al-Malik, says that the early phase of Aḥmad Raḍwān's spiritual development was characterized by extreme restlessness and "contradictory dispositions succeeding one another. . . . In his ecstasies *(wagd)* he spent long periods standing, sitting and getting up again, and he wept frequently. He slept little, if at all."[10] It is clear from his own account, described in chapter 7, that his spiritual vicissitudes alienated many of his neighbors, who saw him as a *magzūb*.

He spent much time in the desert, wandering aimlessly for nights at a time, without fear, for, as he liked to quote from the poet al-Buṣīrī,

> He whose help is in the Apostle of God,
> If lions meet him, he will rest in their jungle.[11]

It is said that when he recollected God in the desert, he heard all of creation, even inanimate rocks, glorifying God, for the Qurʾan affirms that all things glorify God in their own language. On one occasion he could not find a place to urinate because he could not urinate on rocks that were audibly glorifying God. He had to plead with God and His Apostle to silence the rocks in order to relieve himself.[12]

During what ʿAbd al-Malik describes as Aḥmad Raḍwān's second stage, he began to speak the mystical language of "*Suryānī*," and began to communicate with other saints, some of them still living, others having passed away. It was in the third stage of his spiritual development that he founded the "Raḍwān school" and his *sāḥa*, where much of his teaching consisted of interpreting the Qurʾan according to his own inspiration. Although Aḥmad Raḍwān made no organizational provisions for the establishment of an Order, a number of his disciples went on to attract disciples of their own: Maḥmūd Abū Shāmīh of Asyūṭ, Shaykh Faraj of Aswān, Shaykh Aḥmad Abū 'l-Ḥasan of Kom Ombo, also in Aswān province, and of course, his son, Muḥammad.

Aḥmad Raḍwān frequently warned his followers against any attachment to the things of this world, and the brief biography in *Al-Nafaḥāt al-rabbāniyya* affirms that he himself cared nothing for his own sustenance, happily went without food for days at a time, and was satisfied with only half a watermelon rind. Shaykh ʿIzz said that Aḥmad Raḍwān was physically weak because he ate only dates and milk. In one of his teachings he confessed that God had cut off all means of subsistence other than God, who alone was the source of his provision.[13] It is an ancient Sufi virtue to trust in God alone, who, according to the Qur'an, provides sustenance for all creatures (11:6). Nonetheless, unexpectedly, Aḥmad Raḍwān's personal circumstances were reversed, and he became personally wealthy. His biography simply says that "God provided for him from unimaginable sources, in accordance with His Word: 'Whoever fears God will be given a way out, and [God] will provide him with sustenance from sources he could never imagine' (Qur'an 65:2–3)."[14]

Aḥmad Raḍwān's generosity with his wealth is too well-substantiated to doubt and is reflected in the continuing ministry of his *sāḥa* after his death. Hundreds came to his *sāḥa* to eat, drink, sleep, and bask in its aura of holiness. "The people knew no one equal to him in generosity in his day, and they found no one equal to him in this. . . . He turned no beggar away. He gave like one who has no fear of poverty, from all the wealth, food or clothing that God gave him, so that visitors left dazed by meeting him and by his generosity."[15] This description is similar to an account from life of the Prophet, who, it is said, gave so generously even to the most rude and demanding of people that one recipient of his generosity urged his countrymen to become Muslims, "for Muhammad gives like one who has no fear of poverty."[16] Also like the Prophet, he is described as returning ill-treatment with kindness, treating his neighbors and sons with impartiality, and extending hospitality to the neglected elements of society. During an epidemic of malaria and typhoid in 1944 he demonstrated extraordinary courage and compassion, reminiscent of the contemporary Christian saint, Mother Theresa of Calcutta: he personally and fearlessly delivered food, drink, and medicine to families prevented by disease from caring for themselves.[17]

It is said that on one occasion he sent away large numbers of visitors from his *sāḥa* without feeding them, because, looking into their hearts with the *baṣīra* of a gnostic, he saw that they did not meet the stipulations set by the Prophet, who said, "Do not befriend any one except a believer, and do not let any one eat your food except a pious person." Farid Mahir, writing of this incident, says, "This caused some people to oppose him and say that Ahmad Radwan throws people out of his assembly and is harsh with some of those who come to him. If those opponents had looked into the Book of God and understood what is in it, they would know that this is a Muhammadan ethic and the practical application of the Book of God and Sunna of His Apostle."[18]

Shaykh ʿIzz told me a different story, which indicates an interesting struggle between his spiritual state and the standards of hospitality dictated by the Egyptian culture: One time he ordered his sons not to feed some visitors, saying, "Away from me! You come only to eat!" Later he asked his sons whether the visitors had been fed, and was chagrined to learn that they had not been offered any hospitality. But when food was again set before them, his former state returned to him and the food was ordered removed before the visitors could eat it.

Aḥmad Raḍwān's charisma was such that I was often told that if I had ever met him in person I would have been "abducted" and never able to leave Egypt, so captivated would I be by the force of his personality. "His eyes were very attractive," said Shaykh ʿIzz, "so that if he looked at you, you became his prisoner. You wouldn't be able to leave until he dismissed you." The power of his spirituality was keenly felt by those who sat in his assemblies and constituted a living proof for his assertions of the benefits of merely sitting with a gnostic. Aḥmad Raḍwān taught *awrād* and administered oaths to only a handful of disciples, but his influence has extended to thousands. The disciple who wrote Aḥmad Raḍwān's biography at the beginning of *Al-Nafaḥāt al-rabbāniyya* testifies to the spiritual awakening experienced by those privileged with attending his assemblies—living proof of the truth of Radwan's teaching concerning the value of merely sitting with a gnostic.[19]

Aḥmad Raḍwān is credited with many miracles, especially miracles of knowledge, such as knowing people before they are introduced to him, seeing events that happen far away, and being able to communicate with the spirits of other saints. Like all saints, he is someone whose prayers are answered.

Aḥmad Raḍwān sometimes made extravagant claims for himself. He claimed to be able to see all the saints, both living and dead.[20] Other saints were restricted in their access to the Prophet's presence, he said, but he alone had constant access to it.[21] This is a characteristic of the *ghawth* alone. Aḥmad Raḍwān believed that he had become *ghawth* and was presented by the Prophet to all the saints at a great congress of spirits so that no true saint could ever think that he had appointed himself. The suffering he had endured for so many years was a necessary preparation for such a high calling.[22]

Yet, despite such statements of apparent self-assurance, Aḥmad Raḍwān was also often remarkably humble, indeed fearful of God's wrath because of his own sinfulness. His teachings in *Al-Nafaḥāt al-rabbāniyya* are intensely emotional, often interspersed with proclamations of his sinfulness and fear, and with fervent prayers that depict fear and abject humility. "Why do we sleep all night?" he demanded of his hearers. "Why do we slander? Why do we sow dissension? Why do we fill our bellies? Has some news reached us to remove our anxiety? The answer is no! . . . What do we have to do with attachment to this world? My God, prepare us for attachment to You alone. . . . My God, strip our hearts of anything else beside You, and preserve our limbs from rebellion! . . . I always pray, 'My God, do not make anyone enter hellfire because of me!' "[23] He asks rhetorically, "How can a man be proud when an ant can bother him? On what basis can he be proud when he is so weak?"[24]

Recalling the prayer of the Prophet during his farewell speech, he pleads, "Be kind to me, my God! Be kind to me, my God, concerning what has been foreordained for me! I am the deficient, the hopeful, I am the miserable, the poor!"[25] Like the early Sufis, he speaks of his dread at meeting God, uncertain of the outcome for him in the Judgment, though he "will remain between fear and hope." Reflecting his father's sternness, he proclaims, "By God, I have rejoiced in nothing but God for forty years!"[26]

Some of Aḥmad Raḍwān's utterances in *Al-Nafaḥāt al-rabbāniyya* are clearly spoken under the influence of a spiritual state and might appear either extravagantly boastful or doctrinally extremist to some Muslims. He testifies, "By God, I do not collect the words I speak. They are an effusion from God and gifts given in each moment of spiritual realization *(waqt)*, a provision from God."[27] Despite his admonitions to his listeners not to believe that their association with a shaykh guarantees them immunity from hellfire, on one occasion he assured his disciples that, contrary to other saints, he had "no restrictions with the Messenger of God," that he alone was given the privilege of ushering into Paradise with him those who loved him, "without ticket or permit."[28]

During a visit to the *sāḥa* of Shaykh Muḥammad al-Ṭayyib in Qurna in October 1988, the shaykh's eldest son Muḥammad expressed doubts that the book really reflected the words of Aḥmad Raḍwān, because Aḥmad Raḍwān was a humble man. Shaykh ʿIzz, however, affirmed that most of the words recorded there were genuine and that he himself had heard many of them. Shaykh Muḥammad Zakī Ibrāhīm, shaykh of the Muḥammadiyya Shādhiliyya Order and head of the ʿAshīra Muḥammadiyya, one of the best known spokesmen for moderate, reformed Sufism, wrote a note at the end of *Al-Nafaḥāt al-rabbāniyya,* in which he cautions the reader that Shaykh Aḥmad Raḍwān did not himself compose the book and that the method of transmission allowed for the possibility of error.

Nonetheless, he affirms the overwhelming benefit of the book, calling it a "most holy divine effusion," of which some may be likened to a divine revelation. He claims that the original idea for gathering the teachings of Aḥmad Raḍwān into the book was his own, and he says that Aḥmad Raḍwān was the *ghawth* of his time.[29]

Although Aḥmad Raḍwān admired his father's eschewal of contacts with political authorities, the one aspect of controversy that touched his own life, ironically, was his relationship with President Gamal Abdul Nasser. It is difficult to ascertain the extent of this relationship. President Nasser apparently had a deep respect for Aḥmad Raḍwān, visited his *sāḥa,* and built the Raḍwāniyya train station near the *sāḥa* to facilitate his visits. Aḥmad Raḍwān was not one to seek out contact with the politically powerful, and he extended to him no special privileges; ʿIzz points out, for example, that Nasser did not dare smoke in the shaykh's presence. Raḍwān's followers stress that it was Nasser who sought him out, not the reverse. Nonetheless, his association with the architect of the subordination of the religious establishment to secular policies often perceived as un-Islamic was disturbing enough to another shaykh of the region to make him comment that although Aḥmad Raḍwān had performed "countless" miracles, he did not see how somebody could be a true shaykh and yet associate with a "Communist," who was by implication an atheist. Nasser was, however, personally religious, despite his suppression of the Muslim Brotherhood and his subordination of the Islamic religious establishment to serve the objectives of "Arab socialism."

Most controversial of all was Aḥmad Raḍwān's alleged encouragement of Nasser to enter the Six-Day War in June 1967, a war that was an unmitigated disaster for Egypt. Nasser apparently did seek Aḥmad Raḍwān's advice concerning whether or not to enter the war. Aḥmad Raḍwān's response cannot be known for a fact, since the accounts vary widely. Biegman reports, on the authority of Raḍwān's son, Shaykh Muḥammad, that when Raḍwān learned that Nasser intended to visit him to ask his advice, he preempted that visit by rushing to Cairo himself, so he would have no obligations as a host to be polite but could offer him "real" counsel. "During his audience with Nasser, the sheikh allegedly told him that his future held no victory, but apparently this was not enough to deter the President from launching the war."[30] Shaykh ʿIzz said that Raḍwān told Nasser, "You will enter the war," which was not a word of advice but a statement of fact, and that he warned Nasser that he would be defeated, but Nasser ignored this warning. In the wake of defeat, perhaps it was natural for the shaken news media to search for a scapegoat and to blame the popular and progressive president's obvious misjudgment on the advice of a conservative shaykh from Upper Egypt, whose counsel on political and military issues must have seemed irrelevant to many of Nasser's partisans.

Although Biegman says that Aḥmad Raḍwān was granted his wish to die before Egypt's defeat, *Al-Nafaḥāt al-rabbāniyya* gives the date of his death as 11 June 1967, directly after the end of the Six-Day War, which lasted from the fifth to the tenth of June 1967.

Shaykh Aḥmad Abū 'l-Ḥasan

In this section I include the stories of two of Aḥmad Raḍwān's disciples who went on to become shaykhs in their own right: Aḥmad Abū 'l-Ḥasan and ʿIzz al-ʿArab al-Hawārī. Because they are both spiritual sons of Aḥmad Raḍwān, they reflect some of his style and method and are not considered as separate models of sainthood. Nonetheless the separate accounts of their journeys into Sufism are extremely interesting because each of them experienced a radical moral conversion. They are good illustrations of a theme commonly found among the Sufis, that Sufism effected a genuine change in their personalities and life orientation.

Aḥmad Abū 'l-Ḥasan of Kom Ombo was the more successful of the two. His tent at the moulid of Ḥusayn in December 1988 was filled with several hundred devotees. His authoritarian public style (his demand for absolute attention, not tolerating any to rise or for food to be distributed while he spoke) contrasts with a humble and gentle demeanor in person. He was tall and dark, bearing the slender build and refined features typical of people in extreme southern Egypt and the Horn of Africa. An enormous turban perched on his head, which swayed to the music interspersed throughout his teaching. He was a truly impressive man of enormous charisma. When he came to see me in the rear section of the tent, reserved for women, I asked him my usual question, "What is the essence of Sufism?" He replied, "Sufism is the essence of Islam." He asked permission to answer my question by addressing the entire crowd and went to the front of the tent. Although his words were intended for the benefit of everyone, he spoke as if we were having a private conversation, addressing me as "*Duktūra*" ("Doctor"). For several days I returned to the moulid during the day to hear him speak, and he always asked first whether the *duktūra* was present. I will allow him to tell his story in his own words.

"I was one of the people of the night who always stayed up at night and drank forbidden things, with a hard heart that knew no fear. One night we went to a friend's house to drink and spend a 'red night.' When we sat and began to drink, talk, and laugh, my eyes fell on a picture on the wall of a man. When I looked at the picture I felt afraid, because I found the picture looking at me as if it were speaking to me. I began to tremble, and my heart filled with fear. I began to move from one place to another without attracting attention. Every time I moved and looked at the picture, I found it still looked at me as if it wanted to talk to me.[31] My fear increased, although at the time I was never afraid of anything. I remained this way until I sat under the picture. At that time I saw one of my friends move the same way I had. Soon he was sitting next to me. I poked him and asked, 'Are you afraid of the picture?' He said, 'Sh! Yes, just like you, but if we say so, the others will say we are drunk!' The night ended, and as we left we shook the hand of the owner of the house. I asked him about the picture. 'Who is that? Your father?' He said, 'No, that is our lord, al-Ḥājj Aḥmad Raḍwān.'

"I had heard of him but had never seen him. When I knew it was his picture, my fear and dread doubled, and I wanted to see him. Each day my desire to see him increased, as well as my fear of the meeting. Finally the day came when I met him. When he saw me he called me by name and greeted me and sat me by his side and said, 'Why are you late, Ahmad? We've been waiting for you a long time!' I stayed with the shaykh, drawing nourishment from his milk and being illuminated by his lights, until he met the Highest Companion. Of course, when I first met the shaykh I left all my former friends. I recited the *Fātiḥa* and my desire for the Messenger of God increased.

"After the shaykh's passing I felt as if I were an orphan, and my heart turned to the Messenger of God. My love increased and I remained calling him and talking with him, until one day I saw him and asked, 'Where is mystical revelation *(fatḥ)*, Messenger of God?' He pointed, and the mountains and valleys were suddenly closer, until I saw the town of al-Kilḥa in Aswān, and I saw the home of Muḥammad Abū 'l-Futūḥ al-ʿArabī. The vision changed, and I saw two people with the same appearance and dress. I didn't know which was the Messenger of God and which was Shaykh al-ʿArabī. I felt confused. Then the shaykh manifested an aspect of weakness, and I knew he was the shaykh and the other was the Prophet. I turned to him and kissed him and stayed with him until he passed away.[32]

"This is my story with Sufism and the Sufis. If anything remains of Sufism, we are among what remains of the miracles of the Sufis."

Aḥmad Abū 'l-Ḥasan's story is interesting for a number of reasons. It is evident that he lived in a cultural environment deeply tinged with Sufism, as indeed is most of the culture of Upper Egypt. Although he was leading a life that by the standards of his culture was irreligious (not neglecting, however, the standard etiquette of shaking hands with the owner of the house and thanking him for his hospitality), he had heard of Aḥmad Raḍwān and had sufficient faith in the man's stature to feel afraid when he knew of his identity. He felt, in fact, called to him. His actual meeting with the shaykh required an instantaneous change in his lifestyle: leaving old friends, devoting himself to the Qur'an, to prayer, and to love for the Prophet. It was a genuine moral conversion, though apparently not a dramatic change in his beliefs. He died in Spring 1994.

The vision in which the Prophet directs him to Shaykh al-ʿArabī exemplifies a theme discussed in chapters 5 and 7, the role of visions in directing seekers to a particular spiritual guide. The physical resemblance between Shaykh al-ʿArabī and the Prophet, to the point where only a slight aspect of weakness distinguishes the one from the other, signifies that his attachment to Shaykh al-ʿArabī was tantamount to his attachment to the Prophet, and leads him directly into the Prophet's presence. The merging of the account of the vision into the account of his actual service to the shaykh ("I turned to him and kissed him and stayed with him until he passed away") is typical of the reality that visions possess for the Sufi. As experiences in the Sufi path, visions are no less real than what we would call objective experience.

Aḥmad Abū 'l-Ḥasan is illiterate, although he is able to quote extensively from literary works, an attribute that reflects both the often oral quality of teaching in the traditional religious milieu, as well as his gift of divine inspiration. Despite his illiteracy, he drew a diverse crowd that includes many Cairenes of social distinction and higher education, and some, such as a young woman in blue jeans and long, loose hair, who do not look like they belong in any religious circle—if we allow ourselves to be swayed by inaccurate stereotypes. The attraction of all these people to a very traditional, unlearned man from the extreme south of Egypt goes against all the logic of social status in contemporary Egypt, and indicates that in

Figure 11. Shaykh Aḥmad Abū ʾl-Ḥasan (d. 1994) leading his followers in dhikr on 3 December 1988 at the moulid of Ḥusayn.

Sufi circles social standards continue to be subordinate to extraordinary spirituality.

Shaykh ʿIzz al-ʿArab al-Hawārī

Shaykh ʿIzz grew up in a middle-class family of butchers in the province of Qinā in the city of Farshūṭ, which was described by a seventeenth-century Egyptian historian as the stronghold of the rebellious Hawara tribe. ʿIzz explained to me that the name Hawāra, which means "wild" or "rash," was a nickname given the tribe, the most recent nomadic invaders in Upper Egypt, because they were virtually untamable by any government. This tribe considers themselves superior to the surrounding population, who were called (somewhat contemptuously) "peasants" *(fallāḥīn)*. The mayors of the towns and landowners in the area even today are mainly from the Hawāra tribe, while the rest of the population, said Shaykh ʿIzz, "are our servants." In Nasser's day it came to be considered insulting to call people—at least in Upper Egypt—peasants. As Nasser said, "We are all Arabs." The ironic result is that the local population in the Qina region is divided between "the Hawāra and the Arabs," although the Hawāra consider themselves to be of pure Arab stock. ʿIzz's wife, however, comes from the Delta province of Manūfiyya, near Cairo, and people from the rural Delta are, by definition, *fallāḥīn.* ʿIzz loves to amaze visitors from Upper Egypt with the news that he had married a *fallāḥa.* Since the Hawāra consider themselves a noble tribe, the preferred marriage is always within the tribe, and for a woman this preference becomes a virtual mandate. Shaykh Muḥammad Muḥammad al-Ṭayyib joked, "Even if the Prophet himself asked the hand of one of their women in marriage, the Hawāra would say no!" ʿIzz and his brother, however, had no female cousins of appropriate age to marry, and they each married women who were of lower social status by the standards of their own tribe—ʿIzz because his wife was from the Delta, and his brother because his wife was black.

ʿIzz was the eldest of three surviving children. His contact with Sufi shaykhs began very early. He was, he says, a very handsome boy, and his parents were afraid that he would fall victim to the envy of less fortunate families. (Their fear was no doubt exacerbated by the fact that nine of his mother's children died as infants.) They entrusted him to the care of various local saints, that he might be sheltered by their baraka from all evil influences. ʿIzz was greatly affected by what he saw and heard among them. He attended Qurʾanic school and continued to have close contact with local shaykhs.

ʿIzz's contact with Aḥmad Raḍwān came in his youth, starting when he was only eight years old. It was, he said, a type of "adoption." No one else could interrupt Aḥmad Raḍwān when he was in solitary meditation, but he had constant access to him. Although he never gave Aḥmad Raḍwān an official oath, Raḍwān taught him *awrād,* and they had an interior oath, "by a glance," that is, by mutual, unspoken understanding. Aḥmad Raḍwān's impact on him was profound; he calls him *ʿammī,* which literally means "my uncle" but here means "my teacher." He began to receive divine inspiration when he was only eleven, but he did not recognize it as such at that time.

His family moved to Cairo as a result of problems the Hawāra, a large tribe with over one million people, had with the government in the 1950s over the parliamentary elections. In Upper Egypt there were major battles, in which, according to ʿIzz, 180 people were killed in a single day. As a tribal leader, ʿIzz's father was implicated in crimes committed by other tribal members. He decided to escape to Cairo in 1957. ʿIzz was fifteen years old when the rest of the family moved to Cairo in 1958.

"When I came to Cairo, a change occurred in my life, which up till that point had been a very disciplined lifestyle. There were no girls' schools in Upper Egypt at that time, there were no women who went out, there was no cheating or casinos or such things. I had always been first in my class. When I was transferred here, my level began to drop as a result of the change in my environment. I began to turn to evil. I felt that here in Cairo a person only lived by his own strength. I used to terrorize this area, here in the street next to us. In this period I didn't pray or fast or anything else. But I used to go to the moulids. I would take a group of men with me. Some people go to the moulids to play with rifles and other games. I would take fifty piastres from each one who played a game. In those days a half-pound was a lot. If he wouldn't pay, he would get beaten up. I would distribute the money to those who were with me. I would go sit in the place where they do dhikr and weep, without knowing why I was weeping. And I would lose all the money I had taken. This continued about three years."

ʿIzz's father, a domineering man, was disgusted with him and told him he was no good. ʿIzz entered the army in 1963 in order to escape him and continued studying in the army. ʿIzz coerced his wife's family into marrying her to him, although she was already pledged to another man. His wife says that she loved him and that women in her culture love men who are strong. He married in 1966.

After less than a year of marriage, however, ʿIzz fell prey to a mysterious illness that numerous doctors failed to diagnose and that caused him periods of unconsciousness. At the Armed Forces Hospital in the upper-class Cairo suburb of Maʿadi, he was finally diagnosed with an abscess in his right lung and surgery was scheduled to remove half his lung.

"They set the operation for Saturday. On Thursday I heard the call to prayer from the river. There was a mosque in the hospital. This was about eleven o'clock at night, well after the evening prayer, not at the proper time for the call to prayer. But I heard the call to prayer coming from the direction of the river. My room overlooked the river. . . . I was alone in the room. The entire call to prayer was repeated after fifteen minutes. After the second call to prayer had ended, I heard someone calling me by name and say, 'Rise and do ablutions.' I went and filled the bathtub and washed well and did the ablutions. I dressed and found a clean place, where I prayed the evening prayer and then a number of other cycles of prostration. Then I sat in bed and read the Qurʾan.

"While I was reading the Qur'an, I found that the wall that looked out over the river had opened up. I saw a strong beam of light, stronger than the sun. I covered my eyes. When I uncovered them, I looked and saw that doctors had come in, wearing surgical clothes. They rose out of the water. An old man was at their head and he said, 'Don't worry, we are going to do the operation now.' The operation was supposed to be Saturday. This was Thursday. I couldn't see any surgical tools. Twelve people came in, men and women. One man came forward, not the old one who had come first, and he opened the buttons of my shirt and rubbed my chest and closed the buttons again. That was the operation.

"I stayed up perhaps all night. And in fact I did feel comfortable."

When he was examined the following day in preparation for surgery, the X rays revealed no abscess. After repeated X rays, the operation was postponed. Over the next month the doctors searched in vain for the abscess. Finally a puzzled doctor asked ʿIzz to tell him what had happened. When ʿIzz told his story, the doctor replied, "This is the third time this has happened in the last four years!" But, says ʿIzz, he was too shy to report this to his superiors. After another month's rest, he was discharged from the hospital.

ʿIzz explained to me the identity of these visitors who healed him. "First Ḥusayn, the old man. The one who did the operation was Sīdī ʿAlī Zayn al-ʿĀbidīn. The others were Sayyida Nafīsa, Sayyida Sakīna (Sukayna), and Sayyida Ruqayya. And Sayyida Zaynab was there as well, but she was standing by Ḥusayn and didn't do anything. They were all *ahl al-bayt*. All this happened before I had my children. Since that time I have prayed."

After his healing, ʿIzz initially turned to Islamic legalism, and joined the well-known association, al-Jamʿiyya 'l-Sharʿiyya 'l-Islāmiyya. He attended an institute run by that group and graduated with a preacher's certificate and began to teach in the mosque. In the army he pursued more studies to obtain another certificate as a preacher. He served the armed forces as a preacher until he began to receive divine inspiration and to depart from the norms of public preaching. He was dismissed from the army, and continues to receive a monthly pension for his service.

It was at this time that he read Qushayrī's *Risāla fī ʿilm al-taṣawwuf*, in the edition that was edited by Dr. ʿAbd al-Ḥalīm Maḥmūd, then Rector of the Islamic University of Al-Azhar.[33] ʿIzz sought out Dr. Maḥmūd and enjoyed weekly study sessions with him for about a year. He suffered at this time from mild *gazb*, not entirely out of touch with the world, but having little concern for his own body or his family responsibilities. ʿAbd al-Ḥalīm Maḥmūd gave him the surprising advice to go to the cinema, normally considered an irreligious, even immoral pursuit, to "get your feet back on the ground." ʿIzz's weekly lessons began in 1972 and continued until Dr. Maḥmūd was appointed Shaykh of Al-Azhar in 1973.

ʿIzz also received an inner initiation into Sufism through a vision from Ḥusayn himself, in which Ḥusayn gave him a glass of milk, a common symbol of initiation in Islamic visionary narratives. He claims to be in special spiritual contact with Ḥusayn, Sayyida Zaynab, and Abū 'l-Ḥasan al-Shādhilī. It was Shādhilī who forced him to abandon pursuing Sufism through books, with the command, "Do not be Sufi in speech, but be a Sufi word." ʿIzz comments, "A Sufi in speech transmits [knowledge about Sufism], but the Sufi word is the stage in which he speaks out of his own self." Since that time, the only book he has been able to see clearly is the Qurʾan.

He attended the meetings of another Shādhilī shaykh because he enjoyed their dhikr, but he soon came to feel that his own spiritual awareness was greater than that of the shaykh. Nonetheless, when the shaykh asked him to give him his oath, since he had not had actually given a verbal oath to any other living shaykh, he did so, out of politeness. But when his own inspiration and charisma began to attract members of the shaykh's group, the shaykh became jealous, and he left. For a while he held regular meetings for a small group of disciples in which he taught them the inner meaning of the Qurʾan. He claims to have disciples not only in the area where he lives but also in Alexandria and overseas. He says, "I have few disciples but many who love me." It appears, however, that some of his spiritual intensity became dissipated when he devoted his energies and concerns to building a mosque, *sāḥa*, school, and clinic complex, which he calls *sāḥat al-anwār al-dhātiyya*, "court of the lights of God's essence."

One day an old man loudly gave the call to prayer from a pile of burning garbage at the end of ʿIzz's street, pounding the ground with his stick. He walked to the door of ʿIzz's house, where again he gave the call to prayer and pounded the ground with his stick. ʿIzz rushed downstairs to invite the man in, and he shared lunch with the family. He told ʿIzz that he was to build a mosque on the location that was at that time part of the massive garbage heap adjoining the railroad tracks at the end of his street. After lunch as ʿIzz escorted the man from the house he suddenly vanished. At that moment ʿIzz's wife remembered that she had seen this man in a dream the night before and that he was Khiḍr. For this reason, ʿIzz believes that he is building his mosque complex at the command of God given through Khiḍr.

Although ʿIzz has stories of miraculous financial provision for the mosque, and many friends contribute to its construction, there is no doubt that the enormity of his ambitions for the complex has taken a considerable toll on his finances as well as his energy. His time and money are rarely his own; by virtue of his standing in the community as shaykh of the mosque and political officer over his district, as well as the social status of his family, he is expected and indeed expects himself to give generously to all who ask him for money or food. He often longs for the day when the construction will be completed and he can devote himself to more spiritual endeavors, including entering into solitude for meditation. He is torn between his natural sociability and his spiritual longings. He often expressed supreme confidence in his high spiritual standing, saying he was spiritually complete, although on one occasion this was expressed as frustration that he found no shaykh who could "crush me under his feet." He felt that his current trying circumstances were a trial from God sent to humble him, for "I am not as unaware of my faults as you imagine."

It was my bad fortune to arrive at a time when ʿIzz was engaged in construction rather than regular instruction of disciples. On the other hand, it was my good fortune to be connected to a shaykh who had broad contacts and genuine spiritual experience but who had not yet acquired such a large following as to have no time for me or be unwilling to travel. He is not yet well-known, although he may yet become so, for he has a rare combination of gifts that could eventually qualify him to become a great Sufi shaykh. Many of the Sufis whom I met in my travels wondered why I bothered to travel at all to find out about Sufism from other shaykhs when I had such a master as he right there with me. The effect he has on strangers is sometimes magnetic. Perhaps the trials he now endures are indeed a preparation for a higher spiritual calling.

SUFI INTELLECTUAL: AḤMAD ABŪ 'L-WAFĀʾ AL-SHARQĀWĪ (1879–1961)

Modern Egypt has produced a number of Sufi intellectuals who have dedicated their lives to reviving the links of Sufism with mainstream Islam, who have been both scholars of Islam and teachers of Sufism.

Among the most eminent of these personalities are Abū 'l-Wafā' al-Sharqāwī and his father, Abū 'l-Maʿārif Aḥmad ibn Sharqāwī (1834–1899).

It is virtually impossible to discuss the method and influence of Abū 'l-Wafā' al-Sharqāwī without reference to his even more famous father, who was nicknamed Abū 'l-Maʿārif, "father of (esoteric) knowledge." Abū 'l-Wafā' al-Taftāzānī, head of the Supreme Council of Sufi Orders, called Abū 'l-Maʿārif "the most outstanding Sufi of Upper Egypt in modern times."[34]

Figure 12. Shaykh Abū 'l-Wafā al-Sharqāwī (d. 1961) (photograph courtesy of Aḥmad al-Sharqāwī).

Their ancestors lived in a village called al-Khalafiyya near the city of Jirjā in the province of Sūhāj. Six generations before Abū 'l-Maʿārif, an ancestor named ʿAbd al-Salām Jāmiʿ moved with his family to a village near Farshūt that was known as Dayr Sawāda, which literally means "monastery of blackness," in the township of Najʿ Ḥammādī. Abū 'l-Maʿārif established a *sāḥa* in the area and renamed it Dayr al-Saʿāda, "monastery of happiness," still a somewhat unusual name for a Muslim center, since *dayr* connotes a Christian monastery. Later, however, the village came to be called Najʿ al-Shaykh al-Sharqāwī. ʿAbd al-Salām's paternal ancestry went back to Muhammad's caliphal successor, Abū Bakr, while his mother's family was descended from the Prophet via Husayn. The family bore a reputation for piety and soundness in the practice of their faith.

Dayr al-Saʿāda was itself a Qurʾanic school. Abū 'l-Maʿārif studied the Qurʾan under the tutelage of his father, and then in schools in Farshūṭ and Bahjūra. He went on to study the Islamic religious sciences in Jirjā, which was then a center for Islamic learning in Upper Egypt. After mastering the Islamic sciences, he turned to Sufism, devoting himself to it completely. Although he had learned *awrād* from a local shaykh,[35] he was guided through a vision at the age of thirty to seek out Shaykh Aḥmad al-Khuḍayrī, then a prominent Khalwatī shaykh in the spiritual lineage of the famous scholar and reformist Sufi, Aḥmad al-Dardīr (d. 1786/7). In Abū 'l-Maʿārif's vision, the Prophet commanded him to become a spiritual guide, which puzzled him, because such an ambition had never occurred to him, and he felt far from able to carry out this mission. But he began to notice that whenever he merely thought of Shaykh Aḥmad al-Khudayrī, his heart would be filled with light. He came to realize that al-Khuḍayrī was the "father of his spirit and the source of his spiritual elevation and mystical opening *(futūḥ)*." He turned toward the shaykh's town of Ṭahṭā, fearing rejection by a shaykh who seldom accepted disciples, but he was warmly received. He says, "I was drawn to him with my entire self." Shaykh Aḥmad al-Khuḍayrī gradually initiated him into the *wird* of the seven divine Names used by the Khalwatis in dhikr: *Qawī* (Strong), Allah, *Hū* (He), *Ḥaqq* (True Reality), *Ḥayy* (Living), *Qayyūm* (Self-Subsistent), and *Qahhār* (Subduer). He gave him permission to guide disciples in 1868 and eventually named him his successor. Abū 'l-Maʿārif nonetheless states that besides this external journey into Sufism, there was an inner journey in which he was guided by God in a manner he is not able to express.[36]

Biographies of Abū 'l-Maʿārif emphasize that popular religion at the time was "deviant and superstitious," to the point where, according to a line of poetry quoted by Ḥasanayn Muḥammad Makhlūf in his short biography, "perhaps they are unbelievers." Among the deviations Makhlūf cites as prevalent among the Sufis were the mispronunciation of divine Names in dhikr and the utterance of blasphemy or questionable statements under the influence of a spiritual state *(shaṭaḥāt)*.[37] Abū 'l-Maʿārif became a major spokesman for a new, reformed interpretation of Sufism. For many people he embodied and modeled the best of Sufism, a combination of sound religious education, spiritual depth, and the cultivation of traditional Islamic virtues. He is called a reviver of the Sunna, because of his insistence on following the Prophet's virtues and patterns of behavior in his own life.

It appears that he traveled often to spread his message of spirituality and reform throughout Egypt, and despite some opposition by Sufis who felt his message threatened their traditions, he was widely admired by the religious elite of his country. He lived in the time of Muḥammad ʿAbduh (d. 1905), the famous Islamic reformer and associate of Jamāl al-Dīn al-Afghānī. Despite the well-known condemnation by ʿAbduh and his disciple Rashīd Riḍā (d. 1935) of aspects of traditional Sufism, Abū 'l-Maʿārif was much admired and indeed appears to have become a close friend of ʿAbduh. Biographies stress the large numbers of prominent members of the Egyptian religious elite who came to visit him both in his *sāḥa* in Nājʿ Ḥammādī and in the Cairo suburb of ʿAyn Shams, where he maintained an apartment. Ḥasanayn Makhlūf writes, "His *sāḥa* was an institute of learning visited by many ulama, scholars of the law, righteous men and sons of the [Sufi] Way, from all regions."[38] In addition to functioning as a traveling preacher and a Sufi shaykh in the Khalwatī Order, he wrote both didactic treatises articulating a reformed interpretation of Sufism and poems on Sufi themes, the most famous of which treats the Most Beautiful Names of God.[39] His sharp intelligence and learning, his spiritual experiences and demeanor, and his literary eloquence all combined to make him stand out among the religious personalities of modern Egypt.

He died on one of his journeys in a village near Asyūṭ. He had not appeared to be ill, and it appears that he suffered a heart attack from overexertion during dhikr. He was carried to a houseboat, where he continued to recite the name of Allah until his spirit left him.[40]

Abū 'l-Maᶜārif had three sons, each of whom became an outstanding Sufi in his own right. The youngest, Abū 'l-Faḍl, was born in 1881 and took the Sufi oath from his father when he was only sixteen years old. According to Hajjājī, he was initiated into the dhikr of the seven Names and "reached the highest ranks" of spiritual realization before he died at the age of thirty in 1911. Makhlūf describes him as a "gnostic and a poet." Abū 'l-Majd (1893–1929), who is nicknamed "Sulṭān Abū 'l-Majd," was a *magzūb* who manifested signs of sainthood from his childhood. When he was born, he emerged from the birth canal covered by something resembling a cloak, so that none of his limbs appeared, "and they did not know what was in the cloak, a boy or a girl." Forty days after his birth, he was heard reciting the divine name *Ḥaqq*. Ḥajjājī says, "He used to do things that shook heads and confounded minds." He was raised illiterate, remaining in a state of *gazb* all his life and achieving fame for his miracles. Ḥajjājī says that because of this he earned "the respect of the people who came to receive his blessing and enter his solitude."[41]

His nephew, Aḥmad al-Sharqāwī, took a dimmer view of the significance of this uncle. In an interview on 11 November 1988, he said, "He was very famous, even more famous than my father. He had this ability [to work miracles]. He would speak of things from the world of the unseen and knew of things that were happening far away at a time when there was no radio or television or telephone or any way to know such things. He would do such unusual things, which go against the pattern of nature. The stories told of him are too numerous to be counted, and they come from truthful people. My father did not have this ability. My uncle's mind was not sound, he was not responsible for what he did." Shaykh Aḥmad implies here that working miracles, although a natural result of a strong spirit, was also a sign of deficiency, which could be excused in the case of his uncle, since he was *magzūb*.

The Ḥajjājiyyīn, descendants of the famous saint Yūsuf Abū 'l-Ḥajjāj, whose shrine is embedded into the now uncovered Pharaonic temple of Luxor, celebrate the moulid of Abū 'l-Majd every year on the night of the middle of the Islamic month of Shaᶜbān *(nuṣṣ Shaᶜbān)*, the date of his death, an auspicious time with Pharaonic antecedents when many moulids are celebrated. Aḥmad al-Sharqāwī's reaction to this was, "I don't know why they would celebrate the moulid of someone who is *magzūb*." Like Abū 'l-Faḍl, Abū 'l-Majd died relatively young, at the age of thirty-seven.

Abū 'l-Wafā' al-Sharqāwī (7 May 1879–13 June 1961) was the eldest son of Abū 'l-Maʿārif and his successor in spiritual leadership. When he was born his father was already famous and highly esteemed. When his father died, he was only twenty years old. Raised and educated in his father's *sāḥa,* Abū 'l-Wafā' became, like his father, a religious scholar and a Sufi, continuing his mission of reformist preaching and teaching. Nonetheless, it appears that he pursued this mission with some reluctance. He inclined toward seclusion for periods of time, spending days and nights at a time far from home, cut off from all people, occupying himself with dhikr, Qur'an recitation, meditation, and reading. He also traveled to Medina and stayed there for more than a year, intending to remain there permanently in proximity to the Prophet's tomb. However, a group of his disciples and followers went to him to complain that the people were in need of his guidance, and he returned unwillingly to assume the mantle of leadership his father had left.[43]

He wrote his booklet of guidance for his disciples, *Miṣbāḥ al-arwāḥ fī sulūk ṭarīq al-Fattāḥ,* when he was very young, in 1903, at the age of twenty-four. In it he describes his reluctance to assume the role of Sufi shaykh. "My father gave me permission to give guidance about one month before he passed away. God blessed many people with the desire to cling to this (Khalwatī) path. Some asked me to

Figure 13. Author with Shaykh Aḥmad al-Sharqāwī on 22 March 1989.

guide them. . . . I saw that corruption had entered the hearts of people, and the spirits of the seekers were taken with heedlessness. All their limbs and senses acted as veils cutting them off from God. . . . I excused myself as too weak to carry such heavy burdens and guided them to someone more worthy than I. Still, many urgently requested me. . . . It amazed me that people requested me to guide them, without knowing that my father had given me permission to do so." When he began to fear that his refusal to accede to their request would cause some to turn further from the Way of the Truth, he agreed to lead a small group of disciples into the Path.[43]

Nonetheless, his booklet expresses his dim view of the spiritual level of many practicing Sufis. Most of them, he said, seemed to know nothing of the Way except the recitation of *awrād* and verbal affiliation to their shaykh. The result, he said, was an inability to "taste the pleasure of seeking their Lord's presence, and an aversion to what is best."[44] He nonetheless affirms the centrality of the recitation of *awrād* for spiritual progress and insists that they must be recited correctly and with concentration and awareness of their meaning. Other common faults he found among disciples were excessive speaking, which is "the worst deficiency in seekers," and an inability to receive counsel and correction from spiritual brothers. Disciples neglect mutual admonition because they fear it will create difficulties in their relationships, he said, but the giving and receiving of counsel are necessary for travelers on the Sufi path. He also inveighs against the use of dhikr assemblies for simple enjoyment, devoid of spiritual purpose, and the pursuit of Sufi singing as a career instead of for devotion to God. He mentions in passing the need to avoid dhikr assemblies that use heretical methods, by now such a familiar theme in reformist circles that it warrants only a passing warning rather than extensive discourse.

What gives life to the Sufi Way, wrote Abū 'l-Wafā', is the adoption of high morality, which he describes as "the gateway to its splendid gardens" and "a necessary prerequisite for coming to God." He insisted on the necessity of observing proper etiquette with all people, including those who are uneducated and poor. Concerning etiquette in general, he wrote, "One way that Satan has crushed the majority of disciples and corrupted their hearts is that they think that etiquette is merely an external manner. However, this pillar is an act for God and a way to draw near to Him."[45]

Abū 'l-Wafā' was no hypocrite in writing these words, for those who knew him attest to his meticulous observance of rules of etiquette and his humble, respectful demeanor with all people. His son, Shaykh Aḥmad al-Sharqāwī, told me during a visit to Dayr al-Saʿāda, "My father is the only person I have ever met who was genuinely unselfish in everything he did. He was irreproachable in his relations with everyone—his family, his disciples, and strangers. He never got angry, was always extremely polite and considerate, and never acted out of self-interest." This testimony from someone who certainly would have had the opportunity to observe any character flaws in Shaykh Abū 'l-Wafāʾ was not difficult for me to believe, for Shaykh Aḥmad himself is a man who has clearly perfected the art of Sufi *adab*—unfailing humility, grace, and hospitality. By his presence an atmosphere of quiet dignity and gracious hospitality permeates Dayr al-Saʿāda, leaving an indelible impression on the mind.[46]

Under Abū 'l-Wafā's leadership, says Ḥajjājī, Dayr al-Saʿāda became famous, visited by the great and the poor alike. "In his spiritual guidance he was the highest example of adherence to the rules of the Sharīʿa and the teachings of the Way. . . . He was known for the nobility of his morals, his help for the troubled, his assistance to the oppressed, his encouragement of faithfulness among all people, and his unique compassion and understanding, which combined the knowledge of the first teachers with a lofty humanism that encompassed every opinion, respected every principle, and honored every belief. The people all loved him, and especially the Christians, whom he received with affection, love and brotherhood."[47]

Ḥasanayn Makhlūf writes, "Despite its humble appearance, his blessed *sāḥa* was a Kaʿba for those who came, a circle of learning, religion, morals, etiquette, worship and guidance." He also cites the strong sense of brotherhood that existed among the disciples and others who came.[48] The *sāḥa* served as an institute for Qurʾanic studies in the morning, while from midafternoon until nightfall, Shaykh Abū 'l-Wafāʾ held his assembly and received visitors. Many of his visitors were ulama and Sufi shaykhs from all over Egypt and even from other Muslim states in the Arab world, Africa, and Asia. Shaykh Aḥmad Ḥasan al-Bāqūrī described his assembly as "pervaded by thought freed from the shabbiness of blind adherence to tradition *(taqlīd)* and a spirit purified from the leanness of literalism, and a perspective that could almost expose things hidden behind a delicate curtain."[49]

No one who speaks of Shaykh Abū 'l-Wafāʾ fails to mention the many luminaries who visited him at Dayr al-Saʿāda, which is somewhat amazing, considering its remoteness. Among the long list of well-known religious dignitaries who visited the *sāḥa* was Shaykh Muḥammad Ḥasanayn Makhlūf, rector of the Islamic University of Al-Azhar and father of Shaykh Ḥasanayn Muḥammad Makhlūf, who became Mufti of Egypt and authored a short biography of Shaykh Abū 'l-Wafā' and his father. The famous reformer Muḥammad ʿAbduh also visited Dayr al-Saʿāda, no doubt because of his friendship with Abū 'l-Maʿārif, as well as his best-known disciple, Muḥammad Rashīd Riḍā. Many members of Egypt's political and intellectual elite also visited Dayr al-Saʿāda, including the author ʿAbbās Maḥmūd al-ʿAqqād, the nationalist leader Saʿd Zaghlūl, prime ministers ʿAlī Māhir and Muṣṭafā al-Naḥḥās, and the famed scholar and author Dr. Ṭāhā Ḥusayn. As Shaykh Aḥmad al-Sharqāwī said, "He had contacts with all the great men of the republic," including men of the royal family. "Perhaps what distinguished him more than anything else was his intellectual maturity. Al-Sayyid al-Mujaddidi, Egyptian ambassador to Afghanistan and Saudi Arabia, was a Sufi. He said he did not find anyone like my father among all the personalities of the Islamic world. He always spoke the truth and gave sound counsel on any matter that was presented to him but always in a manner that won people's hearts, without in any way embarrassing the person to whom the advice was given. He was respected by all."[50]

His function as Sufi shaykh, however, formally ceased at the beginning of the First World War. Although Shaykh Abū 'l-Wafā' never revealed to his son, Shaykh Aḥmad, why he ceased administering oaths and guiding disciples through *awrād,* he says his father felt that circumstances were inappropriate for this method of education and guidance. He speculates that perhaps it was because he was under observation by the government at that time and because his disciples were insufficiently responsive. It was, however, merely a change in tactic, not an end to his career as spiritual guide. He continued to give guidance, counsel, and education through his assemblies at Dayr al-Saʿāda. But his writings—both his booklet of guidance to his disciples and his poems in praise of the Prophet—are also confined to his early period.

Although local people claim that Shaykh Abū 'l-Wafā' performed miracles, including simultaneous appearances as preacher in mosques in different villages, his son Aḥmad denies this. He does not deny that his father might have been able to perform miracles, citing as proof of this a visit to a psychotherapist in Switzerland for nervous tension (which indicates that his legendary calm demeanor was more a matter of self-control than inner placidity), during which the therapist asked him to concentrate on a metal coin (in order to hypnotize him, perhaps?). Abū 'l-Wafā' was able, by the strength of his spirit, to move the coin. Shaykh Aḥmad insisted, however, that his father was thoroughly intellectual in his methods and approach. Shaykh Aḥmad's understanding of Sufism is also thoroughly intellectual and fairly unmystical. The gnostic, he says, operates by his intellect. Shaykh ʿIzz felt that such statements were deliberately misleading, following the Sufi tradition of publicly affirming the Sharīʿa and privately following mystical interpretations. He also felt that Shaykh Aḥmad's denial that Abū 'l-Wafā' performed miracles was simply humility—refreshingly different and "honest," though not entirely accurate. However, he said, Abū 'l-Wafā' belonged to a school that disdained the working of miracles, regarding them as the "menstrual blood" of saints.

After this interview with Shaykh Aḥmad al-Sharqāwī, ʿIzz took me to see a man in a nearby town whom he said was a *khalīfa,* or successor, of Abū 'l-Wafā', who would give me a different story. But this man told us he had never met Abū 'l-Wafā' personally, although his father had; his acquaintance with Abū 'l-Wafā' was entirely in the spirit. Nonetheless, he too denied knowing of any miracles attributed to Abū 'l-Wafā'.

Shaykh Abū 'l-Wafā' maintained a keen interest in politics and publicly supported Saʿd Zaghlūl during his trip into Upper Egypt to gain support for his anti-British agitation, traveling with him and hosting an elaborate reception for him at Dayr al-Saʿāda. Contemporary Egyptians see Abū 'l-Wafā''s support as critical for helping Egyptians to present a united front behind Zaghlūl's leadership and regard his stance as courageous in view of the political pressures of the time.

Despite his political opposition to the British and his skepticism over the wisdom of supporting the British in World War I, Abū 'l-Wafā' admired aspects of British culture—their scientific and technological achievements, their punctuality, truthfulness, and good manners. Abū 'l-Wafā' was well-traveled. Besides making frequent pilgrimages to Mecca and trips to the Prophet's tomb in Medina, he traveled to India in 1929, where he met Muhammad ʿAli Jinnah, the "father" of Pakistan, and he also visited Europe. Shaykh Aḥmad says, "In Europe he wanted to see all aspects of European society, so he even went to nightclubs. At one nightclub in Paris he talked with a woman reporter who asked him why Muslims were opposed to dancing, which is so nice. He asked if she felt any arousal when dancing with a man, and she said yes. He said, 'That is why Islam forbids it, for whatever leads to corruption must be prevented.' "

Abū 'l-Wafā' al-Sharqāwī is clearly the type of Sufi the government and the Supreme Council of Sufi Orders would consider exemplary, combining religious learning with sober realism, intellectualism, lofty moral standards, and spiritual depth. Yet at the same time as he had close contacts with government figures, he maintained his independence and a certain distance that was reinforced by his geographical remoteness. People came to him for advice, but he did not implicate himself in any way into the affairs of government. Furthermore, he relinquished the role of Sufi shaykh in its proper sense, eschewing inscription into the ranks of the increasingly bureaucratically controlled shaykhs. His method of spiritual guidance remained informal, casting a wide net that touched the lives of many people, and exerting an influence on personal life and national affairs that is difficult to calculate.

ENIGMATIC SELF-EFFACEMENT: SHAYKH MAḤMŪD ABŪ 'L-ʿAZM (1910–1983)

Aḥmad Raḍwān and Abū 'l-Wafā' al-Sharqāwī were both well-known figures who felt called to take active roles in the social and religious life of Egypt and who exerted an influence on important public figures. They have each educated thousands of people in the ways of Sufism and Islam, and some of these have gone on to become teachers of others. Maḥmūd Abū 'l-ʿAzm is an entirely different sort of figure. Although the small band of his devotees that I met in Cairo insist that his followers are many, he is little known in Sufi circles. He never functioned as shaykh of an Order, never pursued the role of teacher, rarely administered oaths, and did not even own a place of residence. He was a mysterious person, and the stories told about him by those who knew him suggest a loner who was initiated into the Sufi path without human agency. His life was an extraordinary series of miraculous occurrences, which became so commonplace that they became normal for him. His story bears the marks of legend, like the stories told of saintly figures from other religious traditions. What is extraordinary is that this legendary-type account is narrated by those who were closest to him in life. He is included here not because of his influence on Egyptian religious life, which was restricted to a small group of individuals, but because he represents another type of Sufi that, removed from the parameters of ordinary social life, nonetheless occupies an important place in Sufi tradition.[51]

Shaykh Maḥmūd was born in 1910 in the village of Kafr Brāsh in the Delta province of Sharqiyya, and he died in al-Manāyir, a village approximately seven to eight kilometers from his birthplace, in 1983. His was a simple peasant family with no known Sufi contacts. He was born with the name Muḥammad ʿAbdallāh. He was named Maḥmūd Abū ʾl-ʿAzm by the legendary Khiḍr, and his mother then remembered that someone had told her this name while he was still in the womb. He began attending Qurʾan school at the age of four, and by the age of six had memorized the entire Qurʾan. His father worked for a foreign-owned wine company, and the boy refused to eat at home because the family's income was derived from a source prohibited by Islamic Law. Other villagers would invite him to eat in their homes.

At the age of eight the boy simply disappeared for nine years, and no one knows where he was. Many years later Laylā, his closest disciple, asked about this time, and he told her he was in a solitary place, where God had appointed two creatures to feed him. She asked if this was a frightening experience, and he replied, "Why should I be afraid, when God was my Provider?" Although he returned to society at the age of seventeen, and he would visit his village, he did not stay there. Once by chance he met his sister on the bus, and she could scarcely believe it was he. At the age of twenty-five he returned to his home village, where a marriage was arranged for him, from which he had a daughter. But his wife was afraid to live with him because strange things would happen: spirits would come and talk with him, and he would be raised off the bed; he would be lying by her side and suddenly he would be gone. After their daughter died at the age of three, his wife left him. He divorced her and did not remarry.

His initiation into Sufism is a mystery. No one knows of anyone who taught him. When asked about this, he merely replied that his shaykh was the Prophet himself.

After his divorce the shaykh came to Cairo and stayed in the homes of various disciples, rarely lingering very long in one place, until the last few years of his life, when he would spend the entire winter with Laylā and her husband, Mamdūh.

Laylā's connection with Shaykh Maḥmūd began with her father, a prosperous landowner. "My father loved the shaykhs. He inclined toward Sufi things. One of his friends told him there was a shaykh at his home, a very good man. My father went to that friend's house, and Shaykh Maḥmūd was there. They sat together without saying anything at all except the usual greetings. But my father knew Shaykh Maḥmūd would be going to the airport at the time of the dawn prayer to perform the pilgrimage. My father returned home at 1:00 A.M., and he began to reproach himself for neglecting to offer to drive him to the airport. He used to offer to take everyone to the airport, so how could it have escaped his mind to offer Shaykh Maḥmūd a ride? When he went into his bedroom, he turned on the lamp and was about to get into bed when he heard someone say, 'Peace be upon you.'[52] He found it was Shaykh Maḥmūd. He came to tell Shams [her father] not to be angry with himself and to assure him that he had the means to get to the airport. This was Shaykh Maḥmūd's first miracle with my father. He sat with him for about fifteen minutes and talked to him. When he was about to leave, Shaykh Maḥmūd told my father he would be visiting frequently. I still wasn't born, only my brother ʿAbd al-Qawī and my sister Mervat. My father offered to take him wherever he wanted to go, but he said, 'No. I will go the same way I came.' He left, and my father didn't see him."

Shaykh Maḥmūd frequently practiced this traditional saintly miracle of appearing suddenly in distant places or appearing in more than one place at a time, but not in an ostentatious manner. Laylā said, "He didn't like to do it in front of anyone. Not just anyone could bear to see it. He didn't talk about it, but, for example, he would be with me and someone would say, 'I saw Shaykh Maḥmūd yesterday in Mecca,' though he was at our house." During Ramaḍān he would simultaneously break the fast with different people in different cities. Four different people might claim that Shaykh Maḥmūd was with them at the same time on the same day, and he could be in Cairo at the same time as he was in Mecca.

The shaykh had many miracles. A widow in his village wanted to go on the pilgrimage but had no means to go there. The shaykh pulled his car up in front of her house and asked if she wanted to go on the pilgrimage. She said yes, and he said, "Then get in the car right away and don't tell anyone." She got in the car and went with him by plane to Mecca. He had all the papers she needed, including her passport, although she had never had her picture taken. She stayed with him in Mecca for twenty-one days. She was not listed among those granted permits by the Egyptian government for the pilgrimage that year, and when she met the other Egyptians they wondered how she had come.

There were many other stories of Shaykh Maḥmud's miraculous provision of the paperwork and finances for various people to go on the pilgrimage. Ḥāgga Laylā tells the following story: "One of the shaykh's 'daughters' was going on the pilgrimage with my mother. He had her money with him. When the preparations for the pilgrimage were finished, he gave me her money, which was LE 700. She needed LE 300 more. He said, 'I'll give you the rest of the money later.' I thought this would mean some time later. He got up, went into the bathroom, and came out laughing and out of breath. He pulled an envelope out of his pocket and said, 'Count the money.' I found it to be the correct amount. I said to myself, 'Does that make sense? Just a minute ago he didn't have it.' He said, 'Laylā, phone so-and-so,' who lived in Heliopolis. 'Ask her how she is, but don't tell her I am here, because I want to sit with you a while more.' I phoned her and asked her how Shaykh Maḥmūd was. She said, 'He was here less than five minutes ago. There was something entrusted to him that he left here, so he took it and left.' He did this so I wouldn't doubt him any more and wonder what was going on. This was how he taught me."

On another occasion, when Laylā was about to go to bed, Shaykh Maḥmūd told her to wait five more minutes. Five minutes later her brother Sami telephoned from California. "He never told me not to go to bed if I wanted to sleep, but this time he did because he knew Sami would phone."

Shaykh Maḥmūd knew a family whose children, according to Laylā and Mamdūḥ, "were totally irreligious, leaning toward the ways of the West." Their son went to London for a heart operation and his father gave him money to go. But when he went he did not take account of the hospital expenses, and he spent all the money on pleasures. He was in his hotel room worrying about this and thinking he would have to go home and tell his father the situation and return again for the operation, when a knock came at the door. The young man called out in English, "Who is it?" and the answer came back in English. (The shaykh allegedly could speak English and French, indeed any language, perfectly, and was familiar with the plays of Shakespeare.) The shaykh entered the room and said that his father had sent him with money for the operation, and he told him not to tell anyone about this. The son nonetheless called home and asked his father if he had sent Shaykh Maḥmūd with some money, and the father said no. "The children of the family did not believe in saints or miracles or anything," explained Mamdūḥ. When the boy returned from London, Shaykh Maḥmūd met him at the bottom of the stairs as he stepped off the plane, and said emphatically, "Didn't I tell you not to tell anyone?" He then vanished, and the young man searched the airport for him in vain.

Shaykh Maḥmūd never returned in the same day to a place where he had visited, except on one occasion when he returned suddenly to Laylā's house, which he had left that morning. Laylā's three-year-old daughter had woken from a nap with a severe allergic reaction, and Laylā was frantically trying to call her doctor, but in vain. Suddenly Shaykh Maḥmūd appeared to reassure her that the rash was nothing serious. This was how she knew that he was aware of the circumstances of his followers. On another occasion, when she went to the moulid of Fāṭima al-Nabawiyya and someone threw some candies into the crowd, she tried to get a piece for her daughter but was unable because of the crush of the crowd. When she returned home, there was Shaykh Maḥmūd, and in his hand was the candy she had been wanting. "Here," he said, "take the *bonbon* you wanted."

In his earlier years he might do a miracle in front of people, said Laylā, but the older he became, the more he tried not to let people see his miraculous powers. He even went to the extreme of asking other people to pray for him if they asked him to pray for them—although the least attribute of a saint is that his prayers are answered. His method was extreme self-effacement. "He had no self at all," said Laylā. "The saint shouldn't show you the path to himself, but to God. He would never say, 'I did such-and-such.' There was no 'I' at all. I would love to see such morals in somebody else, but I have not." Although she often heard him reciting the Qurʾan seemingly all night long, if she asked him in the morning how he had slept, he would say he had slept the entire night. His private practices of worship and meditation were never divulged.

His self-effacement was reflected in his methods of interaction with other people. He never criticized other people, no matter how much he might dislike them or disapprove of their way of life. He spent a good deal of time with Laylā and Mamdūḥ, who, in their younger years, would go out frequently to the Sheraton or some other luxury hotel and spend LE 30 or 40 a night, drinking and dancing. Laylā would spend at least an hour getting her hair and makeup ready before going out. But the shaykh left everyone just as he was. His influence on her was subtle but total, says Laylā. Eventually, after performing the pilgrimage, she decided to abandon her former lifestyle, wear Islamic dress, and devote her nights to Qurʾan reading, prayer, and attending the moulids of the *ahl al-bayt*. (This change also made it necessary for her to quit her job as a French teacher in a secondary school.) She was going to pray all the prayers the Prophet customarily prayed, but Shaykh Maḥmūd told her to do only the five obligatory prayers. After this had become a habit for her, he told her she may pray other prayers as well. He always preferred a few prayers done with sincere devotion over much repetition. He did not like much talk and rarely spoke at all. When he stayed with her, Laylā said, "I would sit for hours holding his hand, like a stupid person." If she asked him a question about a religious matter, he would usually not answer her at that time but would appear to her later in a dream and answer her question. If other people asked him questions about religion, he would tell them to go to a shaykh of al-Azhar. He administered no oaths except to her. He held no regular meetings with his followers, and when there were dhikr assemblies he would not speak. He was a very calm and patient person who rarely became angry, she said, but when he did it was frightening: he was a very tall, large man, even fat, with a red complexion. When he became angry his face became redder and he seemed to become taller so that she feared he would go through the ceiling. His method of correction was by example. She used to eat only the crusts of bread, removing the inner part and leaving it in little pieces on the table. One day he took those little pieces and ate them. She protested that they had other bread for him to eat, but he said, "Better to throw this into my stomach than to throw it in the garbage." In this way, she learned not to do this.

He attracted people by his manners and by his spirit. He was a man of extraordinary humility. Laylā said, "If he met anyone young, although he could be his grandfather, he treated him with great respect. He respected the young more than the old. He never said a word against anyone, no matter what he had done. If anyone asked him about anyone, he would say, 'He is good. They are all good.' I have never seen anyone like him. I have never seen his morals in any other shaykh." It was his character, not his miracles, that attracted him to her. Despite her closeness to him and the fact that he spent more time with her than with anyone else, she was in awe of him and acted with extreme circumspection in front of him, not wishing to anger or annoy him. Occasionally she could joke with him, but his moods of jocularity were limited. While sitting with other people watching television, his mind would wander elsewhere. If everyone laughed, his attention would return to the situation and he would try to figure out why they were laughing.

Laylā always knew when Shaykh Maḥmūd was about to visit, for his aroma would enter the house before he appeared, a distinctive smell that even her young daughter recognized. For the first two years after his death, Laylā said, "I felt like he was with me more than when he was alive. I felt him everywhere. Perhaps I wasn't equipped to see him, but I felt him all the time. I would see him in visions, smell his aroma. After that it began to recede. Maybe it was just my reaction to his death." By the time he died, she said, they were one spirit. She knew little about the doctrine of annihilation in the shaykh but knew only that he was her way to God and that she loved him completely.

When Shaykh Maḥmūd died, both the village of his birth and the village of his early married life wanted to have his body buried in their borders, so his blessing could spread to the entire village. He had left no instructions concerning his burial, so the villagers decided that the shaykh should himself indicate where he should be buried. When he was carried to Kafr Brāsh, the bier stood still and would not enter the village. The bier went on until the pallbearers reached the place in al-Manāyir where he is now buried. There his followers have built a shrine, where they hold dhikr assemblies. His "children," who include both peasants and a number of highly educated young people from the middle and upper classes, are loyal to him alone. He has no successor, and they seek no other shaykh. Nonetheless, many of them clearly feel a need for guidance and seized upon Shaykh ʿIzz when they met him to ask him numerous questions. Mamduh has gone on to take the oath from a Rifaʿi shaykh.

ʿIzz's opinion is that Shaykh Maḥmūd was unquestionably a great saint who had enormous spiritual power and exemplary morals, but his practice of self-effacement left him unproductive as a teacher, in that no one was trained to take his place after him. It is a different kind of mission, he said. One cannot say that one is better than the other, it depends entirely on one's calling by God. Nonetheless, it was ʿIzz's assessment that he was a "barren" shaykh who did not "conceive." His spiritual children were left like orphans.

"MOTHER OF COMPASSION": ḤĀGGA ZAKIYYA OF CAIRO (1899–1982)

Our final example of modern-day sainthood reflects many of the attributes of some of the other saints we have described: a Sufi ascetic who combined a life of devotion with a life of hospitality, who taught mainly in an indirect fashion but exerted enormous influence, a miracle worker and "one whose prayers are answered." But in one critical respect this saint is different from the others: she was a woman. Her personal qualities and even her method of teaching bear many resemblances to the last two saints I have described, and one of her followers even mentions among her virtues *murūʾa*, which could mean valor or generosity but which literally means "manliness." Yet the epithet most often bestowed upon her is "mother of compassion." Her compassion is almost always the first quality people mention in describing her. It is difficult to know whether this particular quality was cultivated so carefully, or perceived to be so dominant, because it is valued so highly in women. Surely Aḥmad Raḍwān could be characterized as compassionate in his care for his neighbors during the malaria and typhoid epidemic of 1944, yet he is more apt to be described as noble, generous, and righteous. People saw her as a motherly figure, and it would appear that she also saw herself as a "mother" to many "children." She administered no oaths and gave no formal lessons, but the bonds she had with her spiritual children were often intense, and the transformations she effected in their lives were often profound.

Zakiyya ʿAbd al-Muṭṭalib Badawī came from the village of Mit Muraggaʿ Salsīl in the Delta province of Manṣūra. A descendant of Ḥusayn, her family is said to have been pious and exemplary. She married the son of her maternal aunt, Muḥammad al-Mahdi ʿAssāsa, who, according to those who knew him, was a great scholar of al-Azhar as well as a Sufi. He followed, as his parents had before him, a Shādhilī shaykh named ʿAbd al-Raḥīm al-Sabʿ (d. 1947) who

Figure 14. Ḥāgga Zakiyya (d.1982) (courtesy of ʿAbd al-Hādī Mūsā ʿAbd al-Hādī).

lived by the shrine of Ḥusayn in Cairo. Through her husband, Zakiyya also came to follow this shaykh and to assume the life of a devotee of the *ahl al-bayt*. She would come to Cairo and visit all the shrines of the *ahl al-bayt* in a single day, beginning and ending with the shrine of Ḥusayn, and on Friday evenings she would attend the *ḥaḍra* of Shaykh ʿAbd al-Raḥīm, the only woman present, doing dhikr separately on a balcony overlooking the men.

From her marriage she had only one child, her daughter Nafīsa, who was conceived after a number of childless years. When Nafīsa was only four years old, she told her father, "Divorce my mother!" Her father was astonished, because they were very happy together. But he consulted Shaykh ʿAbd al-Raḥīm, who advised him that the counsel was from God. He divorced Zakiyya, and both of them remarried. Zakiyya married another cousin from her village, a merchant who had no strong religious inclinations, but the marriage was not happy, and she eventually left him. One of Ḥāgga Zakiyya's spiritual daughters testifies, "And I saw with my own eyes how much she loved her first husband's second wife." She speculates that perhaps God wanted her to experience life with an irreligious man so she would be able to empathize with the troubled people who were to come to her.

Ḥāgga Zakiyya was, to all appearances, blind—since childhood, according to one follower. "But no one ever felt that she had lost her sight. She could see colors and would comment on them. She would see by the light of God." A young medical doctor, however, said, "People said she was blind, but she wasn't really blind. I was there personally when medical doctors examined her and said there was nothing wrong with her eyes. But she didn't use her eyes, because she moved by inner vision *(baṣīra)*, not physical vision *(baṣar)*."

Her spiritual devotions included much dhikr and recitations of praise, and a daily litany of prayers for blessings on the Prophet. She spent many nights in devotion and rarely needed to sleep at all. After her move to Cairo, she prayed the dawn prayer every morning in the mosque of Ḥusayn.

According to one of Ḥāgga Zakiyya's spiritual sons, "she was overcome by lights, and the *ahl al-bayt* ordered her to come to Cairo." She took an apartment in the Darrāsa district, near the shrine of Ḥusayn, where she began her life's ministry of offering hospitality, kindness, and spiritual guidance to "children of the Way." Her spiritual son continued, "She solved their problems, gave kindness to the needy, and prayed for those in distress. God, may He be exalted, did not disappoint her hopes but met needs at her hands, and she solved the problems of all those who came to her. If a rebellious person came to her, God changed him into something good, both women and men. Many repented at her hands and became saints of God, having shrines and being visited by the pious." Later, when her father died, she used her inheritance to buy a piece of land in the Gamāliyya area even closer to the Ḥusayn mosque, where she built a *sāḥa* complex that includes three buildings with a number of bedrooms, a kitchen, and a mosque, in the words of a follower, "to honor those who love the *ahl al-bayt*."

Her method was spiritual discernment and influence by simple association. "God gave her a light in her heart by which she knew the needs of those who came to her and those who needed her kindness," says one of her followers. She would welcome anyone into her presence, and kept her *sāḥa* open and her kitchen operative twenty-four hours a day. Although she spent a good deal of time in solitary devotion, emerging, according to one follower, only on Fridays to sit with her followers and circulate among all the rooms of the *sāḥa*, anyone could knock on her door at any time. She would become angry if anyone were refused an audience with her. "She welcomed everyone," said one of her spiritual daughters. "Each one felt that she loved him more than anyone else. She would be interested in your problem, and you would feel able to bear it after being with her." She would not correct people openly but would test people secretly to determine their character. She offered her children words of counsel and exhortations to be patient, generous, open-minded, striving for what is good, and obedient to God and His Messenger. Little by little those around her would change for the better. One of her spiritual daughters said this was God's grace to her, that she always obtained the desired moral effect on people without making them feel it.

Other stories tell of dramatic healings from moral defects, mental illness, or spirit possession. One woman who suffered from association with a man whose spiritual power was derived from jinn came to Ḥāgga Zakiyya in great fear of the man's power. He had threatened to harm her and her family if she ever left him, and when she realized that his power was derived not from God but from jinn, she did not know where to turn. But Ḥāgga Zakiyya paralyzed him and stripped him of his power shortly after she first came to know her, and soon the man died. Like so many people healed by Ḥāgga Zakiyya, she became a close follower, visiting her several times each week despite the distance of her home from Ḥāgga Zakiyya's *sāḥa*.

One man tells of his attachment to Ḥāgga Zakiyya: "On a Friday after the death of my mother, I went to the mosque of our lord Imām Ḥusayn, where I saw a man who was one of the leading followers of the gnostic, Ḥāgga Zakiyya. He asked me, 'What is wrong?' I told him, 'I am terribly depressed over the death of my mother.' He said, 'I will show you a mother who has kindness, compassion, and mercy.' I went with him to the *sāḥa* of this virtuous lady. When I saw her I began to weep. She motioned to me to sit next to her. I did, and said nothing, but wept. She felt sorry for me and patted me without saying anything. Then she said to me, 'You are thinking of your mother. I have more compassion for you than your mother of whom you are thinking. I belong to you in this world and the next. Any time you are troubled, remember me with the *Fātiḥa*, and your troubles will vanish.' I have lived my whole life with her since 1952, until she passed to the mercy of God, in compassion and contentment."

His attachment to her became profound, and he developed the habit of visiting her and dining with her every day after work. He says, "I have only had troubles in my life since her death." He accompanied her on the pilgrimage four times. He says, "After the morning prayer in the Prophet's mosque, she would stand for a long time. I became tired, but I said, 'It is better that she is with her grandfather, the Messenger of God,' and I was afraid to talk with her [to tell her of my fatigue]. But she [sensed it and]) said, 'Visitation is over, Ḥāgg ʿAbduh.'

"When she went to the Meccan sanctuary, I saw that the path in front of her was wide open [despite the density of the crowds during the pilgrimage]. When she entered the Kaʿba, people made way for her, and no one touched her. She kissed the Black Stone a long time."

Both Ḥāgga Zakiyya's sensitivity to Ḥāgg ʿAbduh's fatigue ("every one felt that she could feel what they felt," said another follower) and the unobstructed path before her during the pilgrimage are seen as miraculous. Most pilgrims are lucky if they get a chance to touch the Black Stone, but she kissed it a long time, following the example of the Prophet. The fact that no one in the crowd touched her implies not only her spiritual power but the preservation of her female modesty and dignity.

Nonetheless, her female modesty and dignity did not prevent her from embracing men or enjoying emotional intimacy with them. A mother, after all, may do so with her sons. As we have seen, Shaykh ʿIzz says she used to have him lay his head in her lap, and called him her daughter, not her son, to indicate that fleshly labels had become meaningless. Shaykh ʿIzz at that time was a young man, and she was already an elderly woman with an aura of compassion and holiness. I commented to ʿIzz that her appearance in her photographs is formidable, swathed in heavy cloths up to her mouth or even her nose, her eyes covered by sunglasses, her features sharp, her body thin. Such things suggested aloofness to me, not the warmth and openness I heard from those who knew her. ʿIzz agreed that her appearance was formidably dignified and that when he first met her he was afraid of her. But gradually he came to see her as the warm, loving person everyone described.

"*Ḥāgga*" (or "*Ḥājja*") is a title given to a woman who has performed the pilgrimage (ḥajj) to Mecca, just as "*Ḥāgg*" (or "*Ḥājj*") is given to a man. There could scarcely be a woman more deserving of the title than Ḥāgga Zakiyya, who performed the pilgrimage twenty-six times and performed the lesser pilgrimage (*ʿumra)* more than fifty times. Many of her miracles occurred during the pilgrimage. She invited a woman to accompany her on the pilgrimage at the last minute although the woman had neither a passport nor a plane ticket. The woman boarded the plane with her, and although the flight crew and authorities in Saudi Arabia were alerted that an unauthorized woman had boarded the plane, the number of passengers was always correct, and the woman was never detected. On one of her pilgrimages with Ḥāgg ʿAbduh, Ḥāgga Zakiyya pulled fish out of the sand and told him to cook it for the pilgrims. He fried some of it and made soup with the rest, and though many pilgrims ate, the food did not run out. In fact, it lasted for five days in that hot climate unrefrigerated before the supply was finally exhausted, and it always remained fresh.

On one of her pilgrimages performed with a young woman, Ḥāgga Zakiyya instructed the young woman to go on ahead of her at the Kaʿba and find a Ḥāgga Zaynab from Ḥusayn, whom she described as a dark woman wearing a green dress. The young woman did as she was told, confident that despite the crowd the saint's baraka would enable her to find Ḥāgga Zaynab. Soon she saw a woman of this description. Furthermore, the woman ran to her immediately and, hearing that Ḥāgga Zakiyya was there, rushed to find her. The two women embraced and talked at length, head to head. But when the woman had gone, Ḥāgga Zakiyya said to her young companion, "It is not her." The young woman was puzzled but went and found another woman of the same description, spoke to her, confirmed that she was indeed Ḥāgga Zaynab from Ḥusayn, and went with her to Ḥāgga Zakiyya. After that woman had gone, the young woman asked Ḥāgga Zakiyya about the first woman. Zakiyya replied, "She doesn't speak Arabic." "And this," exclaimed the young woman who told me the story, "after they had talked with their heads close together for a long time! She didn't openly admit it, but she could understand all the languages. Once when I was talking with an American visitor I misunderstood something he said, and Ḥāgga Zakiyya gently and subtly corrected me, saying, 'He meant such-and-such,' although she allegedly knew no foreign languages at all! Although Ḥāgga Zakiyya didn't perform miracles openly, she could have turned a wall into gold if she'd so desired!"

Her miracles were many: miracles of knowledge and healing and the ability to transcend spatial limitations and appear in more than one place at a time. Shaykh ʿIzz said that Aḥmad Raḍwān had said that she was one of the *abdāl,* that category of saints who could produce replicas of themselves, and appear and disappear at will. A woman said that one time she placed her hand on top of Ḥāgga Zakiyya's, and found there was nothing there at all.

She also visited the tomb of Sīdī Abū 'l-Ḥasan al-Shādhilī, in the remote mountainous region of Humaythira, near the Red Sea, three or four times a year toward the end of her life. According to one of her followers, Ḥāgga Zaynab, she was the first woman to visit the tomb, in the early 1920s, before she was even married. At that time the way to Sīdī Shādhilī was a dangerous desert journey without any proper road to a place that had no electricity or water and was inhabited only by poverty-stricken Bedouins who were ignored by the government and who in turn shunned the rest of society. Later, when Shaykh ʿAbd al-Ḥalīm Maḥmūd was head of the Islamic University of al-Azhar in the 1970s, he had a beautiful white shrine and mosque complex built in honor of Sīdī Shādhilī. Ḥāgga Zakiyya returned, bringing with her a group of women. A woman who was among the group says, "We found that by merely visiting the shrine, everything changed for us: colors changed, we were able to keep from anger, from passions, our spiritual senses were heightened."[53]

When Ḥāgga Zakiyya saw the poverty of the Bedouins of the region around Sīdī Shādhilī, she decided to build a *sāḥa* to serve them. This *sāḥa* was completed only in the last year of her life, but her generous hospitality became well-known among the local people long before that. Says one of her followers, "The government itself showed no interest in them until after the 1967 war. They had no social services whatsoever, and no conscription. She is the one who

Figure 15. Ḥāgga Zakiyya with her close follower, Ḥāgg ʿAbd al-Hādī Mūsā ʿAbd al-Hādī, and his family (courtesy of ʿAbd al-Hādī Mūsā ʿAbd al-Hādī).

brought electricity there and arranged for trucks to bring in water and food every day. The governor went and visited her because he heard there was a seventy-year-old woman in that harsh climate who had no education and was blind. . . . The Bedouin women never used to let any strange person see them at all. They would go to Ḥāgga Zakiyya, where she sat on her bed, and they would call her 'Mama.' She would give them sweet things and money."

Today, the *sāḥa* built by Ḥāgga Zakiyya is one of several in the area around Sidi Shadhili, which, thanks to paved roads and daily public buses, is visited by pilgrims year-round. Among the *sāḥas* in the area, however, only that of Ḥāgga Zakiyya is constantly open and serving meals to visitors, who also sleep in one of the bedrooms of the *sāḥa* or on the benches on its veranda. Her spiritual children who service the *sāḥa* continue to pay special attention to any of the Bedouin who come for a meal. Indeed, the more ragged and poverty-stricken the visitor, the more he is treated with honor, because these were the ones Ḥāgga Zakiyya especially loved.

It is said that Sīḍi Shādhilī informed Ḥāgga Zakiyya that she would die near him, and indeed this transpired. Ḥāgga Zakiyya was aware of the date of her death seven months before it occurred. Ibrāhīm Ramaḍān ʿAlī, the "Shaykh Fāris" who wrote a book on the virtues of the *ahl al-bayt,* tells in this book that he visited her at the Shādhilī shrine during the feast of the great sacrifice *(ʿīd al-aḍḥā)* shortly before she died, and she requested that he remain twenty days after the feast. He asked why, and she said, "So you can wish me farewell, for I am traveling soon." He excused himself because of prior commitments, and they tearfully embraced before his departure. True to her word, she died twenty days after the feast, on 24 December 1982.[54] She is buried in a shrine adjacent to her *sāḥa* in Humaythira.

CHAPTER 10

The Life and Influence of Shaykh Muḥammad ʿUthmān al-Burhānī

The inclusion of a chapter on the life and influence of a Sudanese shaykh in a book on Egyptian Sufism, mystics, and saints requires some justification. The primary justification is the extraordinary success enjoyed by the Burhāniyya in attracting a following in Egypt, especially in the 1970s. Under the leadership of Muḥammad ʿUthmān ʿAbduh of Sudan (d. 1983), the Burhāniyya Order was enormously successful in an age when the Sufi Orders were allegedly declining. Egypt's cultural ties with Sudan run very deep, although typically Sudan has been subject to Egyptian cultural and political hegemony. The Burhāniyya are an interesting example of the reverse, the extraordinary influence of a single Sudanese Order and its shaykh over the religious life of Egypt. The story of the Burhāniyya also forces us to shelve some of our common attitudes regarding the inability of traditional Sufism to appeal to modern, educated Muslims, for it drew many people from the upper and educated classes.

The second justification for including the Burhāniyya in this book is that no other Sufi Order has been the object of such controversy. Popular Sufism forms a subculture within Egyptian society, with its own doctrines, rules, hierarchy, and worldview. Its doctrines are based on the writings of medieval Sufis like Ibn ʿArabī (d. 1240), ʿAbd al-Karīm al-Jīlī (d. 1408), and Jalāl al-Din al-Suyūtī (d. 1505), writers whose work is suspect in reformed circles. Rarely do these doctrines come to surface and attract public controversy, but with the writing of *Tabriʾat al-dhimma fī nuṣḥ al-umma* (Discharging the duty of counselling the nation) by Muḥammad ʿUthmān ʿAbduh, shaykh of the Burhāniyya, they did just that. Typical attacks on the Sufi Orders concentrate not so much on doctrine as on practice, particularly saint shrine visitation and dhikr. These practices are ably defended in the magazine of the Supreme Council of Sufi Orders by the respected shaykh of the

Muḥammadiyya Shādhiliyya Order, Muḥammad Zakī Ibrāhīm. The controversy over the Burhāniyya, however, brought to light the normally esoteric Sufi doctrine regarding the attributes and cosmic significance of the Prophet and his family. This emerges as a watershed issue in the distinction between reformed (or official) and popular Sufism. In 1976 the Egyptian media waged a relentless campaign against the Burhāniyya, depicting the shaykh as a dangerous cult leader trying to pervert Islam from within.

The Burhāniyya Dasūqiyya Shādhiliyya Order, introduced into Egypt by the Sudanese shaykh Muḥammad ʿUthmān ʿAbduh in the 1930s, attracted adherents from all social classes throughout Egypt, in both urban and rural areas. Muḥammad ʿUthmān eagerly engaged in debate with both atheists and Muslim fundamentalists ("Wahhābīs," as he called them), and taught his followers these techniques of debate in order to encourage the spread of the Order. A good deal of the credit for the Burhāniyya's expansion in Egypt goes to the efforts of Shaykh Gamāl al-Sanhūrī, appointed Muḥammad ʿUthmān's representative in Egypt in 1953, when Burhāniyya membership in Egypt was only seventeen. Sanhūrī, who originally came to Cairo from Sudan to study law, had become a political commentator in the mass media, a polished man in western suits with a working knowledge of English and French, when he met Shaykh Muḥammad ʿUthmān in Cairo in 1931. Muḥammad ʿUthmān impressed him with his ability to explain the hidden meaning of the letters in the Qurʾan and confound the learned by virtue of his inspired wisdom. Sanhūrī also learned from him secret techniques in the healing of diseases.

In the 1970s the government initially encouraged the spread of the Order among university students to counteract both Nasserist and Muslim Brotherhood influences; the Burhāniyya were politically inactive and considered harmless. They benefited from the general malaise and search for spiritual authenticity following the Six-Day War in 1967, and by the mid-1970s had acquired, according to their own census, a membership of three million in Egypt alone. In Sudan as well, the Burhāniyya proved successful, and Muḥammad ʿUthmān became *wakīl* (trustee) of the Sufi Council there. In November 1974 he entered Egypt by train from Khartoum, receiving a hero's welcome at every train stop and a reception from state officials worthy of a visiting dignitary.

But it was in that same year that he published his controversial book, *Tabriʾat al-dhimma*. His first book, *Intiṣār awliyāʾ al-Raḥmān ʿalā awliyāʾ al-shayṭān* (The Victory of the friends of the Merciful over the friends of Satan), published in 1970, was aimed at defending Sufi doctrines concerning the special status of the *ahl al-bayt*, the intercession of the saints and visitation of their tombs, as well as explaining the benefits of the Sufi rites of dhikr and the recitation of *awrād*. The book had not aroused any particular interest outside the followers of the Order, and the second book was likewise clearly intended for followers of the Order, not for general consumption. But a local Burhānī shaykh in Minyā was sufficiently disturbed by its contents to send a copy to the office of Religious Endowments in Minyā, which forwarded it with a warning of its heretical content to the Ministry of Religious Endowments in Cairo. An investigation ensued in the Ministries of Religious Endowments and the Interior as well as in the Supreme Council of Sufi Orders, resulting in the confiscation of the book, the banning of the activities of the Order, and a vituperative media campaign against them. Before we examine the contents of the book and the allegations made against it, let us look at the background of the Order and the life of its shaykh.

THE BURHĀNIYYA AND THEIR SHAYKH

The Burhāniyya Dasūqiyya Shādhiliyya Order claims to be an Order combining the teachings and *awrād* of Abū 'l-Ḥasan al-Shādhilī (d. 1258) and his nephew, Ibrāhīm al-Dasūqī (d. 1297). According to Gamāl al-Sanhūrī, a grandson of Shādhilī named Abū 'l-Mawāhib al-Shādhilī was the first to take the banner of the combined Order. He traveled with it to Morocco, where he taught it to the well-known Shādhilī shaykh and scholar, Aḥmad Zarrūq (d. 1493).[1] Zarrūq later traveled to Sudan, where he taught the Order to someone named Abū Danāna, whose son was ordered by Zarrūq to go to Dongola and teach the Order to one Shaykh Faḍl, an ancestor of Muḥammad ʿUthmān. This story is unlikely to be true in its details. There is no evidence that Zarrūq was ever initiated into the Order of Dasūqī, or that he ever went to Sudan, although it is true that he traveled widely and he did go to Egypt. The Order of Ibrāhīm al-Dasūqī appears to be largely confined to Egypt and Sudan and does not exist in Morocco. This joint Shādhilī-Dasūqī Order was unknown in Egypt until Muḥammad ʿUthmān brought it from Sudan, and most Egyptians consider him founder of the Order. The inclusion of Aḥmad Zarrūq, a Sufi criticized by his own master as too legalistic, in the lineage of the Burhāniyya, was probably intended to bolster the Islamic legitimacy of the Order.[2]

Figure 16. Shaykh Muḥammad ʿUthmān ʿAbduh al-Burhāni (d. 1983) (reprinted from *Dīwān baṭā'in al-asrār*, part 1, 1984, a collection of poems believed to be composed posthumously by Muḥammad ʿUthmān and revealed to his followers; courtesy of Shaykh Gamāl al-Sanhūrī).

My information on the Burhāniyya derives from a number of sources, the most important of which is an unpublished two-hundred-page transcription of the shaykh's own recorded speeches, in which he describes his life and spiritual experiences.[3] One of the more interesting aspects of the shaykh's autobiographical account is the paucity of detail on his early life, occupation, and family background. Muḥammad ʿUthmān ʿAbduh was born in Ḥalfā in Sudan in either 1894 or 1902.[4] He says nothing about his education, but Shaykh Gamāl al-Sanhūrī says he received only a primary school education. He tells us nothing about his parents in his discussion of his early childhood, with the exception of one anecdote that appears later in the collection of his speeches and was apparently not part of his intended autobiography. This anecdote indicates that his relationship with his father was not harmonious. The only one of his immediate family whom he mentions in his account of his early childhood is his grandmother, a Sufi who could speak in inspired tongues and apparently made a deep impression on him. Nonetheless, we are told, all his ancestors were pious *(ṣāliḥīn),* and his genealogy goes back to the Prophet through Ḥusayn.

Muḥammad ʿUthmān independently disciplined himself with nightly worship from his youth, although he had learned no *awrād* and had no shaykh to guide him, which is taken by his followers as a sign of extraordinary divine providence and protection. At about the age of ten he pressured a family friend, Shaykh ʿUthmān Ḥāmid ʿAbd al-Bāqī, to teach him the *awrād* of his Order. Family affairs took ʿUthmān Ḥāmid away from Muḥammad ʿUthmān immediately thereafter, and he was still without guidance. However, every night as he recited his *awrād,* he found himself surrounded by the great deceased chief Sufi saints and founders of the Orders, who joined in the recitation and also recited their own *awrād*. Muḥammad ʿUthmān memorized the *awrād* of all the Orders from these nightly visions and assiduously devoted himself to recitation. According to Gamāl al-Sanhūrī, the recitation of *awrād* is the key to the access to all spiritual secrets. As is clear from Muḥammad ʿUthmān's discourses, the *awrād* are also powerful to combat jinn and demonic forces, and some *awrād* are more powerful than others. These nightly visions indicate the care and interest that all the major saints of the past had in Muḥammad ʿUthmān. Later, when he became shaykh, he claims that he was authorized by all the founders of the major Sufi Orders to teach the *awrād* of their Orders. His mission, therefore, was a comprehensive spiritual mission.

One day Sayyid Aḥmad al-Badawī (d. 1278) appeared to him in a vision and took him to a mountain called Jabal al-Awliyāʾ (mountain of the saints), thirty kilometers from Khartoum. Sayyid al-Badawī struck the mountain with his hand and immediately a cave appeared, in which Muḥammad ʿUthmān was ordered to pray. As Gamāl al-Sanhūrī pointed out, this incident of worship in a cave just before his call indicates that he was following in the footsteps of the Prophet Muhammad, whose mission was preceded by worship in the cave of Ḥirāʾ. By implication, he was entrusted with the mission of the Prophet, since the saints are the heirs of the Prophet.

In response to Muḥammad ʿUthmān's repeated pleas to Ibrāhīm al-Dasūqī that he be sent someone to give him spiritual guidance, a blind man came from Dasūq and instructed him in all the *awrād* and guidance of the Order over a period of several months. He also informed him that the *awrād* and secrets of his ancestors had been buried in a particular place. Muḥammad ʿUthmān dug them up and spent a long period of time writing them and preparing them for his disciples. These scrolls were guarded by angels *(ʿawālim)*, who appeared whenever he recited the *awrād* written on them. Muḥammad ʿUthmān complained to Sīdī Ibrāhīm al-Dasūqī that they distracted him and slowed down his recitation, and Ibrāhīm al-Dasūqī commanded them to leave him alone. In his taped discourses, Muḥammad ʿUthmān often depicts himself as quarreling with his spiritual mentor, Ibrāhīm al-Dasūqī, as if the long-deceased saint were his familiar companion, threatening to leave the Order if Sīdī Ibrāhīm did not yield to his demands. Muḥammad ʿUthmān said that on his next visit to Dasūq he tried to find the blind man, who said he lived near the shrine of Ibrāhīm al-Dasūqī, but no one in the vicinity of the shrine had ever heard of him. The implication is that his teacher was no ordinary human being.

Muḥammad ʿUthmān's calling came in an extended vision that appeared over a period of more than forty days, while sleeping and while awake. In this vision he saw a great funerary procession. The vision eventually became so familiar and real to him that he was able, in his words, to extend his inner vision *(baṣīra)* and see that the funerary train was coming from the shrine of Ibrāhīm al-Dasūqī. He seized the funerary bier and lifted the white shroud that covered it, finding underneath it a green cloth, and underneath that a yellow cloth. These, he explains, are the colors of the Order: white represents the Prophet and the Sharīʿa, green represents Ḥusayn and nobility of birth, and yellow represents Abū 'l-Ḥasan al-Shādhilī. When he lifted all these coverings, he found, to his astonishment, that the feet of the dead man exactly matched his own. He turned and found Abū 'l-Ḥasan al-Shādhilī at his side and asked the identity of the dead man and was told it was Ibrāhīm al-Dasūqī. Muḥammad ʿUthmān began to weep, demanding to know why Sayyid Ibrāhīm was dead while Shādhilī and the other saints were alive, and what was he doing using the *awrād* and calling on the *madad* of Sayyid Ibrāhīm if Sayyid Ibrāhīm were dead. But then Ibrāhīm himself appeared and told him it was not he but his Order that was dead, and Muḥammad ʿUthmān was charged with reviving it. Muḥammad ʿUthmān says he refused and negotiated with the saints over a period of two months before Ḥusayn appeared "and the commands of Ḥusayn are executed." However, Ḥusayn granted Muḥammad ʿUthmān anything he requested in order to take on this tremendous burden. According to Muḥammad ʿUthmān, he made tens of requests on behalf of his future disciples, but of these only five are recorded: that none of his disciples would ever become *magzūb;* that none of his disciples would be possessed by evil spirits; that solitary meditation *(khalwa)* be abolished that traveling in search of knowledge *(siyāḥa)* be abolished; and that his disciples would come from eminent sectors of society. According to Muḥammad ʿUthmān, he possessed a document signed by Ḥusayn and Ibrāhīm al-Dasūqī granting him these concessions. In return, he says, the saints placed conditions on him: none of his disciples would belong to any other Order, none would have wrong doctrine, and they would all faithfully recite *awrād*. He was given permission to teach the *awrād* of all the Orders, and, according to Gamāl al-Sanhūrī, if a member of another Order asked him for advice in overcoming a spiritual obstacle, he would tell him to recite the *awrād* of that person's Order, not those of the Burhāniyya. But in order to enter the Burhāniyya, all other oaths to a shaykh must be renounced. This permission to teach the *awrād* was essential to the spread and prosperity of the Order. According to Gamāl al-Sanhūrī, many Sufi shaykhs fail to teach their disciples *awrād*, so the disciples lack all spiritual discipline and fail to progress.

We may note a number of significant elements in this account of Muḥammad ʿUthmān's biography. First, we note the soundness of his pedigree as seen in that all of his ancestors were pious and that he is descended from the Prophet himself, through Ḥusayn. Second, we note the extraordinary divine protection over Muḥammad ʿUthmān from his childhood, in that he engaged in nightly devotions without any external impetus or guidance. Third, we may note the role of visions in his spiritual formation, so that he learns *awrād* through visions and has a relationship with the saints, particularly Ibrāhīm al-Dasūqī, that is extremely familiar. Indeed, it is often not at all apparent in his discourses that he is referring to a visionary experience, because he reports them as if they are normal occurrences and ordinary conversations. Fourth, Muḥammad ʿUthmān is led to follow the paradigm of the Prophet by worshiping in a cave prior to his call. Fifth, he is taught by a mysterious individual who appears and suddenly disappears. The instruction of a unique spiritual leader could not follow ordinary means. Sixth, he is led to discover hidden and potent scrolls that constitute core teachings of the Order. The discovery of hidden books is a familiar beginning to many religious movements and grants the leader of the movement added sanction and power. Seventh, Muḥammad ʿUthmān is commissioned by the chief saints in a comprehensive mission not only to revive the moribund Order of Ibrāhīm al-Dasūqī but to revive Sufism itself in all its Orders. The identification of the dead man as the Order and Muḥammad ʿUthmān's discovery that the dead man's feet exactly matched his own make plain the identification of Muḥammad ʿUthmān with the Way of Sīdī Ibrāhīm. The implication is that those who wished to follow the path of Ibrāhīm al-Dasūqī, one of the four acknowledged great founders of Orders in Egypt, must acknowledge the spiritual leadership of Muḥammad ʿUthmān.

After so many portents of future greatness, it is no surprise to learn that Muḥammad ʿUthmān also received his coronation as *ghawth*, the Axis of the Age, in a vision. Here he was invited to a great banquet attended by all the prophets and saints throughout the ages, as well as all his future disciples, an immense crowd of millions. There he was commanded to eat all of the food on the table. It was a great table filled with vegetables stuffed with the seven minerals. "The meaning of this," explains Gamāl al-Sanhūrī, "is that the head must comprehend all that is in his kingdom." The symbol of eating or drinking for spiritual initiation or participation is of course common in Islam as well as in other religions.[5]

Muḥammad ʿUthmān claims other miracles in his taped speeches, particularly miracles of healing diseases such as cancer, bringing the dead back to life, expelling jinn, turning lead into gold, finding a missing donkey by miraculously calling forth all the donkeys of the world to a single spot, fixing broken waterwheels, and miraculous financial provision for disciples. With the exception of alchemy, most of these were effected through the recitation of *awrād*, although physical substances were also used to heal diseases. The power of *awrād* is such that Muḥammad ʿUthmān said that whoever has *awrād* and still fears the jinn is ignorant. Since his death in 1983, his disciples attribute to him a more novel miracle: communicating to his disciples, from the realm of *barzakh* where the spirits of the righteous dwell until the Resurrection, odes in both Arabic and German. The Arabic odes have been gathered in a volume called *Dīwān baṭāʾin al-asrār* with the dates of their revelation and are sung by the Burhāniyya in their dhikr. Thirty-seven of them, dated from 13 April 1983 to 14 February 1984, are collected in the first published volume. Others have been revealed afterward: I was given a copy of odes up to number 94, dated 27 December 1987. Such an event has never been heard of before in the history of Sufism, say the Burhāniyya, and is even more extraordinary because in his lifetime Muḥammad ʿUthmān never knew German or wrote poetry in any language. The shaykh has also answered the prayers of one follower who asked God not to cut him off from intimate contact with the shaykh after death; he continues to receive guidance as he did when the shaykh was alive. A final grace is given to the shaykh's lovers *(ʿāshiqīn):* his tomb in Khartoum is a Kaʿba for those who come; visiting his tomb yields the same spiritual benefit as going on the ḥajj.

Shaykh Gamāl al-Sanhūrī's wife, Ḥāgga Mīma, originally did not embrace Shaykh Muḥammad ʿUthmān's teachings as her husband did. Although the Burhāniyya held meetings in their apartment, she kept herself apart. But once when they were in Khartoum, she said, "I will greet *ʿamm al-shaykh.*" Gamāl said, "Then you must cover your hair and kiss his hand." She replied, "No, I'm not going to do that. If he wants to see me, let him come to me as I am." And she sat in the car while Gamal went in with the others to greet the shaykh. But the shaykh himself rose and came out, without a word, to her in the car. When she saw that, she rushed out of the car and went to him, taking his hand and weeping profusely. She had said that she would never kiss the hand of anyone after her father, but when she kissed the shaykh's hand she saw it as white and exactly like the hand of her father, although her father had been Turkish and Muḥammad ʿUthmān was Sudanese. Such was the spiritual message from her heart to his, she said, that he had come out and done this miracle. And so she found what she had been looking for all her life in Shaykh Muḥammad ʿUthmān, and she came to love him more than anyone else.

This is Shaykh Muḥammad ʿUthmān as his followers knew him, a man who was spiritually powerful as well as extremely generous, compassionate, and kind. Even his enemies admitted that he was charismatic and seductive in speech. What, then, attracted such vehement hostility in Sufi circles and in the press?

THE CONTROVERSY OVER THE BURHĀNIYYA

The apparent cause was the publication of *Tabriʾat al-dhimma.* This book lacks publication data and is a very large book, with 326 8¼" X 11¼" pages filled with small type and almost no margins. It sold for an entire Egyptian pound (LE 1) when it was published in 1974, a large sum in those days. The main focus of the book is Sufi doctrine concerning the Prophet Muhammad.

Muḥammad ʿUthmān introduces the book by saying that he wrote it with some urgency, "because some people have diminished the stature of the Messenger of God, peace be upon Him, and have claimed that he is only a man to whom God gave a revelation with a Law and ordered him to deliver it, so he did, and his importance ends after he delivers it. They have claimed that there is no benefit to be derived from him. . . . Indeed, they go further . . . by claiming that he, peace be upon him, was ignorant before Gabriel brought him the revelation."[6]

The book aims, then, to show that the Prophet was not merely a man who had received a message from God but an absolutely unique individual in his nature and the manner of his creation, a man whose cosmic importance far exceeds his earthly mission. The book is divided into four parts:

> I. The excellence and unique characteristics of the Prophet, the preexistence of his Light, and a demonstration that all the heavenly religions are derived from him. This part includes long portions quoted verbatim from the writings of ʿAbd Allāh Abū 'l-Barakāt al-Yāfiʿī (d. 1367), another fourteenth-century Sufi, Aḥmad al-Salawī, Jalāl al-Dīn al-Suyūṭī (d. 1505), and, most important, a twenty-page selection from *Qāb qawsayn wa multaqā 'l-nāmūsayn* by ʿAbd al-Karīm al-Jīlī (d. 1408). He admits that some of al-Jīlī's words are, if taken literally, blasphemous, "although if one knows their proper interpretation *(ta'wīl)*, they are not," as when Jīlī says that Muhammad is the very essence of God. "In this case," says Muḥammad ʿUthmān, "Muhammad's attribution to the divine essence is an honorific attribution *(iḍāfat tashrīf)*, because he is created from the light of His essence, whereas all else was created from the lights of His attributes."[7] This extended quote from al-Jīlī articulates clearly the unique relationship of the Muhammadan Reality to the divine, which, since it is the first thing created, must also be identical with the Pen, which was the first thing created according to some ḥadīths, as well as the First Intellect, from which, according to many mystical and philosophical cosmologies, all else emanated.[8] Al-Jīlī's text includes extended discourse on the appearance and manners of the Prophet in order to facilitate spiritual concentration on him toward the end of annihilation in him.[9]

II. The Story of the Prophet's Night Journey and Ascension into the Heavens, affirming the reality of the Prophet's vision of God and the reality of the hierarchy of saints (the *quṭb, awtād, nujabā'*, and *abdāl*), as indicated by various ḥadīths. This part also defends the reality of the believer's vision of the Prophet.

III. This part includes a seventy-seven-page portion from *Jawāhir al-Biḥār* by Jalāl al-Dīn al-Suyūtī, detailing the ways in which Muhammad was absolutely unique, and a thirty-one-page portion from Ibn ʿArabī's *Meccan Revelations* on the Muhammadan Reality, the special status of the *ahl al-bayt*, and the comprehensiveness of Muhammad's Sharīʿa. This section ends with Ibn ʿArabī's attestation that "to see God in the Muhammadan form through the Muhammadan vision is the most complete vision possible."[10]

IV. This part, where once again we have Muḥammad ʿUthmān's own words, is devoted to explicating the progress of the Sufi on the path to God through the levels of *islām* (submission), *īmān* (faith), and *iḥsān* (right conduct toward others), a common Sufi theme; traveling "to God in God;" Muḥammad ʿUthmān's assessment of the great schism between the ʿAlids and the Umayyads in early Islam; and a justification of the intercession of the saints, worship at the tombs of saints, and seeking blessing from their remains.

It is interesting that these last parts received very little attention in the press and attracted little controversy, perhaps because the Sufi Council's own magazine also defends these practices. The particular points that aroused the most controversy concerned the Prophet's identification with the divine essence, the Sufi doctrine of the Muhammadan reality, and Muḥammad ʿUthmān's use of controversial texts. The most controversial aspects of the book were:

1. The interpretation of the opening lines of Sura 89, which read, "By the dawn and ten nights, by the even and the odd, and the night when it passes away." According to Muḥammad ʿUthmān, the Sufi masters know that the "ten nights" mean the ten veils of splendor in which the light of the Prophet travels, from level to level. "The even" means the Aḥmadan Reality within the Muhammadan Reality, and "the odd" is the combination of the two Realities in the singularity of the Muhammadan essence. "The night when it passes," he says, means when Muhammad reveals himself, for Muhammad can only be known by the Prophet's

own self-revelation.[11] After recounting this teaching in a book written to refute *Tabriʾat al-dhimma,* an author who is suspicious of both Sufism and the religious establishment asks his reader, "Did you understand any of this?"[12]

2. Another point of controversy is the authenticity of the famous ḥadīths from Jābir, in which the Prophet states that the first thing God created was the light of Muhammad out of His own light, and that all else in the universe, even the Throne of God and the Preserved Tablet, was made from that Light. After quoting the ḥadīth, Muḥammad ʿUthmān comments, "a sound ḥadīth," although he acknowledges that many scholars do not rely on it because it is insufficiently substantiated from more than one source (in the language of ḥadīth criticism, it is *āḥād*).[13] One of his critics retorts, "Who has determined that it is sound?" and comments, "It is rejected not because it is an isolated report, but because its content is objectionable."[14] Former Mufti of Egypt, Shaykh Muḥammad Ḥasanayn Makhlūf, wrote in a letter to the daily newspaper *Al-Ahrām* that "the strange hadiths in this book are not found in the books of sound Sunna,"[15] and the general director of the propagation of Islam in the Ministry of Religious Endowments, ironically named Shaykh Ibrāhīm al-Dasūqī, said in an interview that "the book destroys the method of judging sound ḥadīth from what is forged. Thus they open the door to the attribution of many superstitions and fables to the Messenger."[16] We have already seen that Muḥammad ʿUthmān, like Ibn ʿArabī, believed that Sufis, by virtue of their mystical illumination and visionary access to the Prophet, are qualified to make pronouncements regarding the soundness of ḥadīths in a way that supersedes the authority of the ulama.[17]

3. Muḥammad ʿUthmān interprets the Qurʾanic verse, "Do not hasten with the Qurʾan before its revelation is delivered to you" (20:114) to indicate that Muhammad had the Qurʾan before it was revealed to him by Gabriel. He supports this idea by quoting another ḥadīth that indicates that when Gabriel received the revelation from the Frequented Fane, the heavenly Kaʿba *(al-bayt al-maʿmūr),* he was in fact receiving it from the eternal Muhammadan Reality. When Muhammad reveals this fact to Gabriel, Gabriel asks why he should tire himself out with delivering the revelation when it comes from Muhammad and returns to him. Muhammad replies, "For the sake of giving the law *(li 'l-tashrīʿ).*" If Gabriel were an intermediary between God and Muhammad, Muḥammad ʿUthmān reasons, then Muhammad

would not be the Messenger of God but the messenger of the messenger of God.[18] Muḥammad ʿUthmān's view of the revelatory process goes counter to Islamic tradition, which depicts Muhammad receiving his revelations, initially in great fear, by hearing them recited by the angel Gabriel.

4. In an interview in *Al-Ahrām,* Shaykh Muḥammad al-Suṭūhī, then head of the Supreme Council of Sufi Orders, objected to the emanationist philosophy of the book, denouncing it as idolatrous because it postulates an intermediary, the Muhammadan Reality, through which God created the world, whereas the standard opinion of Islamic theology is that God created the world from nothing. "This idolatrous point of view," says Suṭūḥī, "may be found among some philosophizing extremists and in Ismāʿīlī Shiʿi beliefs. In his book, *The Incoherence of the Philosophers (Tahāfut al-falāsifa),* al-Ghazālī destroyed this viewpoint which is foreign to Islam. Ibn Taymiyya also destroyed it."[19]

5. Although many Sufis delight in the illiteracy of their gnostics as a proof of the divine source of their knowledge, and most Muslims uphold the doctrine of the illiteracy of their Prophet, Muḥammad ʿUthmān denies that the word *ummī* in the Qur'an (which describes Muhammad as an "*ummī* prophet") means "illiterate." Rather, the *umm* (mother) of all things is their origin, or that which is comprehensive. Therefore, *umm al-kitāb* (The Mother of the Book) is either the heavenly archetype of the Qur'an, hence its source, or the *Fātiḥa,* which contains the entire meaning of the Qur'an. Muhammad (that is, the Muhammadan Reality) is *ummī* in both these senses, in that he is the source of all things and contains the meanings of all things.[20]

6. The Sufi doctrine of the hierarchy of saints that control events in the cosmos in a hidden kingdom is also found objectionable by al-Suṭūḥī, although it is an extremely common doctrine in Sufi literature.

7. Perhaps most surprising is that Shaykh Suṭūḥī denies the possibility that the Sufi might have a vision of Muhammad while awake, although the reality of such visions is affirmed even by such well-loved orthodox Sufi teachers as al-Ghazālī and is well attested in the teachings of the revered founders of the Orders, such as Abū 'l-ʿAbbās al-Mursī, the Egyptian successor to al-Shādhilī, and Aḥmad al-Rifāʿī, one of the four recognized "Axes" (founding fathers) of Sufism in Egypt.

8. Non-Sufis frequently objected to Muḥammad ʿUthmān's declaration of the ability of the saints to see into the world of the

unseen *(ʿālam al-ghayb)*, the knowledge of which they say belongs to God alone. The Qurʾan says, "The world of the unseen: God does not reveal His unseen to anyone except a messenger He has chosen, and He places before and behind Him watchers" (72:26–27). In response to frequent objections that only God knows the unseen, Muḥammad ʿUthmān points out that it is evident from the verse that God allows his prophets and messengers to see the unseen, and by extension, he says, this includes the saints of God, who are the heirs of the prophets.[21] When asked about this in the interview in *Al-Ahrām*, Suṭūḥī is more guarded than to give an outright denial of this possibility: "He gives a strange defense of this belief by linking them (the saints) to the prophets. This is a subject that gives rise to deception, and we do not agree with it." The relationship of sainthood to prophethood has been much discussed in Sufism, occasionally with results that seem, at least on the surface, to equate the gnostic with the prophet or even to exalt the status of the great gnostic over that of the prophet. But even if the saints are not of the rank of prophets, they are nonetheless their heirs and partake in at least some of their light. Sufism is built on the concept of gnosis and the mystic's access to knowledge that is not available to the common person; without this doctrine, Sufism could hardly be called mysticism. Suṭūḥī does not outright deny the gnosis of the saints but merely says "this is a subject that gives rise to deception," that is, one that could deceive the average person unsophisticated in the subtleties of Sufi doctrine.

9. One of the most commonly raised objections to *Tabriʾat al-dhimma* is Muḥammad ʿUthmān's inclusion of the so-called "Kūfan sermon" attributed to ʿAlī ibn Abī Ṭālib, in which he claims divine attributes in statements like, "I am the driver of the thunder, I am the proof of proofs, I am the essence of eternity, I am the First and the Last, I am the External *(al-Ẓāhir)* and the Internal *(al-Bāṭin)*, I am the Sura of the Cow, I am the Criterion (*al-Furqān*, one of the titles of the Qurʾan)," etc. This six-page "sermon" is delivered in extremely rhythmic, rhymed prose, filled with enigmatic phrases in which ʿAlī allegedly vaunted his exalted status in the cosmos. According to Muḥammad ʿUthmān, this speech proves that ʿAlī was created from the divine names and attributes.[22]

Concerning this speech Shaykh Muḥammad Ḥasanayn Makhlūf retorts, "The word 'I' is repeated 255 times in the alleged sermon, followed by expressions that are too long and boring to publish, in addition to their being corrupt and full of lies and endless objectionable things. . . . It is irrational to attribute such words to Imām ʿAlī."[23] He also objects to the claim that the *ahl al-bayt* and the saints are intercessors for the believers with God.

Suṭūḥī gives a more scholarly response to the Kūfan sermon: "This sermon does not appear in *Nahj al-balāgha,* which contains all the words of Imām ʿAlī. The clearest explanation is that it was forged by Shiʿi historians. The committee has said that its style does not agree with the style of Imām ʿAlī in his sermons that we have confidence are his. Its meanings contradict sound Islamic belief. God forbid that such expressions come from Imām ʿAlī! They are only words of Shiʿis who dabbled in philosophy and described ʿAlī in divine terms."[24]

10. Shaykh Ibrāhīm al-Dasūqī of the Ministry of Religious Endowments believed that the most dangerous aspect of the book is that it subtly encourages belief in the awaited Mahdī, the deliverer who, according to Ḥadīth, will come at the end of this age to "fill the world with justice as it is now filled with injustice." Dasuqi says this doctrine "was believed in by some ancient extremist sects like the Shiʿa and the Bāṭiniyya, and the Bahāʾī sect encouraged by the Zionists, and the Bābīs, and the Qādiyaniyya [Aḥmadiyya]."[25] Belief in the Mahdī, however, is by no means confined to non-Sunni sects and has frequently galvanized legalistically oriented reformist movements, like the nineteenth-century Mahdiyya of Sudan, the twelfth-century Almohad dynasty of Spain and Morocco, and, in 1979, the takeover of the Kaʿba by a group opposed to the Saudi regime. The potential danger of Mahdism to established regimes is clearly a threat inherent in this type of popular Islam, but castigating it as Shiʿi has more to do with politics than reality. As we have seen, more than once Suṭūḥī also accused Muḥammad ʿUthmān of being tainted with Shiʿi ideas. But popular Sufism in general is very close to Shiʿism in its devotion to and exaltation of the Prophet and the *ahl al-bayt,* as we have seen, and some Sufis place a great deal of importance on the Imāms of the Twelver Shiʿa.

11. A number of the articles in *Al-Ahrām* criticize the Burhāniyya specifically for complicating the simple faith of Islam, which is "the religion of human nature" *(fiṭra)* and has no secrets. Shaykh Dasūqī stated that the most important characteristic of Islam is that it is "very easy, simple and clear; any obscurity in matters of faith is itself an indication that it is against Islam." Shaykh Muḥammad Ḥasanayn Makhlūf also wrote in a letter to *Al-Aḥram*

> that the idea that God taught Muhammad knowledge that was revealed only to a select group "is unsound and unprovable from the Book or Sunna."[26] Such critics, of course, are setting themselves against all types of esoteric knowledge in Islam, and even, it would seem, against the possibility that the Qurʾan might yield itself to legitimate interpretations that go beyond what the average person might see in it.

What is striking about *Tabriʾat al-dhimma* is that, for all its apparent eccentricity and extremism, it contains virtually nothing original to Muḥammad ʿUthmān. As we have seen, it contains large sections quoted verbatim from other sources, and the rest of the book consists mainly of quotations from ḥadīths and Sufi authors. In fact, when Gamāl al-Sanhūrī gave me my copy of the book, he said, "Muḥammad ʿUthmān did not write this book. Over eighty Muslim writers wrote this book." And Muḥammad ʿUthmān told his followers that by reading his two books they will have an essential summary of more than two hundred books.

The reporter for *Al-Ahrām* is therefore correct to ask Shaykh Suṭūḥī, "Why did the Supreme Sufi Council oppose the book when most of it is taken from Sufi books?"

Suṭūḥī replied, "The chapters taken from some philosophizing Sufis contain obscure language that can be interpreted in a dangerous way."

Surely Suṭūḥī's response can be construed not as an outright refutation of the contents of these chapters but simply an objection to their dissemination to those not qualified to interpret them correctly. If this is indeed what he meant, he is well within the bounds of Sufi tradition. For concerning the controversial "I am the True Reality" of al-Ḥallāj, "sober" Sufis like al-Junayd and al-Ghazālī did not deny that his words expressed a genuine spiritual state, but felt that it was dangerous to utter such apparent blasphemies in public, where they could be misunderstood and lead the masses into unbelief. Therefore he had to be executed to save the masses from error. It is possible that Muḥammad ʿUthmān al-Burhānī was also such a sacrificial lamb, who had to be publicly vilified and banned from spiritual leadership simply because he had made public Sufi doctrines that should have been kept hidden.

As we have seen, the esoteric doctrines revealed in *Tabriʾat al-dhimma* are not at all unique to the Burhāniyya. Most of what he says concerning the Prophet Muhammad may be found in the teachings of many other Orders. This has not prevented the Burhāniyya from being regarded as extremists, even by Sufis of similar doctrines, simply because they were attacked in the media. The Sufis I heard describe the Burhāniyya as extremists could not, however, justify that characterization. But the story of *Tabriʾat al-dhimma* reveals that some Burhānīs were, as they later put it, seduced into joining Sufism because of its promise of moral purification and a deeper and more powerful spiritual life, only to learn that it contains doctrines that contradict their understanding of Islam. So it was for the Burhānī shaykh in Minyā who read *Tabriʾat al-dhimma,* turned it over to authorities, and resigned from his post.[27] However, as I argued earlier, the alleged opposition between the "sober," "orthodox" Sufism represented by al-Ghazālī and approved by the Supreme Council of Sufi Orders, and the "ecstatic," "extremist" Sufism represented by Ibn ʿArabī may be illusory. But the Sufi Council must make its major concern the maintenance of orthodoxy, says Dr. Taftāzānī, because the majority of members of the Orders are ignorant of the basics of Islam. To go directly to the *Ḥaqīqa* without grounding first in the Shariʿa would be dangerous. Turning this principle into public policy appears to mean that doctrines deemed dangerous for the "ignorant" majority must be publicly suppressed.

However, this does not mean that the distinction between popular Sufism and the Sufism of the Supreme Council of Sufi Orders is necessarily merely camouflage. Clearly, there are differences between such "reformed" Orders as the Ḥāmidiyya Shādhiliyya, studied by Michael Gilsenan and so prominently displayed during the Prophet's Birthday processions, and the Burhāniyya, with its esoteric emphases. Gamāl al-Sanhūrī's clash with the Sufi Council reveals at least one crucial area of doctrinal divergence.

According to Sanhūrī, when he applied for recognition of the Burhāniyya, the Sufi Council informed him that in order to be a recognized Order in Egypt, they had to be under an Egyptian shaykh. They requested that the Burhāniyya join the Egyptian Order of the Burhāmiyya, which also claims to represent the tradition of Ibrāhīm al-Dasūqī. According to the anti-Burhani articles that appeared in *Al-Ahrām,* Muḥammad ʿUthmān founded his Order only when he was unsuccessful at seizing control of the Burhāmiyya Order in Sudan. According to Muḥammad ʿUthmān, on the other hand, he enjoyed a close relationship with the leader of the Burhāmiyya in Sudan, who even agreed that Burhānīs could be given the position of *khalīfa* (deputy, successor) in his Order, until he became jealous over the Burhāniyya's phenomenal success. According to Gamāl al-Sanhūrī, Muḥammad ʿUthmān hated the name "Burhāmiyya," which was allegedly a corruption of the name Ibrāhīm; he used to say that if they wanted, they could call themselves "Ibrāhīmiyya," but not Burhāmiyya. The name Burhāniyya was derived from Ibrāhim al-Dasūqī's nickname, *burhān al-milla wa 'l-dīn* (the proof of the religious community and the faith—that is, the vindication of the faith). Muḥammad ʿUthmān said that since it was God who had given Sīdī Ibrāhīm this nickname, it was more appropriate to use this as the name of the Order, just as the Shādhiliyya used Abū 'l-Ḥasan's nickname for their Order.

According to Sanhūrī, Dr. Taftāzānī asked him before the Sufi Council about the origin of the name Burhāniyya, saying it was an invalid name.[28] When Sanhūrī replied that it was derived from a name given Sīdī Ibrāhīm by God, Taftāzānī retorted, "Is there revelation *(waḥy)* after the Messenger of God?!" to which Sanhūrī replied, "Yes, and before the Messenger of God, to those who were not prophets," and he cited two Qurʾanic examples: one that refers to God inspiring (giving *waḥy*) to Moses' mother, although no woman was ever a prophet (20:38, 28:7), and another that says God inspired the bees (16:68). Taftāzānī was outraged, says Sanhūrī, and on this basis turned him out of the Council. Sanhūrī also suggested that the real reason for the Council's rejection of them was jealousy and greed, because 10 percent of the money contributed to the boxes at saints' shrines goes to the Sufi Council, which is then distributed to the Orders based on their membership. With the Burhāniyya's huge membership (almost equalling the total membership of all other Orders in Egypt), hardly anything would be left for the other sixty-eight Orders. If this is true, however, we would have to ask why the Council encouraged the incorporation of the Burhāniyya into the Burhāmiyya, a registered Egyptian Order, which did in fact occur in 1986, three years after Muḥammad ʿUthmān's death.

The attacks on the Burhāniyya in the press originated with attacks on *Tabriʾat al-dhimma,* but there were also suggestions that Muḥammad ʿUthmān was a cunning manipulator and deceiver engaged in a conspiracy to destroy Islam from within.[29] Some letters written to *Al-Ahrām* focused on aspects of the leadership of the Burhāniyya, namely its hierarchical structure, authoritarianism, and the claims it made of its own importance.[30] These are typical features of the Sufi Orders: absolute submission to spiritual authority was long considered necessary for the proper guidance of the disciple; the Sufi hierarchy is seen as a natural consequence of the unequal distribution of God's gifts; and although extravagant claims by Sufi saints are not commended, they are hardly unusual. But revealed in the context of a press campaign against the Order, these features contribute to the depiction of the Burhāniyya as a demonically inspired cult. Members of the Order help each other out, the letters maintained, so that in order to get a good apartment or a good piece of land one was encouraged to join the Burhāniyya. Indeed, in one unnamed city, the Burhaniyya entirely controlled the city council. A secretary for the council wrote to *Al-Ahrām* anonymously, fearful that her letter would cause her to lose her job or be expelled or worse, for such was the fate of those who opposed the Burhāniyya in her city. Administration employees were almost all members of the Order, who spent all their time reciting *awrād* instead of doing their duties; the bulletin board was devoted solely to the Burhāniyya, and the chief activity of the city council was defense of the Order.[31]

A letter from the Egyptian consul in Khartoum was most damaging. He wrote that he had learned that the original Order of Ibrāhīm al-Dasūqī was the Burhāmiyya and that Muḥammad ʿUthmān tried to force its *khalīfa,* who had inherited the position, out of office through court action. When this failed, "Muḥammad ʿUthmān spread the word that in his sleep he had seen that Ibn Batīt would die if he didn't give the *khilāfa* over to him. When this didn't work, he founded an independent Order called the Burhāniyya. This time he succeeded and quickly became wealthy. He now owns commercial companies and a great deal of land, in addition to the financial gifts showered upon him by his disciples in Egypt and Sudan. He has victims in Sudan, including Mr. Ḥasan Maḥmūd Bakr Qāsim, who told many people that Shaykh Muḥammad ʿUthmān took almost L 25,000 from him." The consul went on to complain that despite Muḥammad ʿUthmān's humble beginnings, he now lived in a palace, and that he allowed no outsiders into his retreat centers, something that itself attracts suspicion. Furthermore, he allows his followers to smoke (hardly a rarity among Sufis), and he himself uses snuff, "in opposition to all the Sufi Orders."[32]

The campaign in Egypt against the Burhāniyya did not cease with its official denunciation and the banning of *Tabriʾat al-dhimma.* The Sufi Council of Egypt under Sutuhi pressured the Sufi Council in Sudan to force Muḥammad ʿUthmān out of his position as *wakīl* of that council, and a letter from the general director of religious and cultural guidance in the Sudanese council, dated 18 May 1981, assured the Egyptian Sufi Council that they had complied with this request.[33] Letters to *Al-Ahrām* and *Majallat al-taṣawwuf al-islāmī* expressed outrage that, despite the ban, the activities of the Burhāniyya continued.[34] Suṭūḥī explained that, as the Order was not registered with them, they had no real jurisdiction over them, and they had already had possession of their headquarters by the Ḥusayn mosque.[35] Their *ḥaḍra* in the Ḥusayn mosque on Thursday nights also continued.

Some letters to *Al-Ahrām* complained that the Burhāniyya clearly had friends in high places who enabled them to continue their activities,[36] a claim partially substantiated by Gamāl al-Sanhūrī who said that he brought along some ministers of government who were members of the Order when he had his inquisition before the Sufi Council, in order to ensure that he would be allowed to speak. The fact is that the Burhāniyya attracted many followers among the educated and upper classes in addition to those classes that had been traditional adherents of the Orders, the lower urban and rural classes, despite the newspapers' claim that the Burhāniyya drew most of its members from among the ignorant and uneducated. As Muḥammad al-Sammān complains, the followers of the Burhāniyya "have spread like the plague, in palaces and hovels alike."[37] He points out that when Muḥammad ʿUthmān came to Egypt in late 1974 all the major media devoted much attention to him, and high-ranking personalities rushed to meet him. He points out that although the administration of the Ministry of Religious Endowments knew about the book since 1974, the "sudden, violent" media campaign against the Order began only in 1976, prompting him to ponder the real political reason for this sudden change. He blames the religious authorities in Egypt for failing to take action soon enough.[38]

THE FOREIGN BURHĀNĪS

The Burhāniyya were successful in attracting many Muslims to the Order who had no previous contact with Sufism as well as many non-Muslims, primarily from Germany and Austria but also from America, Australia, Asia, and even southern Sudan, where missionary work was carried out in the local languages. In 1981 the Sudanese magazine *Al-Muslimūn* reported a visit by fifty German converts to Shaykh Muḥammad ʿUthmān in Khartoum. It is striking that the vast majority of these converts were women, who spoke of the spiritual void in Europe and the dignity that Islam offers women.[39] The Burhāniyya publish their *awrād* in Latin letters for those who cannot read Arabic. The Burhāniyya have had centers in

Vienna and in the countryside south of Hamburg.[40] The Vienna center publishes a newsletter instructing its followers concerning Islamic festivals, the meaning of the Names of God, and aspects of Burhānī doctrine. Seeing what an impressive following the Burhāniyya have in the West, one naturally wonders what can make such a Muhammad- and saint-oriented mysticism attractive to Europeans. Is Sufism presented differently to them than it is in a Muslim context?

I had the opportunity to meet four European Burhānīs during the initiation of one of them into the Order by Gamāl al-Sanhūrī, and later I traveled with them to visit the shrine of Ibrāhīm al-Dasūqī. Gamāl al-Sanhūrī addressed himself to the new candidate for initiation by explaining that Muslims believe in 124,000 prophets, four of whom were most important—Abraham, Moses, Jesus, and Muhammad—each of them better than his predecessor. He said that the Muslims loved Jesus much more than the Christians did and that they believed in the religions brought by Moses and Jesus, although the only true religion today was Islam. He advised the new initiate always to have a smile on his face, for to be mild-mannered and gentle was the way of Muhammad. Although people might be rude to him because of his conversion and might be offensive to Islam, he should always be kind and mild-mannered. If he felt the heat of anger, he was advised to have something to eat or to satisfy his need with any woman but not to get angry. The initiate was a divorced man in his forties, and the implication that adultery was a better alternative than anger is certainly interesting. This reflects the apparent absence of emphasis on the Sharīʿa in Gamāl's initiation of Europeans into the Order.

Gamāl told the initiate that after Muhammad, Ḥusayn was the greatest Sufi, and "he is our master." He assured him that the spirits are still alive, so that some people visit the shrine of Ḥusayn and see him sitting there above the tomb. All spirits are still alive, until at the end of time when the angel of death, Isrāfīl, by order of the divine name *al-Mumīt* (that is, by order of God in His aspect of "the One who gives death"), will kill them all and in turn be killed by *al-Mumīt,* so that nothing will remain but God alone (because the Qurʾan says that everything on earth perishes, "but the Face of your Lord remains, full of splendor and nobility," 55:26). He could tell others about the Order, but he should leave it to God to defend them, for even the Prophet and Muḥammad ʿUthmān suffered opposition in their lifetimes; the closer one is to God, the more one must suffer on earth.

For the actual initiation, the shaykh called on the Prophet, Ḥusayn, Ibrāhīm al-Dasūqī, and all the saints, reciting the *Fātiḥa* on their behalf, and expressing his hope that this would be the start of much happiness for the new initiate. He instructed him to recite the *awrād* daily, because this would open his heart to the light of God. The way to God was through the *awrād,* although reciting them without permission would produce madness because they are full of light. Then he told him to close his eyes and recite in his heart "Allah, Allah, Allah." As he did so, tears flowed down the initiate's cheeks. After a while he was instructed to open his eyes. They all recited the *Fātiḥa* together, verse 33:56 from the Qurʾan ("God and His angels pray blessings on the Prophet; you who believe, pray blessings on him and greet him with respect"), and a formula of blessings on the Prophet. Then the shaykh embraced the initiate, and they kissed each other's hands.

As we drove to Dasūq, I asked the new initiate if he had converted to Islam before joining the Burhāniyya. He said no, but he felt spiritually close to the Muslims. It is unlikely that most Muslims would reciprocate that feeling of spiritual closeness, despite their eagerness to convert non-Muslims to Islam, since the form of Islam he had embraced was doubtful, if not repugnant, to many Muslims. I asked him what had led him to join the Order, and he said he had been searching for spiritual fulfillment and found it here. The church in Europe is generally divided and devoid of spirituality, he said, and most people had left it.

This particular group of European Burhānīs displayed an almost total lack of Islamic acculturation: they had picked up some of the polite gestures of the Muslims, and when they entered the shrine of Sīdī Ibrāhīm they fell upon the *maqṣūra* with great emotion (although one woman spent a long time at the tomb of Mūsā Abū 'l-ʿUmrān, housed in the same shrine, before she realized that this was not the tomb of Sīdī Ibrāhīm), rubbing and kissing it. When they were done, they spent a long time reciting their *awrād* together in the mosque. But they did not perform the Muslim prayer when the call to prayer came, and when I asked about their observance of various aspects of the Sharīʿa, it appeared that they were not even particularly aware of common Muslim religious obligations and had no intention of embracing them. It is ironic that in finding "Islam," these representatives of modern European culture embraced the very aspect of Islam that is considered by many contemporary Muslims, including some Sufis, to be the mark of degradation, backwardness, and superstition.

Not all European Burhānīs separate their Sufism from allegiance to Islam and observance of its laws. The newsletter *Al-Burhān,* issued in Vienna, lists the times of prayer and does seem to make some effort to give its readers a rudimentary education in the basics of Islam, alongside some much more complex reading on the meanings of the divine Names, though there is no emphasis on the Sharīʿa itself. The Burhānīs at Haus Schnede, the center near Hamburg, rigorously adhered to all aspects of Islamic law.[41] Alfred Hüber says that the lack of insistence on adherence to the Sharīʿa belongs to the later phase of Shaykh Gamāl's leadership in Egypt; earlier in his career he was much less open to foreigners and much more insistent on being Islamically correct. It is clear from Muḥammad ʿUthmān's words that, regardless of the European Burhānīs or the accusations leveled against him in the press, he never disregarded the Sharīʿa or considered it obsolete once one had entered into the Sufi Way. Discipline in the way of the Sharīʿa never ends, he told one Sufi who suggested they should "leave the Sharīʿa and enter the Way *(ṭarīqa).*"[42]

A cursory reading of the allegorical tale written by a German Burhānī, Kari Kloth, to describe her experiences with Muḥammad ʿUthmān reveals an emphasis on techniques and transcendental awareness of the unity of all being, but nothing that could be regarded as specifically Islamic. The basic message is that by following the spiritual guidance of the "owl," the "little turtle" gradually learned to see things not through the mists of her own limited perspective but through "heavenly eyes" and to realize her essential unity with God; God is known by concentrating on one's own heart, and so one enters into the light.[43] It would appear that the European Burhāniyya I met bore some of the marks of what Elwell-Sutton calls the "pseudo-Sufism" propagated in the West,[44] but not entirely: for, true to the Sufi tradition, Muḥammad ʿUthmān apparently did tell Kloth that in order to live in unity with God one must live in total surrender to His will,[45] and clearly there is some training, at a minimum the discipline of daily recitation of *awrād,* and at times even fairly rigorous training, if one is to take the allegory seriously. However, we cannot know how representative Kloth's experiences are: Shaykh Gamāl said she had learned as much from Muḥammad ʿUthmān as anyone, but she told me that the Burhāniyya in Germany were against her books,[46] and she has almost no contact with them anymore. Muḥammad ʿUthmān's son Ibrāhīm, who became shaykh of the Order after the founder's death in 1983 and subsequently deposed Gamāl al-Sanhūrī from headship over the Order in Egypt, also is not kindly disposed toward her. Were it not for Shaykh Gamāl's support, she said, she would not have had the strength to carry on. She told me that after suffering from bulimia for seven years, coming close to death, she wandered around Upper Egypt and Sudan looking for herself. She found what she was looking for when she met Muḥammad ʿUthmān.

ASSESSING MUḤAMMAD ʿUTHMĀN: SELF-IMAGE AND PUBLIC IMAGE

Writing the life story of a major religious personality poses inherent difficulties for the scholar, because the story of that person's life is likely to be adorned with material that, from an academic point of view, appears to be merely legendary. The more removed the person is from the contemporary scene, the more justified we feel in dismissing stories of supernatural or miraculous intervention as the fabrications of excessively devoted followers. When that material derives from a contemporary autobiographical account, it cannot be as easily dismissed. Our treatment of such phenomena will depend largely on our assessment of the character and psychological state of the speaker, as well as the social role he or she is trying to fill. When the personality in question also becomes the focus of major controversy in his own society, the task of scholarly assessment becomes much more challenging.

Given the very diverse sources that are available to us about Muḥammad ʿUthmān—autobiographical, anecdotal, hagiographical, hostile, and allegorical—what can we say about the man himself? Is it possible for us to write what could be considered an objective, scholarly biography? Given the fact that most of our data concerning his early life lie in the realm of the miraculous and supernatural, and we can only infer from one of his many anecdotes that he originally worked as a baker, the answer would have to be "no." In fact, it would be difficult for a social scientist to account for many of the experiences of the Sufis, for whom visions and miraculous events are almost ordinary. Such stories strike at our assumptions concerning the social linkages that are critical in a person's spiritual formation. Yet if we remove the visionary experiences from our account, we are left with inexplicable gaps.

If, however, we approach the life story of Muḥammad ʿUthmān not in the hope of gaining standard social science objectivity, but focusing on the projection of image, we find that the image of Muḥammad ʿUthmān projected by his own anecdotes and by the Burhāniyya Order contains a number of important elements for analysis, especially concerning his uniqueness and his relationship with his community. We have seen that Muḥammad ʿUthmān attributes his early Sufi practices to internal impetuses, not to external stimuli. He seems to want to emphasize that his social milieu is not to be given credit for the spiritual practices that led to his visions and ultimately to his special calling. No doubt he does this in order to stress the role of divine providence and appointment.

Yet despite his emphasis on his independence and uniqueness, it is important to situate him in an ancient spiritual lineage in order to establish the legitimacy of his claim to its headship. For this, divine commission is not sufficient because custom dictates that headship of the Orders be passed from father to son or at least within a certain family line to its most distinguished candidate. Therefore, the editor of the transcription of Muḥammad ʿUthmān's taped speeches begins the two-hundred-page text with the origins of the Order and emphasizes that the one who initially established the Burhāniyya in Sudan was an ancestor of Muḥammad ʿUthmān. Therefore the powerful, secret texts of the Burhāniyya had been hidden by his ancestors and were available for him to find. The biography of the shaykh read at his anniversary celebration also stresses Muḥammad ʿUthmān's physical descent from the Prophet. In fact, his spiritual descent is from one of the Prophet's grandsons, Ḥasan, and his physical descent is from the other grandson, Ḥusayn, thus granting Muḥammad ʿUthmān an impeccable spiritual pedigree through both his ancestral connection with the Order and his genealogy. For Gamāl al-Sanhūrī, who authored the biography of Muḥammad ʿUthmān read at his moulid and who was likely the editor of the transcription of his speeches as well, Muḥammad ʿUthmān's "community," his social referent that establishes his legitimacy as a Sufi shaykh, is to be situated in these ancestral lineages. For Muḥammad ʿUthmān himself, it would seem, his "community" is that of the great saints whom he sees in his visions. Although he initially learned *awrād* from a family friend, his spiritual guidance was derived from visions and the mysterious blind man from Dasūq. He is without a shaykh in the usual sense, so he lacks the usual spiritual lineage. However, by receiving his guidance and commission directly from the greatest saints that ever lived, his status is even greater than that of the Sufi who learns by ordinary means.[47]

Although Muḥammad ʿUthmān projects an image of himself that is designed to stress his uniqueness, he nonetheless fits a paradigm that is familiar to those acquainted with Sufism, a paradigm that is at least partially modeled on that of the Prophet Muhammad himself. It is this very model that grants him authority to interpret the Qurʾan, perform miracles, and give spiritual guidance. As is evident from the discussion of his depiction in the press, this same model is not meaningful to outsiders, who find his claims ridiculous, his Qurʾanic interpretations dangerous, and his authoritarianism manipulative. In fact, the very attributes that made him a potent and charismatic Sufi shaykh lent themselves to accusations by outsiders that he was a cunning deceiver and dangerous cult leader. The complete disparity between his self-image and the image projected by the press suggests the gap that has grown in Egyptian society between traditional popular religion, which is heavily Sufi, and Islamic reformism, which is promoted by the government and flourishes in the cities. The fact, however, that Muḥammad ʿUthmān was able to win followers from the very social groupings that had, since early in this century, been active in various reformist movements (of the Wahhābī, Muslim Brotherhood, or modernist types) also suggests that traditional spiritual models have not entirely lost their potential for appeal to the educated, modern elite. Evidently, the imperfections and spiritual void perceived by many in modern technological culture make recourse to higher power based on a potent and culturally authentic spirituality very appealing. The reality of science and the material realm exists alongside that of the spiritual realm. The spiritual realm is in fact more powerful and real than the material realm. Physicians cannot cure cancer, but Muḥammad ʿUthmān can. The potent words of the Burhānī *awrād* lead to enlightenment, spiritual protection, and healing.

It is obvious from Muḥammad ʿUthmān's recitation of his commission that he regarded his mission as a comprehensive spiritual one not only to revive the Order of Ibrāhīm al-Dasūqī but to revive Sufism itself. He engaged in debates with those whom he calls "Wahhābīs" (fundamentalists) and atheists, and he taught his followers techniques that would enable them to do the same. He was not trying to appeal merely to a traditional Sufi milieu and an already available clientele. He felt himself called to turn Muslim society as a whole back to the spiritual tradition of Sufism and the veneration of the Prophet. He no doubt saw himself as something of a renewer of Islam.

It would appear that the Burhāniyya's spread to Europe is thanks at least in part to an ability to concentrate on universal themes of mysticism rather than specifically Islamic doctrines. In this way the Order has been able to attract a number of Europeans because of the spiritual void felt by many in the West. The image of Muḥammad ʿUthmān projected by Kari Kloth in the allegory of her experiences with the shaykh is that of a wise, compassionate clairvoyant, who is able to instruct her in the disciplines that lead to transcendental awareness. There is no reference here to the Prophet or saints, or to the Qurʾan, but to more universal mystical images like light, truth, and finding God in one's self. There is no communal reference here at all, neither physical nor spiritual ancestors, nor the larger community of saints that presides over his career in the world of visions. Muḥammad ʿUthmān appears as a solitary wise man in a world of suffering, and Kloth's own experience is, despite Muḥammad ʿUthmān's guidance, one of deep personal effort and solitary awareness. This contrasts sharply with most contemporary Sufi experience in Egypt. As we have seen, for most Egyptian Sufis, the sought-for knowledge is not abstract but is founded in relationships—deep love relationships for one's shaykh, the Prophet, the Prophet's family, and the great saints. The experience of unity they describe is not unity with God but the dissolution of the boundaries of individuality between the Sufis themselves, culminating in an experience of entering into the presence of the Prophet. It is a deeply personalistic, communalistic mystical experience. Although Kari Kloth undoubtedly loved Muḥammad ʿUthmān deeply, the image projected in her allegorical tale is of a fairly solitary struggle, under the guidance of a compassionate, but distant, wise spiritual master, an image that conforms more to Western expectations than to contemporary Egyptian or Sudanese expectations. Muḥammad ʿUthmān's image is therefore able to be molded to a more European model of a mystic, an image that apparently exerts a certain appeal in an atmosphere felt by many to be devoid of true spirituality.

The potency of image lies in its ability to draw on accepted and meaningful cultural models that communicate positive values to those who receive it. The story of Muḥammad ʿUthmān reveals the gap in contemporary Egyptian society between its traditionally-oriented, Sufi sectors and its reformist and secular sectors, in that the image he projected was meaningful to the one and not to the other, except in a negative sense. Yet his story also reveals that some sectors of society usually labeled "modern" still find the traditional model appealing, even if they are not personally deeply rooted in the Sufi culture. The cultural authenticity of Sufism made it an appealing religious alternative, and its lack of political aspiration made it safe and perhaps more genuinely spiritual. At the same time, Muḥammad ʿUthmān was able to project an image that was meaningful and attractive to Europeans, whose spiritual yearnings are less communally oriented. In objective terms, both Muḥammad ʿUthmān's claims of uniqueness and spiritual supremacy and the press's claims that he was a cult leader, a cunning deceiver, and a manipulator are exaggerations of the truth. Yet this very discrepancy of images is perhaps the best indicator of the cultural complexity and discontinuity in contemporary Egyptian society.

Muḥammad ʿUthmān died on 7 April 1983 and is buried in Khartoum. He was succeeded by his son Ibrāhīm in Sudan, while Gamāl al-Sanhūrī remained shaykh over the Egyptian branch until he was forcibly retired by Shaykh Ibrāhīm in 1986, allegedly out of jealousy over Gamāl's success as a leader. Although this was clearly a difficult experience for Shaykh Gamāl, he insists that he does not want to promote division within the Order, so he acquiesced despite many suggestions that he found his own Order. And, he says, life is much calmer this way. He even passes out pictures of Shaykh Ibrāhīm and tells Burhānīs that they must love him, because no one can love a man and hate his son; he will not say a word against him. But Shaykh Ibrāhīm could not expel him from the Order, he said, for his recruitment was at the command of Sīdī Ibrāhīm al-Dasūqī and our lord Ḥusayn, as Muḥammad ʿUthmān himself testified on tape.

With Shaykh Gamāl's retirement, the Burhāniyya also acquiesced in the demands of the Supreme Council of Sufi Orders and under Shaykh Ḥāmid al-Guindī, an Egyptian, became a branch *(bayt)* of the Burhāmiyya Order. The Burhāniyya also began to decline in numbers, although they still have an impressive membership. As one Burhānī told me, Shaykh Ibrāhīm is a very nice, cheerful man, but he does not possess his father's charisma or leadership ability.

CHAPTER 11

Coptic Christianity and Popular Islam in Egypt

Elements of a Common Spirituality

Muslims constitute the great majority of the people of Egypt, but an older faith continues to hold the hearts and minds of a significant minority. The Coptic Orthodox Church, which traces its origin to the apostolic mission of the gospel writer St. Mark, claims a following of at least five million in Egypt, or about 10 percent of the country's population. Some estimates place the number of Copts at as many as ten million, out of a total Egyptian population of fifty-eight million.[1] They are scattered throughout all the provinces of Egypt, although they are best represented in some of the provinces of the heartland of Upper Egypt, Asyūṭ, and Minyā. These are the same provinces that have lately been the center of Islamic militancy, including a campaign to assassinate and terrorize Copts and drive them from the land. Although many Egyptians say that Copts and Muslims have always lived in harmony and that friendships frequently cross confessional lines, suspicions also run deep. I was frequently warned by both groups not to trust members of the other, and each side has its store of tales to attest to the treachery of the other. The Copts see themselves as the "true" Egyptians, direct descendants of the ancient Egyptians, the artifacts of whose glorious civilization draw millions of tourists each year, whereas the Muslims are seen as at least partially descendants of the Arab invaders. However, there are no racial or linguistic distinctions between the two communities, and the traditional sectors of both groups wear the same dress and employ the same architectural features in their homes. Egyptian national policy has stressed the common Arabness and Egyptianness of both communities.

Sufi spirituality has much in common with Coptic spirituality; specifically, they share some of the features that distinguish Sufism from reformist types of Islamic spirituality, be they fundamentalist or modernist. Since Islamic reformism assumed prominence in

Egypt only since the nineteenth century, the common spirituality of Sufism and Coptic Christianity represents a spiritual core that constitutes traditional popular religion in Egypt. Investigating their similarities might bring us closer to an understanding of what, if anything, constitutes—to rob a term used by the Islamists—"authentic" (that is, indigenous) spirituality in Egypt. The links of Sufism with Coptic Christianity are a seldom explored dimension that is essential to delineating Sufism's place in contemporary Egyptian spiritual life.

But there are also differences between Egyptian Sufism and Coptic spirituality. The Coptic Church was subjected to severe persecution during the period of Roman rule, reaching a peak of ferocity during the reign of Diocletian (284–305). During this time many Christians were put to death for their faith, and their stories have etched themselves indelibly into the collective memory of Copts today, who continue to see themselves as a persecuted people. Martyrdom became a coveted prize for those whose hope for real life lay beyond this world. Tales of the early Christians include stories like that of two brothers who went to Alexandria and requested an audience with the governor specifically in order to be martyred.[2] Martyrs included men, women, and children. Such martyrs are automatically granted the status of saint by the church.

The Coptic Orthodox Church has its own pope, seated in the ancient Mediterranean port city of Alexandria. Doctrinally, the church is closely related to the Greek Orthodox and other Eastern Orthodox churches. According to Bishop Athanasius of Bani Suef, the Coptic Church has wrongly been regarded by the West as adherents of the Monophysite creed, which holds that Christ is of a single, divine nature. On the contrary, he says, the Copts "have always believed in God Incarnate with His Divinity and Humanity fully present and united without mixture, confusion or change."[3] Egypt is the land where monasticism began, and its monasteries became the focal point of Coptic spirituality and learning. Priests marry in the Coptic Church, but monks and nuns lead a life of celibacy that is strongly focused on asceticism and contemplation. Although by the nineteenth century, monasteries had declined both in numbers of monks and in the quality of their intellectual life, in recent decades the Coptic Church has enjoyed a revival of monasticism. There are twelve inhabited and officially recognized monasteries in Egypt, and the numbers of monks rose from 214 in 1960 to 630 in 1986.[4] This should not be seen as an isolated phenomenon but as part of the general resurgence of interest in religion among both Coptic and Muslim communities in Egypt since the late 1960s. Many of the new monks are well-trained professionals in such secular occupations as medicine and engineering. The pope is always selected from among the monks, a strong indication of the priority given to the celibate lifestyle.

Copts by and large recognize the contemplative, often reclusive lifestyle as the appropriate model for monks and nuns to follow. This lifestyle consists of long hours of private and communal devotion, fasting, and manual labor that can be accompanied by silent, continuous prayer. This model appears not to have been greatly affected by the new social attitudes promoted among the educated classes to orient energies toward social activism. Since 1965 there has been a new order of "active" Coptic nuns who engage in community welfare activities, but this model is not seen as authentic to many Copts, who say, "They are not nuns."[5] As we have seen, Sufism has often been criticized since the late nineteenth century for being introspective, passive, and quietist rather than promoting socially constructive activity. Non-Sufis criticize the practice of dhikr as a meaningless repetition of words and a dissipation of energies that could better be spent building the society. (Sufis, however, recognize that non-Sufis rarely use their energies for such socially constructive activity and that dhikr is a substitute not for social activism but for sitting in cafes, theaters, or nightclubs.) The Sufi Orders today seldom encourage ordinary disciples to spend extensive periods in solitary meditation as was the norm in medieval Islam. Nonetheless, those who emerge as paragons of holiness among the Sufis are all individuals who have spent considerable amounts of time in solitary devotion and ascetic practices. The contemplative life is considered spiritually superior to social activism by both Sufis and Copts, despite the new social values. This may be a mark of the status of both groups as subcultures within modern Egyptian society.

The Copts have institutionalized ascetic practices for their monastic communities, and even ordinary laypersons are expected to engage in a good deal of fasting. The Muslim fast during the daylight hours of the month of Ramaḍān is well-known, but Copts spend more than half the year in fasts ranging from total fasts for several hours a day to abstinence from all food coming from an animal source or "containing spirit." Copts fast for two weeks before Lent. The Lenten Fast, which is called the Great Fast, begins the day after the feast of the Epiphany and lasts forty days until Palm Sunday. During this time Copts may consume no meat, eggs, fish, wine, or coffee, and may have nothing at all between sunrise and sunset. The Fast of the Apostles lasts forty days after the feast of the Ascension of Jesus into heaven. The fast in honor of the Assumption of the Virgin Mary (who did not die, according to church tradition, but was taken up bodily into heaven) lasts the first fifteen days of August; and the fast of the Nativity of Jesus Christ lasts the twenty-eight days before Christmas.[6] Western observers have sometimes seen the severity of Coptic fasts as a cause of failing health and even blindness.[7] As a contemporary Coptic priest writes, "It is well known that the Coptic Church is a church of asceticism and mysticism from her very beginning."[8] Sufism is the mystical dimension of Islam, and it is not far-fetched to characterize Coptic spirituality as a whole as tinged with asceticism and mysticism. This would be reason enough to explore links between the spirituality and religious experiences of Sufis and Copts in Egypt. As it turns out, the links are many, and reflect in many aspects a common spirituality that is the true popular religion of Egypt.

THE SAINTS IN COPTIC SPIRITUAL LIFE

Saints, the archangel Michael, and the Virgin Mary all play crucial roles in the everyday life of ordinary Copts. People seek the intercession of saints with God and report fantastic miracles at their hands. Although sanctity may be defined through lives of ascetic devotion, its proof, as among the Sufis, is through demonstrations of power. The miracles of living Christian saints include miracles of knowledge, which predominate in the accounts of modern Muslim saints described in chapter 9, but miracles of healing are yet more pronounced and fantastic among the Copts. The healing powers not only of Christian saints but of ordinary Coptic priests are well known and acknowledged in Egypt, among Muslims as well as among Christians. One Muslim told me that Coptic priests are able to heal because they are "closer to nature" than Muslims, which implies that it is their very inferiority that confers on them superior power, a power derived from contact with spiritual beings.

Regardless of the rationale, Muslims have had no trouble venerating Coptic saints and attending Coptic moulids, just as, less often, Copts venerate Muslim saints and attend their moulids. The popular religious lives of the two communities often intersect. The early-nineteenth-century British observer of Egyptian life, Edward Lane, commented, "It is a very remarkable trait in the character of the people of Egypt and other countries of the East, that Muslims, Christians and Jews adopt each other's superstitions, while they abhor the leading doctrines of each other's faiths. In sickness, the Muslim sometimes employs Christian and Jewish priests to pray for him: the Christians and Jews, in the same predicament, often call in Muslim saints for the like purpose."[9] The Jewish community of Egypt has been largely driven out since the 1950s because of tensions between Jewish and non-Jewish communities engendered in Arab countries by the Arab-Israeli conflict. But Coptic-Muslim contacts often converge around saint veneration.

Copts and Muslims hold a common belief concerning the living reality of deceased saints and the efficacy of their intercessions, particularly for those who visit them at their tombs at the most propitious moments. Both confessional groups celebrate their saints on the day of their moulid, and although the word literally means "birthday," for both groups the moulid is celebrated on the anniversary of the saint's death. For Copts, the date of death is the date of the saint's "rebirth" into eternal life. For Muslims, the death of a saint is conceived as his or her union with God, following the pattern of a marriage consummation.

For both groups, in a very real sense the saint does not die. Copts and Muslims believe strongly that the saints are virtually alive, not only in spirit but in body as well. Just as the Muslims say, "God has forbidden the earth to consume the bodies of the saints," a privilege extended in popular belief to the saints, the Copts say in virtually the same language, "The worm does not consume the bodies of the saints." In Latin and Greek Orthodox Christianity, sanctity was demonstrated in the lack of putrefaction surrounding the bones of Christian saints. Although the flesh had vanished from the bones (and in some cases was actually cleansed away from the bones), the remaining bone possessed a pleasing odor, known as the "odor of sanctity." The skeletons of saints were often dismembered in order to be used as relics conveying spiritual power and used for healing.[10] The Copts, however, like the Sufis of Egypt, believe that the flesh of the saints is preserved from corruption. Bodies of saints exhumed after almost two thousand years have allegedly been found entirely uncorrupted, as if they were merely sleeping. One Coptic story of the transfer of a body of a saint says the foot of the saint hit a rock and began to bleed, many hundreds of years after the saint's death. Even the dismembered bodies of the martyred Christians of the Roman era are uncorrupted, remaining "living flesh" in their many parts. At the church of Sitt Rifqa (St. Rebecca) in Sunbat, in the Buhayra province of the Delta, the bodies of the saint and her five children, all of whom were martyred and dismembered by the Romans, are preserved as bloody remains that are uncovered each year during their moulid between the fourteenth and seventeenth of September so that visitors can testify to their incorruptibility.[11] Like the Catholic and Eastern Orthodox churches, the Copts preserve the body parts of saints as relics employed for the purpose of healing.

Despite their common attachment to the visitation of saints' tombs, customs pertaining to saint shrine visitation differ somewhat between Copts and Muslims. Some of these differences arise from the architectural features of the shrines: the Muslim practice of circumambulation of the tomb simply is not possible in most Coptic shrines. Muslims shun pictorial depictions of their saints, whereas Coptic veneration of icons is central to their spiritual life. Both groups cling to and kiss articles associated with the shrine, whether the *maqṣūra* (gridwork barrier) around the tomb, the cloth draped over the tomb, or plaques. Both believe that such objects contain the baraka, or holy power, of the saint. Copts leave votive offerings in the form of bits of clothing or handkerchiefs, a practice less often observed among Muslims in Egypt.[12] Both Copts and Muslims believe in the healing properties of well water associated with their shrines. Both groups write letters to the deceased saints asking them to intervene on their behalf in matters ranging from major illness or injustice to final examinations. Such letters often are not signed because it is taken for granted that the saint knows who has written them.

Many Muslims attend Coptic moulids, and in at least one case there is some popular merging of two personalities from the two traditions: Mārī Girgis, the popular St. George the dragon-slayer and martyr for whom four different moulids are celebrated at four different Egyptian shrines, is sometimes identified with Khidr. Coptic moulids have many of the features of Muslim moulids, including the mounds of roasted chickpeas at moulids in the Delta, the proliferation of merchants' stalls, and the attractions for children, such as rides and stalls selling inexpensive toys. But there are some major differences as well. The Sufi Orders, which figure so prominently in Muslim moulids, are absent from Coptic moulids, and there is no analogous institution among the Copts to transform the moulids into places where the general public may be fed and participate in mystical rites. At Coptic moulids the *khidamāt* are largely private affairs of families camping out or renting a room in a school near the shrine, and they rarely offer hospitality to strangers. The banners that hang over the walkways advertise not the *khidamāt* of Sufi groups but the services of merchants and doctors, including those who specialize in circumcisions—for Coptic moulids, like Muslim moulids, are considered propitious times to perform circumcisions. Tattooers design crosses on wrists or shoulders, or create large emblems, such as St. George on his horse slaying the dragon. It is traditional for Copts to have tattoo crosses on their wrists, which both identify them as Copts and serve as talismans to ward off evil spirits, a function served among Muslims by wearing various charms, including miniature Qur'ans or necklaces with engraved Qur'anic verses. Copts add to their tattoos to mark significant pilgrimages, especially visits to Jerusalem during Holy Week, which would allow them to adopt the title of *Muqaddas* (*Muqaddasa* for a woman), similar to the Muslim practice of adopting the title of *Ḥājj* or *Ḥājja*.

Because there is no organized public religious activity comparable to the dhikrs that might attract people to all-night spiritual celebrations, by midnight the streets begin to empty during Coptic moulids, whereas most Muslim moulids remain very active until the predawn prayer. Secular entertainers have often been among the main attractions at Coptic moulids, although when I attended the largest Coptic moulid, that of St. George in Mīt Damsīs, in the summer of 1988, the church had decreed that such secular entertainment was inappropriate at moulids. I do not know whether this was a local ruling or a new policy.

The focus of activity at the moulid is the church that houses the relics of the saint who is celebrated. There priests pray for healing and blessing for visitors. Of all the saints, St. George is perhaps the most widely associated with spectacular miracles of healing. People come from long distances to be healed of incurable diseases or to have spirits cast out. Many are healed by priests, who lay their hands and a cross on the afflicted persons and recite Psalms over them, but others are healed simply by coming to the shrine. Many visitors report fantastic stories of healing from an assortment of serious afflictions: spirit possession, paralysis, cancer, leprosy, and heart disease, among others. A uniquely Christian sign of healing is the occasional manifestation of crosses of blood appearing on the clothes of the afflicted. During the moulid of St. George in Mīt Damsīs in August 1988, someone had posted "before" and "after" X rays of his lungs to demonstrate how the saint had miraculously healed him of cancer.

THE ROLE OF VISIONS

Visions have played a major role in the history of Coptic Christianity. Otto Meinardus has listed, among the more important apparitions in Coptic history, seven appearances of Christ, thirteen appearances of angels, and three appearances of the Virgin Mary. Yet even this list is not comprehensive. Meinardus notes that these apparitions "are normally related to times of intense personal suffering and anxiety, when the apparition fulfills the role of the healer or the comforter, who offers counsel and advice or makes eschatological promises."[13] However, this refers to apparitions that come to people while awake and does not convey the routineness with which visions are witnessed. Visions of the Virgin Mary, the Archangel Michael, and various saints are common features of the lives of even ordinary Coptic believers. Nearly every spiritually sensitive Copt whom I encountered had stories of visions of deceased saints. Visions may take the form of dreams, appearances of light, or apparitions. As with the Sufis, the most common of these is the dream-vision. These visions, like the visions experienced by the Sufis, serve to give spiritual guidance and are often pivotal in the conversion stories of Copts, which, like those of Sufis, are described as stories of repentance or healing. Apparitions of light appear to be more common among Copts than among Muslims, and in addition Copts have one form of miracle not found among Muslims: apparitions associated with icons, which may speak, heal, weep, bleed, or emit light.

Miracles and supernatural interventions are readily accepted by the Orthodox Church establishment, in contrast to the contemporary Islamic establishment, which encourages a rational approach to faith and classifies most allegedly supernatural events as reflections of an overly imaginative populace that is full of ignorance and superstition. Among the Coptic establishment, disputes concerning papal succession are routinely resolved through visions. The dichotomy between officially endorsed Islam and popular religion appears not to have a precise analogue in the Coptic Church, which acknowledges the beliefs of its adherents in visions and miracles. Perhaps it is for this reason that Sufism, one dimension of popular Islam in Egypt, may rightly be compared with Coptic spirituality as a whole, without differentiation between popular and official aspects.

The most famous and widely seen vision of all in modern Egypt was the apparition of the Virgin Mary over the Church of the Blessed Virgin in the Cairo suburb of Zaytūn, which began in April 1968. The initial appearance came on the Monday of Holy Week, at a time when the Copts were grieved over the loss of Jerusalem to Israel in the June 1967 war, preventing them from performing the pilgrimage to Jerusalem. On 2 April 1968, some mechanics in a garage facing the church were alarmed at the sight of a young woman descending the central dome of the church. They cried out for her to be careful, but when she turned, they recognized her as the Blessed Virgin.[14] Her appearance continued every night for a considerable length of time—the better part of a year, according to Bishop Athanasius, more than two years according to Father Matthias Wahba, and two and a half years, according to Iris el Masri.[15] The length of her appearance prompted an American Catholic priest to call it "unique in the history of Marian apparitions."[16] Her longest single appearance was on 30 April 1968, when the vision remained from 2:45 A.M. until 5 A.M.

The apparition immediately attracted enormous popular attention, and soon there were milling crowds waiting to see her every night, while merchants sold their wares in an atmosphere very much like that of a moulid.[17] The apparition attracted not only Copts, but Muslims as well, for whom Mary is also a saint. In the wake of the devastating defeat of 1967, Egypt was thrown into a major crisis of self-doubt. Many felt that God had abandoned them because they had abandoned Him by following secular ideologies such as the "Arab socialism" of President Nasser. The appearance of the Virgin at this time was seen as a message of comfort to the nation—for to many the Virgin appeared to weep with them over their grief—and as an assurance that God would heal their wounds if they returned to Him. For the Copts, the vision also meant that at a time when they could not visit the Holy Land, the Virgin had chosen to honor Egypt with her own presence.

A papal committee was charged with investigating the matter, and at length Pope Kyrillos VI made a public statement concerning the significance of the vision: "The extraordinary events of the past weeks have been attested to and the Mother of Light, as the Virgin is called in Egypt, came to spread blessing in this country that had welcomed the Holy Family two thousand years ago.[18] It is a phenomenon that is a good sign and it seems that the prevention of the Christian Arabs from visiting the Holy Land in Jerusalem during this pilgrimage time has led the Virgin to appear in Zaytūn."[19]

In a more political vein, the Pope said, "This is a harbinger of peace and speedy victory . . . the salvage of the Holy Land and the entire Arab land from the ends of the enemy. We shall triumph in God's name."[20]

Accounts of the form of the apparition vary. She is always luminous, sometimes visible as a whole person, sometimes in bust form, sometimes merely as light. Meinardus classifies this as a "light-appearance," a type of miracle common in Coptic religious life, rather than an "apparition," because he believes that apparitions are accompanied by verbal messages, and this was not. He believes that the indistinctness of most accounts of the vision, with an emphasis on its luminosity, substantiates this contention. He also notes that Pope Kyrillos VI waited more than a month after the first appearances of the Virgin to visit the site, an indication that he was less enthusiastic than most Copts about the appearance of the Virgin. When asked why he had not gone before, "the Patriarch said that he had been seeing the vision of the Mother of Light, the Dove of Peace, the Virgin Mary, the Mother of Jesus Christ, since his early childhood."[21]

Since the Zaytūn apparition, other visions have also been reported. A thirteen-year-old girl in Beirut who reported a vision of St. George asked the saint about the Zaytūn apparition, to which he replied, "The world has lost faith. The number of unbelievers is increasing ceaselessly. Assure yourself, apparitions will henceforth increase."[22] We may recall that the Egyptian crossing of the Suez Canal in October 1973 was also alleged to be accompanied by visions of angels and the Prophet over the heads of the soldiers.

Besides visions of deceased saints, Copts may also receive visions of a living spiritual preceptor, typically a member of the Coptic clergy. In this case, visions serve to establish the spiritual link between the two, just as it establishes "spiritual connection" between a Sufi shaykh and his disciples. The spiritual children of Elīṣābāt Ibrāhīm, a living Coptic holy woman, have visions of her regularly. The establishment of this contact by vision does not require any formulaic recitation comparable to the Sufi practice of reciting the *Fātiḥa* and a prayer of blessing on the Prophet before calling on the name of the shaykh. One of Elīṣābāt's spiritual children explained to me that we all have the "equipment" to tune in to spiritual things, but receptivity is predicated on the purification of the heart and stilling the mind, just as one stills the mind for sleep. Then one can receive visions and see such beauty that one will be permanently changed. Elīṣābāt herself said, "You see heaven and earth as if you were sleeping while you are awake. It's as if you were watching color television." And she urged me to "let your spirit be linked to mine, that you might see me in a vision."

Figure 17. Muqaddasa Elīṣābāt Ibrāhīm in December 1989.

THE PATH OF SPIRITUAL REFINEMENT

Coptic Christians sometimes experience dramatic personal moral conversions. For all Copts, the pursuit of spiritual refinement begins, like the Sufi path, with repentance and turning from the things of this world. Coptic monks, priests, and nuns, like Sufi shaykhs, often function as counselors for ordinary people who come to them for advice or for blessing *(li 'l-tabarruk)*, and they also may function as spiritual guides in the Sufi sense for those who are not initiated into the clergy. Ordinary Copts may recite daily prayers, the "Hours" or *ajbiyya*, seven times each day. Like the *awrād* of the Sufis, the *ajbiyya* are considered the key to advancing in the spiritual life. Although a few of these prayers are restricted to the clergy, most are open to laymen. They consist of prayers of thanks and praise, the "Our Father," and many passages from the Bible, especially from the book of Psalms. These prayers commemorate events surrounding the death, resurrection, ascension, and anticipated second coming of Christ. They are as follows: 1) the *Prime,* or "Morning Prayer," which commemorates the Resurrection; 2) the *Terce,* or "Third Hour" (9 A.M.) prayer, which commemorates the descent of the Holy Spirit after Christ's ascension into heaven; 3) the *Sext,* or "Sixth Hour" (12 noon) prayer, which commemorates the crucifixion of Jesus; 4) the *None,* or "Ninth Hour" (3 P.M.) prayer, which commemorates the death of Christ and his acceptance of the thief who was crucified beside him and repented of his sins; 5) the *Vespers,* or "Sunset Prayer," which commemorates the time that Jesus' body was taken down from the cross; 6) the *Compline,* or "Sleep Hour" prayer commemorating the burial of Christ and serving as a reminder of the end of one's own life; and 7) three "Midnight" prayers reminding the believer of the second coming of Christ.[23] Edward Lane, writing in the early nineteenth century, says he was assured that hardly any Copt does not pray these prayers.[24] Copts, like Sufis, highly value the life of prayer, fasting, and meditation, considering it key to the dispensing of spiritual blessings. The similarity of Coptic and Sufi perceptions of spirituality and its results may also be seen in their common expectation that holy people are able to transcend spatial limitations. Coptic monks say that one of the goals of the contemplative life is to become *sāyiḥ* or *min al-sawwāḥ*—one who travels freely through space.[25]

As we have seen, Sufis believe that spiritual purification is related to a lack of materiality. People who practice severe austerities may acquire bodies that are "luminous," lacking in materiality by the scarcity of their intake of food. The preservation of the bodies of saints from corruption is sometimes seen as a function of the relative immateriality of their bodies.[26] Coptic ideas regarding spiritual purification are similar but differ in their strong emphasis on sexual abstinence and purity from sexual lust. Whereas Sufis have generally followed the broader Muslim endorsement of marriage, not only to generate children but also to allow for the satisfaction of sexual desires, the Coptic Church has never legitimated the use of sex merely for the satisfaction of natural impulses and regards the sexual act as legitimate only when it is performed for the sake of procreation.[27] The idea that sexual activity interferes with spirituality remains strong in Coptic belief and justifies the church's emphasis on celibacy for its monks and nuns, as well as its ban on sexual activity during periods of fasting, on the eve of feasts, and before and after receiving the Sacrament of Holy Communion. Nonetheless, priests must marry, because their functions place them in direct and constant contact with society at large, in contrast to the largely anchorite existence of the monks and nuns.

The source of impurity lies not in the sexual act itself but in the desire that accompanies it.[28] It is possible for married people to attain true holiness, as we shall see in our discussion of Elīṣābāt. Significantly, it is said that she never experienced sexual desire and that all four of her children were conceived during periods of spiritual intoxication when she was unaware of what was happening. After her fourth child was born, it is said that the Holy Spirit threw her husband off her whenever he tried to approach her. One Coptic man rejected the idea that Muslim saints could be incorruptible after death as Coptic saints are, because Muslims marry, and the very act of marriage involves lust and passion, which defile the body. Presumably, Sitt Rifqa, who was martyred along with her five children, never experienced sexual desire, since her dismembered body is said to be incorruptible.

POPE KYRILLOS VI (1902–1971)

Egyptian Copts have a modern-day saint who exemplifies the model holy life of ascetic detachment and devotion, the monk Mina who became Pope Kyrillos VI. Born in August 1902 with the name of Azer, he entered the monastery of al-Baramus on 27 July 1927. He adopted the name Mina, after a famous Egyptian saint, when he was ordained as a monk on 25 February 1928. After five years at the monastery, he requested permission to go into the desert for solitary devotions. His superiors hesitated to grant him permission to do this, citing his youth and the hardship and dangers of solitude, but Father Raphael Ava Mina, who served as deacon for Pope Kyrillos VI, comments in his brief biographical sketch, "That is the path which all the great saints chose, to fill themselves of God's benedictions and penetrate into God's immense glory, as well as to be in close contact with Jesus Christ. . . . Because he loved the Lord with all his heart and mind, he wanted to think of Him day and night. It was a hidden, internal power which urged him to go to the desert where he could satisfy his love for God."[29] His superiors finally gave him permission to do this, provided he return to the monastery for communal services on Saturdays and Sundays.

After dwelling from 1933 to 1936 in a cave in the Valley of al-Natrūn, home of several well-known monasteries, he moved to a deserted windmill in the Muqattam hills in southeast Cairo. His dwelling place was starkly comfortless, and, we are told, the reptiles and wild animals of the area did not harm him. This attribute of saintliness is typical of both Christian and Sufi tradition and is specifically mentioned of Shaykh Aḥmad Raḍwān, who also dwelled in the desert wilderness for a time.[30]

Miraculous events accompanying this solitude in the desert testify to Father Mina's holiness. At one time the inspector of antiquities attempted to drive him out of the windmill and addressed him disrespectfully. Father Mina appeared to the inspector's wife in a dream, rebuking her, and the next morning the inspector and his wife arrived at the windmill to apologize to the solitary monk. On another occasion, robbers beat him unconscious, but he placed a picture of St. Mina on his injury and stopped his bleeding and was able to walk six kilometers to the hospital, where he astonished the physicians by both his physical strength and the austerity of his diet. Such was the spiritual intensity of this period of his life that he later remarked to his deacon during the pomp of the ceremonies accompanying the return of the body of St. Mark to Egypt from Venice to rest in the newly inaugurated Cathedral of St. Mark, ceremonies attended by President Nasser and Emperor Haile Selassie of Ethiopia, "My son, all these ceremonies are not equal to one day in the windmill in ancient Cairo."[31]

In 1942, during the Second World War, the British forced him to leave his solitary abode, and he moved to a room in Old Cairo, an area with a number of ancient Coptic churches. Many people came to seek his guidance and advice, and with the gifts they gave him he built the Church of St. Mina and a residence for students who came to Cairo to study, "as a shelter for their faith and chastity." Attached to the church were five rooms "dedicated to training the poor sons of the church on various professions: textile, electricity, mechanics, welding and shell work."[32] He lived in this church until his ordination as Pope Kyrillos VI on 10 May 1959.

The reign of Pope Kyrillos VI marked an era of renewal in the church in Egypt and the establishment of Coptic Orthodox churches all over the world. Pope Kyrillos VI was widely regarded as a living saint in the true sense of the word, not merely a carrier of baraka and a living link to the throne of St. Mark but also one who possessed an aura of holiness that rejuvenated the church. His deacon, Father Raphael, said that his daily masses were unique manifestations of spiritual joy and power, his policy of direct accessibility to all people eliminated the problems of alienation caused by the attendants of his predecessors, and his order for all monks to return to their monasteries rejuvenated the spiritual life of those institutions. By virtue of his spiritual influence, many highly educated people entered the priesthood. "Pope Kyrillos restored to the church the illumination of its harmony so that all the world recognized in the church of Alexandria the purity of its metal, and the Sacred Spirit overshadowed it."[33]

Less flattering is the assessment of Otto Meinardus, who wrote, "There is no doubt that he is a genuine thaumaturgos, a deeply pious and religious person with extraordinary spiritual gifts, who, among other things, has stopped the ill-practice of simony, at least on the episcopal level. Many educated and sincere Copts are sadly disappointed and even distressed on account of the inability of the Patriarch to fulfil his administrative responsibilities, as Edward Wakin so pointedly said: 'Not only has a monk become a Patriarch, but the Patriarch has remained a monk.' "[34]

However, the Pope did not manifest the critical attitude and eschewal of political contacts typical of ascetics of both Sufi and Coptic tradition. Noting that both Muslim and Coptic dignitaries hailed the June 1967 war as a "holy war" willed by God, Meinardus comments, "These religious-political demonstrations for national unity should not be regarded simply as unpremeditated, spontaneous acts produced by the crisis. For several months, Cyril VI had proclaimed the basic identity of the goals of the Christian Gospel with the aspirations of the Arab Socialist Society. For years, the Christmas and Easter messages of Cyril VI upheld the right and responsibility of the Arabs to liberate Palestine from the Imperialists and Zionists. As in every national crisis, the Copts have stood solidly behind the Government."[35]

Many testify to the miracles performed by Pope Kyrillos VI, including healings, miracles of knowledge, and the receipt of visions.[36] "One word pronounced by him could solve problems, cure the sick, realize all demands and oust the wicked spirits. He always carried the holy cross which always supported him."[37] Pope Kyrillos's miracles of healing include, in Biegman's words, "an impressive list of complaints and diseases, such as slipped discs, fits, polio, various heart conditions, diabetes, infant mortality, warts, eye disease, kidney stones, chronic chest disease, boils, mental illness, paralysis, spinal fever, cysts, headaches, asthma, lung tumours and post-natal fever."[38] A model of Christian ethics, "he loved even his enemies and entrusted them with important responsibilities." Nonetheless, as in Sufi tradition, God opposed those who opposed His saint. Some of those who plotted against the pope or insulted him met swift accidental death.[39]

Like many Sufi saints, Pope Kyrillos anticipated his death and alluded to it. After he died on 9 March 1971, his body was transported to the Monastery of St. Mina amid unprecedented heavy rains and thunderstorms, which were "considered a participation of nature in declaring its sorrow for the pope's departure." The inhabitants of the area around the monastery welcomed the body of the pope with great joy, because it carried with it great blessing.[40] His tomb is visited by large crowds on Fridays and Sundays, where paper and ballpoint pens are provided for those who wish to make a request of the saint.[41]

It is evident that the model of sainthood offered by Pope Kyrillos VI bears many resemblances to that of Egyptian Sufism. Deep love and devotion to God, expressed in a formative period of solitary prayer and ascetic detachment from material things, purified his spirit and sharpened its receptivity to visions of the spiritual realm. Holiness is expressed through virtue and demonstrated through miracles of healing, knowledge, control over wild beasts, and God's avenging of insults. His sanctity is seen by his followers as infusing the church with new life and is believed to be largely responsible for the revival of the Church in the 1960s.

MUQADDASA ELĪṢĀBĀT IBRĀHĪM

The spiritual life of the Coptic Church is dominated by members of the clergy—monks, priests, and nuns. Sufism, on the other hand, offers the potential for laypersons, both men and women, not only to enter the spiritual life in the full context of family life but even to become spiritual fathers and mothers, saints in their own right without certification or official recognition. This led me to speculate whether Coptic Christianity offers similar opportunities to laymen to advance spiritually and assume informal roles as spiritual fathers and mothers. The phenomenon of lay spiritual leadership appears to be fairly rare, for members of the clergy typically function as personal spiritual guides to laypersons in a manner rarely assumed by members of the ulama, so there is no need for a lay leadership to fill that gap. However, I did meet one outstanding Coptic holy woman and spiritual mother, a miracle worker and teacher without certification or recognition. That was Muqaddasa Elīṣābāt, more commonly called "Mama Elīṣābāt" by her followers.

Elīṣābāt was in her sixties when I met her in August 1988, a woman who eats little, speaks little, and prays much. Today she usually wears simple white clothes resembling the dress of a *ḥājja*, but in her younger days she often wore resplendent garments. She prefers to be photographed holding a cross, in the manner of the Coptic clergy. She was an illiterate peasant from Sūhāj, a province in "middle Egypt," about five hours' drive south of Cairo. Her father was a devout man, whom she described as "a man of baraka, simple as a child," and she followed him in her intense love for Christ. From her youth she was able to work fantastic miracles of healing and had the gift of *shafafiyya*, the "transparency" or clairvoyance that enables her to see visions of the saints and read the hearts of people.

Elīṣābāt describes her life in these words: "When I was ten, I used to see heavenly visions, especially St. George, who gave me many messages. He sent me to many places to preach in the name of Christ in all the towns and cities, performing miracles of healing and exorcising evil spirits, and giving me the gift of a word that would lead to the repentance of people, although I did not know how to read or write. I was happy and used to sacrifice and work with my 'children' to build churches. [And I did] many deeds too numerous to write down." She hoped to enter a convent and live the life of a nun, but "because of the customs of Upper Egypt, my family refused and beat me and forced me to marry. I gave up and submitted to their command and their will, along with God's will."

She married her cousin, a man who had no sympathy for her spiritual inclinations or ministry and treated her cruelly. Nonetheless, she established a ministry as "spiritual mother" to many men and women. Besides her home in Ḥilwān Gardens, a town south of Cairo, she established a residence at Mīt Damsīs in the Delta to serve as a place of ministry during the moulid of St. George. Despite her husband's hostility, she says that St. George himself commanded him to allow her to go to Mīt Damsīs and later to Jerusalem. Her homes at Mīt Damsīs and Ḥilwān Gardens have become virtual chapels of devotion and places of healing, with walls that have been entirely painted with Coptic iconography. A record book at her home in Ḥilwān Gardens records the miracles of healing she has performed, miracles she attributes to St. George.

Nonetheless, her ministry, falling as it does outside the official sanction of the Coptic Church, has aroused some hostility. In the town of Ghayt al-ʿInab near Alexandria, she and her followers built a great church dedicated to St. George. The day that the church was opened, the building was packed with visitors, and a man was crushed to death in the crowd. Elīṣābāt says that her opponents tested her, saying, "If you have a secret *(sirr)*[42] and your deeds are from God, if St. George accompanies you and performs miracles at your hand, then awaken this man from the dead." Elīṣābāt fell into a swoon for an unknown period of time, but when she woke she felt the strength of the Holy Spirit upon her. "I told the dead man, 'Get up!' and he got up immediately. At this point people started yelling and crying, 'Oh hero, St. George!' Glory be to God! I was saved by the blessing of St. George."

By her intercession, a mayor's wife conceived. The mayor became so enamored of her that he wished to marry her and imprisoned her in his home, which she described as a palace. However, St. George set a fire in the house, provoking such a panic that she was able to escape.

Among the many amazing stories associated with her ministry was her association with a man named Isḥāq. Elīṣābāt describes her experience with him as follows: "Every year I had a mission to Mīt Damsīs. God was glorious in curing many diseases and burning evil spirits. I was treating a naked man who didn't look human. He was monstrous—in his face, his hair, and his filth. He was zombielike and was considered a house of devils. He ate grass from the ground, garbage, and wood from trees. For a number of years I saw this man, but I didn't approach him out of fear. Then one day, as I was entering the church of St. George, by his guidance I was commanded to take Ishaq and his wife to Ḥilwān Gardens. When I told the people with me, they were worried and afraid. But at last they tied him up and put him in the car, and brought him to Ḥilwān Gardens, where we imprisoned him in one of the rooms. They locked the doors, fearing his violence. He ate thirty-three loaves of bread at each meal. He ate any meat, even cat meat or dog meat. He didn't know what he was doing.

"One day we opened the door to give him food, but he didn't eat. We wondered what this strange behavior was about. Then they found him on the floor, with his hands and clothes covered with crosses of blood. And on his hand there was writing, written in the Greek handwriting of St. George. [Isḥāq was healed,] and he had a great mission. They took him to the bathroom, made him wear new clothes, and shaved his beard. He was newborn. The letter was on his hand, and his mission surpassed the imagination. He performed signs and wonders and cured many people, and many evil spirits were exorcised by his hand, until he died in 1970."

At the time that I met Elīṣābāt at the moulid of St. George in Mīt Damsīs, she was a widow, and her four children were grown and had children of their own. Her relationship with her spiritual children, who stayed in her house in Mīt Damsīs during the moulid, was similar to the relationships of Sufi shaykhs and spiritual mothers to their followers. She took that relationship very seriously. Her spiritual children regularly have visions of her, and she communes to them through these. She rebuked one of her spiritual sons for his attachment to material things and demanded to know whether he had had visions of her. "All the time," he protested. She appeared not to believe him, saying that she constantly cried out to him in her spirit, but he ignored her.

People lined up at the house at Mīt Damsīs for healing, prayer, and confession. Often she treated them with a roughness that appears startling to someone not accustomed to Coptic methods of healing and exorcism. She greeted one man cordially, but then abruptly began to shout that he should go confess his sin to the priest. When he asked if he should return afterward, she replied that when she knew he had confessed and repented, she would send for him. A girl whispered to her that she had returned to the same sin she had previously committed, and Elīṣābāt slapped her hard on the face and sent her away. The girl looked shocked, and another girl who had accompanied her began to cry. Elīṣābāt patted the other girl on the shoulder and told her to go repent and have faith. Some of Elīṣābāt's followers explained to me that Elīṣābāt was not hitting the girl but the demon within her and claimed that the girl felt no pain.

The lowest level of the house functioned as an informal chapel, the walls painted with images of the saints, where circles of men and women listened to readings from Scripture. Many of them had fantastic stories of healings effected through St. George and Elīṣābāt. One woman had had cancer in her lungs and bones and told me she was healed without anyone touching her or reading a Psalm over her, merely by going to the church of St. George. Another young woman had drunk poison given to her through black magic, and nobody could heal her, but when she came to St. George she was healed. Another woman had a tumor and liver trouble that were cured by St. George. Two men who were former sorcerers told of being healed through repentance and exorcism at the hands of Elīṣābāt. Elīṣābāt's house at the moulid of St. George came the closest to a Sufi *khidma* of anything I have seen at a Coptic moulid, for her spiritual children sat outside and sang hymns into a public address system that broadcast them into the street and attracted more people. Like a Sufi *khidma,* the house offered spiritual and physical nourishment to all who came. Unlike a Sufi *khidma,* it also offered healing and spiritual counsel.

Ḥakīm, one of her close followers told me his story. "My father had twelve children, but they all died. The only ones who survived were my sister and I. That was after my mother had a vision in which she saw a light descending from the heavens onto me and my sister. Even though the town of Maṭariyya had no churches, I loved and feared God. This was despite my bad behavior, for I used to stay up at night drinking, spending time with women of the night, and engaging in other frivolities. This happened until 1969. I became very sick. I went to the doctor, and the diagnosis was that there was no cure. I had a vision of St. George. He had soldiers with him. I felt my body tremble. St. George told me, 'Go tomorrow to Ḥilwān Gardens to Mama the Muqaddasa, because there is a mission for you there.' Immediately I said, 'I am under your command, St. George.'

"I went to Mama Elīṣābāt. Even though I am a relative of her husband, I don't like to deal with him, because he doesn't like me and he treats me with scorn. In the house there was a man whose story was amazing. He had dangerous diseases, but St. George was compassionate with him and healed him by burning the evil spirits that were upon him. His name was Isḥāq. He had a gift that messages would be written on him in blood by the hand of St. George. The message said, 'Ḥakīm is healed, and he has a ministry in this house,' and it called me Amīn. My gift was casting out demons and curing diseases. In this house, any sick person, no matter what his disease, and especially those considered medically incurable, was healed. He would be healed by the baraka of the saints, and especially St. George. The Muslim would be healed, like the Christian, and it is all to the glory of God."

As in the case of Shaykh ʿIzz's story, both healing and visions play an important part in a conversion that implies a new moral lifestyle, but not new beliefs, and a new ministry endued with spiritual power. The healings effected by Elīṣābāt, Ḥakīm, and Isḥāq are all interpreted as healings effected through the power of St. George and the other saints.

An even more remarkable story was narrated by another man at Elīṣābāt's house in Mīt Damsīs, a story that testifies to the terrifying reality of evil spirits in the lives of many people: "In 1967, during the war with Israel, we used to live in an underground shelter, and

I used to pray the Psalms all the time. My relationship with God was very strong. I read from the Bible out loud, and I used to see figures who would talk with me, to the point that my comrades in the shelter thought I was dealing with Israel. One day I lifted my pillow and found one and a half piastres. This recurred for twenty days, and I told my comrades. On the thirtieth day an old man came and told me, 'Take this flower.' I refused, because I didn't want to deal with them [the jinn], because that would anger God. So I refused. Meanwhile a donkey came in carrying about twenty kilograms of gold. He told me to take it as a token of love. But I refused.

"The next day, after I had been finding one and a half piastres under the pillow, they started to take five piasters from me. That went on for forty days. Then a divining spirit came upon me, and it was the daughter of the king of the red jinn. I came to cohabit with her, and she treated me as if I were married to her and brought me whatever I wanted.

"I thought I would marry a relative of mine, so that perhaps the daughter of the king of the red jinn would leave me. But my marriage made her angry and made things more troublesome and complicated. She took me underground and showed me their kingdoms and how they lived. The situation worsened, and I couldn't find anyone to save me from this ordeal, which went on for twelve years. From my cohabitation with her I had a son and a daughter. They used to come visit me in the form of a dog and a cat. One day I let the dog in, so she told me, 'He will live with you above ground.'

"One day my wife went to the market, and when she came home and was entering the house, a dog and a cat came in with her. I knew from their odd behavior that they were my children. They treated my wife very badly. They would eat from my hand but not from hers. They would play with me but not with her. And when she washed the laundry, they tore it to pieces. They greatly annoyed her, so she complained and got so angry that she beat the dog and kicked him out of the house. He got angry and took his sister with him and left. So I started to go to a man named Fahmī for treatment. He had a spirit named Āmāl from the family of King Solomon.[43] She [the spirit] knew everything about me. She told me that since I had beaten and kicked out my son, she would convene a court for me. She went underground and the court convened. They started to question me, and I begged for forgiveness. The judge asked me, 'Why did you beat your child and throw him from the room?' I said, 'How can he be my son, when he is a dog? And he tore up my wife's clothes and threw them into the dirt three times!' So an argument arose between the king of the red army and the army of King Solomon. What is important is that God saved me. They considered me ignorant of their laws and their life.

"One day I went to a doctor, a spiritual doctor. St. George and the Virgin Mary used to appear to him. He began to pray for me, so my wife became pregnant after years without conceiving. A beautiful queen came and put her hand on my wife's abdomen, so she hemorrhaged and miscarried. I spat in her face and wept out of sadness for the loss of the child and for my wife's grief. I got up to pray, crying and asking for the mercy of the saints. When I was in front of the picture of the Mother of Light, she began to blink her eyes, and a voice in my ear said, 'I am with you.'

"One day, brother ʿAṭāllāh came and told me, 'Come, let's pray. Put out the cigarette in your hand.' He asked me, 'Do you want to get rid of your predicament and your sin?' So he took me and my wife to Mīt Damsīs, to the house of Mama Elīṣābāt. Mama began to tell me in the Spirit all that had happened to me. She hit me on the back and told me to go pray in the shrine of St. George. I stayed there for ten days. One day a cross of blood appeared on my clothes and bed sheet. St. George burnt the evil spirits. We went to my home, where there was a woman who looked exactly like my wife to me. But when she lay on my chest, I found that her temperature was two degrees higher than my wife's, so I screamed and cried, 'St. George, save me!' At once she became smoke, and I was healed. God saved me by the prayers of St. George after the torture and journey of slavery that lasted twelve years with the devil. Glory be to God and His saints. In one day He healed me."

This lengthy and—to Western minds—utterly fantastic story was nonetheless very real to the man who told it and to the others in the room, some of whom had been witnesses to some of the events of which he spoke. Popular belief in the jinn extends, as we see here, to Copts as well as to Muslims. Although the Qurʾan says that jinn can hear the Qurʾan and become Muslims, they appear to have a greater propensity for evil than humans, and trafficking with them is forbidden and dangerous. This Islamic belief is very compatible with Christian beliefs in evil spirits, of which the New Testament has much to say. Jinn, those preadamic beings of whose mischief both the Qurʾan and hadith speak, live underground and are created from fire. Hence the young man, despite his devotion to God, was exposed to danger by staying in an underground shelter, and when a jinni impersonated his wife, he was able to recognize the fraud by the difference in her temperature. The only recourse humans have to overcome spirit possession is the power of the saints. Casting out evil spirits is a major ministry of the Coptic clergy, and its legitimacy is fully recognized by the church. Elīṣābāt's ministry proves that this gift is not restricted to those ordained by the church.

Elīṣābāt herself told me the story of a magician who repented at her hands. Magic is performed through the agency of jinn, and while it confers real power, in popular Egyptian belief, it is evil. "A message came on the hand of Ishaq that we should go to the Church of the Virgin Mary in Suez. There was a man who went to that church named ʿAbd al-Malik, who worked in magic. He was deep into magic, and everyone feared him because of his power. Guidance came and said to him, 'Come close, oh chosen one. God wants you.' There were many people around. He was told a second time, 'Repent, oh chosen one.' At once he trembled and stood before me like a peaceful lamb, crying and saying, 'I repent, Lord! Forgive me, Lord!' The dove of the Holy Spirit came and descended on the gathering. ʿAbd al-Malik then took the books he had used for magic and burnt them in the middle of the street, in front of all the people. He declared his repentance and started to preach in God's name. He made people distinguish between the way of the devil and the way of God. Glory be to God!"

The man who introduced me to Elīṣābāt told her that I had a daughter and wanted to have a son. While this was true, I had not expressed any concern over this to him and was surprised to hear the matter being brought before her. She replied that she would see what the Lord had to say. She closed her eyes for a few minutes. Then she told me, in words that sounded like some biblical prophecy, "At this time next year, you will have a son. You shall name him—" I interrupted her to say that my husband and I had agreed that he would be allowed to name our next child. Elīṣābāt smiled and said, "That is fine, you may call him anything you like, but his name will be given to him by God, and it will be Mīkhāʾīl (Michael). But you must promise to bring him to me." I said that I would, although I wondered how this could happen, since I would be in the States at the time of the child's birth and had no plans to return to Egypt any time soon. When I indeed became pregnant two months later, Elīṣābāt's followers saw this as having occurred by her baraka. The following summer I had a son, and, oddly enough, my husband chose the name Michael. When he was four months old I was invited to attend a conference in Cairo, all expenses paid. I accepted the invitation, brought Michael with me, and fulfilled my promise to bring him to Elīṣābāt. Such a series of events would strike even a Western observer as uncanny, but to Elīṣābāt's followers they all substantiated her sanctity.

Elīṣābāt was quite sure that she had had a vision of me some twenty years before, a vision that indicated that God wanted me to share with her in her ministry. She offered to unveil spiritual secrets to me. At one point she grabbed my hand and cried, "You can receive the gift right now!" and remained silently holding my hand with her eyes closed for the next twenty minutes, while I sat in embarrassed silence. One of her followers, a surgeon, told me she had had a vision of St. George and the moment was opportune, and if only I had emptied my mind of all else and yielded to the Spirit, I would have received the gift. I was reminded of how frequently Shaykh ʿIzz chided me for being excessively intellectual, to the detriment of my ability to enter the realm of the spirit.

Elīṣābāt and her followers employ the same vocabulary of spiritual awareness as the Sufis. They speak of inner vision *(baṣīra)*, clairvoyance *(shafāfiyya)*, and spiritual connection *(tarābut rūḥī)*. They communicate through visions. Like the Sufis, they experience spiritual intoxication *(sukr)*. Although saints among the Copts are called *qiddīsīn* (holy ones), and refer to specific individuals canonized by the church, whereas saints among the Muslims are called *awliyāʾ* (friends of God) and are simply any individual popularly recognized as enjoying a close relationship with God, among both Sufis and Copts, saints play a critical role in spiritual life. It is by virtue of their baraka that healings are wrought, repentance procured, and lives touched by the heavenly realm.

Despite the very different perspectives of Islam and Coptic Christianity toward sexuality, some of the attitudes and practices of Elīṣābāt and her followers reflect the specifically Sufi attitudes toward the potential of spiritual individuals to have unusually free and spiritual relationships with members of the opposite sex that would normally be considered prohibited by the society at large. Ordinary legalistic limitations can be transcended by the spiritual person. One of Elīṣābāt's spiritual sons, who left college in order to live with her many years ago, until his family complained to the police that she had kidnapped their son, described the way of life in her house. "We all used to sleep on a single bed, men and women together. When I greeted a sister, it wasn't with a handshake, it was with a hug. Because the flesh had died and there was no lust, as we were living in the spirit." This is comparable to the practices of some Sufis, who sleep, men and women together side by side during the moulids and claim that they experience no sexual desire. "I used to sleep in Mama Elīṣābāt's arms," the man said, "but if I ever thought of her in a lustful way, even for a moment, I would die." I asked him why he said this. He replied that to defile a spiritual relationship by lustful thoughts constituted opposition to the Holy Spirit, "and all sins will be forgiven except opposition to the Holy Spirit."[44]

Although Elīṣābāt never discussed such things openly with me, she did urge me repeatedly to shed my hot, conservative street clothes and wear something more brief and comfortable, since what prevailed in the house was love. She repeated several times, eyeing me to see if I understood, "Love removes obligations. Amen?" Shaykh ʿIzz taught nearly the identical concept, that love is higher than the law, and that once one has entered into the transcendent Truth *(Ḥaqīqa),* there is no *ḥarām*—that is, nothing is strictly prohibited.

It is difficult to know whether Elīṣābāt is entirely unique, or simply unusual. Her own followers assured me that there was hardly anyone else like her and that the clergy believe that all spiritual powers should be confined to their own ranks. For an illiterate peasant girl, wife, and mother to have such a ministry could indeed be interpreted as bucking established authority, just as the Muslim religious establishment has some contempt for the ignorant yet charismatic Sufi shaykhs. But the Sufis, like Elīṣābāt's followers, believe the knowledge gained by inner vision is superior to all other knowledge.

That Elīṣābāt is truly unusual is expressed partly by her attitude toward Muslims, especially Sufis. She has a number of Muslim spiritual children, and she donates money toward the construction of mosques as well as toward churches.[45] She alone among all the Copts I met did not regard my involvement with the Sufis as a betrayal of Christ or the Sufis themselves as utterly devoid of true spirituality and unworthy of my attention. Elīṣābāt told me that there are "high" Sufis who also have *shafāfiyya* and know God. "Don't think that only Christians reach God," she said. "God accepts all those who love and worship Him. Indeed, many Sufis worship and love God more than we do." She mentioned a particular Sufi shaykh whom she much admired, at whose dhikr of the divine name *Ḥayy* (the Living), the entire house shook. Although she believed, as many Copts do, that the Qurʾan was composed by Buḥayra, the Syrian monk who allegedly acknowledged Muhammad's prophethood before he actually received his call, she said we can use the Qurʾan to reach people for God.

That she and the Sufis operate in a very similar mental realm was apparent from her encounter with Shaykh ʿIzz. It was an encounter they had both desired, and it took place at her home in Ḥilwān Gardens, where ʿIzz and I were invited for dinner. After the preliminary formalities, Elīṣābāt barely said a word but sat to the side with her eyes cast down, while ʿIzz conducted a lively conversation with two Muslim men who were Elīṣābāt's spiritual sons. After dinner, Elīṣābāt finally addressed some words to ʿIzz: "When did you enter into the secret?" "At age eight," he replied. She registered mild surprise, but said nothing further. They had apparently been conversing the entire time "in the spirit," and Shaykh ʿIzz told me she was also examining me with her "inner eye" to figure out my relationship with him.[46] Afterward Shaykh ʿIzz told me that she was indeed a "spirit that had arrived" at the divine presence *(rūḥ wāṣila)*, but that she "isn't really a Christian." I asked for an explanation. He said that she, like he, had risen beyond the forms of religion and that her entry into the divine presence was by virtue of her relationship with a Sufi shaykh whom she loved sufficiently to be brought into the Muhammadan presence, although she had never converted to Islam. When I later questioned her about this, Elīṣābāt laughed and replied that the Sufi shaykh had contacted her because of her fame as a healer and that she had not received her gifts through the agency of any man.

COPTS AND SUFIS: MUTUALITY AND EXCLUSION

ʿAmm Amīn, the old dervish who first introduced me to Shaykh ʿIzz, told me he wanted to introduce me to a Christian woman who really had *baṣīra,* who would be able to read my heart. I expressed a willingness to meet the woman, but the meeting was disappointing. Not only was she unable to read my heart but she lacked even ordinary discernment that would recognize that I might still be a Christian despite my intense involvement with the Sufis. When I expressed this observation to ʿAmm Amīn, he acknowledged that she had once had *baṣīra* but had lost it. A Sufi shaykh had told her in his presence that she had lost her gift because she had become attached to material things. She had not denied the truth of his words, but she did deny that Muslims could have any access to things of the Spirit. She concluded that he must have known her spiritual state through unholy means, through a jinni or a demon.

ʿAmm Amīn himself, to my surprise, said that it was true that Christian monks have more spiritual powers than Sufis. He attributed their spirituality to their celibacy. They have no lusts and live in total devotion to God, he said, and God rewards them for this. But they are, in terms of their usefulness to society, no better than a dead man if they live in seclusion.

Copts and Sufis sometimes do recognize their common spiritual terrain. Rare individuals, like ʿIzz and Elīṣābāt, may transcend the forms of their religion and acknowledge their commonality in the realm of the spirit. Yet more often the two communities, though polite and hospitable to each other, deny that true spirituality can be found outside their own. For almost all Muslims, including ʿIzz, Muhammad is the only gateway to God. The only way that a phenomenon like Elīṣābāt could be intelligible to ʿIzz was to rationalize that she had received her gifts by achieving *fanāʾ* in a Sufi shaykh, even if she did not convert to Islam. He hoped for the same for me. Copts, on the other hand, see Muhammad as a false prophet and Jesus as the only way to God. Both groups may invite members of the other to partake of their blessings, and many common people do so. Yet others see participation in the veneration of each other's saints as a grave error. One Muslim woman who went for healing to the Coptic shrine of Amīr Tādros in a largely Muslim quarter of medieval Cairo complained that her affliction merely worsened, and it was her fault for going to a Christian shrine. However, many Muslims do receive healing at the hands of Coptic priests, and Copts occasionally seek refuge in the shrine of a Muslim saint.

Some scholars see in the common Coptic and Muslims beliefs regarding the efficacy of visiting saints' tombs evidence of the endurance of ancient Egyptian beliefs concerning the life of the body after death and the influence of the dead on the fates of the living. They speak of a durable and specifically Egyptian spirituality that has proved constant through the introductions into Egypt of Christianity and Islam. The most forceful argument for this notion is by the late Egyptian sociologist, Sayyid ʿUways, in his book, *Al-Ibdāʿ al-thaqāfī ʿalā 'l-ṭarīqa 'l-miṣriyya* (Cultural Creativity, Egyptian Style), published by the National Center for Sociological and Criminological Studies in 1980. His book concentrates on the custom of writing letters to dead saints, a practice he believes to be directly descended from the ancient Egyptian practice of writing letters to the dead, complaining to them and asking them to meet the needs of the living. The letters addressed to al-Shafiʿi at his tomb assume that by virtue of his status as a descendant of the Prophet and founder of a major school of Islamic law, he presides, along with the Prophet's grandchildren, Ḥusayn and Sayyida Zaynab, over a hidden court that determines the affairs of the living. Shāfiʿī, says Sayyid ʿUways, has taken the place of Osiris as head of the hidden court. The appeal of Ḥusayn, like the appeal of Jesus, he also believes to be directly linked to the pivotal ancient Egyptian myth of Osiris. According to this myth, Osiris was martyred and cut into many scattered pieces, which were gathered and resuscitated by his sister Isis. Isis as a figure of compassionate sibling heroism resembles Sayyida Zaynab, who distinguished herself by her heroism during the massacre of her brother Ḥusayn and his family, and is credited with saving Ḥusayn's sick son, ʿAlī Zayn al-ʿĀbidīn, thereby preserving the line of prophetic descent. Belief in eternal life and eternal responsibility and that the dead affect the living are constants throughout Egyptian history. In the passage of time, according to Dr. ʿUways, the prophets and saints of the Christians and Muslims have acquired the status of the ancient Egyptian gods in their ability to intercede for the living and work miracles on their behalf.

It cannot be doubted that there is a certain amount of continuity in Egyptian religious life since Pharaonic times. It can particularly be seen during certain moulid celebrations, most spectacularly that of Yūsuf Abū 'l-Ḥajjāj in Luxor, in which the procession of boats directly recalls a similar annual procession of Pharaonic times from the Temple of Karnak to the Luxor Temple, atop which the shrine of Abū 'l-Ḥajjāj now rests.[47] Yet the moulid celebrations themselves, in their present form as all-night popular festivals, probably date only from the thirteenth century. The celebration of moulids began with that of the Prophet, as a Muslim response to the celebration of Christmas. The extension of the celebration of moulids to Muslim saints was then likely picked up by the Copts from the Muslims. The two communities have undoubtedly influenced each other, but this influence is not always a direct descent from Pharaonic practices.

That ancient holy places were later associated with Coptic and Muslim saints is extremely probable, and is a phenomenon that can be observed the entire length and breadth of the Muslim world. Goldziher cites numerous examples from Morocco to India, and notes that Egyptians were particularly tenacious in transforming ancient Egyptian legends into modern popular tales.[48] The idea that pre-Islamic holy sites have been transformed into shrines of Muslim saints has even been offered to me by a Coptic man as an explanation for the apparent miracles that have been worked at the shrines of Ḥusayn and Aḥmad al-Badawī: the miracles are worked by Christian saints who are the true inhabitants of the tombs.

The idea of a constant Egyptian personality, however, involves a great deal of romance, a romance that Sayyid ʿUways betrays in his opening lines, which are a quotation from Tawfīq al-Ḥakīm's play, *Return of the Spirit:* "Bring one of those peasants and take out his heart, and you will find in it the deposits of ten thousand years of experience and knowledge which have been deposited one after the other, and he doesn't know!" It is a theme the Egyptians love, and which is frequently discussed in the media. In this same vein, modern Egyptians find an ancient monotheism in the heretical religion initiated by the Pharaoh Akhenaton, which was immediately discarded after his death. Egypt is the origin of monotheism, say the Egyptians, even before the time of Moses.

That a certain amount of cultural continuity exists is scarcely surprising, but that should not blind us to the fact that many of the features mentioned as specifically Egyptian are also found in many other places. One could find many parallels in the religious beliefs and practices of Christians and Muslims all over the world, and one could easily find antecedents in other ancient religions. Egyptian religious life did not develop in isolation. Egyptian Sufism has been strongly influenced by Moroccan and Iraqi Sufism, and many of the major founders of the Sufi Orders in the pivotal twelfth and thirteenth centuries came from those countries. The moulid celebrations in their present form likewise appear to have originated in Syria. Issues of cultural continuity and diffusion are complex, and this book does not aim to provide definitive answers to such questions.

What we can say with some certainty is that there are many parallels in the religious attitudes and experiences of Copts and Sufi Muslims. Clerical, celibate leadership predominates in Coptic Christianity, whereas Sufism allows for many levels of formal and informal leadership by people with no links to the orthodox establishment. The example of Muqaddasa Elīṣābāt, on the other hand, closely parallels the Sufi model of informal spiritual motherhood. Coptic and Sufi practices of pursuing spiritual purity and healing through fasting and private devotions, of visiting saints' tombs, and receiving guidance through visions of saints, point to a common spiritual outlook, perhaps even a distinctively Egyptian type of spirituality, that defies the exclusivity of the official cults.

CHAPTER 12

Conclusion

Sufism in Modern Egypt

Shaykh Aḥmad Abū 'l-Ḥasan defined Sufism as the essence of Islam, and Islam is the religion of the majority of Egyptians. Nonetheless, Egyptian Sufism cherishes values that are the antithesis of those of the larger society in which it is situated. Status in Egyptian society is acquired by wealth, political influence, and education. Sufism, however, demands detachment from material things, disregard for personal reputation, and actions motivated solely by love for God, and it asserts the superiority of mystical illumination over the knowledge of the intellect. While participating in the broader culture, in many ways Sufis embrace a distinctive lifestyle and value system and nurture spiritual insights regarded as secret. For these reasons Sufism may properly be called a subculture within Egyptian society.

If it is a subculture, however, it is one with a very peculiar relationship to the wider society. Historically Sufism has undergirded much of Islamic spirituality and intellectual life, and in previous centuries Sufi shaykhs have wielded political influence and economic power. If much of the political and economic power of the Sufi Orders has faded, their spiritual significance and intellectual contributions to Islamic civilization cannot be erased from the pages of history and continue to be relevant. Many of the great Muslim intellectuals whose works are still read and quoted by the intellectuals of today were profoundly influenced by Sufism. Furthermore, Sufism continues to serve as a main cultural referent for large portions of Egyptian society, especially in the provinces. And though it may be dismissed as irrelevant by modernizers, ignored by secularizers, and attacked by fundamentalists, Sufism nonetheless continues to attract adherents from the very clientele that those groups aim to attract. Many contemporary Sufi Orders have had outstanding success in attracting educated young urbanites. These include reformed Orders like the ʿAzmiyya and the Muḥammadiyya Shādhiliyya, innovative new Orders like the Jāzūliyya Ḥusayniyya Shādhiliyya, and Orders with very traditional orientations like the Burhāniyya. Despite the lack of statistics to prove this contention, it seems very likely that the numbers of active Sufis continue to outnumber members of Islamic fundamentalist associations.

Furthermore, Sufism touches the lives of many who are not members of a recognized Sufi Order, even beyond those who have unofficially taken an oath from a Sufi shaykh. Such people range from the thousands or more who hear dhikrs performed at weddings or other public celebrations, to the many spiritually hungry people who attend religious lessons with a decidedly Sufi perspective, to the wealthy engineer at a wedding in Alexandria who said he went regularly to the dhikr of the Burhāniyya in the Ḥusayn mosque and was deeply involved in Sufism but had decided the Burhāniyya had "gone too far" and therefore declined to take an oath. For this last individual, Sufism had much that attracted him but some things that repelled him as well. His perspective is not unusual for today's social elite, who often have deep spiritual yearnings and find Sufism appealing yet cannot accept its authoritarianism.

Although this suggests that predictions of Sufism's imminent demise are premature, it is not unwarranted to ponder whether Sufism is likely to remain a viable option for a long time to come. The factors affecting the likely outcome for Sufism include the extent of Sufism's incompatibility with the requirements of modern life, the extent to which the ideology of modernism has actually succeeded in dominating thought in Egypt, and the impact of Islamic fundamentalism on Egypt, both now and in the future. Connected with all of these considerations looms the role of the government in regulating, sponsoring, and controlling Egyptian religious life.

MODERNITY, MODERNISM, FUNDAMENTALISM, AND SUFISM

Modernization in Egypt means, as in other places, a greater reliance on technological innovations in daily life, the promotion of industrialization, the bureaucratization of government and industry, the active promotion of education by the central government and its theoretical availability to all income groups, and an increasing role of the central government in all aspects of life. The scientific and technological foundations of modern life have been drawn from Western civilization, and the impact of Western civilization is felt in the proliferation of products imported from the United States, Europe, and Japan, in the availability of films and television shows imported from the United States and Australia, and in the instruction of Western sciences at universities employing textbooks in English.

But if the material effects of modernization are evident everywhere, the impact of what Bruce Lawrence calls the ideology of modernism is less categorical. The value system of modernism is derived from the ideals of the French Enlightenment, emphasizing the autonomy of the individual over and against authoritarianism, the pursuit of empirically derived knowledge without concern for the consequences, and the embrace of progressive change over and against continuity with the past, which is seen as stagnation. The optimistic expectation that scientific advances would yield improvement in the human situation carried with it the corollary that the importance of religion, which represented the oppression and ignorance of the past, was bound to recede in the face of the challenges of science.

The essential incompatibility of Sufism with modernism, understood in these terms, is obvious. Sufism is a system based on submission to authority; it upholds belief in the absolute truths of Islam, and it cares little about material improvement or economic progress. In contrast to the irrelevance of purely spiritual considerations in the modernist system, the entire ethos of Sufism is to live by God, for God, and in God.

Seyyed Hossein Nasr, the Iranian Sufi intellectual presently at George Washington University, described the stark contrasts between the two ideologies by the image of a wheel: the Sufi lives at the center, in touch with his spiritual core, the essential human nature that is the true image of God; "modern man" lives at the rim, occupied with the ephemeral, the changing, the accidental, where "the theomorphic nature of man is either mutilated or openly negated." It is for this reason, he argues, that adherents of Western philosophies feel fragmented and alienated; it is for this reason that psychotherapy, generated as it is from modern behaviorism, can never achieve the total integration of the human personality provided by Sufi training.[1] While Egyptian Sufis rarely speak in terms of finding one's center, they would undoubtedly agree with Nasr's analysis, speaking instead of the basic human need for God; all sense of wholeness derives from moving in the divine will, which is what the very word *Islam* means. All true morality and humanity can derive only from such a connection.

It is likely that the cultural relativism promoted by Enlightenment thought was never entirely embraced in Egypt, where books on comparative religion, for example, aim primarily to demonstrate the superiority of Islam. Nonetheless, the impact of European thought was evident among Muslim intellectuals in the first half of this century;[2] it is less prominent now. Faith in the advantages of a society governed by science has, of course, receded dramatically in the West as well, where modernity is often not perceived as an improvement in the human condition but as an existence, in Marshall Berman's words, "in perpetual disintegration and renewal, trouble and anguish, ambiguity and contradiction."[3] Many Muslims likewise perceive Western civilization as in a state of disintegration, producing human misery through its crass materialism and excessive individualism. The agonies and permutations of Western family life, sexual mores, and rampant crime, as well as political and economic events in Egypt itself, have led many Muslims to feel that both private and public lives are impoverished by ideologies that ignore spiritual needs. The slogan of the Sadat regime (1970–81), "Science and faith," epitomizes the insistence of most Egyptians that both Islam and science form the foundation of their present and future national life. Nonetheless, the Sadat regime did not succeed in convincing many Egyptians that it was sufficiently sincere or thorough in grounding Egyptian public life on faith. The increasing disaffection of middle-class, educated youth from the practices and mores of the government and the Westernized lifestyle of the politically favored classes, the increasingly strident calls for the institution of Islamic law as the law of the state, the fervent distribution of books and pamphlets on aspects of Islamic law that affect daily life, and the spread of Islamic dress for women are all evidences of an important national trend attempting to make traditional Islamic values central to Egyptian life.[4]

Although Islamic fundamentalism, or "Islamism," is the most obvious beneficiary of the turn toward religion since the Six-Day War of June 1967, the trend goes well beyond its borders; it has sparked revival in the Coptic Church and has also prompted some individuals to turn to Sufism. The rapid spread of the Burhaniyya in the 1970s is at least partly owing to this larger national trend. Sufism is in direct competition with Islamic fundamentalism to tap these renewed spiritual yearnings. As we saw in the introductory chapter, Islamic fundamentalism views Sufism very negatively, as promoting passivism, superstition, and the neglect of the Shariʿa, instead of social activism and vigilance against Western ideologies. The attacks on Sufism are not as frequent or as vigorous as the attacks on Western influences in Muslim society, but they are frequent and vigorous enough to prompt detailed rebuttals by Sufi intellectuals such as Dr. ʿAbd al-Ḥalīm Maḥmūd and Shaykh Muḥammad Zakī Ibrāhīm and to lead Shaykh Muḥammad ʿUthmān of the Burhāniyya to instruct his followers in methods of debate with the "Wahhābīs." Sufis take a more benevolent view of the fundamentalists, even when they are under attack: the intention of the fundamentalists, insofar as it is toward producing a godly society, is correct, even if their methods are mistaken. They will be rewarded by God for their good intentions. This attitude has long antecedents in Sufism and can be seen in Ḥallāj's forgiveness of his executors and persecutors and in Ibn ʿArabī's gracious responses to the insults of critical ulama.

Sufis share with Muslim fundamentalists, and indeed with much of Egyptian society, a common dismay over the moral condition of their country. Both Sufis and fundamentalists feel that society is in drastic need of moral reform and that much of its corruption has been caused by the introduction of Western materialism and secularism. The solutions advanced by the two groups for the moral rectification of society, however, are diametrically opposed. Fundamentalists rely on legalistic rigidity and external restraint to impose Islamic norms that will ultimately instill in people Islamic ways of thinking. Sufis, however, rely on methods of inner purification that manifests itself in reformed behavior. Though Sufis share with the fundamentalists a desire to base Egyptian society on Islam, their emphasis on sincerity of action and worship precludes much enthusiasm for its forcible implementation. Fundamentalists wish to reform society by outside imposition. The Sufis want to reform it by inner transformation. These are not, of course, always mutually incompatible goals. Many Sufis would approve of the application of the Sharīʿa and the forced removal of some of the more morally offensive aspects of contemporary society, such as bars, nightclubs, cinemas, and immodest dress for women. On the other hand, such measures would be seen as merely rectifying the appearance of immorality but having little impact on the moral regeneration of individuals or society. If effected through methods of terrorism and intimidation, most Sufis would condemn such reforms, for such methods alienate many sincere believers, who see them as un-Islamic. Fundamentalists, on the other hand, might admire many aspects of Sufi spirituality and no doubt would agree that moral regeneration of the individual is important. Ḥasan al-Bannā, founder of the Muslim Brotherhood in 1928, received his early religious training in a Sufi Order and called the Muslim Brotherhood, among other things, "a Sufi truth."[5] However, insofar as Sufis have promoted introspection and superstition and turned their backs on the great moral crises facing society, fundamentalists condemn them as irrelevant, heretical, and socially regressive. Nonetheless, cooperation between Sufi groups and fundamentalist associations in nonviolent endeavors is not as rare as might be imagined, and I encountered a number of Sufis who belonged or had belonged to such associations.

The increasing willingness of fundamentalist associations to engage in violent public confrontation with the government has recently led the latter to take a more cautious attitude toward allowing public dhikrs and moulids, for fear of attracting the open hostility of the fundamentalists. The recent suppression of the dhikrs behind the Ḥusayn mosque and by the Fāṭima al-Nabawiyya mosque might be a result of such a cautious attitude, though other public justifications are given. If such a trend continues, it could mark the reversal of a policy, in place since Nasser's regime, of permitting the public expression of these popular religious practices.

The Egyptian government attempts to control religious expression while appearing to sponsor it. This is evident not only in the institution of the Supreme Council of Sufi Orders but also in the proliferation of government-sponsored religious meetings and associations and the increasing frequency of religiously oriented television shows. The Supreme Council of Sufi Orders, as an arm of the government, endorses Sufi activities but seeks to control mysticism, which is inherently individualistic, impulsive, and uncontrollable. Ironically, the fact that Nasser sought the advice of a Sufi shaykh who was the consummate mystic indicates that he recognized the usefulness of mystical insight in political decisions, and it recalls the intimate connection of Sufi shaykhs with governments in Mamlūk and Ottoman times. In today's environment, however, the relationship between Nasser and Aḥmad Raḍwān proved controversial from the vantage points of both modernists and Sufis. A majority on both sides appeared to feel that they were best served by mutual avoidance.

Sufis rarely feel the intense alienation from society and militant antimodernism of the fundamentalists. The differences between the Sufi value system and the values of the broader Egyptian society are not sources of alienation and antagonism. They participate fully in all aspects of Egyptian society without difficulty. They rarely participate in antigovernment agitation, and often heartily endorse the moderate stances of the government on larger issues, though they may disapprove of any number of details. Some Sufi Orders are overt participants in the government by their membership in the Supreme Council of Sufi Orders, while other Sufi leaders shun such participation. But their grief over the moral dilemmas of society, which are often perceived by Egyptians to be at the root of the larger social and economic problems, rarely translates into outrage at the government or at any other sector of society.

Sufi awareness of the superiority of spiritual insight over intellectual endeavor has not made them antagonistic to secular education, nor has it prevented them from participating in the educational system with great enthusiasm. Their awareness of the need for detachment from material possessions has not made them resentful of those who possess them, nor has it prevented many of them from acquiring them, though even the wealthy among them typically shun an ostentatiously sumptuous lifestyle. Their distinctive values, which are derived from often profound spiritual conversions and experiences, are seen as a delightful secret that they are privileged to possess and share with others. Their distinctive values make them a subculture, but it is a subculture that is so central to Islam, the professed religion of the majority of Egyptians, that pious Sufis are publicly seen as pious Muslims, an example to be admired and followed, rather than as representatives of a dissenting religious tradition. It is not the individual pious Sufi who is seen as a threat but the successful, authoritarian Sufi shaykh, like Muḥammad ʿUthmān al-Burhānī, who publicly and openly disseminates Islamic viewpoints at variance with the norms of government-sponsored Islamic reformism.

Whereas a major tenet of Islamic fundamentalism appears to be that the government bears responsibility to institute morality in both private and public life, Sufis aim to transform the individual through a combination of divine grace and strenuous personal effort. Sufi Orders provide their own rules for the behavior of their members, but the behavior of people who have not taken an oath to a shaykh is of no concern to them. Their concern is the reform of the individual, not of society at large. Although ultimately this may have repercussions on the larger society—and indeed, it can have enormous repercussions if effected on a wide scale—the Sufi Orders have no more grandiose schemes for the reform of society. It is for this reason that they may be seen as politically and even socially irrelevant, despite the well-known effectiveness of their method.

THE SUFI METHOD: DOES IT WORK IN MODERN SOCIETY?

Sufi shaykhs have long been recognized as the most effective religious teachers and spiritual counselors, reaching many people who remain untouched by the network of the ulama. Sufis have been instrumental in Islamizing vast portions of Central Asia, India, and Africa. They offer counsel and healing to Muslims and non-Muslims alike, and they welcome women and the illiterate. Their method of discipleship, in which the shaykh has intense involvement with a small circle with whom he has spiritual connection and whom he initiates into the divine secrets, with the shaykh's influence radiating out in concentric circles of ever decreasing intensity of attachment, has long been recognized as superbly effective, and has been emulated by modern-day non-Sufi groups such as the Muslim Brotherhood. It is said that the famous modernist reformer Muḥammad ʿAbduh (d. 1905) believed firmly in the Sufi method of religious education and told his disciple, Rashīd Riḍā, "If I despair of reforming al-Azhar, I will take ten students, give them a place with me in ʿAyn Shams, and train them in the Sufi manner, while perfecting their education." He proposed this to his mentor, Jamāl al-Dīn al-Afghānī, when they were in Paris working on the magazine, *Al-ʿUrwa 'l-Wuthqā*. Rashīd Riḍā commented, "If the professor Imam had done what he had wished, it would have been the most beneficial thing he ever did."[6]

Does the Sufi method work in modern society? Has it changed to meet the demands of contemporary society? Many of the Sufis we have encountered through this book were raised in an atmosphere strongly imbued with religiously oriented education and social values. In previous generations, it was not unusual for most people to derive their education solely from religious institutions. Shaykh Aḥmad al-Sharqāwī, his brothers, and their father, Shaykh Abū 'l-Wafāʾ al-Sharqāwī, received their entire education in Dayr al-Saʿāda, the Sufi retreat center that Shaykh Abū 'l-Maʿārif had transformed into a religious institute. Shaykh Aḥmad's sons and nephews, on the other hand, have all gone elsewhere to study, some to al-Azhar in Cairo to study the Islamic sciences, others to secular universities to study secular subjects like engineering. Times have changed, and now the demands of society make salaried employment virtually mandatory for many people, and preparation for a career usually involves education at secular institutions. What the Sharqāwī family has experienced is but a glimpse of events that have altered lifestyles throughout Egypt. It takes more ingenuity to integrate mystical disciplines and meditation into today's pace of life in the urban environment than into the rhythms of agricultural work or the tasks of the traditional artisan. Perhaps it is this as much as the increasing materialism of modern society that led Abū 'l-Wafā' al-Sharqāwī to abandon formal training of Sufi disciples. *Khalwa,* the practice of solitary meditation that used to be routinely encouraged for disciples in the Sufi Way, is now discarded for all but the very few. Nonetheless, the sons of Aḥmad al-Sharqāwī and Aḥmad Raḍwān, studying in the university and taking up urban professions, are still practicing Sufis. Sufi shaykhs are not above pragmatic adaptation to the modern lifestyle. M., a wealthy computer programmer and former presidential bodyguard who was perhaps the only individual I encountered among the Sufis whose frenetic work schedule and lifestyle closely paralleled the hectic lifestyles typical of many overworked Americans, said that he made it clear to his shaykh at the time he took his oath that he would not be able to do his *awrād* on a daily basis. He said the shaykh understood and agreed to a less rigid arrangement than that of traditional Sufism.

Seyyed Hossain Nasr insists that, contrary to popular opinion, Sufism does not demand withdrawal from society. "The most intense contemplative life in Islam is carried out within the matrix of life within society. The Sufi has died to the world inwardly, while outwardly he still participates in the life of society and bears the responsibilities of the station of life in which destiny has placed him. In fact he performs the most perfect action, because his acts emanate from an integrated will and an illuminated intelligence." Nasr insists that the contemplative and active lives complement each other in Islam and that the methods and techniques of Sufism can be performed in any situation.[7] This optimism is warranted only if the individual has perfected that inner solitude that makes actual physical solitude unnecessary. And clearly, not all professions are equally compatible with the incorporation of Sufi spiritual disciplines. Nonetheless, Nasr challenges us to shed some longstanding assumptions about the manner in which the spiritual life must be carried out. Undoubtedly many Sufis would agree that there is a direct link between their spiritual lives and their social actions. But I have little doubt that many also yearn for greater opportunity to be physically alone with God, to perfect their ability to engage in self-examination, prayer, and meditation. The Sufi reformer Shaykh Maḥmūd Muḥammad Khiṭāb al-Subkī recommended that the godly person avoid unnecessary social contacts. He listed love of solitude and little talk as virtues.[8] However, it is more challenging than ever to be alone in Egypt, especially in Cairo, where population has grown dramatically, and it is not at all rare to find large families living in extremely cramped and crowded conditions.

As much as Sufis insist on the importance of time alone with God, they insist on the need to attend spiritual meetings and teaching sessions as well. If anything, Egyptian Sufis place yet more emphasis on the latter, for it is "sitting with a gnostic" that enables one to rise to new spiritual heights. It is also important to note that much of Sufi mystical experience has a communalistic dimension, a point to which we will return shortly. As we have seen, Sufi meetings may be formal or informal, but the associative life of Egypt is in no danger of dying out, and if anything appears to be increasing. This century has seen a rapid rise of Islamic voluntary associations, many offering classes, lessons and social services for all members of society. Sufis have also been active in founding such associations, and the mere proliferation of them has made it more and more acceptable even for women and young people to go out to lessons and activities that have a spiritual dimension. The opportunity for people to enjoy spiritual contacts has never been greater.

THE MESSAGE OF SUFISM: DOES IT SPEAK TO OUR TIMES?

Perhaps more to the point is the question of whether the Sufis have adapted their message to modern social conditions. Do they speak in an archaic language, or do they address concerns seen as relevant to modern Muslims? Often I was impressed with how ʿIzz's perspective not only on spirituality but on psychology, cosmology, and any number of related subjects appeared to reflect a worldview that had not changed since the days of the philosopher and scientist Ibn Sīnā (d. 1037). It is an impressively cohesive, mutually reinforcing worldview, but one that largely ignores modern scientific advances. In a traditional social context, ʿIzz is a learned man. He is still able to impress even very educated young people with his masterful ability to draw many disparate bits of knowledge into a coherent synthesis. New pieces of information are interpreted in light of this system, and made to conform to it or else dismissed. ʿIzz's supreme self-confidence in his understanding of the world is remarkable and to a Westerner somewhat misplaced, despite his profound intelligence and intuition. It always amazed me that in the few situations in which I witnessed him interacting with people whose educational formation was almost entirely secular, he nonetheless was able to impress them with his sweeping analyses. Whether or not I deemed them accurate or relevant to contemporary society, many Egyptians seemed to find them impressive.

But even if ʿIzz's insights and analyses are impressive to educated middle-class Egyptians, are they able to share them? Does ʿIzz represent a perspective that is ultimately bound to die out? This is a question that cannot be answered with any certainty. However, the effects of modern secular education on a religious worldview we now know to be far less absolute than previous generations had imagined. Scholars who have tried to analyze the attraction of Islamic fundamentalism for students educated in medicine, engineering and science have noted that their knowledge of the modern sciences does not affect the essentially traditional orientation of their worldview and cultural values, which have been shaped not by the educational system but by their often deeply religious home environment. Perhaps this also explains why so many Egyptians who lead essentially modern lifestyles and who were educated in secular schools nonetheless find a person like ʿIzz so appealing, even seductive. They have compartmentalized their lives, separating their spiritual yearnings from their earthly ambitions. ʿIzz, on the other hand, leads a life that appears wholly integrated, embracing a lifestyle and worldview that coheres with his spirituality. It seems likely that the number of Sufis who live in such an undented worldview is bound to diminish. But the essentially religious formation provided in the home environment appears, if anything, to be gaining in vigor. The appeal of Sufism has therefore much potential to remain.

This raises the question of whether Sufism's appeal is simply a nostalgic yearning for a simpler, more spiritual age, a refuge in which the socially deprived feel they are somehow unusually privileged by becoming aware of the shallowness of the desire for social and material advantages. It has been suggested that the austerity demanded by Nasser's Arab socialism made a virtue of the necessity of material deprivation. One could argue that Sufism does the same, that, a true "opiate of the masses," it merely removes the desire for things one could not have anyway. I believe such cynicism would be misplaced, but the lack of discontent among the Sufis might lead some critics to such a point of view. Sufism has not, however, anesthetized its adherents from the agonies of modern life, nor has it made them unaware of its problems.

Though many Sufis fail to articulate their message in a new medium, others do. Some Orders, like the Muḥammadiyya Shādhiliyya and the Burhaniyya, tackle the fundamentalists head-on. The arguments they use are based on traditional Islamic texts and do not differ substantially from the defenses of other Sufis of the past, but both their shaykhs expressed an urgency about disseminating such defenses through pamphlets and lectures, because of the new strength of Islamic fundamentalism, or "Wahhābism," as they call it. Other Orders, like the ʿAzmiyya, proselytize with energy and intelligence. Many Sufi shaykhs are able to relate the message of Sufism to the daily crises their followers meet at home, in school, and in the workplace.

Dr. ʿAbd al-Ḥalim Maḥmud, head of the Islamic University of al-Azhar in the 1970s, and therefore the most visible representative of the Islamic religious establishment in Egypt, was an ardent Sufi of the Shādhiliyya Order. He authored a fairly large number of books on Sufism, especially brief biographies of famous Sufis of the past, as well as a lengthy book on the Shādhiliyya and its founder, Abū 'l-Ḥasan al-Shādhili. Although these books are read with some frequency, the book I heard most frequently mentioned in connection with his name was the *Risāla* of al-Qushayri (d. 1072). This *Risāla* has been very influential throughout the history of Sufism, but this version, edited by Dr. ʿAbd al-Ḥalim Maḥmūd and Maḥmūd ibn al-Sharīf, has been cited with great admiration for its clarity. I have even been told that I would never understand the *Risāla* except in this edition. The reasons for the choice of this *Risāla* for publication are obvious in the introduction written by the editors. In Qushayrī's day, Sufism was threatened by antinomians within the movement and critics outside it. Both parties threatened the legitimacy of Sufism as a sound Islamic movement, the first by distorting it while claiming to represent it, the second by distorting it while claiming to understand it. Qushayrī's aim in writing the *Risāla* was, in the first part of the book, to present the biographies of great Sufis from the past who embodied in their lives the very meaning of Islam, in its faith, observance, and the loftiest morality; in the second part of the book, the meanings of Sufi terms are analyzed. Like his predecessor, al-Kalābādhī, Qushayrī presented Sufism not as a movement separate from Islam but as its very essence. Also like al-Kalābādhī, his affiliations with the Ashʿarī school of theology are very evident.[9]

ʿAbd al-Ḥalim Maḥmūd was none other than a modern-day Qushayrī. Lamenting the collapse of morals and faith in modern Egyptian society, he finds no remedy more appropriate than the production of an edited version of Qushayrī's *Risāla,* as well as the production of a series of separate biographies of the great Sufis of the past. These Sufis, he says, embody what Islam is really all about: following the counsel of the Prophet to live at all times as if you see God, knowing that even if you don't see him, he still sees you.[10]

In some respects, Dr. Maḥmūd's defense of Sufism is typical of the defenses made by Sufi intellectuals throughout the centuries. Sufism is shown not only to be compatible with the Qur'an and Ḥadīth but to be the best representation of Islamic piety. But in other respects, Dr. Maḥmūd faces problems specifically associated with the modern age, and these he tackles in virtually all of his books. The first is to show that Islam, and implicitly Sufism as well, is by no means anti-intellectual. The Qur'an makes frequent appeals to people to ponder, contemplate, and examine the evidence of God's existence and power. Citing these as evidence of Islam's positive attitude toward intellectual endeavors, Maḥmūd likewise cites examples of great intellectuals from the Arab-Islamic tradition who excelled in the sciences as well as in spirituality. He finds quotations from Western sources that state that the Arabs were the first empirical scientists. The impetus behind this intellectual inquiry and the great civilization the Arabs built in the medieval period came from Islam. But unlike Western civilization's pursuit of knowledge for its own sake, Muslims pursued it, and all things, in the name of God.

This type of argumentation is entirely typical of the concerns of modern-day Muslim scholars, who wish to prove that intellectual endeavor is not the sole preserve of the West; it is not only compatible with Islam, it emanated from it. But unlike the spiritually bankrupt civilization of the West, Islamic civilization, in its prime, preserved its spiritual values as well. In these types of arguments, Dr. Maḥmūd sounds more like a typical modern-day Muslim intellectual polemicist than like a traditional Sufi. What makes his arguments noteworthy, however, is that they are made in the context of a defense of Sufism. Although Dr. Maḥmūd defends the idea of Sufi gnosis, he is clearly making the point that Sufism is not anti-intellectual, despite the polemics of the Muslim modernists. He even cites Ibn ʿArabī as an example of one of the greatest intellects Islam has ever produced and notes Ibn ʿArabī's intellectual links with the premier Sufi intellectual of the previous century, al-Ghazālī. In contrast to the trend observable among some Muslims of distinguishing between the "extremist" Sufism of Ibn ʿArabī and the "sober, orthodox" Sufism of Ghazālī, ʿAbd al-Ḥalim Maḥmūd sees them as spiritually and intellectually linked.

The other major point that Dr. Maḥmūd reiterates in his writings is that Sufism is not a call for withdrawal from society but incorporates all aspects of life into worship. "The Messenger, blessings and peace be upon him, transformed life into worship; work was worship, and there are sins whose only expiation is the pursuit of a livelihood."[11] Dr. Maḥmūd does not focus on the criticisms various Muslims have made of Sufism—that it entails passivity, excessive introspection, withdrawal from life, and a life of beggary. Instead, he makes the positive statement that Islamic spirituality, which is best exemplified in Sufism, involves work, the pursuit of a livelihood, social action, and the incorporation of all activity into an attitude of servitude or worship.[12] This theme is evident in his individual biographies of Sufi saints as well.

The necessity of observing the Shariʿa is another major point of Dr. Maḥmūd's writings, one that is not exclusively modern but is nonetheless a necessary element in all defenses of Sufism in an Islamic context. Some of the figures he chose to write about do not at first seem to be the best examples to present for Shariʿa-abiding Sufism: figures like Bisṭāmī, who made a number of extravagant boasts about his mystical experiences and his identification with God, and Shiblī, the great lover of God and friend of Ḥallāj.[13] Concerning Bisṭāmī, he suggests that the seemingly blasphemous utterances attributed to him were fabricated by his enemies; and if not, they were said under the influence of a spiritual state achieved by rigorous self-denial and devotion achieved by very few. Bisṭāmī, in his normal state, was a rigorous adherent of the Shariʿa and indeed applied the teachings of Islam with a diligence matched by few. The message is clear: those who criticize the Sufis for failing to observe the Shariʿa have themselves never equaled them in their attachment to the law.

The role of biography in the promotion of a sound interpretation of Sufism is well known in Sufi tradition, as we see in the *Risāla* of al-Qushayrī, and this method is again a favored resort in this century. We see it well exemplified in the works of ʿAbd al-Ḥalīm Maḥmūd, and in many other sources. The Supreme Council of Sufi Orders expresses the hope that moulids will be occasions of contemplation of the exemplary lives of the saints who are celebrated, rather than occasions of disreputable activities and the mingling of men and women. A booklet on the life of Sayyida Zaynab, issued on the occasion of her moulid, was written by Shaykh Manṣūr al-Rifāʿī ʿUbayd, later chief administrator of mosques in the Ministry of Religious Endowments. This booklet takes an approach typical of reformed Sufi shaykhs: after speaking of her life, wisdom, piety, and courage, it exhorts Muslims to make the moulid an occasion of contemplation and imitation of her life rather than of simply crowding together around her shrine. This tactic was also used frequently in the teachings of Shaykh Muḥammad Zakī Ibrāhīm in the women's section of the ʿAshīra Muḥammadiyya.[14]

CONTEMPORARY SUFISM AND ITS CLASSICAL ANTECEDENTS

The extent of continuity between contemporary Egyptian Sufism and the classical Sufism that scholars typically study is considerable and belies the laments over Sufism's demise. Classical Sufism was based on the pursuit of self-examination and self-purification, rigorous ascetic practice, and daily devotions beyond the required Islamic devotions, all under the authority and guidance of a spiritual master. The cultivation of constant recollection of God (dhikr) and the taming of the lusts of the body through self-denial led to an openness to spiritual revelations or inspirations, to a mystical knowledge and insight into the hidden spiritual realm. Sufi theory on the goals and methods of spiritual progress has not changed substantially and is evident in the frequent use of traditional Sufi texts, in both written and oral dissemination. Traditional Sufi sayings and lines of poetry are frequently quoted, and clearly those who quote them believe that these lines express spiritual experiences they have shared but that they are less capable of articulating.

The theory, then, has not altered substantially, but the practices of asceticism so prominent in early Sufism have largely given way to far more moderate means of self-denial and the cultivation of an inner attitude of poverty or need of God, an attitude consistent with the teachings of Abū 'l-Ḥasan al-Shādhilī. The Sufism of contemporary Egypt does not resemble the Sufism of Rābiʿa al-ʿAdawiyya or Bisṭāmī or Junayd or Ḥallāj or even Ghazālī, so much as it resembles the Sufism of Shādhilī and his contemporaries who popularized Sufism by organizing discipleship into the institution we call the Sufi Orders. Even more similar to the Sufism of today is the eighteenth-century work about the life and teachings of the Moroccan shaykh ʿAbd al-ʿAzīz al-Dabbāgh (d. 1717). The popularity of *Al-Ibrīz* and the way in which the experiences narrated in this book resonate with popular belief regarding the miracles of the saints and the function of shaykhs in the lives of their disciples indicate that popular

Sufism in modern Egypt is closely linked with Maghribi Sufism and has not altered substantially in recent centuries.

Perhaps the most noteworthy distinction between the classical Sufism of literature and the Sufism of contemporary Egypt is the permutations in the concept of *fanā'*, or annihilation of the ego. I have argued here that the development of the concept of annihilation in the Messenger of God, and then of annihilation in the shaykh, was accompanied by a transformation of *fanā'* from a mystical state involving psychological "absence" from the world and "presence" with God into a condition of intense love and identification with one's shaykh, and later the Prophet himself. This later meaning of *fanā'* remains largely absent from the literature, not only Western scholarly literature but contemporary Sufi literature as well, which continues to quote from older sources. Some Western scholars have believed that this new focus represented the attempt of reformers to insure the transcendence of God by making the goal of Sufism union with a human being rather than with God. However, the fact that Jīlī (d. 1408), a main expositor of the doctrines of Ibn ʿArabī, provided instructions on the techniques of annihilation in the Messenger, belies this opinion.[15] Annihilation in the Prophet and in the shaykh clearly predate modern reformism and emanate not from reformist concerns but from the doctrine of the Muhammadan Reality articulated by Ibn ʿArabī. Furthermore, this is not a substitution for union with God but a means to it. Nasr appears to be speaking of annihilation in the Prophet when he says that Sufism leads to "the overcoming of the separation between man in his fallen state and man as the Universal and Perfect Man, who is in eternal union with God, because he is the perfect mirror in whom the Divine Names and Qualities are reflected."[16] The shaykh and the Prophet provide the means for ordinary people to participate in a divinity that is beyond their reach.

However, annihilation in the shaykh and the Prophet and the related concepts of "spiritual connection" and "unification" all point to an aspect of Egyptian Sufism that appears to distinguish it from early Sufism: the very communal nature of much of Egyptian mystical experience. For Egyptian Sufis (and Copts), mystical experience involves the dissolution of the boundaries of individuality, connection with each other, with their spiritual masters, with the saints and other holy personages of the past. Mystical experience grants a sense of integration and unity that goes entirely counter to the fragmentation of society and self that appears to epitomize modern society. The Sufi enters a new spiritual community and discovers a sense of wholeness and connection the society at large is unable to offer. Given the very heavy emphasis on social relations in Egypt and the agonies produced by forced separation from loved ones through the pursuit of economic opportunities far from home and the need to find scarce housing, this ability to forge new "families" and "communities" on a spiritual plane meets a need that no purely social institution can offer. This suggests that Sufism's true vitality and appeal lie beneath the surface, unlikely to die out, and ultimately incalculable. The belief system that undergirds this ability to connect spiritually with individuals both living and deceased appears not to be in any danger of collapse, as is evidenced by the very large numbers of books sold on the streets on topics relating to the interpretation of dreams and the life of the spirit after death.

SUFISM, SAINTS, AND SOCIAL CLASS

In an article published in 1976, Frederick de Jong spoke of the "proletarisation" of the visitation of the major saints' shrines, which he saw as the result of the custom of doing dhikr at the shrines of saints on their visiting days. "The slowly growing educated classes tend to dissociate themselves from these public ecstatic forms of religious expression, while social mobility tends also to alienate them from these institutions. Although this is not to say, of course, that the meaning of the saints for them in general is changing or that there would be a change in their belief regarding the *awliyā*ʾ, it has nevertheless changed their religious practice." He nonetheless notes that certain saints "are exclusively visited by and associated with the educated classes."[17]

Many middle-class Cairenes do not attend moulids because they see these as the celebrations of the lower class, and they are repulsed by the oppressive crush of the crowds and the lack of dignity surrounding many of the activities. The association of saint veneration with the poor and uneducated is a stereotype that is not always accurate but is nonetheless consistent with the role of the saint as champion of the oppressed. Despite the frequent association of practices of saint veneration with the lower classes, the cult shows no signs of dying. For one thing, the poor and relatively uneducated continue to predominate numerically in Egyptian society, and we need to be careful about dismissing as irrelevant phenomena pertaining to rural areas or the lower classes. Our models for cultural diffusion presuppose that culture emanates from the urban center to the rural areas and that educated elites set the pace for the rest of society. But as early as 1961 Janet Abu-Lughod noted that the pace of migration from rural to urban areas in Egypt was leading not only to the urbanization of society, but, culturally speaking, to the "ruralization of the city."[18] The values and practices of rural Egypt are perpetuated in the urban setting and ultimately transform it. If rural Islam is strongly tinged with Sufism and saint veneration, then these practices are not irrelevant.

Furthermore, we cannot always judge the social class of those attending moulids or visiting shrines by the clothes they wear. In Cairo it is often assumed that the *gallābiyya* is worn only by peasants and those of the lower class, but in rural areas the *gallābiyya* is universally worn by all social classes, and in Cairo Shaykh ʿIzz and I have sometimes been escorted to moulids in the Mercedes Benz of a government official or a lawyer who had changed into a *gallābiyya* for the occasion. A *gallābiyya* is simply more comfortable than a three-piece suit and is often worn in the evening, especially for religious occasions. Then again, it is not at all unusual to see people in Western clothes or people who are obviously wealthy visiting the shrines in their suits or elaborately decorated forms of middle-class Islamic dress. It is even more common to see women and girls whose dress is identical with that worn by women in Islamic fundamentalist associations. In short, dress is not always a good indicator of religious practice or belief.

THE APPEAL OF SUFISM TODAY

As de Jong points out, even if the educated classes sometimes shun the ecstatic rituals associated with saint shrine veneration, belief in the powers of the saints remains strong. Saints and Sufi shaykhs can exert a very strong appeal for the well-educated, the wealthy, and the modern. This is evident not only by looking at those who visit shrines but also by looking at the followers of contemporary mystics and teachers like Maḥmūd Abū 'l-ʿAzm, Gābir al-Jāzūlī, and Elīṣābāt Ibrāhīm.

The appeal of such mystics as Maḥmūd Abū 'l-ʿAzm, Muḥammad ʿUthmān al-Burhānī, Aḥmad Raḍwān, Ḥāgga Zakiyya, Pope Kyrillos VI, and Elīṣābāt Ibrāhīm derives no doubt from their spiritual power. It is not their otherworldliness that attracts but their ability to affect things in this world. They heal, bring about profound moral conversions, and solve all manner of problems. In a society in which many feel helpless, in which the medical establishment appears hostile or impotent, the power of the saints is accessible and culturally acceptable, and it is superior to that of medicine. Many diseases have no medical cure, but there is no disease, indeed not even death, that lies outside the range of the beneficent power of the saints for those who believe in them. In a society in which many people die suddenly of inexplicable causes, in which diseases, barrenness, and mental illness can as easily be caused by spirits as by physiological factors, the power of the saints is a refuge few in crisis would reject.

Esotericism may exert an appeal for some who have genuinely mystical inclinations, but most people are content merely to be in contact with the repository of mystical knowledge. The appeal of Sufism is not so much its mysticism as its power and the relationships that power creates. The intense attachment to the spiritual preceptor and carrier of baraka is often stronger than a person's relationship with his or her own parents, and from this basic relationship others are formed with spiritual brothers and sisters. In an increasingly fragmented society, a new type of family offers a sense of connection and place.

Sufism is appealing to many because it is tolerant, in a society in which religious loyalties are increasingly expressed as intolerance and even violence. Shaykh Muḥammad Zakī Ibrāhīm said that his association, the ʿAshīra Muḥammadiyya, benefited directly from the violence of the Muslim Brotherhood, because the fear of violent political involvement drove the spiritually thirsty to pursue their longings in safer channels. The Sufi Orders' lack of political involvement might make some see them as socially irrelevant, but it also keeps them above the muddy waters of political frays and adds to their spiritual legitimacy.

Although Sufis would be the first to admit that their ranks contain many who bring shame to the reputation of the Orders, Sufis as a whole embrace an impressive morality that makes a deep impact. The etiquette and sincerity of their interactions wield an enormous attraction that might be more convincing than doctrinal exposition. The medieval Sufi al-Ghazālī observed, during his years of searching for the truth, that Sufis were the most moral Muslims. "Their life is the best life, their method the soundest method, their character the purest character; indeed, were the intellect of the intellectuals and the learning of the learned and the scholarship of the scholars, who are versed in the profundities of revealed truth, brought together in the attempt to improve the life and character of the mystics, they would find no way of doing so."[19] It was their moral character that convinced him of the soundness of Sufism. For many devotees of Sufism today, it was likewise the moral character of their teachers that proved convincing. As Layla said, it was not anything Shaykh Maḥmūd Abū 'l-ʿAzm taught or any miracle he performed that attracted her to him but his profound selflessness. Fundamentalists may preach the necessity of a moral society, but Sufis embody it in their own lives.

In the 1950s and 1960s many social scientists believed that the influence of religion in modern society was bound to continue to diminish, as secular values provided new orientations. Predictions of the irrelevance of religion to modern society have now been demonstrated to be patently false. Technological modernization and the homogenization of international culture have not succeeded in removing religious concerns from the minds of people. If anything, they have heightened them, for cultural identity and moral values appear threatened by secular, materialistic civilization. It is among the middle-class recipients of Western education that demands have arisen in Muslim countries for the application of the Sharīʿa and the creation of a modern society that is culturally "authentic," that is, Islamic. Declarations regarding the demise of Sufism and its merger into other Islamic interpretations have also been premature. Sufism displays a remarkable vitality and a spiritual life that is very real.

It is Sufism's experiential dimension that is convincing. As Ghazālī observed during his own search for truth, "what is most distinctive of mysticism is something which cannot be apprehended by study, but only by immediate ecstasy [*dhawq*—literally 'tasting'], by ecstasy and by a moral change. . . . I apprehended clearly that the mystics were men who had real experiences, not men of words."[20] A contemporary young seeker seemed to echo that observation when she told me her story. She was an engineer who had been a Marxist and "an atheist after a fashion," who did not come from a religious family. Although she was not religious, she went to hear the moderate former Muslim Brother Muḥammad al-Ghazālī speak at a mosque, because she had heard that he was against the government. A woman who worked at the Ministry of Religious Endowments befriended her there, and the young woman gradually became intellectually convinced of the truth of the Qurʾan because it accurately described scientific phenomena. However, her real spiritual conversion came through Sufism. As she said, it was her personal experience (*tadhawwuq*, which again means "tasting") of God in Sufism that was the final proof of God's reality. Now she can no longer doubt, for she walks in God and experiences Him every day. Experience is its own internal proof, resistant to the barbs of outsiders.

The story of Muḥammad ʿUthmān al-Burhānī proves that the model of leadership he offered and the image he presented are not uniformly appealing or intelligible in contemporary Egyptian society. To some he was the greatest living mystic and a thoroughly persuasive teacher and miracle worker; to others, he was a great fraud, cult leader, and conspirator. Egyptian society today has a complexity that makes it unlikely that a single form of spirituality will be universally appealing. But Sufism is likely to remain appealing for many, even for many in the educated middle class. It is a nonviolent, apolitical alternative that is culturally authentic, promises profound moral change, and carries with it the proof of power through healing and changed lives. Its influence is often subtle and unobserved, functioning at the level of reform of the individual rather than political activism. Sufism may continue to change and respond to the pressures to reform and eliminate some of its public displays of ecstasy and nonconformity. But it is unlikely to die out.

NOTES

CHAPTER 1: SUFISM IN AN AGE OF CHANGE

1. Aḥmad Raḍwān, *Al-Nafaḥāt al-rabbāniyya,* a collection of his sayings authorized by his son, Shaykh Muḥammad Raḍwān, 48–49. The two divine sayings in this quote are from the body of literature known as *ḥadīth qudsī,* or "sacred narrative." This is a collection of sayings of God reported by the Prophet Muhammad but not contained in the Qurʾan. *Ḥadīth* refers to a narrative concerning something the Prophet said or did, whereas *ḥadīth qudsī* contains a divine saying. *Ḥadīth qudsī* is particularly important among the Sufis. See William A. Graham, *Divine Word and Prophetic Word in Early Islam: A Reconsideration of the Sources, with Special Reference to the Divine Saying or Hadith Qudsi* (The Hague: Mouton, 1977).

2. Arberry, *Sufism,* 119, 122.

3. Ibid., 123.

4. "Sufism and Pseudo-Sufism," 55.

5. Najjār, *Al-Ṭuruq al-ṣūfiyya fī miṣr,* 9, 263.

6. Ṭawīl, *Al-taṣawwuf fī miṣr ibbāna 'l-ʿaṣr al-ʿuthmānī,* 44, 47–48.

7. Interview with author, Cairo University, 27 February 1988.

8. Hujwīrī, *Kashf al-Maḥjūb of Al Hujwīrī,* 44.

9. *Al-Risāla 'l-qushayriyya,* 4.

10. Introduction to Ibn al-Ḥusayn al-Sulamī, *The Book of Sufi Chivalry (Futuwwah): Lessons to a Son of the Moment,* trans. Sheikh Tosun Bayrak al-Jerrahi al-Halveti (New York: Inner Traditions International, 1983).

11. This argument is found in many works, including al-Ghazālī's (d. 1111) *Iḥyāʾ ʿulūm al-dīn,* 4:142–43, and Aḥmad ibn Taymiyya's (d. 1328) *Libās al-marʾa fī 'l-ṣalāt,* published as *Ḥijāb al-marʾa 'l-muslima wa libāsuhā fī 'l-ṣalāt,* ed. Muḥammad Nāṣir al-Dīn al-Albānī (n.p., n.d.), 42. The famous ideologue of this century's Muslim Brotherhood movement, Sayyid Quṭb (d. 1966), likewise described the generation of the Prophet as "the age of purity most favored of humanity in all ages," in contrast with "our sick, defiled, fallen age" (*Fī ẓilāl al-Qurʾān,* 30 vols. [Cairo: ʿĪsā al-Bābī al-Ḥalabī, 1953], 2:13–14).

12. Lings, *What is Sufism?,* 123–24. Lings, *Sufi Saint of the Twentieth Century,* is devoted to the life and teachings of Shaykh ʿAlawī.

13. For example, the Sanūsiyya of Libya, a modern reformed Sufi Order,

formed the backbone of the resistance to French annexation of Chad and the Italian seizure of Libya and provided Libya with its first ruler, King Idrīs, in the postindependence period. The Mahdist movement of Sudan in the late nineteenth century likewise had roots in one of the dominant Sufi Orders of that country.

14. Goldziher, "The Veneration of Saints in Islam," in *Muslim Studies,* 2:255–341.

15. *Defenders of God,* 27.

16. Ibid., 7, 41.

17. On ʿAbduh and other Islamic modernists, see Albert Hourani, *Arabic Thought in the Liberal Age, 1978–1939* (London: Oxford University Press, 1970).

18. "Some Factors in the Decline of the Sufi Orders."

19. For a Sufi intellectual's analysis and response to such charges, see Maḥmūd, *Qaḍīyat al-taṣawwuf,* 237–38.

20. ʿUways, *Al-Ibdāʿ al-thaqāfī,* 108.

21. *Al-Manār* 7 (1904):331–32; quoted in Gilsenan, *Saint and Sufi in Modern Egypt,* 201.

22. Richard P. Mitchell, *The Society of the Muslim Brothers* (London: Oxford University Press, 1969), 214–15. Bannā's allegation that the Sufi Orders divided Muslim society into "factions" is misleading. The Sufi Orders are not doctrinally or politically distinct, but the division of loyalties among various shaykhs may well have impeded the possibility of concerted response to the challenges of modernization and European imperialism.

23. Ghāzī and al-Jidāwī, *Al-Ṣūfiyya: Al-Wajh al-ākhar,* 16–23, 62.

24. See Homerin, "Ibn Arabi in the People's Assembly." Several books attacking Sufism were on display at the Ramadan book fair in Darrasa in 1988, including a scathing book entitled *Hādhihi hīya 'l-ṣūfiyya,* by ʿAbd al-Raḥmān al-Wakīl. Some of the works of ʿAbd al-Ḥalim Maḥmūd (d. 1978), the late Rector of al-Azhar, are designed to counter such criticisms, especially *Qaḍīyat al-taṣawwuf.*

25. *Moulids of Egypt.*

26. *Saint and Sufi in Modern Egypt,* 48–49.

27. De Jong, "Aspects of the Political Involvement of the Sufi Orders," 196–97.

28. Ibrāhīm, *Al-Lawāʾiḥ al-ṣūfiyya,* 3–17.

29. *Majallat al-taṣawwuf al-islāmi,* August 1981, 6–8. "Stations" *(maqāmāt)* and "states" *(aḥwāl)* are technical terms in Sufism, referring respectively to stages Sufi disciples travel along the path and the spiritual conditions they experience on that path. By reducing this to a "science" of character and conduct, Dr. Taftāzānī tries to deflect criticism through a redefinition of Sufism in a purely ethical vein.

30. Author's interview with Dr. Taftāzānī, Cairo University, 27 February 1988.

31. *Saint and Sufi,* 7.

32. Ibid., 6, 44–45.

33. Ibid., 7 n. 1.

34. J. Heyworth-Dunne, *Introduction to the History of Education in Modern Egypt* (London: Luzac, 1938), 10.

35. Interview with Dr. Taftāzānī, 27 February 1988; interview with Shaykh Muḥammad Zakī Ibrāhīm of the Muḥammadiyya Shādhiliyya, 13 January 1981. Many ordinary Sufis likewise told me that interest in Sufism is increasing among young people.

36. "Aspects of the Political Involvement of Sufi Orders," 184.

37. *Saint and Sufi*, 66–67, 69. Gilsenan states repeatedly that multiple membership is extremely widespread in Egypt and that the Ḥāmidiyya Shādhiliyya are unique in demanding exclusive membership.

38. *Al-Futūḥāt al-makkiyya*, 2:366.

39. Ibrāhīm, *Al-Lawā'iḥ al-ṣūfiyya*, 50; ʿUways, *Al-Ibdāʿ al-thaqāfī*, 225.

40. Gilsenan, *Saint and Sufi*, 226–67.

41. *Egypt: Moulids, Saints, Sufis*, 8. This book, which consists mainly of color photographs with detailed commentary, does not pretend to be a scholarly study, but is a valuable documentary made by an avid frequenter of moulids, shrines, and Sufis. The author was a Dutch diplomat in Cairo for four years.

42. *Al-Ibdāʿ al-thaqāfī*, 86.

43. For some definitions of Sufism provided by early Sufis, see al-Hujwīrī, *Kashf al-Maḥjūb*, 30–44.

44. Literally, "the roots of jurisprudence" *(uṣūl al-fiqh)*, which according to traditional formulation are the Qur'an, the Sunna of the Prophet, the consensus of the scholars, and the systematic reasoning of qualified specialists.

45. Sufis often state this, but in fact the term *Sufism* more likely is derived from the root meaning "wool" *(ṣūf)*. The early Sufis were so called because of the coarse woolen cloaks they wore as part of their ascetic practices. "Purity" *(ṣafā')* comes from a different Arabic root altogether.

46. For an analysis of the contents of some of the Sufi songs sung by Egypt's top two *munshidīn*, Yāsīn al-Tuhāmī and Aḥmad al-Tūnī, and the implications of the vagueness of the object of love in their songs, see Waugh, *Munshidin of Egypt*, ch. 4.

47. *Al-Madrasa 'l-shādhiliyya 'l-ḥadītha wa imāmuhā Abū 'l-Ḥasan al-Shādhilī*. The same author has written a series of short books on famous Sufi personalities.

48. *Mystical Dimensions of Islam*, 56, 57.

49. According to Gamāl ʿAbd al-Gawād of the Center for Political Studies at al-Ahram, Cairo, in a paper delivered in Arabic on the Burhaniyya at a conference entitled "Modernisation et nouvelles formes de mobilisation sociale, Egypte-Bresil 1970–1989," at the Centre d'études et de documentation économique, juridique et sociale (CEDEJ) in Cairo, 15–17 December 1989.

50. In a talk with the followers of Shaykh Maḥmūd Abū 'l-ʿAzm, Cairo, 9 March 1988.

51. Maḥmūd, *Al-Madrasa 'l-shādhiliyya*, 29.

52. Graham, *Beyond the Written Word: Oral Aspects of Scripture in the History of Religion* (Cambridge: Cambridge University Press, 1987), 161, 167.

CHAPTER 2: AMONG THE SUFIS: EXPERIENCES, METHODS, AND APPROACH

1. Funded by the Smithsonian Foreign Currency Fund and the International Communications Agency.

2. Muḥammad al-Bahī, *Al-Islām wa ittijāh al-marʾa 'l-muslima 'l-muʿāṣara* [Islam and the Orientation of the Contemporary Muslim Woman] (Cairo: Dār al-Iʿtiṣām, ca. 1979), depicts Western society as dominated by brothels, pornography, casual intercourse, and the total collapse of the family and all its moral values. The book's purpose is to frighten Muslim women into accepting Islamic strictures as the only protection from such depravity and social chaos.

3. "*Sayyidnā*," "our lord," is an honorific term applied to prophets and saints, and in no way implies divinity.

4. This will be discussed more fully under the topics of *fanāʾ* (annihilation of the ego) and *tawḥīd* (unification of spirits) in chapters 5, 6 and 7. Western scholars studying contemporary Egyptian Sufism have failed to note this point. Cf., for example, Waugh's confusion over a line in a Sufi song, addressed to the Prophet, "I am from you and you are from me," *Munshidīn of Egypt*, 145.

5. According to Michael Frischkopf, an ethnomusicologist researching Sufi music in Egypt at the time of this writing, the dhikrs behind the Ḥusayn mosque are no longer being held. He asked Shaykh ʿIzz about this and was told that they were halted when the government planted gardens around the mosque, "within the last couple of years" (personal letter, 6 May 1994). Some people he met at the Sayyida Nafīsa shrine, however, told him the *ḥaḍra* had stopped after a fight had broken out there. Frischkopf also reported that for a while the *ḥaḍra* at Fāṭima al-Nabawiyya was suspended because it was suspected that it provided a scene for illicit drug dealing but that it later resumed its regular schedule on Monday afternoons. Juan Campo, another scholar in touch with the contemporary Egyptian religious scene, suggested to me in a private conversation that the government is clamping down on aspects of popular religious expression likely to be objectionable to the Islamists, in hopes of avoiding public religious confrontations.

6. Fred de Jong ("Cairene *Ziyâra*-Days") and Paul Kahle ("Zar-Beschwoerungen in Egypten," *Der Islam* 3 [1912]: 1–41) both reported a *ḥaḍra* at this shrine on Abū 'l-Suʿūd's visiting day, but by 1981 there were no *ḥaḍras* there. One informant in 1987 told me this was because Abū 'l-Suʿūd was a place for women.

7. "Cairene *Ziyâra*-Days," 34.

8. Ibid. De Jong is mistaken, however, in calling Shaykh ʿAbāṭa founder

of Bayt ʿAbāṭa, which was founded by his son. According to reports from my informants, Shaykh ʿAbāṭa died in 1941, not the early 1950s, as de Jong says.

9. In times of labor shortage in the nineteenth century, Upper Egyptian women did indeed work in the fields or in factories, according to Kenneth Cuno, Department of History, University of Illinois, but this tends not to be the case now.

CHAPTER 3: THE PROPHET MUHAMMAD AND HIS FAMILY IN EGYPTIAN SUFISM

1. On Rābiʿa, see Smith, *Rābiʿa the Mystic,* 99. On Kharrāz, see Massignon, *Essai sur les origines du lexique technique,* 302.

2. Malaṭāwī, *Al-Ṣūfiyya fī ilhāmihim,* 1:50.

3. The song is recorded on a cassette entitled "Dhikr wa madḥ fī ḥubb al-rasūl" (Recollection and praise in love of the Messenger) and was written by Wahba al-Shādhilī.

4. *What is Sufism?* 118. The complete title of the booklet is *Dalāʾil al-khayrāt wa shawāriq al-anwār fī dhikr al-ṣalāt ʿalā 'l-nabī al-mukhtār* (Proofs of the good things and radiation of light to be gained by mentioning blessings on the chosen Prophet) and was written by Muḥammad ibn Sulaymān al-Jazūlī (d. 1465). A partial translation may be found in Jeffery, *Reader on Islam,* 530–36.

5. Jeffery, *Reader on Islam,* 530.

6. Ibid., 533.

7. I use Ḥadīth, with a capital letter, to refer to the corpus of literature that goes by that name. I refer to a single narrative or report as a ḥadīth, with a lowercase letter.

8. Ibn al-Mubārak, *Al-Ibrīz,* 115–19. Despite the inherent difficulty of this book at points, it is popular among Egyptian Sufis with a more literary bent.

9. Al-Malaṭāwī, *Al-Ṣūfiyya fī ilhāmihim,* 1:52.

10. *Al-Nafaḥāt al-rabbāniyya,* 180–81.

11. Shaykh al-Dabbāgh, in *Al-Ibrīz,* 54, also says that the Prophet's body was luminous, as indicated by the fact that he could eat and drink the nourishment of the people of paradise. But in another place (115) he says that food and drink were merely a metaphor for the spiritual strength the Prophet received from God. Bodies of clay, however, cannot be satisfied with tasting spiritual light, they need food, and so all the (other?) prophets ate and drank. It is significant to note that Muhammad's own contemporaries, from the evidence of the Qurʾan, criticized him for being too ordinary, walking in markets and eating food (25:7). They clearly felt that a prophet should be more extraordinary.

12. Qāḍī ʿIyāḍ, a Maghribi jurist of the Maliki school (d. 1149–50), wrote in his book, *Kitāb al-shifā bi taʿrīf al-Muṣṭafā,* that the Prophet's urine and

He says that Muhammad's maid, Umm Ayman, drank his urine one day as a cure for dropsy and that the Prophet told her she would never again suffer stomachache. ʿAli Dashti, an Iranian scholar and statesman (d. 1980), cites this story to illustrate the lengths Muslims were willing to go in order to give Muhammad superhuman status. *Twenty Three Years: A Study of the Prophetic Career of Mohammad,* trans. F. R. C. Bagley (London: George Allen & Unwin, 1985), 66–67.

13. Zakī Mubārak, *Al-madāʾiḥ al-nabawiyya fī 'l-adab al-ʿarabī* (Cairo: Matbaʿat Muṣṭafā al-bābī al-Ḥalabī wa awlādihi, 1935), 154–55. Al-Buṣīrī (1211–1294) was an Egyptian of the province now known as Beni Suef.

14. For an example of a song on the Muhammadan attributes, see *Maʿa tahiyyāt al-ṭarīqa 'l-jāzūliyya 'l-ḥusayniyya 'l-shādhiliyya,* a small handbook for members of the Jāzūliyya Ḥusayniyya Shādhiliyya Order, founded by the still-living Shaykh Gābir Ḥusayn Aḥmad al-Jāzūlī, 169.

15. Abū Jaʿfar Muḥammad ibn Jarīr al-Ṭabarī, *Jāmiʿ al-bayān ʿan taʾwīl āyy al-qurʾān,* 16 vols., ed. Maḥmūd Muḥammad Shākir (Cairo: Dar al-Maʿārif, 1954), 10:143.

16. Nwyia, *Exégèse coranique et langage mystique,* 95.

17. Ibn Hishām, *Al-Sīra 'l-nabawiyya* (Cairo: n.p., 1955), 1:155; cited in Chodkiewicz, *Le Sceau des saints,* 81.

18. Jaʿfar, *Min al-turāth al-ṣūfī,* 1:79–81. See also Gerhard Boewering, *The Mystical Vision of Existence in Classical Islam: The Qurʾanic Hermeneutics of the Sufi Sahl at-Tustarī (d. 283/896)* (New York: de Gruyter, 1980).

19. Jaʿfar, *Min al-turāth al-ṣūfī,* 1:297–98.

20. Goldziher believed that the doctrine of the Muhammadan light was of Neoplatonic origin ("Neuplatonische und gnostische Elemente im Hadit"). Chodkiewicz rejects such theories of borrowing on the grounds that they "reject the specificity and coherence of the spiritual experience of the believers." He goes on to suggest that the idea of a prophetic light traveling through a series of prophets until its final manifestation in Muhammad is not inconsistent with the Qurʾanic presentation of a series of prophets all delivering the same message, of which Muhammad is the final seal and messenger (46:30, 2:4, 2:136). *Le Sceau des saints,* 82–84.

21. Some other ḥadīths say the first thing God created was the Pen (which wrote everything that would happen until the Hour), or the First Intellect, leading some Sufis to identify Muhammad with these.

22. *Al-Nafaḥāt al-rabbāniyya,* 177.

23. Ḥadīths consist of a chain of transmission, which is the chain of authorities who transmitted the narrative, and a text, which is the substance of the report. The soundness of ḥadīths is judged, according to traditional Muslim scholarship, by examining the chain of transmission *(isnād)* for completeness, accuracy, and reliability. A report that is given by more than one sound chain of transmission is considered best, even if there are slight discrepancies in details.

24. Ibn Taymiyya says this ḥadīth was forged but admits the form "I was a prophet while Adam was between spirit and body," which is found in

Ibn Ḥanbal's *Musnad* and Tirmidhī (Taqī al-Dīn Aḥmad Ibn Taymiyya, *Kitāb Majmūʿat Fatāwā Shaykh al-Islām Ibn Taymiyya,* 4 vols., ed. ʿAlāʾ al-Dīn Abū 'l-Ḥasan ʿAlī Muḥammad ibn ʿAbbās al-Baʿlī al-Dimashqī (Cairo: Maṭbaʿat Kurdistān al-ʿIlmiyya, 1908), 4:8, 70–71). Ghazālī interpreted the "water and clay" ḥadīth to mean simply that the Prophet's mission was predestined. *Al-Maḍnūn al-saghīr,* in margin of ʿAbd al-Karīm al-Jīlī, *Al-Insān al-kāmil fī maʿrifat al-awākhir wa 'l-awāʾil* 2:98. Cited in Chodkewicz, *Le Sceau des saints,* 80.

25. No publication data are given in the book itself, but according to Shaykh Gamāl al-Sanhūrī, it appeared in 1974. The reference is to page 9.

26. *Al-Ahram,* 13 February 1976, 12.

27. Shaykh Ibrāhīm al-Dasūqī, interview with Rajab al-Bannā, *Al-Ahrām,* 16 January 1976, 10.

28. Alfred Hüber, an Austrian scholar and former member of the Burhāniyya, allowed me to photocopy a more than two-hundred-page typed transcript of Muḥammad ʿUthmān's taped discourses. I will refer to this as ʿUthmān, unpublished speeches, and the reference here is 73.

29. Ibid., 72.

30. Ibid., 81–82.

31. *Al-Futūḥāt al-makkiyya,* 1:150.

32. The word translated here as "man" is *insān,* which has the broader, gender-neutral meaning of "human" or "humanity." I have retained the potentially gender-specific translation of the word as "man" because Muḥammad ʿUthmān is obviously interpreting *insān* to refer to a specific man, not to humanity as a whole.

33. *Tabriʾat al-dhimma,* 3.

34. W. H. T. Gairdner, "Al-Ghazālī's *Mishkāt al-Anwār* and the Ghazālī Problem," *Der Islam* (1914): 121 ff.

35. *Studies in Islamic Mysticism,* 111 n. 1. As Frederick Denny points out, *al-insān al-kāmil,* traditionally translated into English as "the Perfect Man," may be legitimately translated as "the perfect (or complete) human," because *insān* is a gender-neutral term referring to humanity as a whole. *An Introduction to Islam* (New York: Macmillan, 1985), 291. Although Ibn ʿArabī does say the "perfect human" can be a female, contemporary Egyptian Sufis believe it is always a man. For this reason, I have kept the traditional translation of this term throughout this book.

36. Smith, *Al-Ghazālī the Mystic,* 209–13.

37. Nicholson translates this as "the Idea of Muhammad," and this may convey what is meant more clearly than "the Muhammadan Reality," the more typical translation. For the Muhammadan Reality is indeed the eternal archetype, like the Platonic Idea, from which the specific exemplifications are derived.

38. *Al-Futūḥāt al-makkiyya;* quoted in ʿUthmān, *Tabriʾat al-dhimma,* 252.

39. *Tabriʾat al-dhimma,* 10.

40. *Bāʾ*, the second letter of the Arabic alphabet, is written as a very shallow bowl with a dot underneath it. *Alif,* the first letter of the alphabet,

is a vertical stroke that resembles a pole or axis *(quṭb)*. Sufi tradition assigns great mystical significance to the letters of the Arabic alphabet, seeing in them the keys to the secrets of the universe. See Schimmel, *Mystical Dimensions*, 411–25.

41. Najjār, *Al-Ṭuruq al-ṣūfiyya fī miṣr*, 280. The Prophet's illiteracy (a belief based on a possible misinterpretation of *al-nabī al-ummī* in the Qur'an, 7:157) is a point of honor, not shame. It indicates that Muhammad could not have learned the information contained in the Qur'an by reading other scriptures, and it is also used as proof of the miraculous nature of the Qur'an's superior literary quality. Given the oral nature of literature in Muhammad's time, these points may well be disputed, but they reflect popular Muslim perspectives. From a Sufi point of view, true knowledge is not derived from books but directly from God.

42. Ibid., 282.

43. Aḥmad ibn Muḥammad ibn ʿĪsā ibn ʿIyāḍ, *Al-mafākhir al-ʿaliyya* (Cairo: n.p., 1961), 105; quoted in Najjār, *Al-ṭuruq al-ṣūfiyya*, 200.

44. Najjār, *Al-ṭuruq al-ṣūfiyya*, 200–201.

45. Ibid., 181–83, 249–50.

46. *Al-Islām waṭan*, no. 19 (November 1988): 15, 56–58.

47. "Mirrors of Prophethood," 71.

48. *Al-Nafaḥāt al-rabbāniyya*, 178.

49. Ibid., 183.

50. Interview with the author, Cairo, 3 April 1989.

51. Medina, the "city of the Prophet," is the place where he is buried. Longing for the Prophet is often expressed as longing for Medina.

52. This song, begun and ended with chants of blessing on the Prophet, is very popular. I have used the text as reproduced in *Maʿa taḥiyyāt al-ṭarīqa 'l-jāzūliyya 'l-ḥusayniyya 'l-shādhiliyya*, 153–54. *ṬāHā*, the title of one of the chapters in the Qur'an, is an epithet for Muhammad. The name Aḥmad, which derives from the same Arabic root as Muhammad, is considered a variant of the same name. In the Qur'an, Jesus predicts the coming of a prophet named Aḥmad, and this is universally interpreted as a reference to Muhammad (61:6).

53. *Maʿa taḥiyyāt al-ṭarīqa 'l-jāzūliyya*, 206.

54. *Al-Nafaḥāt al-rabbāniyya*, 185.

55. Schimmel, *And Muhammad Is His Messenger*, 219.

56. Constance Padwick, *Muslim Devotions* (London: n.p., 1960); quoted in Schimmel, *And Muhammad Is His Messenger*, 226.

57. The text by al-Jīlī is *Al-Nāmūs al-aʿẓam wa 'l-qāmūs al-aqdam fī maʿrifat qadr al-nabī ṣallā Allāhu ʿalayhi wa sallam*. This text was originally in forty parts, but Muḥammad ʿUthmān says he found only parts 10 through 12. He reproduces part 10, entitled *Qāb qawsayn wa multaqā 'l-nāmūsayn*, based on three different manuscripts, in Medina, Cairo, and Aleppo, in *Tabriʾat al-dhimma*, 36–57. Brockelmann likewise says *Al-Nāmūs al-aʿẓam wa 'l-qāmūs al-aqdam* is in forty parts, of which parts 10 through 12 exist in Cairo. Carl Brockelmann, *Geschichte der arabischen Litteratur*, supplement, 2d ed. (Leiden:

E. J. Brill, 1949), 2:264; listed in the 1st ed., 2:205–6. Brockelmann did not make an inventory of the manuscripts of Medina or Aleppo. Michel Chodkiewicz of the Ecole des Hautes Etudes en Sciences Sociales has verified for me the authenticity of Muḥammad ʿUthmān's version of Jīlī's text (personal letter, 17 September 1993). Jīlī's text presents evidence that should considerably alter scholarly opinion on the impetus and origin of the concept of annihilation in the Messenger. I discuss and analyze this text and another unpublished work by Jīlī in "Annihilation in the Prophet in Late Medieval Sufism," a paper delivered at the Middle East Studies Association annual meeting, Research Triangle Park, North Carolina, November 1993. I also rely on Chodkiewicz's painstaking research to specify the date of Jīlī's death, which has been given as anything from 1402 to 1426 by various scholars.

58. *Al-Nafaḥāt al-rabbāniyya*, 179–80.

59. *Maʿa taḥiyyāt al-ṭarīqa 'l-jāzūliyya*, 17.

60. Ibid., 18–20.

61. Ibid., 20.

62. Ibn ʿAṭāʾ Allāh al-Iskandari, *Laṭāʾif al-minan;* cited in *Maʿa taḥiyyāt al-ṭarīqa 'l-jāzūliyya*, 20.

63. *Al-Munqidh min al-ḍalāl*, trans. W. M. Watt, *The Faith and Practice of al-Ghazali* (London: George Allen & Unwin, 1953), 61.

64. They are all to be found in *Maʿa taḥiyyāt al-ṭarīqa 'l-jāzūliyya*, 110, 118, and 130, but their popularity extends beyond the Jāzūliyya Order.

65. The *qibla* is the direction of prayer, which for Muslims is the Kaʿba in Mecca. While Muhammad was still in Mecca, however, before moving to Medina in 622, the direction of prayer was Jerusalem, like the Jews.

66. *Al-Amīn*, the Trustworthy One, is a title by which Muhammad was known in Mecca before he received his first prophetic revelations.

67. I.e., nearness to God.

68. The reference here is to Sura 24:35: "God is the Light of the heavens and the earth. The likeness of His light is as if there were a niche in which there is a lamp, the lamp enclosed in glass."

69. See W. Schmucker, "Mubāhala," *Encyclopaedia of Islam*, 2d ed., 7:276.

70. Ibn Taymiyya, *Ḥuqūq āl al-bayt bayn al-sunna wa 'l-bidʿa*, 10.

71. Ibrāhīm ʿAlī (Shaykh Fāris), *Min faḍāʾil wa khaṣāʾiṣ āl al-bayt*, 22; Mūsā ʿAlī, *ʿAqīlat al-ṭuhr wa 'l-karam al-Sayyidā Zaynab*, 16.

72. The Sunni collections of "sound" ḥadīths by Bukhārī and Muslim both contain this hadith; quoted in Tijānī, *Ahl al-qurbā*, 17–18; ʿAlī, *Min faḍāʾil wa khaṣāʾiṣ*, 17.

73. ʿAlī, *Min faḍāʾil*, 17.

74. Ibid., 60.

75. The word translated as "temptation" is *fitna*, which has broader implications, including "discord" and "civil war." *Fitna* is whatever threatens the unity and stability of the Muslim community, so the man's statement is potentially seditious.

76. *Al-Ḥaqq*, which is often used as a name for God.

77. ʿAlī, *Min faḍāʾil,* 60.

78. Ibid.

79. Ḥadīth from Tirmidhī; quoted in ʿAlī, *Min faḍāʾil,* 65, and in Tījānī, 19.

80. ʿAlī, *Min faḍāʾil,* 16; Sharaf al-Dīn, *Al-Sayyida Nafīsa,* 14.

81. Ibrāhīm ʿAlī commends ʿUmar for his desire to be related by marriage to Muhammad, 25; Tījānī even affirms "our lord" Muʿāwiya as a legal scholar, and emphasizes that "one must think well of the Companions," 44. Ḥasan Kāmil al-Malaṭāwī writes that ʿAlī Zayn al-ʿĀbidīn, the son of Ḥusayn, rejected the condemnation of the first three caliphs and told the Muslims to "love us with the love of Islam, and do not exalt us above our right," and that his son, Muḥammad al-Bāqir, insisted on honoring Abū Bakr and ʿUmar. *Al-Ṣūfiyya fī ilhāmihim,* 2:93, 96.

82. Hodgson, "How Did the Early Shiʿa Become Sectarian?" 2. In my article, "Devotion to the Prophet and His Family," I compare aspects of devotional practices and beliefs regarding the Prophet and the *ahl al-bayt* in Egyptian and Shiʿi Islam and note points of ideological and historical contact between the traditions.

83. ʿAlī, *Min faḍāʾil,* 27–28.

84. Ibid., 29.

85. Ḥadīths from al-Ṭabarānī, al-Ḥakīm, al-Bayhaqī and al-Daylamī; quoted in ʿAlī, *Min faḍāʾil,* 31.

86. ʿAlī, *Min faḍāʾil,* 22; Abū ʿAlam, *Ahl al-bayt, 1: Fāṭima al-Zahrāʾ,* 73. According to the latter, Fāṭima possessed all the attributes of the angels and the *ḥūrīs*, the ever-virgin wives of the righteous in Paradise.

87. Tījānī, 20–23.

88. ʿAlī, *Min faḍāʾil,* 109; Ibn Taymiyya, *Ḥuqūq āl al-bayt,* 31.

89. ʿAbd al-ʿAlīm, *Sayyidnā 'l-Imām al-Ḥusayn,* 3–4.

90. This is not the typical Muslim interpretation of the denial of Jesus' crucifixion. Most Muslims believe that God would not allow His righteous prophet to suffer death but lifted him to heaven and replaced him with someone else who was made to look like him and who was crucified in his stead. Speculation as to the identity of that person includes Simon of Cyrene and Judas Iscariot. But for most Muslims, Jesus was very much flesh and blood. ʿIzz's interpretation of the unreality of Jesus' crucifixion is reminiscent of Gnostic and Docetan beliefs rejected by orthodox Christians.

91. The correspondence between Mary and Fāṭima, and between Jesus and Ḥusayn, was also a theme in early Shiʿism. Ayoub, *Redemptive Suffering in Islam,* 35–36.

92. *Ḥuqūq āl al-bayt,* 30.

93. Rāgib, "Al-Sayyida Nafīsa," 61.

94. This is the subject of a famous novel by Yaḥya Ḥaqqī, *Qandīl Umm Hāshim,* published in 1944 and translated as *The Saint's Lamp.*

95. See Ḥaqqī, *Saint's Lamp,* 9–10.

96. *Al-Ṣaḥīfa 'l-sajjādiyya,* translated by William C. Chittick as *The Psalms of Islam* (New York: Oxford University Press, 1989).

97. *La cité des morts au Caire, Bulletin de l'Institut Français d'Archeologie Orientale* 57 (1958): 78; quoted in Rāgib, "Al-Sayyida Nafīsa," 64.

98. Rāgib, "Al-Sayyida Nafīsa," 65–81.

99. Ibid., 61, 63. Rāgib adds (64) that there are authentic ʿAlid tombs in Cairo that are largely ignored.

100. Sharaf al-Dīn, *Al-Sayyida Nafīsa*, 110, 116–17.

101. ʿAlī, *Min faḍāʾil*, 26.

102. Abū ʿAlam, *Ahl al-bayt*, 9.

103. Sharaf al-Dīn, *Al-Sayyida Nafīsa*, 7.

104. ʿAlī, *Min faḍāʾil*, 118–19.

105. Ibid., 6.

106. For example, the commentary given by the Pakistani, A. Yusuf Ali, in his translation of the Qurʾan, *The Meaning of the Glorious Qurʾan* (Cairo: Dār al-kitāb al-miṣrī, n.d.), 2:1312 n. 4560.

107. The Egyptian Qurʾan exegete Ibn al-Khaṭīb, *Awḍaḥ al-tafāsīr* (Cairo: Al-Maṭbaʿa 'l-miṣriyya wa-maktabatuhā, ca. 1935), 594, says that although love for the Prophet's family is an obligation on all believers, this is not meant by the verse because it would imply a reward for delivering the message.

108. Ibrāhīm, *Al-tabṣīr bi mushāhid shahīrāt āl al-bayt*, 5–6; Abū ʿAlam, *Ahl al-bayt*, 9; Ṣayfī, "Manzilat al-rasūl bayn al-rusul wa 'l-wājib ʿalā 'l-umma naḥwahu," 58; ʿAlī, *Min faḍāʾil*, 46.

109. Cited in ʿAlī, *Min faḍāʾil*, 44.

110. ʿAlī, *Min faḍāʾil*, 6.

111. ʿAlī, *ʿAqīlat al-ṭuhr*, 10–11.

112. Al-Ṭabarānī, *Al-Muʿjam al-kabīr*, Ibn Ḥabbān, *Al-Ṣaḥīḥ*, al-Bayhaqī, and Abū 'l-Shaykh; quoted in ʿAlī, *ʿAqīlat al-ṭuhr*, 10.

113. Abū Bakr al-Khwārizmī, *Al-Manāqib;* in ʿAlī, *Min faḍāʾil*, 24.

114. ʿAlī, *Min faḍāʾil*, 23.

115. ʿAlī, *ʿAqīlat al-ṭuhr*, 19.

116. Ibid., 8.

117. ʿAlī, *Min faḍāʾil*, 166.

118. *Al-ʿurwa 'l-wuthqā*, "the most trustworthy handhold," is found in two verses in the Qurʾan: "Whoever rejects evil and believes in God has grasped the most trustworthy handhold that never breaks" (2:256), and "Whoever submits his whole self to God and does good has indeed grasped the most trustworthy handhold" (31:22). Although there is nothing in these verses to indicate that this expression refers to the *ahl al-bayt*, they are frequently called "the most trustworthy handhold."

119. *Min faḍāʾil*, 6.

120. The words are actually *"Allāh, Allāh, Allāh, Allāh ʿalā nūr Allāh!"* which literally means "Allah, Allah, Allah. Allah on the light of God!" In the Egyptian dialect, "Allah!" is a cry of exquisite admiration, so I have translated the repeated refrain of "Allah, Allah on . . ." rather inadequately as "how wonderfully beautiful," in order to capture the intended meaning.

121. *Maʿa taḥiyyāt al-ṭarīqa 'l-jāzūliyya*, 116.

122. For example, in their criticism of Muḥammad ʿUthmān al-Burhānī, Shaykh Muḥammad al-Suṭūhī of the Supreme Council of Sufi Orders and Shaykh Ibrāhīm al-Dasūqī of the Ministry of Religious Endowments both accused him of propagating Shiʿi doctrines, specifically the deification of ʿAlī, an emanationist philosophy of creation, and the return of the Mahdī (*Al-Ahrām*, 9 January 1976, 10; 16 January 1976, 10).

123. *Min faḍāʾil*, 10, 164.

124. Malaṭāwī, *Al-ṣufiyya fī ilhāmihim*, 1:61. Boasting of a reckless love for which one has been reproached is a theme in pre-Islamic Arabian poetry that has been utilized by Sufi poets such as ʿUmar ibn al-Fāriḍ (d. 1235). See Nicholson, *Studies in Islamic Mysticism*, 179.

125. Bannerth, "La Rifāʿiyya en Egypte," 7.

126. *Maʿa taḥiyyāt al-ṭarīqa 'l-jāzūliyya*, 124.

127. Raḍwān, *Al-Nafaḥāt al-rabbāniyya*, 231.

128. Ibid., 190.

129. According to Michael Winter, this practice has its origin in the formation of family Orders in the fifteenth and sixteenth centuries. *Society and Religion in Early Ottoman Egypt*, 137.

CHAPTER 4: THE SAINTS: BEARERS OF THE PROPHETIC LIGHT

1. Tirmidhī's tenth-century collection of Ḥadīth is one of the six "canonical" collections recognized by Sunni Muslims. Tirmidhī is also the author of an important work, *Khātam al-Awliyāʾ* (Seal of the Saints). The ḥadīth is cited in Māhir, *Karamāt al-awliyāʾ*, 57–58.

2. *Al-Risāla 'l-qushayriyya*, 200–201.

3. Recorded by al-Bukhārī. This ḥadīth is included in Ezzeddin Ibrahim and Denys Johnson-Davies, trans., *Forty Ḥadīth Qudsī* (Beirut: Dār al-Qurʾān al-Karīm, 1980), 104–5.

4. See Hermann Landolt, "Walāyah," *The Encyclopedia of Religion*, 16 vols., ed. Mircea Eliade et al. (New York: Macmillan, 1987), 15:316–23.

5. *Al-Ḥukūma 'l-bāṭiniyya*, 145.

6. *Al-Nafaḥāt al-rabbāniyya*, 25, 34, 35.

7. *Al-Risāla 'l-qushayriyya*, 201, 276.

8. *Saint and Sufi in Modern Egypt*, 45.

9. Abū Nuʿaym al-Iṣfahānī (d. 1038), in his ten-volume *Ḥilyat al-awliyāʾ*, offers 689 biographies of Sufi saints, whose hiddenness is emphasized. Chodkiewicz, *Le Sceau des saints*, 52–53.

10. *Al-Nafaḥāt al-rabbāniyya*, 35.

11. Sharqāwī, *Al-Ḥukūma 'l-bāṭiniyya*, 89.

12. *Al-Nafaḥāt al-rabbāniyya*, 27, 39.

13. G. E. von Grunebaum, "The Place of Parapsychological Phenomena

in Islam," in *Malik Ram Felicitation Volume,* ed. S. A. J. Zaidi (New Delhi: The Printsman, 1972), 83.

14. Winter, *Society and Religion in Early Ottoman Egypt,* 185. The quote is from Ibrāhīm al-Matbūlī, although Winter says other Sufis are quoted as saying this as well.

15. Sharqāwī, *Al-Ḥukūma 'l-bāṭiniyya,* 207–8.

16. Chodkiewicz, *Le Sceau des saints,* 73.

17. Shaʿrānī, *Al-yawāqīt wa 'l-jawāhir,* 2:78ff; quoted in Māhir, *Karamāt al-awliyā',* 71–73, and Sharqāwī, *Al-Ḥukūma 'l-bāṭiniyya,* 44.

18. Muḥyī 'l-Dīn Ibn ʿArabī, *Kitāb manzil al-quṭb wa maqāmuhu wa ḥāluhu* (Hyderabad, India: Maṭbaʿat jamʿiyyat dā'irat al-maʿārif al-ʿuthmāniyya, 1948), 2; included in *Rasā'il Ibn al-ʿArabī.*

19. On Ibn ʿArabī's understanding of sainthood and its hierarchy, the best source is Chodkiewicz, *Le Sceau des saints.*

20. *Mudhakkirat al-murshidīn wa 'l-mustarshidīn,* 37–40. Fred de Jong comments, "In some mystical traditions, those belonging to the saintly hierarchy, including the *ḳuṭb,* are held to be identical with the serious mystical teachers present at a certain time but whose spiritual rank remains undivulged to those outside this hierarchy. This tenet may imply the belief that potentially everybody can become *ḳuṭb* by means of following the *ṭarīḳa,* i.e. by means of the method prescribed by a distinct mystical tradition" ("Al-Ḳuṭb," 546).

21. It may seem impossible for there to be more than one *quṭb* in the sense of axis, and that is true if one is talking of the Axis of the Age, the pivot on which the whole world turns. Ibn ʿArabī, however, also spoke of each region and indeed each village or town having its own *quṭb,* as well as speaking of the *quṭb,* or highest representative, of each particular spiritual station.

22. *Al-Nafaḥāt al-rabbāniyya,* 270.

23. Sharqāwī, *Al-Ḥukūma 'l-bāṭiniyya,* 26–27.

24. Māhir, *Karamāt al-awliyā',* 90.

25. Ibid., 91.

26. "Veneration of Saints in Islam," 286.

27. Kalābādhī, *Doctrine of the Sufis,* 58.

28. Nwyia, *Ibn ʿAṭā' Allāh (m. 709/1309),* 35. I do not mean in any way to undermine Père Nwyia's high estimation of the beauty and wisdom of Ibn ʿAṭā' Allāh's aphorisms, or even to deny that they may be considered miraculous, but merely wish to point out the inappropriateness of judging this the last Sufi miracle ever to be performed in Egypt.

29. *Manners and Customs of the Modern Egyptians,* 445–47.

30. *Egypt: Moulids, Saints, Sufis,* 162. Photographs appear on 160–64.

31. "Cairene *Ziyâra*-Days," 34 n. 28.

32. The young man was something of a show-off throughout the moulid celebration, trying to function as a master of ceremony. However, it was obvious that the intended demonstration of immunity to pain in his case

was unsuccessful. Although he did not bleed, the skin around the pin became increasingly red, in an ever-widening circle, and the man's bravado rapidly faded and was replaced by evident pain. Shaykh ʿIzz told me that if the man had "killed his ego," he would not have felt any pain.

33. *Egypt*, 162.

34. Annemarie Schimmel quotes a hadith to the same effect: "Miracles are the menstruation of men" (*Mystical Dimensions of Islam*, 212). Schimmel's book has an excellent section on the miracles of saints and attitudes toward them, 205–13.

35. Interview with the author at his home in Najʿ Ḥammādī, 11 November 1988.

36. Ghāzī and Jidāwī, *Al-Ṣūfiyya: al-wajh al-ākhar*, 22.

37. Mernissi, "Women, Saints, and Sanctuaries," 105. In a somewhat contradictory fashion, the author goes on to discuss the spiritual significance of the shrine with reference to Eliade's ideas of sacred space. It is not clear whether "religious space" means something different to her than "sacred space."

38. In this respect, Egyptian houses cannot be considered "sacred" spaces, although they are "sacred" in some other respects, as discussed in Juan Campo's admirable book, *The Other Sides of Paradise: Explorations into the Religious Meanings of Domestic Space in Islam* (Columbia: University of South Carolina Press, 1991). Houses are sacred spaces not mainly in the sense that they are the locus of contact between God and humanity but in the sense that they are inviolate. The term *ḥurma* has this sense, as does *ḥarīm*—a term meaning either women or the place where women live—and *al-masjid al-ḥarām*, the "sacred mosque" which is the Kaʿba. Houses, it is true, are also places of worship and baraka, but they are not primarily places of spiritual power or the God-human connection. Campo points out that the Qurʾan frequently speaks of prayer in houses and speaks of "house" to apply to places of worship like the Kaʿba. But the fact that prayer is said in houses does not make houses a "sacred space," because in Islamic belief, according to a hadith, one of the distinctions of Muhammad from other prophets is that "all the earth has been given to me as a mosque/place of prayer." This indicates the lack of centralization and sanctity required for a mosque—but not for a shrine. As Campo says, the "sanctity" or inviolability of houses derives from their association with women. But that very association, I contend, forces us to recognize that *ḥurma* here has to do with inviolability, not holiness, for the presence of women, as I will argue later in this book, is often thought to have a desacralizing effect. Houses are associated, of course, not only with the presence of women but with the conjugal act. Although the conjugal act has been called an "alms" in a ḥadīth, and some contemporary polemicists wishing to emphasize conjugal duties even call it an act of worship, no one would say that such an act should be performed in a "holy" place, whether a mosque or a shrine.

39. Fuchs, "Mawlid," 420.

40. Ibn Khallikan, cited in Fuchs, "Mawlid," 420.

41. *Muhammadan Festivals* (New York, 1951), 73.

42. Cornell, "Mirrors of Prophethood," 559–60; Muhammad Umar Memon, *Ibn Taimīya's Struggle against Popular Religion* (The Hague: Mouton, 1976), 2.

43. Some scholars say that Copts celebrate moulids on the date of death and Muslims celebrate the date of birth, but in fact both groups normally celebrate the moulid on the date of death. Some of the prominent members of *ahl al-bayt* are given a moulid on the date of death and a separate "birthday" celebration *(ʿīd al-mīlād)* on the date of birth. Both celebrations feature dhikr at the saint's shrine, but the birthday celebration is confined to Sufi circles for the most part, whereas moulids are major popular festivals.

44. *ʿUrs* is also the term used in Pakistan for saint's day celebrations that are remarkably similar to moulids.

45. On the Abū 'l-Ḥajjāj moulid, see the beautiful film made by Elizabeth Wickett, *For Those Who Sail to Heaven* (Icarus Films, 1989).

46. For a complete description of the activities taking place at the moulids, see Biegman, *Egypt*, 13–24, which is followed by a beautiful series of colored photographs of the moulids, with full commentary.

47. *Saint and Sufi in Modern Egypt*, 50.

48. Ibn Taymiyya's essay is reproduced in *Al-Manār* 25 (1924–25): 357–66.

49. Lane, *Manners and Customs*, 425–26.

50. The Wahhābī movement, which began in the eighteenth century in west-central Arabia, was a militant reform movement that particularly targeted saint veneration and the Sufi Orders and led eventually to the establishment of the Kingdom of Saudi Arabia in 1932. Sufis in Egypt tend to use the term *Wahhābīs* to describe any who follow their ideology.

51. *Qaḍāya 'l-wasīla wa 'l-qubūr*, 5.

52. Ibid., 8–14. Farīd Māhir also denies that the intention of the petitioner is to pray to the saint, regardless of the wording he uses, and emphasizes that in Islam, deeds are judged by their intentions (*Karamāt al-awliyāʾ*, 89).

53. Abū ʿAbd Allāh Muḥammad al-Bukhārī, *Ṣaḥīḥ al-Bukhārī*, ed. L. Krehl (vols. 1–3) and Th. W. Juynboll (vol. 4) (Leiden: E. J. Brill, 1862–68, 1907/08), book 64, chaps. 8, 12.

54. *Qaḍāya 'l-wasīla wa 'l-qubūr*, 19–20. Cf. Smith, "Concourse between the Living and the Dead."

55. *Qaḍāya*, 34–35.

56. Ibid., 38.

57. Shaykh ʿIzz used a similar argument. However, he clearly believed that *maqām Ibrāhīm*, the "place where Abraham stood," was actually his burial place, because the term *maqām* in Egypt is used for the shrine-tomb of a saint. When I pointed out that a site in Hebron is held to be the burial place of Abraham, he replied that that was merely symbolic and that the real burial place was by the Kaʿba.

58. Ibrāhīm, *Qaḍāya*, 40–45.

59. Ibid., 47.

CHAPTER 5: THE SUFI ORDERS

1. *Mudhakkirat al-murshidīn,* 57. This use of the term "Imām of the age" is strongly reminiscent of Shiʿism, as is the urgency of finding him. One is reminded of the Shiʿi ḥadīth, "He who dies without knowing the Imām of his age dies the death of an unbeliever."

2. Ibid., 62.

3. *Al-Nafaḥāt al-rabbāniyya,* 95.

4. Ibid., 39.

5. Ibid., 181–82.

6. Ibid., 38–39.

7. Ibid., 53.

8. Ibid.

9. Ibid., 53.

10. Al-Malaṭāwī, *Al-Ṣūfiyya fī ilhāmihim,* 1:142.

11. *Mudhakkirat al-murshidīn,* 115–16.

12. *Maʿa taḥiyyāt al-ṭarīqa 'l-jāzūliyya,* 3.

13. *Mudhakkirat al-murshidīn,* 132–33.

14. *Al-Ṣūfiyya fī ilhāmihim,* 1:151–52.

15. *Miṣbāḥ al-arwāḥ,* 4–5.

16. "La Rifaʿiyya en Egypte," 11.

17. Ibn Saʿd, *Biographien Muhammeds, seiner gefaehrten under der spaeteren Traeger des Islams bis zum Jahre 230 der Flucht (Al-Ṭabaqāt al-kubrā),* 9 vols., ed. Eduart Sachau et al. (Leiden: E. J. Brill, 1904–40), 8:1ff, 8:2.

18. Nabia Abbott, "Women and the State in Early Islam," *Journal of Near Eastern Studies* 1 (1942): 118.

19. Edward Lane wrote in 1836, "It is a common custom for a man to kiss the hand of a superior (generally on the back only, but sometimes on the back and front), and then to put it to his forehead, in order to pay him particular respect: but in most cases the latter does not allow this, and only touches the hand that is extended toward his: the other person, then, merely puts his own hand to his lips and forehead" (*Manners and Customs,* 205). It was not long ago in Egypt that a son habitually kissed the hand of his father.

20. *Karamāt al-awliyāʾ,* 18.

21. I must admit that on the entire subject of the numerical value and meaning of the letters of the Arabic alphabet, I remain largely in the dark, despite some brief effort by Shaykh ʿIzz to introduce me to this subject. The entire secret of the universe is thought to be contained in the detached mysterious letters that are found at the beginning of a number of chapters in the Qurʾan, so this topic is never divulged in full to novices. It may well be that my own cultural background makes it difficult for me to appreciate this type of cabalism or that I was deliberately made to feel confused in order to force me to acknowledge that Shaykh ʿIzz knew far more than I about the meaning of the universe. Annemarie Schimmel has an appendix

on "Letter Symbolism in Sufi Literature" in *Mystical Dimensions*, 411–25. Part of the reason *Al-Ibrīz* was recommended to me as an introduction to the deeper teachings of Sufism was its emphasis on teaching letter symbolism, although, again, I found these passages difficult to understand.

22. *Miṣbāḥ al-arwāḥ*, 8, 10.

23. Ibid., 10, 12–13.

24. Ibid., 25.

25. *Al-Ṣūfiyya fī ilhāmihim*, 1:262–63.

26. Shaykh Maḥfūẓ, of the Fāsiyya Shādhiliyya Order, speaking at the moulid of Ḥāgga Zakiyya at her *sāḥa* near the shrine of Abū 'l-Ḥasan al-Shādhili, October 1988.

27. Malaṭāwī, *Al-Ṣūfiyya fī ilhāmihim*, 1:148–49.

28. This positive attitude toward family is by no means unanimous among Sufis. In early Sufism in particular, some Sufis regarded a family as an obstacle to concentration on God.

29. *Miṣbāḥ al-arwāḥ*, 14–15.

30. *Al-Ṣūfiyya fī ilhāmihim*, 1:38–39.

31. Ibid., 1:264.

32. An anonymous reviewer for my article, "Devotion to the Prophet and His Family in Egyptian Sufism," when it was under consideration for publication in the *International Journal of Middle East Studies*, wrote in his comments that "no Sufi Order in Egypt today teaches annihilation *(fanā')* in the Prophet." This comment is simply wrong, and I reproduce it here simply to deflect any potential criticism that I have reproduced rare or extremist points of view. I have heard it taught by shaykhs from the Rifāʿī, Shādhilī, and Khalwatī Orders, all mainline Orders in Egyptian Sufism. If I asked shaykhs about it directly at our first meeting, they were often reluctant to discuss it until Shaykh ʿIzz had assured them that I was already initiated into this secret. In other words, it is not something that is publicized outside the Orders, and for the masses of Sufis it is enough that they simply receive some spiritual edification from their shaykh and love him. *Fanā'* in the Prophet is reserved for those who have real spiritual potential, for once one has *fanā'* in the Prophet, one has no further need for one's shaykh. The Sufis are not unaware of how such doctrines are regarded outside the Orders.

33. *Al-Ibrīz*, 30–31.

34. See Schimmel, *Mystical Dimensions*, 237.

35. Ibn ʿIyāḍ, *Al-Mafākhir al-ʿaliyya*, 77; cited in Najjār, *Al-Ṭuruq al-ṣūfiyya fī Miṣr*, 35.

36. *Al-Risāla 'l-Qushayriyya*, 259.

37. *Mudhakkirat al-murshidīn*, 78–79.

38. *Saint and Sufi in Modern Egypt*, 39–40.

39. *Mudhakkirat al-murshidīn wa 'l-mustarshidīn*, 36–37.

40. *Sufi Saint of the Twentieth Century*, 71 n. 3.

41. The word *adab* also has the entirely different meaning of literature, prompting some Sufis to say that the *adab* of this world is poetry and the

like, whereas the *adab* of the Sufi is the morals of the Prophet. One Sufi defined *adab* as observing proper courtesy and reverence with God, in secret and in public, adding, in a deliberate pun, "If you do this, you are an *adīb* [usually, a master of Arabic belles-lettres], even if you are not an Arab" (Qushayrī, *Al-Risāla 'l-qushayriyya*, 220).

42. Ibid., 220.
43. Kuḥayl, *Abū 'l-ʿAynayn al-Dasūqī*, 90.
44. *Miṣbāḥ al-arwāh*, 30.
45. Malaṭāwī, *Al-Ṣūfiyya fī ilhāmihim*, 1:93–94.
46. Ibn al-Mubārak, *Al-Ibrīz*, 44.
47. *Al-Nafaḥāt al-rabbāniyya*, 54, 47.
48. Sharqāwī, *Al-Ḥukūma 'l-bāṭiniyya*, 30.
49. Ibid., 254.
50. *Al-Nafaḥāt al-rabbāniyya*, 23.
51. *Maʿa taḥiyyāt al-ṭarīqa 'l-jāzūliyya*, 6.
52. Ibid., 7–11.
53. *Mudhakkirat al-murshidīn*, 40–46.
54. *Miṣbāḥ al-arwāḥ*, 16–30. The metaphor of the brethren being a single body recalls the first epistle of St. Paul to the Corinthians, chapter 12, but it is also based on sayings of the Prophet Muhammad: "The believers are like a single man—if his eye is in pain, all of him is in pain. If his head is in pain, all of him is in pain." "Believers are like a building with each other, each strengthening the other." These hadiths are both recorded in the *Ṣaḥīḥ* by Muslim.
55. *Al-Nafaḥāt al-rabbāniyya*, 54–55.
56. Abū 'l-Wafā al-Ghunaymī al-Taftāzānī, "Al-Taṣawwuf fī miṣr fī 'l-ʿaṣr al-ḥadīth" (paper presented at conference in Turkey, 17 September 1985).
57. *Al-Nafaḥāt al-rabbāniyya*, 56.
58. *Mudhadkkirat al-murshidīn*, 100.
59. Tāhā Ḥusayn, *Al-Ayyām*, 1:88–96; cited in Gilsenan, *Saint and Sufi in Modern Egypt*, 67.
60. Seyyed Hossain Nasr makes a similar argument in *Islam and the Plight of Modern Man*, 141.

CHAPTER 6: FOUNDATIONS OF THE SUFI PATH

1. Abū 'l-ʿAzāʾim, *Mudhakkirat al-murshidīn*, 49.
2. Ibid., 49–50.
3. Ibid., 75–76.
4. *Karamāt al-awliyāʾ*, 18.
5. Schimmel, *Mystical Dimensions of Islam*, 48.
6. The association of heavens with spiritual stages does not mean, however, according to Shaykh ʿIzz, that the prophets Muhammad met in the lower heavens were spiritually less advanced than those he met in the upper heavens. That, he said, was simply a matter of habitation, not of

spirituality, and indeed some of those in the lower heavens may be of a higher rank than those in the upper heavens.

7. *Karamāt al-awliyā'*, 22–23.

8. ʿUmar ibn al-Fāriḍ is the Egyptian Sufi poet (d. 1235) whose poems are more frequently sung by Sufi singers in Egypt today than any other's.

9. Anyone acquainted with the Persian meaning of *darwīsh* as "poor man" would find this explanation of the meaning of the word laughable. *Wish* is the colloquial Egyptian word for "face," which in classical Arabic is *wajh*. When I pointed out the true derivation of the word, ʿIzz had no problem incorporating this into his explanation, because the Arabic equivalent, *faqīr*, is also used in Sufi circles to mean one who is "poor toward God," that is, recognizing that his true life exists only in God. Since taking refuge in God indeed incorporates this idea of poverty toward God, ʿIzz was unperturbed by my correction of his analysis of the word's derivation.

10. I have used the translation of Ibrahim and Johnson-Davies, *Forty Ḥadīth Qudsī*, 78. The ḥadīth is recorded by al-Bukhārī, Muslim, al-Tirmidhī, and Ibn Māja.

11. Mursī Abū 'l-ʿAbbās was the thirteenth-century follower and successor of Abū 'l-Ḥasan al-Shādhilī.

12. This attitude is in direct contrast with the severe early stage of Sufism, that of the ascetics who were antisocial and ever weeping. It is said that Fuḍayl ibn ʿIyāḍ (d. 803) smiled only once in thirty years, the day his son died (Schimmel, *Mystical Dimensions of Islam*, 36).

13. This is the famous pre-Islamic Arabian poem of Majnūn ("the possessed man") and his extravagant love for Laylā, which becomes a metaphor for the Sufi's love for God.

14. The existence of the *ghawth* is considered necessary for the world. The function of the *ghawth* is so the link between heaven and earth will not be broken. Before Islam, ʿIzz explained in response to my question, there were many prophets—theoretically, there was a prophet in existence at all times until Muhammad, who was the seal of the prophets. Since Muhammad's death, there has always been a *ghawth* to serve as this necessary link. He is like a railroad switch in which are gathered all the connections, which are then distributed to all individuals.

15. The same is said of Abū Yazīd al-Bisṭāmī (d. 874). See Schimmel, *Mystical Dimensions*, 48.

16. Aḥmad ibn Ḥanbal, *Al-Jāmiʿ al-saghīr*, 2:204, no. 6064.

17. A number of ḥadīths concerning the merits of dhikr are cited in al-Ghazālī's *Invocations and Supplications (Kitāb al-adhkār wa 'l-daʿawāt), Book IX of The Revival of the Religious Sciences (Iḥyā' ʿulūm al-dīn)*, trans. K. Nakamura (Cambridge: Islamic Texts Society, 1990), 6–10.

18. *Al-Risāla 'l-Qushayriyya*, 173.

19. Ibid., 173–74.

20. Ibid., 175.

21. *Mudhakkirat al-murshidīn*, 23–24.

22. *Al-Nafaḥāt al-rabbāniyya*, 19.

23. *Mudhakkirat al-murshidīn*, 27.
24. Malaṭāwī, *Al-Ṣūfiyya fī ilhāmihim*, 2:77–78.
25. *Mudhakkirat al-murshidīn*, 27.
26. Interview with the author, 18 February 1988.
27. *Mudhakkirat al-murshidīn*, 28.
28. Ibid., 31–32.
29. Ibid., 32–33.
30. Biegman, *Egypt: Moulids, Saints, Sufis*, 118.
31. The word *samāᶜ* is not used in spoken Egyptian Arabic in its traditional sense of a Sufi musical concert, but the word appears in modern Sufi works that justify the use of music by recourse to medieval defenses of *samāᶜ*, a word that literally means "hearing."
32. For a detailed account of the Sufi musicians and singers of Egypt and their role in dhikr and Egyptian society, see Waugh, *Munshidīn of Egypt*.
33. Michon, "Sacred Music and Dance in Islam," 469–505.
34. Qushayrī, 260–61.
35. A shorter and different version of this story appears in Qushayrī, 262. In his version Abū Bakr enters and protests against the "psalms of Satan," but the Prophet says, "Leave them alone, Abū Bakr. Every people has its feasts, and our feast is today." There is no mention of ᶜAlī or ᶜUmar in this version, and the point concerning differential permissibility is entirely absent. Hujwīrī records a different story: once when ᶜĀʾisha had a singing girl in her house, ᶜUmar asked leave to enter. "As soon as she heard his step she ran away. He came in and the Apostle smiled. 'O Apostle of God,' cried ᶜUmar, 'what hath made thee smile?' The Apostle answered, 'A slave-girl was singing here, but she ran away as soon as she heard thy step.' 'I will not depart,' said ᶜUmar, 'until I hear what the Apostle heard.' So the Apostle called the girl back and she began to sing, the Apostle listening to her" (*Kashf al-Maḥjūb*, 401).
36. *Kashf al-Maḥjūb*, 402.
37. *Al-Risāla 'l-qushayriyya*, 321.
38. On this, see Michon, "Sacred Music and Dance," 476–77.
39. *Munshidīn of Egypt*, 195.
40. *Miṣbāh al-arwāḥ*, 26.
41. *ᶜIlm*, that is, knowledge gained through the intellect, as opposed to *maᶜrifa*, knowledge gained through mystical insight.
42. I assumed the Presence referred to was that of God, but Shaykh ᶜIzz interpreted it to be that of the Prophet.
43. The "young man" is a term for the Sufi disciple; *futuwwa*, which literally means "young manliness," is often used in the sense of Sufi ethics.
44. A reference to Mount Sinai, the place where God was manifested to Moses.
45. In a letter dated 6 January 1994, Michael Frischkopf writes, "The cassette store next to Fīshāwy [a popular cafe near the Ḥusayn mosque] didn't even carry any Tuni, the proprietor telling me that his popularity had declined; but many cassettes of Yāsīn were available."
46. Ḥasan M. El-Shamy sees dhikr (spelled *zikr*) and zār as existing on the

same therapeutic continuum ("Mental Health in Traditional Culture"). The best and most complete study of the zār that I have seen, one that truly reflects the perspectives of its participants, is an unpublished thesis by Cherifa-Nihal Mazloum, "Le *Zar:* Culte de possession dans l'Egypte contemporaine." The original thesis, including photographs, is in the library of the American Research Center in Egypt. Published sources on the zār include Hani Fakhouri, "The *Zar* Cult in an Egyptian Village," *Anthropological Quarterly* 41 (1968): 49–56; Muhammad al-Jawhari, "Al-Zār," in *Dirāsāt fī ʿilm al-ijtimāʿ wa 'l-anthropologiyya,* studies offered in memory of Dr. Ahmad al-Khishāb (Cairo: Dar al-Maʿārif, 1975), 402–20; Kahle, "Zar-Beschworungen in Egypten"; René Khoury, "Contribution à une bibliographie du zār," *Annales Islamologiques* 16 (1980): 359–74; Miṣrī, *Al-Zār;* Soheir A. Morsy, "Sex Differences and Folk Illness in an Egyptian Village," in *Women in the Muslim World,* ed. Lois Beck and Nikki Keddie (Cambridge: Harvard University Press, 1978), 599–616; Nelson, "Self, Spirit Possession and World View"; Lucie Wood Saunders, "Variants in Zār Experience in an Egyptian Village," in *Case Studies in Spirit Possession,* ed. V. Crapanzano and V. Garrison (New York: John Wiley & Sons, 1977), 177–93; Brenda Z. Seligman, "On the Origin of the Egyptian Zar," *Folklore* 25 (1914): 300–323; Ahmed al-Shahi, "Spirit Possession and Healing: The Zar among the Shaygiyya of the Northern Sudan," *British Society for Middle Eastern Studies Bulletin* 11 (1984): 28–44; and A. Thompson and E. Franke, "The Zar in Egypt," *Moslem World* 3 (1913): 275–89.

47. Fred de Jong ("Cairene *Ziyâra*-Days") and Paul Kahle ("Zar-Beschworungen") have both stated that there is a *ḥaḍra* at the Abū 'l-Suʿūd shrine on his visiting day, but this is no longer the case. De Jong speaks of the inseparability of visiting day and *ḥaḍra,* but this idea is contradicted by the fact that most saints have preferred days for visiting their tombs and not all of them have *ḥaḍras* performed at their shrines.

48. Biegman, *Egypt: Moulids, Saints, Sufis,* 118.

49. *Saint and Sufi,* 171, 201. Gilsenan gives a good summary of social attitudes toward dhikr in Egypt and the link between emotionalism and social class, 171–79, 201.

50. *Al-Nafaḥāt al-rabbāniyya,* 55.

51. *Mudhakkirat al-murshidīn,* 29.

52. *Saint and Sufi,* 179.

53. The lute is apparently used for Sufi *samāʿ* in other countries. Aḥmad al-Ghazālī (d. 1126), brother of the famous Sufi scholar Abū Ḥāmid al-Ghazālī (d. 1111), wrote a treatise in defense of the use of music for sacred purposes, which has been translated by James Robson *(Tracts on Listening to Music).* Both Ghazālīs considered stringed instruments to be forbidden "by general consensus" because of their frequent use in early Islam by effeminates. However, Michon says, this "did not prevent the lute, the *ṭanbūr* (pandore), the *rabāb* (rebec) and the *qānūn* (zither) from finding their place next to the drums and the reed flute *(nay)* in the oratorios of several Sufi orders such as the Mawlawīs ("whirling dervishes") and the Baktashīs of Turkey, the Chishtīs of India, and, much later (mid-thirteenth/nineteenth century), the Shādhilis-Ḥarrāqis of Morocco" (Michon, "Sacred Music and

Dance," 478–79).

54. Qushayrī, 175.

55. *Mudhakkirat al-murshidīn,* 24.

56. Ibid., 25, 26.

57. Interview with the author, 18 April 1989.

58. *Mudhakkirat al-murshidīn,* 25–26.

59. *Invocations and Supplications,* trans. K. Nakamura (Cambridge: Islamic Texts Society, 1990), 23.

60. *Mudhakkirat al-murshidīn,* 24.

61. Malaṭāwī, *Al-Ṣūfiyya fī ilhāmihim,* 2:24.

62. *Mudhakkirat al-murshidīn,* 26.

63. Interview with the author, Abū Tīj, 11 July 1988.

64. *Al-Taṣawwuf wa 'l-ṭarīq ilayhi,* 83.

65. Smith, *Rābiʿa the Mystic,* 22.

66. Malaṭāwī, *Al-Ṣūfiyya fī ilhāmihim,* 1:136.

67. Kuḥayl, *Abu 'l-ʿAynayn al-Dasuqi,* 64.

68. Abū 'l-Faraj ʿAbd al-Raḥmān ibn ʿAlī ibn al-Jawzī, *Talbīs Iblīs* (The Devil's Deception), ed. Khayr al-Dīn ʿAlī (Beirut: n.p., 1970), 190; cited in Ernst, *Words of Ecstasy,* 123.

69. Qushayrī, *Al-Risāla,* 249.

70. *Al-Nafaḥāt al-rabbāniyya,* 228–29.

71. Ibid., 44.

72. Malaṭāwī, *Al-Ṣūfiyya fī ilhāmihim,* 1:129, 2:203.

73. *Al-Nafaḥāt al-rabbāniyya,* 28, 45, 48.

74. *Al-Taṣawwuf wa 'l-ṭarīq ilayhi,* 85. *Shaṭaḥāt* has been translated "theopathic locutions" by Annemarie Schimmel, which is precisely what they are, although I have given a more literal translation of the word, since the meaning was already provided by the context. On the *shaṭaḥāt,* see Ernst, *Words of Ecstasy.*

75. Kuḥayl, *Abū 'l-ʿAynayn al-Dasūqī,* 63–64.

76. Malaṭāwī, *Al-Ṣūfiyya fī ilhāmihim,* 2:199.

77. Abū 'l-ʿAzāʾim, *Mudhakkirat al-murshidīn,* 139, 140, 141. Pages 139–49 of this book are entirely devoted to quoting hadiths promoting compassion and mercy for God's creatures and love "in God."

78. Tijānī, *Ahl al-qurbā,* 80.

79. Ibid., 81.

80. Malaṭāwī, *Al-Ṣūfiyya fī ilhāmihim,* 2:202.

81. Ibid., 2:204–5.

CHAPTER 7: MYSTICAL CONCEPTS AND PRACTICES IN EGYPTIAN SUFISM

1. Māhir, *Karamāt al-awliyāʾ,* 23.

2. John Alden Williams, ed., *Islam* (New York: George Braziller, 1961), 139.

3. *Al-Risāla 'l-qushayriyya,* 13.
4. Ibid., 23.
5. Smith, *Al-Ghazāli the Mystic,* 93–94.
6. Nawfal, *Al-Taṣawwuf,* 73.
7. Māhir, *Karamāt al-awliyā'*, 21.
8. *Al-Nafaḥāt al-rabbāniyya,* 238.
9. Ibid., 47.
10. *Al-Madrasa 'l-shādhiliyya,* 132.
11. E.g., Abū 'l-ʿAzā'im, *Mudhakkirat al-murshidīn,* 53–54, 121–31; Maḥmūd, *Al-Madrasa 'l-shādhiliyya,* 133–35.
12. Gilsenan, *Saint and Sufi in Modern Egypt,* 120.
13. Interview at Shaykh Aḥmad's home, 11 November 1988.
14. *Al-Nafaḥāt al-rabbāniyya,* 29–30.
15. Muḥammad Muṣṭafā Ḥilmī, *Al-Ḥayāt al-rūḥiyya fī 'l-Islām,* (Cairo: al-Hay'a 'l-miṣriyya 'l-ʿāmma li 'l-ta'līf wa 'l-nashr, 1970), 15–16; cited in Najjār, *Al-Ṭuruq al-Ṣūfiyya,* 8.
16. *Al-Risāla 'l-qushayriyya,* 61–62.
17. *Al-Nafaḥāt al-rabbāniyya,* 236, 48.
18. Watt, *Faith and Practice,* 60.
19. Helmut Ritter, "Abū Yazīd al-Bisṭāmī," *Encyclopedia of Islam,* 2d ed., 1:112.
20. Schimmel, *Mystical Dimensions of Islam,* 49; Ritter, "Abū Yazīd al-Bisṭāmī," 163.
21. *Al-Nafaḥāt al-rabbāniyya,* 44–45.
22. Ibid., 48.
23. Ibid., 55.
24. Ibid., 238.
25. Ibid., 49.
26. This can also be translated "You are from me and I am from you." In *Munshidīn of Egypt,* Waugh analyzes a performance by Sabra, a female *munshid,* of a song containing a line addressed to the Prophet, which he translates, "I am from you and you are from me." Waugh believes this line is either addressed to God, "in which case it is a reference to her creation by God, and the Sufi idea of the necessity for God of human love, or to her existence as a child of Muhammad (a Muslim), while the Prophet was just like everyone else, that is, born of women" (145). Although this analysis is possible, I believe it is incorrect. I believe Sabra was expressing her sense of oneness with the Prophet in language that is typical of the Sufis and can be understood in the context of the contemporary doctrines of *fanā'* and *tawḥīd.*
27. I earlier transliterated this word as *maḥabba.* The silent *tā' marbūṭa* at the end of the word, which becomes vocalized only in an *iḍāfa* construction (for instance, "the love of God" [*maḥabbat Allāh*]), is often written by contemporary Egyptians as a *hā'*.
28. Cited in Malaṭāwī, *Al-Ṣūfiyya fī ilhāmihim,* 2:171.
29. Ibid., 168, 189.
30. *Doctrine of the Sufis,* 102.

31. Ibid., 147.
32. For example, Sulamī, *Book of Sufi Chivalry,* 51–55.
33. Malaṭāwī, *Al-Ṣūfiyya fī ilhāmihim,* 2:188.
34. *Al-Nafaḥāt al-rabbāniyya,* 33–34.
35. Ibid., 21–22.
36. Ibid., 236.
37. Ibid., 242–43.
38. Ibid., 236.
39. *Mudhakkirat al-murshidīn,* 64.
40. A recent argument against Freudian interpretation of dreams, in favor of an "Islamic view" that dreams are spiritually instructive, may be found in the book by Dr. ʿIṣām al-Dīn Muḥammad ʿAlī, *Tafsīr al-aḥlām: ruʾya islāmiyya jadīda* (Alexandria: Al-Markaz al-ʿarabī li 'l-nashr wa 'l-tawzīʿ, 1987).
41. For a complete discussion of this verse and its interpretation by medieval and contemporary Muslim authors, see Smith, "Concourse between the Living and the Dead."
42. Ibn ʿArabī, *Al-Futūḥāt al-makkiyya,* 2:375–77. See also Graham, *Divine Word and Prophetic Word,* ch. 2, especially 37; and articles by von Grunebaum, Lecerf, and Corbin in *The Dream and Human Societies,* ed. G. E. von Grunebaum and Roger Caillois (Berkeley and Los Angeles: University of California Press, 1966).
43. Ibn ʿArabī, *Al-Futūḥāt al-makkiyya,* 2:377.
44. ʿAlī, *Tafsīr al-aḥlām,* 97, 100.
45. Ibn ʿArabī, *Al-Futūḥāt al-makkiyya,* 2:377.
46. E.g., the story of al-Ashʿarī's "conversion" from Muʿtazilī doctrine to that of Ahl al-Sunna is cast in the form of a dream-vision of the Prophet. The philosopher Ibn Sīnā (Avicenna) also claimed that many solutions to problems appeared to him in his sleep. Aḥmad ibn al-Qāsim Ibn Abī Uṣaybiʿa, *ʿUyūn al-anbāʾ fī ṭabaqāt al-aṭibbāʾ,* ed. Nizār Riḍā (Beirut: Dār maktabat al-ḥayāt, 1965), 438.
47. Sayyid ʿUways, *Al-Khulūd fī ḥayāt al-miṣriyyīn al-muʿāṣirīn* (Cairo: Al-markaz al-qawmī li 'l-buḥūth al-ijtimāʿiyya wa 'l-janāʾiyya, 1972), cited in Smith, "Concourse between the Living and the Dead," 232.
48. Ibn al-Mubārak, *Al-Ibrīz,* 22.
49. Muḥammad al-Suṭūḥī, in *Al-Ahrām,* 9 January 1976, 10.
50. George Swan, "The Matbuli Incident," *Moslem World* 3 (1913): 175–80.
51. See Yvonne Yazbeck Haddad, *Contemporary Islam and the Challenge of History* (Albany: State University of New York Press, 1982), 43; Hassan Hanafi, "The Relevance of the Islamic Alternative in Egypt," *Arab Studies Quarterly* 4 (1982): 54–74, especially 62; Emmanuel Sivan, *Radical Islam: Medieval Theology and Modern Politics,* enlarged ed. (New Haven: Yale University Press, 1990), especially 120–21, 134.
52. Watt, *Faith and Practice,* 25.
53. *Doctrine of the Sufis,* 46. Arberry adds in a footnote, "As against the view of the Muʿtazilites (an Islamic theological school that flourished in the ninth century), who held that God could be known through the intellect."

54. *Al-Taṣawwuf wa 'l-ṭarīq ilayhi*, 36.

55. *Al-Nafaḥāt al-rabbāniyya*, 46.

56. *Al-Taṣawwuf wa 'l-ṭarīq ilayhi*, 36.

57. Ḥāgga Anhār, head of the women's section of the Muḥammadiyya Sharʿiyya order, 28 March 1989.

58. Watt, *Faith and Practice*, 25.

59. Maḥmūd, *Qaḍīyat al-taṣawwuf*, 177–254.

60. E.g., Shaykh Salāma al-Rāḍī, founder of the Ḥāmidiyya Shādhiliyya. Gilsenan, *Saint and Sufi in Modern Egypt*, 22.

61. For the first few days of our acquaintance, this shaykh never tired of calling me "professor," with mock respect, and using the same mock deference to refer to the wisdom of "the Pakistanis" (because I had studied under Professor Fazlur Rahman at the University of Chicago). I finally tired of this and delivered a mild rebuke to him in Arabic in front of a group of Europeans who did not understand the language: "You do not need to scorn me." He seemed genuinely shocked and exclaimed, "No, scorning is prohibited *(ḥarām)!*" From that point on, he abandoned this behavior and treated me in a more friendly manner.

62. Nawfal, *Al-Taṣawwuf wa 'l-ṭarīq ilayhi*, 35.

63. Ibid.

64. Ibid., 36.

65. Kalabādhī, *Doctrine of the Sufis*, 50–51.

66. Ibn al-Mubārak, *Al-Ibrīz*, 47.

67. *Mudhakkirat al-murshidīn*, 50.

68. Ibid., 18.

69. *Al-Ibrīz*, 45–46. This particular definition illustrates well the concept of the spirit as heavenly and the soul and body as earthly, and the necessity of removing the obstacles of these last in order to free the spirit's receptivity to its original home.

70. *Al-Liwāʾ al-islāmī*, no. 328, 5 May 1988, 3.

71. *Al-Nafaḥāt al-rabbāniyya*, 49.

72. Ibid., 75.

73. The third Caliph, who ruled from 644 to 656. Although he is one of the four "rightly-guided Caliphs," he is seldom used in Sufi tales as a model of piety or insight. He was assassinated in a conspiracy among the Muslim armed forces in Egypt over alleged violations of Qurʾanic norms in his administration.

74. Watt, *Faith and Practice*, 61.

CHAPTER 8: WOMEN AND SEXUALITY IN SUFI LIFE AND THOUGHT

Portions of this chapter were previously published in "Mysticism and Sexuality in Sufi Thought and Life," *Mystics Quarterly* 18, no. 3 (1992): 82–93. That article was written at the invitation of the editor of *Mystics Quar-*

terly, with the prior understanding that this material was later to appear in this book.

1. Dr. Taftāzānī told me in an interview in April 1989 that he personally favored opening up membership in the Orders to women but that the shaykhs of the Orders were not generally open to such a proposal. He suggested that one must prepare the way for such a move. At this time (contrary to our interview in October 1980) he admitted that women do function in the Orders in an informal fashion.

2. See Valerie J. Hoffman-Ladd, "Polemics on the Modesty and Segregation of Women in Contemporary Egypt," *International Journal of Middle East Studies* 19, 1 (1987): 23–50. A recent, well-balanced discussion of women in Islamic discourse and history may be found in Leila Ahmed, *Women and Gender in Islam* (New Haven: Yale University Press, 1992).

3. Ghazālī, *Iḥyā᾽ ʿulūm al-dīn*, 4:142.

4. See Smith, *Rābiʿa the Mystic.*

5. This insight is provided by Elias, "Female and Feminine in Islamic Mysticism," 210–11. This article provides a general overview of female participation in Sufism and also draws an interesting contrast between the cultural debasement of the female and the Sufi exaltation of the celestial feminine.

6. Elias, "Female and Feminine," 213; Nurbakhsh provides a summary of her life in *Sufi Women*, 144–46. Nurbakhsh's book contains the biographies of 124 Sufi women.

7. *Sufis of Andalusia*, 142–46, 154–55.

8. *Muslim Saints and Mystics*, 40. Shaykh ʿIzz, who shared in his culture's generally low regard for women, excepted me from this general judgment with the "compliment" that I was his "brother," not a sister. I was not particularly flattered at being told that I was not bad—for a woman.

9. Smith, *Rābiʿa the Mystic*, 2.

10. "Female and Feminine," 211.

11. "Women in Mystical Islam," 151.

12. *Sunna* means a well-trodden path or custom. In Islam, this refers almost exclusively to the behavior of the Prophet, which is held up as the model of recommended behavior for all Muslims.

13. Goldziher, *Introduction to Islamic Theology and Law*, 122.

14. Ghazālī, *Iḥyā᾽ ʿulūm al-dīn*, 4:97.

15. *Kashf al-Maḥjūb*, 360–66.

16. Ghazālī's "book on marriage," which is part of his larger work, *The Revivification of the Religious Sciences (Iḥyā᾽ ʿulūm al-dīn)*, has been translated by Madelain Farah as *Marriage and Sexuality in Islam*. For a more detailed discussion of Hujwīrī's and Ghazālī's views on marriage, see Hoffman-Ladd, "Mysticism and Sexuality," 83–85.

17. *Iḥyā᾽ ʿulūm al-dīn*, 4:99.

18. Ibid., 98.

19. Ibid., 109.

20. Ibid., 99, 101.

21. Ibid., 108.
22. Ibid., 103–14.
23. Ibid., 116.
24. Ibid., 117.
25. Ibid., 144.
26. Ibid., 148–49.
27. See Winter, *Society and Religion in Early Ottoman Egypt*, 131, and Aḥmad ʿAbd al-Rāziq, *Al-marʾa fī miṣr al-mamālīk* (Cairo: Maktab al-Sharīf wa Saʿīd Raʾfat, 1975), 28–32.
28. *Al-Ṭabaqāt al-kubrā*, 2 vols. (Cairo: Maktabat wa maṭbaʿat Muḥammad ʿAlī Ṣubayḥ wa awlādihi, n.d.), 2:111; cited in ʿAbd al-Rāziq, *Al-marʾa fī miṣr al-mamālīk*, 28–30.
29. Aḥmad al-Ghazālī, *Bawāriq al-ilmāʿ*; quoted in Fritz Meier, "Soufisme et déclin culturel," in *Classicisme et déclin culturel dans l'histoire de l'Islam*, Actes du symposium international d'histoire de la civilisation musulmane, Bordeaux, 25–29 June 1956, ed. R. Brunschvig and G.E. von Grunebaum (Paris: Editions Besson-Chantemerle, 1957), 218.
30. Described by the historian Aḥmad ibn ʿAlī al-Maqrīzī, *Al-Mawāʿiẓ wa 'l-iʿtibār fī dhikr al-khiṭaṭ wa 'l-āthār*, 2 vols. (Bulaq: Dār al-ṭabāʿa 'l-miṣriyya, 1270/1853), 2:428; quoted in ʿAbd al-Rāziq, *Al-Marʾa fī miṣr al-mamālīk*, 28.
31. Ahmed, *Women and Gender in Islam*, 110.
32. Ṭawīl, *Al-Taṣawwuf fī miṣr*, 42.
33. Ibn Ḥajar al-ʿAsqalānī, *Inbāʾ al-ghumr fī anbāʾ al-ʿumr*, ed. Ḥasan Ḥabashī (Cairo: Lajnat iḥyāʾ al-turāth al-islāmī, 1969–72), 2:841; cited in ʿAbd al-Rāziq, *Al-marʾa fī miṣr al-mamālīk*, 31.
34. Goldziher, *Muslim Studies*, 2:274–77.
35. Ibn al-Ḥājj al-ʿAbdarī, *Al-Madkhal*, 4 vols. (Cairo: n.p., 1960), 2:141–42; quoted in ʿAbd al-Rāziq, *Al-Marʾa fī miṣr al-mamālīk*, 32.
36. Cornell, "Mirrors of Prophethood," 501.
37. Hujwīrī, *Kashf al-maḥjūb*, 398.
38. "Eros," 124.
39. Ibid.
40. Al-Bukhārī, *Ṣaḥīḥ al-Bukhārī*, book 67, chap. 85; Ghazālī, *Iḥyāʾ ʿulūm al-dīn*, 4:161.
41. Ghazālī, *Iḥyāʾ ʿulūm al-dīn*, 4:110.
42. *Recognizing Islam: Religion and Society in the Modern Arab World* (New York: Pantheon Books, 1982), 116–20.
43. *Al-Ibrīz* includes an instance of Sīdī Dabbāgh rebuking Ibn al-Mubārak for looking at his wife's private parts during intercourse and other stories indicating his intimate knowledge of everything his disciple did, and in one case his actual presence with his disciple on his wedding night. See the chapter on his miracles, 14–36.
44. One scholar attributes his insights on the spiritual benefits of sexuality to the influence of his wife, the Sufi Miriam bint ʿAbd al-Raḥmān al-Bāj, who "permitted him to attain orgasm through ecstasy and ecstasy through orgasm." A. Bouhdiba, "Amour sacré et amour profane chez Mohidine Ibn

al Arabi," in *Actas del IV Coloquio Hispano-Tunecino* (Madrid: Instituto Hispano-Arabe de Cultura, 1983), 60. Austin suggests that it was Niẓām—the daughter of a Persian shaykh he met in Mecca who inspired the composition of his mystical love poem, *Tarjumān al-Ashwāq* (The Interpreter of Desires)—who led him to gain a new appreciation of the theopany in intercourse. He writes, "Clearly this girl, at once physically and spiritually attractive and fascinating, was a revelation to him in the strictest sense of that word, and I feel sure that what he wrote later of the relationship between man and woman later, in the *Fuṣūṣ*, was inspired by the lasting impression which Niẓām had made upon his whole being" (Austin, "Feminine Dimensions," 11–12).

45. Geoffrey Parrinder, *Sex in the World's Religions* (New York: Oxford Unviersity Press, 1980), 151.

46. *Al-Futūḥāt al-makkiyya,* 1:138.

47. Ibid., 4:84.

48. *Bezels of Wisdom,* 71–81; *Fuṣūṣ al-ḥikam,* 1:214–26.

49. *Bezels of Wisdom,* 274.

50. Ibid.

51. Cf. A. H. Walton, in his Introduction to Shaykh al-Nafzāwī's *The Perfumed Garden for the Soul's Delectation,* trans. Richard Burton (New York: Putnam, 1963), 40: "For the Oriental, orgasm symbolized the ecstasy of the soul possessed by, or in union with God" (quoted in Parrinder, *Sex in the World's Religions,* 168). Parrinder is skeptical of Walton's statement, cautioning that " 'the Oriental' should not be so generalized, and there are vast differences between the pantheism of India and the strict monotheism of orthodox Islam." Parrinder is certainly correct, but his observation that Islamic mysticism indulged in only the "vaguely and symbolically sensual" (172), not the overtly sensual, and failed to make any connection between cosmic reality and sexual practice, reflects a lack of awareness of Ibn ʿArabi on this point. This lack of awareness reflects scholarly neglect of this subject until the mid-1980s. Recent studies of Ibn ʿArabī's views on women and sexuality may be found in Sachiko Murata, *The Tao of Islam: A Sourcebook on Gender Relationships in Islamic Thought* (Albany: State University of New York Press, 1992); Austin, "Feminine Dimensions"; Bouhdiba, "Amour Sacré et Amour Profane chez Mohidine Ibn al Arabi"; and Lutfi, "Feminine Element." Of these, Lutfi's emphasis and interpretation most closely approximate my own, although I wrote this section on Ibn ʿArabī before I became aware of her article. Murata's book deals with the way that gender concepts are implicit in the cosmology and psychology of Sufi and Shiʿi philosophical traditions, an important subject previously neglected in scholarship on Islam.

52. *Bezels of Wisdom,* 274.

53. *Al-Futūḥāt al-makkiyya,* 1:365.

54. *Bezels of Wisdom,* 275.

55. Ibid., 276.

56. *Fuṣūṣ al-ḥikam,* 2:323, 332–33.

57. *Al-Futūḥāt al-makkiyya*, 1:138 ff.
58. *Bezels of Wisdom*, 274.
59. Ibid., 276.
60. *Al-Futūḥāt al-makkiyya*, 2:573–74.
61. "Feminine Dimensions," 13.
62. *Al-Futūḥāt al-makkiyya*, 2:574.
63. Ibid., 2:189–90. One is reminded of the ḥadīth in which Muhammad honored early fruits for the same reason.
64. There are two different ḥadīths in which Muhammad reports his vision of hellfire, in which the greater number of the inhabitants were women. See Jane I. Smith and Yvonne Y. Haddad, "Women in the Afterlife: The Islamic View as Seen from Qur'an and Tradition," *Journal of the American Academy of Religion* 43 (1975): 39–50.
65. *Al-Futūḥāt al-makkiyya*, 2:190.
66. Ibid.
67. Ibid., 191.
68. Ibid., 192.
69. Ibid., 365.
70. Wakīl, *Hādhihi hīya 'l-ṣūfiyya*, 39–42.
71. See Homerin, "Ibn ʿArabi in the People's Assembly."
72. *Al-Futūḥāt*, 3:512. William Schoedel, my colleague at the University of Illinois, pointed out to me that this point of view is very reminiscent of viewpoints attributed by Irenaeus to the Gnostic Valentinians. *Adv. haer.* 1.6.2 and 3. Some contemporary scholars believe, however, that the "spiritual marriage" of the Valentinians referred actually to a type of cohabitation without sexual intercourse (Williams, "Uses of Gender Imagery in Ancient Gnostic Texts"). This article studies two contrasting attitudes toward sexuality that existed in ancient Gnosticism, cautioning against characterizing Gnosticism in a monolithic manner.
73. Schimmel, "Eros," 122.
74. *Al-Futūḥāt al-makkiyya*, 4:125.
75. *Majallat al-taṣawwuf al-islāmī*, April 1981; his comments are reprinted in "Al-Burhāniyya ila mata?" *Majallat al-tasawwuf al-islami*, May 1981, 13.
76. *Al-Risala 'l-qushayriyya*, 323.
77. *Al-Nafaḥāt al-rabbāniyya*, 48–49.
78. "Women, Saints and Sanctuaries."
79. Gilsenan, *Saint and Sufi in Modern Egypt*, 54
80. *Manners and Customs of the Modern Egyptians*, 425–26.
81. John G. Kennedy and Hussein Fahim, "Nubian Dhikr Rituals and Cultural Change," *Muslim World* 64 (1974): 207.
82. On women in *baladī* Cairo and their distinctiveness from other women, see Sawsan el-Messiri, "Self-Images of Traditional Urban Women in Cairo," in Beck and Keddie, *Women in the Muslim World*, 522–40.
83. "La Rifaʿiyya en Egypte," 9.
84. Waugh, *Munshidīn of Egypt*, 19–20.
85. The prevalence of clitoridectomy among women and girls of the

lower classes of Egypt could affect the feelings of Egyptian women concerning intercourse, for it obstructs sexual stimulus to the organ most typically associated with orgasm. Women who have had clitoridectomies nonetheless assure me that they do feel pleasure in intercourse.

86. Mernissi, *Beyond the Veil.*

87. M. E. Combs-Schilling, *Sacred Performances: Islam, Sexuality and Sacrifice* (New York: Columbia University Press, 1989), 268.

88. Ibid., 188–89; 197–98.

89. Parrinder, *Sex in the World's Religions,* 52. June McDaniel reports that the Hindu Bauls of Bengal practice a ritualized sexual intercourse in which, on the contrary, the mixing of fluids is essential. "Liquid Visions: The Fluidity of Divine Perception among the Bauls of Bengal," (paper presented at a conference on "Visions and Visionary Experience in Religion," University of Kansas, Lawrence, Kansas, April 1991).

90. A ḥadīth from al-Bukhārī, quoted in Williams, *Islam,* 87.

91. Ibn Saʿd, *Al-Ṭabaqāt al-kubrā,* ed. Eduart Sachau et al. (Leiden: E. J. Brill, 1904–40), 8:139. The story, reported by a slave girl, emphasizes that the Prophet bathed himself between each act of intercourse.

92. Muḥammad Ḥusayn Haykal, *The Life of Muhammad,* trans. Ismāʿīl Rāgī A. al Fārūqī (North American Trust Publications, 1976), 289; the Arabic original was published in 1936.

CHAPTER 9: MODELS OF SAINTHOOD

1. *Al-Nafaḥāt al-rabbāniyya,* 9.

2. *Mashrabiyya* is a traditional lattice of interlocking pieces of wood with spaces for air to pass through. Traditional Egyptian houses used *mashrabiyya* over windows, to prevent people from looking in, while allowing residents to peek out and air to pass through. It is often used for the *maqṣūra* surrounding a saint's tomb, although sometimes the wood is rough and unfinished. More elaborate shrines have brass *mashrabiyya*-imitation *maqṣūras*. The shrine of Aḥmad Raḍwān, like the *sāḥa* itself, was in modest good taste but well crafted and clean.

3. *Al-Nafaḥāt al-rabbāniyya,* 10.

4. Ibid., 104.

5. Ibid., 109.

6. Ibid., 10.

7. Ibid., 11.

8. Shaykh ʿIzz says it was Shaykh Abū 'l-Wafāʾ al-Sharqāwī who called him "sultan of the *magāzīb*" after Aḥmad Raḍwān stripped himself naked at Abū 'l-Wafāʾ's *sāḥa* in Najʿ Ḥammādī. Abū 'l-Wafāʾ, a strict adherent of Islamic legal standards, would not tolerate such behavior and sent Aḥmad Raḍwān away. Shaykh ʿIzz said that Aḥmad Raḍwān walked the entire distance from Abū ʾl-Wafāʾ's *sāḥa* to al-Baghdādī—a good hour's drive—entirely naked.

9. *Al-Nafaḥāt al-rabbāniyya,* 11.

10. Aḥmad ʿAbd al-Malik, *Al-Madrasa 'l-raḍwāniyya fī 'l-aḥwāl al-rabbāniyya wa 'l-asrār al-ilāhiyya li 'l-quṭb al-ʿārif bi ʾllāh taʿālā al-Ḥājj Aḥmad Raḍwān* (Kom Ombo: Yūsuf Jaʿlūṣ, n.d.); cited in Biegman, *Egypt,* 76.

11. *Al-Nafaḥāt al-rabbāniyya,* 11. Muḥammad al-Buṣīrī (1211–94) was author of the famous *Burda,* or "Mantle Ode," in praise of the Prophet.

12. Biegman, *Egypt,* 120.

13. *Al-Nafaḥāt al-rabbāniyya,* 238.

14. Ibid., 12.

15. Ibid.

16. From *Mishkāt al-Maṣābīḥ,* a popular collection of ḥadīths; in Arthur Jeffery, ed., *Islam: Muhammad and His Religion* (Indianapolis: Liberal Arts Press, 1958), 29.

17. *Al-Nafaḥāt al-rabbāniyya,* 14.

18. *Karamāt al-awliyāʾ,* 174.

19. *Al-Nafaḥāt al-rabbāniyya,* 15.

20. Ibid., 113.

21. Ibid., 75.

22. Ibid., 33.

23. Ibid., 97, 98.

24. Ibid., 99.

25. Ibid., 114. The Prophet's prayer was "I am the wretched, the poor, the negligent and hopeful."

26. Ibid., 233–34.

27. Ibid., 99.

28. Ibid., 75.

29. Ibid., 342–44.

30. Biegman, *Egypt,* 77.

31. This particular portrait of Aḥmad Raḍwān is indeed a compelling one. A poster-size copy of it was given to me by his son, Shaykh Muḥammad, and it observes me now even as I write. The eyes of the portrait do follow the viewer no matter where he stands, and the image of the shaykh does appear unusually vivid, as if he were able to watch people through his portrait. This portrait is included in this book.

32. Shaykh al-ʿArabī died in 1984 or 1985. Aḥmad Abū 'l-Ḥasan appears to have succeeded him as spiritual master of his group, which is simply called "the sons of Abū 'l-Futūḥ al-ʿArabī."

33. It was coedited with Maḥmud ibn al-Sharīf and was published in two volumes in 1966 by Dār al-Taʾlīf. Many Egyptian Sufis told me I would never understand the *Risāla* except in this edition, with its extensive notes. Significantly, ʿIzz deemed Dr. Maḥmūd the "author" of the book.

34. Preface to Ḥajjājī, *Min aʿlām al-ṣaʿīd,* 9.

35. Abū 'l-Maʿārif's grandson, Shaykh Aḥmad al-Sharqāwī, believes this shaykh was Shādhilī.

36. This account of Abū 'l-Maʿārif's attachment to Shaykh Aḥmad al-Khuḍayrī may be found in at least two sources, which are in turn appar-

ently quoting from older sources: Makhlūf, *Ṣafaḥāt nāṣiʿa*, 6–8; Ḥajjājī, *Min aʿlām al-saʿīd*, 24–27.

37. Makhlūf, *Ṣafaḥāt nāṣiʿa*, 11.

38. Ibid., 19.

39. The didactic treatises are *Shams al-taḥqīq wa ʿurwat ahl al-tawfīq* (Cairo: Al-Maṭbaʿa 'l-khayriyya, 1307 A.H./1889–90 C.E.); *Naṣīḥat al-dhākirīn* (1291 A.H./1874 C.E.); *Al-Mawrid al-raḥmānī* (1294 A.H./1877 C.E.). The most famous poem is *Al-Wasīla 'l-ḥasnā: manẓūmat asmāʾ Allāh al-ḥusnā*, with commentary by Ḥasanayn Muḥammad Makhlūf (Cairo: Matbaʿat al-madani, n.d.). Abū 'l-Maʿarif also composed a *tashṭīr*—a filling out—of the famous poem *al-Burda* (the "Mantle Ode") in praise of the Prophet by al-Buṣīrī. This was also published with a commentary by Makhlūf (Cairo: Lajnat al-bayān al-ʿarabī, 1961).

40. Ḥajjājī, *Min aʿlām al-ṣaʿīd*, 39.

41. Ibid., 45.

42. Makhlūf, *Ṣafaḥāt nāṣiʿa*, 36–37.

43. *Miṣbāḥ al-arwāḥ*, 4–5.

44. Ibid., 6.

45. Ibid., 27–30.

46. These words were spoken to me during our final meeting, on 22 March 1989. Knowing we would not be seeing each other again before my departure for the United States at the end of April, he told me, "Although I have always liked Americans, you have raised my estimation of them." He said I had "a mature and enlightened mind and a spirit filled with the light of God." I was rather overwhelmed by this compliment from the man whom Shaykh ʿIzz believed to be the *ghawth* of the age, after the passing of Shaykh Muḥammad al-Ṭayyib. I could not help but see it as intended partly for the benefit of a young man accompanying me and Shaykh ʿIzz to Dayr al-Saʿāda, who had earlier doubted the validity of my spiritual experiences and berated me for my unreasonableness and narrowness of mind for refusing to convert to Islam. After eighteen months among the Sufis, it was not difficult to believe that Shaykh Aḥmad could know, through his mystical insight, the young man's opinion of me, and use this method to correct his manners, if not his opinion. Whatever the truth of the matter, I wrote in my journal, "It filled me with a glow, as my meetings with Shaykh Aḥmad always have. There is a certain bond of love and respect between us which is precious, and I felt that through him my love for Egypt and Sufism were renewed, and the psychological fatigue of the past months vanished." The Sufis, more than other Muslims, appreciate the value of such personal contacts, which they articulate by the exhortation to sit in the company of gnostics. The memoirs concerning the life of Abū 'l-Wafāʾ often do not go beyond praise for his character and descriptions of the marvelous aura of his assemblies at Dayr al-Saʿāda, because it is precisely such an informal method of association that formed the core of his ministry. Only those who have experienced it can fully appreciate its transformative value.

47. Ḥajjājī, *Min aʿlām al-saʿīd*, 47–48. Abū 'l-Wafāʾ's son, Shaykh Aḥmad

al-Sharqāwī, also told me that his father had strong relations with the Coptic Christian community.

48. *Ṣafaḥāt nāṣiʿa*, 24.

49. In Abū 'l-Ḥajjāj Ḥāfiz, "Rajul dīn wa adab wa ʿilm wa siyāsa," *Al-Akhbār*, 15 July 1988.

50. Interview with the author, 11 November 1988.

51. My information concerning Shaykh Maḥmūd is derived almost entirely from Ḥāgga Laylā Shams al-Dīn Aḥmad, who was one of his closest followers. A young woman of the upper class, Ḥāgga Laylā and her husband, Mamdūḥ Abū 'l-ʿAzm (not a relation to the shaykh) graciously offered me and my family both very generous hospitality and friendship, and I remember them with particular fondness and warmth. Shaykh ʿIzz and I also attended a number of meetings of the "children" of Shaykh Maḥmūd, where they did dhikr and Shaykh Maḥmūd's life and manners were discussed.

52. The standard polite greeting in Arabic.

53. This sensation of new appreciation of beauty and a new awareness of the richness of colors by virtue of a spiritual experience has also sometimes been experienced by "born-again" Christians at the time of their conversions. This experience is reflected in the words of an old hymn, "Loved with Everlasting Love," by George Wade Robinson (1838–77):

> Heaven above is softer blue,
> Earth around is sweeter green,
> Something lives in every hue
> Christless eyes have never seen.
> Birds with gladder songs o'erflow,
> Flowers with deeper beauties shine,
> Since I know as now I know
> I am His, and He is mine.

54. *Min faḍā'il wa khaṣā'iṣ*, 179–80.

CHAPTER 10: THE LIFE AND INFLUENCE OF SHAYKH MUḤAMMAD ʿUTHMĀN AL-BURHĀNĪ

1. Author of a commentary on the aphorisms of Ibn ʿAṭā' Allāh al-Sakandarī, *Ḥikam Ibn ʿAṭā' Allāh, sharḥ al-ʿārif bi 'llāh al-Shaykh Zarrūq*, ed. ʿAbd al-Ḥalīm Maḥmūd and Maḥmūd ibn al-Sharīf (Cairo: al-Shaʿb, 1978?), and *Qawāʿid al-taṣawwuf*, ed. Muḥammad Zuhrī al-Najjār (Cairo: Al-Nahḍa 'l-Jadīda, n.d.). A brief summary of his life may be found in Maḥmūd and Ibn al-Sharīf's introduction to his commentary on the *Ḥikam*, 20–22, and a biography exists in English by Ali Khushaim, *Zarruq the Sufi* (Tripoli, Libya: General Company for Publication, 1976).

2. According to Vincent Cornell, in a personal communication, later Shādhilī Orders that want to appear to be very Sharīʿa-abiding included

Zarrūq in their spiritual lineage. This type of fabrication of *silsilas* is believed to have been very common in the history of the Sufi Orders. Given the possibility of mystical connection through visions, the lack of physically substantiated connection has consequences less grave for Sufism than for Ḥadīth transmission.

3. This was loaned to me by Alfred Hüber, an Austrian resident in Cairo and a former member of the Burhāniyya. The transcription does not identify the transcriber, whom I suspect to be Shaykh Gamāl al-Sanhūrī because of the similarity of wording with Shaykh Gamāl's account of the shaykh's life read on the occasion of his moulid. I was a guest on several occasions in the home of Shaykh Gamāl al-Sanhūrī and his wife, who graciously provided me with copies of Shaykh Muḥammad ʿUthmān's writings, the story of the shaykh's life read on the occasion of his moulid, personal accounts of their own experiences with the Shaykh, and a magazine article concerning Germans who had converted to Islam through the efforts of the Burhāniyya. They also invited me to meet some European followers of the Order and to witness the initiation of a Swiss man into the Order.

4. According to Gamāl al-Sanhūrī and the official Burhānī pamphlet that briefly summarizes the life of the shaykh, he was born in 1902. However, in one of his taped discourses as transcribed, he says that he was born in 1894 and founded his Order in 1917.

5. During his Ascension into Heaven, the Prophet Muhammad was also offered wine, milk, or honey to drink. He chose the milk, which marked the "median" character of his community. Shaykh ʿIzz became a disciple of Abū 'l-Ḥasan al-Shādhilī in a vision in which he was seated on Shādhilī's lap and given a glass of milk to drink, which symbolized spiritual adoption. Drinking is often used to indicate taking in spiritual realities, as is indicated by the fact that the different Orders or teachers of Sufism are commonly called *mashrabs*, literally "drinking places." The metaphor of "drinking the cup" is also familiar to us in the Gospels of Matthew (20:22–23; 25:39) and John (18:11), and the symbolism of eating and drinking is most evident in the Christian ritual of the Eucharist.

6. Muḥammad ʿUthmān ʿAbduh al-Burhānī, *Tabriʾat al-dhimma fī nuṣḥ al-umma wa tadhkirat ūlī al-albāb li 'l-sayr ilā 'l-ṣawāb* (n.p., n.d.), 3.

7. Ibid., 36.

8. Ibid., 41.

9. Ibid., 47.

10. Ibid., 252.

11. Ibid., 8.

12. Sammān, *Taʾthīm al-dhimma*, 45.

13. *Tabriʾat al-dhimma*, 9.

14. Sammān, *Taʾthīm al-dhimma*, 49.

15. *Al-Ahrām*, 13 February 1976, 12.

16. Interview with Rajab al-Bannā, *Al-Ahrām*, 16 January 1976, 10.

17. Above, 61.

18. *Tabri'at al-dhimma,* 10.

19. *Al-Ahrām,* 9 January 1976, 10. This point of view is nonetheless not entirely defensible from the Qur'an, in which God "lifted Himself to heaven when it was smoke, and said to it and to the earth, 'Come willingly, or unwillingly!' They said, 'We come willingly.' So He determined them as seven heavens in two days" (41:11). The philosopher Ibn Rushd (d. 1198), in his *Tahāfut al-tahāfut* in response to al-Ghazālī's (d. 1111) *Tahāfut al-falāsifa,* pointed out the ambiguity of the Qur'an on this point.

20. *Tabri'at al-dhimma,* 16. Shaykh Suṭūhī also objected to this point in his interview.

21. *Tabri'at al-dhimma,* 277.

22. Ibid., 294. The sermon is reproduced on 294–99.

23. *Al-Ahrām,* 13 February 1976, 12.

24. *Al-Ahrām,* 9 January 1976, 10.

25. *Al-Ahrām,* 16 January 1976, 10. The Bāṭiniyya (a name that literally means "esotericists") was a name sometimes applied to the Ismā'īlī Shi'a. The Bābī and Bahā'ī sects both developed in nineteenth-century Iran, and the Qādiyāniyya or Aḥmadiyya developed in nineteenth-century India. All of these movements had a heavy Mahdist emphasis in their origins, though it became less marked as they developed. The status of the Aḥmadiyya, who consider themselves Muslims but are considered by Sunnis to have apostated from Islam, has been problematic since the formation of Pakistan as an Islamic state in 1947. In Iran, the Bahā'īs are likewise considered to have apostated from Islam and are subjected to persecution under the Islamic Republic. There is a major Bahā'ī center in Haifa—a possible explanation for the reference to Zionist encouragement, although this may reflect the widespread perception among Muslims in Egypt that Zionists are engaged in a worldwide conspiracy to destroy Islam, and the Bahā'īs might be seen as a fitting tool in that regard. Bahā'ism has become a universalistic religion and bears little evidence today of its Islamic origins.

26. *Al-Ahrām,* 13 February 1976, 12.

27. Sayyid Aḥmad Shaḥḥāt, a lawyer and president of the city of Malwā in Minyā province, as told in his letter in *Al-Ahrām,* 23 January 1976, 12. The series, "Memoirs of a Former Burhānī," in Jamā'at Anṣār al-Sunna 'l-Muḥammadiyya's monthly magazine, *Al-Tawḥīd,* reveals this at the less involved level of a regular attender at the Burhānī lessons.

28. 'Āmir al-Najjār gives the name of Dasūqī's Order as the Burhāniyya and names its branches (*Al-Ṭuruq al-ṣūfiyya,* 245–50).

29. This was indicated in the report prepared by the Ministry of Religious Endowments, according to Shaykh Ibrāhīm al-Dasūqī, *Al-Ahrām,* 16 January 1976, 10. This is also suggested in a letter from the Egyptian consul in Khartoum, *Al-Ahrām,* 6 February 1976, 12.

30. Especially the letters written by 'Ādil Aḥmad Muḥammad of Sinūris, Fayyūm, 30 January 1976, 12.

31. *Al-Ahrām,* 27 February 1976, 12.

32. ʿIṣmat Abū 'l-Qāsim al-Qāḍī, in *Al-Ahrām*, 6 February 1976, 12.

33. A photocopy of this letter is found in *Majallat al-taṣawwuf al-islāmī*, June 1981, 16.

34. Especially the letter addressed by "F.S." to *Majallat al-taṣawwuf al-islāmī*, May 1981, 13.

35. *Al-Ahrām*, 9 January 1976, 10.

36. 6 January 1976, 10.

37. *Taʾthīm al-dhimma*, 6.

38. Ibid., 13–15.

39. "Khamsūna musliman almāniyan fī 'l-Sūdān," *Al-Muslimūn* no. 83 (1981): 36–38.

40. The center near Hamburg is called Haus Schnede and is described by Khalid Duran in an as yet unpublished manuscript, *Muslims in the West*. In chapter 19, which is entitled "Sufism—Will it reap the fruits of the 'youth revolt' against established religion?" Duran points out that most Western converts to Islam (with the exception of African Americans) are Sufis and not "fundis" (fundamentalists/Islamists). As his title suggests, he sees the attraction of Sufism (or "pseudo-Sufism," as Elwell-Sutton calls it, a description with which Duran would appear to agree) as part of the disaffection of Western youth from the church establishment. It was members of the Haus Schnede who went to Khartoum to pledge allegiance to Muḥammad ʿUthmān in 1981. They were led by Salāh al-Dīn ʿĪd, described by Duran as an "Egyptian spiritualist" and a teacher at a local high school in Germany. Up till that point, Duran says, "the *burhānī* fraternity did not transcend the borders of Sudan and Egypt," but the European Sufis "believed the story that the *burhāniya* was the world's largest Sufi order." Duran describes the Burhaniyya as "starkly obscurantist and one of the least intellectual Brotherhoods as far as its leadership is concerned." The Haus Schnede existed as a Sufi center from 1981 to 1986, with six resident nuclear families and weekend activities with forty to fifty participants. During these five years, four hundred people are said to have embraced Islam there.

41. According to Khalid Duran, in a personal communication. Duran, a Moroccan scholar, functioned for a while as their *imām*. In *Muslims in the West*, Duran presents adoption of Middle Eastern habits and dress as an early phase in the conversion process, followed by attempts to incorporate aspects of one's indigenous culture into the new Islamic identity.

42. Unpublished speeches, 67.

43. Kloth, *Die himmlischen Augen*.

44. "Sufism and Pseudo-Sufism."

45. *Die himmlischen Augen*, 30.

46. She had written another book, as yet unpublished, entitled *Alif Lam Mim*, about the words the shaykh had spoken to her and in 1982 was working on an expanded book on the life of the shaykh.

47. As we have seen, visionary initiation is not as rare in Egypt as might be supposed, but headship of an Order still requires social connections. In other parts of the Muslim world, this "*ʿUwaysi*" type of intiation might

be more common and accepted. See Julian Baldick, *Imaginary Muslims: The ʿUwaysi Sufis of Central Asia* (New York: New York University Press, 1993).

CHAPTER 11: COPTIC CHRISTIANITY AND POPULAR ISLAM IN EGYPT: ELEMENTS OF A COMMON SPIRITUALITY

1. The exact figures are a matter of debate between the church and the government. See Solihin, *Copts and Muslims in Egypt*, 12–14. A recent *New York Times* article by Youssef M. Ibrahim ("Muslims' Fury is Falling on Egypt's Christians," 15 March 1993, A-1, A-4) places the number of Coptic Christians in Egypt at ten million, or 17 percent of the population. This is a good deal higher than most estimates.

2. Al-Shammās Samīr Shawqī, *Siyar al-shuhadāʾ wa 'l-qiddīsīn al-āthār* (Biographies of the Martyrs and Pure Saints) (Gharbiyya province: Nasimko li 'l-tabaʿa, 1985), a booklet sold near the church of Sitt Rifqa (St. Rebecca) in Sunbāṭ, based on a manuscript in the church.

3. "The Copts through the Ages." This is a booklet distributed by the Egyptian Ministry of Information, and its pages are not numbered.

4. Meinardus, *Monks and Monasteries*, x.

5. Nelly van Doorn, "Mother Martha and Sister Hannah: Two Female Models of Piety in the Coptic Orthodox Church" (paper presented at the International Conference of Asian and North African Studies in Toronto, August 1990, 13).

6. Kamil, *Coptic Egypt*, 58.

7. Watterson, *Coptic Egypt*, 168–69.

8. Wahba, "Coptic Orthodox Church," 32.

9. *Manners and Customs*, 241.

10. See Lionel Rothkrug, "The 'Odour of Sanctity,' and the Hebrew Origins of Christian Saint Veneration," *Historical Reflections* 8 (1981): 95–142.

11. A booklet distributed by the church of Sitt Rifqa says that she and her children were told in a vision that they would be martyred. They gave all their belongings to the poor and went to testify of their faith and be tortured and killed. Although the booklet says that "Jesus kept their bodies preserved without corruption," it also specifies that every year during their moulid "the bodies are medically treated and processed. They are merely wrapped in thirteen layers of cloth, not in wooden containers as is usually done. Many come to the church to receive baraka, and many miracles have appeared from the body parts" (Shawqī, *Siyar al-shuhadāʾ*, 6). Otto Meinardus, the premier scholar of Christianity in Egypt, wrote that "in the Coptic Church there are only two saints who did not decompose, St. Bishoi and St. Makarius" (*Christian Egypt*, 156). But the accounts I heard from ordinary Copts, including caretakers at the shrines, indicated that all the pure saints are uncorrupted.

12. However, I have seen a rural shrine near Fez in Morocco with a tree

adjoining it, to which were attached bits of cloth from the clothing of pious visitors.

13. Meinardus, *Christian Egypt,* 265–66.

14. El Masri, *Story of the Copts,* 557.

15. Bishop Athanasius, "The Copts through the Ages"; Wahba, "Coptic Orthodox Church," 4; El Masri, *Story of the Copts,* 557.

16. Fr. Jerome Palmer, *Our Lady Returns to Egypt* (Bernardino, Calif.: Culligan Publications, 1969), 1.

17. Nelson, "Stress, Religious Experience and Mental Health."

18. According to the Gospel of Matthew, when King Herod of Judea plotted to kill the baby Jesus, his parents fled with him to Egypt until King Herod was dead (Matt. 2:13–15). Egyptian Christians take great pride in the fact that Egypt gave the Holy Family safe haven, and like to recite the verse, "Out of Egypt I have called my son" (Matt. 2:15). This verse, which originally comes from the Old Testament book of Hosea (11:1), referred in that context to the deliverance of the Israelites from slavery in Egypt. The Gospel of Matthew gives this verse an entirely new meaning, one that is obviously more flattering to Egypt and favored by the Egyptians. Egyptian Christians also like to quote Isaiah 19:25, "Blessed be Egypt my people," ignoring the fact that this refers to a future blessing that will follow a calamitous punishment brought on Egypt for its sins.

19. Nelson, "Stress," 50–51.

20. Meinardus, *Christian Egypt,* 269.

21. Ibid., 268.

22. Ibid., 269.

23. Wahba, "Coptic Orthodox Church," 32–33.

24. *Manners and Customs,* 529.

25. According to Nelly van Doorn, in a private conversation, November 1991.

26. Some scholars have suggested that there may actually be a physiological basis for the belief that reducing one's food intake to a minimum aids in the incorruptibility of the body, as in the case of Japanese ascetics who, it is said, "self-mummify" in this manner (Carmen Blacker, *The Catalpa Bow: A Study of Shamanistic Practices in Japan* [London: George Allen & Unwin, 1975], 87–90).

27. Meinardus, *Christian Egypt,* 300–15.

28. This is reminiscent of Ibn ʿArabī's statement that the gnostic who performs a sexual act in a spiritual manner need not perform ablutions afterward, for it is lust that pollutes, not the act itself. See above, 250.

29. Mina, "Pope Kyrillos VI and the Spiritual Leadership," 8, 9.

30. Shaykh ʿIzz once told me that he wished to test his own saintliness by going to live among wild animals.

31. Mina, "Pope Kyrillos VI," 10–11.

32. Ibid., 22.

33. Ibid., 18.

34. *Christian Egypt,* 45.

35. Ibid., 49–50.

36. A collection of testimonies concerning his miracles may be found in a booklet entitled *Muʿjizāt al-Bābā Kyrillos al-Sādis* (Cairo: Abnāʾ al-Bābā Kyrillos al-Sādis, 1988). The word *muʿjiza* is used by Copts for all miracles, whereas Muslims distinguish between the miracles of Prophets, which are called *muʿjizāt* (literally, "rendering impotent," that is, stopping the mouths of critics) and the miracles of saints, which are called *karāmāt* ("graces").

37. Mina, "Pope Kyrillos VI," 25.

38. Biegman, *Egypt,* 89.

39. Mina, "Pope Kyrillos VI," 25–26.

40. Ibid., 28.

41. Biegman, *Egypt,* 89.

42. "Secret" is not the best translation here, for it refers to a spiritual core that is, nonetheless, inaccessible to other people. Sufis use the same term.

43. In the Qur'an, as in the Midrash, Solomon is represented as a magician who had jinn and birds in his army under his command.

44. The apparent reference is to Matt. 12:31–32, "Every sin and blasphemy will be forgiven men, but the blasphemy against the Spirit will not be forgiven. And whoever says a word against the Son of man will be forgiven; but whoever speaks against the Holy Spirit will not be forgiven, either in this age or in the age to come" (Revised Standard Version). Cf. Mark 3:28–29, Luke 12:10.

45. One young man told me that this was not that unusual among the Copts in Upper Egypt.

46. This encounter between ʿIzz and Eliṣābāt recalls the first meeting of Ibn ʿArabī with another famous Sufi, Shihāb al-Dīn ʿUmar al-Suhrawardī, author of a Sufi treatise called *ʿAwārif al-maʿārif.* "Both of them bowed their heads for an hour without uttering a word to each other, and then parted. When Ibn ʿArabī was asked his opinion of al-Suhrawardī, he said, 'He is embued from head to foot with the norm of the Prophet.' When asked for his opinion of Ibn ʿArabī, al-Suhrawardī said, 'He is an ocean of divine truths' " (R. A. Nicholson, "The Lives of ʿUmar Ibnu 'l-Farid and Muhiyyu'ddin Ibnu'l-ʿArabi," *Journal of the Royal Asiatic Society* [1906]: 812).

47. The beautiful film by Elizabeth Wickett, *For Those Who Sail to Heaven,* about the moulid of Abū 'l-Ḥajjāj, makes use of scenes from the walls of the ancient Egyptian temples to emphasize this continuity.

48. "Veneration of Saints in Islam," 305–11.

CHAPTER 12: CONCLUSION: SUFISM IN MODERN EGYPT

1. *Islam and the Plight of Modern Man,* esp. 4–19, 59.

2. Intellectual dependence on the West, with its corollary of feelings of inferiority, never reached the heights in Egypt that it did in Algeria and Tunisia, where French thought succeeded in dominating intellectual life to the point that it was commonly assumed that a progressive, intellectual atti-

tude demanded outright atheism. Egypt's long history as a cultural center of the Arab world and its pride in the achievements of Arabic literature and thought contrast with the total domination of French language and thought in France's North African colonies.

3. *All That is Solid Melts into Air: The Experience of Modernity* (New York: Simon and Schuster, 1982), 345; cited in Lawrence, *Defenders of God,* 1.

4. Many articles have been published on this topic, making it unnecessary to explore it in detail here. Bruce Lawrence describes Islamic fundamentalism in a comparative context in *Defenders of God.* The five volumes on fundamentalism produced by the Fundamentalism Project, edited by Martin E. Marty and R. Scott Appleby, and published by the University of Chicago Press, contain a number of articles on Islamic fundamentalism, its ideology, roots, and impact on Muslim societies. Articles by John Voll and Andrea Rugh in *Fundamentalisms and Society,* the second volume of the series (1993), argue that Islamic fundamentalism has succeeded, in the 1990s, in shaping much of Egyptian public discourse and individual thought.

5. Richard P. Mitchell, *Society of the Muslim Brothers* (London: Oxford University Press), 14.

6. Abū 'l-Wafā' al-Taftāzānī, in preface to Ḥajjājī, *Min aʿlām al-ṣaʿīd,* 8.

7. *Islam and the Plight of Modern Man,* 58–59.

8. *Al-ʿAhd al-wathīq li-man arāda sulūk aḥsana ṭarīq* (Cairo: Al-ʿAshīra 'l-Muḥammadiyya, 1980), 14.

9. See Hamid Algar's introduction to B. R. von Schlegell's translation of the *Risāla,* which is entitled *Principles of Sufism.*

10. Introduction to *Al-Risāla 'l-qushayriyya,* 12.

11. Ibid., 11.

12. In Arabic, there is no distinction between the two words, which are both *ʿibāda.* Worship is nothing other than serving God.

13. *Sulṭān al-ʿarifīn, Abū Yazīd al-Bisṭāmī* (Cairo: Dār al-Maʿārif, 1985); *Abū Bakr al-Shiblī* (Cairo: Dār al-Maʿārif, 1985).

14. I attended these meetings almost every week from January through October 1981. During my research from 1987 to 1989, the shaykh was too feeble to teach on a regular basis.

15. I have described Jīlī's discussion of this in detail in "Annihilation in the Prophet in Late Medieval Sufism."

16. *Islam and the Plight of Modern Man,* 74.

17. "Cairene *Ziyâra*-Days," 42.

18. Janet Abu-Lughod, "Migrant Adjustment to City Life: The Egyptian Case," *American Journal of Sociology* 67 (1961): 23.

19. Watt, *Faith and Practice of al-Ghazali,* 60.

20. Ibid., 54–55.

GLOSSARY

Ahl al-bayt: "People of the House," the family of the Prophet Muhammad. Most interpretations limit the *ahl al-bayt* to ʿAlī and Fāṭima and their descendants, but some include the wives of the Prophet as well.

Aḥwāl: See *ḥāl.*

Al-Azhar: The Islamic university founded in 972 by the Fāṭimids, it remains the center of the Islamic religious establishment in Egypt and is probably the most prestigious university for the study of Islamic sciences in the world.

Ashʿarī: School of theology, founded by Abū 'l-Ḥasan al-Ashʿarī (d. 935) in response to the Muʿtazilī school of thought, to uphold the doctrines of Aḥmad ibn Ḥanbal with the methods of the Muʿtazila. They are particularly famous for their doctrines of the reality of the attributes of God, the eternity of the Qurʾan, and predestination.

ʿĀshūrāʾ: The tenth day of the Islamic month of Muḥarram, it is the anniversary of the martyrdom of Ḥusayn and is a day of voluntary fasting.

Awliyāʾ (plural of *walī*): Literally meaning "friends" (of God), it is usually translated as "saints."

Awrād (plural of *wird*): These are the special daily prayers of the Sufis, which are said in addition to the five daily *ṣalāt* prayers required of all Muslims. *Awrād* generally consist of prayers for forgiveness, prayers of blessing on the Prophet, supplications for spiritual illumination, and dhikr.

Badr: The first major battle between the Muslims of Medina and the polytheists of Mecca, in 624. The Muslims, though outnumbered more than three to one, won a decisive victory.

Baraka: Literally "blessing," it is a spiritual power associated with holy people, times, places, or things. It is communicable and can bring disaster on evildoers or unbelievers, just as it brings blessing on believers.

Baṣīra: Inner vision, obtained through mystical illumination rather than physical sight *(baṣar).*

Bayt: Literally "house," it means a branch of certain Sufi Orders, such as the Burhāmiyya and Rifāʿiyya, who do not split into separate Orders but allow spiritual teachers within the Order to operate under such nearly autonomous branches.

Caliph: The English rendering of *khalīfa,* it means the "successor" of Muhammad in his political functions and is the title of the ruler of the Islamic state. The institution is called the Caliphate *(khilāfa)*.

Darwīsh/Dervish: In its original Persian it means a "poor" person, but it came to mean a Sufi. In Egypt, the word *dervish* can be a great compliment, meaning someone who is thoroughly devoted to God, or it can be a pejorative, meaning a ragged beggar who makes a show of spirituality but follows practices not condoned by the Sharīʿa.

Dhikr: Literally "remembrance" or "recollection," it is a ritualized recitation or recollection of the Names of God. It is part of the individual Sufi's daily *wird,* and it may also be done communally. Communal dhikr is often accompanied by music.

Fanāʾ: "Annihilation" of the ego or individual self. In early Sufism, its meaning was restricted to annihilation in God and carried connotations of being "present" with God and "absent" from, or unaware of, this world. In later Sufism, one needed first to achieve annihilation in one's shaykh and then in the Prophet, implying not a trancelike state but intense love and identification.

Faqīr: A "poor" man, or a Sufi.

Fātiḥa: The opening chapter of the Qurʾan, it is only seven verses long. It is recited in the daily prayers of the Muslims and is also used as a prayer of blessing on behalf of individuals. It is thought to contain the entire meaning of the Qurʾan.

Fāṭimids: An Ismāʿīlī Shiʿi dynasty that ruled Egypt from 969 to 1171.

Fundamentalism: A religious interpretation based on the absolute authority of the literal interpretation of sacred scriptures. Islamic fundamentalists demand that a conservative interpretation of Islam form the foundation of all public life.

Gallābiyya: A light, cotton robe or dress that is the common garment of many Egyptians.

Gazb (in classical Arabic, *jadhb*): Literally "attraction" or "abduction," it is a mental impairment, temporary, intermittent, or permanent, that occurs as a result of a flash of divine revelation.

Ghawth: Literally "help," it is the word most commonly used in Egypt for the supreme saint in the saintly hierarchy.

Gnostic: In Arabic, *ʿārif bi 'llāh,* "a knower of/in God," one whose knowledge is derived from mystical experience rather than just from ordinary education.

Ḥadīth: An account of something the Prophet Muhammad said or did. The same word is used to refer to the entire body of literature containing these narratives. I use a capital *Ḥ* when referring to this literature in general and a lowercase *ḥ* when referring to a particular narrative.

Ḥadīth qudsī: A divine saying communicated through *ḥadīth* rather than in the Qurʾan.

Ḥaḍra: An assembly for the purpose of dhikr, prayers of invocation, and possibly recitation of the Qurʾan.

Ḥajj: The ritualized pilgrimage to Mecca that is required of all Muslims at least once during their lifetime, if they are financially able.

Ḥājj (feminine *Ḥājja*): Someone who has performed the ḥajj. In the dialect of Cairo and the Egyptian Delta, this is pronounced *Ḥāgg* and *Ḥāgga,* but the *j* is retained in Upper Egypt.

Ḥāl (plural, *aḥwāl*): A spiritual state. Although a spiritual state can refer to virtually any divinely induced psychological or emotional state, a person who is said to be "in" a spiritual state is one whose actions emanate from it rather than from rational thought. Such a person might be an inspired teacher or leader, or might be unable to keep his responsibilities before the Shariʿa.

Ḥaqīqa: "Truth," it means the transcendent spiritual Truth that may be apprehended only through mystical experience and personal illumination.

Imām: A leader. In everyday life, anyone who leads a group of two or more in communal prayer is the *imām* of that group. Imām is also used to mean the leader of the community (the Caliph) and in Shiʿism is used almost exclusively in that meaning. In Sunni Islam, Imām is also a title informally applied to spiritual leaders of great standing. In Ibn ʿArabī's hierarchy of saints, the *quṭb* is assisted by two *imāms*.

Islamists: The name preferred by some for Muslim fundamentalists.

Jihād: Literally "struggle." In the Qurʾan, Muslims are told to struggle in the path of God with their bodies and with their goods. Although the word often is used to mean warfare on behalf of Islam, Sufis use it most frequently in the sense of each person's struggle against the evil in his own soul.

Jinn (a collective plural with the singular *jinnī*): These are beings made of fire who were created before humans. They have a greater propensity than humans to do evil. In the Qurʾan, they eavesdrop on the heavenly council and whisper what they learn to their "friends" on earth, but God has chased them away from heaven by means of meteors. A group of jinn overheard the Qurʾan being recited and became Muslims. Jinn possession of people and houses is a frightening reality for many Egyptians, who avoid walking alone near water or dark places to avoid being susceptible to jinn possession.

Kaʿba: The shrine in Mecca that Muslims believe is built under the Throne of God. Circumambulation of the Kaʿba is the central ritual of the hajj, and Muslims face the direction of the Kaʿba in prayer.

Khalīfa: Literally "successor" or "deputy," in Sufism it means one who functions as spiritual director of a part of a Sufi Order and who may be heir to the shaykh's position when he dies.

Khalwa: Seclusion for the purpose of meditation and spiritual devotions.

Khidma (plural, *khidamāt*): A "service," or hospitality station (in a tent, room, or simply on the sidewalk) at a moulid offering, at minimum, drinks to passersby. Many *khidamāt* offer food as well, and pilgrims coming to the moulids often sleep in *khidamāt*.

Khilāfa: The position of *khalīfa.*

Madad: Literally "assistance," it means the spiritual aid granted by saints, which can also have very tangible physical benefits. Visitors to saints' shrines cry out for *madad,* and refrains of *"Madad, madad"* are frequent in the songs of the *munshidīn.*

Magzūb (plural, *magāzīb*): A person in a state of *gazb.*

Mamlūks: Slave soldiers, usually of Turkish origin, who ruled Egypt from 1250 to 1517. The period of Mamluk rule is divided between the Baḥrī Maluks (1250–1382), who were Turkish military rulers, and the Burjī Mamluks (1382–1517), an oligarchy of military slaves. The Sufi Orders flourished during the Mamlūk period.

Maqām (plural, *maqāmāt*): A stage or station on the spiritual journey. The word is also used in Egypt to mean the manner in which one practices one's spiritual life, even if it is not a generally recognized stage on the Sufi path.

Maqṣūra: The barrier erected around the *tābūt* of a saint. It may be made of wood or metal and is typically done in a lattice style. Devotees may kiss the *maqṣūra,* touch it, or rub it with perfume.

Modernism: An ideology that embraces evolutionary change. "Modernism" can refer to an ideology derived from the European Enlightenment, but "Islamic modernism" is a movement among some Muslim intellectuals to reinterpret the Qurʾan according to its enduring principles and spirit rather than the letter of the Sharīʿa, thereby allowing for an adaptive principle to make Islam better meet the needs of modern life.

Mosque: In Arabic, *masjid,* or *jāmiʿ* if it is a mosque for Friday prayer. The Muslim place of worship.

Moulid: In classical Arabic, *mawlid.* A "saint's day celebration." Although the word literally means "birthday," it is usually held on the anniversary of the saint's death. The celebration may last anywhere from three days to two or three weeks and culminates in a "great night."

Muftī: A scholar of Islamic law whose opinions are sought on legal issues. The Mufti of Egypt is the chief authority on the Sharīʿa.

Munshid (plural, *munshidīn*): Literally, "one who sings praises." It is the word used among Sufis for a professional Sufi singer who sings praises to God and the Prophet or other songs expressing the Sufi experience. *Munshidīn* usually sing during a dhikr, but they may also sing independently of dhikr.

Muslim Brotherhood: A fundamentalist organization founded by Ḥasan al-Bannā in 1928 with the slogans, "The Qurʾan is our constitution" and "Islam: Religion and State." Appealing to the desire of many Muslims to have Islam play a more central role in public life and offering social services not offered at that time by the state, they garnered a membership in virtually every town of Egypt in the 1940s. In 1952 they assisted in the coup led by Gamal Abdul Nasser that overthrew the monarchy, but after a falling-out with Nasser they were banned. They have nonetheless continued to play an important opposition role in Egyptian politics to this day.

Muʿtazila: a school of theology that flourished in Baghdad and Basra in the late eighth and ninth centuries, upholding the efficacy of human reason in matters of theology and the absolute unity and justice of God. The school's scholars were the first Muslims to utilize Greek philosophical methods of reasoning, but they were ultimately rejected by Sunni Muslims as unorthodox.

Ottoman Empire: Originating in the late thirteenth century in Anatolia and the Balkans, the Ottomans conquered Constantinople in 1453 and made it their capital under the new name of Istanbul. They conquered Egypt and Syria in 1517. In the nineteenth century, the Ottoman governor of Egypt, Muhammad ʿAli, ruled virtually independently of Istanbul. The Empire was defeated in World War I and came to a formal end in 1922, when Mustafa Kemal Ataturk abolished the Sultanate.

Qurʾan: Often rendered in English as *Koran*. This is the sacred scripture of the Muslims that is believed to be the word of God, revealed piecemeal to the Prophet Muhammad over a period of twenty-three years (610–632). Recitation of the Qurʾan is done in a distinctive cantillated style and is prominent in Muslim worship. The beauty of the language of the Qurʾan also makes a skillful recitation very pleasurable to hear.

Quṭb: Literally "axis" or "pole," often translated here as "Axis of the Age," this is the supreme saint in the hierarchy of saints. In Egyptian Sufism the word *quṭb* is also used to refer to the founders of the major Sufi Orders: ʿAbd al-Qādir al-Jīlānī, Aḥmad al-Rifāʿī, Aḥmad al-Badawī, and Ibrāhīm al-Dasūqī.

Rakʿa: A cycle of prostration in *ṣalāt*. A *rakʿa* consists of postures of standing, bowing from the hips, and prostration with the forehead on the floor. The various *ṣalāt* prayers each contain a specified number of *rakʿa*s. Proper etiquette of saint shrine visitation includes praying two *rakʿa*s in honor of the saint.

Sāḥa: Literally "court," in Egypt this is the word used for a Sufi center of spiritual retreat, teaching, and hospitality.

Ṣalāt: The ritual prayer required of all Muslims five times daily—dawn *(fajr)*, noon *(ẓuhr)*, midafternoon *(ʿaṣr)*, sunset *(maghrib)*, and evening *(ʿishāʾ)*. *Ṣalāt* must be performed in a state of purity and facing the *qibla*, or direction of the Kaʿba in Mecca.

Sayyid (feminine, *Sayyida*): An honorific title meaning "lord" (or "lady"). It is used for members of the *ahl al-bayt* and others who have acquired a great reputation for sanctity.

Shafāfiyya: Literally "transparency," it is clairvoyance, the ability to see "through things," beyond ordinary perception. It may refer to something as unspectacular as character discernment, which is the first stage in the development of this gift.

Sharīʿa: Islamic law, which is built on the Qurʾan, Ḥadīth, the consensus of the scholars *(ijmāʿ),* and the opinions of individual scholars *(ijtihād).* There are four legal schools in Sunni Islam that follow the same legal principles and recognize each other as valid interpretations of the law. Shiʿi sects of Islam have separate legal schools.

Sharīf (plural, *ashrāf*): A descendant of the Prophet.

Shaykh (feminine, *shaykha*): Sometimes rendered in English as *sheikh.* In Sufism, a spiritual master. In Egypt this is also the title given to graduates from the Islamic University of al-Azhar and is applied informally as an honorific title for anyone whose religious knowledge is respected. The word literally means an elder and in tribal Arab societies is also the title of an elder of a tribe or clan.

Shiʿa (a collective plural of which the singular is *Shiʿi*): The Shiʿa began as a political movement, the partisans of ʿAlī ibn Abī Ṭālib in the struggle over the Caliphate that began in 656, but they developed into a distinct sect of Islam. They believe that the Caliphate—or Imāmate—belongs in the family of the Prophet. The Twelver and Ismaʿili Shiʿa developed distinctive doctrines concerning the Imām: that he was privy to spiritual knowledge by virtue of the portion of the divine light he had inherited from the Prophet; that the Imām is necessary for the guidance of the community; and that the Imām is immune from error. The Islamic Republic of Iran has made Twelver Shiʿism its official creed.

Sufi Order: A method of practicing Sufism, as well as a social institution that teaches this method at the hands of a shaykh who has learned it from another shaykh, in a spiritual lineage *(silsila)* that goes back to the Prophet.

Sunni: The majority of Muslims, approximately 89 percent, consider themselves "people of the Sunna (good example of the Prophet) and the community" *(ahl al-Sunna wa 'l-jamāʿa),* that is, Sunnis. Egypt's Muslims are entirely Sunni. The other major sect of Islam are the Shiʿa.

Tābūt: An oblong wooden structure over the vault in which the body of a saint is buried. The *tābūt* is covered with embroidered silk or linen. At the end of some moulids, the *tābūt* of the saint who is celebrated, and possibly those of other local saints as well, is processed around the town.

Taṣawwuf: The Arabic word for Sufism.

Tawḥīd: "Unification." In Islam in general, this refers to the belief in one God, the main doctrine of Islam. In Egyptian Sufism, it is also used for the belief that the spirits of individuals who love each other in a spiritual manner may become so linked that they "become one" and can communicate without words and share a common inspiration.

Ulama: The scholars of Islam, who specialize in knowledge of the Qurʾan, Ḥadīth, and the Sharīʿa. The singular is *ʿālim,* and the Arabic plural is more properly rendered *ʿulamāʾ.*

Wahhābīs: Members of a movement that began in eighteenth-century Arabia and aimed to eradicate all aspects of popular Islam deemed incompatible with the original form of Islam. In particular, it targeted the veneration of saints and visitation of their tombs. Egyptian Sufis use the word *Wahhābī* to mean "fundamentalist."

Wakīl: A trustee or official in charge of an organization.

Walī: See *awliyā*ʾ.

Wird: See *awrād*.

Zār: A spirit possession ceremony that is particularly associated with women.

Zuhd: Asceticism/self-denial.

BIOGRAPHICAL DICTIONARY

ʿAbāṭa, Muḥammad Ḥasan (d. 1941), a Sufi master and *magzūb* who is the eponym of Bayt ʿAbāṭa, a branch of the Rifāʿiyya founded by his son, Shaykh Hāshim ʿAbāṭa (d. 1985).

ʿAbduh, Muḥammad (1849–1905). The founder of Islamic modernism in Egypt, he devoted himself to efforts to reform Al-Azhar University and the Islamic educational system. He also became Mufti of Egypt. At one time in exile for his political agitation in association with Afghānī, he and Afghānī jointly published a magazine from Paris, *Al-ʿUrwa 'l-Wuthqā*.

Abū Bakr (d. 634), the first Caliph after the death of Muhammad (632–34). Known as "The True" *(al-ṣiddīq),* he was an early convert to Islam and one of Muhammad's closest Companions. During Muhammad's illness, he was appointed *imām* of the communal prayers, which was interpreted by some as an indication that he was intended to succeed Muhammad in his political functions as well.

Abū 'l-ʿAzā'im, Muḥammad Māḍi (d. 1937), former professor of Islamic law at Khartoum University and founder of the ʿAzmiyya Shādhiliyya Order.

Afghānī, Jamāl al-Dīn al- (1838–97). The father of Islamic modernism and modern Muslim nationalism, he was a Persian who traveled widely throughout the Muslim world stirring the Muslims against European imperialism and encouraging the renewal of intellectual life.

Aḥmad Abū 'l-Ḥasan (d. 1994). disciple of Aḥmad Raḍwān (d. 1967) and Muḥammad Abū 'l-Futūḥ (d. 1985), he became spiritual head of the "sons" of Abū 'l-Futūḥ after the latter's death.

Aḥmad ibn Ḥanbal (d. 855), founder of the Ḥanbalī school of Islamic law, often seen as the strictest and most literal interpretation of the law. He championed the authority of Ḥadīth over the capacity of human reason to discern truth on divine matters and became a symbol of popular resistance to efforts by the Caliph al-Ma'mūn (813–33) to force the ulama to recognize Muʿtazilī doctrine. He symbolizes, perhaps more than any other person, the articulation of Sunni doctrine.

ʿĀ'isha, daughter of Abū Bakr. The youngest wife of Muhammad, she may have been only sixteen when he died, and many hadiths have been recited on her authority. She was the only one of Muhammad's wives who was a virgin when he married her, and according to tradition, she was his favorite wife among the wives he took after the death of his first wife, Khadīja, in 619.

ʿAlī ibn Abī Ṭālib (d. 661), the cousin and son-in-law of the Prophet Muhammad. An early Muslim, he was named Caliph after ʿUthmān's murder in 656, but the period of his rule was marred by civil war, and he too was assassinated in 661. He is deemed the first Imam of the Shiʿa, who believe that Muhammad intended him to be the first Caliph after his death, and that the Caliphate/Imāmate belongs among his descendants. Both Sufis and Shiʿa believe he was privy to unique mystical knowledge.

Badawī, Aḥmad al- (d. 1276), a Moroccan who settled in Egypt, is buried in Ṭanṭā, and founded the Aḥmadiyya Order. His moulid is among the largest in Egypt.

Bannā, Ḥasan al- (1906–1949), a schoolteacher who founded the Muslim Brotherhood in 1928.

Bisṭāmī, Abū Yazīd al- (d. 874), also known in Persian as Bāyezīd. He was a Sufi given to ecstatic experiences and epitomizes the classical Sufi experience of *fanāʾ*—annihilation of the ego in God.

Dasūqī, Ibrāhīm (d. 1297), an Egyptian who founded the Burhāmiyya Order and is buried in Dasūq.

Fāṭima, daughter of the Prophet Muhammad and wife of ʿAlī ibn Abī Ṭālib, she is the only one of Muhammad's children to have children.

Fāṭima al-Nabawiyya, allegedly the daughter of Ḥusayn and "mother of orphans," who are buried with her in her mosque-shrine in Cairo.

Gābir Ḥusayn Aḥmad al-Jāzūlī, founder and present shaykh of the Jāzūliyya Ḥusayniyya Shādhiliyya Order.

Gabriel, the archangel said to be the agent of the Qurʾan's revelation to Muhammad.

Gamāl al-Sanhūrī, head of the Egyptian branch of the Burhāniyya from 1953–1986.

Ghazālī, Muḥammad Abū Ḥāmid al- (1058–1111), the consummate Sufi intellectual. An Ashʿarī theologian and scholar of law, a successful college professor with close ties to the government in Baghdad, he underwent a midlife ten-year retreat and converted to Sufism. He authored a large number of books, including *Tahāfut al-falāsifa* (The Incoherence of the Philosophers), *Iḥyāʾ ʿulūm al-dīn* (The Revival of the Religious Sciences), a compendium of knowledge for the religious Muslim, *Al-Munqidh min al-ḍalāl* (Deliverer from Error), which contains the story of his conversion and his arguments for the validity of mystical insight, and *Mishkāt al-anwār* (The Niche of Lights), a thoroughly Sufi work analyzing the meaning of light in intellectual and spiritual life, based on the famous "Light Verse," Qurʾan 24:35. He is thought to exemplify the "sober" Sufism of the intellectual.

Ḥallāj, Ḥusayn ibn Manṣūr al- (d. 922), a famous ecstatic Sufi who uttered the immortal "I am the Truth" *(anā 'l-ḥaqq),* and whose love for God led him to embrace suffering and martyrdom.

Ḥasan, first son of ʿAlī ibn Abī Ṭālib.

Hujwīrī, ʿAlī ibn ʿUthmān al-Jullābī (d. ca. 1071), author of *Kashf al-Maḥjūb,* the earliest Persian treatise on Sufism.

Ḥusayn (d. 680), second son of ʿAlī ibn Abī Ṭālib and grandson of the Prophet, he was martyred at Karbalāʾ in southern Iraq along with his family and followers when he was en route to Kūfa to lead a Shiʿi revolt against the Umayyad empire. His martyrdom is recollected by Twelver Shiʿis with group recitations, passion plays, and mournful processions accompanied by self-flagellation. His head is said to be buried in the mosque-shrine of Ḥusayn in Cairo, and he is much loved among the Sufis of Egypt, many of whom consider him their spiritual master.

Ibn ʿArabī, Muḥyī 'l-Din (1165–1240), sometimes called Ibn al-ʿArabī. Known as "the greatest shaykh" *(al-shaykh al-akbar),* his works have exerted a profound influence on Sufism throughout the Muslim world, though that influence is often mediated through the works of other Sufis of his school, such as Ṣadr al-Dīn al-Qūnawī (d. 1274), ʿAbd al-Karīm al-Jīlī (d. 1423), or ʿAbd al-Wahhāb al-Shaʿrānī (d. 1565). For many modern Muslims, he epitomizes Sufi extremism. His system of thought is often known as the unity of existence *(waḥdat al-wujūd).* He articulated the concept of the Muhammadan Reality, and his writings on the hierarchy of saints and many other topics is the most complete Sufi exposition available. His most important work is the very lengthy and difficult *Al-Futūḥāt al-makkiyya* (The Meccan Revelations), but his most widely read work might be the later *Fuṣūṣ al-Ḥikam* (Bezels of Wisdom).

Ibn Taymiyya, Aḥmad (d. 1328), a Ḥanbalī scholar famous for his vehement and articulate opposition to popular Islam and aspects of Islamic theology, philosophy, and mysticism that he felt contradicted the "pure," early form of Islam. He is the inspiration for a number of modern reform movements, including the Wahhabis, and his writings are disseminated in the streets of Cairo today in booklet form.

Ibrāhīm, Muḥammad Zakī, elderly shaykh of the Muḥammadiyya Shādhiliyya and founder of a well-known voluntary association entitled al-ʿAshīra 'l-Muḥammadiyya (1930). He has been favored by the Egyptian government as a spokesperson for reformed, moderate Sufism, but he has also been a staunch defender of the validity of such popular Sufi practices as the visitation of saints' tombs.

Jīlī, ʿAbd al-Karīm (d. 1423), expositor of the doctrines of Ibn ʿArabī and author of *Al-Insān al-kāmil* (The Perfect Man).

Junayd, Abū 'l-Qāsim Muḥammad al- (d. 910), one of the first Sufi theoreticians, a great authority and representative of "sober" Sufism, who articulated the doctrine of *baqāʾ*—"remaining" in God but present to the world after the experience of "absence" from the world in *fanāʾ*. He figures in the spiritual chains (*silsila*s) of many Sufi Orders.

Khiḍr, the mythical immortal spiritual guide who was Moses' teacher and companion in the Qurʾan (18:65–82).

Maḥmud, ʿAbd al-Ḥalīm (d. 1978), former Rector and then Shaykh of al-Azhar. An important modern interpreter of Islam and author of a number of books on Sufism, he held degrees from al-Azhar (1932) and the Sorbonne (Ph.D., 1940).

Muḥammad Ḥasanayn Makhlūf, Muftī of Egypt in the 1970s.

Muʿāwiya (d. 680), nephew of ʿUthmān ibn ʿAffān, governor of Syria during ʿUthmān's rule, he led the most important opposition to ʿAlī's rule and founded the Umayyad dynasty, which ruled the Islamic empire from Damascus from 661 to 750.

Muḥammad son of ʿAbdallāh, the Prophet of Islam (570–632 A.D.). He was born and raised in the trading town of Mecca, in west-central Arabia. The period of his prophethood (610–632) is divided between the Meccan period (610–622) and the Medinan period (622–632). He was buried in ʿĀʾisha's apartment in their home in Medina, which faced the courtyard of the mosque.

Muḥammad ʿUthmān ʿAbduh (d. 1983), shaykh of the controversial Burhāniyya Dasūqiyya Shādhiliyya Order.

Nafīsa, Sayyida, great-granddaughter of Ḥasan. She is known in Egypt for her piety and wisdom, and her mosque-shrine has been recently and splendidly renovated.

Nasser, Gamal Abdul (d. 1970). Leader of the Free Officers' coup which overthrew King Faruq in 1952, he was president from 1954 until his death in 1970. Architect of "Arab socialism," a policy based on Arab unity, anti-imperialism, and socialist reform, he was regarded as a major hero by many in the Arab world after he ousted the British and French from the Sinai in 1956, until Egypt's defeat in the June 1967 Six-Day War with Israel led many to question his policies. However, his often brutal suppression of the Muslim Brotherhood and his subordination of the Islamic religious establishment, which was assigned the duty of teaching that Islam was a socialist revolution, alienated many religious Muslims.

Qāḍī ʿIyāḍ (d. 1150), a judge of the Mālikī school from Ceuta, Spain, and author of a book articulating a popular and much glorified image of Muhammad.

Qushayrī, Abū 'l-Qāsim al- (d. 1072). An Ashʿarī theologian and scholar of Nishapur whose importance for Egyptian Sufism is his authorship of the most widely read manual on Sufism, *Risāla fī ʿilm al-taṣawwuf,* generally known as *Al-Risāla 'l-qushayriyya.*

Rābiʿa al-ʿAdawiyya (d. 801), a Sufi woman ascetic and celibate credited with developing the idea of selfless love for God.

Raḍwān, Aḥmad (1895–1967), an independent Khalwatī shaykh who lived in the village of al-Baghdādī, near Luxor, and whose spiritual counsel was sought by Gamal Abdul Nasser.

Riḍā, Rashīd (1865–1935), disciple of Muḥammad ʿAbduh and editor of an Islamic journal called *Al-Manār.*

Rifāʿī, Aḥmad al- (d. 1178), an Iraqi Sufi who founded the Rifāʿiyya Order.

The Rifāʿiyya is possibly the largest Order in Egypt and is particularly well known for its miracles, especially its ability to handle snakes and other poisonous creatures.

Sadat, Anwar (d. 1981). President of Egypt from 1970 to 1981, he initially encouraged the revival of Islamic associations on the university campuses but in 1981 cracked down on all religious organizations following violent confrontations between Muslim fundamentalists and Coptic Christians. He was assassinated in October 1981 by a group of Muslim fundamentalists belonging to an organization known as Jihad.

Sahl al-Tustarī (d. 896), developer of the doctrine of the Muhammadan light in Sufism.

Shādhilī, Abū 'l-Ḥasan al- (d. 1258), a Moroccan Sufi who founded the Shādhiliyya Order. He is buried in Egypt by the Red Sea, where he died en route to Mecca. The Shādhiliyya is known as a middle-class Order and is considered among the most scrupulous in observing the precepts of the Sharīʿa.

Shaʿrānī, ʿAbd al-Wahhāb (1493–1565), an Egyptian mystic of the Shādhiliyya and a scholar whose works remain popular in Egypt today.

Sharqāwī, Abū 'l-Wafāʾ (1879–1961), a Sufi intellectual of the Khalwatiyya Order who taught at a center called Dayr al-Saʿāda in Najʿ Ḥammādī, in Qinā province.

Sharqāwī, Aḥmad, son of Abū 'l-Wafāʾ al-Sharqāwī and present head of Dayr al-Saʿāda.

Suṭūḥī, Muḥammad al- (d. 1982), former head of the Supreme Council of Sufi Orders.

Taftāzānī, Abū 'l-Wafā al-Ghunaymī al-, present head of the Supreme Council of Sufi Orders, as well as a vice president and professor of philosophy at Cairo University.

Ṭayyib, Muḥammad al- (d. 1988), a Khalwatī shaykh of Qurna, in Qinā province, who lived on a mere three spoonfuls of milk a day. Many Sufis in the region considered him the *ghawth* after the death of Aḥmad Raḍwān.

ʿUmar ibn al-Khaṭṭab (d. 644), the strong and strictly devout Companion of Muhammad whose leadership was felt even during the Prophet's life. He was the second Caliph of Islam (634–44), and during his rule Muslims conquered vast territories. He is known for his strict but totally just application of the law.

Umm Salama, a wife of the Prophet.

ʿUthmān ibn ʿAffān (d. 656), the third Caliph of Islam (644–56). He was a Companion and son-in-law of the Prophet, but financial inequities and nepotism during his rule provoked a revolt among Arab soldiers stationed in Egypt, who assassinated him. His death marks the beginning of the great civil war that produced the Shiʿi sect.

Zayn al-ʿĀbidīn, ʿAlī, son of Ḥusayn. He was saved from death by his aunt, Sayyida Zaynab, thanks to her singular heroism during the slaughter at Karbalāʾ. He is author of a book of devotional poems. His mosque-shrine is in southern Cairo, not far from that of Sayyida Zaynab.

Zaynab, Sayyida, sister of Ḥusayn and granddaughter of the Prophet. In Egypt, she is heralded for her wisdom, piety, and courage in protecting ʿAlī Zayn al-ʿĀbidīn from death at the hands of the Umayyads. Her mosque-shrine in Cairo is the focus of much devotion.

SELECT BIBLIOGRAPHY

ʿAbd al-ʿAlīm, Muḥammad Muḥammad. *Sayyidnā 'l-Imām al-Ḥusayn*. Cairo: Maṭābiʿ sharikat al-Shamarlī, 1983.

ʿAbduh, Muḥammad ʿUthmān. *Tabriʾat al-dhimma fī nuṣḥ al-umma wa tadhkirat ūlī 'l-albāb li 'l-sayr ilā 'l-ṣawāb*. Khartoum ?: Al-Ṭarīqa 'l-burhāniyya 'l-dasūqiyya 'l-shādhliyya, 1974?

Abū ʿAlam, Tawfīq. *Ahl al-bayt, 1: Fāṭima al-Zahrāʾ*. Cairo: Dār al-maʿārif, 1972.

Abū 'l-ʿAzāʾim Muḥammad Māḍī. *Mudhakkirat al-murshidīn wa 'l-mustarshidīn*. 2d ed. Cairo: Dār al-madīna 'l-munawwara, 1983.

ʿAlī, Ibrāhīm Ramaḍān [Shaykh Fāris]. *Min faḍāʾil wa khaṣāʾiṣ āl al-bayt*. Cairo: Maṭbaʿat dār iḥyāʾ al-kutub al-ʿarabiyya, 1985.

ʿAlī, Mūsā Muḥammad. *ʿAqīlat al-ṭuhr wa 'l-karam al-Sayyida Zaynab*. Cairo: Dār al-turāth al- ʿarabī, 1984.

Arberry, A. J. *Sufism: An Account of the Mystics in Islam*. London: George Allen & Unwin, 1950.

Athanasius, Bishop of Bani Suef. *The Copts Through the Ages*. 4th ed. Cairo: Egyptian Ministry of Information, 1976.

ʿAṭṭār, Farīd al-Dīn. *Muslim Saints and Mystics*. Translated by A. J. Arberry. Oxford: Oxford University Press, 1966.

Austin, R. W. J. "The Feminine Dimensions in Ibn al-ʿArabi's Thought." *Journal of the Muhyiddin Ibn ʿArabi Society* 2 (1984): 5–14.

———. "Meditations on the Vocabulary of Love and Union in Ibn ʿArabi's Thought." *Journal of the Muhyiddin Ibn ʿArabi Society* 3 (1984): 6–19.

Ayoub, Mahmoud. *Redemptive Suffering in Islam: A Study of the Devotional Aspects of ʿĀshūrāʾ in Twelver Shīʿism*. The Hague: Mouton Publishers, 1978.

Bannerth, Ernst. "La Khalwatiyya en Egypte: Quelques aspects de la vie d'une confrérie." *Mélanges de l'Institut Dominicain d'Etudes Orientales* 8 (1964–66): 1–74.

———. "La Rifaʿiyya en Egypte." *Mélanges de l'Institut Dominicain d'Etudes Orientales* 10 (1971): 1–35.

———. "Aspects humains de la Shādhiliyya en Egypte." *Mélanges de l'Institut Dominicain d'Etudes Orientales* 11 (1972): 237–50.

Biegman, Nicolaas H. *Egypt: Moulids, Saints, Sufis*. The Hague: Gary Schwartz/SDU; London: Kegan Paul International, 1990.

Chodkiewicz, Michel. *Le Sceau des saints: Prophétie et sainteté dans la doctrine d'Ibn Arabi*. Paris: Editions Gallimard, 1986.

Cornell, Vincent. "Mirrors of Prophethood: The Evolving Image of the Spiritual Master in the Western Maghrib from the Origins of Sufism to the End of the Sixteenth Century." Ph.D. diss., University of California at Los Angeles, 1989.

de Jong, Frederick. "Cairene *Ziyâra*-Days: A Contribution to the Study of Saint Veneration in Islam." *Die Welt des Islams* 17 (1976): 26–43.

———. "Aspects of the Political Involvement of the Sufi Orders in Twentieth-Century Egypt (1907–1970—An Exploratory Stock-Taking)." In *Islam, Nationalism and Radicalism in Egypt and the Sudan*, edited by Gabriel R. Warburg and Uri M. Kupferschmidt, 183–212. New York: Praeger Publishers, 1983.

———. "Al-Ḳuṭb." *Encyclopaedia of Islam*. 2d ed. Leiden: E. J. Brill, 1954– . 4:543–46.

Eliade, Mircea. *The Sacred and the Profane: The Nature of Religion*. Translated by Willard R. Trask. San Diego: Harcourt Brace Jovanovich, 1959.

Elias, Jamal. "Female and Feminine in Islamic Mysticism." *Muslim World* 78 (1988): 209–24.

El Masri, Iris Habib. *The Story of the Copts*. Cairo: Middle East Council of Churches, 1978.

El-Shamy, Hasan M. "Mental Health in Traditional Culture: A Study of Preventive and Therapeutic Folk Practices in Egypt." *Catalyst* 6 (1972): 13–28.

Elwell-Sutton, L. P. "Sufism and Pseudo-Sufism." In *Islam in the Modern World*, edited by Denis MacEoin and Ahmed al-Shahi, 49–56. New York: St. Martin's Press, 1983.

Ernst, Carl W. *Words of Ecstasy in Sufism*. Albany: State University of New York Press, 1985.

Fuchs, H. "Mawlid." *Encyclopaedia of Islam*. 1st ed. 3:419–22.

Ghazālī, Abū Ḥāmid Muḥammad al-. *Iḥyā' ʿulūm al-dīn*. 5 vols. Cairo: Maṭbaʿat lajnat nashr al-thaqāfa 'l-islāmiyya, 1937.

———. *Marriage and Sexuality in Isalm*. Translated by Madelain Farah. Salt Lake City: University of Utah Press, 1984.

Ghazālī, Aḥmad al-. *Tracts on Listening to Music*. Translated by James Robson. Oriental Translation Fund n.s. 34. London: Royal Asiatic Society, 1938.

Ghāzī, Muḥammad Jamīl, and ʿAbd al-Munʿim al-Jidāwī. *Al-Ṣūfiyya: al-wajh al-ākhar*. Cairo: Al-Maṭbaʿa 'l-fanniyya, 1980.

Gilsenan, Michael D. "Some Factors in the Decline of the Sufi Orders in Modern Egypt." *Muslim World* 57 (1967): 11–18.

———. *Saint and Sufi in Modern Egypt: An Essay in the Sociology of Religion*. Oxford: Oxford University Press, 1973.

———. *Recognizing Islam: Religion and Society in the Modern Arab World*. New York: Pantheon Books, 1982.

Goldziher, Ignaz. "Neuplatonische und gnostische Elemente im Hadit." *Zeitschrift für Assyriologie und verwandte Gebiete* 22 (1909): 317–44.
———. *Etudes sur la tradition islamique*. Translated by Leon Bercher. Paris: Adrien Maisonneuve, 1952.
———. *Muslim Studies*. 2 vols. Translated by C. R. Barber and S. M. Stern. London: George Allen & Unwin, 1971.
———. *Introduction to Islamic Theology and Law*. Translated by Andras Hamori and Ruth Hamori. Princeton: Princeton University Press, 1981.
Ḥajjājī, Muḥammad ʿAbduh al-. *Min aʿlām al-ṣaʿīd fī 'l-qarn al-rābiʿ ʿashar al-hijrī: Abū 'l- Maʿārif Aḥmad ibn Sharqāwī al-khalafī al-imām al-qudwa*. Cairo: Dār al-taḍāmun, 1969.
Ḥaqqī, Yaḥyā. *The Saint's Lamp*. Translated by M. M. Badawi. Leiden: E. J. Brill, 1973.
Hodgson, Marshall G. S. "How Did the Early Shiʿa Become Sectarian?" *Journal of the American Oriental Society* 75 (1955): 1–13.
Hoffman-Ladd, Valerie J. "Devotion to the Prophet and His Family in Egyptian Sufism." *International Journal of Middle East Studies* 24 (1992): 615–37.
———. "Mysticism and Sexuality in Sufi Thought and Life." *Mystics Quarterly* 18, no. 3 (1992): 82–93.
Homerin, Th. Emil. "Ibn Arabi in the People's Assembly: Religion, Press, and Politics in Sadat's Egypt." *Middle East Journal* 40, no. 3 (1986): 462–77.
Hujwīrī, ʿAlī ibn ʿUthmān al-Jullābī al-. *Kashf al-Maḥjūb of Al Hujwīrī*. Translated by Reynold A. Nicholson. E. J. W. Gibb Memorial Series vol. 17. London: Luzac, 1911.
Ibn ʿArabī, Muḥyī al-Dīn ʿAbd Allāh Muḥammad ibn ʿAlī. *Al-Futūḥāt al-makkiyya*. 4 vols. Beirut: Dār Ṣādir, 1966.
———. *Fuṣūṣ al-ḥikam*. 2 vols. Edited by Abū 'l-ʿAlā ʿAffifī. Beirut: Dār al-kitāb al-ʿarabī, 1966.
———. *Rasāʾil Ibn al-ʿArabī*. Beirut: Dār iḥyāʾ al-turāth al-ʿarabī, n.d.
———. *The Sufis of Andalusia: The Rūḥ al-quds and Al-Durrat al-fākhira*. Translated by R. W. J. Austin. London: George Allen & Unwin, 1971.
———. *Bezels of Wisdom*. Translated by R. W. J. Austin. New York: Paulist Press, 1980.
Ibn al-Mubārak, Aḥmad. *Al-Ibrīz*. Cairo: Maktabat ʿAlī Ṣubayḥ wa awlād-ihi, n.d.
Ibn Taymiyya, Taqī al-Dīn Aḥmad. *Ḥuqūq āl al-bayt bayn al-sunna wa 'l-bidʿa*. Edited by ʿAbd al-Qādir Aḥmad ʿAṭāʾ. Cairo: Muʾassasat al-miṣrī li 'l-kitāb, 1981.
Ibrāhīm, Muḥammad Zakī. *Qaḍāyā 'l-wasīla wa 'l-qubūr*. Cairo: Al-ʿAshīra 'l-Muḥammadiyya, 1979.
———. *Al-Tabṣīr bi mushāhid shahīrāt āl al-bayt bi 'l-qāhira*, 2d ed. Cairo: Al-ʿAshīra 'l- Muḥammadiyya, 1980.
Ibrāhīm, Muḥammad Zakī, ed. *Al-Lawāʾiḥ al-ṣūfiyya 'l-rasmiyya 'l-jadīda*. Cairo: Al-ʿAshīra 'l- Muḥammadiyya, 1978.

Jaʿfar, Muḥammad Kamal Ibrāhīm. *Min al-turāth al-ṣūfī: li Sahl ibn ʿAbd Allāh al-Tustarī.* 2 vols. Cairo: Dār al-maʿārif, 1979.

Jāzūlī, Gābir Ḥusayn Aḥmad al-. *Maʿa taḥiyyāt al-ṭarīqa 'l-jāzūliyya 'l-ḥusayniyya 'l-shādhiliyya.* N.p., n.d.

Jeffery, Arthur, ed. *A Reader on Islam.* 's-Gravenhage: Mouton, 1962.

Jīlī, ʿAbd al-Karīm al-. *Al-Insān al-kāmil fī maʿrifat al-awākhir wa 'l-awāʾil.* Cairo: Muṣṭafā al- Bābī al-Ḥalabī, 1949.

Kahle, Paul. "Zâr-Beschwörungen in Egypten." *Der Islam* 3 (1912): 1–41.

Kalabādhī, Abū Bakr al-. *The Doctrine of the Sufis.* Translated by Arthur J. Arberry. Cambridge: Cambridge University Press, 1935.

Kamil, Jill. *Coptic Egypt: History and Guide.* Cairo: American University in Cairo, 1987.

Kloth, Kari. *Die himmlischen Augen: Die Geschichte einer anderen Wirklichkeit.* Hamburg: Verlag Scarabaus, 1987.

Kuḥayl, ʿAbd al-ʿĀl. *Abū 'l-ʿAynayn al-Dasūqī.* Cairo: Maṭbūʿāt al-shaʿb, 1983.

Lane, Edward William. *Manners and Customs of the Modern Egyptians.* The Hague: East-West Publications, 1836.

Lawrence, Bruce. *Defenders of God: The Fundamentalist Revolt against the Modern Age.* San Francisco: Harper and Row, 1989.

Lings, Martin. *A Sufi Saint of the Twentieth Century.* Berkeley and Los Angeles: University of California Press, 1971.

———. *What Is Sufism?* Berkeley and Los Angeles: University of California Press, 1975.

Lutfi, Huda. "The Feminine Element in Ibn ʿArabi's Mystical Philosophy." *Alif: Journal of Comparative Poetics* no. 5 (1985): 7–19.

Māhir, Farīd. *Karamāt al-awliyāʾ.* Cairo: Al-Maṭbaʿa 'l-ʿālamiyya, 1971.

Maḥmūd, ʿAbd al-Ḥalīm. *Al-Madrasa 'l-shādhiliyya wa imāmuhā Abū 'l-Ḥasan al-Shādhilī.* Cairo: Dār al-naṣr li 'l-ṭabāʿa, n.d.

———. *Qaḍīyat al-taṣawwuf.* Cairo: Dār al-maʿārif, 1977.

Maḥmūd, ʿAbd al-Ḥamīd, and Maḥmūd ibn al-Sharīf, eds. *Al-Risāla 'l-qushayriyya.* 2 vols. Cairo: Dār al-Taʾlīf, 1966.

Makhlūf, Ḥasanayn Muḥammad. *Ṣafaḥāt nāṣiʿa min tārīkh al-imāmayn ʿalamay al-Islām, al- ustādhayn al-ʿārifayn bi 'llāh, Shaykh Aḥmad ibn Sharqāwī wa Shaykh Aḥmad Abī 'l- Wafāʾ al-Sharqāwī.* Cairo: Maṭbaʿat al-madanī, 1968.

Malaṭāwī, Ḥasan Kāmil al-. *Al-Ṣūfiyya fī ilhāmihim.* 2 vols. Cairo: Al-Majlis al-aʿlā li 'l- shuʾūn al-islāmiyya, 1969.

Massignon, Louis. *Essai sur les origines du lexique technique de la mystique musulmane.* Rev. ed. Paris: Librairie Philosophique J. Vrin, 1968.

Mazloum, Cherifa-Nihal. "Le *Zâr:* Culte de possession dans l'Egypte contemporaine." thesis, Ecole Pratique des Hautes Etudes en Ethnologie, Sorbonne, Paris, 1975.

McPherson, J. *The Moulids of Egypt.* Cairo: N. M. Press, 1941.

Meinardus Otto F. A. *Christian Egypt: Faith and Life.* Cairo: American University in Cairo Press, 1970.

———. *Monks and Monasteries of the Egyptian Desert*. 2d ed. Cairo: American University in Cairo Press, 1989.

Mernissi, Fatima. "Women, Saints, and Sanctuaries." *Signs: Journal of Women in Culture and Society* 3 (1977): 101–12.

———. *Beyond the Veil: Male-Female Dynamics in a Modern Muslim Society*. Rev. ed. Bloomington: University of Indiana Press, 1987.

Michon, Jean-Louis. "Sacred Music and Dance in Islam." In *Islamic Spirituality, II: Manifestations*, edited by Seyyed Hossein Nasr, 469–505. New York: Crossroad, 1991.

Mina, Father Raphael Ava. "Pope Kyrillos VI and the Spiritual Leadership." Translated by Pope Kyrillos VI Publications. Cairo: Sons of Pope Kyrillos VI, n.d.

Miṣrī, Fāṭima al-. *Al-Zār: Dirāsa nafsiyya wa anthropologiyya*. Cairo: Al-Hay'a 'l-miṣriyya 'l- 'āmma li 'l-kitāb, 1975.

Mu'jizāt al-Bābā Kyrillos al-Sādis. Cairo: Abnā' al-Bābā Kyrillos al-Sādis, 1988.

Najjār, 'Āmir al-. *Al-Ṭuruq al-ṣūfiyya fī miṣr: Nash'atuhā wa nuẓumuhā*. Cairo: Anglo-Egyptian Bookstore, 1978.

Nasr, Seyyed Hossein. *Islam and the Plight of Modern Man*. London: Longman, 1975.

Nawfal, 'Abd al-Razzāq. *Al-Taṣawwuf wa 'l-ṭariq ilayhi*. Cairo: Al-Sha'b, 1972.

Nelson, Cynthia. "Self, Spirit Possession and World View: An Illustration from Egypt." *The International Journal of Social Psychiatry* 17 (1971): 194–209.

———. "Stress, Religious Experience and Mental Health." *Catalyst* 6 (1972): 48–57.

Nicholson, Reynold A. *Studies in Islamic Mysticism*. Cambridge: Cambridge University Press, 1921.

Nurbakhsh, Javad. *Sufi Women*. New York: Khaniqahi-Nimatullahi Publications, 1983.

Nwyia, Paul. *Exégèse coranique et langage mystique*. Recherches de l'Institut de Lettres Orientales v. 49. Beirut: Dar el-Machreq, 1970.

———. *Ibn 'Aṭā' Allāh (m. 709/1309) et la naissance de la confrérie sadilite*. Recherches de l'Institut de Lettres Orientales, vol. 2. Beirut: Dar al-Machreq, 1972.

Parrinder, Geoffrey. *Sex in the World's Religions*. New York: Oxford University Press, 1980.

Qushayrī, Abū 'l-Qāsim al-. *Al-Risāla 'l-qushayriyya*. Cairo: Maktabat wa maṭba'at Muḥammad 'Alī Ṣubayḥ wa awlādihi, n.d.

———. *Principles of Sufism*. Translated by B. R. von Schlegell. Berkeley: Mizan Press, 1990.

Raḍwān, Aḥmad. *Al-Nafaḥāt al-rabbāniyya*. 3d ed. Kom Ombo, Egypt: Yūsuf Ja'lūṣ, 1986.

Rāgib, Yūsuf. "Al-Sayyida Nafīsa, sa légende, son culte et son cimetiére." *Studia Islamica* 44 (1976): 61–86; and 45 (1977): 27–55.

Sammān, Muḥammad ʿAbd Allāh al-. *Taʾthīm al-dhimma fī taḍlīl al-umma, fī 'l-radd ʿalā kitāb "Tabriʾat al-dhimma fī nuṣḥ al-umma" li 'l-shaykh al-burhānī.* Cairo: Dār al-thaqāfa 'l- ʿarabiyya 'l-ṭabāʿa, 1977.
Ṣayfī, ʿAbd al-Ḥamid al-. "Manzilat al-rasūl bayn al-rusul wa 'l-wājib ʿalā 'l-umma naḥwahu." *Al-Islām waṭan* (November 1988): 56–58.
Schimmel, Annemarie. *Mystical Dimensions of Islam.* Chapel Hill: University of North Carolina Press, 1975.
———. "Eros—Heavenly and Not So Heavenly—in Sufi Literature and Life." In *Society and the Sexes in Medieval Islam,* edited by Afaf Lutfi al-Sayyid-Marsot, 119–41. Malibu, California: Undena Publications, 1979.
———. "Women in Mystical Islam." *Women's Studies International Forum* 5 (1981): 145–51.
———. *And Muhammad is His Messenger: The Veneration of the Prophet in Islamic Piety.* Chapel Hill: University of North Carolina Press, 1985.
Sharaf al-Dīn, Aḥmad al-Shaḥāwī Saʿd. *Al-Sayyida Nafīsa, bint Sayyidī Ḥasan al-Anwar.* Cairo: Maṭbaʿat al-ta'līf, n.d.
Sharqāwi, Aḥmad Abū 'l-Wafāʾ al-. *Miṣbāḥ al-arwāḥ fī sulūk ṭarīq al-Fattāḥ.* 2d ed. Cairo: Maṭbaʿat al-madanī, 1962.
Sharqāwī, Ḥasan al-. *Al-Ḥukūma 'l-bāṭiniyya.* Cairo: Dār al-maʿārif, 1982.
Smith, Jane I. "Concourse between the Living and the Dead in Islamic Eschatological Literature." *History of Religions* 19, no. 3 (1980): 224–36.
Smith, Margaret. *Rābiʿa the Mystic and Her Fellow-Saints in Islam.* Cambridge: Cambridge University Press, 1928.
———. *Al-Ghazālī the Mystic.* Oxford: Oxford University Press, 1944; Lahore: Hijra International Publishers, 1983.
Solihin, Sohirin Mohammad. *Copts and Muslims in Egypt: A Study on Harmony and Hostility.* Leicester: Islamic Foundation, 1991.
Ṭawīl, Tawfīq al-. *Al-Taṣawwuf fī miṣr ibbāna 'l-ʿaṣr al-ʿuthmānī.* Al-Jamāmīz: Maktabat al- adab, 1962?
Tijānī, ʿAbd al-ʿAzīz al-ʿĀyidī al-. *Ahl al-qurbā hum ahl Allāh wa khāṣṣatuhu.* Cairo: Maṭbaʿat al-amāna, 1984.
Trimingham, J. Spencer. *The Sufi Orders in Islam.* Oxford: Oxford University Press, 1971.
ʿUways, Sayyid. *Al-Ibdāʿ al-thaqāfī ʿalā 'l-ṭarīqa 'l-miṣriyya: Dirāsa ʿan baʿḍ al-qiddīsīn wa 'l- awliyāʾ fī miṣr.* Cairo: National Center for Sociological and Criminological Studies, 1980.
Wahba, Father Matthias Farid. "The Coptic Orthodox Church of Egypt." 3d printing. San Francisco: St. Antonius Coptic Orthodox Church, 1992.
Wakīl, ʿAbd al-Raḥmān al-. *Hādhihi hīya 'l-ṣūfiyya.* Beirut: Dār al-kutub al-ʿilmiyya, 1984.
Watt, William Montgomery. *The Faith and Practice of al-Ghazali.* London: George Allen & Unwin, 1953.
Watterson, Barbara. *Coptic Egypt.* Edinburgh: Scottish Academic Press, 1988.
Waugh, Earle. *The Munshidīn of Egypt: Their World and Their Song.* Columbia: University of South Carolina Press, 1989.

Williams, Michael A. "Uses of Gender Imagery in Ancient Gnostic Texts." In *Gender and Religion: On the Complexity of Symbols*, edited by Caroline Walker Bynum et al., 196–227. Boston: Beacon Press, 1986.

Winter, Michael. *Society and Religion in Early Ottoman Egypt: Studies in the Writings of ʿAbd al-Wahhāb al-Shaʿrānī.* New Brunswick: Transaction Books, 1982.

INDEX

ʿAbāṭa, Hāshim Muḥammad, 31, 32, 33, 247, 427
ʿAbāṭa, Muḥammad Ḥasan, 31, 32, 115, 382n.8, 427
ʿAbāṭa, Sayyid Hāshim, 33
Abbott, Nabia, 131, 394n.18
ʿAbd al-ʿAlīm, Muḥammad Muḥammad, 388n.89
ʿAbd al-Gawād, Gamāl, 381n.49
ʿAbd al-Ḥamīd al-ʿAryān, 188
ʿAbd Allāh, father of Muhammad, 54
ʿAbd al-Nabī, 245, 251
ʿAbd al-Qādir al-Jīlānī, 150, 423
ʿAbd al-Raḥīm al-Sabʿ, 292, 293
ʿAbd al-Rāziq, Aḥmad, 405n.27-8,n.30,n.33,n.35
ʿAbd al-Salām al-Ḥilwānī, 85, 136
ʿAbd al-Salām Muḥammad, 87
ʿAbduh, Muḥammad, 6, 7, 8, 278, 283, 364, 380n.17, 427, 430
abiding in God *(baqāʾ)*, 200-201, 429
ablutions, 136, 160, 236, 272, 416n.28
Abraham, 53, 68, 72, 320, 393n.57
absence (from the world, present with God), 161, 170, 185, 200, 202, 211, 372, 420
Abū ʿAlam, Tawfīq, 388n.86, 389n.102, 389n.108
Abū 'l-ʿAbbās al-Mursī, 65, 161, 312, 397n.11
Abū 'l-ʿAlāʾ (Abul Ela), 37
Abū 'l-ʿAzāʿim, Sayyid Muḥammad Māḍī, 61, 94, 124, 126, 127, 145, 148, 151, 156, 157, 165, 166, 168-9, 183, 185, 187, 188, 213, 221, 257, 396n.1, 400n.77, 401n.11, 427
Abū 'l-ʿAzm, Maḥmūd, xiv, 140, 209-10, 255, 256, **285-91,** 374, 376, 381n.50, 411n.51
Abū Bakr, 70, 71, 72, 96, 126, 173, 200, 277, 388n.81, 398n.35, 427
Abū 'l-Futūḥ al-ʿArabī, Muḥammad, 127, 268-9, 409n.32, 427
Abū 'l-Ḥadīd (a *magzūb*), 210-11
Abū 'l-Ḥasan, Aḥmad, xiii, 53, 127, 137, 139, 143-4, 212, 262, **267-70,** 357, 409n.32, 427
Abū 'l-Ḥajjāj, Yūsuf, 60, 106 moulid of 109-10, 111, 279, 355, 393n.45, 417n.47
Abū Khalīl of Zaqaziq, 139, 194
Abu-Lughod, Janet, 374, 418n.18
Abū 'l-Maʿāṭī, Burhāmī shaykh, 87, 109
Abū 'l-Maʿātī, Sāmiya, 249
Abū Madyan al-Tilmisānī, 60
Abū Magd, brother of Abū 'l-Wafā al-Sharqāwī, 100-101
Abū 'l-Qumṣān of Qurna, 99, 100
Abū 'l-Suʿūd, 32, 115, 179, 244, 382n.6
adab (Sufi etiquette), 129, 144, 145-9, 165, 281-2, 289, 290, 320, 375-6, 395n.41; with God 146-7, 183, 396n.41; with one's shaykh, 147-8, 394n.19; with fellow disciples, 147, 148-9; with family members, 149, 394n.19
Adam, 56, 58, 236, 384n.24

INDEX

ʿAffīfī, Abū 'l-ʿAlā, 237

Afghānī, Jamāl al-Dīn al-, 278, 364, 427

ahl al-bayt (family of the Prophet), 21, 22, 30-31, 32, 33, 68-87, 105, 111, 122, 127, 153, 161, 171, 176, 178, 188, 193, 194, 246, 256, 273, 289, 293, 294, 299, 301, 302, 310, 314, 388n.82, 389n.107, 389n.118, 393n.43, 419, 423; definition of, 69; hadiths concerning, 69; love for, 77-87, 389n.107; Muhammadan light in, 68; Qurʾanic references to, 68-9; tombs of in Cairo, 76-7

Aḥmad ʿAbd al-Malik, Ḥāgg, 262, 409n.10

Aḥmadiyya Idrīsiyya Shādhiliyya Order, 108, 184

Aḥmadiyya Order, 150, 152, 182, 428

Aḥmadiyya sect, 314, 413n.25

Aḥmad, Laylā Shams al-Dīn Aḥmad, xiv, 286-91, 376, 411n.51

Ahmed, Leila, 404n.2, 405n.31

Ahrām, al-, newspaper, 56, 57, 311, 312, 313, 314-9, 385n.26, 402n.49, 412n.15-6, 413n.19,n.23-7,n.29-31, 414n.32,n.35

ʿĀʾisha, daughter of Abū Bakr and wife of Muhammad, 70, 96, 121, 200, 398n.35, 427-8, 430

ʿĀʾisha, Sayyida (daughter of Jaʿfar al-Sadiq), 32, 77

ajbiyya (Coptic daily prayers), 338-9

Akhenaton, 356

ʿAlawī, Aḥmad al-, 4

Algar, Hamid, 418n.9

Algeria, 417n.2

Ali, A. Yusuf, 389n.106

ʿAlī ibn Abī Ṭālib, cousin and son-in-law of Muhammad, 69-73, 74, 77, 79, 87, 93, 107, 108, 173, 207, 313-4, 398n.35, 424, 428, 430

ʿAlī, Ibrāhīm Ramaḍān. *See* Fāris, Shaykh

ʿAlī, ʿIṣām al-Dīn Muḥammad, 402n.40,n.44

ʿAlī, Muḥammad, 423

ʿAlī, Mūsā Muḥammad, 389n.111-2

Almohad dynasty, 314

American Research Center in Egypt, 25, 82

American University in Cairo, 25, 38, 82, 211

ʿAmm Amīn, xiv, 29, 30, 34, 42, 93, 220, 353-4

ʿAmriyya Rifāʿiyya, 87, 130

angels, 125, 132, 153, 166, 169, 199, 213, 217, 224, 234, 305, 320, 321, 331, 335, 337, 388n.86. *See also* Gabriel

Anhār, Ḥāgga, 403n.57

animalistic, 238-9

animals, 341, 416n.30

annihilation of the ego *(fanāʾ)*, ix, 1, 11, 36, 67, 176, **200-204,** 212, 213, 236, 238-9, 241, 252, 289, 372, 382n.4, 420, 428; annihilation in the Messenger *(fanāʾ fī 'l-rasūl)*, 62, 64-65, 67, 140-1, 203-4, 309, 372, 387n.57, 395n.32, 401n.26; annihilation in one's shaykh *(fanāʾ fī 'l-shaykh)*, 140-1, 203-4, 216, 291, 353-4, 372

Anṣār al-Sunna 'l-Muḥammadiyya, Jamāʿat, 8, 413n.27

Appleby, R. Scott, 418n.4

ʿAqqād, ʿAbbās Maḥmūd al-, 283

Arab socialism, 7, 266, 336, 342, 367, 430

Arberry, A. J., 2, 3-4, 379n.2-3, 402n.53

asceticism *(zuhd)*, 97, 135, 156, 157, 196-200, 207, 231, 255, 257, 260, 262, 291, 329-31, 340, 342, 343, 371, 381n.45, 397n.12

Ashʿarī, Abū 'l-Ḥasan al-, 66, 402n.46, 419

Ashʿarī school of theology, 368, 419, 428

INDEX

ʿAshīra ʾl-Muḥammadiyya al-, 12-13, 99, 226, 265, 371, 375, 418n.14
ʿAshūrāʾ, 245, 419
ʿAsqalānī, Ibn Hajar al-, 405n.33
ʿAṣṣāṣa, Muḥammad al-Mahdī, 292
Ataturk, Mustafa Kemal, 423
Athanasius, Bishop, 329, 336, 416n.15
ʿAṭṭār, Farīd al-Dīn, 229-30
Austin, Ralph W. J., 237, 239, 406n.44,n.51
authoritarianism, 267, 317, 325, 358, 359, 363
awrād. See wird
Axis of the Age. *See quṭb*
Ayoub, Mahmoud, 388n.91
Ayyūbid period, 108
Azhar, al-(mosque and university), 6, 7, 10, 39, 74, 117, 123, 129, 227, 273-4, 283, 290, 292, 364, 368, 380n.24, 419, 424, 427, 430
ʿAzmiyya Shādhiliyya Order, 60, 94, 151, 152, 357, 368, 427

Bābī sect, 314, 413n.25
badal, pl. *abdāl* ("substitutes," a rank in the saintly hierarchy), 94-95, 297, 310
Badawī, Aḥmad al-, 9, 28, 59, 60, 90, 92, 95, 101, 107, 150, 178, 304, 356, 423, 428; moulid of, 110, 248
Badr, battle of, 120, 419
Baghdādiyya Order, 232
Bahāʾī sect, 314, 413n.25
Bahī, Muḥammad al-, 382n.2
Bakrī, Aḥmad Murād al-, 150
Bakrī family, 150
Baktashī Order of Turkey, 399n.53
Baldick, Julian, 415n.47
Bannā, Ḥasan al-, 6, 7, 8, 361-2, 380n.22, 422, 428
Bannā, Rajab al-, 385n.27, 412n.16
Bannerth, Ernst, 130-1, 390n.125
baqāʾ. *See* abiding in God
Bāqir, Muḥammad al-, 388n.81
Bāqūrī, Shaykh Aḥmad Ḥasan al-, 282
baraka, 4, 16, 92, 95, 105, 107, 110, 112, 114, 120, 128, 152, 209, 249, 257, 271, 296, 310, 333, 341, 344, 347, 350, 351, 375, 392n.38, 419
barzakh, 1, 214, 307
baṣīra (inner vision), 35, 83, 87, 92, 162, 220, 221, 263, 293, 305, 351, 353, 419
Baṣrī, Ḥasan al-, 196
bāṭin, 13
Bāṭiniyya, 314, 413n.25
Bayhaqī al-, 388n.85
bayt, 419
Bayt ʿAbāṭa, xiv, 32-33, 37, 81, 99-100, 122, 149, 152-3, 247, 382n.8, 427
Bayyūmī, Sīdī ʿAlī al-, 109
Bayyūmiyya, 152, 182
beauty, 1, 239, 337, 338, 411n.53
becoming one, 41, 140, 141, 204-5, 251-2, 291; one with God, 163, 204
Bedouins, 297-8
Bengal, 408n.89
Berman, Marshall, 360
bewilderment, 261
Bible, 24, 53, 187, 200, 236, 338, 348, 349, 412n.5, 416n.18, 417n.44
bidʿa (heretical innovation), 20, 184-5
Biegman, Nicolaas, 18, 99, 100, 170, 182, 261-2, 266, 267, 342, 381n.41, 393n.46, 398n.30, 399n.48, 409n.12,n.30, 417n.38,n.41
Bilāl (Muhammad's Companion who gave the call to prayer), 202
biographies, 368-71
Bishoi, St., 415n.11
Bisṭāmī, Abū Yazīd al-, 142-3, 158, 197, 201-2, 221, 229, 370, 371, 397n.15, 401n.19, 428
Blacker, Carmen, 416n.26
bodies of saints, 96-97, 108, 217, 332-3, 339-40, 415n.11, 416n.26
body, connectedness with spirit, 167, 251-2, 253

INDEX

Boewering, Gerhard, 384n.18
"born again," 131, 411n.53
Bouhdiba, A., 405n.44, 406n.51
Brockelmann, Carl, 386n.57
brotherhood, 148-9, 152-3, 194, 204-5, 282, 375, 396n.54
Buḥayra, 352
Bukhārī, Abū ʿAbd Allāh Muḥammad Ismāʿīl al-, 387n.72, 390n.3, 393n.53, 397n.10, 405n.40, 408 n.90
Burāq, 125
Burda, al- ("Mantle Ode"), 54
Burhāmiyya Order, 60, 109, 150, 182, 189, 248, 249, 316-7, 318, 327, 419, 428
Burhāniyya Order, 14-15, 17, 23, 56, 57, 133, 155, 186, 209, 243-4, 248, 300-327, 358, 360, 368, 381n.49, 385n.28, 412n.3, 413n.27-8, 428; controversy over, 308-19; foreign Burhānīs, 319-23, 326, 412n.3, 414n.40; lineage of, 302-3, 324, 411-2n.2
Buṣīrī al-, 54, 262, 384n.13, 409n.11, 410n.39

Cairo, 45, 47, 48, 171, 178, 210, 247, 260, 266, 271-2, 278, 285, 286, 293, 301, 354, 366, 421
Caliph/Caliphate, 70-1, 96, 419-20, 421, 424, 427, 428, 431
Campo, Juan, 382n.5, 392n.38
capacity *(istiʿdād)*, 135, 136
celibacy, 193, 229, 230, 354
charity, 255
children, 28, 44, 46, 110, 136, 148, 193, 210, 211, 231, 234, 237, 244, 248, 249, 250, 291, 292, 293, 329, 333, 339, 347
Chishti Order of India, 399n.53
Chittick, William C., 388n.96
Chodkiewicz, Michel, 3, 384n.17, n.20, 385n.24, 387n.57, 390n.9, 391n.16,n.19
Christians, Muslim relations with, 39, 49, 117, 230, 233, 282, 320. *See also* Coptic Christians
circumcision, 334
clitoridectomy, 407-8n.85
Combs-Schilling, M. E., 252, 408n.87
communal nature of Egyptian mysticism, 30, 116, 133-4, 169-70, 203-5, 326, 366, 372-3
compassion, 263, 282, 291-2, 295, 296, 326, 400n.77
confession, 346
contemplative vs. active spiritual life, 330, 365-6, 370. *See also* seclusion
continuity with classical Sufism, 371-3
contraction *(qabḍ)*, 160
conversion, 131, 217, 224, 267, 268-9, 272-3, 289-90, 293-4, 320-1, 338, 347, 363, 374, 411n.53, 412n.3, 414n.41, 428
Coptic Christians/Coptic Church, xi, 48, 328-56; attitudes toward Muslims, 49, 328, 352, 354; doctrines and organization of, 329-30; interactions with Muslims, 106-7, 282, 328, 331-2, 347, 354, 411n.47, 431; membership of, xi, 415n.1; moulids, 117, 331, 332, 333-4, 346, 393n.43; path of spiritual refinement, 338-40; prayers, 330, 338-9, 348, 349; reactions to author, 48-49; revival in, 360; saints in Coptic spiritual life, 331-7, 344-7, 349, 350, 351, 354; sexuality among, 339-40; similarity with Sufis, xi, 351-6; spiritual guidance in, 337-38, 341, 346; visions, 335-7, 344, 346, 347, 349, 351, 415n.11; vocabulary of spiritual awareness, 351. *See also* exorcism; Kyrillos VI, Pope; Ibrahim, Muqaddasa Elisabat; Isḥāq
Corbin, Henry, 402n.42
Cornell, Vincent, 61, 393n.42, 405n.36, 411n.2

criticism of Sufism, 1-4, 5, 7-8, 171, 174-5, 183-5, 191, 241, 300-302, 360-1, 368-9
Cuno, Kenneth, 383n.9

Dabbāgh, ʿAbd al-ʿAzīz al-, 22-23, 52, 140-1, 146, 161-2, 163, 215, 221, 222, 371, 383n.11, 405n.43
dabbūs, used to cut the body as proof of baraka, 99
Dalāʾil al-khayrāt, 51
dancing, 174-5, 179, 181, 285
Daqqāq, Abū ʿAlī al-, 190
Dard, Khwaja Mir, 64
Dardīr, Aḥmad al-, 277
Dashti, ʿAli, 384n.12
Dasūqī, Ibrāhīm al- (saint), 60, 95, 101, 146, 150, 157, 189, 302, 305-7, 316-7, 318, 320-1, 325, 327, 413n.28, 423, 428
Dasūqī, Ibrāhīm al- (of the Ministry of Religious Endowments), 311, 314, 385,n.27, 390n.122
David and Bathsheba, 53
Daylamī al-, 388n.85, 389n.112
Dayr al-Saʿāda, 277, 278, 280, 282-3, 284, 364, 410n.46, 431
death, 1, 96-7, 126, 320, 332, 343, 354-5, 373. *See also* martyrs/martyrdom
de Jong, Frederick, 14, 32, 99, 373, 374, 380n.27, 382n.6,n.8, 391n.20, 399n.47
Delta of Egypt/Lower Egypt, 29, 45, 47, 59, 60, 87, 95, 109, 110, 150, 175, 271, 286, 292, 421
Demirdāsh, Muḥammad, 32
Demirdāshiyya Khalwatiyya, 32, 185
demons, 89, 178, 187, 198, 213, 304, 346, 347, 353
Denny, Frederick, 385n.35
dervish, dervishism *(darwīsh, darwasha)*, 17, 111, 112, 160, 197, 207, 251, 353, 397n.9, 420
dhikr (recollection of God), 7-8, 9, 12, 17, 21, 25-26, 31, 34, 41, 76, 82, 83, 105, 110, 111, 112, 113, 118, 119, 124, 125, 131, 132, 133-4, 138, 139, 143, 145, 147, 153, 157, 163-88, 191, 194, 198, 201, 209, 211, 233, 245-9, 250, 255, 260, 261, 274, 277, 278, 280, 281, 290, 291, 293, 302, 307, 352, 371, 411n.51, 419, 420; controversy over, 183-5, 278, 300, 330, 399n.49; individual and group dhikr, 166-70, 205, 244; music in dhikr, 171-8, 398n.32, 422; psychological states in, 185-8, 211, 213; public dhikrs, 179-182, 183, 188, 272, 334, 358, 362, 373, 382n.5, 393n.43; techniques and benefits of, 164-70, 397n.17; and *zār*, 178-9, 181, 244, 398n.46. *See also* women
Dhū 'l-Nūn al-Miṣrī, 185, 229
Diocletian, 329
disciple. *See murīd;* shaykh-disciple relationship; Sufi path
dosa ceremony, 99-100
dreams, 40, 66, 135, 139-40, 143-4, 213-8, 221, 290, 335, 373, 402n.40,n.46
dress, Islamic (for women), 228, 289, 360, 374
drinking, 25, 34, 114, 115, 153, 154, 180, 181-2, 191, 192, 205, 222, 259, 263, 268, 274, 307, 347, 383n.11, 412n.5, 421. *See also* hospitality
Duran, Khalid, 414n.40-1

eating. *See* food
ecstasy, 162, 167, 170, 173, 174, 176, 182, 183, 186, 187, 206, 213, 262, 376, 377, 405n.44, 406n.51, 428
education, 23-4, 137, 220, 231, 269, 278, 283, 285, 291, 298, 300, 301, 303-4, 319, 325, 357, 358, 363, 364-5, 367, 373, 374, 377, 427
Egypt, ancient, 279, 354-6, 417n.47
Egyptian personality/spirituality (idea of its endurance through ages), 354-6
Egyptian society, complexity of, 326-7, 377

INDEX

Eliade, Mircea, 103-4, 117, 392n.37
Elias, Jamal, 230, 404n.5-6
Elijah, 94
elite/elect, spiritual *(khawāṣṣ)*, 159, 166, 203
El Masri, Iris, 336, 416n.14-5
El-Messiri, Sawsan, 407n.82
El-Shamy, Hasan M., 398n.46
Elwell-Sutton, L. P., 2, 322
Enlightenment, French, 359, 360, 422
Ernst, Carl, 400n.74
Ethiopia, 179, 341
Eve, 236
exorcism, 345-6, 347, 349, 350
expansion *(basṭ)*, 162

Fahim, Hussein, 407n.81
Fakhouri, Hani, 399n.46
fallāḥ (peasant, someone from the Delta), 270-1
fanā'. *See* annihilation of the ego
faqīr, pl. *fuqarā'* (poor man, Sufi), 92, 397n.9, 420
Fārābī, Abu Nasr al-, 58, 61
Farah, Madelain, 404n.16
Faraj, Shaykh, 262
Farghal, Sultan, 41
Fāris, Shaykh (Ibrāhīm Ramaḍān 'Alī), 22, 83-84, 298-9, 387n.71, n.73, 388n.77-81,n.83,n.88, 389n. 101,n.104,n.108-10,n.113-7
fasting, 97, 196-8, 229, 272, 330-1, 339, 419
fatḥ, pl. *futūḥ* (mystical "opening" or unveiling), 220-1, 268, 277, 371
Fātiḥa, opening chapter of the Qur'ān, 97, 105, 117, 131, 132, 135, 142, 170, 216, 268, 295, 312, 321, 420
Fāṭima al-Nabawiyya, 25, 31, 33, 76, 81, 108, 179, 246, 289, 362, 382n.5, 428
Fāṭima, daughter of Muhammad, 69, 73, 74, 75, 79, 107, 108, 388n.86,n.91, 428
Fāṭima of Nishapur, 229
Fāṭimid period, 85, 107, 419, 420
fear of God, 157, 160-1, 263, 264-5, 268, 286
female/receptive, 237, 240
firāsa (reading hearts), 221, 224
fitna, 387n.75
food/eating, 45, 46, 97, 110-2, 115, 143, 147, 148, 160, 161, 196, 198, 205, 211, 229, 259, 260-1, 262, 263, 275, 286, 289, 290, 296, 298, 307, 320, 330-1, 333, 339, 344, 345, 383n.11, 412n.5, 421, 431. *See also* hospitality
forgiveness, asking for *(istighfār)*, 131, 139, 159, 169, 186, 198, 419
Franke, E., 399n.46
France, 417-8n.2
Frischkopf, Michael, 382n.5, 398n.45
Fuchs, H., 392n.39-40
Fuḍayl ibn 'Iyāḍ, 397n.12
fundamentalism/Islamism, fundamentalists/Islamists, xi, 6-7, 16, 40, 121, 152, 210, 226, 301, 325, 328, 329, 357-8, 360-3, 367, 368, 376, 382n.5, 414n.40, 418n.4, 420, 421, 425, 431
futuwwa (Sufi chivalry), 229, 398n.43

Gabriel, the archangel, 54, 55, 57, 59, 73, 221, 224, 253, 311-12, 428
Gairdner, W. H. T., 385n.34
gallābiyya, 34, 181, 374, 420
gazb, 31, 32, 208-13, 261, 273-4, 279, 420. *See also magzub*
generosity 147-8, 164, 263, 275, 292, 297, 411n.51
George, St. *See* Mārī Girgis
ghawth, 159, 162, 207, 258-9, 264, 266, 307, 397n.14, 410n.46, 420, 431. *See also qutb*
Ghazālī, Abū Ḥāmid Muḥammad al-, 22, 58, 66, 174, 187, 193, 197, 201, 219, 224-5, 229, 231-2, 249, 312, 315, 316, 369, 371, 375-6, 379n.11, 385n.24, 397n.17, 404n.3,n.14,n.16, 405n.40-1, 413 n.19,428

Ghazālī, Aḥmad al-, 232, 399n.53, 405n.29
Ghazālī, Muḥammad al-, 376
Ghāzī, Muḥammad Gamīl, 8, 101, 380n.23, 392n.36
Ghunaymiyya Khalwatiyya Order, 10
Gilsenan, Michael, 7, 9, 11-12, 13-14, 15, 90, 113, 183, 234, 316, 380n.21, 381n.37,n.40, 396n.59, 399n.49, 401n.12, 403n.60, 407n.79
Girgis, Yūsuf Sulaymān, xiv
gnosis *(maʿrifa)*, 13, 123, 126, 156, 158, 218-25, 234, 313, 369, 371, 398n.41
gnostic, 90, 91, 95, 123, 124, 125, 126, 127, 135, 139, 145, 147, 156, 170, 171, 202, 208, 209, 213, 220-1, 221, 222, 235, 236, 238-43, 255, 260, 263, 264, 279, 284, 295, 366, 410n.46, 416n.28, 420
Gnosticism (ancient), 407n.72
God: as male and female, 237; Names of, 117, 164, 165-9, 171, 183, 186-7, 201, 220, 235, 236, 239, 277, 278, 320, 321, 352, 372, 387n.76, 420; qualities of and Sufi manners with, 146-7; reflected in creation, 237
Goldziher, Ignaz, 96, 355, 380n.14, 384n.20, 404n.13, 405n.34
government involvement in religion, x, 4, 5, 8-10, 14-5, 28, 301, 312-9, 325, 362-3, 382n.5. *See also* Supreme Council of Sufi Orders
Graham, William A., 24, 37-39, 379n.1, 382n.52, 402n.42
Guindi, Hāmid al-, 327

Haddad, Yvonne Yazbeck, 402n.51, 407n.64
Hadīth: authority of, 52, 133, 228-9; collections of, 387n.72, 388n.79, n.85, 390n.1,n.3, 397n.10, 408 n.90, 409n.16; critiquing soundness of, 56-57, 311, 384n.23-4, 412 n.2; definition of, 379n.1, 383n.7, 420; in Islamic education, 218; quotations from/teachings of, 52, 55, 61, 66, 69, 71-3, 78-80, 95, 96, 118-21, 134, 135, 136, 146, 164, 194, 207, 214, 221, 228-9, 234, 235, 236, 239, 245-6, 250, 309, 311, 314, 349, 384n.21, 392n.34,n.38, 394 n.1, 396n.54, 397n.17, 400n.77, 407n.63-4; role in daily life, 23, 24, 52, 133, 198; role in law, 423, 424, 427; transmitters of, 427; use in defending Sufi doctrines, 85, 95, 118-21, 315, 369.
ḥadīth qudsī, 1, 62, 89-90, 161, 163, 164, 190, 204, 379n.1, 420
haḍra, 31, 32, 62, 99, 167, 179, 180, 181, 183, 244, 248, 293, 319, 382n.5, 382n.6, 399n.47, 420
Ḥāfiẓ, Abū 'l-Ḥajjāj, 411n.49
ḥajj. *See* pilgrimage to Mecca
Ḥajjājī, Muḥammad ʿAbduh al-, 279, 282, 409n.34, 410n.36, n.40,n.47
Ḥajjājiyyīn (descendants of Yūsuf Abū 'l-Ḥajjāj), 279
Ḥakīm, Tawfīq al-, 356
ḥāl, pl. *aḥwāl*, 80, 91, 137
Ḥallāj, Ḥusayn ibn Manṣūr al-, 3, 30, 55, 58, 201, 202, 206-7, 220, 315, 361, 370, 371, 428
Ḥāmidiyya Shādhiliyya Order, 11-12, 17-18, 198, 244-5, 316, 381n.37, 403n.60
Ḥanafī, Ḥassan, 402n.51
Ḥanbalī school, 58, 190, 427, 429
Ḥaqīqa (transcendent Truth), 12, 63, 146, 161, 242, 316, 352, 421
Ḥaqqī, Yaḥyā, 388n.94-5
Ḥasan, grandson of the Prophet, 31, 69, 73, 76, 77, 87, 257, 324, 429
Hawāra tribe, 270-1
Haykal, Muḥammad Ḥusayn, 408n.92

healing, 154-5, 178-9, 217, 272-3, 294, 297, 301, 307, 325, 331, 332, 334, 335, 342, 344-7, 349, 354, 364, 374-5, 377
heart, purification of. *See* soul, purification of
heavens, the seven, 158, 396n.6, 413n.19
Heyworth-Dunne, J., 14, 381n.34
hiddenness of saints, 90-92, 93, 390n.9
hidden truths, 241
hierarchy: of saints, 93-95, 310, 312, 421, 423; in Sufi Orders, 149-50, 300, 317; of tribes, 47
Ḥilmī, Muḥammad Muṣṭafā, 401n.15
ḥizb (prayers recited by Sufi Orders), 59, 132, 153
Hodgson, Marshall, 72, 388n.82
Hoffman-Ladd, Valerie J., 404n.2, n.16
Homerin, Th. Emil, 380n.24, 407n.71
hope, 161, 265
hospitality, 33, 34-35, 36, 37-38, 47, 82, 111, 112, 113-4, 115, 134, 147, 152, 154, 181-2, 198, 226, 245, 247, 250, 255, 259, 263, 264, 269, 282, 286, 291, 293-4, 297, 334, 347, 411n.51. *See also khidma*
Hourani, Albert, 380n.17
Hüber, Alfred, xiii, 322, 385,n.28, 412n.3
Hujwīrī, ʿAlī ibn ʿUthmān al-Jullābī, 3, 173, 231, 379n.8, 381n.43, 398n.35, 404n.16, 405n.37, 429
humility, 157, 168, 173, 191, 264-5, 267, 275, 281, 282, 284, 290
ḥūrīs, 388n.86
Ḥusayn, grandson of the Prophet, 25, 30, 31, 39, 53, 69, 73-76, 77, 82, 84-87, 101, 104, 105, 107, 108, 109, 111, 117, 119, 129, 136, 171, 180, 181, 209, 210, 211, 227, 244, 245, 246, 250, 267, 273, 274, 277, 292, 293, 294, 295, 296, 304, 305, 306, 319, 320, 321, 324, 327, 355, 356, 358, 362, 382n.5, 388n.81,n.91, 419, 429
Ḥusayn, Ṭāhā, 152, 283, 396n.59

Ibn ʿAbbās, cousin of the Prophet, 231
Ibn Abī Uṣaybiʿa, Aḥmad ibn al-Qāsim, 402n.46
Ibn Adham, Ibrāhīm, 196
Ibn ʿArabī, Muḥyī 'l-Dīn, 8, 16, 30, 55, 57, 58, 61, 64, 91, 93-94, 97, 229, 234-43, 249, 251, 300, 310, 311, 316, 361, 369, 372, 380n.24, 385n.35, 391n.18-9,n.21, 402n.42-3,n.45, 405-6n.44, 406n.51, 416n.28, 417n.46, 421, 429
Ibn al-Fāriḍ, ʿUmar, 160, 175, 390n.124, 397n.8
Ibn al-Ḥājj al-ʿAbdarī, 233, 405n.35
Ibn al-Jawzī, 190, 400n.68
Ibn al-Khaṭīb, 389n.107
Ibn al-Mubārak al-Sijilmāsī, Aḥmad, 23, 140-1, 383n.8, 396n.46, 402 n.48, 403n.66, 405n.43
Ibn al-Qayyim al-Jawziyya, 56
Ibn al-Sharīf, Maḥmūd, 368, 409n.33, 411n.1
Ibn ʿAṭāʾ Allāh al-Sakandarī/al-Iskandarī, 22, 98, 387n.62, 391n.28, 411n.1
Ibn Batīt, *khalīfa* of Burhāmiyya in Sudan, 318
Ibn Ḥabbān, 389n.112
Ibn Ḥanbal, Aḥmad, 78, 79, 120, 385n.24, 397n.16, 419, 427
Ibn Hishām, 384n.17
Ibn Isḥāq, 54
Ibn ʿIyāḍ, Aḥmad ibn Muḥammad ibn ʿĪsā, 386n.43, 395n.35
Ibn Khaḍrūya, Aḥmad, 221, 229
Ibn Khallikān, 392n.40
Ibn Māja, 397n.10
Ibn Mashīsh, ʿAbd al-Salām, 60
Ibn Rushd, 413n.19
Ibn Saʿd, 253, 394n.17, 408n.91

Ibn Sālim, disciple of Sahl al-Tustarī, 54, 59
Ibn Sīnā, 58, 61, 366, 402n.46
Ibn Taymiyya, Aḥmad, 56, 58, 69, 75, 118, 120, 312, 379n.11, 384n.24, 387n.70, 388n.88, 393n.48, 429
Ibrahim, Ezzeddin, 390n.3, 397n.10
Ibrāhīm, Muqaddasa Elīṣābāt, xiv, xv, 337, 343-53, 374, 417n.46
Ibrāhīm, Muḥammad Zakī, 12-13, 99, 119-21, 131, 226, 265-6, 301, 361, 371, 375, 380n.28, 381n.35, 381n.39, 389n.108, 393n.58, 429
Ibrāhīm, son of Muḥammad ʿUthmān al-Burhānī, 322-3, 327
Ibrahim, Youssef M., 415.1
Ibrīz, al-, 22, 52, 140-1, 162, 163, 371, 383n.8,n.11, 395n.21,n.33, 396 n.46, 402n.48, 403n.66,n.69, 405 n.43
Idrīs, the prophet, 94
illiteracy, 269, 279, 312, 344, 352, 364, 386n.41
illumination, mystical, 29, 30, 35, 90, 218, 268, 311, 357, 419, 421
Imām, 71, 73, 76, 94, 107, 124, 126, 201, 314, 364, 394n.1, 414n.41, 421, 424, 427, 428
India, 284, 355, 399n.53, 406n.51, 413n.25
inspiration *(ilhām)*, 23-24, 35, 141, 175, 211-3, 214, 221, 222, 233, 252, 262, 269, 271, 273, 301, 371
Institute of Sufi Studies, 11
intellect, 42, 71, 136, 173, 208, 211, 212, 218-20, 222, 224, 228, 240, 242, 250, 277-8, 283-4, 285, 351, 357, 369, 398n.41, 402n.53, 427; First Intellect, 61, 309, 384n.21
intercession, 81-2, 119-21, 144, 310, 314, 331, 332, 333, 345, 354-5, 393n.52
intoxication, 161, 174, 180, 185, 191, 192, 200-201, 203, 211, 213, 340, 351
Iran, 413n.25
Iraq, x, 60, 70, 73-74, 150, 224, 356, 423, 429, 430
Irenaeus, 407n.72
Iṣfahānī, Abū Nuʿaym al-, 390n.9
Isḥāq, 345, 347, 350
ʿishq (passionate love), 162, 180, 190, 241, 261, 308
Isīs, 355
Islamism. *See* fundamentalism
ʿiṣma (prophetic infallibility), 53, 90
Israel, 217, 332, 348, 413n.25
istikhāra (prayer seeking guidance), 36-37, 160, 214-5
ʿIyāḍ, Qāḍī, 58, 383n.12, 430
ʿIzz al-ʿArab al-Hawārī, 23, 34-35, 51, 52, 62-63, 64, 65, 74-75, 80, 81, 86, 87, 90, 92, 93, 94, 95, 96-97, 100, 107, 108, 110, 112-3, 117, 125, 128, 129-30, 134, 135, 136, 138, 141-2, 144-5, 151, 153-5, 158, 159-63, 165, 170, 171, 173, 175, 176-7, 182, 184, 186, 188, 189, 191-2, 193-4, 198, 199, 204-5, 208, 209, 210, 211, 212, 215-7, 218, 221, 222, 223-5, 243, 249, 250, 251, 252, 255, 257-9, 262, 263-4, 265, 266, 267, 270-75, 284, 291, 295-6, 297, 347, 352, 353, 354, 366-7, 374, 382n.5, 392n.32, 393n.57, 396n.6, 397n.9,n.14, 408 n.8, 409n.33, 410n.46, 411n.51, 412n.5, 416n.30, 417n.46; author's relationship with, xiii, xv, 34-49, 64, 136-7, 351, 394n.21, 404n.8

Jābir, companion of the Prophet, 55, 56, 311
Jaʿfar, Muḥammad Kamāl Ibrāhīm, 384n.18,n.19
Jāmiʿ, ʿAbd al-Salām, 277
Jamʿiyya ʾl-sharʿiyya ʾl-islāmiyya al-, 273
Japanese ascetics, 416n.26
Jawharī, Muḥammad al-, 399n.46
Jāzūlī, Gābir al-, xiii, 65, 127, 147-8, 151, 167, 184-5, 374, 384n.14, 428

Jazūlī, Muḥammad ibn Sulaymān, 233, 383n.4
Jāzūliyya Ḥusayniyya Shādhiliyya Order, 18, 20, 127, 147-8, 152, 247, 357, 384n.14, 386n.52-53, 387n.62, n.64, 390n.121,n.126, 428
Jeffery, Arthur, 383n.4,n.5, 409n.16
Jerusalem, pilgrimage to, 334, 336
Jesus Christ, 29, 75, 94, 157, 187, 192, 320, 331, 335, 339, 340, 344, 354, 355, 386n.52, 388n.90-1, 412n.5, 415n.11, 416n.18
Jews, 236, 332, 387n.65
Jidāwī, ʿAbd al-Munʿim al-, 380n.23, 392n.36
jihad, 8, 164, 196-200, 231, 421
Jīlī, ʿAbd al-Karīm al-, 58-59, 64, 300, 309, 372, 385n.24, 386n.57, 418n.15, 429
jinn, 21, 154-5, 238, 294, 304, 307, 348-50, 353, 417n.43, 421
Jinnah, Muhammad ʿAli, 284
Job, 206
Johnson-Davies, Denys, 390n.3, 397n.10
Joseph, son of Jacob, 73, 202, 214, 219-20, 241
Junayd, Abū 'l-Qāsim Muḥammad al-, 89, 130, 189, 200, 231, 315, 371, 429
June 1967 war (Six-Day War), 7, 266-7, 297, 301, 336, 342, 347, 360, 40
jurisprudence, roots of, 381n.44

Kaʿba, 43, 59, 64, 72, 104, 121, 201, 245, 282, 295, 296, 308, 314, 387n.65, 392n.38, 393n.57, 421, 423
Kahle, Paul, 382n.6, 399n.46-7
Kalabādhī, Abū Bakr al-, 206, 218, 368, 391n.27, 403n.65
Kamil, Jill, 415n.6
Karbalāʾ, 74-75, 429, 431
kashf (mystical unveiling), 29, 57, 162, 176, 213, 219-25, 240
Kennedy, John G., 407n.81
Khadīja, wife of Muḥammad, 428
khalīfa, 421
Khalīliyya Order, 139
Khalwatiyya Order, 133, 139, 150, 152, 182, 199, 261, 277, 278, 280, 395n.32, 430, 431. *See also* Ghunaymiyya Khalwatiyya, Musallamiyya Khalwatiyya
Kharrāz, Abū Saʿīd Aḥmad al-, 383n.1
Khawārij/Khārijīs, 70
khidma, pl. *khidamāt* (hospitality tent), 33, 37, 82, 108, 110-1, 112, 116, 198, 210, 226, 227, 247, 251, 333-4, 346-7, 421
Khiḍr, al-, 34, 54, 61, 94, 125, 130, 160, 208, 217, 220, 242, 275, 286, 333, 429
Khoury, René, 399n.46
Khuḍayrī, Shaykh Aḥmad al-, 277, 409n.36
Khushaim, Ali, 411n.1
Khwārizmī, Abū Bakr al-, 389n.113
Kloth, Kari, xiv, 322-3, 326, 414n.4,n.46
Kufa, 74-75
Kuḥayl, ʿAbd al-ʿĀl, 396n.43, 400n.67,n.75
Kyrillos VI, 336-7, 340-3, 374, 417n.36

Landolt, Hermann, 390n.4
Lane, Edward William, 99, 119, 245, 393n.49, 394n.19
Laylā and Majnūn/Qays, 162, 397n.13
Laylā, Ḥagga, 227, 249
law, Islamic. *See* Sharīʿa
Law No. 118, 9-10
Lawrence, Bruce, 5, 6, 359, 418nn.3 and 4
Lecerf, Jean, 402n.42
letters of Arabic alphabet, significance of, 206, 234, 301, 385n.40, 394n.21
light, 277, 293, 326; decorating shrines, 103, 114; divine light/light of God, 66, 104, 105, 114, 125, 161, 170, 187, 188, 191, 208, 209, 212,

light (*continued*)
220, 221, 274, 309, 311, 321, 387n.68, 389n.120, 410n.46, 424; of dhikr, 169, 186, 187, 188; festooning streets in moulid, 110; fire as light to Moses, 176; in visionary experiences, 163, 213, 335, 337; luminosity of bodies of ascetic saints, 97, 339, 383n.11; Mother of Light, 336, 349; as spiritual knowledge, 136, 294; of the Truth, 196, 200, 218, 222. *See also* Muhammad, Prophet of Islam
Lings, Martin, 3-4, 51, 145, 379n.12
Logos doctrine, 58
longing, 157, 158, 162, 190, 261, 386n.51
loss of control, 208-13
love: for the *ahl al-bayt*, 21, 78-82; for brethren, 21, 147, 148-9; for God, 50, 157, 162, 166, 170, 187, 189-92, 202, 206-7, 213, 221, 352, 357, 370, 397n.13, 428; for Muhammad, 21, 50-1, 56, 61-3, 67-68, 401n.26; for a shaykh 126, 138, 140-1, 151, 203, 282, 327, 410n.46; for the world, 146, 197; as basis for *fanā'*, 372; as foundation of piety, 118; as foundation of Sufism, 21, 136, 152, 153, 188-9, 192; God's love 89, 190, 198, 223, 237, 401n.26; in God, 193-4, 400n.77; in Sufi poetry and songs, 178, 184, 192, 233, 241, 248-9, 381n.46, 390n.124; leading to unification of spirits, 204-5, 251-2; of Muhammad and the Sufi gnostic for women, 235-9; of Muslim for Christians, 282; as station in the Sufi path, 158; unlimited by law, 242, 352; without lust between men and women 250-1, 351-2; women's love for Muhammad and gnostic men, 239-40, 353
lust, 160, 196, 224, 234, 239, 240, 250, 251, 253, 340, 351-2, 354, 371, 416n.28
Luṭfī, Hudā, 406n.51
Luxor 1, 28, 257, 355, 430

madad (assistance given by holy person), 96, 99, 134, 175, 176, 177, 180, 422
madness. *See gazb*
Maghrib. *see* Morocco
magic, 350, 417n.43
magzūb, pl. *magāzīb*, 100-101, 112, 208-13, 261, 262, 279, 306, 408n.8, 422, 427
Mahdī, 314, 390n.122, 413n.25
Maḥfūẓ, Shaykh of Fāsiyya Shādhiliyya, 395n.26
Māhir, ʿAli, 283
Māhir, Farīd, 22, 131, 157, 158, 263, 390n.1, 391n.17,n.24, 393n.52, 400n.1, 401n.7
Maḥmūd, ʿAbd al-Ḥalīm, 22, 129, 198, 211, 219-20, 248, 273-4, 297, 361, 368-70, 380n.19,n.24, 381n.51, 401n.11, 403n.59, 409n.33, 411n.1, 430
Maḥmūd Abū Shāmiḥ, 262
Majallat al-taṣawwuf al-islāmī, 10, 11, 30, 380n.29
Makarius, St., 415n.11
Makhlūf, Ḥasanayn Muḥammad, 278, 279, 282, 283, 410n.36-8,n.42
Makhlūf, Muḥammad Ḥasanayn, 56, 283, 311, 313-5, 430
Makkī, Abū Ṭālib al-, 23
Malāmatiyya, 5, 241
Malaṭāwī, Ḥasan al-, 128, 133-4, 138-9, 383n.2,n.9, 388n.81, 390n.124, 394n.10, 395n.27, 396n.45, 398n. 24, 400n.61, n.66, n.72, n.76, n.80, 401n.28, 402n.33
Malik al-Nāṣir Muḥammad ibn Qalāwūn al-, 77
Mālik ibn Anas, 172
Mālikī school of jurisprudence, 383n.12
Mamdūḥ Abū 'l-ʿAzm, xiv, 286, 288, 289, 291, 411n.51
Mamlūk period, 2, 77, 232-3, 362, 422

Ma'mūn, Caliph, 427
manifestations of God *(tajalliyāt)*, 63, 175, 187, 221, 406n.44
maqām, pl. *maqāmāt*, 80, 91, 92, 156-63, 243, 380n.29, 393n.57, 422
Maqrīzī, Aḥmad ibn ʿAlī al-, 232, 405n.30
maqṣūra (grid surrounding saints' tombs), 103, 105, 107, 113, 117, 259, 321, 333, 408n.2, 422
marginalization of Sufism in Egyptian society, 16-18
Mārī Girgis (St. George), 333-4, 337, 344-7, 349
Mark, St., 328, 341
marriage, 40, 42-43, 69, 143, 230-32, 239, 249, 250, 251-3, 271, 272, 286, 293-4, 339-40, 348; as metaphor, 41, 109, 189, 235, 237, 240
Marty, Martin E., 418n.4
martyrs/martyrdom, 74-6, 329, 332-3, 340, 415n.11, 419, 428, 429
Mary, mother of Jesus, 75, 217, 230, 331, 335-7, 349, 388n.91
mashrabiyya (traditional interlocking woodwork), 259, 408n.2
Massignon, Louis, 77, 383n.1
Matbūlī, Ibrāhīm al-, 391n.14
Mazloum, Cherifa-Nihal, 399n.46
McDaniel, June, 408n.89
McPherson, J. W., 8-9
mediation of disputes, 153-4
Medina, 51, 63, 65, 74, 280, 284, 386n.51, 419, 430
Meier, Fritz, 405n.29
Meinardus, Otto, 335, 337, 342, 415n.4,n.11, 416n.13,n.20-2,n.27
Memon, Muhammad Umar, 393n.42
memorization of texts, 24
Mernissi, Fatima, 101-2, 244, 252, 392n.37, 408n.86
Michael, archangel, 331, 335
Michon, Jean-Louis, 398n.33,n.38, 399n.53
Mīma, Ḥāgga, xiv, 308
Mina, Raphael Ava, 340, 341, 416n.29,n.31-3, 417n.37
miracles, 2, 77, 90, 98-101, 106-7, 118, 128, 218, 250, 255, 260, 261, 264, 266, 269, 275, 279, 283-4, 285, 287-9, 292, 296-7, 307-8, 323, 325, 331, 334, 335, 337, 341, 342, 344-5, 355-6,371,386n.41,391n.28, 392n.34, 405n.4, 417n.36, 431
Mirghāniyya Order, 21
Miriam bint ʿAbd al-Raḥmān al-Bāj, 405n.44
Miṣrī, Fāṭima al-, 399n.46
Mitchell, Richard P., 380n.22, 418n.5
moderation, 160, 168-9, 371
modernism/modernist, xi, 5-6, 7, 16, 325, 328, 359-60, 362, 369, 380n.17, 422, 427
modernization, xi, 5, 357, 358-63, 367
modesty and morality, 27-28, 241, 250-1, 252, 295-6. *See also* women
monks, 160
Monophysite creed, 329
moral corruption of modern society, 359-61, 368-9, 382n.2
Morocco, x, 52, 60, 101, 108, 146, 150, 163, 215, 219, 244, 252, 302, 314, 355, 356, 372, 399n.53, 415n.12
Morsy, Soheir A., 399n.46
Moses, 53, 125, 176, 192, 208, 221, 317, 320, 356, 398n.44, 429
mosques, 34-35, 38, 101-2, 104, 110, 113, 117, 118, 120, 121, 130, 134, 136, 143, 144, 175, 177, 180, 181, 210, 212, 217, 226, 227, 229, 244-6, 247, 259, 273, 274-5, 283, 294, 295, 319, 358, 376, 382n.5, 422, 430
moulids, 2, 5, 8-9, 18, 21, 28, 30, 33, 37-38, 41, 74, 81-83, 87, 99, 100, 105, 107-17, 119, 122, 127, 136, 140, 151, 173, 178, 181, 182, 184, 188, 197, 208-9, 210, 226, 242, 245, 247-9, 250, 251, 259, 260, 267-8, 272, 279, 289, 324, 332, 333-4, 346, 352, 355, 356, 362, 370-1, 373, 374, 391n.32, 393n.43-6, 395n.26, 421, 422, 424
Muʿāwiya, 70, 71, 73, 388n.81, 40

Mubārak, Zakī, 384n.13
muftī, 422, 427, 430
Muḥammad, ʿĀdil Aḥmad, 413n.30
Muhammad, Prophet of Islam: ascension of, 53-4, 120, 125, 158, 221, 222, 310, 412n.5; attitude toward marriage, 230-1; attitude toward poetry and song, 172-3; attitude toward work, 370; birthday/moulid of, 107-9, 151, 247, 316, 355; blessing the Prophet *(al-ṣalāt ʿalā 'l-nabī)*, praising the Prophet *(madīḥat al-nabī)*, 50-51, 65-6, 67, 110, 131, 137, 142, 169, 171, 179, 180, 244, 260, 261, 283, 293, 321, 383n.3-4, 386n.52, 419, 422; and Buḥayra, 352; centrality of devotion to, ix, 50-1; color associated with, 305; controversy over Sufi doctrine of, 309-13, 315-6, 325; descent from, 87-8, 277, 304, 324; as exemplar, 3, 23, 51-2, 146, 172, 230, 263, 278, 295, 304, 320, 396n.41, 404n.12, 417n.46; as gateway to God, 43, 203-4, 354; honoring M. through compassion on *magāzib*, 213; illiteracy of, 24; intercession of, 51, 81-2, 119-20, 175, 262, 321; life of, 153, 430; love for, 21, 50-1, 56, 61-4, 67-8, 178, 188-9, 193, 268, 326, 401.26; mercy to all creatures, 51; Muhammadan light, 54-56, 57-61, 67, 78, 89, 105, 125, 153, 161, 221, 309, 310, 311, 383n.11, 384n.20, 431; Muhammadan path, 61; Muhammadan presence, 36, 57, 162-3, 167, 203-4, 264, 269, 353, 398n.42; Muhammadan Reality, 58-9, 61, 141, 236, 309, 310, 312, 372, 385n.37, 429; mystical experience of, 208; oaths to, 130-1; oneness with, 116, 382n.4, 401n.27; perfection of, 3; professing ignorance of unseen world, 222; prayer of, 265; Prophet's mosque in Medina, 295; saints as heirs of, 304; sayings of, 1, 23, 160, 193, 200, 223, 253, 263, 369, 396n.54, 398n.35, 409n.25; Sayyida Zaynab's respect for, 86-7; seal of prophets, 53, 397n.14, sexuality of, 253; as shaykh, 286; sinlessness of, 52-3; suffering of, 320; Sufi doctrines of, 301, 384n.21; as teacher, 1, 135-6; tomb of, 121; trained by God, 145; uniqueness of, 52-4, 383n.12; visions of, 65-66, 129, 162-3, 214, 216, 217, 268-9, 277, 310, 311, 337, 402n.46; and women, 226, 235, 239. *See also ahl al-bayt*, annihilation in the Messenger, Ḥadith
Muḥammad ʿUthmān ʿAbduh, shaykh of the Burhāniyya, xiv, 56-57, 64, 104, 133, 155, 216-7, 257, 300-327, 361, 363, 374, 377, 385n.28,n.32, 385n.38, 386n.57, 390n.122; life of, 303-8, 412n.3-4,n.6, 430; self-image and public image of, 323-7
Muḥammadiyya Shādhiliyya Order, 17, 99, 131, 152, 185, 226, 265, 301, 357, 368, 381n.35
Muḥammadiyya Sharʿiyya Order, 248, 403n.57
Mujaddidī, al-Sayyid al-, 283
munshidīn (Sufi singers), 8, 21, 67, 111, 112, 137, 168, 171, 174-8, 179, 180, 181, 182, 192, 194, 248-9, 251, 381n.46, 397n.8, 398n.32, 401n.26, 422
Muqātil, 54
Murata, Sachiko, 406n.51
murīd (disciple), 131, 138, 185, 208. *See also* shaykh-disciple relationship
muruwwa/murūʾa (manliness), 229, 292
Mūsā Abū ʿAlī, shaykh in Karnak, 92, 109, 198, 216
Mūsā Abū 'l-ʿUmrān, 321
Musallamiyya Khalwatiyya Order, 227, 249
music, 7-8, 12, 18, 31, 113, 148, 168,

171-8, 185, 209, 248-9, 267, 346-7, 382n.5; controversy over, 171, 172-4, 399n.53
musical instruments in dhikr, 171-2, 181, 185
Muslim Brotherhood, 7, 12, 14, 242-3, 248, 266, 301, 325, 362, 364, 375, 376, 379n.11, 422, 428, 430
Muslim ibn al-Ḥajjāj, 387n.72, 397n.10
Muʿtazila/Muʿtazilism, 66, 402n.46, 402n.53, 419, 423, 427
Muẓaffar al-Dīn Kokböri/Kokbūrū, 108
mystical union, 201-2, 406n.51
mysticism, mystical experience, 1, 156-63, 212-3, 221-5, 227, 233, 234, 241, 253, 330-1
mystics' appeal, 374-5

Nafīsa, daughter of Ḥāgga Zakiyya, xiii, 293
Nafīsa, Sayyida, 30-31, 76-77, 86, 179, 273, 382n.5, 430
Naḥḥās, Muṣṭafā al-, 283
Najjār, ʿĀmir al-, 379n.5, 386n.41, n.43-44, 395n.35, 401n.15, 413n.28
Najrān, Christian delegation from, 69
Naqshbandiyya Order, 74, 152, 182
Nasr, Seyyed Hossein, 359, 365, 372, 396n.60
Nasser, Gamal Abdul, 7, 9, 15, 259, 266-7, 270, 301, 336, 341, 362, 367, 422, 430
Nawfal, ʿAbd al-Razzāq, 188-9, 192, 197, 219, 401n.6, 403n.62
Nelson, Cynthia, 399n.46, 416n.17, n.19
Neoplatonism, 61, 384n.20
New York Times, 415.1
Nicholson, Reynold A., 58, 385n.37, 390n.124, 417n.46
Niẓām, Persian girl Ibn ʿArabī met in Mecca, 406n.44
Niẓāmī, Persian poet, 158
Nubia, 247
numbers/numerology, 158, 166, 394n.21
Nurbakhsh, Javad, 404n.6
Nūrī, Abū 'l-Ḥusayn al-, 190
Nwyia, Paul, 98, 384n.16, 391n.28

oath (*ʿahd, bayʿa*), 127, 129, 130-1, 139, 140, 142, 143, 144, 151, 274, 283, 285, 290, 291, 292, 358, 363, 365
obliteration (*maḥw*), 161
October 1973 war, 217, 337
Osiris, 355
Otto, Rudolf, 103
Ottoman period, 2, 232-3, 362, 423

Padwick, Constance, 386n.56
Pakistan, 284, 389n.106, 393n.44, 403n.61, 413n.25
Palmer, Fr. Jerome, 416n.16
Parrinder, Geoffrey, 406n.45,n.51, 408n.89
passions, 1, 196, 198, 200, 201, 208, 236, 238, 250, 297, 340. *See also ʿishq*
patience, 206, 231
Paul, St., 187, 200, 396n.54
Pen, the, 384n.21
People's Assembly of Egypt, 241
Perfect Man, 58-9, 236, 252, 372, 385n.35, 429
personal relations in Egypt, 28-9
pilgrimage to Mecca (*ḥajj*), 120, 192, 245, 284, 287, 289, 295, 296, 308, 421
poetry and song, 63-4, 67-8, 79, 80-1, 84-6, 114, 115, 137, 148, 151, 158, 175-6, 177-8, 189, 194, 206-7, 233, 278, 279, 283, 307-8, 371, 384n.14, 390n.124, 395n.41, 397n.8
politics, 261, 266, 275, 283, 284, 301-2, 314, 342, 357, 360, 362-3, 375, 422-3. *See also* government involvement in religion
pollution, ritual, 244, 247, 383n.12, 416n.28

poverty, 196-7, 209, 262-3, 265, 297-8, 397n.9
prayer (*ṣalāt, duʿā*), 31, 90, 102-4, 105, 110, 118-21, 125, 131-2, 133, 143, 148, 151, 155, 163, 164, 167, 187-8, 192, 194, 209, 227, 229, 231, 235, 245-6, 248, 255, 264-5, 269, 272, 274, 289, 290, 292, 293, 321-2, 365, 419, 421, 422, 423, 427. *See also hizb, istikhara, rakʿa*
predestination, 160, 176, 200, 419
presence, divine, 161-2, 174, 189, 214, 221, 281, 353
presence with God, 161-2, 167, 170, 175, 185, 188, 189, 200, 202, 372, 420
Preserved Tablet, 59, 143, 223, 311
pride, 265, 275
Primordial Covenant, 36, 134
Prophet, the. *See* Muhammad, Prophet of Islam
prophetic medicine, 154-5
prophets, 53, 96, 125-6, 142, 170, 207, 222, 224, 307, 313, 317, 320, 355, 384, 397n.14,n.20
psychology and psychological states, 154-5, 158, 159-63, 169-70, 179, 180, 182, 184, 185-8, 366, 372

Qāḍī, ʿIṣmat Abū 'l-Qāsim al-, 414n.32
Qādiriyya Order, 150
Qāsimiyya Shādhiliyya Order, 140
Qays/Majnūn and Laylā, 162, 397n.13
qibla, 387n.65, 423
Qināwī, ʿAbd al-Raḥīm al-, 60, 108, 111, 247
Qūnawī, Sadr al-Dīn al-, 429
Qurʾan, 423; doctrines concerning, 419; importance and authority of, 10-11, 12, 78-9, 86, 185, 220, 255; independent letters of, 394n.21; interpretation of, 11, 54, 57, 86, 142, 158, 208, 212, 214, 220, 222, 234, 236, 274, 301, 310-11, 312, 313, 315, 317, 320, 325, 369, 376, 389n.106-7, 422; memorization of, 24, 261; on tomb decorations, 103; political uses of, 422; reading of, 23, 106, 110, 198, 248, 269, 272-3, 289; recitation of, 44, 133, 147, 155, 280, 289, 420, 421, 423; relation to Ḥadīth, 69; revelation of, 59, 120, 352; role in education and law, 381n.44, 423, 424; study of, 118, 153, 218, 271, 277, 282, 286; teachings of, 20-1, 53-4, 75, 114, 120, 125, 127, 138-9, 146, 163-4, 167, 171, 187, 189, 190, 193, 200, 202, 206, 214, 217, 219, 221, 222, 228, 230, 231, 233, 236, 241, 262, 349, 383n.11, 384n.20, 386n.41,n.52, 392n.38, 417n.43, 421, 429; use of for healing, 154-5; use in dhikr, 169; verses of, 20, 36, 51-2, 54, 57, 67, 68-9, 72, 78, 89, 90, 119, 124, 125, 130, 136, 158, 160, 162, 193, 198, 222, 263, 320, 387n.68, 389n.118, 413n.19, 428. *See also Fātiḥa*
Qushayrī, Abū 'l-Qāsim al-, 3, 22, 89, 90, 142, 146, 164-5, 172-4, 190, 201, 206, 243, 273, 368-9, 370, 396n.41, 398n.34-5, 400n.54,n.69, 409n.33, 430
quṭb, 60, 93-95, 97, 104, 130, 150, 157, 238-9, 310, 386n.40, 391n.20-1, 421, 423
Quṭb, Sayyid, 379n.11

Rābiʿa al-ʿAdawiyya, 50, 189, 229-30, 250, 371, 383n.1, 430
Rāḍī, Shaykh Salāma al-, 403n.60
Raḍwān, ʿAbdallāh Aḥmad, 259-60
Raḍwān, Aḥmad, 1, 15, 20, 45-46, 52, 55-56, 61, 65, 87, 90, 91, 95, 107, 111, 124-5, 126, 128, 144, 145, 146, 147, 149, 151, 163, 165, 183, 190, 197, 200, 201, 202, 204, 207, 208, 209, 211, 212, 213, 216, 219,

223, 224, 243, 255, 256, **257-67**, 268, 269, 271, 285, 292, 297, 341, 362, 365, 374, 379n.1, 390n.127, 408n.2,n.8, 409n.31, 427, 430, 431
Raḍwān, Muḥammad Aḥmad (son of Aḥmad Raḍwān), xiii, 20, 45-46, 128, 145, 259, 260, 262, 266, 379n.1, 409n.31
Raḍwān, Muḥammad Aḥmad Muḥammad (father of Aḥmad Raḍwān), 260
Raḍwān, Ṣāliḥ Aḥmad, 259
Raḍwān, Zayn al-ʿĀbidīn Aḥmad, 259
Rāgib, Yūsuf, 76, 77, 388n.93, 389n.97-9
Rahman, Fazlur, 403n.61
rakʿa (cycle of prayer), 102, 105, 423
Ramaḍān, 52, 95, 120, 287, 330, 380n.24
Ramlī, Muḥammad al-, 261
reform in Sufi Orders, 17-18, 185, 255, 265, 278, 280-1, 301, 316, 372, 377
refuge in God, 160, 197, 397n.9
relevance of Sufism in modern Egypt, 326-7, 357-77
Religious Endowments, Ministry of, 10, 23, 222, 302, 311, 314, 319, 370, 376, 390n.122
repentance, 156, 159-60, 196, 198, 294, 346, 350, 351
research experiences of author, 25-49, 251, 260, 267-8, 275, 350-1, 395n.32, 403n.61, 410n.46, 411n.51
research methodology, ix-xi, 26-28, 30-34, 37-39
Resurrection, Day of, 36, 80, 214, 307
ribāṭ (Sufi convent), 232-3
Riḍā, Rashīd, 7, 8, 278, 283, 364, 430
Rifāʿī, Aḥmad al-, 60, 65, 99-100, 101, 104, 109, 117, 150, 151, 312, 423, 430
Rifāʿiyya Order, 19, 21, 32, 60, 98-100, 132, 150-4, 170, 182, 395n.32, 419, 430-1. *See also* ʿAmriyya Rifāʿiyya, Bayt ʿAbāṭa
Rifqa, Sitt (St. Rebecca), 333, 340, 415n.2,n.11
Rightly-Guided Caliphs (first four Caliphs), 70, 103
Rīḥānī, Shaykh (teacher of Muḥammad ʿAbāṭa), 32
Ritter, Helmut, 401n.19
Robinson, George Wade, 411n.53
Robson, James, 399n.53
Roman rule in Egypt, 329, 333
Rondi, Ibn al-ʿAbbād al-, 91
Rothkrug, Lionel, 415n.10
Rugh, Andrea, 418n.4
Rūmī, Jalāl al-Dīn, 241
Ruqayya, daughter of ʿAlī, 77, 273
rural-urban dichotomy and relationship, 373-4

sacred space: houses as, 392n.38; perceptions and use of, 116-18; saints' shrines as, 101-7, 118; women and sacred space, 244-6, 392n.38
sacrifice of animals, 105, 252, 299
Sadat, Anwar, 360, 431
Saʿdiyya Order, 99
sāḥa, 34-35, 38, 46, 115, 129, 130, 154, 216, 243, 259, 260, 261, 262, 263, 265, 266, 274, 277, 278, 280, 282, 294, 295, 297-9, 395n.26, 408n.2,n.8, 423
Sahl al-Tustarī, 54-55, 58, 165, 384n.18, 431
Saʿīd al-Daḥḥ, shaykh of Aḥmadiyya Idrīsiyya Shādhiliyya, 108, 184
sainthood, 1, 89-98, 255-99
saint cult, 2, 4, 30-32, 83, 95-96, 101-22, 118-22. *See also* moulids, saints' shrines
saints *(awliyā')*, 68, 89-122, 116, 124, 125, 126, 128, 141, 152, 162-3, 166, 171, 175, 178-9, 189, 193, 199, 202-3, 207, 209, 211, 212, 216, 217, 224,

saints (*continued*)
233, 234, 245, 255-99, 264, 265, 271, 279, 288, 289, 291, 294, 302, 304, 305-7, 310, 312-14, 324, 326, 355-6, 370, 371, 373-5, 392 n.34, 419, 422. *See also* Coptic Christians
saints' shrines/tombs, 4-5, 12, 25-26, 30-31, 32, 33, 37, 51, 76, 82, 83, 86, 101-8, 113-22, 179-182, 183, 209, 210, 211, 217, 227, 244, 256, 259, 279, 291, 293, 294, 297, 305, 310, 321, 332-4, 354, 355-6, 371, 373-4, 389n.99, 393n.43, 393n.57, 399n.47, 422, 429, 431-2; architecture of, 103, 333; controversy over visitation of, 118-21, 300, 302, 393n.50, 429; visitation of, 423
Saladin, 108, 150
Salawī, Aḥmad al-, 309
samāʿ (Sufi musical concerts), 171-4, 232, 398n.31, 399n.53
Sammān, Muḥammad al-, 319, 412n.12,n.14
Sammāniyya Order, 261
Sanhūrī, Gamāl al-, xiii-iv, xv, 62, 133, 155, 186, 209, 211, 220, 261, 301, 302, 303, 304, 306, 308, 315, 316-7, 319-23, 324, 327, 385,n.25, 412n.3-4, 428
Sanūsiyya Order, 64, 379n.13
Satan, 66, 90, 124, 146, 165, 166, 173, 186, 213, 214, 229, 230, 234, 242, 243, 249, 250, 398n.35
Saunders, Lucie Wood, 399n.46
Ṣāwī, Aḥmad al-, 150
Ṣāwī, trustee of Bayt ʿAbāta, 31
Ṣayfī, al-Sayyid ʿAbd al-Ḥamīd al-, 61, 389n.108
sayyid/sayyida (honorific title), 423
Schimmel, Annemarie, 23, 202, 230, 233, 386n.40, 386n.55-56, 392n.34, 394n.21, 395n.34, 396n.5, 397n.15, 400n.74, 401n.20, 407n.73
Schmucker, W., 387n.69
Schoedel, William R., 407n.72
science, 359-60, 366-7, 369, 376
seclusion/solitude *(khalwa)*, 129, 161, 198-200, 271, 280, 286, 306, 340-1, 343, 354, 365-6, 370, 421
secret/s, 1, 23, 34, 41, 72, 78, 83, 128-9, 132, 145, 160, 167, 176, 189, 204, 205, 212, 219, 221, 223, 238, 240, 242, 249, 253-4, 301, 305, 345, 351, 353, 357, 363, 386n.40, 395n.32, 396n.41, 417n.42
Selassie, Emperor Haile, 341
self-denial, 35, 196-200
seven, 158
sexes, segregation of, 3, 25, 44, 46, 110, 111, 119, 131, 226, 229, 232-3, 239-40, 241-3, 245-8, 250-1, 260, 267, 272, 293, 351
sexual temptation, 226, 228, 250-1, 252, 387n.75
sexuality, 94, 143-4, 230-1, 233-42, 251-4, 249, 251-4, 320, 339-40, 354, 360, 392n.38, 405n.43-4, 406n.51, 407n.72, 408n.85,n.89,n.91, 416 n.28
Shabāb Sayyidnā Muḥammad, Jamʿiyyat, 248
Shādhilī, Abū 'l-Ḥasan al-, 11, 23, 51, 60, 65, 104, 107, 115, 127, 129, 142, 146, 150, 162, 197, 245, 260, 274, 297-9, 302, 305, 312, 368, 371, 381n.47, 395n.26, 397n.11, 412n.5, 41
Shādhilī, Abū 'l-Mawāhib al-, 302
Shādhilī, Wahba al-, 383n.3
Shādhiliyya Order, 20, 21, 22, 60, 84, 150, 152, 197, 292, 317, 368, 395n.32, 399n.53, 411n.2, 431. *See also* Aḥmadiyya Idrīsiyya Shādhiliyya, Ḥāmidiyya Shādhiliyya, Jāzūliyya Ḥusayniyya Shādhiliyya, Muḥammadiyya Shādhiliyya, Qāsimiyya Shādhiliyya
shafāfiyya (clairvoyance), 41, 221, 224, 344, 351, 352, 423
Shāfiʿī, Muḥammad ibn Idrīs al-, 77, 86, 120, 172, 354-5

Shaḥḥāt, Sayyid Aḥmad, 413n.27
Shahi, Ahmed al-, 399n.46
Shakar, Farīd al-Dīn Ganj-i, 230
Sharaf al-Dīn, Aḥmad al-Shāḥawī Saʿd, 388n.80, 389n.100,n.103
Shaʿrānī, ʿAbd al-Wahhāb al-, 2, 22, 76, 92, 93, 232, 235, 391n.17, 429, 41
Shaʿrāwī, Shaykh Muḥammad Mutawallī al-, 10, 23, 222-3
Shaʿrāwī, Shaykh (a *magzūb*), 209-10
Sharīʿa, 9, 11, 12, 13, 20, 60, 61, 63, 94, 133, 146, 147, 184, 192, 208, 211, 241-43, 282, 284, 286, 305, 310, 311, 316, 320, 321-2, 352, 360, 361, 370, 376, 381n.44, 411n.2, 420, 421, 422, 423-4, 427, 431
sharīf, pl. *ashrāf* (descendants of the Prophet), 87-88, 424
Sharqāwī, Abū 'l-Faḍl, 279
Sharqāwī, Abū 'l-Maʿārif Aḥmad ibn, 276-9, 283, 364, 409n.35-6, 410n.39
Sharqāwī, Abū 'l-Majd, 279
Sharqāwī, Abū 'l-Wafā al-, 100-101, 128, 133, 138, 144, 146, 148-9, 174, 255, 256, 257, 258, 275-85, 364, 365, 408n.8, 410n.46-7, 431
Sharqāwī, Aḥmad al-, xiii, 100-101, 199, 203, 279, 280, 282, 283-4, 364, 365, 409n.35, 410n.46-7, 431
Sharqāwī, Ḥasan al-, 90, 390n.11, 391n.15,n.17,n.23, 396n.48
shaṭḥ, pl. *shaṭaḥāt* or *shaṭḥiyyāt* (theopathic locutions), 278, 400n.74
Shawqī, al-Shammās Samīr, 415nn.2 and 11
shaykh-disciple relationship, 36, 116, 123-7, 134-45, 147-8, 163, 174, 185-7, 188, 194, 199-200, 203-4, 205, 213, 215-6, 217, 224, 240, 251, 265, 268-9, 274, 281, 289-90, 294-6, 306, 317, 364, 371, 405n.43
shaykh of shaykhs *(shaykh al-shuyūkh, shaykh mashāyikh al-ṭuruq al-ṣūfiyya),* 150. *See also* Supreme Council of Sufi Orders; Suṭūḥī, Muḥammad al-; Taftāzānī, Abū 'l-Wafā al-Ghunaymi al-; shaykhs, 3, 4, 9-10, 12, 16, 18, 23, 24, 37, 38, 41, 87-88, 95, 98-101, 112-3, 115, 129-31, 149, 183, 185, 197, 207, 216, 220, 232, 240, 243-4, 271, 277, 282, 286, 352, 374-5, 380n.22; characteristics and qualifications of, 123, 127-9, 234; definition of, 123, 424; finding a shaykh, 130; necessity of, 124-5, 198, 213; oaths to, 127, 129, 130-1, 139, 140, 142, 143, 144, 151, 363, 365; social roles of 153-5, 357, 362; teaching styles, 134-40. *See also* shaykh-disciple relationship
Shiʿa/Shiʿi, 19, 54-55, 58, 69-71, 76, 77, 79, 85, 153, 312, 314, 388n.82, 390n.122, 394n.1, 413n.25, 420, 421, 424, 428, 429, 431
Shiblī, Abū Bakr al-, 370
silsila (spiritual lineage of a Sufi Order), 128, 324, 412n.2, 429
sin, 159-60, 165, 170, 196, 207, 241, 242, 264, 349, 352
Sivan, Emmanuel, 402n.51
Six-Day War. *See* June 1967 war
siyāḥa (traveling in search of knowledge), 306
sleep, 44-5, 96, 111, 261, 262, 289, 293, 298, 332, 351-2, 421
smell, 97, 112, 291, 332, 415n.10
smiling, 162, 261, 320, 397n.12
Smith, Jane I., 393n.54, 402n.41, n.47, 407n.64
Smith, Margaret, 383n.1, 385n.36, 400n.65, 401n.5, 404n.4,n.9
smoking, 116-7, 154, 181, 185, 210, 227, 249, 259, 266, 318
social class and status, 17-18, 39, 47, 48, 112, 121, 145, 152, 179, 181, 182, 184, 197, 210, 247, 269-71, 275, 291, 300, 301, 319, 357, 358, 360, 367, 373-4, 376, 377, 399n.49, 411n.51

Solihin, Sohirin Mohammad, 415 n.1
Solomon, King, 348, 348, 417n.43
songs. *See* munshidīn; poetry and song
soul, 133, 158, 164, 170, 186, 193, 196, 200, 214, 231, 403n.69; purification of, 1, 11, 164, 196-200, 201, 206, 208, 219; killing the soul/ego, 200, 205, 233, 242, 252, 392n.32
spirit, 11, 176, 191-2, 196, 353; communicating with or between spirits, 169-70, 216, 224, 227, 234, 262, 264, 286, 307; dhikr of the spirit, 166; divine spirit/spirit of God, 235, 236, 238; evil spirits, 154-5, 198, 243, 294, 334, 342, 345, 347-50, 421; heavenly origin of human spirits, 126, 251, 403n.69; human spirits created from light, 222; in death, 1, 40, 214, 320, 373; in sleep, 40, 214; "in the spirit," 40, 173, 184, 191, 201, 249, 250, 284, 351, 353; spirits meeting before creation of bodies, 36, 134, 194; world of the spirit, 196
spiritual connection, 41, 116, 134, 138, 142, 194, 208, 337, 351, 364, 372, 375, 412n.2
spiritual discernment, 40, 147
spiritual journey, 1, 42, 124, 125, 157, 158, 196, 202, 213, 267, 277, 422. *See also* Sufi path
spiritual states (*ḥāl*, pl. *aḥwāl*), 80, 94, 138, 141, 157, 160, 173, 189, 200, 211, 240, 243, 253, 263, 265, 278, 370, 380n.29, 421
subculture, 330, 357, 363
Subkī, Maḥmūd Muḥammad Kiṭāb al-, 7, 365-6
Sudan, 154, 179, 244, 257, 300, 301, 302, 303, 308, 314, 316, 318, 319, 324, 326, 413n.29, 427
suffering, 78, 138, 187, 202, 206-7, 231, 240, 264, 320, 326, 335, 388n.90, 391n.32, 428
Sufi method, contrasted with fundamentalist method of moral reform, 361-3, 376; effectiveness in modern society, 364-6
Sufi Orders, 4, 7, 9-10, 17-18, 87-88, 105, 109, 110, 115-6, 123-55, 148, 182, 256-7, 300, 304, 307, 315, 318, 363, 375, 390n.129, 424; membership of, 13-16, 357-8; registered and unregistered, 14-15, 256-7; relations between, 150-2, 183-5; social functions of, 152-5; structure of, 149-50. *See also* women
Sufi path, 80, 83, 123, 131, 156-225, 231, 243, 269, 285, 289, 310; stations on the way (*maqam*, pl. *maqamat*), 80, 156-63
Sufism, definitions of, 1, 19-22, 81-83, 197, 357, 381n.43,n.45
Sufism, historical importance of, 4, 357, 364, 379n.13
Suhrawardī, Abū Najīb al-, 23
Suhrawardī, Shihāb al-Dīn ʿUmar al-, 417n.46
Sukayna, daughter of Ḥusayn ("Sitt Sakina"), 77, 273
Sulamī, Muhammad ibn al-Husayn, 22, 379n.10, 402n.32
Sunna, 10, 52, 185, 219, 230, 263, 278, 311, 315, 381n.44, 404n.12, 424
Sunni Islam, 3, 19, 66, 69-71, 78, 85, 119, 153, 387n.72, 390n.1, 402n.46, 413n.25, 423, 424, 427
Supreme Council of Sufi Orders, 9-11, 14-15, 25, 57, 100, 109, 130, 150, 185, 216, 226, 242-3, 256, 257, 276, 285, 300, 310, 312, 315, 316, 317, 318, 362, 363, 370, 390n.122
Suryānī, language of the angels, 262
Suṭūḥī, Muḥammad al-, 57-58, 66,

312-13, 314, 315, 318-9, 390n.122, 402n.49, 413n.20, 431
Suyūṭī, Jalāl al-Dīn al-, 300, 309, 310
Swan, George, 217, 402n.50
Syria, 356, 423, 430

Ṭabarānī, al-, 388n.85, 389n.112
Ṭabarī, Abū Jaʿfar Muḥammad Ibn Jarīr al-, 54, 384n.15
tābūt (catafalque), 103, 110, 114, 115, 424
Tadhkaray, Princess, 232
Tadros, Amīr (Coptic saint), 354
Taftāzānī, Abū 'l-Wafā al-Ghunaymī al-, 2, 10-11, 12-13, 14, 25, 100, 112, 150, 276, 316, 317, 380n.29-30, 381n.35, 396n.56, 404n.1, 418n.6, 431
Tantric Buddhism, 252
tasting *(dhawq)*, 222, 376
tattoos, 334
tawḥīd, belief in God's oneness, 54, 207, 424
tawḥīd, unification of spirits, 204-5, 230, 251-2, 372, 382n.4, 401n.26, 424
Tawḥīd, Jamāʿat al-, 8
Ṭawīl, Tawfīq al-, 379n.6, 405n.32
Ṭayyib, Shaykh Aḥmad Aḥmad al- (d. 1956), 111, 182
Ṭayyib, Shaykh Muḥammad Aḥmad al-(d. 1988), xiii, 97, 111, 139, 198, 258, 265, 410n.46, 431
Ṭayyib, Shaykh Muḥammad Muḥammad al- (son of Shaykh Muḥammad Aḥmad al-Ṭayyib), 265, 271
testing of disciples, 40, 43, 144
texts and their role in modern Sufism, ix-x, 22-24, 156, 212, 218-20, 234-5, 269, 274, 305, 306-7, 309-15, 324, 368-72
Theresa, Mother (of Calcutta), 263
Thompson, A., 399n.46
Throne of God, 53-54, 55, 62, 65, 72, 104, 125, 132, 154, 201-2, 221, 311, 421
Tijānī, ʿAbd al-ʿAzīz al-ʿĀyidī al-, 387n.72, 388n.79,n.81,n.87, 400 n.78
Tirmidhī, Ḥakīm al-, 89, 119, 385n.24, 388n.79,n.85, 390n.1, 397n.10
Tosun Bayrak al-Jerrahi al-Halveti, Shaykh, 379n.10
tourists, 257, 259
transcendent Truth. See *Ḥaqīqa*
Tuhāmī, Shaykh al (father of Yāsīn al-Tuhāmī), 251
Tuhāmī, Yāsīn al-. *See* Yāsīn al-Tuhāmī
Tūnī, Aḥmad al-, xiii, 172, 175-7, 251, 381n.46, 398n.45
Tunisia, 417n.2

ʿUbayd, Shaykh Mansur al-Rifaʿi, 370
Ulama, 12, 218, 220, 282, 311, 361, 364, 424, 427
ʿUmar ibn al-Khaṭṭāb, 70, 71, 72, 96, 126, 131, 173, 200, 224, 388n.81, 398n.35, 431
Umayyads, 15, 73, 76, 310, 430, 432
Umm Ayman, 384n.12
Umm Fatḥī, 29, 30, 227, 249, 250
Umm Salama, wife of the Prophet, 53, 69
unification. *See tawḥīd*
union with spirit of Muhammad, 62-3
United Nations, 217
unseen, realm of *(ʿālam al-ghayb)*, 139, 176, 221-3, 234, 279, 313, 371
Upper Egypt, 29, 44-45, 46-47, 95, 109, 110-1, 128, 139, 149, 153-4, 171, 175, 182, 210, 216, 245, 247, 255, 257, 260, 267, 269, 270-1, 276, 277, 284, 383n.9, 417n.45, 421
ʿUthmān ibn ʿAffān, 70, 71, 72, 224, 403n.73, 428, 430

ʿUthmān, Muḥammad. *See* Muḥammad ʿUthman ʿAbduh
ʿUways, Sayyid, 18, 354-5, 356, 380n.20, 402n.47
ʿuwaysi initiation, 414-5n.47

van Doorn, Nelly, xiv, 415n.5, 416n.25
veiling of vision/understanding, 29, 83, 146, 192, 242
visions, 40-41, 58, 65-66, 91, 104, 129, 130, 134, 135, 138, 139-40, 200, 207, 211, 213-8, 224-5, 256, 268, 272-3, 274-5, 277, 304-8, 310, 323-4, 326, 335-7, 342, 343, 344, 346, 347, 349, 351, 412n.2,n.5, 414n.47, 415n.11
Voll, John O., 418n.4
von Grunebaum, Gustave E., 92, 108, 390n.13, 402n.42
von Schlegell, B. R., 418n.9

Wāfī, Muḥammad, 98
Wāfī, Wāfī Muḥammad, xiii, 98-99, 151, 154
Wahba, Father Matthias, 336, 415n.8, 416n.15,n.23
Wahhābīs, 119, 301, 325, 361, 368, 393n.50, 424-5, 429
waḥy (prophetic revelation), 221, 223, 224, 266, 311-12, 317
wajd, 162
wakīl, 425
Wakīl, ʿAbd al-Raḥīm al-, 380, 407n.70
Walton, A. H., 406n.51
waqt ("moment" of spiritual realization), 265
Wāsiṭī, Abū 'l-Fatḥ al-, 60
watad, pl. *awtād* ("pillar," a position in the saintly hierarchy), 94, 310
Watt, William Montgomery, 387 n.63, 401n.18, 402n.52, 403n.58, n.74, 418n.19
Watterson, Barbara, 415n.7
Waugh, Earle, 174, 381n.46, 382n.4, 398n.32, 401n.26, 407n.84
wealth, 262-3, 318, 357, 363, 374
West, Egyptian attitudes toward, 28, 40, 284-5, 359-61, 382n.2, 410n.46, 418n.2
West, Muslims in, 414n.40
Wickett, Elizabeth, 393n.45, 417 n.47
Williams, John Alden, 400n.2, 408n.90
Williams, Michael, 407n.72
Winter, Michael, 390n.129, 391n.14, 405n.27
wird, pl. *awrād*, 16, 124, 131-34, 139, 141, 142, 147, 153, 166, 199, 261, 264, 277, 281, 283, 302, 304-7, 318, 319, 321, 322, 324, 325, 338, 365, 419, 420
witness *(mushāhada)*, 1, 83, 157, 159, 161, 162-3, 187, 202, 213, 222, 223, 224, 310
women: attitudes toward, 45-46, 227-30, 231-4, 235-6, 272, 292, 404n.8; in Cairo and Delta, 45, 247-8, 407n.82; in dhikr, 25-26, 164, 180-2, 184, 191, 233, 244-9, 260, 293; education of, 272; fundamentalist pressures on, 382n.2; in the ideas of Ibn ʿArabi, 94, 235-41, 406n.51; keeping the company of women, 239-43, 347; martyrs in the early church, 329; modesty norms, 228, 360; in mosques, 244-6; in moulids 110-1, 113-4, 173, 226, 247-8, 267; musicians, 179; in prayer, 244, 245-6; in the Qur'an, 228; and sacred space, 244-6; at saints' shrines, 25-26, 117, 118-22, 244-6, 297, 382n.6; singers, 173, 248-9, 401n.26; as spiritual leaders, 129, 130, 227, 232, 249-50, 292-9, 343-53, 356; Sufi etiquette with wives, 148-9; in Sufi Orders, 25,

131, 139-40, 142, 226-7, 232-3, 242-51, 319, 364, 404n.1; Sufi women, 229-30, 249-50, 404n.5-6; in Upper Egypt, 44-45, 149, 247, 383n.9; and visionary experiences, 215; and *zār*, 178-9, 244. *See also* sexual segregation
wrath of God, 91, 93, 146, 235, 264

Yāfiʿī, ʿAbd Allāh Abū 'l-Barakāt al-, 309
yaqīn ("certainty"), 221-2
Yāsīn al-Tuhāmī, xiii, 175, 177-8, 192, 194, 381n.46, 398n.45
Yazīd, son of Muʿāwiya, 74, 76

Zaghlūl, Saʿd, 283, 284
Zakiyya ʿAbd al-Muṭṭalib Badawī, Ḥāgga, xiii, 106, 115, 130, 149, 250, 255, 256, 291-9, 374, 395n.26
zār (spirit possession cult), 32, 178-9, 181, 244, 248, 398-9n.46, 425
Zarrūq, Aḥmad, 96, 302, 411n.1-2
Zayn al-ʿĀbidin, ʿĀlī, 25-26, 30-31, 76, 84-85, 108, 115, 171, 174, 179, 181, 246, 355, 388n.81, 431-2
Zaynab, Sayyida, granddaughter of Muhammad, 30, 31, 76, 77, 84, 86-87, 95, 101, 106-7, 114, 117, 139, 140, 180, 244, 245, 273, 274, 355, 370, 431-2
Zaynab, wife of Shaykh ʿAbāta, 32
Zaynab Fāṭima bint al-ʿAbbās, 232
Zaytūn, vision of Mary at, 335-7
Zionists, 314, 342, 413n.25
zuhd, 425. *See also* asceticism
Zulaykhā, 241

Lightning Source UK Ltd.
Milton Keynes UK
UKOW03f2355280514

232493UK00002B/47/P

9 781570 038495